INTRODUCTORY LINGUISTICS

Robert A. Hall Jr.

Professor of Linguistics
Cornell University

INTRODUCTORY

LINGUISTICS

CHILTON BOOKS

A DIVISION OF CHILTON COMPANY
PUBLISHERS   PHILADELPHIA   NEW YORK

To
Frances Adkins Hall

PREFACE

A POSSIBLE SUBTITLE for this book might be "Linguistics Made Accessible."
Not "Linguistics Made Easy:" this latter goal would be both impossible and
undesirable. It has been my aim, however, to present the basic findings of
linguistics in such a form that they will be understandable to the general
public, with as little as possible of the complication and obscurity which
unfortunately characterize many presentations of this subject, even in works
intended for beginners.

The word *introductory* in the title must also be emphasized. This book is
not intended as an exhaustive presentation of all branches of linguistics—a
task which, by now, would call for a number of volumes and which would,
in view of the high degree of specialization which has been reached in this
field, probably be beyond the capabilities of any single scholar. Nor does this
book contain anything new or original. My aim has been simply to present
the fundamentals of linguistics, and especially those aspects which are accepted by most or all scholars, in such a way as to serve as a basis either for
obtaining a basic understanding of the nature and functioning of language,
or for going on to advanced study with the help of more detailed and technical presentations.

My approach has been resolutely eclectic, not adhering exclusively to
any one "school" of linguistic analysis, but rather, choosing from each
those approaches and techniques which seem to be most helpful in making
linguistics understandable. I have made a special effort to illustrate every
phenomenon discussed, preferring to restrict my presentation and to afford
thorough exemplification, rather than to cover a wider range of topics with
insufficient documentation. Believing that it is beneficial for the beginner to
become acquainted with as many and as divergent linguistic structures as
possible, I have ranged as widely as possible in choosing examples; I have
tried to avoid using English for my basic exemplification, normally bringing
English in only after a wider perspective has been afforded from other
languages. I also believe firmly that it is harmful to the beginner to cite
English or other languages only in conventional spelling, and therefore I
have, for the most part, given a phonemic and/or phonetic transcription

vii

wherever it is at all relevant. I have followed the traditional order of presentation: phonetics, phonemics, morphology, syntax, considering each of these as the indispensable preliminary to the study of the ensuing ones.

The book is divided into eighty chapters of approximately 2400–3000 words each, intended for use in a two-semester college course with approximately eighty-five to ninety class hours available (of which five or ten can be used for testing or for further assignments), or for a two quarters' course with approximately forty hours per quarter. In summer sessions, language institutes, etc., the book can be covered in eight five-day weeks by assigning two chapters per day, or in six by assigning three per day. After considerable reflection, it has been decided not to include problems or to provide a workbook, primarily because, to be solved accurately and to serve as effective illustrations of linguistic techniques, problems must be longer and greater amounts of data must be furnished than is practicable within the limits of a single textbook or short workbook. The individual teacher will undoubtedly wish to supplement this presentation with further illustrative material and problems of his own choosing.

My indebtedness to numerous authors, for general approach and specific examples, will be evident from the references at the end of each chapter; I have drawn especially on Bloomfield (1933a), Hockett (1958), and Gleason (1961), although I have diverged from their views in many respects. I follow Hockett in not including a chapter on the history of linguistics—for which see Bloomfield (1933a), Joos (1957), and Pedersen (1932)—nor an enumeration of the world's languages—for which see Meillet-Cohen (1952).

Acknowledgments for permission to reproduce material are due to:

1) the editors of the journal *Language:* material from articles of mine and from Grimes and Agard (1959), Joos (1948 and 1960), Twaddell (1948), and Whorf (1936);

2) the editors of the *Journal of the American Oriental Society:* the table of the Old Persian syllabary from Kent (1950);

3) the International Phonetic Association: the tabular presentation of the *International Phonetic Alphabet;*

4) Holt, Rinehart and Winston Inc.: several brief passages and a map from Bloomfield (1933a);

5) D. C. Heath and Co.: the diagram of the organs of speech from my phonetic introduction to Ma. de Lourdes Sá Pereira's *Brazilian Portuguese Grammar,* and a reproduction of a page from the Oxford manuscript of the *Chanson de Roland* from T. A. Jenkins' edition of that poem;

6) Professor Hans Kurath: maps from Kurath (1939 and 1949);

7) Professor Morris Bishop and Miss Lorine Niedecker: excerpts from their poems.

Certain passages of my *Linguistics and Your Language* (Hall, 1960b; copyright by Robert A. Hall Jr.) have been adapted for use in several of the chapters of this book.

I am grateful to Cornell University for facilitating the use of this text in a preliminary edition in their elementary linguistics course; and to Professors J M. Cowan and C. F. Hockett for valuable criticism and suggestions. My wife, Frances Adkins Hall, has been a constant source of inspiration and help; to her this book is gratefully dedicated.

R. A. H. Jr.

Ithaca, N.Y.
November, 1963.

CONTENTS

INTRODUCTION

Why Analyze Language?

WE HUMAN BEINGS spend our entire lives using language as a means of communication. We are surrounded by language and enveloped by it, much as we are by the air which we breathe. Similarly, just as we disregard the air around us ninety-nine percent of the time, so we tend to take the existence of language for granted. We become aware of its presence and importance only when difficulties arise in our use of it or of its derivatives such as writing. We may meet with such minor problems as a mispronunciation or a malapropism, or even a more severe difficulty like a bad case of speech disturbance (e.g., stuttering or aphasia). Or perhaps we may have trouble with spelling or punctuation:—do we write *o* or *ou* in the last syllable of *glamo(u)r?*—do we or don't we put a comma before the last element in a series like *honor, praise* (,) and *glory?* Yet the problems which arise in connection with mispronunciation, misspelling, and such matters have only a superficial importance, and usually have little significance for the deeper functioning of our language as a whole.

As a result, we are not normally in the habit of analyzing our use of language, except in the framework which we learned in school for dealing with relatively superficial problems like the ones mentioned above. Yet, this framework is incomplete and faulty, because it deals almost wholly with the way language is written or with what is to be considered "correct." Hence, when we are faced with the necessity of carrying our discussion to levels deeper than those of writing and "correctness"—for instance, of examining the way we make sounds when we speak, or the structural patterns into which our speech falls—our reaction is frequently one of indifference or bafflement. We even tend to reject indignantly, in our conception of language, any innovation which goes beyond what we have been taught in school, and of whose existence and necessity we have not hitherto been aware.

Yet a moment's reflection will show us that we do need a newer and deeper understanding of language than our culture has given us to date. We need a more effective analysis of language—both of language in general and of our own language in particular—for a number of purposes in the modern world. Such a new approach is necessary for:

1. **Understanding our own language.** Our schools do a woefully poor job of teaching reading, spelling, and the facts of the English language. As long as education was confined to a small number of favored persons be-

longing to the leisure class, it was not a major loss to society if they wasted time and energy, and acquired inaccurate notions, in studying their native language. In fact, as the economist and sociologist Thorstein Veblen pointed out long since, such inefficiency epitomized "conspicuous waste," and such erroneous ideas were part of the "trained incapacity" by which the elite demonstrated both their superiority to those of the common herd and their freedom from the need for vulgar efficiency. In modern times, however, the situation is radically different. We can no longer afford to waste anyone's time or energy in needless acquisition or display of inefficiency, and especially not in our schools, where we are engaged in a massive effort to educate the entire population to literacy and to accuracy in thinking. Thus we need the light which thorough and complete analysis can throw on our language: how it is spoken and written, how it is constructed, and how it functions. This knowledge is of fundamental impoitance for constructing new texts and training our teachers, and for insuring that schools do a satisfactory job in teaching reading, spelling, grammar, and intelligent attitudes towards our language.

2. **Foreign language teaching.** Similar considerations hold true for the way in which foreign languages are taught in our schools. Linguistic analysts have long known that the traditional methods by which foreign languages have been taught are highly unsatisfactory—either the parroting of grammatical paradigms (*je suis, tu es, il est* . . .) and rules ("Five Latin verbs take the ablative instead of the accusative: *utor, fruor, fungor, potior* and *vescor*"), or the word-for-word translation of stories and poems. Persons trained by traditional methods have normally been unable to understand, speak, read, or write the foreign language, even after years of study. If they have succeeded in doing so nevertheless, it has been in spite of, rather than because of the way they were taught, and they have had to waste considerable time and energy. Classical Latin and Greek, even more than modern languages, have suffered from such mishandling.

Here again, modern conditions and techniques have brought the problem to a head. We can no longer afford to waste years of anyone's time in fruitless effort, when, with the help of linguistic analysis, effective results can be achieved in a shorter time. Present-day methods, and especially the use of mechanical recording devices, have made it evident that foreign languages must be taught first of all on a basis of hearing and speaking, and that ability to read and write must be built up on the foundation thus established. Yet in order to teach languages in this way, a sound knowledge of linguistic structure is necessary—not only of the language to be learned, but of the learner's native language as well, so that we can contrast the two and identify the points of structural difference which are likely to cause us trouble. Traditional "grammar" has shown itself completely insufficient to meet this need; only a scientific analysis of language can do so.

3. **The social function of language.** A better understanding of language and its functioning is necessary, not only for our schools, but also for our everyday life. This is especially true for our understanding of the way lan

guage functions in society. That every human society is held together by language, is a truism. Differences in language, however, are also important in social structure, and serve as means of establishing and maintaining social distinctions. Such differences are often real (e.g., *hain't* in the sense of "have not", marking its user as having inferior socio-economic status), but they are often imaginary (e.g., the use of *it's me* instead of *it is I*, supposedly a mark of inferior education, but actually widespread at all levels of society and of intellectual ability and training). Whether our culture wishes to continue social discrimination based on real or imaginary linguistic differences is a matter beyond the power of the linguistic analyst to decide (though he may have his own personal attitudes, democratic or anti-democratic as the case may be). However, only a complete picture of the facts, as provided by linguistic analysis, will be a satisfactory basis for intelligent and realistic decisions.

4. **Language and intellectual life.** How does language function in intellectual (literary, philosophical, scientific) expression, and how does a deepened understanding of the nature of language affect our conception of intellectual activity? Our traditional philosophy of language regards it as wholly the expression of individual personality. To a large extent, this view is based on an old-established confusion (reinforced by the aesthetics of the philosopher Benedetto Croce and his followers) between "languages" as systems of conventional, culturally transmitted symbolism, and "language" in general as the use made of such a system and the meanings conveyed thereby. A fresh, complete analysis of linguistic systems and their functioning reveals hitherto unsuspected relationships. In literature, we find that both the intellectual and the aesthetic content of a work (e.g., Gerald Manly Hopkins' poetry or Racine's dramas) are far more dependent upon the structural characteristics of the language in which it is written, than we usually think. Similarly, many philosophical "concepts" (e.g., Aristotle's ten categories of predication) and systems of logic have an intimate connection with the language the philosopher uses for his analysis of the universe. It has been suggested that our entire world-view is, if not wholly determined, at least colored to a large extent by the structure and categories of the language we speak (the so-called "Whorfian hypothesis," set forth by the late Benjamin Lee Whorf). An even more extreme view suggests that most or even all of what we usually term "ideas," "concepts," or "thought" is not due to some nonmaterial, supernatural entity ("mind," "spirit," or the like), but is simply our language and its meanings—i.e., the phenomena of the world about us with which our grammatical structure and the words of our language are correlated.

5. **Human and nonhuman beings.** The human race is usually referred to as *homo sapiens:* "man capable of wisdom," because of the observation, familiar since ancient times, that only mankind thinks and philosophizes. However, an even better characterization of the human race would be as *homo loquens:* "man capable of speech." Many types of living beings have systems of communication which they use among themselves: deer and

other animals, for instance, give cries by which they warn each other of approaching danger; birds and animals have mating calls; and bees have systems of movement (normally called "dancing") whereby they tell each other, through often complicated representations, of the location of sources of nectar. However, human language is unique, because (as Hockett has pointed out) it has seven characteristics, all of which are shared by no other communicative system:

a. **Duality:** every language has a system of significant units of sound (*phonemes*) and also, on another level, a system of significant units of form (*morphemes*), which consist of meaningful arrangements of phonemes. The structure of language is thus *dual*.

b. **Productivity:** the structural elements of human language can be combined to produce new utterances, which neither the speaker nor his hearers may ever have said or heard before and yet which both sides understand without difficulty.

c. **Arbitrariness:** there is no inherent, necessary relation or similarity between any given feature of a language and its meaning. (In bee dancing, on the other hand, the different movements of the bee represent actual directions and distances to the source of nectar; the system is therefore said to be *iconic*, i.e., directly representative and giving, as it were, a picture of what is referred to.)

d. **Interchangeability:** any person using a linguistic system can both send and receive messages, by speaking and being understood, and by understanding what he hears from other speakers.

e. **Specialization:** each human language is a special system, suitable for conveying messages within its own framework of structure and meaning, and having very little direct physical relation to the meanings or acts which it involves.

f. **Displacement:** human language can be used, not only in the direct context to which reference is made, but also at places and times in which the context referred to is not present. Thus, I can talk about apple pie, the Holy Roman Empire, abstract justice, or unicorns, and my hearers—provided they are familiar with the context—can understand me, without its being present or without their even having experienced it (nobody ever saw a unicorn!).

g. **Cultural transmission:** human language is transmitted from one individual to another, not by physical inheritance, but by learning. When we are young, we learn by imitation from those who are older than we are (and also from others of our own generation!); the knowledge thus gained, plus any new knowledge we may have obtained, we then pass on to our successors. It is only through the use of language that human knowledge can be cumulative, so that each new individual does not have to start from scratch in acquiring familiarity with the world about him, but can learn from past generations (through the accumulated knowledge of the tribe and race) more quickly than they themselves learned.

No other living beings have communication systems embodying all these seven characteristics. It is his use of language that has given man his unique position in the world of living beings, so that we can say that the human race started to be human when its use of language began, and not until then. Nonlinguistic culture and language are interdependent, in that neither one can exist or develop without the other—both are part of human culture as a whole.

If an accurate and thorough analysis of linguistic phenomena is as important as we have just seen it to be, it would seem highly desirable for a knowledge of linguistic analysis to be as widespread as possible. Yet, even now, relatively little attention is paid in our society to linguistics and its findings. In the mid-twentieth century, the results of linguistic analysis have indeed come to be somewhat better known than they were in previous times; but their diffusion is still blocked by a large body of unscientific beliefs and attitudes that are widespread in European and Anglo-Saxon culture. Before proceeding to a discussion of the nature of linguistic systems and the place of language in society, we shall therefore devote a chapter to the prevailing obstacles to the acceptance of linguistic analysis, so that the reader may approach linguistics without misconception or prejudice.

NOTES

Thorstein Veblen: Hall, 1960d.
The teaching of English: Sledd, 1959; Smith, 1956.
The teaching of foreign languages: Brooks, 1960; Hall, 1945.
Language and intellectual life: Whorf, 1956.
Benedetto Croce: Hall, 1963.
Gerald Manly Hopkins: Hill, 1955.
Aristotle's categories and logic: Sayce, 1880, vol. 2, p. 329.
Seven characteristics of human language: Hockett, 1958, Chap. 64.

2

Obstacles to Linguistic Analysis

THERE ARE MANY obstacles to an objective and scientific analysis of language. Most of these are deeply rooted in our culture's folklore concerning language, which we often accept and follow without even being aware that we are doing so. Other, more overtly expressed misconceptions often rest on folkloristic bases, even where they have received academic sanction and social standing.

Perhaps the most extensive misconception concerning language—at least in the English-speaking world—involves the relation of writing to speech. When we are children, we learn to speak without being analytically aware of the processes involved; in fact, we normally do not remember the earlier stages of our learning to speak. By the time we go to school at the age of five or six, the basic linguistic habits of our native speech have been formed, and we use them in everyday play and other activities without being aware of them. In school, all our conscious attention in language matters is directed towards learning to read and write, and all the analysis that we ever normally perform on language—in school or out—is concerned with its linguistic manifestations. Consequently, from our earliest schooling onwards, neither we nor our elders and teachers have any idea of how to deal with language except in terms of writing.

From this bias which is thus imparted from the outset, and from the great importance which writing has in our culture (especially in the more complicated aspects of our technology), it is easy to derive the idea that writing is more important than speech, that writing is "primary" and speech only "secondary." Our schools lay tremendous emphasis on the "correct" spelling of words, and give no training at all in understanding how sounds are produced or how our language is constructed in terms of the phonemic units involved. Hence we are shocked at such harmless "misspellings" as *cloke* for *cloak*, or *smoak* for *smoke*, without realizing that they make no difference at all in the readability of the words or their comprehensibility when spoken (as a matter of fact, *cloke* and *smoak* were normal alternate spellings for these words as recently as two hundred years ago). We are also horrified at the idea of changing the spelling of a word (e.g., in "spelling-reform"), because we think that somehow, if the spelling is altered, the word itself will be deformed or debased. In fact, however, the spelling of a word is never more than a reflection (in English orthography, often a very imperfect reflection) of the way it is pronounced; changing the spelling of a word does not change the word itself, any more than photographing someone from a new angle changes the person photographed.

Once we have made the effort required to turn our attitude right side out, and realize that, in language, speech is fundamental and writing (despite its undeniable importance in modern life) only a secondary derivative and representation of speech, then whole new vistas are opened up to us. A thorough analysis of the way we speak reveals many phenomena that are not represented at all, or are represented only incompletely, in our orthography: e.g., the role that stress plays in forming our words, and the extensive system of intonation patterns that every language manifests. Some problems are shown to be only apparent, rather than real, because they deal only with orthography, rather than speech: for instance, the question whether we should write a space, a hyphen, or no space between the two parts of, say, *street car* (*street-car, streetcar*). Such a compound as this is the same word, pronounced with the same type of stresses (full on the first element, intermediate on the second), and may be symbolized in phonemic transcription in some such way as /stríjt+kàr/, no matter which way it is written. The major problem here is to bring ourselves to realize that no written form, be it our conventional spelling or a phonetic or phonemic transcription, is anything but a representation of what is spoken, and that hence our attention must go first of all to the facts of language as an oral and auditory phenomenon.

Closely connected with our culture's overemphasis on writing is the widespread, but erroneous, belief that there is such a thing as absolute "right" and "wrong" in language matters. We are taught, especially in school, that any given usage, if it is not unquestionably "correct," must be equally unquestionably "incorrect." If such an expression as *I'm all tuckered out* or *Get a load of this* is not acceptable at the highest levels of formal literary usage, we are told that it is "slang," "bad English," or even "not English"—even though it may be used by many millions of speakers in their normal everyday conversation. This bias in favor of an imaginary absolute standard is reinforced by our insistence on regarding spelling as something which must be completely fixed; many people go to a dictionary, not to find the actual facts of usage, but to ascertain, in case of doubt, which spelling is "preferred" (*through* or *thru? check* or *cheque?* etc.). When the editors of the third edition of the *Webster-Merriam International Dictionary* placed its description of pronunciation, spelling, and usage on a basis of actual fact rather than of dogmatic prescription, loud howls went up from outraged purists who considered that the dictionary, by telling the truth, was "debasing the English language!"

The actual facts regarding "correct" usage are much more complicated than our purists would have us believe. Of course, at any given time, there are usages which many consider "incorrect"; but "correctness" or "incorrectness" is relative, not absolute, in that it consists only in acceptability or unacceptability to a certain group of persons, and may vary from one group to the next. The only time we can call any usage totally incorrect is when it would never be used by any native speaker of the language, no matter what his social or intellectual standing—for instance, a word beginning in *pfsk-*, or a combination like *men the* for "the men." Even this type of "incorrectness" is subject to change over the course of time, and what was formerly incorrect in the absolute (because no one would ever have said it) can become correct and vice-versa, as when the Old French *ce suis je* ("it am I") was replaced by the Modern French *c'est moi* ("it's me"). Furthermore, purists go to great extremes in condemning, as "incorrect," usages which are in fact perfectly acceptable and in widespread use by the community, including people of the highest social and intellectual rank. We have already mentioned *it's me* as one of these constructions which are falsely labelled "incorrect," and there are many others, including *ain't* in the meaning of "am not, is not, are not" (which is completely acceptable socially in many parts of the English-speaking world), *due to* in the sense of "owing to, because of," and so forth.

The same is true of expressions under special taboos, including the so-called "Anglo-Saxon" or "four-letter" words referring to sexual and excretory functions, and also words referring to holy personages or religious beliefs (e.g., *Jesus! Christ! My God! Damn it to hell!*) when used humorously or as swear-words. Here again, the taboo itself is very real, and in our society violations of such taboos are punished severely. Yet we must realize that even these taboos are observed only in some strata of society, not on all levels; and that not all societies have the same taboos. In France or Italy, for example, *mon Dieu!* or *Dio mio!* are only mild expletives and have nothing like the force of their English counterpart, *My God!*; and similarly for *Madonna mia!* and like expressions. On the other hand, such an expression as *bloody*, which to speakers of American English seems quite harmless, is under a severe taboo in England and the British Commonwealth.

Our entire complex of puristic attitudes is an inheritance from the seventeenth and eighteenth centuries, when social and political factors combined to make the then rising upper bourgeoisie an easy mark for unscrupulous correctness-mongers. An authoritarian, absolutist attitude towards all aspects of life—political, religious, linguistic, literary—was inculcated in France from the time of Cardinal Richelieu (1585–1642) onward, and reached its height in the reign of Louis XIV (1660–1715). Richelieu set up the French Academy in 1635 with the avowed purpose of regulating, down to the minutest detail, French language and letters—an unrealistic and impossible aim, but one which French intellectuals have ever since been educated to accept as an ideal. The upper middle class of seventeenth-century France wished to imitate their "betters," in speech as well as in other matters, and were very ready to take lessons from puristic language teachers who based their precepts on the "authority" of the French Academy and classicizing grammarians (as witness the scene of the grammar lesson in Molière's *Le Bourgeois Gentilhomme*, in which the newly-rich Monsieur Jourdain learns that all his life he has been talking prose and never knew it).

In eighteenth-century England, the middle classes were engaged in a similar process of social climbing, and were, likewise, easily victimized by grammarians who taught "correct" speech and writing (for a consideration).

Some of the seventeenth- and eighteenth-century English grammarians' rules were even made up out of whole cloth (such as the notorious *shall* and *will* rule, which has plagued English grammar ever since its invention by one John Wallis). The authoritarian, absolutist attitudes and prescriptions of eighteenth-century purism were imported into the United States and became widely diffused in the nineteenth century, due to the delusion that they led to the "best" English. By now, however, our inherited purism is badly out of date in its unfounded authoritarianism and absolutism, and is of no benefit to anyone except those who have a financial interest or gain a sadistic pleasure in enforcing their dicta (no matter how unrealistic or downright false) on others. Still worse, he who mistakenly accepts puristic doctrines is thereby rendered incapable of perceiving or even wanting to perceive the truth concerning language.

A further, indirect effect of purism, against which we must be on our guard, is found in certain misconceptions to which we may be subject once we have accepted the basic principles that language is primarily an oral phenomenon and that purism is a false and harmful doctrine. The notion is widespread that whatever is spoken is vague, inexact or fluctuating, in contrast to the apparent fixity of what is written (in accordance with Horace's dictun. *littera scripta manet*, "the written word is permanent"). Hence new adepts in linguistics often tend to think that they are now justified in relaxing their standards of accuracy in observation and description. Quite the opposite is true: linguistics demands more, not less, care in hearing and recording the facts of language, which are more, not less, complex than our conventional orthography would lead us to believe. We also tend to feel, when we find that linguistics opposes a purism which we may have already wished to reject without quite daring to do so, that we are now justified in considering that "anything goes," both in our own usage and in our attitudes towards other people's linguistic behavior. However, simply because linguistic analysts deny the existence of absolute rules of "correctness," they do not deny that, in our society, some language behavior (such as *hain't* "have not") is disfavored and hence to be avoided by anyone who wishes to be socially acceptable. When we are learning a foreign language, the abandonment of the old grammar-and-translation method does not mean that we can now throw grammatical forms around any which way, or pay no attention to the exact meaning of what we are saying. Linguistics imposes a stricter, not a laxer, intellectual discipline than has previously been customary in language analysis—but this new discipline has to come from within, from our own heightened percep-tions of actual facts, instead of being imposed from outside by authoritarian fiat.

On close acquaintance with linguistic analysis, we often find that its tech-nical procedures and vocabulary are quite complicated, and demand a great deal of hard work if we are to learn and apply them successfully. Hence, if we have been expecting linguistics to afford us a "royal road" to an under-standing of language without any work on our part, we may be severely disappointed. Matters are not helped by the fact that some linguistic analysts apparently make a virtue out of being as esoteric and incomprehensible as possible, introducing needless complications into their analysis and presentation. Extreme compression is another favorite goal of some linguistic analysts, who thereby render even the most valid conclusions inaccessible to any but their fellow experts. However, a just mean does exist; it is possible to learn the basic techniques and findings of linguistic analysis without having to be frightened away by excessive rigor on the part of its practitioners. Nor need we be afraid of unfamiliar terminology, e.g., of words like *morpheme*, *allomorph*, *plus-juncture*, etc. Every science has to have its own special terminology, either using new terms (such as *neutron*, *proton*, *electron* in atomic physics) or redefining old ones (as economists do with *demand*, *supply*, etc.). If newcomers to such fields as physics and economics have no trouble learning and using the terminology of these fields, we should have none with that of linguistics.

It is not an easy task to rid ourselves of all the misconceptions and prejudices concerning language which beset our society, since all of us have been exposed to them since our earliest childhood and have absorbed them both in school and out. Hence we need not be disappointed if we are not completely "converted" at the outset, and if we find difficulty in squaring certain findings of linguistics with deep-rooted notions which die hard. The effort is worth making, however, since the knowledge to be gained from an understanding of linguistics is more complete and more useful than the notions about language which we learn from our schools and our folklore.

NOTES

"Correctness" and *"right vs. wrong"* *in language:* for a more discursive treatment cf. Hall, 1960b, Chaps. 1–4.

English spelling: Hall, 1961b.

Webster's Third International Unabridged Dictionary: Gunderson (ed.), 1962; MacDonald, 1962; Pei, 1962; Read, 1963.

Eighteenth-century purism: Leonard, 1929.

Shall *and* will *rules:* Fries, 1925.

3

The Nature of Linguistic Systems

BY OUR DEFINITION of *homo loquens* (see p. 5), all human beings have the use of language. It used to be thought, however, that people of the lower classes must have a markedly inferior vocabulary and linguistic structure to that of educated persons. A German professor who taught comparative philology at Oxford in the nineteenth century, F. Max Müller, was responsible for spreading the story that a peasant would not have a vocabulary of over three hundred words. This figure has passed into our folklore about language, and we often hear "three hundred words" cited as the extent of the vocabulary of a waitress, a day-laborer, or anyone else who is considered socially or intellectually inferior. An Italian scholar once referred to the speakers of everyday Latin in the Late Roman Empire as "talking without syntax"—a contradiction in terms, if taken literally, since *syntax* means the "putting together" of linguistic elements, and no one can talk without putting elements together. Modern research has shown definitely that the distance between the linguistic resources of an educated person and those of an uneducated person is relatively slight. A complete study of the vocabulary of a Swedish peasant showed a total of 23,000 words, whereas it has been estimated that a university professor has perhaps 35,000 or 40,000 words in his active usage. A team of Japanese investigators once followed a workman, a business-man and a university professor around in Tokyo for a whole day, noting down every single thing that each of the subjects said. A careful count showed that, in the course of one day, the workman used 15,000 different words, the business-man 17,000, and the professor 18,000. As for the speakers of Late Latin, what the Italian scholar clearly meant was, not that their linguistic structure had absolutely no syntax, but that it did not show the syntactical complexities of classical Latin.

It is also widely believed that the languages of "primitive" peoples must somehow be inferior to those of more advanced, "civilized" communities. The old "three hundred words" myth often appears in this connection, and so does the idea that "primitive" languages have no articulated sounds, consist of nothing but grunts, have no grammar, have words for specific objects but not for abstract concepts, etc., etc. Here again, careful investigation has shown these notions to be unfounded. Every study that has been made to date on a "primitive" language has shown it to have the same type of structure and as rich a vocabulary as do other languages. Many of our misconceptions concerning "primitive" languages go back to the reports of early missionaries, whose techniques of investigation were poor and who misinterpreted the answers their informants gave them. If we start with the notion that Latin grammar is the only valid kind of linguistic structure, and then find that other languages cannot be forced into the Latin mould, then of course we will conclude that they "have no grammar." In short, there is no such thing at the present stage of human development as a truly "primitive language." There must have been a stage at which human speech was much less developed than it is at present, but that period was at least hundreds of thousands of years ago, and no traces of it have survived anywhere. All languages spoken at present, even those of American Indian, African, or Australian Bushman tribes, have reached substantially the same stage of development and are equally susceptible to linguistic analysis. Hence, also, we are completely justified in citing data from "primitive" languages, whenever they are relevant, in our exposition of the principles of linguistics.

All human linguistic systems share certain basic characteristics. They are all primarily oral and auditory in their nature, i.e., they are produced with the organs of speech (see Chap. 9), and are perceived with those of hearing. For many languages, systems of writing have been devised, and in some types of discourse (e.g. advanced mathematics), writing is essential to discussion; but this does not alter the basically oral–auditory nature of language. As a matter of fact, extensive literacy among the general public, even in the so-called "civilized" nations, has existed for only the last hundred and fifty years or so; before about 1800, the great majority of humans everywhere were illiterate. Even now, at a generous estimate, not over half of the human race are literate or semi-literate (think of all the tribes of South America, Africa and Asia). But those who do not read and write, nevertheless speak and listen; they send forth and react to linguistic communications, and that is what makes them human.

All languages are systems of symbolism. The symbolism involved in linguistic communication is not iconic (cf. p. 6), but arbitrary. One example will do for many thousands: the word for "dog" in French is *chien;* in Italian *cane;* in Spanish *perro;* in Portuguese *cachorro;* in German *Hund;* in Russian *sobáka,* etc. All the languages of the earth taken together would probably show well over a thousand different words for "dog;" yet there is no reason in the nature of the animal itself why it should be referred to by one sequence of phonemes in one language, and another one in another. This is true even of our onomatopoeic words, which supposedly represent noises made by animals or coming from other sources: for instance, the cat says *meow* in English and *miau* in German, but *gnao* in French and Italian. Despite a certain amount of direct phonetic imitation, onomatopoetic words always fit into the phonemic system of the language in which they occur and are always stylized at least to a certain degree.

That which is symbolized by any given feature of a language is the *meaning* of that feature. Language, as we saw in Chapter 1, functions on two levels: that of a small number of units of sound (*phonemes*), which are combined into larger units of meaningful linguistic form (*morphemes*) and their further combinations. The phonemes of a language are simply like building-blocks, of which utterances are composed; in themselves, phonemes have no meaning. Morphemes, on the other hand, are the minimal units which carry meaning; particular types of combinations of morphemes (compound words, phrase-types, clause-types) also carry meanings of their own. To define the meaning of a word or a grammatical construction, we must be able to state all the contexts in which it occurs or to which it refers. We need not enter here into the debate over the philosophical import of meaning, whether it is a reflection of abstract "ideas" that have their *locus existendi* in a nonphysical "mind," about which much ink has been spilled without arriving at any conclusive result. Linguistics should be independent of any school of psychology or philosophy, and self-contained in its object of investigation (human language) and its findings.

Every human language is a system with a very complicated organization—far more complicated than we normally realize. In addition to a certain number of phonemes, each language has a large number of morphemes, and an almost infinite number of combinations thereof. The grammatical system of any language, strictly speaking, consists of a number of elements which do not necessarily have "dictionary meaning," but which indicate the function of other elements with which they are combined (for example, our noun-plural suffixes written with -*s* and -*es* in such words as *books, bags, roses;* the past-tense suffix written with -*t*, -*d* and -*ed* in such verbs as *slept, marked, created;* the definite article *the* and the indefinite article *a, an;* etc.). These elements which indicate grammatical functions are termed "function-words" or "functors"; those which have specific "dictionary meaning" (e.g. *table, smooth, ride,* etc.) are called "content-words" or "contentives." The expressions *functor* and *contentive* are perhaps somewhat preferable, in that the elements to which they refer are often not words, but prefixes, suffixes or other features which do not occur independently and hence are not normally termed "words."

Although human languages are systematic, they are not completely so. No linguistic system is absolutely complete and regular; in every language there are irregularities of one kind or another (like our noun plurals *men, geese, children* in contrast with *faces, bags, books*) and incompletenesses (for instance, in English we have the set of terms *father-in-law, mother-in-law, brother-in-law,* etc., but no terms to refer to the reciprocal relation of two couples whose children have married each other). As Edward Sapir remarked in his book *Language:* "Unfortunately—or luckily—no language is tyrannically consistent. All grammars leak." Every language will show a certain amount of looseness somewhere in its organization: at any given point of time, there will be alternative choices within the system to express certain particular meanings, and the usage of those who speak the language will fluctuate between the alternatives. Thus, in Italian, when a family name is used alone without modifiers, it occurs in some instances with a preceding definite article (*il Machiavelli, il Petrarca*), and in some instances without (*Mussolini, Gronchi, Segni,* etc.). In such cases, the alternative usages usually have slightly different connotations; at present, using the definite article with a family name in Italian implies emotional detachment, and the construction with article (*il Machiavelli*) occurs primarily in a context of literary or artistic discussion (where the person referred to is regarded as a historical figure) or in a bureaucratic context, especially that of crime reporting. Hence an ordinary person, a public figure, etc., will normally be referred to without the article; using the definite article in such an instance carries an overtone of hostility or contempt. For any such fluctuation, statistical studies will show the frequency and context of the alternatives at any given point of time.

Human language serves much the same type of purpose as does a control system, a so-called "servo-mechanism" such as a thermostat, an electric or pneumatic door-control or a motor-control system on a train. These "servo-mechanisms" act to set off reactions, often on a large scale, not by performing them directly, but simply by "triggering" them. When a motorman pushes a button to open or close the doors on a subway train, the act of pushing the button does not, in itself, exert all the energy required to open them or close them; all that it does is to release a small amount of energy, which in its turn activates the controls of the motors which do the actual work. In much the same way, linguistic systems operate with quite a small expenditure of energy, so far as the actual effort of talking and listening is concerned (if someone is too sick even to talk, he must be really on the ragged edge of death). The interchange of messages by means of language serves to "trigger" actions on the part of the hearer or hearers, whether these actions involve motions on the part of the latter or simply further speech, externalized or not. This is what enables humans to extend the activity of their own brains over the whole world, and down through time even long after they are dead, by the transmission of linguistic messages (either auditorily or as recorded in writing), whereas nonhumans have to rely exclusively on abilities built into their own physical structure to obtain any given result. I can ask someone else to open the door, to shut the window, to cook my supper and even, if necessary, to feed me; I can order goods from half-way across the world, either by telephoning or by writing; I can write a book or record a message on tape, and have it reach my descendants decades or centuries hence; but a dog or a bird can do none of these things, because only humans have language at their disposal with which to transmit messages.

We mentioned, in the preceding paragraph, the externalization of speech. It has been known for many centuries, especially through introspection on the part of individual speakers, that speech goes on, not only when we are talking to others, but also when we are "thinking," either speaking under our breath ("talking to ourselves") or not uttering any audible sound at all. It is often thought that the latter type of "internal speech" does not involve the use of language at all, but simply some kind of abstract "thought" which places "concepts" in relation to each other within our "minds." However, physiological research has shown that, even when we are "thinking" without uttering audible sound, nerve impulses are still starting out from our brains, as if we were going to speak; the nerve impulses are then inhibited, on the level of the muscles of the organs of speech. When we are children, and have not yet learned to inhibit these impulses, we talk to ourselves, even when alone, and especially when we are first learning to read; then we learn to inhibit our nerve impulses and not to externalize our speech at all. (Some cultures are much less severe than others against persons who "talk to themselves." In Italy, for instance, it is not uncommon to see people of all ages going down the street talking and gesturing to themselves.) Consequently, "silent thought" involves nonexternalized speech far more than we customarily realize, and "silent reading" is always built up on a basis of inhibited speech. Every time anyone "reads silently" or "writes silently," an act of inner speech takes place, even when its externalization is completely blocked on the muscular level. This consideration is important for our consideration of the role that language habits play in "thought," and also for the very practical question of how we are to teach "silent reading" in our schools (cf. Chap. 73).

Languages are systems of habits. The habitual nature of language is, in general, insufficiently realized in our normal thinking on the subject; especially philosophers and aestheticians tend to treat language as if it were wholly the product of conscious reflection and purposive behavior. In fact, we acquire very extensive linguistic patterns when we are children, and use them in adult life, without becoming aware of their almost wholly habitual nature. Our linguistic behavior is comparable to an iceberg, of which more than nine-tenths is below the level of our awareness. In Twaddell's words, our language habits are "both below and above the control of the individual" —below, in that they are so extensively habitual; above, in that they are not the product of individual free will, but are common to the entire group of persons who use the language.

Languages are then, as we have seen in this chapter, systems of oral–auditory habits, used by humans for conveyance of messages through arbitrary symbolism; they function as low-energy communication systems for "triggering" actions which are often on a far higher level of energy. However, their systematicity is not complete or watertight, and every language shows a certain amount of looseness of organization. The *locus existendi* of any given linguistic system is in the brains of the people who use it, and only secondarily in the written documents which represent it or the grammatical codifications which describe it. Hence language is at the same time an individual and a social phenomenon; in the next chapter we shall discuss the relation between these two aspects of language, and its function in human society.

NOTES

The supposed three-hundred-word vocabulary of rustics: "Now we are told on good authority, by a country clergyman, that some of the labourers in his parish have not 300 words in their vocabulary" (Müller, 1862, vol. 1, p. 271).

"Talking without syntax": Pepe, 1942, quoted by Maurer, 1951, p. 166.

Vocabulary of Tokyo speakers: Grootaers, 1958.

"Primitive" languages and Latin grammar: Boas, 1911, Introd.: pp. 35–43.
Meaning: Fries, 1954.
Functors and contentives: Hockett, 1958, Chap. 21.
"Watertightness" of language: Sapir, 1921, Chap. 2.
Definite article + family name in Italian: Hall, 1941, 1964.
Silent speech and silent reading: Edfeldt, 1960.
Control exercised by individual over language: Twaddell, 1948.

4

Language, Individual and Society

LANGUAGE IS, as we have remarked, both an individual and a social phenomenon. It is individual because it manifests itself only in the habits—potential or actualized—of each individual speaker. Since these habits are controlled in the brain—though it is not yet known for certain in which part of the brain, or even if there is a specific part of the brain which controls language habits—we may speak of linguistic activity as having its *locus existendi* in the individual brain. At the same time, language is intimately connected with society through its function, which is primarily that of communicating messages from any given individual to one or more others; nor could human society exist without language. These two aspects of language, the individual and the social, are therefore extremely closely interconnected. Language forms the major link between the individual and society, and makes it possible for him to live at the same time as an individual personality complete in himself, and as a fully functioning member of his social group.

By the age of twelve or thirteen, the normal individual has a fully developed and functioning linguistic system, and may be referred to as a linguistic adult. (We are referring here to the *structure*, not to the *vocabulary*, involved in the linguistic system; one's stock of vocabulary items can of course undergo even considerable expansion after the age of twelve or thirteen.) Each person's total set of language habits is termed his *idiolect*, and is peculiar to him as an individual. This does not mean that the individual invents his idiolect out of thin air. On the contrary, the individual "creates" nothing in his idiolect, except in the sense that he has been building it up, in his behavior patterns, since his earliest childhood; but every idiolect is developed through imitation of other idiolects. The individual normally imitates very closely those models with whom he has been in continual and intensive contact, especially in his early years (parents, playmates, teachers), and less closely those with whom his contacts have been less intimate. Yet, since each individual has different experiences from those of every other individual, in language as in other matters, each idiolect is different, at least in slight details, from every other. No two idiolects are absolutely identical in every respect, any more than any two sets of fingerprints.

Yet of course, humans are able to communicate with each other, by virtue of the similarity of idiolects. Whenever two or more individuals are able to talk together and understand each other, the resultant group is termed a *speech-community*. The degree of closeness of similarity between two or more idiolects—and hence the degree of mutual comprehension, and of cohesiveness of the speech-community—is relative. In small, closely-knit groups, all of whose members are in continual contact with each other, the cohesiveness of the speech-community is correspondingly great, and the differences between idiolects are minor. This is the case in small families, tribes, or communities which live isolated from other groups while having intense contacts within their own group (e.g., the Amish in eastern Pennsylvania, or many mountain tribes in Central and South America). At the opposite extreme is the type of large, even immense modern speech-community like those of English, French, or Chinese, with hundreds of millions of speakers and numerous sub-divisions. In such large groups, the speakers within each major sub-division (say, North America, Great Britain, Australia, etc., within the English-speaking world) have little difficulty in understanding each other, and even speakers from neighboring sub-divisions (e.g., Australia and New Zealand). At the extremes of linguistic divergence, however, even those who belong to the same over-all speech-community (say, a Georgia "cracker" and a Scottish Highlander, or a North Chinese and a Cantonese) have considerable difficulty in achieving mutual comprehension.

It follows that all the terms which refer to linguistic groupings (*language, dialect, sub-dialect*) larger than the individual idiolect are likewise all relative. (Here we must avoid a widespread confusion of terms: linguistic analysts use the term *dialect*, not in its popular pejorative sense of "vulgar, uneducated, foreign, or rustic speech," but to refer to any sub-division of a language, even the most prestigious literary variety.) Usually, the term *language* is reserved for the largest linguistic grouping within any speech-community (e.g., English, French, German, Italian, Spanish). The term *dialect* refers to any sub-division thereof, such as Tuscan, Lombard, Piedmontese, etc., in Italian; and *sub-dialect* refers to a lesser division within a dialect, such as Milanese, Bergamasque, and so on among the varieties of Lombard. At the other extreme of size, larger groups of related languages which have developed by differentiation out of a common source (cf. Chap. 51), are called *families*, and a group of related families is a *stock*. Thus, Spanish, Italian, French, and the other Romance languages, which have developed out of Latin, form the Romance family; and the Latin, Celtic, Germanic, Balto-Slavic, Indo-Iranian, and several other families make up the Indo-European stock. However, since these terms too are relative, considerable variation exists in their use, and some scholars will even refer to the language families which make up the Indo-European stock as "the Indo-European dialects" because, at one time, they undoubtedly were simply varieties of one language.

Within any given speech-community, there are lines of greater or lesser *density of communication*—in other words, any given individual talks more to some people than to others. In theory, those individuals who talk most to each other—between whom the density of communication is greatest—should influence each other most and should therefore show the greatest similarity in their speech. Actually, however, otʰer factors enter into play as well, especially that of prestige, so that any given speaker may be influenced more (say, in following a given pronunciation, grammatical feature, or item of vocabulary) by one or more prestige-bearing persons who are relatively removed from him socially, than by a much larger number of close everyday associates. The interplay of social contact and prestige groups, in influencing any given idiolect, is often very complicated, especially in modern times, when prestige figures are beginning to exert considerable influence through newspapers, radio, and television.

In analyzing the reflection of social structure in the differentiation of a speech-community, we must distinguish two planes: that of dialectal divisions, and that of functional levels of usage. Leonard Bloomfield's statement of the relation between dialects is classical (*Language*, p. 52):

"The main types of speech in a complex speech community can be roughly classified as follows:

(1) *Literary standard*, used in the most formal discussion and writing (example: *I have none*);

(2) *Colloquial standard*, the speech of the privileged class (example: *I haven't any* or *I haven't got any*—in England only if spoken with the southern "public school" sounds and intonation);

(3) *Provincial standard*, in the United States probably not to be differentiated from 2, spoken by the "middle class," very close to 2, but differing slightly from province to province (example: *I haven't any* or *I haven't got any*, spoken, in England, with sounds or intonations that deviate from the "public school" standard);

(4) *Substandard*, clearly different from 1, 2, and 3, spoken in European countries by the "lower middle" class, in the United States by almost all but the speakers of types 2 and 3, and differing topographically, without intense local difference (example: *I ain't got none*);

(5) *Local dialect*, spoken by the least privileged class; only slightly developed in the United States; in Switzerland used also, as a domestic language, by the other classes; differs almost from village to village; the varieties so great as often to be incomprehensible to each other and to speakers of 2, 3, and 4 (example: *a hae nane*)."

Intersecting with these lines of dialectal division, and especially with that between standard and nonstandard, is the difference in functional level, between formal and informal, first formulated by the late John S. Kenyon, one of the ablest observers of American English speech. Kenyon established a four-way distinction, between:

(a) *Formal standard:* Normally used only in very "correct" situations and elegant writing, oratory, and what used to be termed "elocution" (e.g., *it is I*).

(b) *Informal standard:* Used by socially acceptable people in their ordinary everyday contacts (e.g., *it's me; he went away; that's yours*).

(c) *Informal nonstandard:* Essentially equivalent to Bloomfield's "substandard" (e.g., *he beat it; he took it on the lam; that's yourn; you and me better go home*).

(d) *Formal nonstandard:* A variety which arises when those whose native speech is informal nonstandard try to achieve the formal level, and often create forms or combinations which no standard speaker would ever use on any level (e.g. *between you and I*).

The boundaries between dialectal divisions and between functional levels are, of course, subject to many gradations and are constantly shifting in space, time, and social level. Features of usage are constantly passing from one status to another, either rising or falling in prestige. Thus, *leisure* used to be pronounced with the vowel of *beat* in the first syllable throughout the English-speaking world, as it still is in the United States; in British standard usage, this pronunciation has been replaced by one rhyming with *measure*, and the earlier pronunciation has been relegated to the status of a rather archaic provincialism. To pronounce the names of the days of the week (*Sunday, Monday,* etc.) with the full vowel of the word *day* in the second part of the compound (e.g., *Sún-dày* instead of *Súndy*) used to be an outstanding example of formal nonstandard usage; Kenyon cites the instance of a broadcaster who announced "Sún-dày will be Móther's Dày," which many of his hearers interpreted as "Some day will be Mother's Day." Similarly, the use of *presently* in the sense of "at present" instead of "soon" used to be formal nonstandard, with a connotation of rather vulgar, pretentious journalese. Both of these usages, however, and many others like them, have by now become so widespread that they have passed from the status of formal nonstandard to that of informal standard, even though many members of the speech-community (the present writer included!) still dislike them.

In a geographical sense, too, the boundaries of speech-communities or of their subdivisions are almost never absolutely sharp or fixed. Even in the case of different languages (e.g., French and Flemish in Belgium, French and German in France and Switzerland, or French and English in Canada), there are often tiny islands or enclaves of one language within the territory along the frontier. In a city like Brussels, which lies athwart the boundary between French and Flemish, the interpenetration of the different speech-communities becomes extremely complicated. Furthermore, there are continual shifts taking place from day to day and from hour to hour, not only with the casual movements of individuals along the frontier and beyond it, but also with changes of residence on a more or less permanent basis. Many individuals, both in and out of border zones, are bilingual or multilingual, and hence can be said to have two or more idiolects and to belong to more than one speech-community. The same considerations hold true, with even greater force, for the boundaries between dialects within a single speech-community; here, social mobility is a further factor tending to blur the divisions even more. Consequently, any lines which we may draw between one dialect and another, or even one language and another, can never be more than an approximation. However, in this as in many other aspects of mass phenomena, we must use approximations, *faute de mieux,* simply because a complete and detailed description would be beyond any possiblity of achievement.

Linguistic features serve both centripetal and centrifugal purposes in social structure. Without the cement of communication through language, humans could never have achieved anything like the complicated methods of cooperation on which even the simplest society depends. On the other hand, most social divisions, although not caused by language, are accentuated by the existence of linguistic differences and the use which many persons make of these latter for enhancing their social position, a process of linguistic snobbery. Both positively and negatively, our use of language is inextricably interwoven with our existence both as individuals and as members of human society.

NOTES

Idiolect: Bloch, 1948; Hall, 1951a; Hockett, 1958, Chap. 38; Sapir, 1921, Chap. 7 (without use of the term *idiolect*).

Speech-community and density of communication: Bloomfield, 1933a, Chap. 3.

Cultural levels and functional varieties: Kenyon, 1948.

5

Analytical Techniques

To a considerable extent, the techniques used in analyzing any given phenomenon are determined by the characteristics of the phenomenon itself. In the case of language, we must take into account, above all, the duality of linguistic systems (cf. Chap. 3), with the division of language into a phonological and a morphologico-syntactic level, and then the distinction between the raw material of speech and its organization into functional units. For the latter, we shall need to have specific criteria for their identification and classification.

In analyzing the phonological aspects of language, we must first be able to describe the raw material, the sounds which make up the actual events of speech. In speaking, we produce sounds with certain parts of our bodies, the so-called "organs of speech" (cf. Chap. 8); and these sounds consist of disturbances in the air between us and our hearers. Our task here is to identify the characteristics of these sounds, in the study of *phonetics*, which can be based (as we shall see in Chap. 7) either on the organs of speech used in the production and articulation of the sounds, or on the physical characteristics of the sounds themselves. In phonetic analysis, our task is similar to that of the natural sciences, in that we must find adequate and clearly defined categories into which the physical events can be classified. In articulatory phonetics, these will be based on the identification of the organs of speech and combinations thereof which are used in producing sounds; in acoustic phonetics, on the physical characteristics of the sounds as revealed by machines, especially the sound-spectrograph.

Phonetics, whether *articulatory* or *acoustic*, deals only with events as such; but the main task of linguistics is to go beyond the level of raw material and to describe the patterns, the configurations, into which the raw material falls in the system of any given language. In so doing, the linguistic analyst identifies points of contrast in the patterns, and the relations between them; these contrasts are to be identified in terms of the *functional units* into which the raw material can be classified. There is a series of technical terms, all formed with the suffix *-eme*, referring to such units; this suffix is added to Greek or Latin roots, making words with the meaning of "functional unit of . . . ". Thus:

phon-: "sound"	*phoneme:* "functional unit of sound"
ton-: "tone"	*toneme:* "functional unit of tone"

morph-: "form"	*morpheme:* "functional unit of form"
tagm-: "position"	*tagmeme:* "functional unit of relative position"
sem-: "meaning"	*sememe:* "functional unit of meaning"
graph-: "writing"	*grapheme:* "functional unit of writing or of visual shape"

Any functional unit such as a phoneme, morpheme, etc., is made up of one or more elements of linguistic behavior which, in this context, function as raw material. Many linguistic analysts use, to denote such elements in this function, a series of English words which approximate the Greek or Latin roots given above, in their simple form: *phone:* "a sound", *tone:* "a tone", *morph:* "a form", *seme:* "an element of meaning", *graph:* "an element of visual shape". For instance, the form *a* (English indefinite article before consonants) is one morph, and *an* (indefinite article before vowels) is another morph; the two taken together, however, function as one unit, the indefinite article, which therefore constitutes a single morpheme. Similarly, in the Tuscan dialect of Italian, the sound [h]* is one phone, which we find only when ·it is short and between two vowels, as in [la'hasa] "the house", [dihoha'hola] "of Coca-Cola". In Tuscan, the sound [k] is another phone, which we never find between two vowels when it is short, but which we do find under other conditions (long between two vowels, or short and not between two vowels), e.g., in [ak'kasa] "at home", [pẹrkoha'hola] "for Coca-Cola". These two phones function in Tuscan as one unit, a single phoneme, which we may transcribe as /k/† wherever it occurs, regardless of whether the actual phone involved is [h] or [k]. The expressions cited above would be given in phonemic transcription, respectively, as /lakása/, /lakokakóla/, /akkása/, and /perkokakóla/.

When we classify elements together in functional units in this way, the process of classification can be looked at from either of two points of view. If we start our analysis from the point of view of the functional unit, the elements which make it up appear as *positional variants* of the phoneme, morpheme, or whatever type of unit is involved. We call them "positional variants" because they vary according to the position in which they occur. Thus, in the cases described in the previous paragraph, we can say that the English indefinite article has the positional variants *a* (before consonants) and *an* (before vowels); and that the Tuscan phoneme transcribed /k/ has the positional variants [h] when single between vowels, and [k] elsewhere.

Looking at the relationship from the other direction, we see that the classificatory process involves subsuming certain elements under the heading of a given unit, and we say that such elements are *members* of the functional unit. It is convenient to have a series of terms to refer to elements subsumed under functional units in this way; to do so, we use a special prefix, *allo-*, which is

---

* Square brackets around one or more letters indicate that the letter(s) is being used as part of a phonetic transcription (cf. Chap. 7); the superior vertical tick ' indicates that the following syllable is stressed.

† Slant lines around one or more letters indicate that the letter(s) is being used as part of a phonemic transcription (cf. Chap. 14); in such a transcription, the acute accent indicates stress.

used before the various Greek or Latin roots mentioned earlier. Thus, we have such a series as:

phone: "sound"	*allophone:* "sound which functions as a member of a phoneme"
tone: "tone"	*allotone:* "tone which functions as a member of a toneme"
morph: "form"	*allomorph:* "form which functions as a member of a morpheme"
seme: "meaning"	*alloseme:* "meaning which functions as a member of a sememe"
graph: "writing"	*allograph:* "graph which functions as a member of a grapheme"

We would, therefore, describe the forms *a* and *an* as allomorphs of the English definite article morpheme, and the sounds [h] and [k] as allophones of the Tuscan phoneme which is transcribed as /k/.

How do we know whether any given element is to be classified under one functional unit rather than another? There are three criteria which are normally observed in the process of classification: distribution, similarity, and identity of function. By *distribution*, we mean the conditions under which the various elements (allophones, allomorphs, etc.) occur, i.e., the positions in which they are found with respect to each other and to other elements. If two elements occur in the same position with respect to each other (in the same *environment*), with different function or meaning, they are said to be in *contrast* with each other. Thus, in English, *a (an)* and *the* both occur in approximately the same environment, especially before nouns: *a book, the book; an apple, the apple;* and *a (an)* has a different meaning from *the* in this position. Hence the indefinite article in English is in contrast with the definite article, and cannot be said to form part of the same morpheme; they must, therefore, be different morphemes. Similarly, in Tuscan, the sounds [p] and [k] occur in the same environment, e.g., at the beginning of a word, as in ['pappa] "he eats (like a child)" vs. ['kappa] "the letter *k*". They thus contrast with each other and hence cannot belong to the same phoneme. Whenever two elements occur in such a way as to contrast with each other, we say that they are in *contrastive distribution*.

But when two or more elements occur in such environments as not to contrast with each other, we say that they are in *noncontrastive distribution*. This is the case, as we have seen, with the morphs *a* and *an* in English, and with the sounds [h] and [k] in Tuscan. A noncontrastive distribution is one of the pre-requisites for elements to be classed together as members of the same functional unit. If one element occurs where the other does not, and vice versa, so that they complement each other, we say that (as in the two examples we have been using), they are in *complementary distribution*. On occasion, however, we find that, although they are not in contrast, they are not wholly in complementary distribution. Often, elements alternate freely with each other, as do the sounds [s] and [z] between vowels in Central Italian pronunciation, so that in *casa:* "house" we find either ['kasa] or ['kaza]. In such cases we speak of *free alternation*, and of *noncontrastive* rather than complementary distribution.

The criterion of similarity applies to phonetic resemblance in the case of phonetic features, and to meaning in the case of other types of variants. Thus,

Tuscan [k] and [h] have in common the fact that they are both voiceless (cf. Chap. 8), and both are pronounced in the back part of the mouth. English *a* and *an* both have the same meaning, approximately "one unspecified member of the class referred to by the noun modified." On occasion, some linguistic analysts stretch the criterion of similarity rather far, and doubt can arise as to whether certain sounds are really similar enough to warrant their being grouped together as allophones of the same phoneme (as in the instance of [ə] and [h], which we shall discuss in Chap. 16).

The requirement of identity of function serves to prevent the grouping together of disparate elements on the basis of complementary distribution and similarity of sound or meaning alone. Thus, we would hardly class together under the same morpheme the French particle *y* (a form which takes the place of phrases introduced by *à*: "to" and other prepositions) and phrases such as *à lui:* "to him" (dative, and also used instead of *y* when a person is referred to, as in *je pense à lui*, not *j'y pense*, for "I'm directing my thoughts towards him"). Although these two elements are in complementary distribution (*y* refers to things, phrases like *à lui* to persons), and they share similar meanings, nevertheless they do not have the same function, since *y* is an enclitic form attached to verbs, and is a morpheme, whereas combinations like *à lui* function on a different level, being phrases consisting of preposition + object and functioning as a complement of verbal phrases (cf. Chap. 34).

A parallel from a nonlinguistic situation may perhaps be of use in understanding our criteria. At Yale University in 1943–44, as director of the Italian language program for the A.S.T.P. (cf. Chap. 77), I had to find teachers for three sections of an elementary Italian class meeting at the same hours. For each of two of the sections, I found a single teacher; for the third, I found someone who could come Monday, Wednesday, and Friday, but not Tuesday, Thursday and Saturday. For these latter three days of the week, I had to find a fourth person, so that the schedule of the sections and teachers was as follows:

	M	Tu	W	Th	F	S
Section 1	A	A	A	A	A	A
Section 2	B	B	B	B	B	B
Section 3	C	D	C	D	C	D

To describe this situation, we might refer to each functional unit of teaching load as a "teachereme", and to each variant of a "teachereme" as an "alloteacher". Each section was covered by one "teachereme", and in the cases of Sections 1 and 2, the "teacheremes" had only one "alloteacher" apiece (A and B, respectively). The "teachereme" covering Section 3, however, had two "alloteachers", C three days a week and D the other three. C and D were positional variants of the same "teachereme" in that, although they were different persons, they met our three classificational requirements. They were in noncontrastive (in this case, complementary) distribution, **since C came Monday, Wednesday, and Friday, and D came Tuesday,**

Thursday, and Saturday. They were similar, in that both were native speakers of Italian; and, taken together, they fulfilled the same function (of teaching a section of the elementary Italian class) as did the other two teachers, A and B.

Another frequently-cited parallel, perhaps somewhat more frivolous, is from the detective story When a given character (say, the butler) is always off the scene when the murderer is on, and the murderer always off the scene when the butler is on, we begin to suspect that the butler and the murderer are the same (they are in complementary distribution). But they must also have a certain degree of physical similarity (in sex, height, size, etc.) to be identified as the same person. Moreover, if there is a choice among several possibilities, in order for the butler to be the murderer he must fit into the pattern of the story and have the same function therein as the murderer (in a detective story, he must have some motive to commit the crime). The art of a good detective story writer consists in hiding the clues to such an identification, in a welter of conflicting or irrelevant evidence, so that the detective in the story and the reader are playing a game of wits throughout as to which can arrive earlier at an identification of the guilty person by the criteria we have just been discussing.

The distinction between the nonfunctional and the functional viewpoints, which are fundamental in modern linguistics, first became evident in the contrast between phonetic (raw material) and phonemic (functional) analysis. Since the words *phonetic* and *phonemic* both contain the first part *phon-*, this element has been "peeled out" of the two words, and what is left has been used to refer to these two viewpoints: *etic* (pronounced as in "phon-etic") for the nonfunctional, and *emic* for the functional. This pair of terms is widely used to refer to the contrast between nonfunctional and functional levels of analysis in other parts of linguistics (e.g., in morphological and syntactic study). It has also proved very useful in nonlinguistic studies as well as linguistics, especially in anthropology and other behavioral sciences. Thus, it is helpful to distinguish between the etic and the emic levels in analyzing the structure of meals, of religious services, of political activities, etc. This distinction may well prove to have been one of the most important contributions of linguistics to the social sciences.

NOTES

Fundamental assumptions of linguistics: Bloomfield, 1926. For a very different approach, see Hjelmslev, 1953.

Technical procedures: Bloch and Trager, 1942; Harris, 1951.

Suffix -eme: Hall, 1951c.

"Etic" and "emic": Pike, 1954–1955–1960, Vol. 1, Chap. 3, et passim.

For some hostile reactions to current analytical approaches, see, for example, Messing, 1951; Pei, 1946; Sperber, 1960.

PART I

THE DESCRIPTION OF LANGUAGE

6

The Structure of Language

As we have seen, the sounds of speech are correlated with features of the world around us (meanings), and by making sounds which other speakers hear and interpret, we send linguistic messages and (when we ourselves play the role of hearers) react to them. This correlation of sound and meaning takes place through a system which is quite complex, inasmuch as it involves several levels of organization. The material of our speech habits falls into various sub-sets, which are usually represented in a vertical listing, implying the existence of hierarchical levels, as shown in Fig. 1.

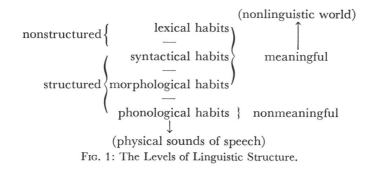

Fig. 1: The Levels of Linguistic Structure.

On what is normally considered the lowest level of linguistic structure are our phonological habits, which include both the raw material of speech-sounds themselves (to be analyzed on the etic level, in phonetics) and their structural organization (which we study on the emic level, in phonemics). Our speech-habits are structured, but the units of our phonological behavior, the phonemes of our language, have in themselves no meaning. The term *linguistic form*, in its broadest sense, can refer to any meaningful sequence of phonemes, from the shortest prefix or suffix to the longest sentence; but the morphological level of our linguistic habits involves the organization of *minimum* forms, both as morphs on the etic level, and as morphemes on the emic level. The organization of morphemes into longer combinations is dealt with in the analysis of *syntax* (from Greek *syn-* "together" and *taxis* "a putting or placing," literally the "placing together" of forms), whereas the various elements which in themselves carry only "dictionary meaning," i.e., are correlated directly with the features of the nonlinguistic world (e.g., *table, chair, lamp; eat, drink, walk;* etc.) function on the level of vocabulary or *lexicon*. Like our phonological habits, our morphological and syntactic habits are highly structured in themselves; but, unlike phonological habits, they are also meaningful (forms and constructions have meanings of their own, apart from the meanings of the lexical items which enter into them: thus, the noun plural formation in English means "more than one" of whatever is referred to; the English present-perfect verb-phrase refers to action lasting up to or involving the present time; etc.). Our lexical habits, however, are not structured except in terms of their meanings.

Linguistic analysis is concerned primarily with the central three of these structural levels: phonology, morphology, and syntax. We must deal, under phonology, with both phonemics and phonetics, since the latter has a structure of its own, describable in terms of the production or characteristics of the sounds themselves (cf. Chaps. 7 to 13). On the outer edge of phonetics, the analysis of the molecular disturbances in the air which are involved in the production of speech-sounds as well as other noises, leads off in the direction of general physics; and the study of the parts of the body involved in speaking and hearing leads into human anatomy and physiology. On the other end of our series of levels, the study of meaning leads to that of the entire universe around us, since our linguistic forms can, at least in theory, refer to all the phenomena that can possibly be observed by human beings (and if we have no term for a hitherto unknown phenomenon, we can always coin a new word or phrase for it). Hence the meanings of lexical items cannot, in general, be organized into clearly definable structural units such as can be established in phonology, morphology, and syntax, because the structure of the world around us and of our reactions to it does not, in most instances, lend itself to such neat and well organized classification. Linguistic analysts do indeed use the term *sememe* for "functional unit of meaning," but sememes cannot be established with the same type of precision as can phonemes, morphemes, and syntactic units; for this to be possible, our knowledge and analysis of the world around us and of our own inner reactions would have to be far more advanced than it is at present or is likely to be in the conceivable future.

Since linguistic analysts are, in general, interested primarily in the structure of language habits, they have tended to concentrate their attention on the three levels of linguistic behavior which, as we have seen, are structured (phonology, morphology, syntax), and to declare themselves less interested in the border zones of phonetics on the one end of the spectrum and of meaning on the other. Some have even gone so far as to declare, not only that they themselves are completely uninterested in meaning, but that linguistics as a discipline should (at least in theory) have no concern with meaning, and that the analysis of language structures should be carried out with complete disregard of meaning. Such scholars will, at the most, admit grudgingly that the meanings of linguistic forms may be allowed to enter into consideration only as a short-cut to a quick and approximative analysis, since the detailed study and description of patterning which (according to them) would enable the analyst to dispense with consideration of meaning would demand an impossible amount of time and energy. Such an extreme attitude is open to considerable objection, from the theoretical point of view. In addition, it has done a great deal of harm to linguistics in the picture which it has presented to the general public, since it has laid linguistic analysts open to the charge that they are interested only in language as sound, and neglect what gives language its major function in human life, namely meaning. This criticism is valid as applied to the extremists whom we have just mentioned, but not to the linguistic analysts whose viewpoint is more moderate. Semantics (the analysis of meaning) forms the bridge between linguistics and the study of the nonlinguistic world, and as such, although on the border line, forms an integral and essential part of linguistics.

In the analysis of linguistic structure, however, considerations of form must take precedence over considerations of meaning. These latter do play a role, but it must of necessity be a subordinate one. In phonemics, we have to make use of meaning for the differentiation of functional units: if a difference in sound is correlated with a difference of meaning in any given pair of words (e.g., *pit* vs. *bit; bit* vs. *bat; bat* vs. *bad*), then that difference is significant and hence the two sounds which are thus in contrast must belong to different phonemes. What the difference in meaning may be, is not relevant on the phonological level. If, for instance, I am analyzing a hitherto unknown language, and its speakers tell me that [pa] (with no puff of breath or *aspiration* following the [p]) means one thing and [p'a] (with aspiration following the [p]) means something quite different, then I conclude that the unaspirated [p] and the aspirated [p'] must belong to different phonemes, even if I have no idea what [pa] and [p'a] mean. On the morphological and syntactical levels, the various morphemes and syntactic constructions have meanings of their own, which must be carefully studied and formulated as part of the linguistic analyst's task (cf. the example of the Italian family name used with or without the definite article, pp. 15–16). On the other hand, we will not group disparate phenomena together just because they can on occasion have the same meaning, as did one scholar who lumped together in an (otherwise excellent) study on the syntax of the Italian imperative, not only the imperative form of the verb itself (e.g., *parla:* "speak!") but also such structurally different forms as the subjunctive (e.g., *parli:* "let him speak; you [formal]: speak!"), the infinitive (*parlare:* "to speak") and even phrases like *Vi prego di parlare:* "I beg you to speak", because of their use in commands or requests.

Graphemics—the study of writing systems—is also tangential to linguistics, since, as we have repeatedly pointed out, speech is fundamental in human linguistic activity, whereas writing is not. The function of writing is to give a partial representation of speech. For native speakers of a language, the purpose of a writing system is simply mnemonic, to call to mind something that they already know; but, for purposes of learning or analysis, no written record of speech, even the most detailed and narrow phonetic transcription, can be more than partial. The locution "to reduce a language to writing" is not a figurative expression, and in itself indicates why writing is an unsatisfactory point of departure for the analysis of linguistic structure. On the other hand, we have to depend on written records for our notation of linguistic phenomena, and for our knowledge of all human speech in past epochs (up to the invention of phonographic and magnetic recording devices), so that graphemic analysis is an indispensable ancillary study in historical linguistics (cf. Chap. 44).

The structure of language is constantly changing throughout time; in the usage of every individual, some minute change takes place even from day to day, as he learns new words, new forms, new pronunciations, and allows older habits to fall into desuetude. When taken in the aggregate over the centuries, these minute innovations add up to major changes in the habits of entire speech-communities, so that, say, the English language of our day is very different from that of King Arthur's or even of Chaucer's time. Yet it is useful to describe a language *as if* it existed at a given point of time without any changes taking place; in fact, this approach (which is termed *descriptive* or *synchronic*) is not only helpful but necessary both for the historical (*diachronic*) study of successive stages of a language, and for the application of linguistics in practical ways. We therefore adopt a fiction, treating a linguistic system as if it could be described without reference to the time factor, or, more specifically, without reference to permanent changes which take place in the system over the course of time. This is the same type of fiction as that adopted by, say, the makers of maps, even though in a modern metropolis the pattern of streets and transportation is constantly changing (the publishers of a map of Hamburg state that, on the average, some alteration takes place every other day).

With regard to the elements being described, there are two schools in descriptive linguistics: those analysts who believe in eliminating all consideration of the time factor, including the time used by the analyst in passing from the observation of one phenomenon to that of another; and those who believe in taking into account this latter type of passage of time. The first group wish to limit their description strictly to an enumeration of items and the arrangements or sequences in which they are found. Thus, for instance, they will describe the relation between the singular *book* and the plural *books* as involving simply the noun *book*, the plural suffix -*s*, and the order NOUN + PLURAL SUFFIX. For the irregular plural *men*, in an effort to be thoroughly consistent, they will describe the relationship between *man* and *men* as involving the singular *man*, a plural suffix consisting of nothing at all ("zero"), and an alternation between the vowels *a* and *e*. On occasion, this insistence on limiting descriptions to a listing of items and their arrangements can lead to highly artificial results.

The other group of analysts take into account the passage of time when the observer moves from one part of his material to another, and hence speak of even purely synchronic relationships as involving processes or change. Thus, they will treat the plural *books* as being formed by the "addition" of the suffix -*s* to the singular, and the formation of *men* as involving a "replacement" of one vowel by another. This approach is based on a listing of items involved and of "processes" which the items "undergo." For this type of description, it is always necessary to choose some one member of a set of forms and to describe it as basic and the others as derived from it—a choice which is on occasion difficult and can also lead to highly arbitrary or artificial results. In some respects, the item-and-process (IP) approach is closer to our traditional type of grammatical description than is the item-and-arrangement (IA) approach. Each has its own usefulness: the IA approach in determining the constituent elements of complex forms and syntactic constructions (in mapping the territory, as it were); the IP approach in presenting a language which has already been explored and analyzed, especially in preparing teaching materials (comparable to making a guide-book). The IP approach, carried to its logical extreme, is the basis of the transformation type of grammar (cf. Chap. 38). In this presentation we shall not base our treatment exclusively on either the IA or the IP approach, but shall utilize both, as may prove most appropriate for whatever material is being discussed.

In describing linguistic structure, the analyst can proceed either "from the bottom upward" (in terms of the levels shown in Fig. 1, p. 31), i.e., starting from phonology and proceeding thence to morphology and syntax, or in the inverse direction, starting at the "top" with syntax and working downward to morphology and eventually to phonology. Each of these procedures has its advantages and disadvantages. The first is useful for a presentation using the IA approach, and makes it possible to give a thorough description of the underlying phonological structure of a language before proceeding to describe, in terms of the phonemic units involved, its morphology and syntax. Some analysts consider that each level of linguistic description must be kept absolutely separate from the others, and that each must be described exhaustively before proceeding to the next higher level, in order to avoid aprioristic procedures (i.e., assuming that the reader knows in advance what is coming next). The opposite approach, starting with syntax, is favored by other scholars, including the practitioners of transformation grammar, who do not mind aprioristic techniques of description and who wish to describe structure in terms of unfolding and increasingly complex expansions of syntactic kernels and their "realization" in forms and sounds. The first of these approaches, starting from phonology and going "upward" to morphology and syntax, is on the whole preferable, and will be followed in our presentation.

NOTES

Levels of linguistic structure: Hockett, 1958, Chap. 16.

Role of meaning in linguistic analysis: Bloomfield, 1933a, passim; Fries, 1954, 1961; Harris, 1951.

Italian "imperative": Huber-Sauter, 1951.

Synchronic vs. diachronic: De Saussure, 1916, passim; Wells, 1947.

IA and IP approach: Hockett, 1954.

7

Phonetics

IF WE ARE to "start from the bottom" (pp. 31–32), our first concern must be to analyze the sounds with which humans speak. Clearly it will not do, for several reasons, to begin our analysis simply with the letters used in our conventional spelling. The twenty-six letters of the Roman alphabet are by no means sufficient to represent even all the sounds of the English language, to say nothing of all those which the human vocal apparatus is able to produce. Furthermore, the use which our conventional spelling makes of these twenty-six letters is, in many instances, inconsistent and capricious, so that we could not base any rational or accurate analysis on them, either in alphabetical order or in any other. How, for example, would we go about analyzing "the sound of the letter *c*," when it is used in so many different values (as in *carrot, cent, indict,* etc.) and when the sounds for which it stands are also represented by other letters, as in *karat* and *scent?* The result could only be a hopeless hodgepodge.

To analyze sounds, we must have a completely different basis, one connected in some way with the physical properties of the sounds themselves. Our folklore about language does include a series of terms based on general impressions and approximate comparisons of the effects produced by sounds with those produced by other phenomena on our senses of touch or vision. Thus, we often call a given sound "flat" or "broad" or "smooth" or "harsh" or "soft" or "hard" or "bright" or "dark." But these terms are unsatisfactory, simply because they are purely impressionistic, and do not mean the same thing to one person as they do to another. Speaking of a "broad *a*" may suggest one thing (e.g., the vowel sound of *ah*) to one person, and another (perhaps the vowel sound of *flat*) to someone else. In French, the word *grasseyer*, meaning literally "to fatten", has been used for a great many different kinds of *r*-like sounds, so that in the end there was no way of knowing what was meant by it; the phonetician Kr. Nyrop suggested that the best definition would be "a term, generally contemptuous, which people apply to other people's pronunciation; those who pronounce *r* in any given way, use the word *grasseyer* to describe any other way of pronouncing the said consonant." Trying to describe sounds in auditory, impressionistic terms is likely to give about as accurate results as describing chemical elements in terms of their smells. The impressions we get through our senses of hearing and smell cannot be stated in clear and analyzable enough terms to be of any use in scientific work.

These impressions are, however, produced by certain specific properties of the sound-waves in the air, as they strike our ear-drums. It has always seemed, to phoneticians, desirable to analyze the properties of the sound waves themselves, in their acoustic qualities. However, until recently, all efforts to find a satisfactory basis for such a study have been vain, because the human ear alone is not equipped to do so, and adequate machines have not been available. On the other hand, from the mid-nineteenth century onward, analytical techniques, based primarily on the study of human anatomy, have been available for analyzing sounds in terms of the parts of the body used in producing them. From the fact that we analyze the physiology of the articulation of sound, this kind of analysis is known as *physiological* or *articulatory* phonetics. It affords a reasonably exact basis for the analysis of sounds, since it is far more exact to classify a sound as being made, say, with the top of the tongue raised against the rear of the palate than it is to call it "hard" or "scratchy."

The study of articulatory phonetics is, therefore, based first of all on a detailed enumeration and classification of the organs of the body used in making speech-sounds, the so-called "organs of speech" (see Chap. 8). The knowledge of the organs of speech, their relation to each other, and the way in which they are used in speaking, affords a universal framework in which the sounds of all languages can be classified. This is possible because all human beings, no matter what race or other sub-division they belong to, have the same organs of speech, and can make whatever sounds are customary in the language they are brought up speaking. Our folklore about language includes the notion that some sounds are "impossible to pronounce," or that innate differences of physiological structure make people of a certain group inherently incapable of pronouncing certain sounds found in languages spoken by people of other groups. Thus, some whites believe themselves "unable" to make the differences in the pitch of individual syllables found in Chinese and in many Southeast Asian, African, and American Indian languages; Tuscans believe themselves hereditarily unable to pronounce word-final consonant sounds; etc. These notions are quite unfounded. A white child brought up in China among speakers of Chinese will learn to speak exactly as they do; a child of Tuscan parents brought up speaking English from his earliest years will have no difficulty at all in pronouncing word-final consonants. A slightly more sophisticated version of this same folkloristic notion is found in a recent attempt by a physiologist to show a statistical correlation between blood-group types and the presence or absence of the "th" sounds in the world's languages; the effort failed, because of naïve misunderstanding of the distribution of national languages and their dialects.

In analytical work, and in presenting the findings of phonetic analysis, it is convenient to have a written representation correlated with the sounds we observe and classify—a representation in which each graphic symbol will be used in a one-to-one correspondence with the sound it represents, without the inconsistencies, "silent letters," or other caprices which trouble our conventional orthographies. A set of graphic symbols giving a consistent representation of speech-sounds is a *phonetic transcription;* to make it clear that letters used as part of a phonetic transcription do not represent conventional spelling or any other kind of transcription, they are usually set off by square brackets, [   ]. The symbols used in phonetic transcriptions are usually those of our familiar Roman alphabet, expanded, wherever necessary, by the addition of new letters or by the alteration of familiar letters. (There have been a few systems of phonetic transcription whose authors tried to avoid all use of the Roman alphabet, insofar as it represents sounds; but such systems have proven too complicated and unwieldy for general use.) For the newcomer to linguistics, the greatest hurdle to overcome, in using a phonetic transcription, is the difficulty he experiences in realizing that its symbols must be used consistently, e.g. that *cent* must always be transcribed as ['sɛnt], even when the resultant transcription goes counter to our deeply ingrained habits of orthography.

To provide new symbols for phonetic transcriptions, letters can be taken over from other alphabets, such as the Greek or the Old English: for instance, we use the Greek theta [θ] to stand for the first sound of *thin*, and the Old English letter [ð] for the first sound of *this*. We can turn a letter upside down or on its side, e.g. in using [ə] for the last sound of *sofa*, or [ɔ] for the vowel sound of *law*. Small capital or italic letters may be assigned special values, as in the use of [ɪ] for the vowel sound of *bit*. We can change some part of a letter's shape, e.g., lengthening the right-hand leg of the letter *n* to make a special symbol [ŋ] for the sound usually spelled *ng*, or curving the bottom part of the letter *z* down and around to make a symbol for the middle consonant sound of *measure*, the *zh*-sound [ʒ]. We can put various small marks (often called "diacritics" or "diacritical marks") such as accent-marks, dots, small straight or curved lines, etc., either above, below, alongside or through a letter. In this way, we can use the letter *s* with an inverted circumflex accent (a "wedge"), forming the symbol [š], standing for the last sound of *mash;* or the letter *o* with two dots over it to stand for the vowel sound of French *peur:* "fear" [ö]. Sometimes a line is written through a letter to indicate some special kind of sound, as in the symbol [ł] to stand for an *l*-sound pronounced in the back of the mouth, as we usually do in American English *full.*

There have been many phonetic transcriptions devised in the last hundred and fifty years, such as Lepsius' alphabet, designed in Germany in the mid-nineteenth century and used very widely for recording native languages in former German colonies; the alphabet of the American Anthropological Association, used for American Indian languages; the International Phonetic Alphabet (abbreviated IPA); and others, including quite a number of partial modifications of the IPA, such as Kenyon's version adapted to American English (and further modified by Pike), or Trager and Smith's. The designers of the IPA originally intended it to be full enough to cover all the possible sounds of human speech; at the end of the last century and the beginning of this, it attained very wide currency among phoneticians and language-teachers, and is used in most beginning language books, in a great many foreign-language dictionaries, and in a few English-English dictionaries, such as the Kenyon-Knott *Pronouncing Dictionary of American English*. (Most ordinary dictionaries, however, do not use a true phonetic transcription, but resort to the makeshift expedient of simply putting one kind of mark or another over conventional spelling.)

The IPA, however, is not *the* phonetic alphabet, in the sense of being the only possible or permissible one, as some phoneticians and language teachers seem to think. It has certain drawbacks, especially in its original promulgators' insistence on avoiding diacritical marks (which has led to a tremendous proliferation of variations in graphic shapes for phonetic symbols, as more and more unfamiliar sounds had to be represented). The IPA or any other phonetic transcription can be modified as necessary, as long as the fundamental principle of consistency in representing sounds is observed. In our chapters on phonetics (7 through 14), we shall use a modified IPA, as is the practice of most present day linguistic analysts.

Even during the period when articulatory phonetics was developing most rapidly (at the end of the nineteenth century and the beginning of the twentieth), some scholars were dissatisfied with a classification of sounds wholly in terms of the mechanism used in their production. Such a classification, it was suspected, was not complete or wholly accurate, because observers noted that sounds could often be produced in more than one way. For instance, the French *u*-sound (as in *mur:* "wall") is usually described as a "high-front-rounded" vowel, because in its production the top of the tongue is normally high in the front of the mouth and the lips are rounded; yet many Frenchmen make a perfectly normal *u* with lips rounded only partially or not at all. Hence some analysts tried to set up, even before techniques of accurate measurement were available, a set of categories of acoustic characteristics by which to classify sounds. This primitive acoustic classification involved setting up such oppositions as "acute" vs. "grave," "compact" vs. "diffuse," etc., which were uncomfortably reminiscent of the impressionistic terms like "smooth," "harsh" and so forth whose merits we have already discussed (p. 36).

In the nineteen-forties, greatly improved techniques of mechanical analysis became available for the acoustic study of speech-sounds, especially with the *sound spectrograph*. This machine produces *sound spectrograms*, or schematic representations of the intensity and the frequencies of the harmonics (the *formants*) involved in vowel sounds (vocoids), and also of the types of interruptions which constitute consonant sounds (contoids). It was expected, when the sound spectrograph first became available, that the results of acoustic phonetics would disprove many of the theories hitherto held by phoneticians of the articulatory school, and would provide a more satisfactory basis for the classification of sounds in terms of their inherent characteristics. Actually, sound spectrograms have revealed many new and unsuspected facts concerning the nature of the sounds themselves and the transitions between them in the flow of speech. However, the acoustic approach has not brought about the complete revolution in phonetics that was expected of it. On the contrary, its results have, by and large, confirmed the validity of the articulatory approach, especially in showing that the position of articulation of vowel sounds (Chap. 9) correlates closely with the characteristics of the formants of these sounds. Articulatory and acoustic approaches work hand in hand, not in opposition to each other, in modern phonetic analysis.

The terms which are used in articulatory phonetics to describe the positions and manners in which sounds are produced serve essentially to label the processes by which the phonetician or his pupils learn to imitate the sounds they are describing; hence these terms have been described as "imitation-labels." Thus, when we speak of French *u* as a "high-front-rounded" vowel sound, we are saying that it is the type of sound which we imitate with the top of our tongue and our lips in the position referred to by that label. The "imitation-label" technique, based on articulatory analysis with additional data from acoustic research, is still the most effective approach to phonetic description, and is that which will be followed in the ensuing chapters.

NOTES

General Phonetics: Heffner, 1952; Kaiser (ed.), 1957; Pike, 1943; Smalley, 1961–62; Wise, 1957.

French "grasseyer": Nyrop, 1902, p. 48.

"Th" groups: Darlington, 1947, 1961; Brosnahan, 1961.

Phonetic transcriptions appear regularly in *Le Maître Phonétique; American Speech* used to have a section of each issue devoted to transcriptions of different varieties of American English.

History of IPA alphabet: Albright, 1958.

Acoustic phonetics: Hockett, 1958, Chap. 5; Joos, 1948; Pulgram, 1959.

8

The Organs of Speech

THE PROCESS OF SPEAKING involves modifying the column of air which enters and leaves our lungs as we breathe, thus producing audible sounds. Hence essentially all of the human respiratory tract is included in the "organs of speech." In general, speech-sounds are made on outgoing breath, although in a few languages (such as Hottentot), there are genuine speech-sounds, often called "clicks," made on ingoing air, and even whole syllables pronounced on entering breath have been attested from Maidu, an American

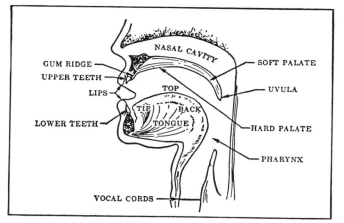

FIG. 2: The Organs of Speech (Cross-Section).

Indian language. The column of air or *breath-stream* is modified, on its way to or (usually) from the lungs by various portions of the respiratory tract through which it passes. Fig. 2 gives schematic representation of a cross section of the parts of the body involved, from the vocal cords upward.

We shall trace the course of the breath-stream on its way upward and outward from the lungs, and shall enumerate and discuss the organs of speech in the order in which the breath-stream passes them. We must begin, however, below the lungs, with the diaphragm, which controls the expansion and contraction of the lungs in breathing and, according to some phoneticians, is involved in the production of the chest-pulses on which the division of syllables is based (cf. Chap. 11). The lungs themselves simply serve as a source for air, which passes upward out of the lungs through the bronchial tubes and the trachea (or windpipe). On its way through the trachea, the air passes through a box-like structure of cartilage called the larynx (more commonly known as the "Adam's apple") which contains the vocal cords.

The vocal cords are two movable membranes—not really cords like the strings of a piano or violin, but mucous membranes, attached to the sides of the larynx. They can either lie along the side of the larynx without making any sound; or be brought together completely to shut off the passage of the breath; or be brought together partially, letting the breath-stream pass but vibrating as it passes and thus setting up sound waves. The adjective referring to the larynx is *laryngeal* or *glottal;* a complete stoppage of the breath-stream by the vocal cords is called a *glottal stop* or *glottal catch* (such as we make between the two *oh*'s of "Oh-oh!" when said in surprise or reproof). The sound waves resulting from the vibration of the vocal cords are known as *voice;* a sound accompanied by voice (usually all vocoids and many contoids, like English *b, d, v, z*) is called a *voiced* sound; one not accompanied by voice (like English *p, t, f, s*) is termed *voiceless.* The tension of the vocal cords determines *pitch;* the force with which air is expelled from the lungs determines the *volume* of a sound.

Once it has passed the vocal cords on its way out of the lungs, the breath stream passes various points in the pharynx, nose, and mouth, at any which the column of air can be modified and sound-waves can be set up, either by the formation of resonance-chambers or by specific obstructions of one kind or another. At the top of the throat, the *pharynx* can be constricted, by the back of the tongue being brought close to or in contact with the back wall of the throat; sounds made in this position (known as *pharyngeal* sounds) are found, for example, in Arabic. Above the pharynx, at the back of the oral and nasal cavities and serving to close off or admit air to the nasal cavity, is a flap of flesh known as the *velum*, from which there hangs down a movable tip, the *uvula*. A sound made by contact with or near the velum is termed *velar*. The backmost part of the velum is known as the *velic*, and is involved in shutting off the nasal cavity (see next paragraph).

In the nasal cavity there are no points at which an obstruction can be made or the breath-stream otherwise modified, but the whole nasal cavity can be brought into play as a resonance-chamber by lowering the velum and opening the velic so as to allow the breath stream to pass into the nose; a sound with nasal resonance thus added is called *nasalized*, and the effect produced is *nasalization*. Those who have just had adenoids removed find it impossible to close off the nasal cavity completely with the velic, and some speakers (not only of American English, as our folklore has it, but of other languages as well) never acquire the habit of closing the velic completely, so that they give a certain amount of nasalization to all their speech (they "talk through the nose," like the old comedy figures of New England farmers such as Uncle Josh or Farmer Hayseed). On the other hand, if we have a cold and cannot let the breath into the nose at all because the uvula is inflamed or the nasal passages are blocked by mucus, we cannot use the nasal cavity as a resonance chamber even in such sounds as *n* and *m* which are normally nasalized, and we say, for instance, "sprig is cubbig" instead of "spring is coming."

Most of the points at which the breath stream can be modified are located in the mouth or *oral cavity;* sounds made in the mouth without nasalization are hence called *oral,* in contradistinction to *nasal* sounds, which involve nasalization in addition to other types of modification. The chief movable organ inside the oral cavity is the tongue, whose importance is so great as to have caused speakers of many languages to consider it as the prime factor in speech (as witness the widespread identity between words for "tongue" and those for "language," including Latin and Italian *lingua,* French *langue,* Spanish *lengua,* Russian *jazýk,* etc., and even English *tongue* in expressions like "the German tongue"). The tongue is an extremely mobile fleshy organ, which can be raised and lowered; we can raise and lower either the front or the middle or the back of the tongue, and we can do this either in the center of the tongue, on its sides, or all at once. Articulations made with the tongue are called *lingual,* although this term is not much used.

Since so many parts of the tongue are used in articulation, we have special nouns and adjectives to refer to them. Phoneticians distinguish four parts of the upper surface of the tongue as being important in making contact or near-contact with the roof of the mouth: from back to front, they are the back; the rear of the top part, or *dorsum;* the *front* of the top part; and the tip or *apex.* (Do not confuse the "front," which is on the top of the tongue, with the tip, which is the part that makes contact with the lower front teeth when the tongue is depressed.) To the three italicized terms correspond the adjectives *dorsal, frontal,* and *apical,* respectively. In pronouncing some types of sounds found in languages of India and elsewhere, the tip of the tongue is curled upward and backward, in a *retroflex*—or *domal*—articulation. In sounds like English *s* and *sh,* the center of the tongue is depressed, forming a trough or rill through which the air passes, making a hissing sound; such sounds are called *sibilants.* In pronouncing *l,* on the other hand, we normally keep the center of the tongue pressed against the roof of the mouth but depress one or both sides of the tongue, in a *lateral* articulation. Any articulation in which the tongue is raised towards the roof of the mouth is called *high,* and one in which it is lowered is of course called *low.* Similarly, the terms *front* and *back* refer to articulations in which the tongue is moved to those parts of the mouth.

Corresponding to the areas of the upper surface of the tongue which we have just mentioned, are a series of regions in the roof of the mouth. From back to front, these are: the velum, or "soft palate"; the front or "hard" palate; the gum-ridge or alveolum; and the upper front teeth. (It is rare for the lower teeth to be involved in the articulation of sounds within the oral cavity.) For sounds made in the region of the velum, the customary adjective is *velar,* but *postpalatal* and *guttural* are also widely used. For sounds made in the other three regions which we have just mentioned, the normal adjectives are *palatal*, *alveolar*, and *dental*. On occasion, it is necessary to distinguish also the middle region of the palate between the soft palate and the hard palate; articulations made here are called *medio-palatal*. If the tongue is pushed out of the oral cavity between the upper and lower teeth (as in the English sounds spelled *th*), the resultant sounds are termed *interdental*. Out beyond the front teeth are the lips; if both lips are involved in the articulation, it is called *bilabial*, but if only one (usually the lower) lip is involved, the adjective *labial* is used. We find, on occasion, combined adjectives to indicate that more than one region is involved in an articulation simultaneously: thus, *labio-dental* refers to a sound involving both lips and teeth at the same time (normally the upper teeth against the lower lip, as in English *f* and *v*), and *labio-velar* to one in which lips and velum are both brought into play at once (e.g. [kw], usually spelled *qu* in English, as in *quick*).

It must be emphasized that, except for the vocal cords, all of the regions of the organs of speech which we have been discussing have no sharply defined limits. They are, rather, areas in the anatomical tracts involved, which can be identified approximately, but which (especially in the case of the tongue and roof of the mouth) shade off imperceptibly into each other. As a result, it is not possible to identify the place of articulation of any given sound with mathematical precision; we often speak of "points" of articulation, but this is simply a somewhat loose use of the term, which sometimes gives rise to the impression that more exactness can be attained in phonetic description than is actually the case. The number of separate "points" of articulation is virtually infinite, and hence it is not possible to establish a definite number of sounds which the human vocal apparatus is capable of producing. We shall see (cf. Chap. 14) that this situation in phonetics contrasts sharply with the fact that each language has a clearly definable, limited number of functional units of sound (phonemes), and is one of the major reasons why linguistic analysts find it advisable to separate sharply the treatment of phonetics from that of phonemics. Specifically because of the infinite gradation possible within the raw material of speech-sounds, some linguists have even declared that phonetics does not belong to linguistics proper; but such an attitude depends on an excessive restriction of the field of linguistics to an exclusive analysis of functional units on the emic level.

It is also important to note, from the point of view of general linguistic theory, that none of the organs of speech have linguistic use as their prime or original function. The diaphragm, lungs, and nose serve the purpose of breathing; the vocal cords, that of shutting off the passage of breath out of the lungs (as we can observe when pushing hard against some object we are trying to move). The oral cavity serves primarily for the intake of food; the lips for shutting off the oral cavity from the outside; the velum for shutting off the nasal cavity from the oral cavity, and thus preventing particles of food from getting back up into the nose; and the teeth and tongue for maneuvering food, one for chewing it, the other for moving it backward in the mouth. It is quite clear that, in the long-range development of mankind, the function of the "organs of speech" is only secondary, and hence must have developed quite late in the evolution of the human race. The use of oral–auditory signalling was aided by the fact that it is perceptible under many more conditions, and less favorable ones (e.g., darkness), than other types of signalling (e.g., visual, to say nothing of tactile or olfactory). Its specialization in the respiratory tract was clearly helped by the presence there of so many movable organs, located close together in a relatively small portion of the human anatomy, whose movements can be closely coordinated together so as to produce an almost infinite number of modifications of the breath-stream. It has been said that each of us, in everyday speech, performs all the time an even more complicated and even more delicately adjusted series of movements than does a "one-man orchestra" in playing a whole ensemble of instruments at once on the vaudeville stage.

NOTES

Organs of speech: Gleason, 1961, Chap. 15; Hockett, 1958, Chap. 7.

Terminology and symbols: Trager, 1958 (with, however, a not always fortunate choice of symbols).

9

Vocoids

IT HAS BEEN CUSTOMARY in phonology to speak of "vowels" and "consonants," on no matter what level (phonetic, phonemic, or orthographic), and then, if necessary, to distinguish, as we have been doing so far, between, say, "vowel sounds," "vowel phonemes," and "vowel letters" (and likewise for consonants). However, this procedure often leads to confusion, so that at present many phoneticians prefer to have special terms for what are normally called "vowel sounds" and "consonant sounds." These two terms are *vocoid* and *contoid*, respectively; we shall henceforth use these words when referring to sounds on the strictly phonetic level.

In classifying speech-sounds, we distinguish two main types: those in which the organs of speech (primarily the tongue) are used to form resonance chambers through which the breath-stream passes without any audible friction being produced; and those in which the breath-stream is obstructed in one way or another to produce audible friction, either by stopping the passage of air entirely for a fraction of a second or by forcing it into narrow channels. The type of sound which involves only resonance is termed a *vocoid* ("vowel sound"); that involving audible friction, a *contoid* ("consonant sound"). There are also intermediate stages between these two types, which may be called *semivocoids* or *semicontoids*.

In the production of vocoids, the most important single factor is the position of the top (not the tip!) of the tongue in the oral cavity. It is most convenient to start our description with what may be called "purely oral" vocoids, i.e., those whose quality depends only on the positions assumed by the top of the tongue inside the mouth and on the position of the lips. The top of the tongue may vary in its position along two axes, that of *tongue-height* (from *high* to *low*) and that of *tongue-advancement* (from the *front* to the *center* to the *back* of the mouth); the lips may be either *rounded* (puckered out) or *unrounded* (drawn back). Vocoids are therefore normally classified according to these three criteria: tongue-height (high, mid, low); tongue-advancement (front, central, back); and lip-rounding (rounded, unrounded). In representing the position of vocoid articulations relative to each other, we normally set up charts or diagrams (e.g., Fig. 3 ff.) in which the various phonetic symbols are placed higher or lower on the page in accordance with the height of the top of the tongue, and to the left if the sound is articulated in the front of the mouth and to the right if in the back of the mouth.

If the top of the tongue is raised high in the front of the mouth, with lips unrounded and rather sharply drawn back, the resultant vocoid is that spelled *i* in French *machine* [ma'ʃin] or *ici* [i'si] "here", or Italian *vita* ['vi:ta] "life". Such a vocoid is termed *high-front-unrounded*, and is normally transcribed [i]. A vocoid pronounced with the top of the tongue high, but raised in the back of the mouth, and with the lips sharply rounded, is the sound spelled *ou* in French (e.g., *bout* [bu] "end", *mou* [mu] "soft") and *u* in Italian (as in *muro* ['mu:ro] "wall"), and customarily transcribed [u]. With the top of the tongue low in the mouth, in central position, and with lips unrounded (but markedly drawn back), we produce a vocoid transcribed [a], as in Italian *amare* [a'ma:re] "to love". If we arrange these three symbols [i], [u], [a] in a schematic representation such as that described at the end of the preceding paragraph, we obtain a triangle-shaped diagram (Fig. 3), which is often known in traditional phonetics as the "vowel triangle." We may perhaps redub it the "the vocoid triangle," for the sake of consistency.

The vocoid triangle furnishes the basic framework within which the other oral vocoid articulations can be fitted. A vocoid with front and unrounded articulation, but with the top of the tongue in the mid-range of height, is a

	FRONT UNROUNDED	CENTRAL UNROUNDED	BACK ROUNDED
High	i		u
Low		a	

FIG. 3: The Vocoid Triangle.

mid-front-unrounded vocoid, usually transcribed with the symbol [e] or a variant thereof (cf. below). The parallel vocoid in the mid-back range, with lips rounded (but usually not so much as for [u]), is normally assigned the symbol [o] or a variant thereof. The mid-range of tongue-height can be subdivided further into two main varieties: high-mid and low-mid. The high-mid sounds are often articulated with nearly the same type of lip-rounding as the high vowels, but with the top of the tongue somewhat lower. The symbol [e] is usually reserved for the high-mid-front-unrounded vocoid, as in French *été* [ète] "summer", or Italian *vero* ['ve:ro] "true"; and [o] is assigned to the high-mid-back-rounded sound of French *beau:* "beautiful", or Italian *voce:* "voice". The "broken" symbols [ɛ] and [ɔ] are assigned to low-mid varieties, in which the top of the tongue is in a lower position and the lips less markedly drawn back or less markedly rounded than for [e] and [o], respectively. We find [ɛ] in such words as French *bête* [bɛ:t] "animal", or Italian *festa* ['fɛsta] "feast"; and [ɔ] in Italian *forte* ['fɔrte] "strong". Fig. 4 shows the vocoid triangle expanded by the addition of these four high-mid and low-mid vocoids.

The vocoids pronounced with low tongue-height are not limited to [a], either. If the top of the tongue is raised rather slightly and brought towards the front of the mouth, a vocoid like that of English *hat*, *bat* results, normally transcribed [æ]: [hæt], [bæt]. However, if it is moved towards the back of the mouth, slightly raised, and with the lips rounded slightly, the resultant vocoid is like that of French *pâte:* "paste", for which the special symbol [ɑ] is used: [pɑːt]. The top of the tongue can also be raised in the center of the mouth; a vocoid produced in low-mid-central position, such as the last sound of English *sofa*, is transcribed [ə]: ['soᵘfə]. A somewhat higher variety, occurring in English only under stress, is often transcribed with an upside-down v, [ʌ], as in English *but* [bʌt]. A vocoid produced in high-central position, such as the Russian sound written ы in Cyrillic characters and named "yeri" in Russian terminology, transcribed [ɨ] (and often called, from the shape of the symbol, "barred eye"): e.g., Russian быть [bɨtʲ] "to be". These examples which we have cited for the centrally-articulated vocoids involve nonrounded lips, but lip-rounded central vowels also occur,

	FRONT UNROUNDED	CENTRAL UNROUNDED	BACK ROUNDED
High	i		u
High-Mid	e		o
Low-Mid	ɛ		ɔ
Low		a	

Fig. 4: The Vocoid Triangle (Expanded).

	FRONT UNROUNDED	CENTRAL UNROUNDED	BACK ROUNDED
High	[i]	[ɨ]	[u]
High-Mid	[e]	[ʌ]	[o]
Low-Mid	[ɛ]	[ə]	[ɔ]
Low	[æ]	[a]	[ɑ]

Fig. 5: The Vocoid Quadrilateral.

as in the [ӧ] of French *le* [lӧ] "him—it" (as in *faites-le* [fɛt'lӧ] "do it!"). Central rounded vocoids are often transcribed with a diaeresis (two dots) placed over the symbol for the nonrounded variety. When we add the vocoids discussed in this paragraph to our schematic representation, the resultant diagram is no longer a triangle but a quadrilateral, as shown in Fig. 5.

Nor is the correlation of front articulation with unrounded lips, or of back articulation, always the only kind found. In many languages (e.g., French, German, the Scandinavian languages, Hungarian, etc.), there are vocoids which are uttered with the tongue raised in the front of the mouth but with the lips rounded at the same time. For the high-front-rounded variety, the IPA symbol is [y]: e.g., French *mur* [myr] "wall", or German *Hüte* ['hyːtə] "hats"; for the high-mid-front-rounded vocoid, it is [ø], as in French *feu* [fø] "fire", or German *König* ['køːniç] "king"; and for the low-mid-front-rounded sound, it is [œ], as in French *peur* [pœːʀ] "fear", or German *Köln* [kœln] "Cologne (the city)". Some phoneticians, however, prefer the symbols [ü], [ö], and [öˇ], respectively (for the symbol of lowering,

[ʼ], see later in this chapter). It is also possible to have the opposite type of correlation, back articulation with unrounded lips; certain types of British and Commonwealth English show back-unrounded vocoids. For the high-back-unrounded variety, the upside-down *m* is used: [ɯ], as in some British or Commonwealth pronunciations of *room* [rɯm]. For the mid-back-unrounded vocoids, if necessary, [ɣ] can be used, with or without signs of raising or lowering. The complete set of symbols for the positions and correlations we have been discussing, in an expanded vocoid quadrilateral, is shown in Fig. 6.

To the basic types of vocoid articulation discussed so far, other elements are on occasion added. The most frequent of these is *nasalization* (cf. p. 42): any vocoid can occur nasalized as well as non-nasalized. In most languages, there is at least a slight degree of nasalization in vocoids adjacent to nasal contoids (cf. Chap. 10), but in many (e.g., French, Portuguese, Polish), there are clear contrasts on the phonetic level between some vocoids that are virtually free from nasalization and others that have it. The most widely

	FRONT UN-ROUNDED	FRONT ROUNDED	CENTRAL UN-ROUNDED	CENTRAL ROUNDED	BACK UN-ROUNDED	BACK ROUNDED
High	[i]	[y] ([ü])	[ɨ]	[ɨ]	[ɯ]	[u]
High-Mid	[e]	[ø] ([ö])	[ʌ]	[ӣ]	[ɣ]	[o]
Low-Mid	[ɛ]	[œ] [(öˇ)]	[ə]	[ɜ]	[ɣˇ]	[ɔ]
Low	[æ]		[a]			[ɑ]

Fɪɢ. 6: The Vocoid Quadrilateral (Expanded).

used phonetic symbol for nasalization is the til [~], written over the symbol for the corresponding oral vocoid, e.g., [ẽ] for the mid-high-front-unrounded nasal vocoid, as in Portuguese *bem* [bẽ] "well". Occasionally we find, to indicate nasalization, a small raised n following the phonetic symbol, or a hook written under it, e.g. [eⁿ] or [ę] for the sound just discussed.

Retroflexion can occur with some vocoids, especially those in the mid-central range; here, retroflexion involves, not the bending back of the tongue tip, but the bunching of the tongue muscles upward and backward so as to raise the dorsum of the tongue towards the velum, at the same time as the mid-central articulation is maintained. This type of sound is heard in the various vocoids which are spelled *er, ir, ur* (e.g., in *berth, mirth, curse*) in those varieties of English where the [r] contoid is no longer pronounced at the end of a syllable (e.g., in standard British English, in the eastern part of New England and in much of the southeastern United States). The symbol for such a retroflexed [ə] is [ɚ], and the words given above, pronounced with this vocoid, would be transcribed [bɚθ], [mɚθ], [kɚs] respectively.

Another dimension of variation in vocoids is the contrast between *lax* and *tense* articulation. In some languages—English being the best example— there are series of vocoids in which the muscles of the tongue are lax, as opposed to other series in which they are held tense. (The difference between a lax vocoid and a tense one can be felt by putting the thumb and index finger around the bottom of the tongue muscles underneath the jaw, and feeling the difference in tension when pronouncing *bit* as opposed to *beat*.) In English, the vocoid of *beat* is tense, that of *bit* is lax; a parallel difference exists in the back-rounded series, with a tense vocoid in *boot* and a lax one in *book*. For the lax vocoids, small capital letters are often used as phonetic

	FRONT UN- ROUNDED TENSE	FRONT UN- ROUNDED LAX	CENTRAL UN- ROUNDED TENSE	CENTRAL UN- ROUNDED LAX	BACK ROUNDED LAX	BACK ROUNDED TENSE
High	[i]					[u]
		[ɪ]		[ɨ]	[ʊ]	
High-Mid	[e]		[ʌ]			[o]
Low-Mid		[ɛ]		[ə]	[ɔ]	
Low	[æ]			[a]	[ɑ]	

Examples:

VOCOID	PHONETIC TRANSCRIPTION	CONVENTIONAL SPELLING
[i]	[bit]	*beat*
[ɪ]	[bɪt]	*bit*
[e]	[bet]	*bait*
[ɛ]	[bɛt]	*bet*
[æ]	[bæt]	*bat*
[ʌ]	[bʌt]	*but*
[ɪ]	[dʒɪst]	*jist* *
[ə]	['sofə]	*sofa*
[a]	[hai]	*high*
[ɑ]	['fɑðr̩]	*father*
[ɔ]	[bɔt]	*bought*
[o]	[bot]	*boat*
[ʊ]	[bʊk]	*book*
[u]	[but]	*boot*

FIG. 7: English Vocoids (with Examples).

symbols, [ɪ] for the vocoid of *bit* [bɪt], and [ʊ] for that of *book* [bʊk]. According to some analyses of English, the [ɛ], [ɔ], and [ə] sounds are also lax in their articulation and belong in the same series with [ɪ] and [ʊ]. The entire range of English vocoids is shown Fig. 7, with examples in phonetic transcription and conventional spelling for easy identification.

Both vocoids and contoids can occur *short* or *long*, i.e., with an actual difference in the number of milliseconds taken in their articulation. In German, for instance, the vocoids of *Stadt:* "city" and *Staat:* "state" differ only in that the second is approximately twice the length of the first. A long sound is

* As in some people's pronunciation of *That's jist too bad!*.

normally marked by a colon [:] written after the symbol for the sound involved: thus, Ger. *Stadt* is transcribed [ʃtat] and *Staat* [ʃtaːt]. Apparently the vocoids of Latin were ten, five short and five long, each pair differentiated only in length: e.g., *vīta* ['wiːta] "life", but *fidēs* ['fideːs] "faith", and similarly for the other four pairs of vocoids. This distinction was so fundamental in Latin phonology as to have served for the basis of the prosodic system according to which Latin poetry was written. In English, many speakers make differences in the length of vocoids, but normally these differences are correlated either with the nature of the following contoid (voiced or voiceless), or with stress or other types of emphasis: e.g., *pick* [pɪk] (with short vocoid before voiceless contoid), but *pig* [pɪːg] (with longer vocoid before voiced contoid). If a sound is somewhat longer than "short," but not fully "long," it is termed "half-long," and indicated by a raised dot [·] placed after the phonetic symbol involved: some speakers of English say [pɪ·g] rather than [pɪːg]. In the other direction, in some languages (e.g., Esthonian), we find vocoids which are even longer than ordinary "long" vocoids; such "over-long" sounds are marked with a colon and a raised dot, or with two colons, following the symbol for the sound involved: e.g., [eː·] or [eːː]. Needless to say, there are infinite gradations in phonetic length, and the colon and the raised dot are only approximate indications of the main phonetic contrasts which are possible.

On occasion, to indicate even finer shades of difference in tongue height and advancement than those we have been describing, phoneticians use special marks in phonetic transcription, placing these marks after the phonetic symbols to which they refer. To indicate a sound with a slightly higher articulation than normal, we use a raised carat [ˆ], and for a slightly lower one, the same mark inverted [ˇ]. The raised carat placed on its side serves to indicate a slight change in tongue-advancement, with the point facing left to indicate fronting: [ˈ], and facing right for backing: [ʼ]. With these marks, it is possible to indicate fairly minute shades of difference in sound; but no phonetic transcription can ever afford an exact indication of all the most minute degrees of shading, especially in vocoids. (The English phonetician Henry Sweet, the prototype of Henry Higgins in Shaw's *Pygmalion* and *My Fair Lady*, is said to have been able to distinguish around 120 different vocoids by ear.)

The vocoids we have been discussing so far serve as centers of syllables (cf. Chap. 14). It is also possible for vocoids to occur, not as syllable-centers, but adjacent to other vocoids which have this function; in such instances, the vocoids which are not acting as syllable-centers are termed *semivocoids* if they do not involve audible friction, or *semicontoids* if they do. A combination of full vocoid (i.e., one acting as the center of a syllable) plus a semivocoid or semicontoid is termed a *phonetic diphthong;* if two semivocoids or semicontoids are involved, we have a *phonetic triphthong.* Usually, the semivocoids or semicontoids involved are those corresponding to the high vocoids [i], [y], and [u]; on occasion, however, lower positions of articulation are also found.

To indicate the semivocoids in transcription, the mark [ˬ] is usually placed under the symbol for the corresponding vocoid: thus, [i̯] as in English *high* [hai̯], [u̯] as in *how* [hau̯]. For [y̯], we may cite Dutch *huis* [hœys] "house"; for [ɛ̞], Roumanian *seară* ['sɛ̞arə] "evening"; and for [ɔ̞], Roumanian *poartă* ['pɔ̞artə] "door". British English has semivocoid [ə̯], corresponding to American English [r] after certain vocoids, e.g., *here* [hɪə̯]. For semicontoids, separate phonetic symbols are customarily used, especially [j] for that articulated in the position of [i], as in Eng. *yet* [jɛt] (some phoneticians, those whose use [ü] for the high-front-rounded vocoid, prefer to use [y] for this semivocoid); [w] for the one corresponding to [u], as in English *wet* [wɛt]; and [ɥ] (an upside-down h; some phoneticians prefer [ü̯]) for the semicontoid corresponding to [y], as in French *huit* [ɥit] "eight". Voiceless semicontoids, indicated by a little circle placed underneath the phonetic symbol, or else by a separate character, also occur widely, as in French *Pierre* [pjɛ̥ːr] "Peter", *toit* [twḁ] "roof", and *puis* [pɥ̥i]: "then". The German "Ich-Laut" is a voiceless high-front-unrounded semicontoid [j̊] (in manuals of German phonetics, normally transcribed [ç], as in *ich* [ij̊] or [iç] "I").

After the tense vocoids [i] and [e], English has "off-glides" involving the gliding forward and upward of the top of the tongue, and after [u] and [o], similar "off-glides" involving a gliding backward and upward. There has been an extensive debate among phonologists—not yet fully resolved—about the status of these tense vocoids, from both the phonetic and the phonemic point of view: are English [i], [e], [u] and [o] diphthongs or are they not? Those who insist that they are, emphasize the existence of the off-glides and equate these latter with the semivocoids [i̯] and [u̯], respectively; on the other hand, those who prefer to consider English [i], [e], [u] and [o] as simple vocoids (monophthongs), minimize the existence of these off-glides and point out that in some varieties of English (especially North Central American) these vocoids have virtually no off-glides at all. In transcribing these four vocoids, we may perhaps, in very narrow transcription, indicate the off-glides by small raised characters, and thus avoid committing ourselves definitively one way or the other: e.g., *beat* [biʲt], *bait* [beʲt], *boot* [buʷt], and *boat* [boʷt].

In diphthongs, the semivocoid or semicontoid element can occur either before or after the full vocoid, as can be see in the examples cited in the next to the last preceding paragraph. In triphthongs, normally one semivocoid or semicontoid element precedes the center of the syllable and one follows, as in English *wow* [wau̯] or in Italian words like *mièi* [mjɛi̯] "my, mine (m. pl.)", *tuòi* [twɔi̯] "thy, thine (m. pl.)", or *Chièuti* ['kjɛu̯ti] (name of a town). It is rare for two semivocoids to occur together following a vocoid, but such a combination is occasionally found, as in the Australian pronunciation of words which in American English have [o], e.g., *no* [nai̯ɯ̯], *soda* ['sai̯ɯdə].

NOTES

Vocoids: Hockett, 1958, Chap. 9.
Vowel-length in American English: Heffner, 1937–40.

10

Contoids

CONTOID ARTICULATIONS, as pointed out earlier, involve the production of audible friction, by the obstruction of the breath stream at one or more points along its passage outward from the lungs. We classify contoids according to three major criteria: the point at which the obstruction is made (*place of articulation*), the way in which it is made (*manner of articulation*), and the presence or absence of vibration in the larynx (*voicing*). Furthermore, it is often necessary to distinguish the various ways in which a contoid is articulated at one or more of the three stages of its pronunciation: the *onset* (attack, start), the *hold*, and the *release*. We have already enumerated (cf. Chap. 8) the main regions of the organs of speech which serve for distinguishing the point of articulation; in this chapter we shall be concerned primarily with the different manners in which contoids can be articulated.

The major division, in manner of articulation, is between those contoids in which the passage of air is entirely stopped for a fraction of a second (*stops*) and those in which the air continues to pass through some kind of restricted channel (*continuants*). A pure stop, or *plosive*, is one in which the release involves simply allowing the air to resume its passage with a slight explosion. Plosives can be made at any of the points of articulation we have discussed. One made in the larynx, normally voiceless, is symbolized by [ʔ]. It is possible to stop the breath-stream at the pharynx, by pressing the rear of the tongue against the back wall of the throat; such pharyngeal plosives occur in Arabic. The voiceless pharyngeal plosive is symbolized by [q] and the voiced variety by a special shape of the letter g, [ɢ]. In the back of the mouth, most articulations against the velum are made with the dorsum of the tongue, producing *dorso-velar* contoids such as the voiceless plosive [k] and the voiced plosive [g]. If necessary, we can distinguish between [k'], [k] and [k'], and between [g'], [g] and [g'] (for the marks ['] and ['], cf. p. 51).

In the forward part of the mouth, the top of the tongue can articulate stops against the palate (symbol for the voiceless frontal-palatal plosive, [c]; for the voiced variety, [ɟ]), although pure plosives in this position are fairly rare. Most stops in the forward part of the mouth are made with the tip or apex of the tongue: against the gum ridge (*apico-alveolar*), as in English [t] and [d] (voiceless and voiced, respectively); or against the inside of the upper front teeth (*apico-dental*), as in the [t] and [d] of French, Italian, Spanish, and many other languages. If necessary, these two articulations can be distinguished by adding the backing symbol ['] when transcribing the English apico-alveolars and writing them [t'] and [d'], but this distinction is rarely called for. The tip of the tongue may be retroflexed, as found in many languages of India, to make contact behind the gum ridge with the front part of the palate; a *retroflex apico-palatal voiceless* plosive is transcribed [ṭ], and the corresponding voiced plosive [ḍ]. In theory, stops could be made in the labio-dental position, with the upper teeth against the lower lip (or vice-versa), but in actuality, such stops occur only as substitutes for bilabial stops when a speaker is laughing so hard he cannot close his lips. Bilabial plosives are symbolized, the voiceless variety by [p], and the voiced by [b].

Among the continuants, we must distinguish a number of different types of contoids in accordance with the various ways in which the breath stream may be channeled to constrict it and produce audible friction. If the organs of speech are brought nearly together and the breath is forced out equally over the entire area of near contact, the resultant sound is a *fricative*. In English, we have voiceless and voiced fricatives in labio-dental position ([f] and [v] respectively) and in apico-interdental position. We have both voiceless and voiced apico-interdental fricatives, but the contrast between the two is masked by the use of *th* to represent both in spelling. The voiceless variety, as in *thin*, is transcribed with the Greek theta, [θ]; the voiced, as in *this*, either with Greek delta [δ] or with the letter "eth" borrowed from Old English orthography, [ð]. Fricatives can also be uttered at many other points, from the larynx all the way out to the lips. A voiceless glottal fricative is involved in "aspiration" (as at the beginning of *hit*, *hard*, etc.), transcribed [h], and its voiced counterpart (found in some languages of India), transcribed [ɦ]. Pharyngeal fricatives, voiceless [ḥ] and voiced [ɡ],* are found in Arabic. The voiceless velar fricative (transcribed [x] or with Greek chi [χ]) is found in many languages, e.g., Castilian Spanish, Russian, and German (in which latter it is called the "Ach-Laut"; the corresponding voiced fricative (transcribed [ɣ] or with Greek gamma [γ]) is less common, but is found in many varieties of Spanish, e.g. in *agua* ['aɣu̯a] "water". A palatal fricative is very close to the semicontoids [j] and [j̊] in articulation (cf. p. 52). Not only labio-dental, but also purely bilabial fricatives occur, the voiceless variety (transcribed with Greek phi [Φ] or with [p]) as in Japanese, and the voiced (transcribed with Greek beta [β] or with [ƀ] or with [b]), as in Spanish *haba* ['aβa] "bean".

Sibilants involve the depressing of the center of the tongue to form a channel or rill through which the air passes, making a hissing sound (cf. p. 43). The chief points of articulation for sibilants are the dental, alveolar, and palatal regions. English has the voiceless apico-dental sibilant [s] and its voiced counterpart [z], as in *sin* [sin] and *zebra* ['zibrə]; and the voiceless frontal-palatal sibilant, usually spelled *sh* but transcribed phonetically either with

---

* A bar is often written across a phonetic symbol for a plosive to indicate a fricative produced in the same position. Greek letters are also widely used for fricatives in phonetic transcription.

"long s" [ʃ] or with s with a wedge over it [š], as in *shin* [ʃɪn], [šɪn], and the corresponding voiced sound, often spelled *zh* at the beginning of Russian names like *Zhukov*, and transcribed [ʒ] or [ž], e.g., in *measure* ['mɛʒr̩], ['mɛžr̩]. (For continuants as syllable-centers, transcribed with dots underneath the phonetic symbol, cf. ch. 11.) In some languages, e.g., Castilian Spanish and the North Italian dialects in the Po valley, we also find voiceless and voiced apico-alveolar sibilants, transcribed [ŝ] and [ẑ] respectively. On occasion, the palatal sibilants are referred to half in jest as *shibilants* or as *hishing* sounds.

In *laterals*, the air passes out over one or both sides of the tongue. Here again, most laterals are made in the dental and palatal regions; furthermore, most are voiced. At the beginning of a syllable, most speakers of English have a voiced apico-dental or apico-alveolar lateral (symbol [l]): e.g., *like* [laɪk], *look* [lʊk]; most continental European languages have only this type of *l*-sound, often termed "bright *l*" from its acoustic effect. At the end of a syllable, however, most varieties of English have a "dark *l*" or "back *l*," made by bunching up the back of the tongue towards the velum, so as to allow the air to pass over the side(s) of the tongue in the rear of the mouth (symbol [ɫ]), as in *full* [fʊɫ], *fill* [fɪɫ]. There are some varieties of English (especially in Scotland) in which the "back *l*" occurs in all positions, e.g., *like* [ɫaɪk], *look* [ɫʊk]. A palatal *l*, usually articulated with the top rather than the tip of the tongue, occurs in many Romance languages (phonetic symbol (ʎ), [λ], [ĺ], or [ļ]), as in Spanish *calle* ['kaʎe] "street", Italian *figlia* ['fiʎ:a] "daughter", or Portuguese *filha* ['fiʎə] "daughter". This palatal [ʎ] often produces on the ears of speakers of English an effect similar to that of our [l] plus [j], as in *million* ['mɪljən]; however, a true palatal [ʎ] is a single contoid (not a sequence of two) and is made with the top of the tongue against the hard palate from the onset through the release. Voiceless laterals are found corresponding to all the voiced laterals just described, and are transcribed by placing a small circle underneath the appropriate phonetic symbol, as in French *peuple* [pœpl̥] "people".

In *nasal* continuants, the breath stream is interrupted at some point in the oral cavity or at the lips, while being allowed to enter the nose and create resonance there; almost all nasal contoids are voiced. The dorsal-velar nasal, spelled *ng* in English, is a single sound transcribed [ŋ], e.g., in *sing* [sɪŋ]; the frontal-palatal nasal [ɲ] is likewise a single sound, occurring in many Romance languages, e.g., Italian *vigna* ['viɲ:a] "vineyard", Spanish *daño* ['daɲo] "harm", Portuguese *minha* ['miɲə] "my (f. sg.)". English [n] is normally articulated in apico-alveolar position, with the tip of the tongue against the gum ridge, but in most continental European and many other languages it is apico-dental; both varieties are usually transcribed [n], but the alveolar nasal can be given the transcription [n˲] if necessary. A retroflex apico-palatal nasal [ṇ] is found in Sanskrit and many languages of India. We are familiar with the bilabial nasal [m] in English; Italian has also a labio-dental nasal [ɱ] in such words as *inferiore* [iɱfe'rjo:re] "lower". Voiceless nasals are theoretically possible in all these positions, and would be transcribed, as usual, placing the symbol for voicelessness [̥] below the appropriate phonetic symbol; in actuality, any voiceless nasal sounds simply like a snort. In certain interjections, we do use voiceless bilabial nasals, as in [m̥m], usually written *mf!* (expressing contempt), or ['m̥m̥m], written *mphm!* (indicating agreement, often grudging).

In *trills*, a movable organ of speech is made to beat very rapidly and repeatedly in the same position, either flapping loose in the stream of air (in the uvular trill) or striking against some other organ, as in apico-alveolar or apico-dental trills. The voiced uvular trill, transcribed [ʀ], is commonly found in German, e.g. *rund* [ʀunt] "round". French used to have a similar uvular trill, but now normally has only a weak uvular fricative [ʁ] in its place, as in *peur* [pœʁ] "fear". A dental or alveolar trill is widespread for *r* in many languages, and is transcribed [r:] or [r̄], e.g. Span. *carro* ['kar̄o] or ['kar:o] "cart". We have a voiced bilabial trill in our English interjection *brrr!* expressing cold. Here again, voiceless trills are possible in all positions, as in French *meurtre* [mœʁ̥tʁ̥] "murder".

A single beat, like those which when repeated constitute a trill, and not long enough to constitute a stop, is known as a *flap*. The most common position for a flap is apico-dental or apico-alveolar; the voiced dental alveolar flap is transcribed [r], and found as the normal *r*-articulation between vocoids in standard British English, Italian, Spanish, etc., as in the British English articulation of *very* ['vɛrɪ]. A great many speakers of American English have a different type of *r*-sound (see below) and use a voiced apico-alveolar flap instead of a voiceless or voiced apico-dental stop in such words as *writing* and *riding*, both ['ɹairɪŋ] in many varieties of American pronunciation.

The American variety of the *r*-contoid is difficult to classify. It involves bunching of the tongue muscles so as to raise the back of the tongue upwards towards a dorso-velar position, and (in my pronunciation, at least) a lowering of the central part of the tongue at the same time. One hesitates to term it a dorso-velar sibilant (!); perhaps *voiced dorsal fricative* would be a satisfactory term, since the sound seems characterized by some special quality given to the air waves by the bunching up of the tongue muscles and the resultant conformation of the dorsum rather than by the velar region of the roof of the mouth. The customary phonetic symbol for the American *r* is the letter r upside down: [ɹ].

As in the case of the vocoids, we can set up a chart representing the relative positions of the articulations of the various simple contoids we have discussed so far (Fig. 8). In such a chart, the horizontal dimension represents the various points of articulation, with the lips on the extreme left and the larynx on the extreme right; and the vertical dimension, the different manners of articulation, usually beginning with stops and ending with trills. Voicing is a third dimension, normally shown by placing the phonetic symbols for voiced contoids in a different plane from those for the voiceless sounds.

In addition to simple contoid sounds, whose articulation is performed in the same point and manner throughout their onset, hold, and release, there are also complex contoids, involving a combination of more than one type of pronunciation (in respect to voicing, point or manner) between onset and

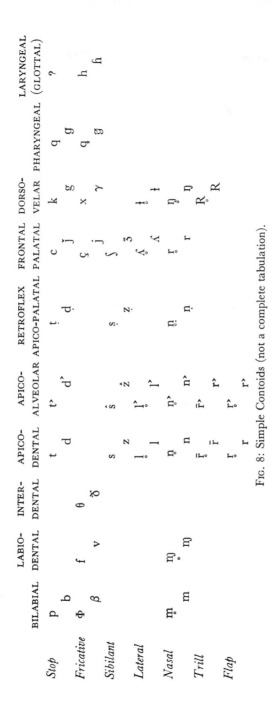

FIG. 8: Simple Contoids (not a complete tabulation).

release. A sound may begin voiced and end voiceless, or vice-versa; such phenomena are usually associated with the transition between neighboring words, and will be discussed in more detail later (cf. Chap. 12). The most common type of combination of manners of articulation involves a stop onset and hold, and either sibilant or affricate release. A stop contoid with sibilant release is known as an *assibilate*. The apico-dental assibilate (voiceless [tˢ], voiced [dᶻ]) is found, for example, in Italian, in such words as *zio* ['tˢi:o] "uncle" and *zùcchero* ['dᶻuk:ɛro] "sugar". We do not have this type of assibilate in English, but the corresponding contoids articulated in frontal-palatal position are found in English. The voiceless frontal-palatal assibilate, usually written *ch* in our orthography, is transcribed [tʃ] or [tˢ̌]; and the voiced variety (which we spell *j* or else with *g* before *e* and *i*) is transcribed [dʒ] or [dᶻ̌]. Examples: Eng. *church* [tʃʌɹtʃ] or [tˢ̌ʌɹtˢ̌]; *judge* ['dʒʌdʒ] or [dᶻ̌ʌdᶻ̌]; Ital. *cena* ['tʃe:na] or ['tˢ̌e:na] "supper"; *gita* ['dʒi:ta] or ['dᶻ̌i:ta] "excursion". The choice between [tʃ] and [tˢ̌], and similarly between [dʒ] and [dᶻ̌], is wholly arbitrary, since neither set of characters has any intrinsic superiority over the other, and typographical considerations (e.g., the availability or nonavailability of a given character on the typewriter or in the print-shop) may be allowed to determine our choice.

Assibilates are often referred to as "affricates," a confusing usage, since the latter term is also used for complex contoids in which a stop onset and hold are followed by a fricative release, of the type of [Φ], [θ] or [x]. Such true affricates are found, for example, in German and its dialects, e.g., German *Pfennig* ['pΦeniç]; Swiss-German also has the dorso-velar affricate [kˣ]. We also find stop onset and hold with lateral release, e.g., in many American Indian languages; symbols [tˡ] and [dˡ], as in such Mexican place-names as *Tlaxpan* ['tˡaspan]. Not only stops, but other types of contoids as well, occur with an extra puff of breath accompanying the release, in which case they are known as *aspirated* and are transcribed with a small raised h following the phonetic symbol: e.g., [pʰ], [tʰ], [kʰ] etc., as in English *pin* [pʰɪn]; an alternative type of transcription is with a raised comma following the phonetic symbol, e.g., [p'], etc. In some languages of India, not only voiceless contoids but also voiced ones occur aspirated, with a voiced laryngeal fricative [ɦ] following the release of the contoid.

In other types of complex contoids we find simultaneous articulation at two points of contact, and not infrequently with two different manners of articulation at the same time. In some African languages we find [kp] and [gb] as single but complex contoids; nearer home, our own [kw] and [gw] involve labio-velar articulation, i.e., the combination of a dorso-velar stop with a lip-rounded semicontoid, as in English *quick* [kwɪk] and Italian *quanto* ['kwanto] "how much", and Italian *guanto* ['gwanto] "glove". More extensive series of contoids involving simultaneity of articulation are found in languages which have *palatalized*, *labialized*, or *glottalized* contoids. In Russian and other Slavic languages, in Marshallese (a language of the Micronesian region), and elsewhere, we find whole series of contoid articulations involving a simultaneous raising of the top of the tongue towards the palate, as in Russian здесь [zdᶦesᶦ] "here", быть [bitᶦ] "to be". Palatalization is indicated either by a raised ᶦ following the phonetic symbol involved (as in the examples given) or by a comma placed underneath the symbol (e.g., [zďeş], [biţ]). Labialization, in which the articulation of a contoid is accompanied by lip-rounding, is usually indicated by transcribing the appropriate phonetic symbol with [ˌ] underneath it or with a small raised [ʷ] following: e.g., [ţ] or [tʷ]. An articulation is glottalized if it is accompanied by a simultaneous stoppage of the breath at the vocal chords, and is indicated by the sign for the glottal stop [ʔ] written after the phonetic symbol: e.g. (tʔ].

A contoid articulation may also be preceded by some secondary feature, especially nasalization; if this latter is present, the contoid is termed *prenasalized*, and the phonetic symbol is preceded by a raised letter indicating a nasalization in the appropriate position: e.g. the bilabial plosives [p] and [b] with prenasalization will be transcribed [ᵐp] and [ᵐb], respectively; and similarly for [ⁿt] and [ⁿd], [ᵑk], and [ᵑg], etc. Such prenasalized contoids are found widely in African and Melanesian languages, and also in Brazilian Portuguese, as in *grande* ['grɔ̃ⁿdʒi] "big".

NOTES

Contoids: Hockett, 1955, §25, 1958, Chap. 8.
Releases of final stops in English: Malécot, 1958.

11

The Syllable

THE SYLLABLE is perhaps the most extensively discussed of phonetic phenomena, and at the same time that on which there is least agreement among
phoneticians. All are agreed that such a thing as the syllable exists—in
speech as well as in writing—and all utilize the concept of the syllable in
analyzing speech-sounds; but concerning its nature there is considerable
debate. Here we shall simply attempt to synthesize what is definitely known
concerning the syllable.

In any stream of speech, there are differences in *sonority* from one point to
the next; these differences are caused, not only by the amount of voicing
furnished by the vocal cords, but also by the actual amount of air coming
from the lungs and of resonance produced by its passage through the organs
of speech. In general, of course, vocoids are the most sonorous sounds, since
they are normally voiced and are by definition produced with no obstruction other than that involved in the formation of resonance-chambers which
give each vocoid its specific quality. Among vocoids, the low-central [a]
(which has the greatest opening and hence the most resonance) is the most
sonorous, and the high-front [i] and [y] are the least. However, contoids also
can show a certain amount of sonority, though to a lesser degree than vocoids;
naturally, the voiced contoids are more sonorous than the voiceless, and the
con inuants are more sonorous than the stops. Hence, even in an interjection
like our *pst!*, which contains no vocoid and only three voiceless contoids,
there are differences in sonority: the [s], being a continuant, is more sonorous
than either of the two voiceless stops which surround it. With the aid of
various mechanical devices, it is possible to plot, for any given stretch of
speech, the differences in sonority, which appear as a curve with peaks and
troughs (shown in schematic form for a few sample words in Fig. 9).

It has been a matter of common observation since antiquity that in Greek,
Latin, and our modern European languages, the number of vocoid sounds
in any utterance was correlated, at least approximately, with the number of
syllables which native speakers would instinctively recognize in that utterance. In an Italian word like *telègrafo*, for instance, everybody recognizes
four syllables: [te-'lɛ-gra-fo]; in Spanish *desembolsado* "disbursed", five:
[de-sɛm-bɔl-'sa-ðo]; etc. If more than one vocoid occurs in the same syllable,
in a familiar language, one is more sonorous than the other(s), and those
which are less sonorous are classed as semivocoids or semicontoids (cf. pp.

51–52), forming a diphthong with the full vocoid. Thus, in Italian *buono* ['bwɔ-no] "good," there are two syllables, with a diphthong in the first, and there are five syllables in the Spanish form *diciéndoselo* [di-'θ jɛn-do-se-lo] "saying it to him (her)". The sound articulated with the peak of sonority of a syllable is known as its *nucleus* or *center*.

On the basis of this correlation between the number of full vocoids and that of syllables, it was long since proposed to define the syllable as a segment of speech containing a peak of sonority, or, conversely, as that stretch

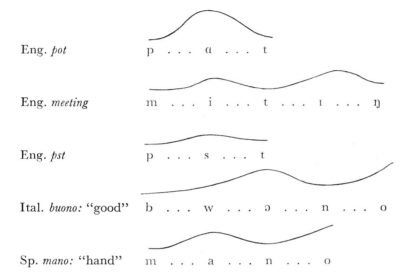

Eng. *pot*	p . . . ɑ . . . t
Eng. *meeting*	m . . . i . . . t . . . ɪ . . . ŋ
Eng. *pst*	p . . . s . . . t
Ital. *buono:* "good"	b . . . w . . . ɔ . . . n . . . o
Sp. *mano:* "hand"	m . . . a . . . n . . . o

FIG. 9: Peaks and Troughs of Sonority (the vertical dimension shows increase of sonority, the horizontal dimension shows passage of time).

between two troughs of sonority. Such a definition is reasonably satisfactory for our familiar European languages; but it is insufficient to take care of the situation in other languages, where this correlation does not necessarily hold true. We are accustomed to each syllable having a full vocoid as its center, and to each full vocoid acting as the center of a separate syllable, as in Italian *traendo* [tra-'ɛn-do] "bringing"; but in some languages we find that what defines the syllable is not necessarily the peak of sonority. It is necessary to have further distinctions in the structure of syllables; we may use Hockett's terms of *onset* (the beginning of the articulation of the syllable), *peak* (the center), and *coda* (what comes after the peak and before the onset of the next syllable). If the coda of one syllable cannot be clearly separated from the onset of the next, the two together can be called an *interlude* (i.e., that which comes between the peaks of the two syllables involved).

In most languages, a syllable is to be defined by its possession of a vocoid as center, often accompanied by other characteristics such as tone, stress, or length. In at least one language, however, many syllables and even whole sequences of syllables ("words") can occur without any vocoid at all, and set off from each other simply by their distinctive onsets. This language is Bella Coola (an American Indian language of British Columbia), and the classic example, containing no vocoids and only four contoids, all voiceless, is the four-syllable "word" [ɬ-k'ʷ-t-xʷ] "make it big!". This is a limiting case, but not a mere curiosity, in that other languages (e.g., Kota, spoken in southern India) show similar but not such extreme characteristics.

To explain the possibility of syllables being pronounced even without vocoids, we must examine the way in which the air is brought forth from the lungs. The diaphragm serves to contract the lungs and force the air out; the muscles between the ribs (intercostal muscles) reinforce this movement of expulsion and add further slight contractions and expansions which split a single expulsion of air into a series of smaller pulses. The amount of speech uttered on a single expulsion of air from the lungs is a *breath-group*, and the separate chest-pulses within each single expulsion of air serves as the carriers of the separate syllables. In most languages, peaks of sonority normally coincide with chest-pulses in forming the centers of syllables, but the examples of Bella Coola and Kota show that it is not absolutely necessary, in the nature of things, that this be the case.

In Bella Coola, a syllable can occur without anything resembling a vocoid in it; but in many languages (including English), syllables occur with peaks not consisting of full vocoids. We have numerous syllables in which [m], [n], [ŋ], [l], ([ɫ]), and [r], although contoids, act as the centers of syllables in words such as *bottom* ['bɑtm̩], *button* ['bʌtn̩], *baking* ['bekŋ̩], *bottle* ['bɑtl̩], and *butter* ['bʌtɹ̩]. I have [ɹ] under stress in at least one word, *pretty* ['pɹ̩ti]. When a contoid acts in this way as the center of a syllable, it is known as a *syllabic* contoid, and is indicated in transcription by a vertical tick [ˌ] placed underneath the appropriate phonetic symbol, as in the examples given above. The rather forbidding term *syllabicity* is used to refer to the functioning of a contoid as the center of a syllable. The nasals and "liquids" ([r] and [l] and their different varieties) occur most frequently as syllabic contoids, but we find other continuants also as centers of syllables, particularly in interjections, as when we imitate the noise made by a fly or bee with *bzzz* [bz̩:], or "shush" someone with *sh!* [ʃ̩:], or call someone's attention quietly with *pst* [pst̩].

Although, in most languages, it is perfectly easy to identify the number of syllables in any given utterance, it is not always so easy to establish the boundaries between syllables. In the Romance languages, at least those of a conservative type (e.g., Portuguese, Spanish, Italian, Roumanian), the onset of a syllable is clearly marked in contrast to what has gone before. In these languages, if a single contoid, or a cluster consisting of contoid + [r] or of contoid + [l], comes before the center of a syllable, then the boundary of the syllable falls before the contoid or cluster involved. In other clusters, the first contoid belongs in the syllable of the preceding vocoid, the second in that of the following. In such languages, the native speakers have little or no difficulty in knowing almost instinctively where the syllable-boundaries lie, and hence have no problems in the orthographical division of words (e.g., at the end of a line).

In English, however, the situation is quite different. A single contoid between two vocoids belongs to the syllables of both (is *ambisyllabic*), in that its onset comes before the end of the first syllable involved, the syllable-boundary (lowest point of sonority, or beginning of next chest-pulse) falls during the hold, and the release comes after the beginning of the next syllable, as shown in the samples in Fig. 10. (This observation holds true whether we define the

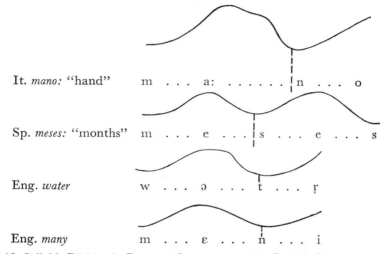

It. *mano:* "hand"   m   . . .   a: . . . . . .   n   . . .   o

Sp. *meses:* "months"   m   . . .   e   . . .   s   . . .   e   . . .   s

Eng. *water*   w   . . .   ɔ   . . .   t   . . .   ɹ

Eng. *many*   m   . . .   ɛ   . . .   n   . . .   i

Fɪɢ. 10: Syllable Division in Romance Languages and in English (the dotted vertical lines show where the syllable-divisions fall).

English syllable in terms of sonority or of chest pulse.) This is one of the reasons why speakers of English have a hard time learning to place the syllable-division before, not during, an intervocalic contoid in Italian or Spanish. It is also the reason underlying our perplexity with regard to many syllable-divisions in the spelling of English, where the morphologic structure of a word gives us no clue to its division. For instance, how are we to divide a work like *water* or *many*—should we write *wa-ter* or *wat-er*, *ma-ny* or *man-y?* Some will divide one way and some the other, and endless, irresolvable disputes will result; irresolvable, because the facts of our pronunciation (of which the spelling is only a reflection) afford us no basis on which to found our orthographical division, since the syllable-division in these words falls in the middle of the [t] in *water* and of the [n] in *many*.

If a syllable ends in a vocoid or diphthong, with no contoid following in the same syllable (i.e., if the syllable has no coda or interlude at the end), it is known as a *free* syllable; but if there are one or more contoids in the syllable after the vocoid (i.e. if a coda or interlude follows the center of the syllable), then the syllable is called *checked*. The expressions "open" and "closed" syllables are also used where we have spoken of "free" and "checked;" but it is perhaps preferable to avoid these terms, since *open* and *closed* are also used by some scholars to refer to the lower varieties of mid-range vocoids (cf. Chap. 9). However, we do use the terms *open syllabification* to apply to the state of affairs in a language like Italian or Spanish which has a predominance of free syllables, with syllable-division falling clearly between sounds, and *closed syllabification* for a language like English with a predominance of checked syllables, due especially to the prevalence of interludes instead of codas and onsets between vocoids.

There is a great variation in the rate at which the speakers of any given language utter syllables. The fastest flow of syllables verges on the incomprehensible; and thus, for example, the art of George Baker or Martyn Green in delivering Gilbert and Sullivan patter songs depends on their skill in ultra-rapid articulation of syllables while keeping them clearly audible. The slowest flow is found in over-careful, oratorical delivery, especially before large groups in acoustically poor surroundings. Between these two extremes lies the rate of most of our ordinary utterances. Even then, in ordinary speech, we do not normally utter all our syllables at exactly the same rate, but change very frequently, even within the same breath-group, and particularly when we are "hemming and hawing" to search for what we are going to say.

The way in which the utterance of syllables is timed, i.e., the *rhythm* of their utterance, differs from one language to another, and there are at least two distinct types of timing. In one type (as found in Italian, French, Spanish, etc.), the rate of utterance of a succession of syllables remains approximately the same no matter how many stresses there are or where they fall in the stream of speech; an utterance of, say, ten syllables will take approximately twice as long as one of five syllables. This type of rhythm is known as *syllable-timed*, since it is determined by the number of syllables (stressed or unstressed). In another type of rhythm (such as we have in English), the stressed syllables in an utterance come at evenly spaced intervals, and any unstressed syllables falling in between the stressed ones are simply fitted in with greater or less speeding up as may be necessary. In this type of rhythm, which is known as *stress-timed*, a breath-group containing, say, two stressed syllables will take up the same amount of time no matter whether there are no, one, or five unstressed syllables in between. (Cf. Fig. 11 for examples.) A stress-timed language like English sounds very choppy and jerky to speakers of French or Spanish, since they expect to hear an even succession of syllables, with approximately the same amount of time allotted to each; but to us, the syllable-timed utterances of those languages sound as if they were being fired from a machine-gun.

An example of the stress-timed rhythm of English pushed to the very limits and beyond is found in the limerick:

> There wás a young mán of Japán
> Who wrote vérses that néver would scán;
>   But when péople asked "Whý?"
>   He would álways replý:
> "Well, you see, I almost always do my very living bést to squeeze
> just as many extra syllables into the last líne as I feel that I possibly cán!"

The last line depends for its humor on the fact that, although it seems to violate the metric rules of English entirely, with an impossible number of syllables, it nevertheless fits the basic rhythmic pattern of the limerick, having only three main stresses, and, if it is read at an ultra-fast rate, the unstressed syllables will fit into the pattern in a relatively normal way.

ENGLISH (stress-timed) RHYTHM:

| · · | · | · · · · | · · | · · | · · | · |

the in-di-vi- dual syl- ⌐come in a high-ly ir-re-gu-lar rhy-thm
                    ⌐la-bles seem to ⌐

ITALIAN (syllable-timed) RHYTHM:

· · · · · · | · · · · | · · | ·

Con la Me-tro-po-li-ta-na non si va a San Pie-tro   "with the subway one doesn't go to St. Peter's"

FIG. 11: Stress-Timed and Syllable-Timed Rhythm (English and Italian examples).

In stress-timed languages, the degree of stress and rate of pronunciation have a marked effect on the position of articulation and resultant distinctness of sounds, especially in the unstressed syllables. Thus, in English, the more rapid is our speech, the more our unstressed vocoids are articulated towards the center of the mouth, and the more fusion there is between adjacent contoids, so that the pronunication of *Don't you want to go to lunch?* may range anywhere from ['doᵂnt ju 'wɔnt tu 'goᵂ tu 'lʌntʃ] (if we are talking very slowly, e.g., under bad acoustic conditions or to a foreigner who knows little English), all the way to [ɳtʃwɔŋg'lʌntʃ] (thrown out, say, as a quick passing question). In Italian, French, or Spanish, on the other hand, the unstressed syllables show the same type of articulation as do the stressed ones, and their characteristics are changed little, if any, by an increase in the rate of pronunciation. This state of affairs does not reflect any particular demerit of English speech-habits, or any special merit of those of Italian or the other Romance languages; it is a normal concomitant of stress-timed rhythm on the one hand and of syllable-timed rhythm on the other. Our traditional school grammars and even many conservative linguistic analysts base their discussions exclusively on the slow, ultra-careful rate of speech, but a satisfactory, thorough discussion of the structure of any language should take into account whatever changes occur in pronunciation (and, as a result, in grammatical forms and syntactic combinations) as the rate of speech is increased.

NOTES

The syllable: Hála, 1960, 1961; Rosetti, 1959; Stetson, 1945.

12

Basis of Articulation and Phenomena of Transition

IT IS EASY, on the basis of the analytical approach to speech-sounds that we have outlined in the last four chapters, to adopt an "atomistic" attitude, even without realizing it, and to consider that when we have described a set of speech-sounds in terms of the physiological mechanism of the production of each one of them, we have done all that is necessary. Actually, what we term "speech-sounds" are simply the most easily identifiable features in a stream of sound which includes many other phenomena and is conditioned by a number of factors besides those of the specific place and manner of articulation of the speech-sounds themselves. Some of these other phenomena are irrelevant for linguistic activity, and constitute simply what communications engineers call "noise" (disturbing extraneous elements in a message being conveyed), as when we sniffle, sneeze, cough, groan, or make other noises in the midst of our speech. Certain such "noise"-like elements have a semi-linguistic status, in that they are more or less conventionalized in any given speech community and differ from one language to the next. Even so, it is well known that many of our "interjections" are marginal to our linguistic systems, in that they consist, wholly or in part, of sounds which are not part of the normal phonetic inventory of the language with which they are associated, as in the case of our *mf!* [m̥m̥] or *mphm!* ['m̥m̥m̥] (cf. p. 56).

Certain other aspects of our production of speech sounds, however, are intimately related to the speech-sounds themselves, although they do not necessarily serve to distinguish one phoneme from another. This is especially true of our habits of holding the entire mechanism with which we articulate our sounds. These habits differ from one language to another, and are at the root of a large part of what is termed, loosely, one's "accent" in speaking a language. Collectively, these habits are known as the *basis of articulation*. They involve especially the over-all position in which the organs of speech are held when one is not talking (and hence which serve as a point of departure when starting to talk); the way in which we tense the muscles of the throat and face; and the manner and rate in which we make the transition from one sound to the next.

For speakers of English, the normal position for the tongue in repose is in the center of the mouth and somewhat raised, more or less in the position of [ə]. Hence, when we merely open our mouths and let more or less unformed sound issue forth (as when we are hesitating as to what to say next), our hesitation-formula is [ə . . . ə . . . ə], which we usually transcribe as "uh . . . uh . . . uh." A speaker of Italian, on the other hand, will have the tongue in repose somewhat raised in the front of the mouth and will express hesitation with [ɛ . . . ɛ . . . ɛ] "eh . . . eh . . . eh." Not only hesitation-formulas, but the entire articulation of speaking will be affected by the point of departure for the tongue-position. In Italian, there are even social differences in the position in which the tongue is held: it is considered plebeian and socially inelegant to have a back articulation, and especially upper-class women affect a very fronted style of articulation. American English speech is articulated more towards the center of the mouth than is Italian. When American English vocoids are reduced in length and intensity, due to the stress-timed rhythm of our speech (p. 64), their position tends towards the mid-central (although they do not by any means always merge with [ə], as some have mistakenly thought).

There are also differences in the way in which speakers of different languages pass from one sound to the next. The entire problem of transition in the stream of speech tends in general to be neglected, because we are misled by the fact that when we write down an utterance—be it in conventional spelling or the narrowest of phonetic transcription—we use a sequence of letters written one after the other in a horizontal line. The linearity of such a sequence, and the fact that our letters are discrete entities, is likely to lead us to think of each sound as an entity in itself, separate and distinct from what has gone before and what comes after. Basing their precepts on the separateness of letters in writing, purists have for centuries been urging us: "Be sure to pronounce all the letters distinctly, and don't slur your sounds into each other, else you can't be understood." Phoneticians, too, tend to pay so much attention to individual sounds that they too often think of them as coming exclusively one after the other.

Even before the development of acoustic phonetics, some scholars suspected that this was far from being the case. If we distinguish clearly between the onset, the hold, and the release of sounds, we find that in many instances the onset of any given sound reaches far back into the release and even into the hold of the preceding one, and that its release may continue well into the onset of the next. The stream of speech does not consist of neat, clearly split segments of sound each sharply distinct from the other; on the contrary, it is like a kaleidoscopic procession of intermingled features, the transition between which is constantly taking place even as the features themselves seem to be at their clearest. Acoustic phonetics confirmed this view, by demonstrating that there is no such thing as an absolutely clean break between one speech-sound and the next; on the contrary, between each sound and what follows there is an intermingling known technically as *slur* (without, however, the unfavorable connotation often given this word). Hence the phenomena involved in the transition between sounds have considerable importance both for phonetics as such and (as we shall see in Chap. 18) for phonemics in the analysis of juncture.

To date, we have been speaking of sounds within the breath-group, but for the study of transition phenomena it is also valuable to include the element of *pause*, or the silence from which a speaker starts in making an utterance and to which he returns when the utterance is finished. (If necessary, we use the symbol # for pause.) On starting to speak after pause, the speaker of English normally does not set his vocal cords vibrating until a fraction of a second after he has made the onset of a vocoid or a voiced contoid. This makes his [b] sound as if it were [ᵖb], and likewise his [d] = [ᵗd], [g] = [ᵏg], [z] = [ˢz], etc. In French, Italian, and Spanish, on the other hand, vocoids and voiced contoids are fully voiced from the very start, or the voicing may even start a tiny fraction of a second before the onset of the rest of the articulation. Speakers of these languages identify a voiced sound by the voicing, which they expect to hear from the start, and assign to the voiceless category any sound whose onset is voiceless, even though voicing may start later. An American may think, in speaking Italian, that he is pronouncing an initial [zb] in, say, [zbaˈʎaːre]: "to make a mistake", but if he says [ˢzbaˈʎaːre], he will be heard as having said [spaˈʎare] no matter how hard he may try to voice the rest of the [z] and the [b].

Before a pause, too, we find various special phenomena. On occasion, we may find that the habits of one language are exactly the opposite of those of another. In French and Italian, for instance, a final contoid before pause has a very clear and distinct release, voiceless (written [°] after the appropriate phonetic symbol) after a voiceless contoid, and voiced (transcribed [•]) after a voiced one. Thus: French [pip°] "pipe", [bɔb•] "bomb". This clear release is not an aspiration, nor, in the case of the voiced contoids, is it the vocoid [ə], since it does not involve an extra syllable. A speaker of French or Italian identifies a final contoid by this clearly audible release, and if he does not hear the release he concludes that no final contoid has been pronounced. In English, on the other hand, our final contoids in such words as *pap, pat, pack, sab,* * *sad, sag* are regularly pronounced, when before pause, without any release at all; we simply put our tongues in the appropriate contact-position and allow the breath-stream to cease. Hence, to us, the Frenchman or Italian who puts a full release on a final contoid and pronounces, say [pæt°] seems to be adding an extra vocoid.

And yet, to speakers of English, the final contoids of *pap, pat* and *pack*, or of *sab, sad* and *sag*, are perfectly distinguishable from each other, even though they all end without any audible release. How is this possible? The answer is that, in the case of our final contoids, our ear identifies them, not on the basis of the way they end, but of the way they begin and of the way the preceding vocoid ends, when the tongue is making the transition from the vocoid to the contoid articulation. In other words, there are slightly different varieties of [æ] before [p], [t], and [k], and before [b], [d], and [g]. This is what might be expected, since the tongue passes rapidly through a number of different positions from the low-front articulation of [æ] either towards the top part of the mouth for [t][d], or towards the top back part for [k][g]. There is, furthermore, the anticipation of the unvoicing in the case of final [p][t][k], which

* As in the old counting-out jingle *Ibbety bibbety sibbety sab.*

differentiates a vocoid preceding them from one preceding [b][d][g]. With the predominantly closed syllabification of English, such phenomena of anticipation are extremely frequent and normal in our pronunciation.

Anticipation and continuation are inevitable results of the fact that speakers of English are constantly keeping their organs of speech, and especially their tongue, on the move throughout any utterance. This is in marked contrast to the transition habits of speakers of Romance languages, who, instead of making a slow, gradual, continual transition as in English, make a fast transition immediately preceding each syllable to the basic position for the organs of speech in that syllable, hold the position (relatively speaking) during the utterance of the syllable, and then make another fast transition to the next. Even though I may have all the individual vocoids and contoids pronounced exactly according to the text-book of phonetics, if I speak French with English transition-habits or vice versa, my hearers will consider that I have an atrocious "accent." Furthermore, although one's "accent" is not, as a whole, phonemically significant, many specific aspects of transition are, in different languages, and furnish the basis for setting up phonemic features of juncture (cf. Chap. 17).

If, then, sounds are so slurred together that their beginnings and ends are inextricably mixed, how is it that we are able to understand speech at all when we hear it? The answer is that our hearing, likewise, is so constructed as to make an inevitable blending, over several hundredths of a second, in our perception of sounds; this is technically termed *smear*. Due to the existence of smear in our perception of sounds, the presence of a certain amount of slur, of the type we have been discussing in connection with transition-phenomena, serves the essential purpose of modifying sounds so as to let us know what is coming next or what has gone before. Contoids, particularly, often consist simply of interruptions in the resonance of the vocoids, and are often so short in duration, that the actual perception of the contoids is lost in the smear of a few hundredths of a second; and if we did not have the special quality of the consonant slurred into preceding or following vocoids, we would not be able to know which contoid had been pronounced. In *Acoustic Phonetics* (1948), Martin Joos says:

"Such identification of consonants [i.e. consonant sounds or contoids—RAHjr.] by their effects on contiguous resonants is apparently depended on by listeners to a far greater extent than commonly supposed. It is not only a voiceless-stop hold that is inaudible to a listener; the majority of consonants make such faint impressions on spectrograms that we must suppose them to be either absolutely inaudible or at any rate so faintly inaudible as to be separately imperceptible. . . . If the speaker trained himself to reduce his slur to, say, one third the customary extent . . . there would be very little profit in this 'improvement' because the listener's smear would still blend the segments together nearly as thoroughly as ever, but there could easily be a considerable loss in it because then the vowels would perhaps not furnish enough evidence to identify the consonants properly."

This is another of the many instances in which a knowledge of the actual facts of language shows the faulty basis on which puristic precepts rest. The purists advise us to separate our sounds and articulate each apart from the others; but this advice, if it were possible to follow it, would render our speech not more, but less intelligible!

NOTES

Basis of articulation: Stetson, 1951.
Juncture, from an acoustic-phonetic point of view: Lehiste, 1960.

13

Intensity and Pitch

NOT ALL SYLLABLES are pronounced exactly alike, with respect to the force with which the air is expelled from the lungs, or to the musical pitch which is imparted to them by the tension of the vocal chords. If they were, we should have a succession of hammer-like blows, all alike, one per syllable, and a series of literally monotone pitches. In every language that has been subjected to accurate analysis, we find that successive syllables are distinguished from each other—either in the intensity of muscular strength with which they are uttered, or in their pitch, or both. The term *accent* is often used as a general cover term for phenomena of intensity and pitch, and frequently a distinction is made between "stress accent" and "pitch accent," but the term *accent* is too often a source of confusion, especially since it is also used to refer to written accent-marks (ʹ ` and the like). Hence we shall, for the phonetic level of our discussion, use the terms *intensity* to refer to the degree of force with which a syllable is uttered, and *pitch* for the musical tone involved; we shall reserve *stress* and *intonation*, respectively, for the discussion of the phonemic organization of these phenomena. Intensity, incidentally, is not to be confused with loudness, which is the degree of strength with which the vocal cords are vibrating. The two are usually correlated, but not always; it is possible to utter a sequence of syllables with very little intensity of lung force but considerable loudness in the vibration of the vocal cords, and vice versa.

The diaphragm and intercostal muscles can exert differing degrees of force in expelling the air from the lungs; these differences are perceived by hearers as differences in the intensity of the syllables. In IPA phonetic transcription, the marks representing intensity are placed before the symbols that stand for the syllable involved. Normally, weak intensity is left unmarked, and "full" is marked with a superior vertical tick [ʹ], as in Eng. *paper* [ˈpepr̩], *deduction* [diˈdʌkʃn̩], *negligée* [nɛglɪˈʒe], etc. An intensity intermediate between full and weak is marked with an inferior vertical tick [ˌ], e.g., for the third syllable in *elevator* [ˈɛləˌvetr̩], for the first in *transmigration* [ˌtrænzmajˈgreʃn̩], for the second in *capitulation* [kæˌpɪtʃuˈleʃn̩], etc. An intensity even stronger than "full" is indicated by two superior vertical ticks [ʺ], and is customarily used to mark emphatic, overstrong force, as in *SHUT UP!* [ʺʃʌt ʺʌp]. These four levels of intensity are all that, in practice, it is normally found necessary to symbolize for any given language, though in actuality, here as in almost all other aspects of phonetics, the range of possibilities is almost infinitely great in its minute gradations.

Languages vary greatly in the purely phonetic aspect of the intensity with which their syllables are uttered. Within any given language, also, there can be a greater or lesser extent of difference between the extremes of intensity which the speakers normally use. One extreme, perhaps, is found in French, where (with one exception), all syllables are uttered with virtually the same amount of intensity, and that intensity is quite low in its actual physical strength; speakers of French simply do not expel the air from their lungs at all strongly when they are speaking. The only exception to this rule of uniform, low intensity on French syllables is that certain syllables are uttered with slightly (but only slightly) greater intensity, which we shall here mark with ['] (although it does not stand for an intensity by any means as that which we mark in English with the same sign): e.g., *marcher* [mar'ʃe] "to walk", *vaniteux* [vani'tø] "vain, conceited", *possibilité* [pɔsibili'te] "possibility", etc. The presence of this slightly greater intensity marks these syllables as being at the end of morphological units (not necessarily "words," since combinations of "words" such as *il n'est pas encore venu* [ilnɛpɑzūkɔrvə'ny] "he has not yet come", have only one such intensified syllable at the end of the entire combination). Extra-strong intensity, of the type usually marked with ["], is rare in standard French, in which emphasis is customarily indicated by syntactic rather than phonological means.

At the other extreme, perhaps, is Hungarian, in which some syllables are uttered with very great intensity indeed, and others with very slight force. The force used on the most heavily intensified syllables is as strong as that which we class as extra-strong in English. In between are other levels of lesser intensity. The occurrences of these various levels are automatically conditioned by the number of syllables in the word involved, with an alternation whereby the even-numbered syllables (counting from the first) are weak and the odd-numbered ones are uttered with gradually decreasing force from the beginning of the word. If we mark the heaviest intensity with ["], the next heaviest with ['], the next with [ˌ], and leave the weak syllables unmarked, we find that such a longish Hungarian word as *lehetetlenül:* "impossibly" is to be transcribed as ["lɛhɛ'tɛtlɛˌnyl]. In Hungarian, the occurrence of the heaviest possible intensity on a syllable serves to mark the beginning of a word. Old Latin may well have had a similar situation to that found in Hungarian, as shown by the weakening of vowel phonemes in postinitial syllables in such forms as *cecinī:* "I'm through singing," from an older *ce-can-ī*, to the verb root *can-* "sing." *

English is more or less in between the two extremes of phonetic intensity as represented by French and Hungarian. We have several levels of phonetic intensity, as set forth in the second paragraph of this chapter, ranging from very strong to very weak. In English, furthermore, the onset of intensity is

---

* We use the asterisk * in front of the citation of a linguistic form to indicate that it is not attested but must be supposed to have existed, or must be assumed as an intermediate stage in a process of logical derivation, especially in transformation grammar (cf. Chap. 38).

not determined automatically by the boundary of the syllable, as it is in many other languages (e.g., French, Italian, Hungarian). We have, at least optionally, such differences in the onset of intensity as those between [əˈnem] "a name" and [ənˈem] "an aim"; these differences in onset of intensity serve also as indications of boundaries between morphological elements (cf. Chap. 17).

In every language, there are differences in the level of pitch between any given syllable and those surrounding it. The expression "monotone" has no real meaning as applied to any variety of normal speech; if a succession of syllables is uttered on a real monotone, i.e., staying exactly on the same pitch from beginning to end, we have, not normal speech, but a type of singing such as is found in some varieties of Roman Catholic and Anglican chanting. No normal person speaks in a true monotone, nor are very many people really tone-deaf, i.e. wholly unable to distinguish one pitch from another. In order to be truly tone-deaf, a person would have to be unable to distinguish a sentence uttered with rising and then falling pitch (e.g. *He's going home.*) from the same sentence with pitch rising continually all the way to the end (e.g., *He's going home?*). Such a person would be a pathological case, with impaired hearing due to either physiological or psychological causes. Every normal speaker of a language has a range of from one to three octaves, which lies roughly an octave higher, on the average, for women than for men. Women's and men's pitch ranges overlap, and it often happens that a woman with a low alto speaking voice is mistaken for a man with a high tenor, or vice versa.

In our Western European music, at least that reflecting the "common practice" in tonal harmony of the last three centuries, pitches are organized into a systematic arrangement based on the octave and fixed intervals within it. No such organization is possible in our treatment of pitch in human speech, because we do not keep the successive syllables of our speech on anything resembling fixed pitch. Nor would it be possible to notate the successive pitches of our speech in anything more than an approximate way; even the German *Sprechstimme* or imitation of speech in singing (used, for instance, by Alban Berg in his opera *Wozzeck*) is only a stylization which approaches, but does not reproduce, actual speech. In analyzing the use of pitch in speech, all that we can do is to identify the level of the pitch on a given syllable, either in terms of the direction in which it is moving within the syllable itself, or of its position relative to the pitch of previous and following syllables.

In many languages (including Chinese as the best-known example, but also numerous others in Southeast Asia, Africa and the Americas), the pitch on each individual syllable can be of different types. There are three major possibilities: it may remain level, or rise during the utterance, or fall. These three directions can also be combined in further ways, giving such *compound pitches* as level-rising, level-falling, rising-falling, falling-rising, etc. With respect to each other, syllables can be on various pitch-levels, of which there are theoretically an infinitely graded series, but of which, in practice, we need to distinguish not more than three or four, e.g. low, norm (or low-mid), mid, and high. In phonetic transcription, it is customary to use a short line placed after the phonetic symbols for the syllable involved, and giving an iconic representation of the level and direction of the pitch of the syllable: e.g. North Chinese [ma⁻] "mother", [ma′] "hemp", [ma‿] "horse", [ma˺] "scold". Other types of notation involve use of superscript numbers or accent marks, but these involve a certain amount of analysis of the significant contrasts involved and hence belong under phonemic rather than phonetic notation (cf. Chap. 19).

Our familiar Western European languages do not have this type of variable and significant pitch on individual syllables; rather, the speakers of each language have their own habits, as a speech-community, with regard to the way

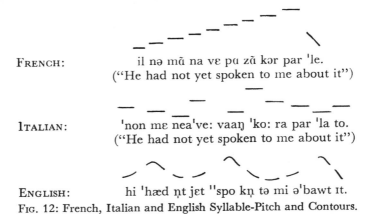

FRENCH: il nə mɑ̃ na vɛ pɑ zɑ̃ kɔr par 'le.
                  ("He had not yet spoken to me about it")

ITALIAN: 'non mɛ nea've: vaaŋ 'ko: ra par 'la to.
                  ("He had not yet spoken to me about it")

ENGLISH: hi 'hæd ṇt jɛt ''spo kṇ tə mi ə'bawt ɪt.

FIG. 12: French, Italian and English Syllable-Pitch and Contours.

pitch does or does not move within the syllable in general. In Italian and the other Romance languages, the pitch remains relatively level on each successive syllable; in French, especially, it normally remains wholly level, except that it may rise upward during the final syllable of a sharply rising sequence, and may fall during the last syllable of a falling or rising-falling sequence. (See examples in Fig. 12.) In English, however, we allow the pitch to move during the pronunciation of each syllable, upward or downward as the case may be, in accordance with several factors, including the general direction of the pitch-contour of the utterance (cf. below) and the intensity with which the syllable is uttered. (In English, the greater the force with which a syllable is pronounced, the higher we tend to make its pitch—a correlation which does not necessarily hold true in other languages.) Styles of singing and of melodic line, especially in spontaneous folk art, are very largely in accord with the pitch-habits of the musician's native language; contrast the even articulation of syllables in a French folk song with the slides and sinuosities of pitch in a rock-and-roll piece.

Over segments of speech longer than a single syllable, we find that in most languages there are directions taken by the successions of pitches on the individual syllables; these successive ups and downs of pitches are known as *pitch-contours*. A segment of speech set off from other segments by a single pitch-contour is on occasion called a *macrosegment*. In some languages, such as English, pitch-contours can be described in terms of relative *levels* of pitch; all scholars recognize at least four levels of pitch for English (usually numbered from one for the lowest to four for the highest), and some consider that there are one or two more levels as well, making five or six in all. In some other languages, the contours involve a gradual progression of pitch from one syllable to another, applying (as in French) to each successive syllable or (as in Italian) to each successive stressed syllable. In such instances, we cannot speak of relative levels, but simply of *directions* (e.g., rising, falling, falling-rising, etc.) which the pitch-contours take. The organization of both syllable-pitch and pitch-contours into tonemes or tonemic units belongs to phonemics, and will be treated under intonation (in Chap. 19).

Other aspects of pitch, although not phonemically significant, contribute to "accent" in the broadest sense, i.e., a particular way of speaking. Our folkloristic terminology recognizes this in its use of such impressionistic terms as *monotone* and *singsong*, which refer to the *range* within which any speaker or group of speakers move in varying the pitch levels of their speech. This is to a certain extent a matter of individual variation, but differs also from one speech-community to the next. In British English, the range of pitch-variation is rather wider than that of American English, i.e., speakers will either go rather higher or lower in the pitch which they reach. Hence speakers of British English will say that Americans "talk in a monotone," whereas Americans consider that Englishmen use a "singsong" in speaking. Italian has a wider pitch-range than either British or American English; speakers of English confusedly notice this and the fact that Italian pitch-contours correspond to those of Italian opera and of our Western European music in general (which is an outgrowth of seventeenth-century Italian music), and exclaim in awe that "Italians sing even when they speak."

In addition to variations in intensity and pitch, there are also variations in other respects which have not yet been proven relevant to linguistic analysis, particularly in what is known as *voice-quality*. Under this heading come the register in which one speaks, loudness, roughness, and similar qualities. It is possible to establish sets of gradations for each of these (e.g., high vs. low register; loud vs. soft; smooth vs. rough), but there do not, as yet, seem to be any functional units establishable in these categories, nor do these various qualities seem to be associated with any linguistically relevant meanings. At the most, we can say that voice quality serves to identify the speaker as a particular individual, and to convey very vague, general over-all information as to his or her emotional state and attitude.

NOTES

The literature on general analysis of melodic contours is very disappointingly slight. For Romance melodic curves, cf. Sapon, 1958/59.

14

Phonemics

THE ORIGINAL AIM of the International Phonetic Association, in promulgating the IPA phonetic transcription, was to provide a framework and a set of symbols which would be universally applicable to all languages of the world, and to all sounds which the human vocal organs could possibly produce. After half a century or more of intensive analysis of speech sounds, it became evident, around the 1920's, that the goal of the IPA was unrealizable, for two reasons. In the first place, as we have been pointing out at various places in our discussion so far, most of the "points" in the organs of speech (e.g., velum, palate, alveola, teeth, etc.) and the other ranges of possible variation in the articulation of sounds (e.g., in pitch or intensity) are infinitely gradated, so that it is simply impossible to isolate the totality of possible points on these scales. Henry Sweet's ability to distinguish 120 different vocoid sounds (cf. p. 51) was a tour de force of virtuosity, but even Sweet was far from exhausting the total number of possibilities. As hitherto uninvestigated languages have been studied, unsuspected new sounds and shadings of sound-quality have continually been discovered; the history of the IPA transcription, since its beginnings, has been one of continual expansion to meet previously unexpected needs.

Accordingly, some phoneticians tended, at one time, to take a pessimistic view of the possibility of ever reaching a satisfactory over-all classification of speech-sounds. Such pessimism was rendered unnecessary by the realization that this goal was, after all, irrelevant to the main purpose of linguistics, which is the analysis of the structure of languages. Several leading scholars on both sides of the Atlantic—Prince Nicholas Troubetzkoy in Czechoslovakia, and Edward Sapir and Leonard Bloomfield in America—came, largely independently of each other, to realize in the 1920's that, in the phonology of a language, it is more important to identify the functional units of sound, the *phonemes*, and their relation to each other, than it is to attain an impossibly minute detail in describing every single speech-sound which its speakers may use. No single linguistic system ever uses the total range of possible speech-sounds; on the contrary, for every given language, it is necessary only to identify the phonemes which its speakers use to establish meaningful contrasts within the system itself. This is a relatively simple task, since, although the totality of possible speech-sounds is infinite, the number of phonemes in any one language is quite limited, ranging normally from fifteen to forty-five or fifty. This approach does not deny (as some have mistakenly thought) the importance of phonetics as a technique for analyzing the raw material of speech-sounds; such a study is useful itself and indispensable as a basis for further analysis on a higher level. However, the main task of the linguistic analyst lies beyond the phonetic level, in determining the contrastive phonological units of the language, as a basis on which to build up, in its turn, a description of the higher levels (morphologic, syntactical) of the language he is dealing with.

Since each language has its own phonemic structure, we cannot expect that the same sound, or the same group of sounds, will necessarily have the same function in one language as in another. For instance, both English and Castilian Spanish have a pair of interdental fricatives, the voiceless [θ] and the voiced [ð], which from the phonetic point of view are very similar. The relation of the two sounds to each other and to other sounds is, however, very different in the phonologic system of English from what it is in that of Spanish. The English [θ] and [ð] are clearly in contrast with each other, in that they serve to distinguish words of different meaning: cf. pairs like *ether* ['iθɾ] vs. *either* ['iðɾ], *wreath* ['riθ] vs. *wreathe* ['rið], and *thigh* ['θai̯] vs. *thy* ['ðai̯]. The fricative [θ] also contrasts with the voiceless alveolar and bilabial stops [t] and [p], as in *tick* ['tɪk] vs. *thick* ['θɪk] and *pick* ['pɪk]; similarly, [ð] contrasts with [d] and [b], as in *then* ['ðɛn] vs. *den* ['dɛn] and *Ben* ['bɛn]. Our voiceless [θ] fits into a series with the labio-dental voiceless fricative [f], and [ð] parallels the voiced labio-dental fricative [v], so that we can safely say that we have a set of eight phonemes in this part of the English consonant system, with the alveolar-interdental phonemes /t d θ ð/ paralleling the four bilabial and labio-dental phonemes /p b f v/. Fig. 12 shows the pattern into which these eight English phonemes fall with respect to each other.

In Castilian Spanish, however, the situation is different. Speakers of this variety of Spanish have [θ] in clear contrast with [t], as in *ciento* ['θjento] "a hundred", vs. *tiento* ['tjento] "tiento" (a type of musical composition); with [f], as in *cinco* ['θiŋko] "five", vs. *finca* ['fiŋka]: "farm"; and with [p], as in *cesar* [θe'sar] "to cease" vs. *pesar* [pe'sar] "to weigh". But [ð] is not in contrast with [d] in Castilian or any other variety of Spanish, so that the relation of this pair is not parallel to that of [θ] and [t]. There is no instance in Spanish in which [ð] and [d] play a role in keeping the meanings of two words apart; and [ð] and [d] are in complementary distribution (cf. p. 26), since [d] occurs after pause and after [n], [r] and [l] (as in *dado* ['daðo] "given", *cuando* ['kwando] "when", *guardar* [gwar'dar] "to look", *caldo* ['kaldo] "broth"), whereas [ð] occurs elsewhere, including between vowels within a phrase, as in *ha dado* ['a'ðaðo] "he has given", *piedra* ['pjeðra] "stone". Furthermore, the relationship between [ð] and [d] is paralleled by those between [β] and [b], [γ] and [g]; in each of these pairs, the plosive and the fricative are in non-contrastive, complementary distribution. Hence we are justified in considering that in Spanish [d] and [ð] are not two separate phonemes, but positional variants (allophones), and, similarly, that [b] and [β] are to be classed together as belonging to one phoneme, and that [g] and [γ] belong likewise together. How we transcribe these phonemes will depend on several factors, of which IPA phonetic transcription is only one. In this instance, we could use either of the letters d or ð for our phonemic symbol, as might be most convenient typographically; clearly d will be far more available than ð on typewriters and in print-shops, and so we will choose d, and likewise b in preference to β, and g in preference to γ. Spanish has, therefore, in this range, only three dental or interdental phonemes

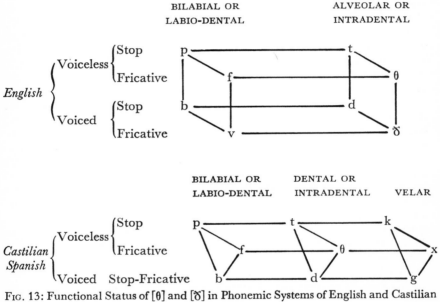

Fig. 13: Functional Status of [θ] and [ð] in Phonemic Systems of English and Castilian Spanish.

/t θ d/, paralleling the three in bilabial or labio-dental position /p f b/, and the three in velar position /k x g/, as shown in Fig. 13.

By contrasting the patterns of English and Castilian Spanish as shown in Fig. 13, we see that where English has two voiced phonemes in alveolar-intradental position, the stop /d/ and the fricative /ð/, Spanish has only one, which we decided to transcribe /d/, which, however, includes the two positional variants [d] and [ð], similar in sound but not in function to the English sounds [d] and [ð]. To make the differences in patterning evident, some scholars like to draw lines along each dimension of phonemic contrast, and to point out the differences in graphic shape that appear in each diagram as a result. English has a contrast in voicing between each of the pairs /p b/, /f v/, /t d/, and /θ ð/, as shown by the vertical lines in the English part of

Fig. 12; in position of articulation, between each of the pairs /p t/, /f θ/, /b d/, and /v ð/, as shown by the horizontal lines; and in manner of articulation, between each of the pairs /p f/, /b v/, /t θ/, and /d ð/, as shown by the lines running in front-vs.-back direction. The resultant geometrical figure is cube-like. In Castilian Spanish, however, there is contrast in manner of articulation only between the voiceless sets /p t k/ and /f θ x/, but not in the voiced series, in which stops and fricatives do not contrast phonemically and we have only the one set /b d g/. Hence the resultant figure is similar to a triangular prism, not to a four-sided shape. Such geometrical comparisons are often helpful to understanding the functional relationships involved, although they are not of the essence of phonemic analysis.

At this point, confusion tends to arise, because we often have difficulty distinguishing between phonetic symbols, phonemic symbols, and letters of the alphabet as used in our orthography. We must keep in mind that the characters between square brackets [ ] refer to sounds, and should, if possible, be read off by making the sound itself: e.g., reading [d] as "the sound —" (here make an alveolar or dental voiced plosive, instead of pronouncing the name of the letter, in this case "dee"). A phoneme is not itself a sound, but a unit of sound, which may include one or more sounds. Hence a phonemic symbol should not be read off with a sound, nor—as even many linguistic analysts do—with the name of the letter which represents it ("the phoneme dee"), but with a longer but necessary circumlocution, e.g., reading off /d/ as "the phoneme transcribed dee". Neither the phonetic symbol nor the phonemic symbol in themselves stand for any feature of our writing system, though there is often a certain amount of correlation, and, in general, both phonetic and phonemic symbols are chosen, where possible, to coincide with the traditional use of such unambiguous letters as b, d, m, etc.

Numerous definitions of the phoneme have been proposed, none of them wholly satisfactory. Depending on the point of view taken, we can define a phoneme as a unit, a rubric, a bundle of sound-features, or a point of contrast. We have already emphasized that a phoneme is a functional unit of speech-sound. In this definition, we are emphasizing the relation of phonemics to phonetics, as also in the related definition of a phoneme as a rubric under which one or more noncontrasting sounds are to be classified according to the criteria discussed in Chap. 5. A phoneme is a combination of features of sound (e.g., stop articulation, bilabial position, and voicing in /b/, or high and front tongue position and absence of lip-rounding in /i/) which render one phoneme distinct from another, and which are therefore known as *distinctive features*. These distinctive features normally occur grouped together in "bundles" of several at a time (tongue height and advancement, and other features, in vowels; place and manner of articulation and voicing in consonants). Any linguistic phenomenon, whether phoneme, morpheme, or syntactic combination, derives its function from being in contrast with other comparable phenomena in the system. Thus, for instance, the English phoneme /b/ derives its special function from the fact that in voicing it contrasts with /p/, in position it contrasts with /d/ and /g/, and in manner of articulation with /v/ and /m/. If, for example, /b/ were wholly isolated as a single unit of sound that was not set off by being in opposition to any other unit of sound, there would be no functional contrast and hence no pattern of any kind. A phoneme is, viewed in this light, a point in a network of functional contrasts in the phonetic material of a language. However, some linguistic analysts go too far in maintaining that contrast in patterning is the only factor that determines the nature of a phoneme.

Much ink has been wasted in a futile discussion as to whether phonemes are "realities," "fictions," or "abstractions." From the point of view of purely physical phenomena, the only "reality" is the single speech-event, which is never repeated exactly the same twice in succession. Every item which we study in our analysis, whether speech-sound or phoneme, whether linguistic form or morpheme, is an "abstraction" on some level, higher or lower. All our study of language is based on the discovery of recurrent partial similarities between utterances; the resultant abstractions have as much "reality" as do any other units and patterns of human behavior, e.g., the pattern-points and relations within kinship-systems, political organizations, or habits of eating and drinking. We do not need to introduce special theories of psychology or philosophy to recognize the "reality" of the phoneme as a unit of human behavior, no matter what our views on metaphysics and its relation to linguistic meaning. Experimentation has shown that naive native speakers of any given language react differentially, not to single speech-sounds, but to phonemic units of their native language, and are normally incapable of recognizing nonfunctional, subphonemic differences in sound: for instance, a native speaker of Spanish usually has no realization that he or she is using [d] as an allophone of /d/ in some positions and [ð] in others, and when native speakers of Spanish learn English, they have to put in special effort on learning to make a phonemic distinction between /d/ and /ð/.

The relation between the phoneme and the speech-sound(s) which is (are) subsumed under it can be viewed from two angles, two directions. If we start from the sounds themselves viewed as raw material, we can consider them as being subsumed or classified under the phoneme as a rubric, and can term the sound(s) the *allophone(s)* of the phoneme. (Every phoneme has at least one allophone, and many have two, three, or more.) If, however, we take the phoneme as our starting point and descend from it to the speech-sounds which it includes, we can consider them as *positional variants* of the phoneme, or we can say that they are *realizations* or *actualizations* thereof. That is, the phoneme is *realized*—or *actualized*—by manifesting itself as one speech-sound when it occurs in a given position (say, Spanish /d/ appearing as [d] after pause, /r/, /l/ or /n/) and as another speech-sound in another environment (e.g., Spanish /d/ varying to [ð] in other positions). The choice of these terms implies, to a certain extent, the direction in which the analyst is moving in his treatment of the topic: the term *allophone* implies passage from speech-sound to phoneme, and the other terms mentioned above suggest that we are passing in the opposite direction. Either direction of analysis is permissible, and each has its usefulness for certain types of approach to phonology.

The process of classifying speech-sounds into phonemes is simply that of applying the criteria discussed on pp. 24–27 and 33. If we wish to know whether any two sounds belong to the same phoneme, we investigate whether there are instances in which the difference between the two makes a difference in meaning. If there are, the two cannot belong to the same phoneme, as in the instances of English *tick* ['tɪk] vs. *thick* ['θɪk], or Spanish *tiento* ['tjento] vs. *ciento* ['θjento] cited on p. 77. For this purpose, linguistic analysts prefer *minimal pairs*, i.e., pairs of forms in which the two sounds involved are the only features that differentiate the forms, as in these and most of the other examples given on p. 77; but minimal pairs are not essential to show that two sounds do not belong to the same phoneme. If we cannot discover any instance in which the two sounds in question are in contrast—and this often involves a long search and investigation of even the least frequent elements of a language—then the pair is "suspicious," i.e., we suspect that they may belong to the same phoneme. We then apply the further criteria of phonetic similarity and identity of function (pp. 26–27). If the two sounds are phonetically similar in some respect, then there is considerable likelihood that they may belong to the same phoneme; however, if they are not similar in any way, then we do not put them together in the same phoneme, even if they are in noncontrastive distribution (e.g., the English sound [h], which is a voiceless glottal fricative or aspirate, and [ŋ], which is a voiced velar nasal continuant).

We normally look for functional parallelisms in other parts of the phonologic system to confirm our assignment of two or more sounds to the same phoneme, as in the Spanish materials discussed on pp. 77–79, where the identity of function of [d] and [ð] is paralleled by that of [b] and [β] and by that of [g] and [γ]. In many instances, the decision is far from clear-cut—especially in the case of some present-day languages with immense speech-communities like English, French and Russian—and it is perfectly possible for scholars to disagree on the phonemic status of a given feature or set of features, even after intensive investigation and discussion (cf. Chap. 20).

Our choice of symbols to represent phonemes is considerably freer than is our choice of phonetic characters. In phonetics, although the use of IPA is not considered obligatory by all scholars, it is very widespread and advisable, even if only for reasons of mutual comprehension across the boundaries of language materials. A phonemic transcription, on the other hand, can, by its very nature, be designed only for one particular language or dialect, since the phonemic system of each language differs from that of every other, and a phonemic transcription must be devised to suit the pattern of the language being investigated and no other. By and large, it would seem advisable to base one's phonemic transcription on IPA wherever possible; but, especially where typographical problems would result, it is perfectly permissible to use characters in ways different from those of IPA and, if necessary, to introduce letters or combinations of letters that are not used in IPA (e.g., č or ch in the value of tʃ). On occasion, a phonemic transcription is adapted, in some respect, to the values assigned to letters in the conventional orthography of some standard language, for practical reasons, as when one follows French spelling in using *ch* for /ʃ/ and *j* for /ʒ/ in the McConnell-Laubach orthography for Haitian Creole, in order to ease the task of speakers of Creole in learning French spelling at a later stage. A phonemically-based spelling adapted in this way to the practical needs of a people or ethnic group is called an *ethnophonemic transcription*.

Confusion often arises over the difference between a phonetic and a phonemic transcription, and over the need for having the latter in addition to the former. Within a short time after the inception of IPA, many phoneticians realized that it was not necessary to mark every minute difference of sound, in a *narrow* phonetic transcription, except in the first stages of phonetic analysis. Reacting against the excessive complexity of narrow transcription, some workers began to simplify their transcription by omitting distinctions that did not seem great to their ears, and evolved a somewhat less complex type of phonetic writing called *broad* transcription. For instance, in a narrow transcription of my own speech, one would transcribe *pool* as ['p'uʷɫ], *empty* as ['emptiʲ], and *idle* as ['aɪdɫ]; a broad transcription would omit notation of the aspirated [p'] in *pool* and of the upward glide following the vowels [i] and [u] in *pool* and *empty*, but would still mark the difference between the front and back *l*-sounds, and would transcribe these same words as ['puɫ], ['empti] and ['aɪdl]. Yet "broad transcription" has never been wholly satisfactory, because phoneticians using it have tended to omit details that seemed to them unessential, without explicit and rigorous criteria for their procedures, on the basis of their own impression of what was essential and what was not. A thoroughly functional approach is necessary, in order to identify the functional units of sound of each language, and a phonemic transcription in order to symbolize them according to a more rigorous procedure than that of a mere broad phonetic transcription.

In other words, in a phonetic transcription our aim is to keep each symbol in a one-to-one correspondence with a specific speech-sound, in a framework of reference of the entire gamut of sounds producible by human beings. In a phonemic transcription, on the other hand, it is still essential to preserve a one-to-one correspondence, but in a much more restricted framework, between each symbol and a phoneme of a particular system, for the purpose of representing only the relatively small number of functional units found in that system. The resultant freedom of choice of characters to represent phonemes, and the fact that a given symbol may symbolize one phoneme in a given system but another phoneme in a different system (e.g., the use of /y/ to stand for a high front rounded vowel in French, but for a high central unrounded vowel in Roumanian) is often confusing to laymen and newcomers to linguistics. As one becomes more familiar with linguistic analysis, however, one has no more trouble shifting from one value of a phonemic symbol to another, or from the use of one symbol to that of another for a phoneme of a particular language, than does a skilled automobile driver in changing from one gear-shift to another as he drives various types of machines.

NOTES

Phonemics in general: Martinet, 1949; Sapir, 1925, 1933; Swadesh, 1934; Twaddell, 1935; Trubetzkoy, 1958.

Relations between phonetics and phonemics: Bühler, 1931; Hockett, 1942; Jakobson, 1956.

Distinctive features: Jakobson, Fant and Halle, 1952.

Statistical description of phonemic characteristics: Cherry, Halle and Jakobson, 1953.

15

Vowel Patterns

LIKE CERTAIN TYPES of speech sound (vocoids and contoids), certain corresponding types of phoneme—vowels and consonants*—come, or seem to come, like segments in an utterance, in a sequence one after the other, and the phonemic symbols representing them can be written in a line from left to right. Vowel and consonant phonemes are, therefore, often referred to as *segmental* or *linear* phonemes. Other phonemic features, such as stress, juncture, and intonation patterns, do not come either "before" or "after" vowels and consonants, but occur at the same time, extending over segments of utterances, either syllables or longer stretches. In phonemic transcription, we represent stress, juncture, and intonation by symbols placed either above those for linear phonemes (e.g. accent-marks over vowel letters) or next to them in accordance with special conventions that they are to be understood as applying to specific stretches of linear symbols (as we do with punctuation marks like the comma or the question mark). Hence phenomena of stress, juncture, and intonation are often called *nonlinear* or *suprasegmental* phonemes. Some prefer to use the general term *prosody* for suprasegmental phonemic phenomena, and *prosodic feature* for individual phonemic aspects of prosody.

Phonemes are classified and their patterns are established in terms of the features by which they stand in contrast with each other, and which, as pointed out on p. 79, we therefore term *distinctive features*. Since phonemes are composed of distinctive features, another term for these latter is *phonological components*. Among segmental phonemes, there is one type whose distinctive features include contrasts in tongue-height and advancement, plus, on occasion, lip-rounding, nasality, length, and other added phonological components; bundles of these features make up *vowel* phonemes, which obviously correspond on the phonemic level to vocoids on the phonetic level. The other major type of segmental phoneme is of course the consonants, whose major distinctive features involve place and manner of articulation, and voicing, and which correspond to contoids. As on the phonetic level semivocoids and semicontoids, so do semivowels and semiconsonants occupy, on the phonemic level, an intermediate functional position between vowels and consonants.

Because all vocoid articulations involve differences in tongue-height and

---

* Whenever we use the terms *vowel* and *consonant* alone, it is to be understood that we are referring to phonemes; if we wish to refer to letters of the alphabet, we shall speak specifically of *vowel letters* and *consonant letters*.

advancement (Chap. 5), these are the two dimensions of contrast which are found in the vowel systems of virtually all languages. There is only one instance reported in which, phonemically, tongue height is the only dimension of contrast (although, phonetically, there are also differences in tongue advancement); this is Adyge, a Caucasian language, which has one high, one mid, and one low vowel phoneme. Such contrasts are usually represented graphically by geometrical diagrams, of the type given in Fig. 12. For Adyge, we have simply a one-line vertical scheme:

ɨ
|
ə
|
a

Apparently there are no instances of languages with contrast only in tongue advancement, of the hypothetical type /i/—/u/ or /i/—/ɨ/—/u/. It has been surmised that stages anterior to Proto-Indo-Hittite (for this and other "proto-languages," cf. Chap. 51) may have had only one purely vocalic phoneme, or even none; but these hypothetical stages are supposed to have had various semivowels as well, which would have functioned both as centers of syllables and as onsets or codas, i.e., as consonants.

Aside from the marginal types just mentioned, most vowel systems involve two or three dimensions of contrast; when there are more than three, it is often convenient to set up separate subsystems rather than complicate the pattern with multidimensional schemes. Of two-dimensional patterns, the most common involve simply a front-vs.-back contrast, and either two levels of tongue-height or three. With two levels of height, high vs. low, we have as the simplest variant a triangular pattern superficially similar to the phonetic vocoid triangle (Fig. 3, p. 47):

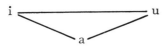

Such a pattern is found in some varieties of Arabic, in Cree (an Algonquian language), Eskimo, and a number of other languages. Within a framework of this type, further intermediate contrasts may be included, e.g., a high-central vowel, as in Amahuaca (a South American Indian language):

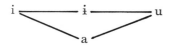

A two-way contrast in the low as well as the high level is also widespread, forming a rectangle rather than a triangle:

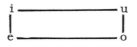

as in Apachean, Fox, Shawnee and other North and South American Indian languages, as well as (probably) in Proto-Germanic.

With three levels of tongue-height contrasting with each other, there are more possibilities for variation. The most frequent pattern is almost "classical," having contrasts of front vs. back at the high and mid levels, but not at the low level, as in Spanish, Modern Greek, Russian, Czech, Fijian, Japanese, and many African, American, and Pacific languages:

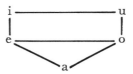

A front-vs.-back contrast can occur at the lowest level as well, though not so frequently; we find this type of pattern in Persian, Ukrainian, Menomini (an Algonquian language), and others:

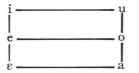

Four levels of tongue-height also occur, although in many instances they may be reanalyzed with a semicomponential technique (see Chap. 20). In such a pattern, we can find either an extension of the "classical" type (see the previous paragraph), with an added pair of contrasts in the central range (high-mid vs. low-mid), as in Italian and Proto-Italo-Western Romance (so-called "Vulgar Latin") and other languages:

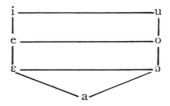

or else, with a front-vs.-back contrast at the lowest level also, as in some
dialects of Polish:

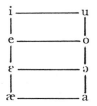

or, in the low range, with /a/ vs. /ɑ/ instead of /æ/ vs. /a/.

If a third dimension of contrast is present, it often involves significant lip-
rounding in addition to tongue-height and advancement. In many languages
(e.g., German, Hungarian, etc.) there is, in addition to the front-unrounded
and the back-rounded vowels, a series of front-rounded vowels:

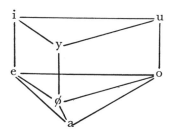

and a similar figure results from an added series, not of front-rounded, but of
back-unrounded vowels, as in Roumanian:

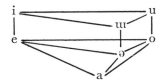

In some instances of this type, there is a further contrast at the lowest level
of tongue-height between a front and a back low vowel, e.g., /æ/ vs. /a/ or
/a/ vs. /ɑ/. On occasion, there is a three-dimensional contrast at only one
level of tongue-height, as in Taki-Taki (the English-based creole of Dutch
Guiana, also called Sranan):

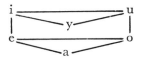

A highly symmetrical pattern is posited by some scholars for English, with a three-way contrast on all three levels:

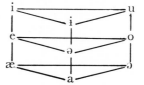

In Esthonian we find a similar nine-vowel pattern, but with the third dimension formed by a front-rounded vowel series:

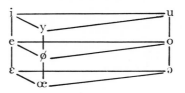

The oral vowel system of standard orthoepic French is like that given here for Esthonian, plus an added level (low) with a contrast between front /a/ and back /ɑ/, and (according to some analysts) a mid-central unrounded /ə/, very defective in its distribution, which does not fit into the pattern:

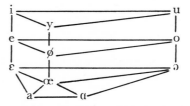

These patterns which we have given do not exhaust the possibilities by any means. Furthermore, not all vowel-patterns are as symmetrical as these, since in many languages there are contrasts in one part of the pattern which are not paralleled in the other. Thus, for instance, for Proto-Continental Romance (intermediate between Latin and "Vulgar Latin"), we have to set up eight vowel phonemes, whose pattern was as follows:

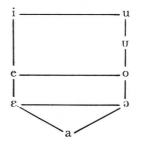

without any /ɪ/-phoneme to contrast directly with /ʊ/. Other varieties of skewness in all the various possible dimensions can be attested from a number of languages, but lack of space prevents a detailed listing.

If other dimensions of contrast are present, it is often economical to extract one or more of them as phonological components and symbolize them separately. We normally do this with Classical Latin, which we know to have had ten individual vowel phonemes, usually written in our textbooks *i e a o u ī ē ā ō ū*, and which we can represent in phonemic transcription as /i e a o u i: e: a: o: u:/. One could, if desired, simply state that we have two subsystems, one with five short vowels and one with five long, and leave it at that, making parallel diagrams for the two subsystems:

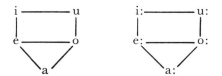

or we could make a single diagram combining the two sets so as to show vowel-length as an additional dimension of contrast:

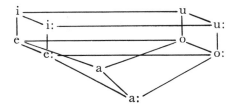

It is more economical, and perhaps more revelatory of the basic structure of the Latin vowel-system, to recognize simply a five-vowel system of the "classical" type described on p. 86, with an added component of vowel-length (symbol /:/) which applies to all five vowels:

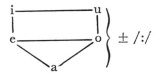

When the vowel-systems of all the Romance languages (which are descendants of Latin, though not directly of Classical Latin) are viewed in this light, their history is seen to involve essentially the addition of such further components as vowel-length, tenseness, or nasalization, or the development of new dimensions of contrast, added to the basic framework of a "classical"-type five-vowel system.

Not only vowel-length, but nasalization, the contrast between high-mid and low-mid tongue-height, that between tenseness and laxness, and any other features which it is desired to treat in this way, can be extracted as separate phonological components, symbolized with appropriate diacritical marks placed over or following the vowel-symbol. Thus, in French, we recognize a subsystem of nasal vowels, which IPA symbolizes in phonetic transcription as [ɛ̃ ɑ̃ ɔ̃ œ̃]; functionally, however, there is no need to identify the nasal vowels with certain contrasts ([ɛ] vs. [e], [ɔ] vs. [o], [œ] vs. [ø], and [ɑ] vs. [a]) which have significance only in the oral vowel subsystem. We can therefore, using /e/ to stand for the mid-front-unrounded vowel range, transcribe [ɛ̃] as /ẽ/, and similarly we can symbolize [ɔ̃] as /õ/, [ɑ̃] as /ã/; [œ̃] can be left as /œ̃/, since it is easier typographically to use this symbol than /ø/ with a til over it. The resultant subsystem of French nasal vowels shows the following pattern:

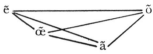

In the usage of many speakers of French, especially Parisians, the nasal vowel /œ̃/ has merged with /ẽ/, so that, for example, /œ̃parfœ̃/ "a perfume" has become /ẽparfẽ/. For these speakers, the nasal vowel subsystem has been reduced from three-dimensional to two-dimensional:

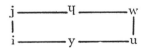

Semiconsonants show the same type of phonologic components as do vowels, and hence are to be classed along with them (normally on the high level of tongue-height). A typical pattern, involving three semiconsonants paralleling three high vowels, is that of modern standard French, in which /j/ is in the same position as the high-front-unrounded /i/, and likewise /w/ corresponds to /u/ and /ɥ/ patterns with /y/:

$$
\begin{array}{ccc}
j & \text{---}ɥ\text{---} & w \\
| & & | \\
i & \text{---}y\text{---} & u
\end{array}
$$

However, a semivocoid or semicontoid is to be classed as a semiconsonant phoneme only if it patterns with the consonants in the system of the language as a whole, rather than with the vowels. In English, the semivocoids [i̯] and [u̯] occur only after vowels, as in *high* ['hai̯] and *how* ['hau̯], and the semicontoids [j] and [w] only before vowels, as in *yes* ['jɛs], *win* ['wɪn]. Since they occur in complementary distribution and are phonetically very similar, fulfilling the same functions in the pattern of the language, [j] and [i̯] clearly belong together in the same phoneme, and so do [w] and [u̯]. Each of the

English phonemes thus constituted behaves like a consonant in many ways in the system of the language, e.g., in having the preconsonantal form of the indefinite article *a* [ə] used before it rather than the prevocalic form *an* [ən], as in *a year* [ə 'jir], *a wife* [ə'waif̣]; hence we shall class the two phonemes under discussion as semi-consonants, transcribing them /j/ and /w/ respectively, as in *a year* /əjír/, *a wife* /əwájf/. In Italian, however, [i̥] and [j] do not contrast in any way with [i], but function simply as allophones thereof before or after other vowels, and the situation is similar for [w] and [u̥] with respect to [u]; hence, for Italian, we do not set up /j/ and /w/ as phonemes separate from /i/ and /u/, and words like *piatto* ['pjat:o] "dish", and *causa* ['kau̥sa] "cause", will be interpreted phonemically as /piátto/ and /káusa/, respectively.

It is often convenient, in describing a language, to give a listing of the phonemes, with, under each, the indication of the allophones, the conditions under which they occur, and examples. Under the examples, it is most informative to cite them, not only in phonemic transcription, but also in phonetic transcription and in conventional spelling (if the language has such), with the meaning in quotation marks. We give a sample of such a listing, for the vowel phonemes of Italian:

PHONEME	ALLOPHONES	CONDITIONS OF OCCURRENCE	EXAMPLES
/i/	[j]	Before a following vowel (other than /i/)	/piátto/ ['pjat:o] *piatto* "plate"
	[i̥]	After a preceding vowel (other than /i/)	/mái/ ['mai̥] *mai* "never"
	[i]	Elsewhere	/vino/ ['vi:no] *vino* "wine"
/e^/	[e^]	Under stress	/mé^no/ ['me^:no] *meno* "less"
/e/	[ɛ]	Under stress, and unstressed before /m n l r/	/béne/ ['bɛ:ne] *bene* "well"; /meló^ne/ [mɛ'lo^:ne] *melone* "melon"
	[e]	Unstressed, elsewhere	/sédé^re/ [se'de^:re] *sedere* "to sit"
/a/	[a]	Everywhere	/guardáre/ [gwarʳ'da:re] *guardare* "to look"
/o/	[ɔ]	Under stress, and unstressed before /m n l r/	/pórta/['pɔrʳta] *porta* "door"; /ométto/ [ɔ'met:o] *ometto* "I omit"
	[o]	Unstressed, elsewhere	/votáre/ [vo'ta:re] *votare* "to vote"
/o^/	[o^]	Under stress	/benó^ne/ [bɛ'no:ne] *benone* "very good"
/u/	[w]	Before following vowel (other than /u/)	/buóno/ ['bwɔ:no] *buono* "good"
	[u̥]	After preceding vowel (other than /u/)	/káusa/ ['kau̥sa], ['kau̥za] *causa* "cause"
	[u]	Elsewhere	/futúro/ [fu'tu:ro] *futuro* "future"

All stressed vowels are phonetically long in free, nonfinal syllables, as in examples just given.

Pattern of Italian vowel phonemes:

$$
\begin{array}{cc}
\text{i} & \text{u} \\
\text{e} & \text{o}
\end{array}
\Big\} \{ \pm \ /^/ \ \text{(contrast between high-mid and low-mid) under stress}
$$

a

NOTES

On vowel patterns in general: Hockett, 1955, §24.
Italian vowels: Hall, 1948b.

16

Consonant Patterns

THE PATTERNS assumed by consonant phonemes are usually rather more complicated and considerably less symmetrical than are those of vowels. There are two main dimensions of phonemic contrast found in all languages studied so far: place and manner of articulation, corresponding to these characteristics of contoids (cf. Chap. 10). In addition, there may also be further contrasts in voicing, glottalization, aspiration, palatalization, pre-nasalization, length, etc.; in any given language, these contrasts may occur singly or more than one at a time as distinctive features of particular phonemes. There are more possible differentiations in place and manner for consonants than there are in tongue-height and advancement for vowels. It is relatively rare, however, to find entire systems of consonants which show even an approximate symmetry throughout; almost all consonant-systems show some gaps.

In regard to place of articulation, all languages seem to show at least a three-way contrast, even though in sub-sections of the system (e.g., oral consonants) there is only a two-way contrast. In Hawaiian, for instance, the vowel system involves a "classical" five-vowel pattern (p. 86), plus two semiconsonants /j w/, which pattern with the top vowels, and six consonants: two stops /p k/, two nasals /m n/, the lateral /l/, and the laryngeal affricate /h/. At an earlier stage, apparently, the /k/ was pronounced farther front in the mouth, as a /t/, in the same position as for /n/, so that the small consonant-system of Hawaiian was relatively symmetrical:

	Extra-oral	Oral	Laryngeal
Stop	p	t	?
Fricative			h
Nasal	m	n	
Lateral		l	

In modern times, the /t/ has become /k/, but without changing its functional status, since the essence of either /t/ or /k/ in this pattern is that it is simply an oral (i.e., neither labial nor laryngeal) articulation. That we choose to write /k/ rather than /t/ for modern Hawaiian [k] is due primarily to an ingrained residuum of alphabetic conservatism, in that only the most sophisticated and uninhibited phonemicist would be willing to fly so violently in the face of our graphic tradition.

The consonant-pattern of Hawaiian is extremely simple, and yet it takes somewhat of a tour de force of artificiality to make it appear completely symmetrical, involving, in its modern form, only a three-way contrast in place and a three-way contrast in manner. In virtually all other languages, the contrasts are more numerous (in that they may also include such dimensions as voicing, glottalization, etc., as mentioned above) and more extensive within each dimension. In their over-all consonant-patterns, most languages would seem to have more than a three-way contrast in place of articulation. For instance, Latin, which apparently had a fairly simple consonant-system, had in its stops a three-way contrast, involving bilabial, dental, and velar positions:

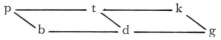

but its fricatives included a labio-dental /f/ and a laryngeal /h/.

Here again, it depends on how far we wish to depart from phonetic reality, whether we recognize for Latin a three-way or a four-way contrast. Most phonemicists would probably be willing to collapse bilabial and labio-dental place of articulation into one functional grouping, "labial" position, since they are in complementary distribution in Latin and do not contrast with each other; one would therefore place /f/ together with /p b/ under the heading of "labial" consonants. But as to /h/, some would be willing, for Latin, to lump laryngeal and velar place of articulation together into one functional grouping which might be called simply "guttural" position, and others would not. If we group /h/ along with /k g/, we then have a three-way contrast, for Latin, between labial, purely oral, and "guttural" stops and fricatives:

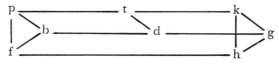

However, if we do not group /h/ with /k g/, we have a four-way contrast (labial, dental, velar and laryngeal), with two holes in the pattern:

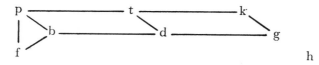

In many other languages, there is indisputably a four-way or even a five-way over-all contrast in position. In German, the stops, taken alone, show a three-way contrast (labial, alveolar, velar), and the fricatives alone likewise

show a three-way contrast (labial, velar, laryngeal), but one which intersects
with the stop contrasts so much as to render it impossible to collapse velar and
laryngeal into one position even if we wanted to:

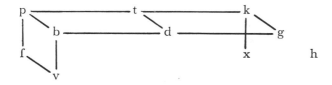

The greatest number of contrasts in position ever found seems to be on the
order of five, as in Kota (a Dravidian language of southern India), which has
labial, interdental, dental, apico-palatal (retroflex), and (dorso-) velar. The
issue is often confused by the question as to whether it is desirable or not to
take palatalized, assibilated or affricated sounds as constituting single phonemes or clusters of two phonemes each. Thus, in English, are the [tʃ] of
church and the [dʒ] of *judge* to be interpreted as single phonemes, /č/ and /ǰ/
respectively, or as clusters /tʃ/ and /dʒ/? Our answer will depend on what
we make of these sounds' status with respect to distribution (cf. Chap. 17)
and to juncture (Chap. 18); but on our answer will depend, in turn, our
interpretation of the English consonant-pattern: shall we recognize four positions of articulation (labial, dental, velar, and laryngeal) or five (adding
palatal between dental and velar)? If we adopt the former solution, we have
fewer positions (thereby being more economical) and a more compact pattern
for the stops and fricatives:

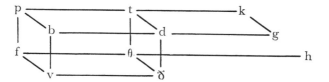

but we have more clusters of consonants (/tʃ/ and /dʒ/). If we recognize
/č/ and /ǰ/ as unit phonemes (assibilates), we have more positions in the
stop series, but fewer clusters and a palatal position for stops corresponding to
that which we have to set up for sibilants anyway (see Fig. 14).

What we have said for contrasts in position holds also for contrasts in manner. In almost all languages, the contrasts in manner are three-, four-, or
even five-way. In English, for instance, we have stops, fricatives, sibilants,
nasals, and the lateral /l/ and dorsal retroflex /r/, so that the total pattern
(if we accept /č/ and /ǰ/ as stop phonemes) is as shown in Fig. 14. For some
varieties of English, /r/ is not a dorsal retroflex continuant but (between
vowels) a tongue-tip flap (British English "veddy"), and so for these varieties we should perhaps place /r/ in the dental column under /l/, thus
making a six-way rather than a five-way contrast in manner.

In some languages, additional dimensions of contrast enter into the pattern, creating more or less neat additional sets. For instance, in Russian virtually all consonants appear both palatalized and nonpalatalized ("soft" and "hard" in traditional terminology), and we have to assume that a similar situation existed in Proto-Gallo-Romance. For Russian, we set up a pattern as shown in Fig. 15, in which the subscript /,/ (others prefer a little superscript /ʲ/) stands for palatalization, and the palatalized correspondents of

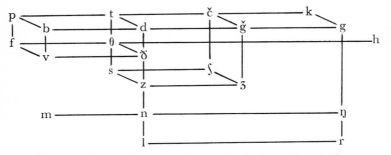

Fig. 14: English Consonant Pattern (Including /č/ and /ǧ/).

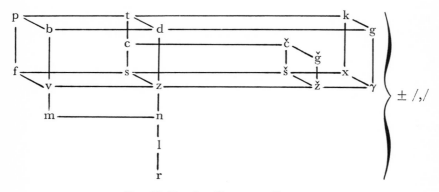

Fig. 15: Russian Consonant Pattern.

each of the phonemes listed here will be transcribed phonemically with a subscript comma, e.g. /p/ and /ț/ in /piț/ "to drink". (We can, for Russian and many other languages, combine the fricative and the sibilant into one functional manner of articulation, because they are, in such languages, in complementary distribution.)

Sometimes the final results of such tabulations are fairly symmetrical, as in the consonant system of orthoepic French (Fig. 16). In the case of French, we can, on the grounds of complementary distribution, bring bilabial and labio-dental together under "labial" position; palatal and velar together under "palato-velar"; and fricative and sibilant together under "spirant" manner, without doing violence to the phonetic facts of the language and without forcing completely disparate elements into artificial parallelism or pushing recalcitrant elements "out into the cold." For Russian, for instance, /c/ and /č ǧ/ have the same manner of articulation, assibilate: /c/ is phonetically [tˢ], and /č ǧ/ are [tˢ] and [dᶻ] respectively. They form, taken together, a set of assibilates which introduce a rather asymmetrical element into an otherwise regular pattern. One can take care of /č ǧ/ by putting them into the row of stops along with /p t k b d g / and calling them "palatal stops"; one is then left with /c/, which can be taken care of, in such a solution, only by "sweeping it under the carpet," i.e. by treating it as a "left-over."

The consonant-patterns of most languages, when taken as wholes, simply do not lend themselves to formulation in overly neat patterns. As Edward Sapir said, no language forms a water-tight system, and we should be suspicious if too pretty a picture results from the phonemic analysis of a phonetically asymmetrical situation. In despair of ever achieving complete symmetry for over-all consonant-patterns, some phonemicists prefer to separate

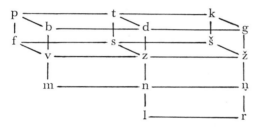

FIG. 16: Consonant System of Orthoepic Standard French.

out numerous sub-systems, such as the obstruents (those in which the passage of the breath is obstructed in some way, i.e., plosives, affricates and assibilates, and spirants), the laryngeals (those produced in pharynx or larynx), and the sonorants (all others). Under these sub-headings, much prettier pictures can often be obtained, but at the expense of any easy recognition (at least for the beginner) of over-all complexity.

An extreme instance of artificiality is found in the treatment which some phonemicists give to English /h/. The distribution of the sound [h] in English is defective, being limited to initial and intervocalic position: *hit* ['hɪt], *aha* [a'ha]; it is not found in postvocalic position. In some varieties of English, there are long vocoids contrasting with short (e.g., *bomb* ['bɑm] vs. *balm* ['bɑːm]), or vocoids followed by an inward, centering glide which we can transcribe as [ə], as in *real* ['riəl]. For such speakers, vowel length [ː] and/or the centering glide [ə] are in complementary distribution with [h]. On the basis of this distribution, one analysis of English treats [ː] and [ə] as postvocalic allophones of /h/, and calls this phoneme a "semivowel," even though the phonetic similarity of the allophones thus established is so tenuous as to be virtually nonexistent, and only one of the three, [ə], has any semivocoid

characteristics phonetically. In this system, *balm* would be transcribed phonemically as /báhm/, and *real* as /ríhl/. This formulation has the apparent
advantage of being highly patterned, of making a very neat system (nine
vowels /i e æ i ə a u o ɔ/ plus three semivowels /j w h/), even though it has
little or no relation to reality. It would be preferable, as being more in accord
with the facts, to recognize vowel-length as phonemically distinct for those
speakers who have a contrast between *bomb* /bám/ and *balm* /bá:m/, and
[ə̣] as an allophone of /ə/ for those who say *real* /ríəl/, even though the
resultant picture is much less neat. Unfortunately, the formulation of "post-
vocalic /h/" as a "semivowel" has become very widely known and accepted,
and hence is likely to be difficult to dislodge.

Earlier in this chapter we mentioned the problem of treating certain phonetically complex contoids, especially assibilates like [tˢ], [dᶻ], [tˢ̌], and [dᶻ̌].
The solution will vary from one language to another, according to the distribution in which these contoids are found in the language and the situation
with respect to juncture (Chap. 18). In Italian, for instance, all four of these
complex contoids are found, and they contrast both with each other and with
other obstruents, at the beginning and in the middle of words: e.g. *zio* ['tˢi:o]
"uncle", *zùcchero* ['dᶻuk:ɛro] "sugar", *mezzo* ['metˢ:o] "overripe", *mèzzo*
['mɛdᶻ:o] "half", *cielo* ['tˢ̌ɛ:lo] "heaven", *gelo* ['dᶻ̌ɛ:lo] "frost", *faccio* ['fatˢ̌:o]
"I do", *faggio* ['fadᶻ̌:o] "beech". There is a /s/-phoneme in Italian, which,
however, includes both [s] and [z] as allophones, so that there is no separate
phoneme /z/; similarly, there is a phoneme /š/ but no /ž/. In this situation,
it is best to recognize [tˢ dᶻ tˢ̌ dᶻ̌] as separate phonemes, using (for convenience'
sake), the somewhat simpler phonemic symbols /c z̧ č ǧ/ respectively. The
resultant pattern for Italian stops (including both plosives and assibilates)
and spirants (fricatives and sibilants) is as follows:

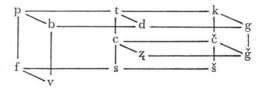

In English, on the other hand, there are no assibilates [tˢ] or [dᶻ]; there are
only [tʃ] and [dʒ], which some observers maintain are phonetically combinations of [t] plus [ʃ], [d] plus [ʒ], respectively, rather than single assibilate
sounds [tˢ̌] and [dᶻ̌]. We have the contoid clusters [ts] and [dz], but in limited
distribution, since they occur only in the middle and at the end of words (as
in *Stetson, cats, Edsel, adze);* only a few people, in a relatively few learnèd
words, use initial [ts-], in such German words as *Zeitgeist* ['tsait‚gaist] "spirit
of the times", or the ultimately Chinese *tse-tse* ['tsi‚tsi] *fly.* Most American
phonemicists at present prefer to take ⌜tʃ⌝ and [dʒ] as unit phonemes /č/ and
/ǧ/, arguing that they are not parallel in distribution to the clusters /ts/ and
/dz/, as pointed out above. However, there are many other parallel sets of

clusters which are equally defective in their distribution (e.g., /tr/ and /dr/ at the beginning of words and in the middle, but not at the end; or /tl/ and /dl/ only in the middle). Such contrasts as that between *Why choose?* ['hwaị 'tʃuz] and *white shoes* ['hwaịt 'ʃuz] can be taken care of by recognizing that there is a difference in transition between the [t] and the [ʃ] in the first and the second of these examples, and treating it as one of juncture. We therefore need not set up extra phonemes /č/ and /ǧ/ to take care of such cases (transcribing these expressions, say, as /hwáj čúz/ vs. /hwájt šúz/), but can simply insert a mark of disjuncture in the second and transcribe them as /hwáj+tʃúz/ (/hwáj+tšúz/) vs. /hwájt+ʃúz/ (/hwájt+šúz/), respectively.

Long contoids are usually to be interpreted as geminate consonants, i.e., involving a two-consonant cluster consisting of the consonant followed by itself. Thus, in Italian, most consonants occur in both short and long varieties, the long being from one and one-half to two times the length of the short. That this contrast is significant, is shown by many minimal pairs, e.g. *fatto* [fat:o] "done", vs. *fato* ['fa:to] "fate"; *carro* ['kar:o] "cart", vs. *caro* ['ka:ro] "dear", and many others. We could, conceivably, set up /:/ as a separate phonologic component for such contrasts, but this would find no parallel elsewhere in the system, and it is more economical to treat the long consonants as geminates, transcribing e.g. /fátto/ and /kárro/ vs. /fáto/ and /káro/. Certain palatalized contoids (e.g. [r] and [ʎ]) occur only long in Italian, and the assibilates [tˢ] and [dᶻ] are always long when in the middle of a word between vowels, as in *meglio* ['meʎ:o] "better", *bagno* ['baɲ:o] "bath", *pazzo* ['patˢ:o] "crazy", *razzo* ['radᶻ:o] "jet". That these contoids are also to be treated as long and hence phonemically geminate, is shown by the presence of short vocoids as allophones of the vowels preceding them. Hence we transcribe phonemically the four words given, as /méḷḷo/, /báṇṇo/, /pácco/,* and /rázẓo/.

In other instances of the opposition between long and short, however, considerations of pattern congruity and economy fail us, and our decision has to be more or less arbitrary. In Spanish, for instance, there is a contrast between long and short only in the case of [r] vs. [r:], in such pairs as *caro* ['karo] "dear", vs. *carro* ['kar:o] "cart"; but in Spanish, the preceding vocoid is short before both [r] and [r:], and there are no other contrasting sets of long and short contoids in the present-day language. Some analysts therefore prefer to set up two separate phonemes, with some type of symbolism to show the phonetic resemblance but nothing more, e.g. /r/ and /ʀ/, for short and long respectively; others prefer to treat them as single and geminate, transcribing /r/ and /rr/ respectively; and still others (the present writer included) prefer to extract a phonological component of length, applicable only to the contrast /r/ vs. /r:/ (or, if one prefers to use a macron instead of a colon with the consonant letter, /r̄/), and significant only between two vowels within a word.

A special problem is posed by syllabicity (cf. p. 62), as in the English

* Do not confuse this phonemic transcription of *pazzo*, in which /c/ stands for [tˢ], with the Italian spelling of *pacco* /pákko/ "package"!

syllabic contoids [m̩], [n̩], [r̩], and [l̩]. Almost all phonemicists, in dealing with these, prefer to treat them as clusters of /ə/ plus consonant, on grounds of distribution (because unstressed [əm] does not occur, and unstressed [m̩] takes its place, and similarly for the other syllabic contoids). According to this interpretation, *bottom* ['bɑtm̩] is to be transcribed phonemically as /bátəm/, and similarly for *button* ['bʌtn̩] /bə́tən/, *baking* (as in *baking-powder*) ['bekŋ̩] /békəŋ/, *butter* ['bʌtr̩] /bə́tər/, and *bottle* ['bɑtl̩] /bátəl/. There are a few inconvenient little facts, however, which have to be swept under the carpet to make such an interpretation wholly acceptable, e.g., the fact that in at least some persons' speech (the present writer's included), some of these syllabic contoids occur not only unstressed but stressed, as in *pretty* ['pr̩ti] (not ['prɪti] nor yet ['pʌrti]) and such (admittedly marginal, but frequent) exclamations as *hm!* ['hm̩]. Analogous, and considerably stronger, objections may be raised against theories which would interpret nasality, in the standard French nasal vocoids [æ̃ ɑ̃ ɔ̃ œ̃], as an allophone of /n/, transcribing, say, French *bain* [bæ̃] "bath" as /ben/ instead of /bẽ/, *sang* [sɑ̃] "blood" as /san/ instead of /sɑ̃/, etc.

We have tried to show in this chapter that patterning does exist in the organization of consonant systems, although it is not so easy to demonstrate as in the case of vowel patterns, and in many instances the pattern is much more irregular and disjointed. Especially for consonant systems, the phonemicist's job is to take the phonetic material as he finds it, analyze it by eliminating all the nonfunctional contrasts, and formulate the result as neatly as he can—without, however, distorting relationships or omitting uncomfortable facts in order to obtain a pretty picture. To achieve the aim of making phonemics the functional analysis of phonetics, the analyst must steer a difficult middle course between the Scylla of too literal an adherence to the nonfunctional, purely raw material of phonetics, on the one hand, and the Charybdis of an excessive desire for neat, elegant, symmetrical, and aesthetically pleasing but phonetically unrealistic patterning on the other.

We give here a sample listing of the consonant phonemes of a specific language (again Italian), according to the principles used in the listing of Italian vowel phonemes at the end of Chap. 15.

PHONEME	ALLOPHONE	CONDITIONS OF OCCURRENCE	EXAMPLES
/p/	[p]	Everywhere	/pé^pe/ ['pe^:pe] *pepe* "pepper"
/t/	[t]	Everywhere	/tánto/ ['tanⁿto] *tanto* "so much"
/k/	[k]	Everywhere	/káki/ ['ka:ki] *kaki* "persimmon"
/b/	[b]	Everywhere	/bábbo/ ['bab:o] *babbo* "dad"
/d/	[d]	Everywhere	/dádo/ ['da:do] *dado* "die (one of a pair of dice)"
/g/	[g]	Everywhere	/gagá/ [ga'ga] *gagá* "dandy"

PHONEME	ALLOPHONE	CONDITIONS OF OCCURRENCE	EXAMPLES
/f/	[f]	Everywhere	/fífa/ [ˈfiːfa] *fifa* "fear"
/v/	[v]	Everywhere	/avvánvera/ [avˈvaŋvera] *a vànvera* "at random"
/s/	[z]	Before voiced consonant	/sdentáto/ [zdenˈtaːto] *sdentato* "toothless"
	[s] or [z]	Between vowels: in free alternation in Central Italy; [s] in South Italy; [z] in North Italy	/káusa/ [ˈkausa], [ˈkauza] *causa* "cause"
	[s]	Elsewhere, including when geminate	/sentíre/ [senˈtiːre] *sentire* "to hear"; /pasta/ [ˈpasᵉta] *pasta* "paste"; /kássa/ [ˈkasːa] *cassa* "cashier's office"
/š/	[ʃ]	Everywhere; only geminate between vowels	/šáme/ [ˈʃaːme] *sciame* "swarm"; /fášša/ [ˈfaʃːa] *fascia* "band"
/c/	[tˢ]	Everywhere; only geminate between vowels	/cío/ [ˈtˢiːo] *zio* "uncle"; /pácco/ [ˈpatˢːo] *pazzo* "crazy"
/z̧/	[dᶻ]	Everywhere; only geminate between vowels	/z̧áino/ [ˈdᶻaino] *zàino* "knapsack"; /báz̧z̧a/ [ˈbadᶻːa] *bazza* "pointed chin"
/č/	[tˢ]	Everywhere	/čéˆna/ [ˈtˢeːna] *cena* "dinner"; /káčo/ [ˈkaːtˢo] *cacio* "cheese"
/ǧ/	[dᶻ]	Everywhere	/ǧénte/ [ˈdᶻenⁿte] *gente* "people";/maǧía/[maˈdᶻiːa] *magìa* "magic"
/m/	[m]	Everywhere	/máno/ [ˈmaːno] *mano* "hand"; /z̧ámpa/ [ˈdᶻamᵐpa] *zampa* "paw"
/n/	[ɱ]	Before /f v/	/inferióˆre/ [iɱfeˈrjoːre] *inferiore* "lower"
	[ŋ]	Before /k g/	/bánka/ [ˈbaŋᵑka] *banca* "bank"
	[n]	Elsewhere, including when geminate	/náno/ [ˈnaːno] *nano* "dwarf"; /pánna/ [ˈpanːa] *panna* "whipped cream"
/ṇ/	[ɲ]	Everywhere; occurs only geminate between vowels	/ṇókki/ [ˈɲɔkːi] *gnocchi* "potato dumplings"; /báṇṇo/ [ˈbaɲːo] *bagno* "bath"
/l/	[l]	Everywhere	/lillá/ [lilˈla] *lillà* "lilac"
/ḷ/	[ʎ]	Everywhere; occurs only geminate between vowels	/fíḷḷo/ [ˈfiʎːo] *figlio* "son"
/r/	[r]	Everywhere	/ráro/ [ˈraːro] *raro* "rare"; /kárro/ [ˈkarːo] *carro* "cart"

The continuants /s m n l r/ are allophonically slightly longer (indicated in phonetic transcription by raised consonant letters) before a following consonant than elsewhere.

Italian consonant phoneme pattern:

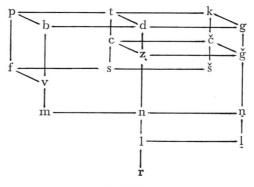

NOTES

Consonant-patterns: Hockett, 1955, §25.
French: Hall, 1948d.
Italian: Hall, 1948b.
Proto-Gallo-Romance: Hall, 1950.
English /h/: Trager and Smith, 1951, §1.32.
The phonemic interpretation of long consonants: Swadesh, 1937.

17

Limitations on Occurrence

IN ANY GIVEN language, not all phonemes occur in all positions with respect to the syllable on which they are uttered or with respect to each other. The statement of these limitations is part of the analyst's task in describing the phonological pattern of the language. Their existence is, furthermore, of major importance for the recognition of a fundamental characteristic of human language, redundancy (cf. the end of this chapter).

When we have determined the vowel and consonant phonemes of a language, we pass to its syllable-structure. This is to be stated in terms of the permissible combinations of vowel (V) and consonant(s) (C) in the syllables of the language; if necessary, further symbols can be used, such as V́ for stressed vowel. It is often convenient to state the possible combinations in a list, keeping the symbol V in the center, and giving examples for each type of syllable, as in the following list for Italian:

PERMISSIBLE COMBINATIONS	EXAMPLES
V	/o-/, e.g., in /omé^tto/ "little man"
CV	/di/ "of"
CCV	/tre/ "three"
CCCV	/stra-/, e.g., in /stragránde/ "very big"
VC	/in/ "in"
VCC	/sámp/, nickname of /sampdória/ "Sampdoria (Genoese soccer team)"
CVC	/kon/ "with"
CCVC	/tras-/, e.g., in /trasmé^ttere/ "to transmit"
CCCVC	/strak-/, e.g., in /strakkíno/ "a kind of cheese"

A statement of this type tells us, in positive terms, the types of combinations of phonemes that do occur in Italian syllables; in its implications, it is also negative, in that it tells us that other combinations do not occur, and that hence syllables like */strúmpf/ or */akst/ would be foreign to Italian phonological patterns. Some languages have syllable structures much simpler than those of Italian: in Hawaiian and some other South Sea island languages, syllables have only the structure V or CV. At the other extreme, some languages (e.g. English and German) can have syllables with as many as three consonants at their onset and four as their coda: CCCVCCCC, as in some people's pronunciation of *strengths* /stréŋkθs/. Such limitations on syllable-structure are quite important in second-language learning (cf. Chap.

77), since the speaker of any one language is likely to have difficulty mastering the unfamiliar syllable-types of a second language.

In addition to the limitations imposed by syllable-types, there are also, in most languages, quite stringent limitations on the sequences of phonemes that can occur either within syllables or across syllable-boundaries. There are often limitations on the occurrence of single phonemes in syllable-initial or syllable-final position: thus, in English, all phonemes except /ŋ/ can occur initially, and all English consonants except /h/ can occur in word-final position; but in Tuscan, no consonant occurs in word-final position. Modern standard non-Tuscan Italian has greatly relaxed this principle, and most consonants occur in word-final position, especially due to three factors: (1) large numbers of loan-words from foreign languages, such as /náilon/ *nailon* "nylon", /líder/ *leader*, /gól/ *gol* "goal" (in soccer); (2) borrowings from North Italian dialects, particularly in proper names such as /rumór/ *Rumor*, /merlín/ *Merlin*, /saragát/ *Saragat;* and (3) coined words, especially trade-names such as /ítalmilk/ *Italmilk* (name of a frozen-custard machine), /fónit/ *Fonit* (name of a brand of gramophone record), and many others.

Permissible combinations, both of vowels and diphthongs, and of consonants, are best listed in positive terms, in any one of several ways. Perhaps the simplest, but the least revelatory of pattern, is to make a simple enumeration, in either alphabetical or some other order, of all the combinations found: e.g., for English, /fr- tr- kr- br- dr- gr- fr- θr- šr-; pl- kl- bl- gl- fl- sl-; tw- kw- dw- gw- θw- sw- hw-/ and so forth. One can also set up a table with all the phonemes of the languages listed both across the top and down the side, and then, at the intersection of each pair of lines where a cluster occurs, either mark an x or write in the symbols for the cluster itself. Such a procedure is quite graphic, but rather clumsy. Still another procedure is to list the possible combinations in terms of their occurrence in the syllable-structure of the language, once this has been set forth. One then makes a listing of the following type (here exemplified only partially for Italian consonants):

Syllable Initial:

C: Any C, e.g., /piétra/ *pietra* "stone"; /ǧállo/ *giallo* "yellow", etc.

CC: /p/ + /t n s l r/: e.g., /pterodáttilo/ *pterodàttilo* "pterodactyl"; /pneumátiko/ *pneumàtico* "tire"; /psikósi/ *psicosi* "psychosis"; /plástico/ *plastico* "plastic"; /prátika/ *pràtica* "practice".

  /b/ + /d l r/: e.g., /bdéllio/ *bdellio* "bdellium"; /blu/ *blu* "blue"; /brávo/ *bravo* "fine".

  /s/ + any C: e.g., /spíllo/ *spillo* "needle"; /sǧeláre/ *sgelare* "to unfreeze, thaw"; (etc.).

CCC: /s/ + /p/ or /t/ + /r/: /spreǧáre/ *spregiare* "to despise"; /strilláre/ *strillare* "to yell".

  /s/ + /p/ + /l/: /spléndido/ *splèndido* "splendid" (etc.).

A full listing of the possibilities of phonemic combinations for any given language normally takes up several pages. In preparing such a listing, the phonemicist must take into account, not only the words and forms approved by purists, but all that are in normal, general, everyday use by the ordinary speakers of the language. For a heavily purist-ridden language like Italian, this involves recognizing the existence and widespread use of such learnèd words as /politeáma/ *politeama* "theater"; of such foreignisms as /básket/ *basket(ball)*, /sprínt/ *sprint* "trade-name of an automobile and of a gasoline", /míting/ or /mítinge/ or even /mítiŋ/ "meeting"; etc. Nor should names of dialectal or foreign origin, e.g. Slavic names in /-iˇ/ *-ich* in Italian, or German names beginning in /šn- šm-/ like *Schneider, Schmidt* in English, be omitted on puristic grounds. Often such borrowings (which, especially under modern conditions, are going on all the time) introduce previously unfamiliar features, not only combinations of phonemes, but even new phonemic contrasts (e.g., that between /n/ and /ŋ/ in Italian) where they have not been present before. Admittedly, for large modern speech-communities it is hard to know where to draw the line; a fair number of speakers of New Zealand English have /ŋ-/ in initial position, as in the feminine name /ŋájo/ *Ngaio*, but not many people in other parts of the English-speaking world have this feature. A fair number of speakers of English, even not knowing any German, use /x/ in certain words and names of German origin, particularly in the name of the composer /báx/ *Bach;* a few probably achieve an approximation of Chinese tones on the syllables of names like *Mao Tse Tung;* etc. Yet, at least in theory, all these dialectal and even idiolectal peculiarities should be taken into account in order to attain a complete picture of current usage at any given time.

From our consideration of the limitations on the occurrence of phonemes emerges a point of salient importance for the functioning of language as a whole: the existence of *redundancy* in linguistic structure. The term *redundancy* is normally somewhat pejorative in our everyday usage, implying the presence of needless and hence undesirable features (especially verbiage, like *for the main and simple reason that*, a favorite expression of Booth Tarkington's small-boy hero Penrod, instead of *because*). In communications engineering, however, *redundancy* is used with no pejorative connotations, to refer to the availability of greater resources than are strictly necessary for the conveyance of a message. If all the possible combinations of phonemes in any given language were used by its speakers, with none left over, the amount of redundancy would be zero. However, there are large gaps in the phonologic structures of most languages, in that far from all the theoretically possible combinations of phonemes occur. In general, it is estimated that the redundancy of most languages is around fifty percent, i.e., that their structures utilize only about half of the available phonologic combinations. Redundancy thus enables a considerable amount of variation from the norm of ordinary speech without the conveyance of the message being seriously impaired.

Phonological redundancy is of several types. On the lowest level is that of the absence of certain allophones in certain environments, which makes for a looseness in the distribution of phonetic material: for instance, in English, since aspirated [p'] does not occur normally after [s], there is room for it to occur in abnormal speech (emphatic, foreign accent, etc.) without its making any difference in meaning. Within the framework of available combinations of phonemes, there are many which just happen not to occur, such as (to make a few up on the spur of the moment) English */klɔ́p/ *clup*, */dríb/ *drib*, */vɔ́rd/ *verd*, etc., etc. It is on this extensive reservoir of normally un-utilized combinations that our advertisers draw for inventing new trade-names such as *Fab*, *Dreft*, *Preem*, and the like. On occasion, such combinations are used humorously or onomatopoetically, become part of the special dialect of some particular group, and then pass into general usage, e.g. /blíp/ *blip*, which before the invention of radar was a nonsense-syllable, but now refers to a spot on a radar screen.

On a higher level of phonological significance is the non-occurrence of particular combinations of phonemes. A speaker of English has no difficulty in reading off such orthographic sequences as *gluf, *murl, or *fliff, because the corresponding phonemic sequences /glɔ́f/, /mɔ́rl/, /flíf/ fit into our familiar phonological patterns; for the same reason, a speaker of Spanish can deal easily with such nonsense-words as *nucho /núčo/ or *doncar /donkár/. But we cannot deal so easily with, say, *zbin, *zmile, *mratf, **ntugl;* we simply do not have, in our phonemic inventory, /zb-/, /zm-/, /mr-/, /-tf/, /nt-/, /-gl/ in the positions called for in these "words," and hence find it difficult or impossible to "twist our tongues around" the phonemic sequences /zbín/, /zmájl/, /mrǽtf/, or /ntɔ́gl/. Not only the combinations, but the positions in which they occur, may cause difficulty. We have no trouble pronouncing, say, /tf/ in *Catford* /kǽtfərd/, /nt/ in *hunt* /hɔ́nt/, or /gl/ in *glow* /glɔ́/; but /tf/ and /gl/ in final position, or /nt-/ in initial position, are too unfamiliar to us, because our phonemic combination pattern does not include them in those positions.

Naturally, since the permissible occurrences of phonemes and their com-binations differ from one language to another, what seems "difficult" to speakers of one language will seem not only "easy," but the only possible way of handling a particular phonological situation, to speakers of another. For an Italian, the phoneme /s/ has a voiced allophone [z] which is, for him, the only variety of sibilant contoid that can possibly occur before a voiced contoid, and hence an Italian speaking English cannot keep from pronounc-ing *smile* as ['zmail̦], which to our ears contains the "impossible" initial con-sonant cluster */zm-/. No serious trouble results in our understanding of the Italian "accent" in this case, because */zm-/ is simply nonexistent in English. A speaker of English using [sm-] in Italian, e.g. in a word like /smuóvere/ "to displace", sounds equally peculiar; but if we use [sd-] in-stead of [zd-] in an Italian word like /sdentáto/ "toothless", we run the risk of being misunderstood, because our Italian hearers will (as pointed out on p. 68) identify the voiceless onset of [sd-] as signalling the cluster [st-] and will think we have said /stentáto/ "forced".

These differences in redundancy and in its location in the phonemic pat-tern from one language to another are not due to lack of intelligence or planning on the part of speech-communities, nor are they due to perversity or "cussèdness." On occasion, the absence of certain habits does get made into a prized characteristic, and the members of particular groups pride them-selves on their inability to make certain sounds or to produce certain phonemes in certain positions, as in Tuscans' supposed "inability" to pronounce final consonants (p. 37), a case of Veblenian "trained incapacity" (p. 4). Nor are these differences due to heredity. A child of English-speaking parents brought up, say, in Florence and speaking only Tuscan, will have all the Tuscan habits of speech, including the "inability" to produce final consonants; but a child of Tuscan origin, brought up speaking exclusively English, will have no difficulty at all in doing so. These differences in phonological limitations, like other characteristics of linguistic structures, are simply culturally-transmitted sets of habits, which inevitably differ from one speech-community to another, without there being any question of deliberate intent or of superior or inferior merit involved at any time.

Redundancy in language, especially in phonological structure, is not at all to be regretted or condemned. On the contrary, it is what enables language to be understood under situations of less (often, considerably less) than perfect communicability. This can be understood from the parallel situation existing in writing. In one of his novels, P. G. Wodehouse mentions office-windows on which old, half-effaced lettering announces the firm name "J-v- -nd S-m-tr- R-bb-- -mp-rt--g C--p-ny"; even though nearly half the letters are gone, we still have little difficulty supplying the missing ones and identifying the full name as "Java and Sumatra Rubber Importing Company". Similarly, when we hear speech under unfavorable conditions (e.g., in a noisy room, in a factory, over a low-fidelity loud-speaker as in a railway station), we may not hear by any means all of the sounds that have left the speaker's lips, but we can none the less get most or all of his message. It is redundancy that gives flexibility to human speech, and which makes it adaptable to use in less-than-perfect surroundings. It is also (as we shall see in Chap. 49) one of the major factors contributing to linguistic change.

NOTES

The syllable from a phonemic point of view: O'Connor and Trim, 1953; Sommerfelt, 1931; Stetson, 1936.

Redundancy: Hockett, 1958, Chap. 10.

Stress and Juncture

IN CHAPTER 13 we discussed the phonetic characteristics of the intensity with which syllables are uttered. Phonemically significant intensity is customarily termed *stress*, which is indicated in phonemic transcriptions by accent marks (e.g., the acute accent ´, the grave accent`, or the circumflex ^) written over the symbols standing for vowel phonemes. This change in symbolization enables us to represent stress separately from phenomena of syllable onset and transition (juncture), and thus frees us from the presumption, implicit in IPA's marking of intensity, that the onset of intensity relative to syllable-division is always important no matter with what language we are working.

As the prevalence of intensity, on the phonetic level, varies from language to language, so does that of phonemically significant stress, but in different ways. At one extreme is French, which simply does not have any stress-system at all. The usual misconception that "French words are always stressed on the last syllable" is due to the fact that there is a slight increase in phonetic intensity on the last syllable of a breath-group (cf. pp. 64, 72); when any word is pronounced separately in French, it of course forms an independent breath-group and automatically receives a slight increase in intensity on its last syllable. (This is the origin of the Frenchified pronunciation of such non-French names as *Capri*, which in Italian is /kápri/ but which, pronounced in French fashion, has become /kaprí/ in popular parlance; and similarly with the name of the Greek port *Patras* and with that of the Louisiana city *New Orleans*.) French does have a so-called "accent d'intensité," which consists in pronouncing each syllable separately with a certain amount of intensity on each, as in *impossible!* ['ˈæˈpɔˈsibl]. This phenomenon can be symbolized in phonemic transcription with an acute accent-mark, e.g. /épósíbl/; but it does not constitute a normal stress-system in the language.

It is not necessary, however, for a language to have faint or nearly non-existent phonetic intensity for stress to be absent from its phonologic system. Hungarian, as mentioned on p. 72, has quite strong intensity on the initial syllable of each word; but, from the very fact of its being automatic, this intensity is not phonemically significant. This is true for any language where the position of intensity can be stated in terms of automatic occurrence. In Classical Latin, for instance, a word was stressed on the next to the last syllable if that syllable was long "by nature" (i.e., contained a long vowel, as in *monēta:* "coin") or "by position" (i.e., was checked, as in *amantem:* "loving"), but otherwise stress fell on the third from the last syllable (as in *littera:* "letter"). In such languages as Hungarian and Latin, stress serves rather as a marker to indicate word-division: in Hungarian, each time we hear a heavy stress, we know that a new word has begun; the speaker of Latin, on hearing a heavy stress, knew that the end of the word was going to fall on the next or the second-next syllable.

What makes stress phonemic in a language is, not the strength with which the air is expelled from the lungs, but the existence of contrasts based on the position of the intensity. If its position is not automatic, but makes a difference in meaning, then stress is phonemic. In English, for instance, there is a difference between such verbs as *contráct* /kantrǽkt/, *survey* /sərvéj/, *permit* /pərmít/, *subject* /səbdʒékt/, etc., with stress on the second syllable, and the corresponding nouns *contract* /kántrækt/, *survey* /sə́rvej/, *permit* /pə́rmɪt/, *subject* /sə́bdʒɛkt/, with stress on the first. In Italian, there is a contrast between such verb-forms as *canto* /kánto/ "I sing" and *cantò* /kantó/ "he sang", and between such words as *prìncipi* /prínčipi/ "princes" and *princìpi* /prinčípi/ "principles". Hence we conclude that English and Italian, because of these and many other similar contrasts, have phonemic stress. (Naturally, the presence or absence of accent-marks in the writing system-connected with a language has nothing at all to do with the phonemic status of stress in that language.)

If stress is phonemic in a language, there must be at least two contrasting levels of stress, which are usually termed *weak* and *primary*, respectively. This is the situation in the conservative Romance languages such as Italian, Spanish, Portuguese, Roumanian, etc., and all that is needed to indicate phonemic stress in transcribing these languages is the acute mark /´/, for primary stress, as in the Italian examples cited so far, or in Spanish *cantar* /kantár/ "to sing", *huérfano* /uérfano/ "orphan", etc. In such languages, if an intermediate level of phonetic intensity is present, its occurrence is automatic, and it can be interpreted as an allophone of primary stress occurring under certain junctural conditions, e.g., Italian *stuzzicadenti* /stúccika+dénti/ [ˌstutˢːika'dɛnti] "tooth-pick".

In more complicated stress systems, if the level of stress between primary and weak is also unpredictable in its occurrence, it is necessarily phonemic. The term *secondary* is usually reserved for significant stress between primary and weak, and it is indicated with the grave accent /`/, as in German /ájzen+bà:n/ *Eisenbahn* "railroad, (lit., iron-road)", /fá:r+kàrte/ *Fahrkarte* "ticket (lit., travel-card)", /kàjzers+láwtern/ *Kaiserslautern* (town-name), etc.

The stress situation in English has long been the object of debate. For individual words in English, we need set up no more than three levels of stress. To avoid confusion with the Trager-Smith nomenclature (cf. below), we shall use the terms *full* and *intermediate* for the traditional two top levels of English stress, and shall use the traditional acute accent-mark for full phonemic stress and the grave for intermediate. The words given on p. 71

would be transcribed, according to this interpretation, as follows: *paper* /pépər/, *deduction* /didə́kʃən/, *negligée* /nɛglɪʒé/, *elevator* /éləvètər/, *transmigration* /trǽnzmajgréʃən/, *capitulation* /kæpìtʃuléʃən/. A double acute accent can be used for the emphatic or over-full degree of stress: *SHUT UP!* /ʃə́t ə́p/. At least one of these extra-strong stresses appears in every utterance; often, there are two or more of them in longer utterances, and we term that part of an English utterance which contains one extra-strong stress a *phonemic phrase.*

In recent years, an alternative formulation, originally proposed by Trager and Smith, has gained widespread acceptance. In this treatment, the four levels of stress mentioned above are recognized, but what we have termed "extra strong" is called "primary," the symbol /´/ is used for it, and it is claimed that one is present in every word. "Secondary" is the term used by Trager and Smith to cover the cases in which a stress which in an isolated word would be primary is reduced somewhat because of the presence of another primary stress occupying a position of priority in a compound or a phonemic phrase: Trager-Smith symbol /ˋ/. For what we have termed "intermediate," Trager and Smith use the term "tertiary" stress, and the circumflex accent-mark /ˆ/; weak stress is, as usual, left unmarked. The words given in the preceding paragraph would be transcribed in the Trager-Smith system as /péypər/, /diydə́kʃən/, /negližéy/, /éləvèytər/, /trǽnzmaygréyšən/, /kæpîčuwléyšən/. Examples of reduction of primary to secondary stress in compounds or phonemic phrases would be: *elevator* /éləvèytər/ plus *operator* /ápərèytər/ giving *elevator-operator* /éləvèytər+àpərêytər/; or the sentence *Where does he think he's going to?* /hwèr+dəz+iy+θìŋk+iy+z+gówiŋ+tûw/.

The supporters of the Trager-Smith formulation argue that it is necessary to recognize four types of stress on the level of the individual word because of the existence of compounds like *elevator-operator,* each of whose component parts themselves include the three levels of stress that all analysts recognize. However, the "reduced primary," or what Trager and Smith call the "secondary" stress in such compounds can perfectly well be interpreted as an allophonic variety of "primary" or "full" stress after internal open juncture (cf. our discussion below), occurring under certain specifiable conditions. Longer stretches of "reduced primary" stresses can occur without our having to postulate extra intermediate degrees of phonemically significant stress to take care of them, as in *elevator-operator-union-meetings* (one compound, with one full or "primary" stress and then successive, gradually weakening, "reduced primary" stresses), which we would suggest transcribing as /éləvètər+ápərètər+júnjən+mítɪŋz/. The occurrence of what Trager and Smith call "primary" stress in each phonemic phrase is a matter of phrasal, not of word, stress, and should be treated as such; the full stress inherent in each word in English should not be confused with the extra-strong stress which always occurs on one element of a phonemic phrase, and which is therefore always present when a word is cited in isolation (cf. the analogous situation in French, cited on p. 108).

Closely allied with problems of stress are those of *juncture*, the way in which phonemes follow each other or are "joined" in the stream of speech. In all languages there are at least two types of juncture: *close juncture*, in which each phoneme follows closely on the other without any interruption or other type of special transition; and *prepausal juncture*, in which the stream of speech ceases before a pause. The Romance languages have this type of situation, so that in normal, everyday speech no distinction is made (e.g., in syllabification) between expressions or sentences of different meaning but involving the same sequence of phonemes. This gives rise to many notorious puns, such as French *il est tout vert:* "he (it) is all green" = *il est ouvert:* "he (it) is open", both /iletuver/; or the Italian joke *Qual'è il colmo per un sarto?—Di dover cucire le falde dell'Appennino col lago di Como* (= *coll'ago di Como):* "What's the last straw for a tailor?—To have to sew up the folds of the Appennines with the lake (= with the needle) of Como", in which *col lago di Como:* "with the lake of Como" and *coll'ago di Como:* "with the needle of Como" are both /kollágodikó^mo/. Only very educated speakers of French or Italian will make any junctural distinctions within the pairs given, and even then only when they are attempting to make the distinction over-clear, as when speaking with foreigners. Elizabethan English would seem to have had a junctural situation of this type, to judge from the frequency of such formations as *an apron, an adder* from *a napron, a nadder,* and the frequency, in Shakespeare and other Elizabethan authors, of puns depending on misunderstanding of word-boundaries.

Present-day English, however, as well as many other languages, has more than these two types of juncture. It is convenient to subsume, under the general heading of "internal open juncture," a number of types of transition between sounds and between syllables, as discussed in Chap. 12. Among these phenomena are: prepausal type of articulation of a contoid, including absence of final release and slight lengthening of [m n r l]; the drawling of prepausal vocoids and diphthongs; and differences in syllable onset. A frequently-cited three-way example of junctural contrast in English is:

nitrate "a type of mineral" /nájtrèt/ [ˈnajˌtʼɹet] or [ˈnajˌtřet]. In this word, the element [aj] is of normal length, not drawled; the [t] can be either aspirated before [ɹ] or merged with a special palatal allophone [ř] that many speakers of present-day English use in the clusters /tr/ [tř] and /dr/ [dř]. The onset of the second syllable comes before the cluster /tr/.

night-rate (e.g., for telegrams) /nájt+rèt/ [ˈnaitˌret]. Here the onset of the second syllable comes between the /t/ and the /r/. For /t/, we have the allophone which comes before pause, without audible release; the /r/ has the normal dorsal retroflex allophone [ɹ], never the [ř] which appears in close juncture after [t] and [d]. The [ai̯] is short, not drawled.

Nye-trait (a trait or characteristic of a Mr. Nye) /náj+trèt/ [ˈnaːi̯ˌtʼɹet] or [ˈnaːi̯ˌtřet]. In this compound, the /áj/ is slightly drawled (represented in our phonetic transcription by [aːi]) as is the case at the end of single words (e.g. *buy* /báj/ [ˈbaːi], *high* /háj/ [ˈhaːi]); the /tr/ is either [tʼɹ] or [tř], as at the beginning of a word; and the onset of the second syllable comes before this cluster.

Other notorious pairs or trios of compounds which illustrate internal open juncture (or, as some prefer to call it, internal *disjuncture*) are *syntax* /síntæks/ vs. *sin-tax* (a tax on sin) /sín-tæks/, in which the [n] is slightly lengthened as it normally is at the end of a word; and the set *light housekeeper* /lájt háws+kìpər/ (a housekeeper who is light, not hefty) vs. *light-housekeeper* /làjt+háws+kìpər/ (someone who does light housekeeping) vs. *lighthouse-keeper* /lájt+hàws+kìpər/ (someone who keeps a lighthouse).

Similar phenomena of juncture occur in German, where the occurrence of certain allophones in unexpected positions is best subsumed under the heading of internal disjuncture. The phoneme /x/ (written *ch*) has two allophones, [x] (the "Ach-Laut") and [ç] (the "Ich-Laut"); the former occurs normally after back vowels, and the former after other phonemes and pause. However, there are a few instances in which [ç] occurs after a back vowel, as in ['ku:çən] *Kuhchen* "a little cow" (as opposed to ['kuxən] "a cake"). Here, it would be most inconvenient, and contrary to the "Sprachgefühl" or feeling for the language which its native speakers have (which is not to be despised, although certainly not to be taken as our only or even our primary guide in linguistic analysis), to set up two separate phonemes /ç/ and /x/ just on the basis of this and one or two similar cases. We can subsume the use of this unexpected allophone [ç] in this position under the phenomenon of internal disjuncture, and transcribe *Kuhchen* as /kú:+xen/. In other words, internal disjuncture does not necessarily involve only "openness" of transition; it is a heading under which various phenomena can be subsumed, including the appearance of allophones "out of place."

There must be some further justification, however, aside from mere "out-of-place-ness" of an allophone, for setting up a disjuncture in such an instance; we find it in the fact that virtually all cases of internal disjuncture in compounds, there is a morphological boundary at the points where the phonological separation occurs. The Prague phonologists, Prince Nicholas Troubetzkoy and his followers, went so far as to consider this type of disjuncture as a primarily morphological phenomenon, referring to it as a *Grenzsignal* or "boundary-marker." Others, especially some American phonologists, have objected to this procedure, considering that morphological criteria should never be introduced into phonological analysis, since, according to them, this would constitute an undesirable, almost heretical "mixing of levels." In support of this position, they cite such English examples as the alternative pronunciation of the name *Plato* as not only /pléto/ but /plé+tò/, presumably homonymous with *play-toe (a toe for playing with, or an unreal toe), in which, according to them, the internal disjuncture marks no morphologic boundary. In this latter instance, however, it would seem that the very presence of the disjuncture makes the name *Plato* into a compound and divides it into two separate elements, even though neither of them has any meaning by itself.

Juncture, close or open, is also a very useful heading under which to subsume a great many automatic phonologic replacements, on both the phonetic and the phonemic level. In many languages, assimilations take place, i.e. one sound is made partially or wholly like the preceding or the following one, in certain combinations. Thus, in French, the liquids and nasals /l r m n/ are automatically devoiced at the end of a breath-group after a preceding voiceless plosive, as in *peuple* /pœpl/ [pœpl̥] "people". This can be treated as a phonetic concomitant of breath-group-final disjuncture. On the phonemic level, we have such instances (still in French) as the combination *chemin de fer:* "railroad (lit., road of iron)", in which the separate elements are /ʃəmɛ̃/ "road" + /də/ "of" + /fer/ "iron;" in rapid speech, the first element loses its /ə/ and so does the second, and in the resultant cluster /df/ the /d/ loses its voicing and is automatically replaced by /t/, so that the normal pronunciation of this expression is /ʃmɛ̃tfer/, with loss of /ə/ and assimilation of /d/ to /f/ in voicing as results of close juncture. On occasion, the loss of a phonological component or distinctive feature (p. 79) is involved. Thus, in German, whenever there is a pair of consonants which contrast as to voicing (e.g. /p b/, /t d/, /k g/, /f v/), the voiced one of the pair is automatically unvoiced at the end of a word: e.g. *Bund:* "league", pl. *Bunde* /búnde/, has the singular /búnt/, homonymous with *bunt* /búnt/ "many-colored, bright" (whose plural, however, is *bunte* /búnte/). The component of voicing, which in other positions is functionally significant in German, is lost here, a phenomenon which can be subsumed under the heading of overriding effects of prepausal or internal open juncture. Here again, the effect of juncture also serves to mark a word-boundary, since this is one of the ways the speaker of German knows that the end of a word has come.

NOTES

English stress-patterns: Trager and Smith, 1951.
Juncture: Sommerfelt, 1936; Trager and Smith, 1951.
German [x] *and* [ç]: Moulton, 1947; Leopold, 1948.
"Grenzsignale:" Trubetzkoy, 1958.

19

Intonation

PITCH, SINCE IT EXTENDS over at least one syllable and—in longer contours—over more than one, is a suprasegmental phenomenon, and so are the phonemic units of intonation which are composed of pitches. The term *toneme* has been proposed for such units (and, presumably, one would use *allotone* for a positional variant of a toneme), but has not received as widespread acceptance as have other terms in *-eme*.

In many languages, as pointed out in Chap. 13, varying pitch on individual syllables makes a difference in meaning. To the Chinese examples listed there, we can add many others, e.g., the following from Ewe (a West African language): /tó/ (with high tone) "ear", vs. /tò/ (low tone) "buffalo", and /tǒ/ (gliding tone) "mortar". In Norwegian, differences of pitch are significant on stressed syllables, as in the contrast /bǿner/ (with rising pitch on the first syllable, in addition to stress) "peasants", vs. /bø̀ner/ (with falling pitch) "beans". The combinations of tones on single syllables can become very complicated, and Cantonese is said to have between nine and twelve altogether.

Some scholars have objected to using the expression "tone-languages" for Chinese, Ewe and others of this type, considering that the function of tone is no more distinctive than that of, say, nasalization, in furnishing an added phonemic feature to a given vowel. However, this view seems to result from a somewhat naive misinterpretation of our phonemic representation with accent marks written over vowel letters to symbolize tone. Tone phenomena apply, not to individual vowels as does nasalization or lip-rounding, but to entire syllables. There is thus a major difference between the functioning of tone in our familiar languages such as English (in which it does not have phonemic significance on individual syllables) and those like Chinese (in which it does). The term *tone-languages*, as used at present, refers to languages of this latter type, which not only present special practical problems but are structurally different as well.

For English and probably most (if not all) other languages, sequences of pitches over longer stretches have a fundamentally different function from that of pitch on individual syllables in tone-languages. An intonation contour does not, in itself, make any difference in the "dictionary meaning" of an utterance; it tells the hearer something concerning the emotional attitude of the speaker. As such, the intonation patterns of a language are among the very first patterns which a child learns to respond to and to imitate. According to some theories, when animals (e.g., dogs) respond to human speech, they are reacting, not to segmental phonemes, but to intonation contours alone.

The phonemic organization of intonational contours has been investigated thoroughly only for a few languages, especially English and French. Even what little has been done to date shows, however, that there are not only one, but various ways in which intonation-contours are structured. For English, it is possible to set up a system involving four relative pitch-levels and three terminal directions of pitch (which some call "clause-boundaries"). The pitch-levels are normally referred to by numbers from 1 (low) to 2 (mid), 3 (high) and 4 (extra-high); some also use 0 for extra-low and 5 for super-extra-high (as when a speaker squeaks in excitement). Almost all writers on English intonation now follow the system just described; unfortunately, one of the most extensive discussions (Pike, 1946) uses the numerals in the opposite order, with 1 for extra-high and 4 for low, but the systems are mutually convertible, so little harm is done. The three terminal directions involve either a rise in pitch at the very end of a sequence of pitches, a fall in pitch, or the pitch staying on the same level. Some scholars use a double vertical bar ‖, and others use graphic devices like ↵ or ↑ for the rising terminal direction; ‖ or → for level; and # or ⌢ or ↓ for falling. We shall use ↵, →, and ⌢, as the simplest, most iconic, and hence most easily comprehensible.

The intonation-patterns of English utterances are describable in terms of sequences of these relative pitch-levels, organized into intonational contours, each followed by one of the three terminal directions. For ordinary statements, the normal sequence is (2)31 ⌢, e.g.:

$$\overset{2}{\text{He's}} \text{ reading } \overset{3}{\text{a}} \text{ time-}\overset{1}{\text{ta}}\text{ble.} \quad ⌢$$

As shown by the parentheses around the (2), this part of the contour is less important than the combination of 3 followed by 1, which is all that is present when the utterance involves no elements preceding the final emphatic (Trager-Smith "primary") stress of the phonemic phrase:

$$\text{(What's he reading?) A } \overset{3}{\text{time-}}\overset{1}{\text{ta}}\text{ble.} \quad ⌢$$

If the utterance consists of only one syllable, then more than one level of pitch occurs on the same syllable (in this case, 3 and 1), and if there is no unstressed syllable at the end to receive the terminal direction, this too is telescoped onto the single available syllable:

$$\text{(Where's he going?) } \overset{3}{\text{Home}}\overset{1}{\text{wards.}} \quad ⌢$$

$$\text{(Where's he going?) } \overset{3}{\text{Ho}}\overset{1}{\text{me.}}⌢$$

The primary function of the terminal directions (which some call, rather confusingly, "junctures") is to tell the hearer where the speaker stands with respect to his utterance and what is to follow. The terminal ⌢ seems to tell the hearer "this is the end of at least this part of what I have to say"; →, "there is something more coming"; ⌣, "I want you to say something in reply". Hence ⌐ often (though not always) comes at a place where a period is written in our conventional punctuation; it is often called "period juncture" or (from the shape of the symbol #) "double-cross juncture." Similarly, → is often termed "comma juncture" because it frequently corresponds to a comma in punctuation, or a "single-bar juncture" from the symbol |; and ⌣, often "question-mark juncture" or "double-bar juncture" from the symbol ‖.

Of the intonation-contours and terminal directions of English, proper, the most frequent is probably the (2)31⌐ just described; (2)23⌣, as in

2   2   3⌣
Is he working?

is also very frequent. This contour, but followed by → instead of ⌣, is also used to elicit grunts or other indications that the hearer is listening:

2   23→
We went to Verona . . .
Uh-huh . . .

2   23→
. . . then on to Florence . . . .
Yeah . . .

2   31 ⌐
. . . then to Rome.

The contour (2)32→ is the normal intonation for prefinal sections of an utterance, and the → tells the hearer that this is not the end:

2   32→   32→   2   31 ⌐
We went to Verona, then to Florence, and then to Rome.

There are a number of other possible combinations, most of which indicate either intensification (especially if the pitch is raised) or moderation (with lowering of the pitch). These intonation-patterns are not always associated with specific types of grammatical structure, and it is erroneous to speak of "declarative intonation," "interrogative intonation," etc. For instance, the (2)23⌣ intonation is not the only one to be used with interrogative sentences in English. In American English, it is used with those which require a yes-or-no answer, whether they have "interrogative" (inverted) word-order or not:

2   2   3⌣
Is he coming?
2   2   3⌣
He's coming?

On the other hand, those calling for information have the (2)31⌐ contour:

2   31⌐
What do you want?

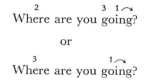

2   3 1⌐
Where are you going?

or

3   1⌐
Where are you going?

Not all varieties of the language have the same intonation patterns, or the same use even of those which they have in common. British and American English use the (2)31⌐ pattern differently in questions, inasmuch as British English uses this contour (and even more frequently, the [3]21⌐ contour) on yes-or-no questions:

3   2   1⌐
Are you going home?

The existence of such differences is, in general, not realized by naive speakers, since (as mentioned on p. 114) intonation-patterns are among the earliest linguistic features we learn and hence those of which we are least consciously aware. (In general, our unawareness is made even greater by the inadequate representation which our orthography gives to intonation, and the almost total neglect of the topic in our schools' teaching of English.) Yet our reactions to intonation are very deep-rooted and intense, because it is so closely associated with what it tells us (or what we interpret it as telling us) concerning the emotional attitude of the person(s) we are listening to. For Americans, use of the (2)31⌐ or (3)21⌐ intonation contour on a "yes-or-no" question implies an extremely patronizing attitude. On the other hand, speakers of British English associate the use of the (2)23⌣ pattern on such questions with impudence or aggressiveness. The unconscious use and equally unconscious reactions to such uses of intonation-patterns is one of the major sources of cross-cultural misunderstandings—in this case, the different emotional connotations of the intonation-contours involved have contributed in no small measure to the American's image of the British as patronizing snobs, and to the Englishman's stereotype of the American as an impudent, aggressive boor.

Not all languages have intonational patterns which can be described in terms of relative pitch-levels. (One of the greatest mistakes in recent linguistics has been the attempt to force the description of all languages into the mould of patterns first worked out for English.) In French, for instance, the pitch on successive syllables either rises gradually, rises sharply, or falls (cf. Chap. 13). If there is a sequence of gradually rising pitches, and the sequence is interrupted only to resume rising, each successive sequence starts slightly higher than did the preceding one; in a long series of such sequences, the last one may begin on a level of relative pitch considerably higher than the end of the first sequence. For French, we must set up our intonation-contours according to the direction they take: gradual-rising, sharp-rising, falling, rising-falling. Terminal directions are not of significance in French intonation, and their use produces the effect of a strong foreign accent. The intonation contour in French is not coterminous with the breath-group (pp. 74–75), since with one breath group there can be one or more interruptions in the direction of the pitch. This happens frequently in longer sentences: for example (representing gradual-rising intonation by $\nearrow$ at the end of the sequence, and rising-falling by $\frown$):

mafam$\nearrow$ eparti$\nearrow$ səmatẽ$\nearrow$ purale$\nearrow$ alekol$\frown$

(*Ma femme est partie ce matin pour aller à l'école:* "my wife left this morning to go to school").

The intonational structure of Italian is similar to that of French in its basic outlines, except that Italian has a phonemic contrast between stressed and unstressed syllables (p. 109) which French does not have. The unstressed syllables of Italian are allophonically on a lower pitch than that of adjacent stressed syllables; but, phonemically, all that counts in determining the intonation-contours is the pitch on the stressed syllables. Italian, like French, has contours of gradually and sharply rising, falling, and rising-falling intonation. The other Romance languages are probably similar to French and Italian in this respect, rather than to English with its four or more relative pitch-levels.

The full description and formulation of intonation-patterns is as important for syntactic patterns as is that of the linear phonemes and the stress and juncture phenomena of a language. The divisions of a longer utterance are to be marked off in terms, first of the over-all intonation-contours which carry them, and then of the terminal directions or other types of interruption (e.g. French pitch-direction changes) which set off the lesser sub-divisions. In the case of earlier stages of languages, for which we have no auditory documentation (gramophone records date only from the beginning of this century), we have to depend on such meager information as the often capricious punctuation can afford. The comparative study of the intonation of related families of languages (e.g. Romance, Germanic) should provide the possibility of reconstructing ancestral and intermediate stages of intonational as well as other phonemic patterns; to date, however, the lack of adequate descriptions of the various intonational systems has rendered comparative work impossible.

NOTES

Intonation: Daneš, 1960.

Tone languages: Pike, 1948.

English intonation: Wells, 1945, 1947c; Trager and Smith, 1951.

French intonation: Coustenoble and Armstrong, 1934 (phonemic in practice though not in overt terminology).

Meanings conveyed by intonation contours: Uldall, 1960.

20

Alternative Formulations

AT VARIOUS POINTS in Chaps. 15 to 19, we have mentioned the existence of more than one solution for certain problems. It must not be thought that linguistic analysis, and especially phonemics, is a cut-and-dried series of procedures for arriving at rigidly formulated results. In many instances, it is possible for analysts to start from the same data, and, because of differences in premises and procedures, to arrive at differing conclusions. This "non-uniqueness of phonemic solutions" (as it was called in the title of a famous essay) distresses beginners unduly, because they feel that it confuses them and because they are often still under the spell of our authoritarian, absolutist tradition, which teaches us to expect an unrealistic single solution to all problems. However, once the differences in premises are realized and stated, and the resultant analyses compared, it is often possible to establish mutual convertibility between the different solutions, so that little practical difficulty need exist beyond the superficial trouble of learning to interpret more than one formulation for the same set of facts.

Differences in graphic symbolization need not detain us long. As mentioned in our discussion of IPA phonetic transcription (pp. 38–39), many linguists are dissatisfied with some of its symbols, and have made certain substitutions, such as š for ʃ, ž for ʒ, č for tʃ, ğ or ǰ for dʒ, etc. In some instances, these are purely graphic differences; in others, they imply a different approach to the analysis of the phenomena involved. Thus, those who consider the sound written *ch* in *church* and that written *j* in *judge* to be a unit phoneme desire unit symbols (č for [tʃ], ğ, or ǰ for [dʒ]), instead of the IPA transcription, which suggests that [tʃ] and [dʒ] are clusters, not unitary contoids. The same is true of the IPA transcription of nasal vowels, using the symbols ã, ɔ̃ etc., which imply that nasalization is a concomitant phonologic component added to the oral vocoid, rather than (as some analysts would insist for certain languages such as French or Portuguese) a sequence of vowel phoneme plus an allophone of a nasal consonant: /an on/.

These latter instances are examples of a desire which some phonemicists evince, in the direction of "linear" solutions for phonemic problems, i.e., for solutions which permit the symbolization of as many phonemic features as possible by means of letters which can be written one after the other. On occasion, this desire leads to an emphasis on nonsignificant phonologic features at the expense of those which are significant and which should, in the nature of phonemic analysis, underlie one's formulation. In Brazilian Portuguese, for instance, there are five nasal vocoids [ĩ ẽ ɔ̃ õ ũ], the second of which, before pause, can be followed by an optional closure of the dorsum against the velum to produce a faint dorso-velar nasal epilogue: [eᵑ]. Clearly, this epilogue [ᵑ] is secondary in importance to nasality, which is the true distinctive feature of all five of these vocoids. One analyst, however, proposed to treat the [ᵑ] as the phonemically significant feature in Brazilian Portuguese nasality; to use the symbol /ŋ/ for nasality; and to transcribe these five nasal vowel phonemes as /iŋ eŋ aŋ oŋ uŋ/. At best, such a solution simply substitutes a symbol which follows the vowel letter for one written above it, and is at most a contribution to typographical convenience. At worst, it involves a misanalysis of the situation, neglecting what is significant for all five of these vowel phonemes (their nasalization) in order to symbolize what is optional, in only one position (prepausal), and occurring with only one of the five nasal vowels, in [eᵑ].

Which of the two main formulations of English vowel structure we accept, will depend on our attitude towards linearity of representation and the importance of post-vocalic glides. In IPA, and the adaptations of it made by Kenyon (p. 38) and later by Pike, the individual vocoids are used as a point of departure, and, in the case of [iʲ], [eʲ], [uʷ] and [oʷ], the glides which follow them are considered secondary in importance to the distinction between tenseness in [i e u o] and laxness in [ɪ ɛ ʊ ɔ] (cf. our discussion on p. 50). For followers of the Bloomfield tradition (as developed later by Bloch, Trager, Hockett and Smith), the contrast between tenseness and laxness is considered secondary, simply a function of the presence or absence of glide elements following the vowel. Accordingly, these analysts treat [iʲ] or [ij] as functionally equivalent to [ɪj], and similarly equate [eʲ] or [ej] with [ɛj], [uʷ] or [uw] with [ʊw], and [oʷ] with [ow]. However, if no phonemic contrast is recognized between [ɪ] and [i] etc. as such, there is no need of using the special letters ɪ ɛ ʊ for the high-front, mid-front and high-back lax vowels, and the ordinary letters i e u can be used instead. (For [o], the "New England short *o*" of *road*, *coat* is called into play, which gives the pattern [as set forth on p. 88] greater symmetry and avoids the necessity of equating [oʷ] with /ɔw/.) Thus the road is now open to treating the vowel nuclei of *beat*, *bait*, *boot* and *boat* as diphthongs: /ij ej uw ow/, and transcribing, say, these words as /bíjt béjt búwt bówt/ respectively. Yet, of course, such linearity may bring apparent "economy" in one way (reducing the number of unit phonemes), but at the cost of greater complication elsewhere (increasing the number of diphthongal combinations to be recognized).

An excessive desire for symmetry also enters into the Trager-Smith formulation of English vowel pattern, since the analysis described above yields (with the addition of /æ a ə ɔ/) eight vowels, which pattern as follows:

i		u
e	ə	o
æ	a	ɔ

There is an obvious gap at the top in the center, which in the Trager-Smith formulation is filled in with the high-central vowel /ɨ/. The vocoid [ɪ] is fairly common in many people's speech as an unstressed allophone of /ɪ/ (Trager-Smith /i/), especially in words like *Ithaca* /íθɪkə/ ['ɪθɪkə], a pronunciation reflected in the frequent spelling *Ithica*. But contrast between [ɪ] and [ɪ] is very rare, and occurs only in a few people's speech. Its functional load, in other words, is extremely low. Yet its inclusion fills a gap in the pattern, and so the Trager-Smith formulation makes this rare, unusual vocalic contrast into the keystone of the "nine-vowel" system posited for English. Phonetic realism is here sacrificed to linearity of symbolization and symmetry of pattern.

A higher level of analysis is involved in problems of complementation which arise when speech-sounds occur partially, but not wholly, in contrast. In American English east of the Alleghenies, speakers have a contrast between /æ/, /ɛ/ and /e/ in such words as *bat* /bǽt/, *bet* /bɛ́t/ and *bait* /bét/ respectively, and also before /r/ in say, *carry* /kǽri/, *kerry* /kɛ́ri/, and *Carey* /kéri/. West of the Alleghenies, however, most speakers have the three-way contrast everywhere except before /r/, but have only one vowel phoneme (normally /ɛ/) in *carry*, *kerry* and *Carey*, so that the Carey Insurance Company can advertise punningly "Carry /kéri/ insurance with Carey /kéri/." When a contrast is significant in some positions but not in others (as with that between /æ/, /ɛ/ and /e/ before /r/ in American English west of the Alleghenies), it is said to be *neutralized* in the positions where it is not significant. Other instances of neutralization are: the absence of contrast between high-mid and low-mid vowels in unstressed position in Italian, in contradistinction to its presence in stressed position, e.g., in /véˆrde/ ['veˆrde] "green" and /béne/ ['bɛːne] "well"; the absence of contrast between voiced and voiceless consonants in word-final position in German, in contrast to its presence in other positions, as in the examples cited on p. 113 (the plural forms /búnde/ "leagues" and /búnte/ "varicolored" both have the singular /búnt/); and the absence of contrast between /r/ and /r:/ in Spanish everywhere except when between vowels (p. 99).

The solutions proposed for this type of partial contrast have differed, often according to the school of linguistics to which the analyst adheres. In case there is no difficulty in assigning the sounds involved to specific phonemes, on the basis of their phonetic similarity, we need recognize only that there are gaps in distribution. Thus, German *Bund:* "league" clearly has a final /t/, not /d/, and it may clearly be transcribed /búnt/; we need worry no more except to observe that /b d g v/ just happen not to occur in word-final position in German. But in case the sounds involved in the neutralization are not clearly assignable to one phoneme or the other, we are in trouble as long as we assume that every phonemic contrast identifiable for the language must be clearly identifiable at every point in the language ("once a phoneme, always a phoneme," in an aphoristic formulation of the principle). For instance, unstressed [e] and [o] in Italian vary along a gamut of vowel color, in rather free alternation, but decidely more open before liquid and nasal contoids, and closer elsewhere: e.g., /tené^re/ [tɛ'ne^:re] *tenere* "to hold", /affolláto/ [af:ɔl'lato] "crowded". To assign these varieties of unstressed [e] and [o] to either the tense /é^ ó^/ or the lax /é ó/ which occur stressed, would be quite arbitrary, and in some instances, for varieties of sound lying directly in between, well-nigh impossible.

In this situation, the Prague phonologists (cf. p. 112) would set up a special phonemic entity called an *archiphoneme* to cover ranges of sound where phonological contrast is neutralized. Usually, capital letters were used to represent archiphonemes in phonemic transcription, e.g. /E/ for English /æ ɛ e/ before /r/, as in *Carry* /kÉri/ *insurance with Carey* /kÉri/; /T /for German /d/ neutralized to /t/ in word-final position, as in /búnT/, singular of both /búnde/ "leagues" and /búnte/ "vari-colored (pl.)"; or /E O/ for Italian unstressed [ɛ] ranging to [e] and [ɔ] ranging to [o] as described in the previous paragraph, for instance in /tEné^rE/ "to hold", /affOllátO/ "crowded". This solution provides ample representation for such instances of absence of contrast, and is sufficiently ambiguous to cover situations where the phonetic facts themselves are ambiguous. However, it can be objected that too many archiphonemes spoil the broth, in that a flock of archiphonemic symbols complicates transcription and serves a basically negative, rather than positive, purpose, in symbolizing absence rather than presence of contrast.

We can overcome the dilemma of neutralization, and avoid setting up archiphonemes in such cases, by recognizing what might be termed "the converse of the archiphoneme." This involves treating as basic phonemes of a language those bundles of distinctive features which are clearly identifiable and which occur unambiguously combined throughout the language. In instances of partial contrast or neutralization, each case of contrast can be treated as involving one of the basic phonemes plus a further phonological component or distinctive feature which is significant only in particular positions, but not elsewhere. Thus, for the Italian vowels, as shown in the pattern on p. 92, we can recognize an underlying five-vowel system, with a three-way contrast in tongue-height and a two-way contrast in tongue-advancement, which is valid in all positions, stressed as well as unstressed; and a further contrast between high-mid (or tense) and low-mid (or lax) which is significant only when the vowel is stressed. We afford alphabetical symbolization, in our transcription, only to the basic phonemes of the language (in this instance /i e a o u/) and indicate the added phonological components with other marks, e.g., accent-marks, shift-signs, etc. Which aspect of an added component we choose to symbolize, and which we choose to leave unmarked, is determined wholly by practical considerations. For the Italian stressed vowels, in texts for teaching, it is probably most helpful to mark the open (lax) stressed vowels with a grave accent, and to leave the close (tense) ones unmarked in conventional orthography: e.g. *bène:* "well", but *verde:* "green". In phonemic transcription of this same system, primarily for considerations of comparability with the vowel-systems of other Romance languages and Latin in historical work, it is more convenient to mark the stressed close (tense) vowels with the mark /^/ following the phonemic symbol, and to leave the others unmarked: /vé^rde/ "green", /gó^la/ "throat", but /béne/ "well", /buóno/ "good".

This type of phonemic transcription, which might be called "semicomponential," is especially helpful in instances where the phonemic status of a contrast is doubtful because only a few speakers make it. In the table of Italian consonants on pp. 100–102, we presented [s] and [z] as being in wholly noncontrastive distribution. Yet according to conservative dictionaries and in a few individuals' pronunciation, there seems to be a contrast between [s] and [z], only when they are single and between vowels, in a few words, e.g., *ròsa* ['rɔːza] "rose", vs. *rosa* ['roːsa] "gnawed (past participle f. sg. of *ródere:* "to gnaw")". Here, it would clearly be most uneconomical to recognize /s/ and /z/ as contrasting phonemes throughout the entire system of the language and the entire Italian speech-community only to take care of these few individuals' contrast between [s] and [z] in one position in a few words. It would be only somewhat less uneconomical to set up an archiphoneme /S/ to mark in every position except that where [s] and [z] contrast for a few individuals in a few words. It is far more economical and convenient to recognize the contrast between voiced and voiceless, in Italian sibilants, as having phonological significance only in this highly restricted environment; to mark it with some device, e.g., a subscript dot under the letter s to represent the addition of voicing, e.g., in /rósa/ "rose", vs. /ró^sa/ "gnawed"; and to use this indication in our phonemic transcription only in the positions and for the speakers in whose idiolects it is relevant, omitting it elsewhere.

At the present stage of development of linguistics, it is not possible to say flatly that one type of phonemic analysis is superior or inferior to another. However, some type of organization of speech-sounds into functional units or phonemes does exist in every language, and it is the linguist's task to isolate them and formulate the system inherent in them. It has been fashionable to distinguish, facetiously, between two approaches to linguistics, the "God's truth" school (which supposedly considers that there is one fundamental truth to be expressed concerning every linguistic system), and the "hocus-pocus" school (which treats linguistics as simply a set of game-like manoeuvres to be carried out according to the analyst's preconceived principles, and using the linguistic facts only as a set of data to be manipulated at will). In these terms, we can perhaps say that "God's truth" in language (as in other matters) does exist, but that it is not given to man to discover it and formulate it in any but approximate terms, which can have only relative validity; and that hocus-pocus is basically foreign to the aims of linguistics or any other science, except as a perhaps unavoidable part of the "philosophy of *as if*" inherent in all scientific analysis.

NOTES

Non-uniqueness: Chao, 1934.
Brazilian Portuguese: Hall, 1943b, d; Reed and Leite, 1947.
Neutralization: Martinet, 1936; Hall, 1960a.
Componential analysis: Harris, 1944.
"God's truth" and "hocus-pocus": Householder, 1952; cf. also Hockett, 1948c.

21

Grammar and "Inner Form"

Every language—be it English, French, Latin, Hindustani, Navaho or Hottentot—has a grammar of its own. This statement (to which, I believe, every linguistic analyst would subscribe) is sharply contradictory to our traditional attitude towards grammar. We are usually brought up to think that there is only one type of grammar, applicable most of all to Greek and Latin, and also to modern "languages of civilization" such as English and French, but not very well to "exotic" languages like Hindustani and certainly not at all to the tongues of "primitive" peoples like the Navaho or Hottentots. However, this confusion is due to the numerous senses in which the term *grammar* is used. In order to understand the difference between the traditional senses of this word and the way in which the linguistic analyst uses it, we will do well to make a quick survey of its historical developments.

The first meaning of Greek γραμματική was "the art of writing," especially as opposed to ῥητορική or "the art of speaking (in public)." From this, the Greek term and the form which is assumed when borrowed into Latin, *grammatica*, passed to mean also "a set of rules for writing," particularly as codified by such late Latin grammarians as Priscian and Donatus. In medieval times, when the Romance vernaculars had diverged from Latin but were not the object of formal study, a boy going to school came into contact with grammar only when he started to learn the rules of Latin. From this correlation there developed a third meaning of *grammatica*, identifying it with Latin as a language, as opposed to the vernaculars, which (because they were learned by everyone in childhood by trial and error, and had not been codified in rule-books) were thought to be "devoid of grammar."

In the seventeenth and eighteenth centuries, the social-climbing bourgeoisie of the period were trained to regard a command of "grammar" as one of the accomplishments essential for achieving higher social status (cf. pp. 10–11). In this situation, *grammar* came to mean "socially acceptable usage," as when *isn't* is called "grammatical" and *ain't* "ungrammatical." When grammar is taught in our modern schools, the term acquires a fifth sense, that of "the terminology of traditional grammatical analysis." Teachers often complain of children's not knowing such definitions as "a verb is a word which expresses action, being or condition" by saying "the children don't know any grammar." The modern linguistic analyst does not shy away from the term *grammar*, despite all the various senses that have been attached to it. However, he redefines it in still a sixth way, as involving simply the statement of the structure of a language, as it is actually used rather than as somebody says that it ought to be used. For modern linguistics, a grammar is far more than a mere set of rules; it is the statement, in as much detail as possible, of an extensive network of relationships among habits of linguistic behavior, including their meanings. From this point of view, as we saw in Chap. 3, every language has its own structure and hence its own grammar.

It is possible, therefore, to write various types of grammar, some of which will meet with the linguistic analyst's approval and others of which will not. A *prescriptive* grammar, which gives injunctions as to how to speak and how not, will receive approval only insofar as it corresponds to the actual facts of the situation. Unfortunately, almost all prescriptive grammars are highly unrealistic in their injunctions, which is why modern linguists tend to treat them with scorn. A *descriptive* grammar, on the other hand, is the end-product of an analytical study of the structure of a language; it may range in size from an extensive description covering hundreds of pages, to a highly compressed *structural sketch* of only fifty to a hundred pages. If the grammatical structure of one language is set against that of another (e.g., to see what the differences in structure are and hence what difficulties there will be for native speakers of the one in learning the other), we have a *contrastive* grammar. The historical development of the structure of a language (e.g., from Latin to French, or Spanish, or Portuguese) is present in a *historical* grammar; if the discussion involves the comparative study of the history and divergence of several languages or dialects from a common ancestral source, we have a *comparative* grammar.

The "man-in-the-street" tends to confuse the grammatical structure of a language with its vocabulary, its contentives (p. 15). In Germany, for instance, purists are violently opposed to the use of words of Latin or French origin. Consider the following German sentence: *Die Koordination der Funktionen wird direkt von den autorisierten Büro-Chefs determiniert* "the coordination of the functions is determined directly by the authorized bureau chiefs," which I found in a recent discussion of the organization of part of the German bureaucracy. The reaction of German purists to such a sentence is immediately "That's not German; that's a mishmash of Latin and French," because all the contentives have come from Latin (*Koordination, Funktion, direkt, determinieren*) or French (*autorisieren, Büro, Chef*).* Yet compare this German sentence with its English equivalent and with sentences containing the same contentives in other languages:

French: La coördination des fonctions est déterminée directement par les chefs de
    bureau autorisés.
Italian: La coordinazione delle funzioni viene determinata direttamente dai capi-
    ufficio autorizzati.
Latin: Functionum coordinatio immediate ab officiorum capitibus determinatur.

* In "pure" German, this would read: "Die Beiordnung der Aufgaben wird unmittelbar von den Amtsvorgesetzten bestimmt," but nobody except ultranationalist purists would ever use such expressions nowadays.

Each one of these sentences is unmistakably French, Italian, English, and Latin, respectively, not German. What makes them belong to these various languages is the functors that are used, the system into which they fit in relation to each other, and the order of the significant combinations of the language. As soon as we have *die* (def. art. f. sg. nominative), *der* (def. art. pl. genitive), the noun-plural suffix *-en*, *wird* + past participle in a passive construction, *von* indicating agent, *den* (def. art. pl. dative), and the past participle separated from its auxiliary by an intervening complement, we know that we have German structure and no other. Simply, we recognize French structure by the presence of such forms as *la*, *des*, the plural suffix (written *-s*, but zero here in pronunciation), *est*, etc.; English structure by *the*, *of*, *is*, *-ed*, *-ly*, *by*; and Latin by the absence of definite article, by the genitive pl. suffix *-um*, the adverb-forming suffix *-ē*, the passive 3.sg. present suffix *-tur*, and so forth.

Of these elements, some have a certain amount of "dictionary meaning," e.g., German *wird* "becomes, gets (passive)," English *is*, Italian *di* "of"; but others serve only to indicate grammatical relationships, e.g., English *and*, which tells us simply that two grammatical elements are connected on an equal functional level. Inasmuch as the former type of functors indicate both grammatical relations and "dictionary meanings," Sapir termed them "mixed-relational" elements, and those which indicate only grammatical relations he called "pure-relational." That even "pure-relational" elements do have meaning, can be seen from the well-known *Jabberwocky* in Lewis Carroll's *Through the Looking-Glass*, whose beginning is often and rightly cited in this connection:

> 'Twas brillig, and the slithy toves
> Did gyre and gimble in the wabe;
> All mimsy were the borogoves,
> And the mome raths outgrabe.

Carroll explains certain of these terms in the following text, e.g. *gyre* as "turn, gyrate," and *outgrabe* as the past of a verb *outgribe*. Yet most of the contentives in *Jabberwocky* are meaningless, or at best vaguely suggestive of words in normal use.

In the passage immediately following this stanza, Alice exclaims: "Somehow . . . it seems to fill my head with ideas—only I don't know exactly what they are!" In part, the "ideas" with which it fills her head are the vague associations with existent contentives, such as *gyre* has with *gyrate*, or *gimble* with "(turn like a) gimlet"; but mostly, they were the grammatical relationships indicated by the pure-relational and mixed-relational elements:

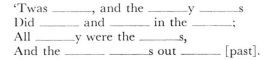

'Twas _____, and the _____y _____s
Did _____ and _____ in the _____;
All _____y were the _____s,
And the _____ _____s out _____ [past].

These grammatical elements serve as a kind of framework on which meaningful contentives may be hung, provided they fit the structural pattern (others prefer the simile of a skeleton of functors and grammatical relationships, which may be clothed with the flesh of contentives); we could construct any number of stanzas on this same pattern, such as

> 'Twas morning, and the snowy trees
> Did shine and glitter in the air;
> All sunny were the mountain-tops
> And the lone peaks outflared.

Conversely, we may not know what the contentives mean, but we can tell what their relations to each other are and a good deal about their probable nature and activities, simply from the functors which connect them and the order in which they are arranged. In *Jabberwocky*, we may not know what *toves* are, but we know that they are *slithy*, that they *gyre* and *gimble*, and that the place where they do their gyring and gimbling is the *wabe*—whatever that may be. Furthermore, we know the parts of speech to which these various meaningless or semi-meaningless contentives belong: *tove* is a noun (it is preceded by *the* and has the plural suffix -*s*, and has the element *slithy*—a typical formation with the adjectival suffix -*y*—preceding it), *gyre* and *gimble* are verbs (they occur in the phrase-type *did* + VERB), and so forth. One of the most frequent observations of modern linguistic analysts is that the traditional pseudo-philosophical definitions of parts of speech ("a noun is a word that names a person, place, or thing," etc.) are poor because they do not correspond to facts. Thus, such undoubted nouns as *reflection* or *electricity* are not names of persons, places, or things, but rather of actions (motions of particles); but they are none the less nouns, not because of what they name, but because of their linguistic characteristics. *Reflection* and *electricity* are nouns for the same reason that *tove* and *wabe* are nouns—because they can be preceded by *the*. In fact, we would do well to turn the traditional definition around, and say that a "thing" is whatever is referred to by a noun, be it *table*, *chair*, *electricity*, *justice*, or the non-existent *wabe*.

The grammatical system of a language is constituted by its functors, their relations to each other (in the form-classes or parts of speech which they serve to establish, and the grammatical categories which they mark) and the significant orderings of grammatical elements. This system, and the meanings which it expresses, are by some called the "grammatical core," and by others, more vaguely, the "inner form" of the language. The former term concentrates our attention more on the structural elements themselves, the latter more on their meanings. The meanings of the structural elements, although often hard to define, have a real existence and are very important in determining our understanding of the relation of the contentives in any utterance. Certain jokes depend on deliberate use of the meanings attached to functors or grammatical constructions, as in the remark attributed to a Georgia "cracker:"

If the dog would only catch a rabbit, we could have rabbit pie for supper, if we had a dog.

The wry humor of this remark consists specifically in the contradiction between the use, first of the definite article *the* (indicating that a specific member of the class referred to by the noun *dog* does exist) and later of the indefinite article *a*, indicating that it does not exist with the definiteness previously specified. Many poetical effects, too, depend on such apparently insignificant grammatical features, e.g., the use of the definite article in the third line of Coleridge's *Kubla Khan:*

> Where Alph, the sacred river, ran.

The use of the definite article here assures us of the reality of Alph, which the poet is assuming in advance that we know and are willing to accept. Think how flat not only this line, but the whole beginning of the poem, would be if Coleridge had written *Where Alph, a sacred river, ran.*

Other jokes depend on violation of syntactic habits, as in the five-word Spanish dialogue: *¿Se fué?—No, lo fueron.* "Did he go away?—No, they made him go away". The point of this very compressed joke is entirely lost in translation, because it depends on an unusual use of the past absolute of the verb *irse* "to go away (of one's own accord)". This verb normally occurs only in the reflexive, as in *se fué*, literally "he went himself"; it does not usually occur with a direct object, and hence the construction *lo fueron*, literally "they went him = they kicked him out, expelled him, made him go away" has a strong shock-value because of its unusual grammatical construction.

In describing the grammatical core of a language, the linguistic analyst's task is, first of all, to isolate the functors and to ascertain their meanings, and also to identify the different possibilities of combinations, of both functors and contentives, in meaningful order (especially, but not exclusively, syntactic combination). Then, using them as his guide lines, he determines which classes of forms occur in combination with which other forms, whether contentives or functors; the grammatical categories of the language (e.g., number, person, tense, etc.) are to be stated in connection with the classes of forms established in this way. On occasion, the meanings of form classes, grammatical categories, or constructions are not necessarily those which our traditional grammar assigns them; and their customary names are often quite misleading. We must determine their meanings as accurately as we can by examining all the contexts in which they occur, nor must we be afraid to rename them if necessary in order to avoid confusion.

A good example of this type of reanalysis and renaming is furnished by the English "present perfect" (*he has come*, etc.), which is radically different in both structure and meaning from the Latin present perfect (e.g., *vēnit*, to *venīre:* "come"). A Latin form like this is usually labelled "present perfect" and translated "he has come," but its real meaning is "his coming is over and done with." The "present perfect" verbal phrase in modern continental European languages, which superficially resembles the English construction, e.g., French *il est venu* or German *er ist gekommen*, means rather "he came." But the English phrase *he has come* refers to an action which lasts, or whose effects last, up to the present time, and which are "open-ended," i.e., still subject to change. The best example of this meaning, in contrast with that of the English simple past ("action completely in the past"), was given in a dialogue in a detective story I once read, where the inspector of police is interrogating the daughter of the victim, immediately after the murder, as to his connections with France:

I. Was your father ever in Paris?
D. Yes, he has been . . . [suddenly realizing he is now dead and the situation is no longer subject to further developments] he was in Paris three or four times.

This basic meaning of the English "perfect phrase" construction is the cause of the common mistake made by continental Europeans when they equate it with their phrases of similar structure but different meaning, so that they produce sentences like "The treaty of Versailles has been signed in 1919." The linguistic analyst insists on our recognizing, for the so-called "present perfect" in English, that it is not a simple tense (on the order of *came, went,* etc.), but a verbal phrase consisting of auxiliary + past participle; and that it is not a "perfect" in the sense of referring to an action definitively over and done with, but just the opposite. A new name might be indicated, e.g., "past incompletive verbal phrase" or the likes.

Instances of this sort show us that we should not base our descriptions and comparisons of the "inner form" of languages either on meaning or on form alone, but on both, starting from formal characteristics and then proceeding to the semantic features which are symbolized thereby. If we base our discussion on meaning alone, we are likely to bring together structurally disparate phenomena. This was recognized as early as the time of the sixteenth-century Italian philologist Benedetto Varchi, who, in his linguistic dialogue *L'Ercolano*, has one of his interlocutors compare Italian *è amato:* "he is loved" with the synonymous Latin *amātur;* whereupon another interlocutor points out that the Latin is a single verb form, whereas the Italian expression is a phrase consisting of the auxiliary *èssere:* "to be" + past participle, a fact which makes the Italian structurally different from the Latin. On the other hand, if we go by structural characteristics alone, we run the opposite risk, that of putting together features which are similar in shape but different in meaning, as in the case of English *he has come* and French *il est venu* which we have just discussed.

NOTES

Types of grammar: Gleason, 1961, Chap. 13.
"Inner form": Leopold, 1929.
On vocabulary and language, cf. Sapir's remark "The linguistic student should never make the mistake of identifying a language with its dictionary" (Sapir, 1921, Chap. 10).
Benedetto Varchi: Hall, 1942a, Chap. 4.

22

Morphology

ANY MEANINGFUL UTTERANCE carried by a single intonation contour is termed a *linguistic form*. The length of linguistic forms can range from a single word (e.g. *Fire! Help!*) to very long sentences. Our immediate concern in morphology, the study of forms, is not with longer linguistic forms, but with the structure of minimum units of form, *morphemes*. We arrive at these minimum units by thorough and careful comparison of all the material at our disposition, as contained in the *corpus* which we have. A corpus of linguistic material is a collection of utterances in a language (preferably recorded in careful, narrow phonetic transcription), which may range from a few words or sentences to a very large collection of books. For the languages in which a great literature has been written, the literature serves as an extensive corpus— whose validity, however, is restricted to the literary variety of the language and is also further diminished by its being written in a conventional orthography. The best situation is that in which the linguistic analyst is also a native speaker of the language he is working on; in this case, he has at his disposal an unlimited stock of forms which he can make up as needed, with a native speaker's knowledge of what is and what is not normal in the language.

At the initial stages, the comparison of elements in a language to determine their morphemic structure involves, at least in theory, making a series of successive cuts and investigations by trial and error to see if the resultant sequences of phonemes have independent meaning. In an Italian sentence like *Sono venuto stamattina* /só^novenútostamattína/ "I came this morning", we obtain, by making such successive cuts, the following results:

/s/	Does not occur separately and with meaning.
/só^/	" " " " " " "
/só^n/	Occurs as a free alternant of /só^no/, e.g. in /só^nvenúto/ "I came".
/sóñov/, /só^nove/, /sóñoven/	Do not occur separately and with meaning.
/só^novenúto/	Means "I have come, I came", but we suspect and find, on checking, that it consists of two elements, /só^no/ "I am" plus /venúto/ (see below).
/ó^/, /ó^no/ etc.	Do not occur separately and with meaning.

/ve/	Means "to you", and also "there" in combinations like /velodó/ "I give it to you", /velomándo/ "I send it there"; obviously no relation to the form we have here.
/ven/	Only a poetic variant of /vene/ "some to you".
/venú/, /venút/	Do not occur separately and with meaning.
/venúto/	Means "in the condition of having come (m. sg.)"; together with /só^no/, means "I have come, I came", and the m. sg. form /venúto/ tells us that /só^no/ is here the form meaning "I am", not the one meaning "they are".
/venútos/ etc. etc., until we come to	Do not occur separately and with meaning.
/sta/	As a verb-form, means "is located, stands, is (with regard to health)", but is always accompanied by doubling of the following consonant and so cannot be involved here.
/stam/, /stama/ etc.	Do not occur separately and with meaning.
/stamattína/	Means "this morning".
/mattína/	Means "morning" (sg.).
/tína/ etc.	A girl's name, obviously not involved here.

By a procedure of this sort, too long to exemplify here *in toto*, we find that the "words" contained in this short Italian sentence are: /só^no/ "I am", /venúto/ "in a condition of having come (m. sg.)", and /stamattína/ "this morning". This latter "word" consists of two elements, /sta/ "this" (occurring also in /stamáne/ or /stamáni/ "this morning", /stasé^ra/ "this evening", and /stanótte/ "this [last] night") and the form /mattína/ "morning", which is found independently in many combinations.

Our work has not finished with the identification of separate "words"; however, because many so-called "words" consist of even smaller elements which are also meaningful as either contentives or functors, but which do not occur independently. In the Italian example just given, each of the separate "words" breaks down this way: /só^no/ into /só^n-/, a positional variant of /éss-/ "be" + /-o/ indicating first person singular present; /venúto/ into /ven-/ "come" + /u/ (a vowel which normally accompanies this particular stem of verbs of this class) + /t/ (suffix forming the past participle) + /o/ (ending indicating masculine grammatical gender and singular number); /mattína/ into /mattín-/ "morning" + /-a/ (ending indicating singular number but not, in itself, the grammatical gender of the word, which happens in this instance to be "feminine"). The element /sta/ "this", in present-day standard Italian, does not lend itself to a further breakdown of this type, although we can see by a comparison with dialectal usage and Old Italian that it, too, earlier consisted of /st-/ "this" + /-a/ (stem vowel indicating singular number and, in this instance, feminine grammatical gender).

The fact that some minimum forms, in almost any language, can occur alone, and others cannot, is of cardinal importance in determining the relation of morphemes to each other, because it enables us to state which morphemes occur in connection with which. Forms which do not occur alone are termed *bound* forms, and those which do occur alone are *free*. In the abstract, we speak of the *bondage* and the *freedom* of forms. It is often useful to distinguish between *minimum forms* (whether bound or free) and *minimum free forms*, which (according to the language involved) may or may not contain one or more bound forms among their constituent elements. Languages vary greatly in the prevalence of bound forms: in some (which are said to include Chinese and Ewe) there are very few, if any; in others (like English) most minimum forms are free but some are bound; and in still others (like Eskimo and French) almost all minimum forms are bound. A good example of the prevalence of bondage in French would be any longer sentence such as /ilnəmãnavepazãkorparle^/ "he hadn't yet spoken to me about it". In this sentence, only /ãkor/ "yet" and conceivably also /parle^/ "spoken" are free, and all the rest of the forms are bound. We must not let ourselves be deceived by spelling in this type of instance, or by the use of spaces between "words" in conventional orthography. The French conventional spelling of this sentence, *il ne m'en avait pas encore parlé*, would make us think that we were dealing here with eight separate free forms, whereas actually all but two of the forms are bound.

Bound forms are customarily thought of as occurring primarily in morphological structure, i.e., in inflection (Chap. 24) and derivation (Chap. 28). However, some forms are bound on higher levels of grammatical structure, i.e., occur only in connection with one type of syntactic construction or another. It is instructive, in this respect, to examine the difference between the English noun-plural suffix (written -*s*, -*es*, but consisting in its phonemic shape, of the allomorphs /-əz -s -z/) and the possessive suffix (consisting of the same allomorphs but written '*s*). Both are bound, but they occur on different levels of bondage. The plural suffix occurs only with individual nouns: e.g., /háwzəz/ *houses*, /kǽts/ *cats*, /ájz/ *eyes*, /dɔ́gz/ *dogs*; or with combinations (compounds) functioning as individual nouns, e.g. /bə́s+tìkəts/ *bus-tickets*, /skáwt+mǽstərz/ *scout-masters*, etc. We do not normally add it to combinations larger than individual nouns or compounds (e.g., */ðəkǽthwɪtʃkɔ́tðəmàwsəz/ *the-cat-which-caught-the-mouse-s* for "the cats which caught the mouse"). If we do find it in such combinations, we normally interpret it as belonging to the last element, and would tend to take this hypothetical phrase as due simply to a slip of the tongue which had substituted *mouses* for *mice* in "the cat which caught the mice." On the other hand, the possessive suffix is freely added to both individual nouns and compounds, and to longer phrases which fulfill the function of nouns in syntactic constructions (cf. Chap. 34): e.g., /ðəlɔ́rdméjərəvlɔ́ndənzʃó/: *the Lord Mayor of London's show;* /ðəmǽnajsɔ́jéstərdezdɔ́tər/ *the man I saw yesterday's daughter;* etc. We can therefore speak of the English noun-plural suffix as being bound on the level of inflection, or *inflectionally bound;* and of the possessive suffix as being bound on the level of phrase structure, or *phrasally bound.*

Other examples of phrasally bound forms are, for English, the definite article *the* and the indefinite article *a*, *an*. In French, Spanish, Italian, and the other Romance languages, the articles are phrasally bound as in English, and also a number of other forms, such as prepositions (Fr. /d(ə)/ *de, d'* "of"; Italian /daˣ/ *da* "from";† Spanish, Italian /kon/ *con* "with"; etc., etc.). Under this same heading come also the "conjunctive" elements of the Romance languages—pronouns and other particles which occur with verbs in the formation of a kind of superconjugation or "verbal core," e.g., French /m(ə)/ *me, m'* "me"; /ã(n)/ *en* (replacing phrases introduced by /d(ə)/ *de, d'* "of, from, about") etc., as in /ilmãparl/ *il m'en parle* "he speaks to me about it". On the clausal level, such conjunctions as Eng. /ðət/ *that*, Fr. /k(ə)/ *que, qu'* "that", or conjunctional phrases like Eng. /kənsídərɪŋðət/ *considering that*, or Italian/benkéˣ/ *benché* "although", are clausally bound. On occasion, we find bound elements restricted in their occurrence to certain particular types of structures, such as the Neo-Melanesian (Melanesian Pidgin English) form /i-/, which occurs only with a third-person predicate, as in /i-ren/ "it's raining", /dɪsfɛlə pɪkɪnɪni i-krajawt tuməs/ "this child (is) crying a great deal", or /əl i-hardwok/ "they work". Such a form can be termed a "third-person predicate marker," and is *predicatively bound*. Other more specific types of bondage can of course be recognized as may be necessary.

In our discussion to date, we have normally put the term "word" in quotation marks, to show that we regard it as an expression which, although widely used, is not to be taken seriously as a useful concept in linguistic analysis. A *word* is popularly thought of as "a separate, independent element of language," and as one which is written with a space before and after it. However, the concept of a "word" has no universal applicability in linguistic analysis.‡ In some instances, a "word" can be roughly equated with a minimum free form, as is usually done for English, German, Spanish, etc. Such a procedure gives approximate satisfaction when we are dealing with forms like Eng. *chair, chairs, come, comes, go, went*, etc., or their German equivalents like *Stuhl, Stühle, kommen, kommt, gekommen, gehen, ging*. However, it fails in the case of "words" which, although written separately, are not free forms, such as Eng. *a, an, the, that* (conjunction), or the other examples cited above in our discussion of phrasally and clausally bound forms. It also fails when a language has few or no free forms at all, as in the case of French (cf. above); in such an instance, as already pointed out, conventional orthography is very deceptive.

Some efforts have been made to salvage the notion of "word" by trying to find linguistic criteria for identifying, say, the "phonologic word" or the "morphologic word." This procedure may be useful for individual languages,

† The small raised /ˣ/ in the phonemic transcription of an Italian form indicates that the form causes the doubling of a following consonant phoneme (so-called *raddoppiamento sintàttico* or "syntactic doubling"); cf. Chap. 23.
‡ There have been hundreds of definitions proposed for the term *word*, none of them satisfactory.

but has no universal validity, as does the identification of phonemes, morphemes, or syntactic constructions. The term *lexeme* has also been proposed, to refer to a word-like unit, but has not proved to be of any usefulness in linguistic analysis. If the concept of *word* is to be used in linguistics at all, it must be with considerable circumspection; some have even suggested that it be deliberately restricted to graphemics (cf. Chap. 44) and used only in the redefined sense of "a form written in conventional spelling with a space preceding and following it." We shall avoid the word *word* as much as possible, preferring to couch our discussion in terms of *forms* (free and bound) and significant units of form or *morphemes*.

The analyst's task in describing the morphological and syntactic structure of a language is to isolate, list, and formulate the partial resemblances which exist between utterances, with respect to both form and meaning. In morphology, this involves observing which forms occur in combination with which others. In Italian, for instance, the endings /-a/ (sg.), /-e/ (pl.); /-o/ (sg.), /-i/ (pl.); etc., occur only with a certain category of forms such as /matíta/ "pencil", /inkióstro/ "ink", which we may call "substantives (= nouns and adjectives)," whereas other endings like /-o/ (1.sg.), /-i/ (2.sg.), zero (3.sg.), occur only with another category of forms like /kánto/ "I sing", /pássi/ "thou passest", /mánǧa/ "he eats", which are usually called "verbs." There seems to be no language in which all forms may occur equally freely in combination with all others; apparently in all languages there are limitations on the combination of some forms with others. The limitations applying to any given form or set of forms, with regard to the combinations in which it may occur, are known as its *privileges of occurrence*. We depend largely on the privileges of occurrence of forms, especially bound forms, for the determination of form-classes on a morphologic basis (Chap. 24) and of syntactic combination-types (phrases, clauses; cf. Chap. 31 ff.).

In morphological analysis, our concern is with the patterning of bound forms and minimum free forms into classes and sub-classes, as determined first of all by their morphological characteristics and also by their syntactical privileges of occurrence. Our normal procedure is to find elements which remain relatively constant in form and meaning throughout sets of morphologically related forms. Thus, the English element /kæt/ *cat* is common to the singular /kæt/ *cat*, the plural /kæts/ *cats;* the derivatives /kætɪʃ/ *cattish*, /kætdəm/ *catdom* ("the cat world"), /kæti/ *catty*, etc.; and the compounds /kæt+fùd/ *cat food*, /kæt+làjk/ *catlike*, and so forth. The element /rájt/ *write*, with certain changes, is common to the simple verb-form /rájt/ *write*, the 3.sg. /rájts/ *writes*, the past /rót/ *wrote*, the "*ing*-form" /rájtɪŋ/ *writing*, the past participle /rítən/ *written*, and such compounds as /ə́ndər+ràjt/ *underwrite*, /hǽnd+ràjtɪŋ/ *handwriting*, or /tájp+ràjtər/ *typewriter*.

One normally takes one particular form as basic and then treats the other forms of the set as being formed on it, as with /kæt/ *cat* and /rájt/ *write* in the sets just listed. On occasion, this procedure has to be somewhat arbitrary, as in the case of English /tébəl/ *table*, noun and verb: which is to be regarded as basic? Most of us would probably treat the noun /tébəl/ *table* as basic and the verb ("to place something on the table") as derived from it. Our decision would be reached, however, whether consciously or unconsciously, on the analogy of other instances, where the decision is clearer, such as /gréz/ *graze,* derived from /grǽs/ *grass* with change of vowel and voicing of final consonant. Some analysts, despairing of ever finding a wholly nonarbitrary criterion for such instances, have tried to work out procedures whereby such relationships may be described without having to treat some one form of a set as "basic" and the others as "formed on" it. In such an approach, for instance, /tébəl/ *table* would be regarded as being neither noun (N) or verb (V), but belonging to a separate category of "noun-and-verb" (NV). Such procedures involve, however, an equally arbitrary assumption that our analytical technique can and should be completely static, purposely removing the time-factor from consideration even as applied to the analyst's passage from one item under analysis to the next. They usually result in setting up an excessive and cumbersome number of extra categories and complicated statements merely in order to avoid identifying the "basic" form of a group.

In describing the relations between forms, most analysts (with the exception of the school just mentioned) do so in terms of *grammatical processes,* which involve the alteration of a form in one way or another so as to produce another, related form. Grammatical processes may involve either the modification of a single form in some way, or the combination of more than one form. Under modification are included processes that involve *addition, subtraction,* or *replacement* of one or more phonemes. An element which is simply added to a form is known as an *affix,* and the process involved is *affixation.* The three main types of affix are the *prefix* (added before a form, as in /prífɪks/ *prefix,* with the element /pri-/ *pre-* plus /fíks/ *fix*), the *suffix* (added after a form, as in most of our familiar endings such as the noun-plural and possessive suffixes discussed on pp. 132–133), and the *infix.* The corresponding processes are of course called *prefixation, suffixation,* and *infixation.* The last-mentioned involves the insertion of one or more phonemes at some point within a form, as when, in Old Latin, a /n/ was inserted in certain verb-roots to form the imperfective stem: e.g., /nigu̯-/ "snow", but /ningu̯-/ (imperfective) "to snow"; /fig-/ "mould", (imperfective) /fing-/ "break"; /frag-/ "break", (imperfective) /frang-/. If some element of a form is repeated, being thus infixed before (or after) itself, the process is called *reduplication.* Thus, in Tagalog, the initial syllable of certain forms is reduplicated to give an additional meaning of "only . . . :" /isá/ "one", /iisá/ "only one"; /dalawá/ "two", /dadalawá/ "only two"; /tatló/ "three", /tatatló/ "only three"; /píso/ "peso", /pipíso/ "only one peso", etc. If, in a given pair of forms, nothing at all is added, in contrast to the addition of an affix in other forms of the same category, we speak of *zero-affixation;* this is a convenient way of handling, say, such English plural formations as /ʃíp/ *sheep* (sg.) vs. /ʃíp/ *sheep* (pl.), as contrasted with /dɔ́g/ *dog* vs. /dɔ́gz/ *dogs.*

In some instances, changes in prosodic patterns take place along with other types of grammatical processes. Thus, in English noun-compounds, the stress-pattern changes as the compounding takes place, in that the full (Trager-

Smith "primary") stress on the second and following elements of the compound is replaced by intermediate (Trager-Smith "tertiary") stress, as in /bə́s/ *bus* + /tíkɛt/ *ticket* → /bə́s+tìkɛt/ *bus-ticket*. In nouns in /-éʃən/ *-ation* derived from verbs in /-èt/ *-ate*, the pattern of stress in the underlying verb is reversed in the derived noun, so that, say, from /fɔ́rmjulèt/ *formulate* we have /fɔ̀rmjuléʃən/ *formulation*. These changes in stress (in tone languages, they are often changes in pitch) may be described under replacements (cf. below), but they are often treated as if they involved an affixation of some kind, and (since they involve suprasegmental phonemes) termed *superfixes*.

Subtraction is, on occasion, a convenient way of stating a relationship that involves the presence of certain disparate elements in one part of a set of forms, and their absence in another part. A familiar example is a certain class of French adjectives:

MEANING	A	B
"cold"	frwa	frwad
"hot"	ʃoˆ	ʃoˆd
"bad"	move	movez
"seated"	asi	asiz
"fried"	fri	frit
"distinct"	distē	distēkt
"false"	fo	fos
"long"	lõ	lõg
"drunk"	su	sul
"light"	leʒe	leʒer
"nice"	ʒãti	ʒãtij
"good"	bõ	bon

To describe the relation of the forms in column B to those in column A by starting from the latter, and treating the former as involving the suffixation of some additional element, would require a whole series of separate statements as to which final consonant is to be added to which adjective: /d/ to /frwa/ and /ʃoˆ/, /z/ to /move/ and /asi/, etc. It is much more convenient to start from column B as basic, and to describe the forms of column A in relation thereto. If we proceed in this way, we can simply say that the forms of column A are derived from those of column B by subtracting the final consonant or cluster of consonants, and, in case the final consonant is a nasal, with concomitant nasalization of the preceding vowel (/bon/ "good" in column B, /bõ/ in column A). This suggestion (which is quite old, going back at least half a century, to the French phonetician Paul Passy) often shocks those who are attached to French traditional grammar, because the forms of our column B are usually termed "feminine" and those of column A "masculine." Traditional grammar, operating in terms of conventional spelling, derives the feminine from the masculine, and any departure from this procedure is felt as a heresy. However, the Lord did not create the feminine grammatical gender after the masculine in the Garden of Eden, nor did St. Paul declare the feminine grammatical gender to be a "weaker vessel." We need not be shocked or have hostile reactions if it proves more convenient to derive masculine adjective-forms from feminine in French rather than vice versa.

In *replacement*, the place of one or more elements is taken by one or more others. This process is very familiar to us in English, with our noun plural formations of the type /mǽn/ *man*, /mén/ *men*; /máws/ *mouse*, /májs/ *mice*; /wúmən/ *woman*, /wímən/ *women*; /gús/ *goose*, /gís/ *geese*. The formation of the past tenses and past participles of most of our irregular verbs is, for the most part, accomplished in the same way, as in /síŋ, sǽŋ, sóŋ/ *sing, sang, sung*; /drájv, dróv, drívən/ *drive, drove, driven*; /tǽr, tór, tórn/ *tear, tore, torn*; etc. Of course, replacement can also apply to consonants, as in /háwz/ *house* (verb) derived from /háws/ *house* (noun), with the replacement of a voiceless final consonant by a voiced one. Frequently, replacement is accompanied by one or more other processes, such as suffixation, in such formations as /slépt/ *slept* (past tense and past participle) on /slíp/ *sleep* (simple form of the verb). If the replacement is so extensive as to involve all or virtually all of the phonemes of a form, we speak of *suppletion*, as in Eng. /gó/ *go* (simple form) vs. /wént/ *went* (past). A well known Latin example is the verb /fer-/ "bear, carry" (imperfective stem), whose perfective stem is /tul-/ and whose past participle is /la:t-/ (principal parts, as usually cited, *ferō ferre tulī lātus*).

NOTES

Morphology: Elson and Pickett, 1960; Nida, 1949; Pickett, 1956.
Levels of bondage: Hall, 1946a.
Lexeme: Hockett, 1958, Chap. 19.
Privileges of occurrence: Hockett, 1958, Chaps. 18, 20, 21.
English form-classes: Hockett, 1958, Chap. 26.
Grammatical processes: Boas, 1911; Sapir, 1921, Chap. 6.
Zero: Haas, 1957; Hoenigswald, 1959.
French adjectives: Beyer and Passy, 1893; Bloomfield, 1933a, Chap. 13.

23

Morphophonemics and Sandhi

THE VARIANTS of a morpheme differ from each other, by definition, with regard to their phonemic shape; if a morpheme has only the one phonemic shape (e.g., Eng. *shape* /ʃép/), it has only one allomorph and no problem of variation arises. It is often valuable to have the phonemic differences between allomorphs taken care of in one's description before entering on the discussion of the structure of the morphemic pattern itself. In phonemically different shapes of allomorphs, the phonemes which differ are said to *alternate* with each other or to be *in alternation* (as when /ɪ/ alternates with /æ/ and with /ə/ in /síŋ sǽŋ sə́ŋ/ *sing sang sung*). The mark ∼ is often used to mean "alternates, alternating, in alternation with," e.g. /ɪ/ ∼ /æ/ ∼ /ə/ or /síŋ ∼ sǽŋ ∼ sə́ŋ/ in the preceding examples. An alternation of phonemes within a given morpheme bridges the gap between the morphological and the phonemic levels, and hence is called *morphophonemic*. It would be perfectly possible to analyze the structure of a language without reference to morphophonemic alternations, but only at the expense of cluttering up the morphological and syntactical description with details which could better be taken care of at a lower level, in a separate section devoted to morphophonemics, and whose elimination would permit us to concentrate more on the essential aspects of purely morphological or syntactical relationships.

In the broadest sense of the term, morphophonemics includes all alternations of phonemes within morphemes, whether these alternations are predictable (automatic) or not, and whether they are meaningful or not. It is useful to distinguish among these various possibilities; in many instances, automatic nonmeaningful alternations can be taken care of on the phonetic or phonemic level, even before we reach the stage of morphophonemics. As pointed out in Chap. 18 (pp. 112–113), phonetic assimilations are best described as concomitant effects of juncture, as in the devoicing of French /l r m n/ at the end of a breath group after a preceding voiceless plosive, e.g., /batr/ [batʀ̥] *battre* "to beat". Such effects of juncture are often known as phenomena of *sandhi*. This term was borrowed in the nineteenth century from Sanskrit, in which it means "a putting together"; in India, it is pronounced /sándhi/ ['sʌndfii], but in English, usually /sɔ́ndi/ or /sǽndi/.*

---

* The grammatical term *sandhi* is thus homonymous with both *Sunday* and *sundae* "a combination, a putting-together of ice-cream and syrup;" for the possibility that the latter term may have been borrowed from Skt. *sandhi* through Anglo-Indian channels around the turn of the present century, cf. Austin, 1945.

Sandhi can be of two varieties: internal, that taking place within a morpheme, and external, that taking place across the boundaries of morphemes. Variations of phonemes in sandhi are termed *sandhi-variations*, and the resulting morpheme-alternants or allomorphs are *sandhi-alternants*.

Automatic sandhi-variation on the phonemic level is also best treated under phonemic effects of juncture. Within individual morphemes (in internal sandhi), there are a great many such effects in English and other modern European languages, particularly in that part of the vocabulary which has been borrowed from Latin or Greek, and in the special form assumed by morphemes in derivation (Chap. 28). Thus, /n/ does not normally occur in close juncture before /p b m/ in English, but is automatically replaced by /m/, e.g. in words like /ɪmprábəbəl/ *improbable*, consisting of the negative prefix /ɪn-/ *in-* (e.g., in /inórdɪnət/ *inordinate*) plus /prábəbəl/ *probable*. The suffixation of our learnèd words shows similar phenomena, as when /áksɪdèt/ *oxidate* + /-jən/ *-ion* gives /àksɪdéʃən/ *oxidation*, with /t/ + /j/ being replaced by /ʃ/. Similarly, in Italian, the parallel suffix /-ió^ne/ *-ione* added to such stems as /dissolút-/ *dissolut-* gives automatically /dissolució^ne/ *dissoluzione* "dissolution", with /t/ replaced by /c/ when followed by /i/ + vowel. Many of the processes of phonemic replacement involved in such morphophonemic alternations are the results of historical development, or simulate such results, and are referred to by the same terms as are used for historical phonological change (Chap. 52), such as *assimilation, palatalization* (as in the instances just given), *dissimilation, metathesis*, etc.

Of more functional significance than these automatic replacements are the nonautomatic morphophonemic alternations which occur, without or with accompanying changes in meaning. The Romance languages manifest, very widely, a type of alternation between simple vowel and diphthong, often correlated with the position of stress. Thus, the Spanish verb /kolgár/ *colgar* "to hang" has two variant shapes of the root, /kolg-/ unstressed and /kuélg-/ stressed, as in /kuélga/ *cuelga* "he hangs"; similarly, /sentár/ *sentar* "to seat" has /sent-/ unstressed and /siént-/ stressed, as in /siénta/ *sienta* "he seats". These alternations, /o/ ~ /ué/ and /e/ ~ /ié/, cannot be treated as automatic, because there are many parallel instances in which /e/ and /o/ remain undiphthongized under stress, as in the verbs /komér/ *comer* "to eat" and /kedár/ *quedar* "to stay", which have root-stressed forms like /kóme/ *come* "he eats" and /kéda/ "he stays". Hence we have to set up /o/ ~ /ué/ and /e/ ~ /ié/ as separate morphophonemic alternations in Spanish. Some Spanish verbs show more extensive vowel alternations than this, as in /sentír/ *sentir* "to feel", which has not only /e/ ~ /ié/ under stress, but also /e/ ~ /i/ when unstressed before /i/ + a stressed vowel, e.g., in /sintió/ *sintió* "he felt", /sintiéndo/ *sintiendo* "feeling". This alternation of /e ~ i ~ ié/ constitutes a different morphophonemic alternation from that of /e ~ ié/ which we observed for /sentár/ "to seat", and would have to be enumerated and symbolized separately in a complete treatment of Spanish morphophonemics.

It is not worth our trouble to set up special symbolization for automatic morphophonemic replacements, because they can be taken care of as effects of juncture or the like. This holds even for instances of neutralization where the result is clearly assignable to a specific phoneme, as in the case of Ger. /búnt/ *Bund* "league" (p. 121). For nonautomatic replacements, it is in theory possible to symbolize each one in the language, using special characters of one kind or another, especially capital letters, italics, and so forth. For Spanish, we could symbolize the /e ∼ ié/ alternation just discussed by //E//,* and could transcribe the root /sent- ∼ siént-/ "to seat" morphophonemically as //sEnt//. Such a morphophonemic transcription conveys the information that this root contains the kind of /e/ which remains as such when unstressed but goes to /ié/ when stressed. For the alternation /e ∼ i ∼ ié/ manifested in /sentír/ "to feel", we might use the italic capital //*E*// and write the root /sent- ∼ sint- ∼ siént-/ in morphophonemic transcription as //s*E*nt-//, a transcription which tells the reader that this /e/ is the kind which goes to /i/ when unstressed before /i/ plus a following stressed vowel, goes to /ié/ under stress, and remains /e/ otherwise. Thus, the two morphophonemic transcriptions //sEnt-// "to seat" and //s*E*nt-// "to feel" give us, in shorthand form, a great deal of information concerning the phonemic shapes which these roots assume under specific conditions.

A parallel situation in English is that of the plural formation of nouns like /lájf/ *life*, /wájf/ *wife*. We have nouns ending in /-f/, with regular plurals in /-fs/, like /mə́f/ *muff* and /mə́fs/ *muffs;* and nouns ending in /-v/ with regular plurals in /-vz/, like /də́v/ *dove* and /də́vz/ *doves*. Alongside of these, however, we have a few whose singular ends in a /-f/ that is replaced, irregularly, by /-v/ in the plural: e.g. /wájf/ *wife* and /wájvz/ *wives*, or /nájf/ *knife* and /nájvz/ *knives*. For the alternation of /f ∼ v/ in these words, we might set up a morphophonemic symbol //F//, and transcribe them morphophonemically as //wájF// and //nájF//, respectively.

In many languages, however, there are a great many morphophonemic alternations which occur in only a few forms, and for which it would be, from a practical point of view, unrewarding to provide special symbolization. In Italian, for example, certain alternations of vowels such as /e ∼ ié/ and /o ∼ uó/ are very frequent, especially in verb-forms, and considerable time and space may be saved by setting up the special morphophonemic symbols //E// and //O//, respectively, for these alternations, using them to transcribe such verb-roots as //vEn-// "come", //tEn-// "hold", //vOl-// "wish," etc. However, a number of other vocalic alternations occur only in one or two forms, e.g. /e ∼ i/ in the root /de-/ *de-* "god" vs. the masculine noun /dío/ *dio* "god"; /u ∼ uó/ in the sg. /búe/ *bue* "ox", pl. /buói/ *buoi* "oxen" and the possessive adjectives /túo/ *tuo* "thy" and /súo/ *suo* "his, hers, its", with m. pl. /tuói/ *tuoi* and /suói/ *suoi* respectively; and /i ∼ ié/ in /mío/ *mio* "my," m. pl. /miéi/ *miei*. In theory, special morphophonemic symbolism for each of these alternations (e.g. //E// for /e ∼ i/, //U// for /u ∼ uó/, //I// for /i ∼ ié/, etc.) would permit each and every morpheme of the language to be cited in a single shape in morphophonemic transcription,

* Morphophonemic transcriptions will be enclosed between double slant lines: //.

e.g. //dE-// "god", //bU-// "ox", //tU-// "thy", //sU-// "his, hers, its", //mI-// "my". In practice, however, such a complete morphophonemiciza-tion of our transcriptions would overload both the morphophonemic section of the description and the reader's memory, with a great many symbols for alternations which occur in only one or a few morphemes; it is more useful to provide special symbolization only for those morphophonemic alterna-tions which are relatively frequent. The boundary between relative frequency and infrequency can be determined only by rule-of-thumb and by practical considerations such as availability of symbols on typewriters or in print-shops.

Morphophonemic analysis often reveals the presence of important phe-nomena which go neglected in the traditional grammar of a language because they are represented only poorly or not at all in conventional spelling. Such a situation exists in English with the derivational relation between *house* (noun) and *house* (verb); since both are spelled alike, we often fail to realize that there is an alternation between voiceless /s/ in /háws/ (noun) and voiced /z/ in /háwz/ (verb). This alternation serves as a grammatical process in deriving a number of verbs from nouns and adjectives, e.g., /ríð/ *wreathe* from /ríθ/ *wreath*, or /sév/ *save* from /séf/ *safe*. In some other forms, this alternation occurs together with other replacements, as in /gréz/ *graze* on /grǽs/ *grass*, /béð/ *bathe* on /bǽθ/ *bath*, etc. Some of these derived verbs seem to us to involve other processes than that of voicing, because we habit-ually think of them in terms of spelling rather than in sound (e.g. *wreathe* as built on *wreath*, or *bathe* on *bath*, by the addition of a final letter *e*).

A much more far-reaching phenomenon of this sort, masked by deficiencies in the conventional orthography, is the Italian "syntactic doubling" of con-sonants (*raddoppiamento sintàttico*) which takes place in external sandhi. After certain elements which, in spelling and when pronounced in isolation, end in a vowel (e.g., prepositions like /da/ *da* "from" or /su/ *su* "on"; con-junctions like /e/ *e* "and" or /o/ *o* "or"; and any word ending in a stressed vowel), the initial consonant of a following element in close juncture within a breath group is doubled. Thus, /da/ *da* "from" + /firénce/ *Firenze* "Florence" gives /daffirénce/ *da Firenze* "from Florence"; /da/ + /ró^ma/ *Roma* "Rome" gives /darró^ma/ *da Roma* "from Rome"; /vá/ *va* "it goes" + /béne/ *bene* "well" gives /vábbéne/ *va bene* "it goes well = all right"; etc. This reduplication, as can be seen in these examples, is not rep-resented in Italian conventional spelling. The only exception to this state-ment is formed by certain combinations which are habitually written together as single words: e.g., /da/ *da* "from" + /kápo/ *capo* "head, beginning", giving /dakkápo/ *da capo* or *daccapo* "from the beginning."

This morphophonemic peculiarity of certain Italian words is not auto-matic; it is limited to certain specific forms, which are not all predictable on the basis of either phonologic or morphologic characteristics. These forms must be indicated specially in some fashion, either by the clumsy procedure (followed in such Italian grammars or treatises on phonetics as pay any attention to the phenomenon at all) of making a complete list, or by the far simpler procedure of putting a morphophonemic mark, such as a small raised

$//^x//$, after them. One would thus transcribe *da:* "from" as $//da^x//$, *va:* "he, she, it goes" as $//vá^x//$, and so forth; and $//da^xró^\wedge ma//$ is phonemically /darró^ma/, $//vá^xbéne//$ is phonemically /vábbéne/, etc. When we have recognized the existence of this morphophonemic phenomenon $//^x//$ in external sandhi, we find that it also plays a role in internal sandhi in verb inflection, and even some verb roots have to be set up as involving $//^x//$, for instance $//tra^x-//$ "to draw", with infinitive /trárre/ *trarre* = $//tra^x-//$ + infinitive ending /-re/.

A morphophonemic alternation can itself be a feature of inflection or derivation (as in the instance of /háwz/ *house* [verb] derived from /háws/ *house* [noun], cf. p. 137), in which case it may be referred to as a *morphophonemic process*. French has a very widespread morphophonemic alternation in which a final consonant or consonant cluster is lost, with nasalization of a preceding oral vowel if the consonant involved is /n/ or /ɳ/. This alternation is exemplified in the list of "feminine" and "masculine" adjectives given on p. 136; it may be symbolized by either a special letter (e.g., $//L//$) or some other symbol, such as a downward-pointing arrow: $//\downarrow //$. It is found, not only in the formation of the masculine of certain classes of adjectives on the respective feminine, but also very widely in verb-inflection. Thus, the ending of the 3.sg. present of all but first-conjugation verbs is $//-\downarrow //$: e.g., /dorm-/ *dorm-* "sleep" + $//-\downarrow //$ gives /(il)dor/ *il dort* "he sleeps". It is also found in many types of derivation, such as that of nouns on verb-roots, as in /abri/ *abri* "shelter" on /abrit-/ *abrit-* "to shelter".

In some instances, it is difficult to decide whether a particular phenomenon is phonemic or morphophonemic in its nature. French has two such problems: that of "aspirate *h*" and that of "mute *e*." A number of French forms which begin with a vowel phoneme are nevertheless treated, in sandhi, as if they began with a consonant, and the preconsonantal allomorph of a preceding element is used before them: thus, before /e^ro^/ *héros* "hero," one uses the preconsonantal form of the definite article /lə/ *le*, not /l/ *l'*, as in /ləe^ro^/ *le héros* "the hero", and similarly with /omar/ *homard* "lobster", /ləomar/ *le homard* "the lobster". In earlier French, almost all of these words were pronounced with an initial /h-/, and the spelling with *h* reflected the pronunciation; later, the phoneme /h/ was lost, but the spelling with *h*, and the term "aspirate *h*" for the letter written at the beginning of such words, were retained. The situation was then confused by the introduction, from Middle French times (roughly the 14th and 15th centuries) onwards, of the letter *h-* into the spelling of many words which had always begun with a vowel phoneme in French, e.g. /om/ *homme* "man", /onet/ *honnête* "honest".

French grammarians accordingly distinguish, on the basis of spelling, between two kinds of "*h*." One kind, the "mute *h*" (as in *homme, honnête*), is treated as nonexistent for purposes of liaison (the use of a prevocalic allomorph of a preceding morpheme), as in /le^zom/ *les hommes* "the men", parallel to /lezãfã/ *les enfants* "the children". The other, or "aspirate," *h*, involves the use of a preconsonantal allomorph of an immediately preceding morpheme, as pointed out in the preceding paragraph. To use a pre-vocalic allomorph before a word beginning with "aspirate *h*" is a boner, and makes its user the object of ridicule, as in the story of the Fourteenth-of-July orator who wished to speak of *les héros de la politique française:* "the heroes of French politics", but referred to them, with more truth than poetry, not as /le^e^ro^/, but as /le^ze^ro^/ "the zeroes" of French politics!

Whether this phenomenon of "aspirate *h*" is phonemic or morphophonemic depends on the phonetic behavior of the speaker involved. Some speakers of modern French use, in words involving "aspirate *h*," a slight muscular constriction of the pharynx (which we may symbolize here by [']), so that [le^e^ro^] "the heroes" is different phonetically from [le^õz] "the eleven". Others make no such difference, having the same kind of transition between the two parts of [le^e^ro^] as between those of [le^õz]. For the first kind of speaker, the existence of an actual phonetic distinction implies that of a distinction on the phonemic level; for them, we should set up "aspirate *h*" as a separate phoneme /'/, with the single allophone ['] (muscular constriction of the pharynx). This phoneme is to be classed among the consonants, and the occurrence of pre-consonantal allomorphs before it is perfectly natural; for those who have /'/ as a phoneme, the problem becomes rather one of "mute *h*," the irrational use of *h* in spelling before words which actually begin with a vowel phoneme. However, a phoneme cannot have the allophone zero (no sound at all); hence, for those who have no distinctive feature of sound corresponding to "aspirate *h*," we cannot set up a phoneme /'/, but must treat this as a morphophonemic phenomenon. For such speakers, //'// is the use, before words which begin with a vowel phoneme but contain this feature, of preconsonantal instead of prevocalic allomorphs of preceding morphemes.

Traditionally, French is described as having a phoneme /ə/, with a single allophone [ə], rather similar to English [ɔ] but involving slightly more lip-rounding. In Old French, this phoneme occurred in all positions, and was written *e* wherever it occurred, as in /ačətǽr/ *acheter* "to buy", /empərǽðrə/ *emperedre* "emperor", /fámə/ *fame* "woman", etc. The writing of *e* for earlier /ə/ has survived in a great many words in modern French, but the occurrence of the phoneme has been greatly restricted. It has disappeared, through a phenomenon of internal and external sandhi, in a great many phonologically determined positions: at the end of words (as in /fámə/ "woman", which has become /fam/, and a host of similar instances); and in the interior of words between two single consonant phonemes each flanked by a vowel, in the sequence VC(ə)CV (as in /ačətǽr/ "to buy", which has become first /aʃəte^/ and then, in normal modern pronunciation, /aʃte^/). In other positions, especially after a cluster of two consonants not at the end of a phonemic phrase, or after one or more consonants at the beginning of a phonemic phrase, or with *"accent d'intensité,"* /ə/ is not lost, as in /ãtrənu/ *entre nous* "between us", /bɔzwḛ/ *besoin* "need", or /fer erɔ́fer/ *faire et refaire* "to do and re-do". There is thus a very extensive alternation between /ə/ and zero; so far, this is to be regarded as simply a semiautomatic morphophonemic alternation, a phonemic concomitant of close juncture.

In many (perhaps, by now, most) modern Frenchmen's pronunciation, however, there is no longer a separate phonetic entity [ə], because it has merged with lax [œ], and hence there is no longer a phoneme /ə/. For these speakers, the presence or absence of [œ] is not a phonemic, but purely a morphophonemic matter: they have two varieties of /œ/, which are different, not phonemically, but morphophonemically. One variety is quite stable and is not subject to loss under any conditions, as in /pœr/ *peur* "fear"; the other is quite unstable, and is subject to loss under the conditions outlined in the preceding paragraph. For such speakers' usage, we can, if we wish, keep the symbol ə, but redefine it, in morphophonemic terms: for them, //ə// is a variety of /œ/ which is subject to loss under certain phonologically definable conditions.

Morphophonemics, as a field of linguistic analysis, is intermediate (as its name implies) between the morphemic and the phonemic levels. It can never take the place, in linguistic analysis, of phonemics proper; but it is very useful as a bridge, for treating and symbolizing, in advance of morphologic analysis, those phonemic alternations which are best gotten out of the way before we proceed to the truly significant relationships in morphologic structure.

NOTES

The morphophonemics of English learnèd words: Bloomfield, 1933b.
Italian morphophonemics: Hall, 1948b.
Italian syntactic doubling: Norman, 1937; Fiorelli, 1958.
French "aspirate h" *and "mute* e": Valdman, 1961.

24

Form-Classes and Inflection

To DATE, no language that has been accurately described has been observed to have only one undifferentiated type of minimum form; in other words, the forms of all languages seem to fall into at least two classes or "parts of speech." (We need not hesitate to keep this traditional term, provided we re-define it as referring to the classes into which the minimum forms of a language fall.) At one extreme seems to be Nootka, a language of the Pacific Northwest, whose forms are simply either uninflected or inflected; at the other, our familiar Indo-European languages, which have four or five main parts of speech and numerous subsidiary classes. The form-classes of a language are determined first of all by morphologic criteria, particularly the privileges of occurrence of bound forms. Often, however, morphologic criteria alone are insufficient, and we must have subsidiary recourse to criteria of syntactic combination as well. The bound forms which occur with one form class or another, and which indicate the grammatical relationships of the form-classes to the rest of an utterance, constitute the *inflection* of a language. (In popular parlance, *inflection* is often used in the meaning of "intonation" or "tone of voice," but linguistic analysts never use the term in this sense.)

A simple example of the determination of form-classes is furnished by Neo-Melanesian (Melanesian Pidgin English). We can set up four lists of typical Neo-Melanesian forms, as follows:

LIST A

/bɪgfɛlə/ "large"
/gʊdfɛlə/ "good"
/najsfɛlə/ "pretty"
/smɔlfɛlə/ "small"
/nufɛlə/ "new"
/səmfɛlə/ "some"
/nədərfɛlə/ "another"
/wənfɛlə/ "one, a, an"
/tufɛlə/ "two"
/trifɛlə/ "three"
/forfɛlə/ "four"
etc., including /sɛvɛnfɛlə/ "seven"

LIST B

| /mi/ "I, me" | /mifɛlə/ "we, us" |
| /ju/ "you (sg.)" | /jufɛlə/ "you (pl.)" |

LIST C

/kʊk/ "cook, burn"	/kʊkɪm/ "cook, burn (something)"
/brɪŋ/ "bring"	/brɪŋɪm/ "bring (someone, something)"
/rɛdi/ "be ready"	/rɛdiɪm/ "make ready"
/gæmən/ "deceive, lie"	/gæmənɪm/ "deceive, lie to (someone)"
/mek/ "do, make"	/mekɪm/ "make (someone, something)"
/fɪnɪš/ "finish"	/fɪnɪšɪm/ "finish (something)"
/kɪč/ "take"	/kɪčɪm/ "take (someone, something)"
/slip/ "lie recumbent"	/slipɪm/ "fell (e.g. a tree)"
/kajkaj/ "feed on, eat"	/kajkajɪm/ "bite"

LIST D

/rəbɪš/	"without standing in the community"
/mæn/	"man"
/meri/	"woman"
/læpun/	"old person"
/ɛm/	"he, him; she, her; it"
/əl/	"they"
/sævi/	"know"
/go/	"go"
/stap/	"remain, be located (Sp. *estar*)"
/kəm/	"come"
/tru/	"really, in truth"
/tæsəl/	"only"
/nogʊd/	"with undesirable results, badly"
/ɪnsajd/	"in, inside"
/bɪlɔŋ/	"in close relation with; of, for"
/lɔŋ/	"in not so close relation with; at, in, to, from, by, with, etc."

In lists A, B, and C, we present morphemes which combine with the three inflectionally bound forms of Neo-Melanesian: the suffix /-fɛlə/, adding no contentive meaning to the form to which it is added, but simply marking it as a member of that class (list A); another suffix /-fɛlə/ meaning "plural," and added only to /mi/ and /ju/ (list B); and /-ɪm/, added to a different group of forms and meaning "a direct object (either present in the utterance or to be inferred in the context) is present" (list C). The fourth list contains forms which never occur with any of these inflectional suffixes, and which, from a purely morphologic point of view, are "indeclinables." As for naming these form-classes, it does not matter what terms we use. We could use the letters A, B, C, D; we could call the classes by neutral names such as "red," "green," "yellow," and "blue"; or we could use the traditional names "adjective," "pronoun," "verb," and "indeclinable." But if we use these latter names, we must be willing to redefine them, for Neo-Melanesian, in terms of the grammatical characteristics which each class manifests. In our first approximation, therefore, we will define "pronouns" as those forms which take the plural suffix /-fɛlə/; "adjectives," those which take the empty suffix /-fɛlə/; and "verbs," those which take the transitive suffix /-ɪm/.

On passing to Neo-Melanesian syntax, however, we observe that some of the forms given in list D behave, in the syntactic combinations into which they enter, like those of Classes A, B, or C. Thus, forms of Class A occur as attributes before the head they modify, as in /bɪgfɛlə haws/ "(a) large house", /najsfɛlə mɪsɪs/ "(a) pretty lady", /nədərfɛlə mæn/ "another man", /trifɛlə diwaj/: "three trees". A form like /rəbɪš/ also occurs in this same construction: /rəbɪš mæn/ "a man without standing in the community, an outcast". Forms of Class B occur as subjects in clauses, as direct objects of forms of Class C, or after /bɪlɔŋ/ and /lɔŋ/ (Class D): e.g., /mi go/ "I go", /jufɛlə gæmən/ "you are lying", /mi lʊkɪm ju/ "I see you", /bɪlɔŋ mifɛlə/ "of us = our, ours". The forms /ɛm/ and /ɔl/ occur in these same constructions: /ɛm i-go/ "he goes", /ɔl i-gæmən/ "they are lying", /mi lʊkɪm ɔl/ "I see them", /bɪlɔŋ ɛm/ "of him, her, it = his, hers, its". Not only the forms of type C, but some of type D occur with forms of type B as subject and modified by such elements as /ɪnsajd/ "inside", or phrases introduced by /lɔŋ/ "at, in, to, etc.": thus, /mi no gæmən/ "I'm not lying" is paralleled by /mi no go/ "I'm not going"; /ɛm i-slipɪm dɪsfɛlə diwaj/ "he fells this tree", by /ɛm i-sævi dɪsfɛlə diwaj/ "he knows this tree"; /motokar i-rɛdi lɔŋ rod/ "the automobile is ready on the road", by /motokar i-stap lɔŋ rod/ "the automobile is standing on the road."

In these instances, we can do one of two things. We can invent special names, such as "adjectivals," "pronominals," "verbals," for forms of Class D which behave like Neo-Melanesian adjectives, pronouns and verbs, but do not take the inflectionally bound forms that characterize them. Or else we can expand our definition of these form-classes to include not only forms which show certain inflectional characteristics, but also those which behave in the same way syntactically. Note, however, that our first approach has to be through morphologic, not syntactic characteristics; otherwise, we are likely to get lost in a welter of conflicting and overlapping patterns of syntactic combinations.

We can therefore remove, say, /rəbɪš/ from Class D and put it with the adjectives; /ɛm/ and /ɔl/ can go with the pronouns; and /sævi/, /kəm/, /go/, /stap/ can go with the verbs, as a special subclass of intransitives. Among the remaining forms, we can establish various further classes purely on the basis of the syntactic combinations into which they enter, especially with forms of the morphologically identified classes which we have already established. Thus, one type of indeclinable, like /mæn/, /meri/, /læpun/, occurs as head in constructions with adjectival attributes: e.g. /gʊdfɛlə mæn/ "(a) good man", /najsfɛlə meri/ "(a) pretty woman", /səmfɛlə læpun/ "some old person(s)"; and also as subjects and objects in verbal constructions, and as objects of /lɔŋ/ and /bɪlɔŋ/: e.g., /wənfɛlə mæn i-wɔkəbawt lɔŋ rod/ "a man was (is, will be) walking along the road"; /nogʊd ju slipɪm dɪsfɛlə diwaj/ "don't fell this tree". This type of indeclinable can be set aside as a separate class, and termed either "Class D¹," "purple form," or "noun." By similar procedures, we can set aside such further subclasses as prepositions (including /lɔŋ/ and /bɪlɔŋ/); adverbs (including /tru/, /tæsɔl/, /ɪnsajd/, /nogʊd/); etc.

Neo-Melanesian is a pidgin language (Chap. 64), and hence has a reduced structure, so that the determination of its form-classes is relatively simple. For "full-sized" languages, the problem is of the same type, but more complicated, and the presentation of our entire procedure in identifying and defining the form-classes of English, French, Spanish, German, Hungarian, etc., would take a considerable number of pages for each. It must be emphasized, however, that our procedure must never involve starting from a preconceived set of "parts of speech" (particularly, as has often been the case, those of Latin), and then finding their equivalents in the language being studied. Our description of the part-of-speech system of any language must reflect the organization inherent in the language itself ("God's truth" as far as we can get at it), and our terminology, even if we use traditional terms like "noun," "verb," "adjective," etc., must be defined wholly in terms of the language itself, not of Latin, English, or aprioristically determined meanings.

An inflectional element serves, first of all, to indicate a grammatical relationship between the forms to which it is attached and other parts of the sentence. Thus, in Latin *boni hominēs:* "good men", the inflectional endings -*i* and -*ēs*, both masculine plural nominative, serve to tie these two forms together (according to the principle of concord, Chap. 33), and also to fit them for certain functions in larger combinations (in this instance, to function as subject of a verb or as vocative). If an element does not indicate a grammatical relationship, it cannot be considered inflectional. For instance, the English adjectival endings /-ər/ -*er* (comparative) and /-ɛst/ -*est* (superlative) indicate no grammatical relationship: the structure of the three phrases *the big house, the bigger house,* and *the biggest house* is exactly the same, DETERMINER + ADJECTIVE + HEAD in each instance. Hence the English suffixes /-ər/ and /-ɛst/ are not inflectional, but derivational. (This fact does not diminish their usefulness in helping to determine the form-class of "adjective" in English, as including any form which can form comparatives and superlatives by adding these suffixes.)

Languages vary greatly in the extent of their inflectional systems and in the complication with which the inflectionally bound forms combine with each other and with the forms to which they are added. An old-fashioned classification of languages used to be into "analytic" and "synthetic," the former being supposedly those which expressed grammatical relationships with few or no inflectionally bound forms and many fixed syntactic combinations (e.g., Chinese, English), and the latter those whose inflection showed many complications and whose word-order was correspondingly free (e.g., Latin, Greek, Sanskrit). This classification has been out-of-date since the beginning of the twentieth century, as is the case also with another slightly more extensive differentiation of language types into "isolating," "agglutinative," "polysynthetic," and "inflecting." An "isolating" language supposedly had no bound forms; in an "agglutinative" language like Hungarian or Turkish, elements come one after the other, e.g. Hungarian /seretlek/ *szeretlek* "love-thee-I, i.e., I love you"; in "polysynthetic" languages, an "excessive" number of elements were joined together into long strings constituting sentence-words, the stock example being Eskimo /a: wlisa-ut-iss?ar-siniarpu-ŋa/: "I am looking for something suitable for a fish-line"; and in "inflected" languages more than one meaning was thought to be expressed in a single bound form, e.g., Italian /kantóˣ/ *cantò* "he sang", with /-óˣ/ showing third person, singular number, past absolute tense, and (in traditional grammar) "indicative" mood.

These classifications are out-of-date because they are only relative (a language like English may be "analytic" in some ways and "synthetic" in others), and because they confuse a number of different criteria of classification: morphophonemic complexity, multiplicity of meanings in bound forms, and the relation of syntactic to morphologic phenomena. Furthermore, those who used such classifications normally based their study on languages as written in conventional spelling, and hence erred greatly in their perception of the facts. The most notorious example is of course French, in which almost every utterance is a string of bound forms, like *Je ne regrette pas de lui en avoir parlé* /ʒǝnrǝgretpadlɥiãnavwarparleˆ/ "I'm not sorry for having spoken to him about it"; French is almost as "polysynthetic" as Eskimo, but it is not usually recognized as such because its orthography does not reflect the way the language is actually spoken.

One axis of comparison for inflectional structures is that of morphophonemic complexity. In Turkish, there is little or no complication at the borders of inflectional elements, and hence the structure of strings of inflectionally bound forms is quite clear, as in a verb form like /kirilmadilarmɨ/ "were they not broken?" = root /kir-/ "break" + /-il-/ "passive" + /-ma-/ "negative" + /-dɨ-/ "past" + /-lar-/ "third person plural" + /-mɨ/ "interrogative." There is a certain amount of variation in the allomorphs of some of these suffixal morphemes, especially due to the morphophonemic requirement of "vowel harmony," i.e., that the vowels in each word be of the same type, back or front; nevertheless, the structure is quite transparent. These Turkish suffixal elements must appear in a particular order with respect to the root to which they are attached and to each other. There is an immense number of combinations of these elements, rather over three thousand, which can occur with any Turkish verb root. Yet, despite its extensiveness, the structure of Turkish verbs is relatively regular, and free from the sub-divisions into "conjugations" and the complicated paradigms of even Latin, Greek, or Sanskrit, to say nothing of Algonquian or Iroquoian languages.

In contrast to Turkish, at the other extreme of morphophonemic complexity, stand many American Indian languages, in which a number of different bound forms include the indication of both subject and object. The stock example is Cree, an Algonquian language, in which we have such verb forms as:

VERB FORM	MEANING	SUFFIX	ACTOR	OBJECT
/nisa:kiha:w/	"I love him"	/-a:w/	1.sg.	3.sg.
/nisa:kiha:wak/	"I love them"	/-a:wak/	1.sg.	3.pl.
/kisa:kiha:w/	"thou lovest him"	/-a:w/	2.sg.	3.sg.
/nisa:kihik/	"he loves me"	/-ik/	3.sg.	1.sg.
/nisa:kihikuna:n/	"he loves us (but not you)"	/-ikuna:n/	3.sg.	1.pl. (exclusive)
/kisa:kihitina:n/	"we love thee"	/-itina:n/	1.pl.	2.sg.
/kisa:kihitin/	"I love thee"	/-itin/	1.sg.	2.sg.

(etc.)

These suffixes can be analyzed into further constituent elements, but only
with considerable difficulty and artificiality. It is hardly worth the trouble
to do so, any more than it is with the (rather simpler) verb endings of Latin,
which indicate only the actor, here exemplified with /ama:-/ "love":

VERB FORM	MEANING	SUFFIX	ACTOR
/amo:/	"I love"	/-/ (with replacement of /a/ by /o/)	1.sg.
/ama:s/	"thou lovest"	/-s/	2.sg.
/amat/	"he loves"	/-t/ (with automatic loss of /:/)	3.sg.
/ama:mus/	"we love"	/-mus/	1.pl.
/ama:tis/	"ye love"	/-tis/	2.pl.
/amant/	"they love"	/-nt/ (with automatic loss of /:/)	3.pl.

Matters are complicated in many languages, especially in the Indo-
European family, by the existence of numerous subcategories into which the
members of form classes fall because of various peculiarities of their inflection.
For nouns and adjectives, these subcategories are usually called *declensions;*
for verbs, *conjugations.* In Latin, the nouns fall into six main declensions,
according to the choice of vowel to which the case- and number-endings
are added (with considerable morphophonemic alternations). We list them
here, in the traditional order, with a slight change in numbering:

DECLENSION	STEM VOWEL	EXAMPLE
I	/a/	/ro:s-a-/ "rose"
II	/o/*	/domin-o-/ "master"
IIIa	/i/	/turr-i-/ "tower"
IIIb	/Ø/†	/ko:nsul-/ "consul"
IV	/u/	/man-u-/ "hand"
V	/e/	/speki-e-/ "appearance"

Latin verbs, likewise, show four conjugations, determined by the "characteristic" or "thematic" vowel used in forming the verb stems. Three of the
four conjugations have two sub-classes each, determined by the presence or
absence of length in the stem vowel:

CONJUGATION	THEMATIC VOWEL	EXAMPLE
Ia	/a:/	/am-a:-/ "love"
Ib	/a/	/st-a-/ "stand"
IIa	/e:/	/mon-e:-/ "warn"
IIb	/e/	/re:g-e-/ "rule"
IIIa	/i:/	/aud-i:-/ "hear"
IIIb	/i/	/kap-i-/ "take"
IV	/Ø/	/pot-/ "be able"

In Latin and the Romance languages, verbs have more than one stem,
to which various endings are added. Latin had one stem whose use indicated

* Automatically replaced by /u/ in the endings /-u-s/ and /-u-m/, so that the nominative sg. of this form is /dominus/ and the accusative sg. is /dominum/.
    † We use the special symbol Ø for "zero" to avoid confusion with either small or
capital O.

that the situation was "open-ended," i.e. not over and done with (imperfective), and another showing that the situation was closed, over and done with (perfective). Thus, *vīvit* /u̯i:u̯it/ (imperfective stem *vīv-* /u̯i:u̯-/) meant "he is living", whereas *vīxit* /u̯i:ksit/ (perfective stem *vīx-* /u̯i:ks-/) meant "his living is over and done with, he is through living = he is dead". When a Roman senator came to the end of a speech, he said *dīxī* /di:ksi:/ "my speaking is finished = that's all I have to say"; the customary way of translating /di:ksi:/ as "I have spoken" misses the point entirely. In the Romance languages, the old perfective stem has come to refer, rather, to exclusively past time (e.g., Italian /vísse/ *visse* "he lived"); the old imperfect, to time not exclusively past (e.g. Ital. /víve/ *vive:* "he lives"); and a new stem (usually called the "future" stem) has developed, formed on the infinitive, referring to probable events (as in Italian /viverá^x/ *viverà* "he will live, he's probably living"). In the forms based on each of these stems, there may be all kinds of irregularities, either in the allomorphs of the stems (as in Ital. /véngo/ *vengo* "I come", on /vEn-/ "come") or in the inflectional elements such as tense markers or personal endings (e.g., /éro/ *ero* "I was", where we might have expected */essé^vo/ on the root /éss-/ *ess-* "to be"). A satisfactory classification of verb-roots in Romance languages has to take into account the relation of the root to the three stems just mentioned, and the presence or absence of irregularities in the forms built on each of the three.

When we speak of "roots" and "stems," we are of course referring to elements which are to be abstracted from sets of related forms (nouns, verbs, etc.) by the process of observing and stating partial similarities. We do not imply, in setting up roots or stems, that they are now or must necessarily have been separate entities or free forms. Speakers of different languages vary greatly in their awareness of the existence and interplay of roots; in the English speech-community, such awareness seems relatively uncommon, whereas it is said that speakers of Russian are very much aware of the role of roots and stems in their language. Nor are "roots" or "stems" determinable by any aprioristic principles; the analyst can define them as best suits his convenience in describing the structure of the language. Our criteria will often differ from one language to another. For instance, we obtain the most consistent results for French by defining the verb root as that element which precedes the ending /-e/ *-ais, -ait* (1., 3.sg.) of the imperfect, as in /mãʒ-/ "eat", to /mãʒe/ *mangeait* "was eating," etc. On the other hand, in Italian it is more convenient to start from the present participle and to define the root as what comes before the /-ándo -éndo/ *-ando -endo* of this form, as in /ved-/ "see" on /vedéndo/ *vedendo* "seeing" or /pass-/ "pass" in /passándo/ "passing." In each case, we make our choice in order to avoid certain irregularities: the French roots /av-/ "have" and /sav-/ "know" show up as /ej-/ and /saʃ-/ in the present participles /ejã/ *ayant* "having" and /saʃã/ *sachant* "knowing," respectively, whereas in Italian the root /ess-/ *ess-* "be" has an irregular allomorph in the imperfect, e.g., /éro/ *ero* "I used to be".

In some instances, it is helpful to present the forms of a language in sets or *paradigms*, as in the familiar Latin models:

SINGULAR		PLURAL	
/dominus/	"master (nominative)"	/domini:/	"masters (nominative)"
/domini:/	"of a master"	/domino:rum/	"of masters"
/domino:/	"to a master"	/domini:s/	"to masters"
/dominum/	"master (accusative)"	/domino:s/	"masters (accusative)"
/domino:/	"from a master"	/domini:s/	"from masters"
/domine/	"o master!"		

In languages with a number of inflected forms and considerable morpho-phonemic complexity, such as Latin, Greek, Sanskrit, or the Algonquian languages, this is probably as effective a way of presentation as any. For other languages with either less morphophonemic complexity or a smaller number of endings, presentation of paradigmatic sets is wasteful. In the case of English, such a listing used to be common in traditional grammars, for example:

a table
of a table
to a table
a table
from a table
o table!

This type of presentation was, of course, worse than useless in presenting the structure of English, and served only to make any intelligent person think "grammar" a waste of time—which, in this form, it was.

NOTES

The form-classes of Neo-Melanesian: Hall, 1943a, 1955b. For a similar procedure for Haitian Creole, cf. Hall, 1962a.

Turkish: Gleason, 1961, Chap. 9.

Parts of speech: Robins, 1952.

25

Categories of Inflection

IN GENERAL, inflectional elements, no matter what the grammatical process involved, serve to indicate not only relationships of forms to other parts of the utterance, but also various meanings, sometimes quite specific and sometimes relatively vague or generic. According to the different types of meaning which they convey, we distinguish various *categories of inflection*. The categories of inflection may be quite separate, each associated with a different morpheme, as in languages traditionally termed "agglutinative" (cf. the Turkish example on p. 149), or they may be tangled together, several at a time, as in the Indo-European and Algonquian languages (cf. pp. 149–150 ff.). A category of inflection may be associated with several grammatical processes at once: e.g., the English noun-plural morpheme, some of whose allomorphs involve suffixation; others involve vowel-replacements, as in /mǽn/ *man* /mέn/ *men;* and others involve further morphophonemic alternations in the stem as well, as in /tʃájld/ *child* /tʃíldrən/ *children.*

A very widespread category of inflection is that of *number*, in which the inflectional variation indicates a distinction, usually in the arithmetical number of the objects referred to. Number is found with various parts of speech—substantives (adjectives and/or nouns), pronouns, verbs. The most familiar distinction in number is that between *singular* (one) and *plural* (more than one), as in Spanish /kása/ *casa* "house", /kásas/ *casas* "houses", but other distinctions are also possible. Greek, Sanskrit, and a number of other languages representing an earlier stage of Indo-European structure have a special form for the *dual* (two), so that a Greek noun may have three forms in any given case, such as /anthrɔ́:pos/ ἄνθρωπος "(one) man", /anthrɔ́:po:/ ἄνθρώπω "two men", and /anthrɔ́:poi/ ἄνθρωποι "(more than two) men". In other languages, there are still further distinctions, with special forms for *trial* (three) and *quadral* (four). These meanings are translated (but with phrasal, not inflectional formations) in such Neo-Melanesian pronominal phrases as /mi tufɛlə/ "the two of us", /ɛm trifɛlə/ "the three of them", /ju forfɛlə/ "the four of you".

On occasion, there are subtle variations in the meaning of number-contrast. In English, our "plural" does not mean simply "more than one," as our traditional grammar would have us believe, but rather "not restricted to one." This is evident from such normal English uses of the "plural" as *Somebody left their books on this table;* in a sentence like this, *their* is a convenient way of indicating that the "somebody" may have been one person or more than one. Compare also the habitual telephone operator's reply *They don't answer*, when by the nature of things only one person can pick up the receiver; she is indicating that no answer is forthcoming from whoever is at the other end of the line—one person, more than one, or nobody. Purists who tell us that we should never use a "plural" with a "singular" indefinite antecedent (e.g. *somebody . . . they, somebody . . . their*) are simply demonstrating their own ignorance and insensitivity to the subtleties of English linguistic structure.

Together with number, we often find *grammatical gender*. This type of inflectional variation manifests itself especially in grammatical concord (Chap. 33): the way that we know that, say, Lat. /homo:/ "man" is masculine in gender, and that /karo:/ "flesh" is feminine, is that, when they are modified by adjectives, the modifiers have to have different forms, e.g., /homo: malus/ "a bad man", but /karo: mala/ "bad flesh". But grammatical gender is not exclusively a phenomenon of concord, since, in a language having gender, the selection of one gender as opposed to another tells the hearer that that particular gender is being referred to: e.g. Spanish /ésboníta/ "she (either some woman or an object referred to by some feminine noun) is pretty".

Grammatical gender may involve any number of contrasts, from two to twenty or more. The Romance languages have two genders, customarily called "feminine" and "masculine," because they agree, in general, fairly well with biological sex, as in Italian /ilragácco/ *il ragazzo* "the boy" vs. /ladónna/ *la donna* "the woman"; but a better term for "masculine" would be "not exclusively feminine" or "non-feminine". In many instances, even in terms referring to living beings, grammatical gender is arbitrarily assigned and has no connection with sex, as in /lavíttima/ *la vittima* "the victim", /lasentinélla/ *la sentinella* "the sentinel" (feminines), but /ilsopráno/ *il soprano* "the soprano", /ilkontrálto/ *il contralto* "the contralto" (masculines). Scandinavian languages also have a two-way contrast, with genders usually termed "common" (e.g., /entídniŋ/ *en tidning* "a newspaper") and "neuter" (e.g. /ethús/ *ett hus* "a house"). In German, Latin, Greek, Sanskrit, etc., in addition to the basic division between feminine and non-feminine, there is a further subdivision of the non-feminine into "masculine" and "neuter." The latter differs from the former, in Indo-European languages, only in the inflectional characteristics of certain forms (e.g. Latin /oppida/ "towns", neuter pl. nom. and acc.; as opposed to /domini:/ "masters (nom.)", /domino:s/ "masters (acc.)").

Other contrasts in gender include animate vs. inanimate, found in many American Indian languages. The Bantu languages have grammatical genders involving as many as twenty different classes, correlated in general both with biological sex and with size, shape, etc., of the objects referred to. In these languages, the gender-concord must be observed not only in nouns and adjectives, but in verbs and other parts of the utterance containing them.

Here again, the English situation is rather different from what it is usually represented as being. Our traditional grammars tell us that not only English

pronouns show gender (*he, she, it*), but also our nouns, in that some are substituted by *he* (e.g., *man, boy, gander*, supposedly "masculine"), some by *she*
(e.g., *woman, girl, goose*, "feminine") and most by *it* (e.g., *table, chair, window*,
"neuter"). Grammatical gender, however, involves obligatory agreement
without regard to the actual sex of what is referred to, as in the Italian examples cited on p. 154, or German /dasvájp/ *das Weib* "the woman", /dasfrój
+làjn/ *das Fräulein* "the young lady" (both neuter, although they refer
to females). In English, however, the pronoun used to refer to any person
or living being is determined, not by arbitrary grammatical classification,
but by the actual sex of what is referred to. Thus, to refer to a woman whose
first name is *Jack, Charles, Gordon*, or *Beaumont*, we still must use *she*, and a
man who happens to be named *Helen* still has to be called *he*. What we have
in English is, therefore, not grammatical gender at all, but sex-reference,
and even this is manifested inflectionally only in our pronoun-system (*he,
she, it* and related forms). Our nouns have no grammatical gender of any
kind, and no inflectional manifestation of their sex-reference (*man, boy,
gander, bull* etc. are not differentiated from *woman, girl, goose, cow* in any way
that correlates with the sex referred to).

Case is a category of inflection by which certain forms are marked as
usable in certain types of syntactic dependence, especially (though by no
means exclusively) on verbs. English manifests case only in its pronouns:
/áj/ *I*, /wí/ *we*, /(h)í/ *he*, /ʃí/ *she*, and /ðé/ *they* for use as subjects ("nominative" or "subjective" case); and the corresponding forms /mí/ *me*, /ás/ *us*,
/(h)ím/ *him*, /(h)ár/ *her*, and /(ð)ém/ *them* for use as objects in verbal
phrases or after prepositions ("accusative" or "objective" case). From Latin,
we are familiar with four additional cases, the genitive or "possessive" (e.g.,
/domini:/ "of a master"), the dative (/domino:/ "to a master"), the ablative (/domino:/ "to a master", in this declension identical with the dative,
but in other declensions different, as in /konsuli:/ "to a consul" vs. /konsule/
"from a consul") and vocative (/domine/ "o master!"). Others, such as the
instrumental ("by means of . . .", as in Russian /stólom/ "by means of
the table", to /stól/ "table") and the locative ("in, at, on", e.g., Russian
/stóļe/ "on the table") are present in other Indo-European languages.

In languages of other families, we find considerably more than these
eight cases; some analysts distinguish as many as twenty or more. If the
language involved has an "agglutinative" type of loose morpheme sequence,
it may be doubtful whether all the forms usually termed "cases" really
deserve this term. Hungarian, for example, has a great many pure-relational
suffixes such as /-nak -nek/* "to", /-hoz -hez -høz/ "towards", /-ban -ben/
"in", as in /ha:znak/ *háznak* "to the house", /køɲvnek/ *könyvnek* "to the
book", /føldhøz/ *földhöz* "towards the ground", /va:rošban/ *városban* "in
the city". However, these suffixes also occur independently of nouns and

---

* Most Hungarian suffixes have two or three forms for use when attached to morphemes
with varying types of vowel structure (back, front-unrounded, and in some instances
front-rounded); Hungarian is like Turkish in having an extensive morphophonemic
requirement of "vowel harmony" (cf. p. 149).

provided with possessive suffixes: e.g., /nekem/ *nekem* "to me", /hozza:/ *hozzá* "towards him". In this situation, it is perhaps better to reserve the term "case" for those few Hungarian pure-relational elements which do not occur with possessive suffixes (e.g. /-t/ accusative, as in /kø̈ɲvet/ *könyvet* "book [acc.]"), thus reducing the number of cases from a presumed twenty to around seven.

In all human speech situations, at least two persons are involved: the speaker and the person(s) spoken to. One or more other persons or things may also be the topic of discussion. This universal situation is the basis of the category of *person*, which always, apparently, includes a distinction between *first* (the speaker) and *second* (the person addressed). There is normally also at least a *third* person, referring to persons or things which are neither speaking nor addressed. In some languages, such as colloquial Brazilian Portuguese, the distinction in verb-forms is simply between first and non-first person: /žátu/ *janto* "I lunch" vs. /žáta/ *janta* "you (sg.) lunch" or "he, she, it lunches", and similarly with the plural /žátámus/ *jantamos* "we lunch" vs. /žátãu/ *jantam* "you (pl.) lunch" or "they lunch". Further distinctions are often made within these persons: for instance, many languages have separate first-person categories to refer to "we = I and somebody else, but not you" (*exclusive*) and to "we = you and I" (*inclusive*), as in Tagálog /kamí/ "we (excl.)" vs. /tá:ju/ "we (incl.)". A distinction within the third person is found in the often-cited Algonquian "obviative," in which one variety of third-person form means "the person or thing referred to most recently, or nearer the center of attention," and another, the obviative, means "the person or thing referred to earlier or of subsidiary importance": e.g. Cree /utástutin/ "his (own) hat", but /utastutínijiw/ "his (some other person's) hat". If the reference is back to the subject of the sentence, the form is said to be *reflexive*, as in Latin /se:/ "himself, herself, itself, themselves".

In such languages as the Finno-Ugric family (Hungarian, Finnish, etc.), the Semitic family (including Hebrew and Arabic) and the Algonquian family, the person and number of a possessor may be shown by an inflectional element. This category of inflection is known as *possession*, exemplified by such sets of forms as the following Hungarian paradigm:

SINGULAR	PLURAL
/kø̈ɲvem/ *könyvem* "my book"	/kø̈ɲveim/ *könyveim* "my books"
/kø̈ɲved/ *könyved* "thy book"	/kø̈ɲveid/ *könyveid* "thy books"
/kø̈ɲve/ *könyve* "his book"	/kø̈ɲvei/ *könyvei* "his books"
/kø̈ɲvynk/ *könyvünk* "our book"	/kø̈ɲveink/ *könyveink* "our books"
/kø̈ɲvtek/ *könyvtek* "your book"	/kø̈ɲveitek/ *könyveitek* "your books"
/kø̈ɲyvyk/ *könyvük* "their book"	/kø̈ɲveik/ *könyveik* "their books"

In Algonquian languages, possession is indicated by prefixes, e.g. Menomini /neto:s/ "my canoe", /oto:s/ "his canoe", and so forth. In Hungarian, Armenian, and Arabic, these possessive elements accompany not only nouns, but also pure-relational elements of the type discussed on pp. 155–156, as in Hungarian /bennem/ *bennem* "in me", /neki/ *neki* "to him" (as if the meaning were something like "my-in", "his-to"). In this situation, some analysts prefer to speak of *allocation* rather than *possession*.

The categories discussed up to this point are usually found with substantive-like form-classes (nouns, adjectives, pronouns), though person is very widely found in verb-systems also. The following are usually associated with verb-like forms, but here again not exclusively. For instance, in Hupa (an American Indian language of California), tense-endings are added to nouns, not to verbs:

> /xonta/ "house now existing"
> /xontaneen/ "house formerly existing, i.e., in ruins"
> /xontate/ "house that will exist, i.e., not yet built"

Contrasts in *tense* refer to the time at which the action takes place (or, as in the example just given, the thing referred to exists). On the basis of Latin, we normally think of tense as involving a three-way contrast between present, past, and future, as in /amo:/ "I am loving", /ama:bam/ "I was loving", /ama:bo:/ "I shall be loving"; /ama:ųi:/ "I'm through loving", /ama: ųeram/ "I was through loving, had loved", /ama:ųero:/ "I shall be through loving, shall have loved". The Germanic and Slavic languages have only a two-way contrast in tense inflection, between past and non-past, e.g. German /ixkóme/ *ich komme* "I'm coming" vs. /ixkám/ *ich kam* "I was coming"; Russian /čitáju/: "I read (present)" vs. /čitál/ "I (m.) read (past)". For the Romance languages, traditional grammars give present, past, and "future" tenses, but their real tense-organization is into past, non-past ("present"), and a tense whose characteristic is that it has no reference to time (timeless, usually called "subjunctive"). Each Romance language has two or three of these tenses built on each of two or three stems (cf. pp. 150–151). It is best, in describing the structure of the Romance languages, to avoid the traditional grammatical terms, and to speak of the tenses simply as "past," "non-past," and "timeless," formed on Stem A (traditionally called the "present stem"), B ("future stem") and C ("preterite stem") respectively. Thus, Spanish has, on Stem A, the three tenses: Past A ("imperfect"), e.g., /benía/ *venía* "he was coming"; Non-Past A ("present indicative"), e.g., /biéne/ *viene* "he is coming"; and Timeless A ("present subjunctive"), e.g., /bénga/ *venga* "(that) he come; let him come". The other Romance languages have similar tense-formations.

Mood is a type of inflection which refers to the speaker's attitude towards the event—whether he regards it as real (*indicative* mood) or unreal, expresses a wish (*optative*) or urges someone to do something (*hortatory*), considers it contingent or subordinate to some other phenomenon (*subjunctive*), etc. Latin had a full set of tenses—past, present, future—for two moods, indicative and subjunctive: e.g. /amat/ "he is loving (indicative)" vs. /amet/ "(that) he love; may he love (subjunctive)". Other languages, like Fox (an Algonquian language), have a great many moods. We have no separate inflectional category of mood in English; the use of the simple form of the verb in the third person singular (also third person plural in *be*, and *were* instead of *was*) takes the place of the subjunctive in conservative usage: e.g., *it is desirable that he come* (not *comes*), *it would be preferable that he keep* (not *keeps*) *his mouth shut.* The traditional Latinizing grammar of the Romance languages treats the "subjunctive" tenses as if they were "moods;" but these forms— although, historically, they are survivals of the Latin subjunctive—are not separate "moods" in present structure, but simply tenses (cf. the preceding paragraph).

The verb in Haitian Creole is to be defined as including those forms which can take two prefixes: /ap-/, indicating continuing or lasting action ("is . . . -ing"), and /fek-/ or /fek-rĕk-/, indicating action recently completed ("has just . . . -ed"), as in /ap-mãʒeˆ/ "am (is, are) eating", formed on /mãʒeˆ/ "eat", and /fek-mãʒeˆ/ "have (has) just eaten". These prefixes exemplify the category of *aspect*, which indicates the way, not that an event is located in time, but that it is distributed. Under aspect are included such contrasts as those of completed (perfective) action vs. incomplete (imperfective); habitual vs. individual events; repeated vs. single; beginning vs. lasting. Latin, as already mentioned (pp. 150–151), had two stems for each normal verb, a perfective stem and an imperfective stem, with a whole set of tenses and moods built up on each. The Romance languages have a survival of this contrast in aspect, but only in the difference between Past A (traditionally called "imperfect") and Past C ("preterite" or "past absolute"), as in Italian /manǧóˣ/ *mangiò* "he ate (at one or more clearly delimitable points of time in the past)", vs. /manǧáva/ *mangiava* "he was eating, used to eat, would often eat (not limited to specific points of time in the past)". The category of aspect is best known from the Slavic languages, especially Russian (from whose grammatical terminology this term comes). In those languages, however, aspect is a phenomenon of derivation, not of inflection, since to the "imperfective" conjugation of each verb corresponds a "perfective" conjugation, the one derived from the other by (usually) addition of a prefix: thus, on /čitát̡/ читать: "to read", with such forms as /čitáju/ "I read", is formed the perfective /počitát̡/ "to have read", with /počitál/ "I have read", etc.

Another widespread category of verb inflection is *voice*, in which the main contrast is between the actor or subject of the verb as the performer of the action (*active* voice) and the actor or subject as the undergoer of the action (*passive* voice). Latin had only these two voices, as in /amat/ "he loves" vs. /ama:tur/ "he is loved". Greek had a three-way contrast between active (/lú:o:/ λύω "I loose"), passive (/lú:omai/ λύομαι "I am loosed"), and *mediopassive*, in which the action falls back on the subject in a reflexive-like way (/érkhomai/ ἔρχομαι "I go"). Allied to voice is *transitivity*, the use of separate inflectional forms indicating that a direct object is or is not involved. The transitive form of the Neo-Melanesian verbs cited in set C on p. 146 indicates that a direct object is involved, whether mentioned explicitly in the utterance or not (/mi kukɪm tɪnmit/ "I'm cooking the meat", /mi kukɪm/ "I'm cooking it"), and the intransitive form has either active meaning without a direct object, or passive meaning (/ɛm i-slip/ "he is recumbent";

/tınmit i-kʊk/ "the meat is cooked"). Hungarian has a similar distinction, but the transitive form of the verb implies only a third person object: /seretek/ *szeretek* "I love (no object specified)", but /seretem/ *szeretem* is "I love (some third-person object, hence) him, her, it or them".

It is not necessary for inflectional variations to have any "dictionary" meaning at all, in order to have the status of "categories of inflection." In modern French, almost all forms show a variation, on the inflectional level, in their sandhi-alternation, since a form can have up to three different phonemic shapes, mostly but not wholly according to the following phoneme (vowel, pause, consonant). Some forms have only one shape, some have two, and some have three, as in the following examples:

	I "city"	II "good (m. sg.)"	III "ten"	IV "four"	V "her"
Before vowel	/vil/	/bon/	/diz/	/katr/	/l/
Before pause	/vil/	/bõ/	/dis/	/katr/	/la/
Before consonant	/vil/	/bõ/	/di/	/kat/	/la/

There are five different combinations in which these possibilities can occur, as shown in columns I–V above; these constitute five different types of sandhi-alternation. It is not possible to predict, on the basis of linguistic structure or meaning, to which type any given French form will belong. Hence the type of sandhi-alternation (numbers I–V, above) constitutes a separate category of inflection which must be stated in advance for each morpheme, along with its other inflectional features such as part of speech, gender, verb-conjugation, etc.; e.g. /vil/ *ville* "city", n/f/I; /diz ∼ dis ∼ di/ *dix* "ten" num/III, etc.

Not only "words," but bound morphemes, such as the noun-plural suffix, manifest sandhi-alternation in French. The noun-plural suffix has several different alternants involving /-z/ and zero, of which the most common shows sandhi-alternation-type II, with /-z/ before vowel (/dəbozarbr/ *de beaux arbres* "beautiful trees") but zero before pause or consonant (/lez-arbrəsõbo/ *les arbres sont beaux* "the trees are beautiful", /dəbogarsõ/ *de beaux garçons* "handsome boys"). It is often convenient to represent the sandhi-variants of a morpheme by some type of morphophonemic symbol, e.g., a raised ᶻ to stand for "/ᶻ ∼ Ø ∼ Ø/", as in //dãᶻ// *dans* "in"; but such morphophonemic symbolization does not take the place of a complete analysis of French sandhi-alternation.

We must emphasize that the various categories of meaning which we have been discussing are not necessarily expressed by inflectional elements in order to be expressed at all. Normally only a few of them find inflectional expression in any given language; but those that are not indicated by morphological means can always be expressed by other devices, especially syntactic. In English, for instance, we have no inflectional contrast between active and passive. All our verbs have active meaning (whether transitive or intransitive) in their simple inflected forms (*eat, kill, write*), and for passive meaning we have phrases consisting of the auxiliaries *be* or *get* plus past participles (*be eaten, get eaten; be killed, get killed; be written, get written*). Conversely, we must be on our guard not to equate syntactically expressed categories (e.g., the passive in English) with inflectional categories of similar meaning (e.g., the passive in Latin). In many instances, our traditional grammars do just this, as when they treat a phrase like Latin /loku:tus est/ "he is in a having-spoken condition, he is through speaking" as if it were an inflectional element because it is, in the verb-paradigm as a whole, in complementary distribution with truly inflected forms like /lokuitur/ "he speaks". Such procedures obscure the distinction between morphology and syntax, and should not be encouraged in linguistic analysis.

NOTES

Sex-reference in English pronouns: Hall, 1951b.
Possible semantic correlations between grammatical gender and biological sex: Ervin, 1962.
Hungarian "cases": Lotz, 1939; Hall, 1944b.
"Allocation": Hockett, 1958, Chap. 27.
Tense: Bull, 1960.
French sandhi-alternation as a morphological category: Hall, 1948d.

26

Substitutes

SUPPOSE THAT, every time we wished to refer to a given person, place, thing, time, etc., we had to do so by repeating in full the complete element of the utterance referring to him, her, or it. We would then have innumerable repetitions and long-winded phrases of this kind, in such a dialogue as the following between John, Ruth and Mary:

J: John wishes Ruth and Mary to tell John the names of the places involved in the desires of Ruth and Mary to go on the morning of January 12, 1963.
R: Ruth and Mary would like to go to the museum.
M: Oh, no, the museum does not have objects of an unspecified type having a possible interest for Mary. Mary would like to go to the hairdresser's shop.
R: The hairdresser's shop is not open on the morning of January 12, 1963. If Mary wants to go to the hairdresser's shop, Mary will have to wait until the morning following January 12, 1963.
M: Mary does not think Ruth is being nice.
J: The entire group of three persons, John, Ruth and Mary, had better go to the museum. In the museum are to be found a lot of interesting things.

In real life, the dialogue would be much shorter and snappier:

J: Where do you want to go this morning?
R: We'd like to go to the museum.
M: Oh, no, it hasn't got anything that would interest me. I'd like to go to the hairdresser's.
R: It's not open this morning. If you want to go there, you'll have to wait until tomorrow morning.
M: I don't think you're being nice.
J: We'd better all three go to the museum. There are a lot of interesting things there.

The comparative brevity of the "real-life" version is made possible by the existence, in every linguistic system, of a number of *substitute* elements which occupy the places that would otherwise be taken by full morphemes or phrases. The most obvious of these are the *pronouns*, which take the place of continually repeated nouns or noun-phrases (*John, Ruth, Mary, the museum,* etc.). However, a number of other elements also belong in the category of substitutes: demonstratives (*this, that, there*); interrogatives (*who? what? where? why?*); relatives (*who, which, what*); and indefinites (*some, somebody, something; any, anybody, anything; no, nobody, nothing*). On occasion, the absence of a usually expected element (a *zero-replacement*) acts as a substitute, as in *the hairdresser's* for *the hairdresser's shop.*

All languages apparently have personal pronouns, which take the place of constant repetition of either "the speaker," "the hearer" and "some person or persons extraneous to both speaker and hearer," or of the personal names (*John, Ruth, Mary*) of each individual involved. When children are first learning to talk, they often pass through a stage at which they have mastered the principle of the proper name but not that of the personal pronoun, and will refer, to themselves and those to whom they are talking, by means of proper names exclusively: *Daddy come play with Johnny? Johnny want to play*, etc. Failure to master the principle of pronominal substitution at an early stage is one sign of major developmental retardation in a child.

Personal pronoun systems show all the variations in person, number, and gender discussed in the preceding chapter. Many languages show the contrast between first person plural inclusive and exclusive in their pronoun systems: thus, Neo-Melanesian has an exclusive first person plural pronoun /mifɛlə/ "we (not including you)" and an inclusive pronoun compound /jumi/ "we (including you)". Gender may be manifested in some, all, or none of a language's personal pronouns. Our familiar Indo-European systems show gender only in the third person, as in German /íx/ "I", /dú:/ "thou", but /é:r/ "he", /zí:/ "she", and /és/ "it" (with related case-forms). English has sex-reference only in the third person singular, in *he, she, it*. Other languages, such as Hungarian, simply have no grammatical gender at all anywhere in their system, including the personal pronoun: Hung. /ø:/ *ő* means simply "the person being referred to: he, she, it", and similarly with /ø:k/ *ők* "they". On the other hand, there is in some languages an obligatory gender distinction in the first and second person pronouns, e.g., in the present day Spanish compound pronouns /nosótras/ *nosotras* "we, us (f.)" vs. /nosótros/ *nosotros* "we, us (m.)", and similarly for the second person plural /bosótras/ *vosotras* "you (f.pl.)" vs. /bosótros/ *vosotros* "you (m.pl.)". The second person pronoun *you* of modern standard English makes no distinction in number, but nonstandard English makes up for this deficiency with various new plural-formations, such as /júz/ *youse* (with the regular noun-plural suffix /-z/) or phrasal formations like /jú+ɔl/ *you-all* or /jəɔl/ *y'all*.

The meanings associated with personal pronouns, especially those of direct address—i.e., the contexts in which the pronouns are used—are often quite subtly differentiated in accordance with social status and barriers between the persons speaking to each other. In many languages, the second person singular is reserved for instances in which there is no social barrier, e.g., between members of the same family, close associates and friends, and when speaking to young children or animals. This is the case with French /ty/, Italian and Spanish /tú/ *tu*; Brazilian Portuguese /vosê^/ *você*; German /dú:/ *du*; Russian /tí/ etc. In more formal social intercourse, all kinds of degrees of deference may find morphological expression, including indication of both humility and condescension. Modern standard Italian has both /vó^i/ *voi* (used as a true second-person plural for /tú/ *tu*; as a pronoun of courtesy in southern Italy; and as a pronoun of condescension to rustics, etc., in northern Italy), and /léi/ *Lei*, plural /lóˆro/ *Loro* for elegant direct address (with third-person grammatical agreement). Eighteenth-century German had a similar use of the third-person pronouns, both singular and plural: /éːr/ *Er* "he" when speaking to a man; /zíː/ *Sie* "she" to a woman; and /zíː/ *Sie* "they" (with plural concord) when speaking to more than one person. In modern German, the last-mentioned has survived in polite address to both one and more than one person; use of /éːr/ *Er* in direct address is extremely archaic and considered so condescending as to be (if understood at all) a virtual insult. In our familiar languages, this feature of personal address is a mild manifestation of what is practised much more extremely in some other speech-communities (Japanese, Ponapean), the use of whole different sets of grammatical forms and vocabulary-items when speaking to exalted persons (e.g., royalty or honored guests).

In many languages, the personal pronouns show enough difference from nouns or adjectives in their inflectional characteristics to be treated as a separate form-class. Personal pronouns often show a certain amount of similarity with noun-inflection, but not enough to warrant breaking the personal pronoun inflection down in analysis as thoroughly as can be done for nouns. Thus, in Italian, one can recognize in the plural forms /nóˆi/ *noi* "we, us" and /vóˆi/ *voi* "you" an element /-i/ which can be equated with the plural ending /-i/ seen in most nouns, such as /líbri/ *libri* "books", /káni/ *cani* "dogs", /móˆḷḷi/ *mogli* "wives". However, if we were to "peel out" this element /-i/ and regard it as a plural ending, we would be left with forlorn stems /noˆ-/ and /voˆ-/, which we could only treat as suppletive allomorphs of the first person singular pronoun stems /í-/ and /m-/ (in /ío/ *io* "I" and /méˆ/ *me* "me") and the second person stem /t-/ (in /tú/ *tu* "thou" and /téˆ/ *te* "thee") respectively. Such a procedure would not really leave us much more advanced than before in our understanding of Italian structure; we would do better to recognize that there are some groups of forms that are not worth tearing apart below a certain level. On the other hand, in some languages, part or all of the personal pronouns are just like nouns in their inflection: e.g., in Hungarian, /øː/ *ő* "he, she, it" takes various noun suffixes, such as the plural /-k/ in /øːk/ *ők* "they", the accusative /-t/ in /øːt/ *őt* "him, her, it", and a combination of these two suffixes in /øːket/ *őket* "them".

The inflection of pronouns often involves special allomorphs for unstressed positions. Among the Romance languages, French has perhaps the most extensively developed system of this type, with separate stressed independent forms such as /mwa/ *moi* "I, me," and unstressed bound forms both for subject (/ʒə/ *je:* "I") and object (/m(ə)/ *me, m'* "me, to me") throughout its pronominal system. English pronouns, too, have extensive sandhi variation, with especially the loss of initial /h-/ in /hí/ *he*, /hím/ *him* and /hór/ *her* and of /ð-/ in /ðém/ *them* when these forms are unstressed: thus, /ájdóntθíŋkizvéribráit/ *I don't think he's very bright*, or /dʒəstlúkətəm/ *Just look at them!*. To represent these unstressed forms in spelling as *'e, 'im, 'er, 'em* is a form of eye-dialect (cf. Chap. 45) and gives a fictitious flavor of illiteracy or homely rusticity (*If you can't lick 'em, jine 'em*). We normally do not spell these forms as we pronounce them, and our spelling habits, here as in many other instances, mislead us as to the actual facts of our linguistic behavior.

Pronouns and similar substitutes refer to some other element of the utterance, usually already uttered, but on occasion still to come (as in *With their rifles on their shoulders, the soldiers marched down the street*). The element referred to is termed the *antecedent* (even if it follows!) and the phenomenon of reference is called *anaphora*. On occasion, a pronominal type of anaphora is obtained with special substitute elements in certain kinds of phrases, as when, in English, to avoid repeating a noun after an adjective, we use a compound formed with unstressed /wən/ *one* as an anaphoric substitute: *I don't want a red pencil, I want a black one* /əblǽk+wən/. Or the anaphora may be accomplished by replacing some element by zero: e.g. *I wanted to go but I couldn't* (i.e., go). This phenomenon is often termed *zero-anaphora*. If a substitute form is used without any antecedent at all, it is said to have *empty anaphora*: e.g., *it's raining* (what is raining?); *beat it!* "run away!" (beat what?).

The personal pronouns involve, normally, pure substitution as their main grammatical and semantic function. Other types of pronouns, adjectives and adverbs involve further elements of meaning, particularly pointing out, in the demonstratives; asking questions, in the interrogatives; tying one clause into another in a dependent relation, in the relatives. The function of pointing out is often called *deixis*, and demonstrative forms are called *deictic*. Deixis may involve a simple two-way contrast, as in English *this* "near the speaker" vs. *that* "away from the speaker"; or it may be more complicated, as in the three-way contrast in Spanish /éste/ *este* "this", /ése/ *ese* "that (near the hearer)", and /akél/ *aquel* "that (away from both speaker and hearer)". In other languages, further distinctions may be made between "in sight" and "out of sight," between "here now" and "formerly here but now out of sight," etc.

In demonstratives, relatives, and interrogatives, the inflectional categories expressed are often conflicting and intersecting, and frequently have no correspondence with categories found elsewhere in the language. Between English *who?* and *what?* (interrogative), and between *who* and *which* (or *that*) (relative), there is a contrast of human vs. nonhuman: e.g., *the man who ate the beef* vs. *the dog which* (or *that*) *ate the beef*. In French, we distinguish between /ki/ *qui* and /kə/ *que* as relatives and the same pair as interrogatives, because the pair shows a different contrast in each of these two functions. As relatives, they contrast with respect to case, /ki/ *qui* being nominative and /kə/ *que* being objective: /lomkievnyjer/ *l'homme qui est venu hier* "the man who came yesterday" vs. /lomkəʒeˆrakotrejer/ *l'homme que j'ai rencontré hier* "the man whom I met yesterday". As interrogatives, they contrast in animation, /ki/ referring to humans (nominative and objective) and /kə/ to nonhumans (accusative only; replaced by an allomorph /kwa/ as object of a preposition, and not occurring as subject): e.g., /kiafesaɛ́/ *Qui a fait ça?* "Who did that?"; /kivwajevuɛ́/ *Qui voyez-vous?* "Whom do you see?" but /kəvwajevuɛ́/ *Que voyez-vous?* "What do you see?" and /dəkwaparlevué/ *De quoi parlez-vous?* "What are you talking about?"

Demonstrative pronouns or adjectives may be combined with other deictic elements (e.g. bound or free adverbial forms) to give more complicated systems. Again in French, all the demonstratives combine optionally with the suffixed elements /-si/ *-ci* "here" and /-la/ *-là* "there" to give a three-way contrast, as shown in Fig. 17. All the forms given in the first column ("without suffix") are bound, since in present-day French usage none of them occur without some following element, either phrase or clause, as in /səkrejõ/ *ce crayon* "this pencil (which I am calling to your attention, without specifying its nearness or farness)", /səlԛidmõfis/ *celui de mon fils* "the one of my son = my son's (e.g., pencil)"; /səlԛikʒeˆaʃteˆjer/ *ӥelui que j'ai acheté hier* "the one (e.g., pencil) that I bought yesterday". One of the major troubles which

	WITHOUT SUFFIX	WITH /-si/ *-ci* "HERE"	—WITH/ -la /-là "THERE"
Noninflected Pronoun	/sə/ *ce* "this, that"	/səsi/ *ceci* "this"	/səla/ *cela* "that"
Inflected Pronoun	/sɛl/ *celle* "the one" f. sg.	/sɛlsi/ *celle-ci*	/sɛlla/ *celle-là*
	/səlԛi/ *celui* m. sg.	/səlԛisi/ *celui-ci*	/səlԛila/ *celui-là*
	/sɛlᶻ/ *celles* f. pl.	/sɛlsi/ *celles-ci*	/sɛlla/ *celles-là*
	/sœˆᶻ/ *ceux* m. pl.	/sœˆsi/ *ceux-ci*	/sœˆla/ *ceux-là*
Inflected Adjective	/sɛt/ *cette* "this, that" f. sg.	/sɛt . . . si/ *cette . . . -ci*	/sɛt . . . la/ *cette . . . -là*
	/sɛt/ *cet* m. sg. before vowel	/sɛt . . . si/ *cet . . . -ci*	/sɛt . . . la/ *cet . . . -là*
	/sə/ *ce* m. sg. before cons.	/sə . . . si/ *ce . . . -ci*	/sə . . . la/ *ce . . . -là*
	/seˆᶻ/ *ces* pl.	/seˆᶻ . . . si/ *ces . . . -ci*	/seˆᶻ . . . la/ *ces . . . là*

FIG. 17: French Demonstratives.

speakers of French and English have in learning each other's languages comes from the use of zero-anaphora in English (e.g., *my son's* = *my son's pencil*) where French uses a bound demonstrative pronoun with anaphoric gender and number reference (as in *celui* [= *le crayon*] *de mon fils*).

We are most familiar with substitution in pronouns (taking the place of nouns) and pronominal adjectives; these two classes often overlap in Indo-European languages. Other form classes can also be replaced by substitutes, as is widely the case with verbs in English. Most English verbs (except *be, have,* and modal auxiliaries) are replaced by *do*: we can say, if we want to, *John does not write books, but I write books,* but such an expression is clumsier than *John doesn't write books but I do,* in which *do* takes the place of *write books.* On the model of the term /pró+nàwn/ *pronoun,* we can coin the term /pró+və̀rb/ *pro-verb* for *do* in this function. Similarly, we might call unstressed /wən/ *one* in *the black one,* etc. (cf. above, p. 164) a /prò+ǽdʒɛktɪv/ *pro-adjective.* Traditional grammar already uses the term "pronominal adverb" to refer to such forms as /ðǽr/ *there*, /ðέn/ *then*, /ðέns* /*thence*, /ðíðər/ *thither*, and others like /náw/ *now*, /jéstərdi/ *yesterday*, /tɛdé/ *today*, /təmárə/ *tomorrow*, etc., which take the place of adverbially used expressions like *on the table*, *at 2:48 P.M.*, *January 12*, etc.

Not only individual parts of speech or their syntactical equivalents, but also specific types of phrases, can be replaced by special substitutive elements. A distinguishing feature of the Romance languages is their use of special particles within the verbal core (Chap. 34). These particles, termed collectively *conjunctive* elements because they are used in conjunction with verbs, are all bound forms (cf. pp. 131 ff.). They include not only unstressed object forms of pronouns, but also forms which tell the hearer that a phrase of a certain type is being referred to as antecedent. French //ãⁿ// *en* substitutes for phrases introduced by /d(ə)/ *de* "of, from; about", as in /ʒeˆdeˆsigaret/ *j'ai des cigarettes* "I have some (lit. of the) cigarettes", replaced by /ʒãneˆ/ *j'en ai* "I have some"; /ilvjɛ̆ttynis/ *il vient de Tunis* "he comes from Tunis", replaced by /ilãvjɛ̆/ *il en vient* "he comes from there"; /nuparlõdlavimodern/ *nous parlons de lav ie moderne* "we're talking about modern life", replaced by /nuzãparlõ/ *nous en parlons* "we're talking about it". Similarly, French /i/ *y* replaces phrases introduced by prepositions whose literal meaning involves "place where or to which", such as /a/ *à* "at, in", //dãᶻ// *dans* "in", //ãⁿ// *en* "in", /syr/ *sur* "on", etc.: e.g., /ilie/ *il y est* "it is there" = /iledãlabwat/ *il est dans la boîte* "it's on the box" or /iletalamezõ/ *il est à la maison* "it's at home", etc.; /ilipãs/ "he's thinking of it" = /ilpãsasonoto/ *il pense à son auto* "he's thinking of his automobile", etc. Particles like French /i/ *y* and //ãⁿ// *en*, and their parallels in the other Romance languages (e.g. Italian /či/ *ci*, /vi/ *vi* and /ne/ *ne*) are misclassified in traditional grammar, whose authors do not know what to do with these elements, and call them by such misnomers as "pronominal adverbs" or even "pronouns." Since their function is that of taking the place of certain types of phrases, they may best be termed /pró+frɛ̀z/ *pro-phrase*.

Another such element in the Romance languages, normally homophonous with the masculine singular conjunctive direct object pronoun, indicates that a predicate complement has been omitted. It is not the same as the m. sg. conjunctive object pronoun, however, since the particle which substitutes for the predicate complement is invariable no matter what the gender and number of its antecedent. Thus, the Spanish sentences /estáskansádo?/ *¿estás cansado?* "Are you (m. sg.) tired?" and /estáskansáda?/ *¿estás cansada?* "Are you (f. sg.) tired?" will both receive an answer like /sí, loestói/ *sí, lo estoy* "yes, I am (i.e., tired)", and the parallel plural questions /estáiskansádos/ *¿estáis cansados?* (m. pl.) and /estáiskansádas?/ *¿estais cansadas?* (f. pl.) will both receive an answer like /sí, loestámos/ *sí, lo estamos* "yes, we are (tired)", with /lo/ *lo*, invariable, replacing the predicate complement in all four instances. This and parallel elements in the other Romance languages (e.g., Fr. //l(ə)// *le, l'*; Italian /lo/ *lo*) have no translational equivalent in English, because we use zero-replacement where this particle would be used in Romance. The best term for this invariable /lo/ (Sp., It.) or //l(ə)// (Fr.), which replaces a predicate complement, would probably be something like /prò+prèdɪkət+kámpləmənt/ *pro-predicate-complement*. All the various conjunctive elements of the Romance verbal core—pronouns, pro-phrases, and pro-predicate-complements—can be given an over-all name like /prò+kámpləmənt/ *pro-complement*, which will indicate their basic function as substitutes for various types of verbal complements.

NOTES

On substitutes in general: Bloomfield, 1933, Chap. 15; Hockett, 1958, Chap. 30.
Italian forms of direct address: Grand, 1930.
Pro-complements: Hall, 1952b.

27

Constituents and Constructions

By DEFINITION, in inflected forms, one or more inflectionally bound elements are present, or else, in such instances as /ʃíp/ *sheep* (pl.) vs. /ʃíp/ *sheep* (sg.), a zero-element which is classified as such by contrast with the presence of phonemically actualized forms in other parts of the inflectional set, like /-z/ in /bǽgz/ *bags*. In complex inflected forms, the inflectional elements are normally not all equal in their relationship to each other, but are arranged in what are usually termed *layers* of construction. Thus, in Italian /venivámo/ *venivamo* "we were coming", the outermost layer involves the person-and-number morpheme, in this instance the suffix /-mo/ of the first person plural. The next layer contains the tense-forming morpheme, the suffix /-va-/ of the past tense formed on Stem A (cf. p. 157); in this particular form, the stress falls on this suffix, whereas in others (e.g., /venívano/ *venivano* "they were coming", it falls on the stem). The next layer involves Stem A itself, /veni-/, which in its turn consists of the root /ven-/ *ven-* "come" (here in its unstressed allomorph) plus a characteristic or thematic vowel /-i-/ *-i-*. Not all complex inflected forms, in Italian or other languages, are as easy to "peel" the layers off of as this particular form; but the principle of layering holds true even if in some or many forms of a language, the layers may be fused at various points, or reduced to zero, as in Italian /venívo/ *venivo* "I was coming" or /veníva/ *veniva* "he was coming".

This principle of layering is fundamental, not only in inflected forms, but also in forms containing derivational elements and in larger combinations involving two or more inflected or derived forms. The minimum forms resulting when all the cuts have been made are termed *ultimate constituents*, the elements which ultimately constitute the form or combination being analyzed: in Italian /venivámo/ *venivamo*, the ultimate constituents are the root allomorph /ven-/, the thematic vowel /-i-/, the Past A tense formant /-va-/, the stress /'/ (here falling on the tense-formant), and the 1.pl. person-and-number morpheme /-mo/. But normally, each complex form or combination is to be divided by making successive cuts; the result of each such cut is termed an *immediate constituent*. The stock example is given with forms like English /ən+dʒéntəlmənli/ *ungentlemanly* or /ən+lédilajk/ *unladylike*. These consist of the ultimate constituents /ən-/ *un-*, plus /dʒéntəlmən/ *gentleman* or /lédi/ *lady*, plus /-li/ *-ly* or /-lajk/ *-like*, respectively; but in each instance, the three ultimate constituents are not of equal importance in determining the structure of the form. These forms must be analyzed by first finding their immediate constituents. For each, the first cut will be made, not before /-li/ -ly or /-lajk/ -like, but after /ən-/ un-. This is because we do not have, in English, the forms */ən+dʒéntəlmən/ ungentleman or */ən+lédi/ unlady; we do not say of anyone *He's an ungentleman or *She's an unlady. But if we made our first cut before the suffixed elements /-li/ -ly or /-lajk/ -like, those are the immediate constituents we would get. This conclusion is further supported by the internal open juncture /+/ after /ən-/, which here is clearly acting as a Grenzsignal or boundary-marker. Then /dʒéntəlmənli/ gentlemanly and /lédilajk/ ladylike each break down further into /dʒéntəlmən/ gentleman + /-li/ -ly and /lédi/ lady + /-lajk/ -like respectively, again because we have no such forms in English as /mənli/ -manly or /ilajk/ -ylike, which would result if we were to cut differently.

The same principle holds true for syntactic constructions (phrases and clauses). It is obvious that in a short sentence like /dʒánwə́rks²³¹⟩/ John works, we have, first of all, the intonation-curve /231⟩/ plus the linear elements /dʒánwə́rks/ John works. This is because intonation-curves occur spread over entire clauses, not split among the individual elements of the clauses which they carry. The immediate constituents resulting from the next cut will have to be /dʒán/ John and /wə́rks/ works; the next (and only further) cut will be on the inflectional rather than the syntactical level, giving us the simple verb form /wə́rk/ plus /-s/ -s, which is the appropriate allomorph of the 3.sg. verb ending. We have to cut this way because this verb-ending is inflectionally, not syntactically, bound, and does not occur attached to phrases or clauses as wholes: we will not cut this sentence into /dʒánwə́rk/ John work + /-s/ -s. In larger constructions, the cutting is more complicated. In English, it will be determined primarily by the types of phrasal combinations which do or do not occur. Thus, for /majbró̌ðərz+ərnát-hírdʒəstnáw²³¹⟩/ my brothers are not here just now, our first cut will have to take away the intonation-curve (again /231⟩/ in this instance) from the linear elements. Our next will be between /majbró̌ðərz/ my brothers and the rest; and then further cuts will separate /maj/ my from /bró̌ðərz/ brothers, /ərnáthír/ are not here from /dʒəstnáw/ just now, and so forth. Often, even in English, immediate constituents are discontinuous; if we had /ərnátwə́rkɪŋ/ are not working instead of /ərnáthír/ are not here, we should have to split it into /ər . . . wə́rkɪŋ/ are . . . working plus /nát/ not.

In English, the detailed analysis of immediate constituents necessitates a great deal of laborious comparison of possible combination-types, especially of phrases and clauses. In other languages, with more complicated inflectional structures and more extensive cross-reference by concord and government (cf. Chap. 33), the determination of immediate constituents is made easier by these more immediately perceivable relationships. In a Spanish sentence like /lasnínaspuertor:ikéɲas áθentrabáxosmuibonítos/ las niñas puertorriqueñas hacen trabajos muy bonitos "the Puerto Rican girls do very pretty pieces of work", we are helped in making our immediate constituent cut by various phenomena of concord. Spanish subjects agree with the verbs of their predicates in person and number, but not in gender, so that we know that our first syntactic cut must be between /lasniṇaspuertor:ikeṇas/ *las niñas puertorriqueñas* and the rest, because the verb form /áθen/ *hacen* "they make" is the only element which meets these specifications with respect to the subject /níṇas/ *niñas*.

In Latin, the syntactic ties of agreement and government were so extensive as to permit widespread use of discontinuous constituents, especially in poetical or oratorical style. In even such simple verses as *Aequam mementō rēbus in arduīs servāre mentem:* "Remember to keep a balanced mind in difficult situations", *aequam:* "balanced" modifies *mentem:* "mind"; the noun phrase *aequam . . . mentem* is the object of *servāre* "to keep", which is further modified by *rēbus in arduīs* (= *rēbus . . . arduīs* "difficult matters" + the preposition *in:* "in"); and the whole construction depends on *mementō:* "remember". This state of affairs in Latin is a great headache to schoolboys trying to decipher Cicero or Vergil from the starting-point of a far more linear syntax like that of English, but it must have provided great interest and suspense to skilled Roman hearers and readers, who must have found Latin poetry and oratory very exciting because of the posing and gradual resolutions of intricate questions of syntactic relationships in the course of each sentence.

In inflected forms, whether they be simple like English /wɔ́rks/ *works* (= simple form of a verb plus one suffix), or complicated like the Italian verb form /venivámo/ analyzed at the beginning of this chapter, there is never any question as to what is the fundamental element of the form, the element which gives it its function with relation to the rest of the utterance. In a verbal form, it is the verb-root; in a nominal form, it is the noun or noun-stem, and so forth. The part of a form or construction (combination of free forms) which determines its function in the utterance may be termed its *center;* an inflected form always contains its center in itself. To describe such a form or construction we use the adjective *endocentric,* meaning "having its center in itself" (Greek *endo-:* "inside" + *centr-* + *-ic*). In derivation, a form like /ən+dʒɛ́ntəlmənli/ *ungentlemanly,* formed on /dʒɛ́ntəlmənli/ *gentlemanly* and having the same adjectival function (i.e., entering into the same range of further constructions) is likewise endocentric.

For larger constructions (phrases), we can illustrate the principle of endocentricity by such a series as:

Men.
The men.
The friendly men.
The friendly Canadian men.
The six friendly Canadian men.
The six friendly Canadian men on the boat.
The six friendly Canadian men on the boat who helped us with our luggage.

In all of these successive expansions, accomplished by adding successive elements to the single noun *men*, the noun itself remains the center of the construction. The construction itself, no matter how much expanded by the addition of further modifiers, can still enter into the same type of further grammatical relationships (e.g., it can act as the subject of a clause, as the object of a verb or preposition, etc.). If we change the various modifiers (adding or removing elements like articles, numerals, adjectives, or phrases or clauses), but do not change the form *men*, the remaining elements of the utterance will not be changed: after *men*, for example, we will always have to have *are*, not *is*; *were*, not *was*; *work*, not *works*. But if we change *men* in some way, say by making it singular and using *man* instead, this change affects both the inner structure of the phrase and the possible further combinations into which it can enter. If we have a singular center like *man*, certain modifying elements cannot be introduced (e.g., numerals higher than *one*); and certain elements in the further combinations must be changed (for instance, such verbs as *are*, *were*, *work* have to become singular likewise: *is*, *was*, *works*). All of these phrases given above are endocentric phrases with a noun as their center, and may therefore be termed endocentric noun-phrases (or nominal phrases). The center of an endocentric construction is often called its *head*, and elements which are subordinate to it are termed *attributes* or *modifiers*.

Not all constructions are endocentric. A phrase like *on the boat* may have anyone of several different functions: it may act as attribute to a noun (*the men on the boat*) or to a verb (*he works on the boat*) or to an adjective or past participle (*hoisted on the boat*). In the instance of other types of elements modifying *men*, *works*, or *hoisted*, it is their form-class or the form-class of their head which determines their function: *the Canadian* (adjective) *men*, *he works often* (adverb), or *hoisted aloft* (adverb). In *on the boat*, however, there is no element which determines its function: *in* is a preposition, *the* is a definite article, and *boat* is a noun; but the phrase as a whole functions as an adjective or an adverb. In other words, the element which determines the function of the phrase (its center) is not contained within the phrase in any of its constituent elements, but is its structure as a whole (preposition plus object); the center of the phrase is thus outside of the phrase itself. Any construction having its center, not inside, but outside of itself is termed *exocentric* (= Greek *exo-*: "outside" + *centr-* + *-ic*). Not only phrases, but derivationally formed elements can be exocentric, e.g., /bítər+swìt/ *bitter-sweet* (noun, name of a plant), since it consists of two adjectives but functions as a noun.

To indicate the relationships of the immediate constituents in an utterance or a part thereof, and the dependence relationships in endocentric constructions, resort is often had to *diagramming*. For the primarily linear relations of a language like English, it is useful to write out the graphic representation (phonemic or orthographical) of the sentence in its normal order, and then to draw lines between and below its elements to show the cuts to be made and the groupings into which the elements fall. For suprasegmental elements like intonation, a horizontal line can be drawn between the representation of the intonation and that of the rest of the utterance. Our first example shows the diagramming of a very simple sentence like *John loves Mary:*

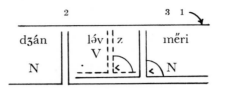

In this diagram, the top line separates out the intonation-curve; the solid lines below the transcription indicate syntactical cuts; and the dash lines indicate cuts on the inflectional level. The arrow within the quarter-circle indicates a relation of attribute to head, with the point of the arrow facing towards the head. This diagram tells us schematically that the utterance consists of the intonation curve /231⟩/ and /dʒán+lə́vzméˑri/; that this latter part has as its elements the noun (N) /dʒán/ and the verbal phrase /lə́vzméˑri/, but that their relation is exocentric, not endocentric (subject-plus-predicate combinations are always exocentric); that /lə́vzméˑri/ has as its head the verb (V) /lə́vz/ and the attribute noun (N) (direct object complement) /méri/, which in this instance happens to bear the sentence-stress /″/; and that /lə́vz/ consists of the simple form of the verb /lə́v/ plus the (necessarily endocentrically dependent) inflectional element /-z/.

At this point, we have space for only one further linear diagram of a somewhat longer utterance, designed to exemplify the use of further features such as a dot-and-dash line for derivational cuts, in the sentence *The store was an absolute mad-house this afternoon:*

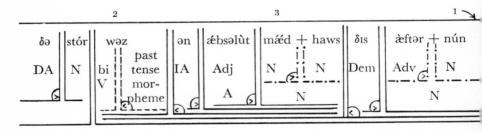

In earlier grammatical discussions and especially in the teaching of Latin (often in that of English as well), a rather different type of diagramming was used, which involved taking the elements of a sentence out of their linear positions, if necessary, and placing them next to or below one another in such a way as to show their grammatical relationships. The sentence just analyzed would have been diagrammed, according to one variety of the traditional treatment, as follows:

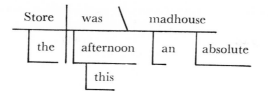

A Latin sentence of somewhat similar structure, e.g., *Gallia est omnis divīsa in partēs trēs:* "All Gaul is divided into three parts" (to take a simple example) would be diagrammed as follows:

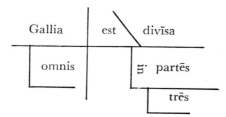

and a rather more complicated sentence like *Caesar ad eam partem pervēnit quae nōndum flūmen transīerat:* "Caesar arrived at that part which had not yet crossed the river" would be diagrammed:

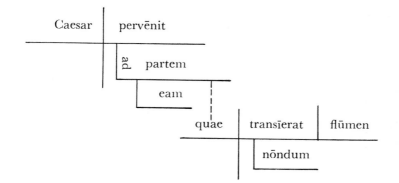

Among the conventions of this kind of diagramming are that the subject is placed above the main horizontal line, on the left of the main vertical line (which extends below the horizontal and indicates the cut between subject and verb); the main verb is placed on the right, and an upright half-line sets off a direct object, whereas a backwards-slanting line sets off a predicate complement. Modifiers are written on lines below the elements they modify, and prepositions on the vertical lines leading to the indication of their objects.

Dependent clauses are connected with dotted lines from the relative elements to their antecedents. In oral exercises connected with such diagrams, the learner states the principles involved in the agreement of each type of modifier, the government of each case, etc.

This latter type of diagram is most useful for a language like Latin (for which it was designed), to make clear the relationships between elements which belong together but are often separated by long intervening stretches (cf. the Latin example given on p. 173)—an especially difficult feature for speakers of a language with string-like, linearly organized constituent structures like those of English. For the purpose for which it was designed, the traditional diagramming of Latin is excellent. It is somewhat less applicable to English; its chief drawback in this connection is that it does not indicate immediate constituent structure clearly. The linear type of diagram shown on p. 172 is better for this purpose, but, in its turn, it is not well adapted to indicating discontinuous structures.

NOTES

Immediate constituents: Hockett, 1958, Chap. 17; Wells, 1947b.
Discontinuous constituents: Harris, 1945, 1962.

28

Derivation

MORPHOLOGY consists of two layers: an outer one, involving inflectionally bound forms, and an inner one (to which we come when we have "peeled off" all the inflectional elements), the layer of derivation. It is rare for this relative order of inflection and derivation to be reversed; one example is afforded by a few words in German, such as /kínderxen/ *Kinderchen* "little children" = /kínder/ *Kinder* "children" (consisting of /kind-/ *Kind* "child" plus the inflectional suffix/ -er/ *-er*, plural) + /-xen/ *-chen* "little . . . (derivational suffix, diminutive)".

When the inflectional elements have been taken away from a form, what is left is a *stem*. Thus, taking away the plural suffix /-z/ *-s* from /pǽnz/ *pans*, we have the stem /pǽn-/; taking away the replacement process /ǽ → ɛ/ from /mɛ́n/ *men*, we have /mǽn-/ *man-*; taking away the past-tense suffix /-əd/ *-ed* from /sáwndəd/ *sounded*, we have /sáwnd-/ *sound-*, etc. (Some analysts, when considering any form in its function as a stem in derivation, always write a hyphen after it, even though it may also exist as an independent free form, such as *pan, man, sound*.) Some examples from Italian, in which virtually every free form ends in a stem-vowel which forms part of an inflectional ending: /kása/ *casa* "house", minus /-a/ *-a* (noun sg. ending) = /kas-/ *cas-*; /kasé^tta/ *casetta* "little house", minus /-a/ *-a* = /kasé^tt-/ *casett-*; /skrivéndo/ *scrivendo* "writing", minus /-éndo/ *-endo* (present participial ending) = /skriv-/ *scriv-*; /preskrivéndo/ *prescrivendo* "prescribing", minus /-éndo/ = /preskriv-/ *prescriv-*; /fré^sko/ *fresco* "cool", minus /-o/ *-o* m. sg. adjective ending = /fré^sk-/ *fresc-*; /freské^tto/ *freschetto* "coolish", minus /-o/ *-o* = /freské^tt-/ *freschett-*; /freskettíno/ *freschettino* "rather coolish", minus /-o/ *-o* = /freskettín-/ *freschettin-*.

Here, as elsewhere, we must observe the principles of immediate constituents; for example, the last form cited does not consist of /fré^sk-/ plus /+ettín-/, but of /freské^tt-/ plus /+ín-/, which in its turn consists of /fré^sk-/ plus /+é^tt-/. (It is convenient to have different separation marks to indicate elements used in derivation as distinct from those used in inflection; we shall write a hyphen in our transcription before or after inflectionally bound forms, and a small raised plus-sign before or after derivationally bound forms.)

If a stem cannot be broken down into any further elements, i.e., if it consists of a single morpheme, it is called a simple stem. All the English forms cited in the preceding paragraph are of this type, as are Italian /kás-/ *cas-*

"house", /fréˆsk-/ *fresc-* "cool", /skrív-/ *scriv-* "write". In determining whether a stem is simple or not, we must depend on its similarity in form and meaning to other elements. Thus, English /síŋər/ *singer* "one who sings" (noun, with plural /síŋərz/ *singers*) is not simple, but derived (see next paragraph), because it consists of two morphemes, /sɪŋ-/ *sing-* and /⁺ər/ *-er*, agentive suffix, meaning "one who . . . -s". We can identify this derivational agentive suffix by its recurrence in many parallel formations having the same structure and meaning, as in /bítər/ *beater* "one who beats", /rájtər/ *writer* "one who writes", /lúzər/ *loser* "one who loses", etc. But such forms as /hǽmər/ *hammer* "instrument for hitting nails" and /bʌ́tər/ *butter* "the yellow substance we spread on bread" do not break down this way; a *hammer* is not "one who hams", and *butter* "the yellow substance" is not "one who butts" (If we coin a word /bʌ́tər/ *butter* "one who butts", it is a different word, specifically by virtue of its derivational structure.) The element /ər/ in *hammer* and in *butter* "yellow substance" cannot be identified with the homonymous /⁺ər/ *-er* of *singer, writer, loser,* because it has no meaning in common with this latter and does not occur attached to the same kind of stems (in this instance, verbs). Hence we must classify *hammer* and *butter* "yellow substance" as simple stems, despite the fact that they contain a sequence of phonemes /ər/ which is superficially similar to the agentive /⁺ər/ *-er* of *singer* etc.

A stem consisting of more than one morpheme is termed a *derived* stem. These, in their turn, break down into *primary* and *secondary* derived stems. In both of these types, we distinguish between *derivatives*, which are formed by the use of affixes of one type or another, and *compounds*, in which two or more elements are joined together without the use of derivational affixes. The intersection of these two lines of division in derived stems may be shown as follows:

PRIMARY DERIVATIVES   PRIMARY COMPOUNDS
(type /risív-/ *receive*)   (type /téləgrǽf/ *telegraph*)
SECONDARY DERIVATIVES   SECONDARY COMPOUNDS
(type /mǽnli/ *manly*)   (type /bébi-sìt/ *baby-sit*)

The term *primary*, in this connection, means "not involving a stem", i.e., involving forms which are bound on the derivational level; *secondary* means "involving one or more stems", i.e., forms which are themselves susceptible of use in inflection.

In a primary derivative, none of its constituent elements is itself a stem, but one is a derivational affix, and the other is a derivationally bound form termed a *base*. Primary derivatives are widespread in our learnèd vocabulary of Greek and Latin origin, in such forms as /risív-/ *receive*, /disív-/ *deceive*, /kansív-/ *conceive*, /idʒékt-/ *eject*, /ridʒékt-/ *reject*, etc. In a secondary derivative, one of its immediate constituents is a stem, and the other is a derivational affix of some kind, as in most of our nonlearnèd derivational formations: e.g. /mǽnli/ *manly* = /mǽn/ *man* + /⁺li/ *-ly*; /ǽktər/ *actor* = /ǽkt/ *act* + /⁺ər/ *-or*; /ǽktrɛs/ *actress* = /ǽkt(ə)r/ + /⁺ɛs/ *-ess*; etc., etc.

If no derivational affix is involved, and the constituents of a derived stem are simply juxtaposed—with or without some meaningless connecting element—the formation is a compound. If two bases (derivationally bound forms, as defined in the preceding paragraph) are joined together in this way, we have a *primary compound* or *base-compound;* as with primary derivatives, most of our English examples of this kind occur in our learnèd Graeco-Latin vocabulary, as in /téləgræf/ *telegraph* = /tɛlə⁺/ *tele-* "far" + /⁺græf/ *-graph* "write". Other languages with learnèd vocabulary of this type have similar formations, e.g., Italian /fonográmma/ *fonogramma* "recorded telephone message" = /fonográmm-/ *fonogramm-* + /-a/ *-a* noun ending (m. sg.), and /fonográmm-/ = /fono⁺/ *fono-* "sound" plus /⁺gramm-/ *gramm-* "writing". If both or all of the constituents of the compound are stems, we have a *secondary compound* or *stem-compound.* English has at least one fairly widespread type of stem compound, in our combinations of noun plus verb such as /bébi+sìt/ *baby-sit*, /gét+kræʃ/ *gate-crash*, /tájp+ràjt/ *typewrite*. Other instances of stem compounds may be cited from Latin, in which two stems such as /fid-/ "faith" and /frag-/ "break" can combine to make an adjective like /fidifrag-/ "breaking one's faith, faithless". In such stem compounds, especially in Greek and Latin (and languages which imitate their derivational procedures), meaningless but automatic connective elements can occur between the stems, e.g., the /⁺i⁺/ in Latin /fidifrag-/ or in Italian /velívolo/ *velivolo* "aeroplane", a term coined by Gabriele d'Annunzio (1863–1938) out of /véˀl-/ *vel-* "sail" + /vol-/ *vol-* "fly".

In many instances, it is hard to determine the exact meaning of a base occurring only in primary derivation. Our English learnèd vocabulary is full of such elements which had a very clear, concrete meaning in their Latin sources, but which have simply lost their meaning as modern English has developed. Thus, in Latin, the stem /kap-/ *cap-* meant "to take", and this meaning was quite clear in its derivatives, such as /akkip-/ *accip-* "to take to (oneself), get, accept", /deˀkip-/ *dēcip-* "to take down, trick, deceive", /inkip-/ *incip-* "to take in, set in, start", or /rekip-/ *recip-* "take back, receive". (The form /⁺kip-/ is a derivationally conditioned allomorph of /kap-/ in Latin.) But in English, the meaning of /⁺sijv/ *-ceive* and of its allomorphs /⁺sɛpt/ *-cept* (as in /æksépt/ *accept*, /risépʃən/ *reception*) and /⁺sít/ *-ceipt* (as in /risít/ *receipt*) has paled out so much as to be, at best, quite vague. Certainly there is no common meaning "take" in *accept, acception, deceive, deception, inception, receive, receipt, reception.* For this reason, some linguistic analysts cast doubt on the identification of such bases as /⁺sív/ *-ceive*, /⁺fór/ *-fer*, /⁺tén/ *-tain*; yet there is enough of a vague common meaning, coupled with extensive derivational parallelism, in the primary derivatives of these elements to make it useful for us to "peel them out" and identify them as bases.

Needless to say, many derived forms are quite complex, involving two or more layers of derivation. As immediate constituents, any of the various types enumerated at the beginning of this chapter can occur. Thus, in /bébi+sìtər/ *baby-sitter*, the stem-compound /bébi+sìt/ *baby-sit* serves in its turn as the base on which a secondary derivative is built with the agentive suffix /⁺ər/ -er. To this, in its turn, could be added a further derivational suffix /⁺ɪʃ/ -ish, forming /bébi+sìtərɪʃ/ baby-sitterish "like a baby-sitter"; and a still further derivational suffix /⁺nɛs/ -ness could be added to this last formation, giving /bébi+sìtərɪʃnɛs/ baby-sitterishness (as in I don't like her eternal baby-sitterishness). Similarly, a primary compound can occur as the base for further derivation: /téləgræf/ plus /⁺ɪk/ -ic gives /tèləgræfɪk/ telegraphic, which in its turn, with the suffixes /⁺əl/ -al and /⁺ɪk/ -ic, gives /tèləgræfɪkəli/ telegraphically. (Since English does not have double consonant phonemes except across disjuncture, //ll// is automatically reduced to /l/.) When primary derivatives, in our learnèd vocabulary, receive further derivational elements, they often undergo considerable allomorphic and morphophonemic variation. Thus, when the suffix /⁺jən/ -ion is added to /risív/ receive, the root /⁺sív/ -ceive is replaced by /⁺sᵉpt⁺/ -cept-, and the resultant formation, morphophonemically //risəptjən// reception, has a replacement of //tj// by /ʃ/, so that we have the actual derived form /risépʃən/.

The instance of /tèləgræfɪkəli/ telegraphically illustrates a fairly frequent occurrence, that of defective derivation. In our presentation in the preceding paragraph, we spoke of this form as being simply "with the suffixes /⁺əl/ -al and /⁺ɪk/ -ic" added, and were purposely vague about the exact relationships involved. There are many instances of adjectival formations in /⁺əl/ -al being extended by the adverbial suffix /⁺li/ -ly, as in /ædʒᵉktájvəli/ adjectivally, built on /ædʒᵉktájvəl/ adjectival, and likewise /mànəgræfɪkəli/ monographically on /mànəgræfɪkəl/ monographical, etc. In the case of /tèləgræfɪkəli/ telegraphically, however, there is (in modern English, at least) no form */tèləgræfɪkəl/ telegraphical, which we could consider as the immediate base on which the adverb in /⁺li/ -ly is built. In a case like this, we can do one of two things: either recognize a hypothetical form */tèləgræfɪkəl/ telegraphical as an intermediate stage in the process of successive derivations, or we can set up a composite suffix /⁺əli/ -ally.

The same problem is posed in the case of such a derived noun as /òrièntéʃən/ maturation, which seems to be parallel to nouns like /màdəréʃən/ moderation (to /mádərèt/ moderate), or /sòrkjuléʃən/ circulation (to /sórkjulèt/ circulate). However, there is no verb */órientèt/ orientate, but only /órièt/ orient. Do we postulate a hypothetical verb */órientèt/ orientate as one of the immediate constituents of /òrientéʃən/ orientation, or do we set up a composite suffix /⁺éʃən/ -ation to account for this and similar instances? The latter procedure seems on the surface more economical; but it savors too much of a merely practical short-cut, and the assumption of hypothetical intermediate forms gives a more thorough-going analysis and a more consistent over-all description. Sometimes, it must be admitted, the results of this latter procedure can seem very artificial, as when it forces us to recognize a zero base in French /ãtjen/ antienne "antiphon", which consists simply of the derivation prefix /ãti⁺/ anti- plus the derivational suffix /⁺en/ -enne (f.), with nothing in between.

Yet the assumption of a zero-element, although it has often been condemned as an artificial procedure, is often very useful, particularly in describing the relations of forms belonging to a given part of speech which are identical, phonologically, with forms of another part of speech. Thus, /rɔ́n/ *run* (noun) is clearly related to /rɔ́n/ *run* (verb); and /tébəl/ *table* (verb) to /tébəl/ *table* (noun); and likewise in a host of other instances. If we do not recognize, say, /rɔ́n/ *run* (noun) as derived from its verbal homonym, we are forced to set up a number of extra form-classes. In addition to N (noun), V (verb), and A (adjective) we must set up NV, AV, NA, and NAV—a procedure which, as pointed out on p. 135, is rigid, clumsy and wasteful, and does not provide for the great amount of day-to-day fluctuation that undoubtedly exists in this type of formation. It is far more convenient, although at first glance more artificial, to assume that /rɔ́n/ *run* (noun) is derived from /rɔ́n/ *run* ('verb) by means of a zero-suffix which has the inflectional characteristics of a regular noun.

Assumption of such a zero-suffix is the only efficient way of dealing with homonymity of stems in languages whose inflected stems are virtually all bound forms. Thus, in Italian, the relationship of such a verb as /acionáre/ *azionare* "to set in action" to its base /ació^ne/ *azione* "action" is best described as involving a derived verb stem /ació^n-/ *azion-* (first conjugation, weak) which is formed on the homonymous noun stem /ació^n-/ *azion-* ("third" declension, feminine) by means of a suffix /⁺Ø-/ which forms first-conjugation weak verbs. That this assumption of a zero-element is not so wholly artificial as it seems is shown by such English derivations as /lájf/ *Life* (name of a magazine), obviously formed on /lájf/ *life* (common noun). These two forms are different morphophonemically, since the latter has the plural /lájvz/ *lives* and hence the morphophonemic shape //lájF// (cf. p. 140). The former, however, has the regular plural /lájfs/ *Lifes* (the news-vendor will always ask his helper *Have this week's Lifes arrived yet?*, never . . . *this week's Lives* . . .), and hence is morphophonemically //lájf//. We will do best to describe the magazine-name as derived from the common noun by means of a zero-suffix /⁺0-/ which includes, as part of its morphological characteristics, the replacement of //F// by //f//.

In our discussion of such derivatives as /màdəréʃən/ on /mádərèt/, and /tèləgrǽfɪk/ on /téləgrǽf/, we have included the phonemic transcription throughout, in order to show certain phenomena of stress-alternation which are not evident in conventional spelling, and which are likely to escape attention if not given special symbolization. In derivation, both by affixation and by compounding, these alternations of stress (termed *modulation* in some discussions) form part of the morphological process, and must be mentioned in our descriptions. It is such a feature of modulation, for instance, that differentiates the phrase /blǽk + bɔ́rd/ (*a*) *black bird* (when pronounced with disjuncture between the two elements) from the compound /blǽk + bɔ̀rd/ *blackbird*. In some languages, e.g., French, features of this type are not found (in this instance, because French has no significant suprasegmental system of stress). Wherever possible, it is well to use special symbols to indicate processes of modulation. In Italian derivation, for instance, the symbol /≤/ can be used to indicate displacement of stress to the third syllable before the last (the antepenultimate); thus, we can describe the Italian compound /piróskafo/ *piròscafo* "steamship" as having the stem /piróskaf-/ *piròscaf-*, which consists of /piro+/ "fire" (= /pir+/ plus the connecting vowel /+o+/) + /skaf-/ "boat", with the suffix /+⁻Ø-/ "noun of the second declension (m.)".

NOTES

Derivation: Bloomfield, 1933a, Chap. 14.
English learnèd words: Bloomfield, 1933b.

29

Affixation

IN DERIVATION by affixation, all types of affixes can be found in one language or another: suffixes, prefixes, infixes. If the derivation involves simply shift of stress, with no affix of any kind, we can speak of a change of superfix. Uncomplicated examples of these various types of derivation follow:

SUFFIXATION: English /tékər/ *taker*, on /ték/ *take;* /slájnɛs/ *slyness*, on /sláj/ *sly*.

PREFIXATION: English /diláws/ *delouse*, on /láws/ *louse;* /prifíks/ *prefix* (verb), on /fíks/ *fix*.

INFIXATION: Tagálog /pumí:lit/ "one who compelled" = /pí:lit/ "effort" with the infix /⁺um⁺/ "one who does . . . ". Reduplication is found in such forms as Chamorro /agagáña/ "to go to Agaña" = /agáña/ "Agaña (town-name)" with /ga/ repeated before the stem.

CHANGE OF SUPERFIX: shift of stress from second to first syllable in English /kántrækt/ *contract* (noun), on /kantrǽkt/ *contract* (verb), or /prífiks/ *prefix* (noun), on /prifíks/ *prefix* (verb).

Both in derivatives formed by affixation and in compounds, the distinction between endocentric and exocentric is of major importance, and furnishes a valuable guide for an initial classification of types of derived forms. Obviously, any formation involving the derivation of one part of speech from another will be considered exocentric, such as /dɛrivéʃən/ *derivation* (noun) on /dirájv/ *derive* (verb); /májti/ *mighty* (adjective) on /májt/ *might* (noun), /slájnɛs/ *slyness* (noun) on /sláj/ *sly* (adjective); etc. etc. In case the derived form is of the same part of speech as the one on which it is based, the decision between endocentricity and exocentricity may be somewhat harder to make. In general, if the derived form manifests the same inflectional characteristics, and shows the same general range of distribution in its syntactic uses, as the one from which it is derived, it will be considered endocentric. This is the case with such Italian forms as /kaséˆtta/ *casetta* "little house", on /kása/ *casa* "house", or /kantikkiáre/ *canticchiare* "to sing under one's breath", on /kantáre/ *cantare* "to sing"; or English /stárlɛt/ *starlet*, on /stár/ *star*. But if the derived form belongs to a different sub-class, or is markedly different in its syntactic uses, from its base, then we must consider it exocentric, as in the case of Italian /donnóˆne/ *donnone* (noun, m.) "big woman", on /dónna/ *donna* (noun, f.) "woman", or the instance of Eng. //lájf// *Life* (magazine-name) formed on //lájF// *life* (common noun) discussed in the previous chapter.

The detailed analysis of derivation by affixation in any given language is likely to take a great deal of time and energy, and its complete description often occupies an apparently disproportionate amount of space. This is due to two factors which are very important in derivational relationships, especially in languages which have extensive learnèd vocabularies which have been borrowed more or less scatteringly from languages of alien structure. (Thus, English, French, and other West European languages have Graeco-Latin learnèd words; Haitian and other French-based creoles have numerous French borrowings; and Burmese, Malay, and other languages of south-east Asia have Sanskrit loan-words.) The first of these factors is the very random and unpredictable distribution of affixed elements in relation to the bases to which they are added; the other is the frequent presence of equally random and unpredictable allomorphic variation in the bases themselves. Each of these phenomena must be described in detail, in order to achieve completeness.

In many instances, there are several affixes which have nearly the same meaning and nearly (but not wholly) complementary distribution, as is the case with the English suffixes /⁺t/ -t, /⁺θ/ -th, /⁺ɪti/ -ity, /⁺nɛs/ -ness, and /⁺dəm/ -dom. All of these form exocentric noun derivatives on adjectives, meaning approximately "the quality of being . . . ," as in /hájt/ height, on /háj/ high; /lép θ/ length, on /lɔŋ/ long; /dénsɪti/ density, on /déns/ dense; /tájrdnɛs/ tiredness, on /tájrd/; and /wízdəm/ wisdom, on /wájz/ wise. Yet speakers of English have the "feeling" that these are not simply variant forms of the same suffix. This "feeling" is justified, because on occasion more than one of these suffixes can be added to the same base: we can speak both of /dénsɪti/ density and of /dénsnɛs/ denseness, with rather a shade of difference in meaning (density applies to the physical characteristics of a substance which is dense [not thin or porous], whereas denseness applies to the psychologic or intellectual characteristics of a person who is dense [not very bright]). Consequently, unless we content ourselves with a summary listing of these various suffixes, we cannot give a thorough and accurate description of their occurrence without entering on an extensive listing of all the combinations in which each of them occurs. There are no phonological or morphological characteristics of the adjectives involved which will enable us to make brief covering statements; the only thing that can be done is to make a listing of all the adjectives to which each suffix is added. For some, the list will be quite short: e.g., /⁺t/ -t is added only to /háj/ high and (perhaps) to /sláj/ sly in /slájt/ sleight(-of-hand); /⁺θ/ -th to a few such as /wídθ/ width on /wájd/ wide, /dépθ/ depth on /díp/ deep, and those cited at the beginning of this paragraph; and /⁺ɪti/ -ity to a certain number of learnèd elements. The suffixes /⁺nɛs/ -ness and /⁺dəm/ -dom are much more freely added to all kinds of adjectives.

In this situation, many grammarians have preferred to establish a distinction between "live" and "dead," or "productive" and "unproductive" derivational elements, in order to justify a relative neglect of those which are seemingly no longer used freely in new formations. Yet such a distinction is hardly justifiable. In some instances, the traditional formulations have simply not been based on accurate observation of the facts. Most grammarians of English, paying attention only to serious, permanently established formations, have treated /⁺dəm/ -dom as a "dead" suffix. Actually, however, it is very widely used in humorous, often short-lived formations (nonce-formations, cf. Chap. 47) such as /fílmdəm/ filmdom, /stárdəm/ stardom, /nátsidəm/ Nazidom, etc., and even /lɔ́rəldəm/ Laureldom (the habitual condition characteristic of the role played by the comedian Stan Laurel—a nonce-coinage made by my wife ca. 1939). Furthermore, no one can tell when an apparently "dead" element will be used as the basis for a new formation. The stock example is the use of /⁺si/ -cy (present only in a few derivatives such as /kə́rəntsi/ currency on /kə́rənt/ current) in the formation, on /nɔ́rməl/ normal, of /nɔ́rməlsi/ normalcy, as the key word in Warren G. Harding's campaign for the Presidency in 1920, with his insistence on a "return to normalcy." Similarly, the apparently learnèd composite suffix /⁺éʃəs/ -acious, -aceous served in the 1920's and '30's for such semi-humorous new-formations as /kə̀rvéʃəs/ curvaceous on /kə́rv/ curve and /bà̀ðəréʃəs/ botheracious on /bá̀ðər/ bother. There is no limit to the extent to which an apparently "dead" derivational element may be suddenly and quite capriciously "resurrected" and become productive. Hence, for describing the state of affairs at any given moment, there is no alternative to a complete, exhaustive listing of all the complicated peculiarities in the privileges of occurrence of every derivational element.

The other major difficulty in giving an exhaustive description of derivation lies in the great variability in the allomorphs of the bases. We must often devote entire pages to a listing of the special variants which occur before individual suffixes or after individual prefixes, especially in learnèd words. Some of the variations in phonemic shape can be taken care of beforehand, in dealing with morphophonemics, under the heading of automatic replacements in one type or another of junctural conditions: e.g., the replacement of /t/ plus /j/ by /tʃ/ when /⁺jər/ -ure is added to a base like /dʒɔ́ŋkt⁺/ junct- in forming /dʒɔ́ŋktʃər/ juncture. Others, however, cannot be taken care of in this way; there is no basis on which anyone can predict that, say, /dʒɔ́jn/ join will be replaced by /dʒɔ́ŋkt⁺/ when it is followed by /⁺jər/ -ure. This situation is especially troublesome with forms like /dʒɔ́jn/ join, which came into English from Latin through French, but which have allomorphs of the type /dʒɔ́ŋkt⁺/ junct-. In a case like this, the allomorphs are so clearly related that they cannot be separated off as distinct morphemes, but they occur in derivatives that were borrowed (usually at a later date) directly from Latin and hence show a phonemic shape closer to that which they had in the ultimate source-language.

On occasion, contrary to the general procedure of making successive immediate constituent cuts, it is useful to consider certain prefixes and suffixes as belonging together, and as constituting (as it were) composite discontinuous affixes. This is the case in a number of French, Italian, and Spanish derivatives where different stems, although formed with the same prefix, fall into different inflectional sub-classes (e.g., conjugations). Thus, in French, with the prefix /a⁺/ *a-* "to" (often, but not always, accompanied in spelling by the doubling of the following consonant letter), we find, on the base /lym⁺/ *lum-* "light", the derivative /alym-/ "to light", a verb of the first conjugation (infinitive /alyme/ *allumer*). On such bases as //but⁺// *bout* "end" or /ter/ *terre* "land", however, we have, with the same prefix, the derivatives /abutis-/ *aboutiss-* "to come to an end, amount to" and /ateris-/ *atterriss-* "to land (e.g. of an aeroplane)"; these verbs belong to a sub-class of the "third" conjugation (parallel to /fəz-/ *fais-* "make") and have the infinitives /abutir/ *aboutir* and /aterir/ *atterrir*, respectively. In such instances, it is best to say that French /alym-/ *allum-* is formed with the prefix /a⁺/ and at the same time the verb suffix /⁺∅-/ with the inflectional characteristics of the first conjugation; but that /abutis-/ *aboutiss-* and /ateris-/ *atterriss-* are formed with /a⁺/ . . . /⁺is-/ vb/IIIb.

In the formation of derivatives with clearly isolable affixed elements, there is relatively little difficulty in establishing at least approximate meanings for the affixes and—in general—for the bases to which they are added. For primary bases, it is often considerably more difficult to do so, as we saw in Chap. 28 for forms like /⁺sív/ *-ceive*, /⁺fɔ́r/ *-fer*, /⁺mít/ and similar elements of our Graeco-Latin vocabulary. The problem becomes even more acute in the case of partial resemblances between bases which seem to share certain phonemes and certain features of meaning, but with a very haphazard distribution. Thus, in English, a considerable number of demonstratives begin with /ð⁺/, such as /ðís/ *this*, /ðǽt/ *that*, /ðɛ́n/ *then*, /ðɔ́s/ *thus*, /ðɛ́ns/ *thence*, /ðíðər/ *thither*, /ðǽr/ *there*. Some of the elements which follow /ð⁺/ recur in a few other forms, like /hwɛ́n/ *when*, /hwɛ́ns/ *whence*, /hwíðər/ *whither*, /hwǽr/ *where;* but we have no forms like */hwɔ́s/ *whus* or */hwís/ *whis* (except in humorous nonce-coinages). In other apparently related forms there are capricious variations such as /⁺at/ instead of /⁺æt/ in /hwát/ *what.* Furthermore, the element /ð⁺/ occurs in other, unrelated forms such as /ðáw/ *thou* and its group. Is it worth while, at this point, to "peel out" such a base as "demonstrative /ð⁺/" and to enumerate all the various apparent formative elements that follow it? Some analysts would answer affirmatively, but others would consider such a procedure excessively rigorous.

The situation becomes even more problematical in the case of so-called "sound-symbolism," in which certain phonemes or clusters (especially initial or final) seem to be associated with certain very vague types of meaning or emotional overtones. Some analysts wish to recognize such "base-forming morphemes" as /bl⁺/ *bl-*, with a meaning something like "make a burbling noise", as in /blúp/ *bloop*, /blǽr/ *blare*, /blǽt/ *blat*, etc.; or, in Italian, a morpheme /bamb⁺/ "child", in /bambíno/ *bambino* "child", /rimbambíre/ *rimbambire* "grow senile (i.e. return to acting like a child)", and, with a "symbolic diminutive" replacement of /a/ by /i/, in /bímbo/ *bimbo* "baby". Each of these cases has to be decided on its own merits; of these two, for instance, the second seems much more probable as an independent morpheme than the first, chiefly because a much more specific meaning can be associated with Italian /bamb+/ than with English /bl+/.

On occasion, theories of "sound-symbolism" have been developed at great length and with great ingenuity, even leading to the setting up of extensive formulas for "onomatopoetic" words, such as:

$$\left.\begin{matrix} \text{Stop or} \\ \text{fricative} \end{matrix}\right\} + \Big\{ /r/ \text{ or } /l/ \Big\} + \Big\{ \text{vowel} \Big\} + \Big\{ \text{nasal} \Big\} + \left\{\begin{matrix} \text{voiceless} \\ \text{stop} \end{matrix}\right.$$

for words such as Eng. /klɔ́mp/ *clump*, /krímp/ *crimp*, /klǽŋk/ *clank*, /príŋk/ *prink*, /frɔ́mp/ *frump*, /grɔ́nt/ *grunt*, etc., of varying degrees of comic or ridiculous connotation. However, the structure identified in this way is so multiform, and the common features of meaning are so vague, as to be too all-inclusive; one can cite many other words such as /plǽŋk/ *plank*, /grǽnt/ *grant*, /flínt/ *flint*, which have no such connotations.

Doubtful in the highest degree are attempts to establish cross-cultural systems of sound- symbolism such as those in which it is maintained that, say, high-front vowels symbolize smallness (as in French /pətit/ *petite*, Italian /píkkolo/ *piccolo* or /piččíno/ *piccino*—all: "little"), and low or back vowels indicate largeness (as in French /grãd/, Ital. /gránde/—both: "large"). In such naïve forms as these, theories of cross-cultural sound-symbolism are easily demolished by pointing to such major exceptions as English /bíg/ *big* and /smɔ́l/ *small*, or German /kláin/ *klein* "little". Any secondary associations of a symbolic type which the forms of a given language may have are due, not to any universal, cross-culturally valid psychological characteristics of the human race, but purely to phonological and semantic similarities within each individual language.

NOTES

The English suffix -dom: Wentworth, 1941; Estrich and Sperber, 1952, Chap. 8.
Sound symbolism: Jespersen, 1922, Chap. 20.

30

Compounding

WITH COMPOUNDING, we are on the borderline between morphology and syntax. Many compound formations show the same type of combination of morphemes, in any given language, as is found in phrasal groupings, for example English /blǽk+bə̀rd/ *blackbird,* similar in the sequence of its elements to /blǽk bə́rd/ *black bird;* or /dréd+nɔ̀t/ *dreadnought,* similar to /dréd nɔ́t/ "fear nothing". Such formations are called *phrasal* or *syntactic compounds,* because of their similarity to phrases or syntactic constructions in some (not all!) of their features. Others, which do not correspond to any phrasal combination of the language, are termed nonphrasal or asyntactic compounds, such as English /dór+nàb/ *door-knob* (we do not have phrases of the type */dór náb/) or /fájr+prùf/ *fire-proof* (a /fájr prúf/, if it meant anything, would be "proof afforded by means of fire"). Some scholars also distinguish an intermediate type of *semi-syntactic* compounds such as /blú+àjd/ *blue-eyed,* which contain phrasal types (in this case /blú áj/ *blue eye*) plus derivational features such as the participle-forming suffix /+(ə)d/ *-d, -ed.*

The first problem in dealing with compounds is how to distinguish phrasal compounds from simple phrases. Recourse must be had to additional nonsyntactic features such as prosodic characteristics of stress, pitch or juncture; the use of special forms of the constituent elements; or the possibility of either interrupting the construction or expanding it by the addition of further modifiers. In languages which have stress-systems, there are often special patterns of modulation signalling compounds as such; in those with sandhi-phenomena such as internal disjuncture (Chap. 18), the presence of this or similar types of juncture-phenomena assists us in identifying compounds. The stock example from English is the contrast between, say, /lɔ́ŋ légz/ *long legs* (noun plural; phrase with two full stresses and only optional disjuncture between the two elements) and /lɔ́ŋ+lègz/ in (*Daddy*) *long-legs* (compound, with only one full stress, and obligatory disjuncture). An old anecdote concerns the confusion of a Frenchman who saw nothing funny in a joke to the effect that the President-elect was going to move from his private residence, a *white house* /hwájt háws/, into the *White House* /hwájt+hàws/; in French, there are no contrasts in stress or internal disjuncture, and the Frenchman, not hearing these differences in English, interpreted the two expressions as being identical.

If criteria of a prosodic nature are lacking, as they are in French, we may invoke others. A French syntactic compound may often be distinguished from a comparable phrase by the use of a particular sandhi-alternant (cf. Chap. 23). For instance, the "preconsonantal," not the "prevocalic" alternant of most nouns is used in constructing phrases, even if a vowel begins the immediately following form. Thus, the noun for "wine", spelled *vin*, has two sandhi-alternants, of which the "preconsonantal" form (under which it is usually cited when pronounced separately) is /vẽ/, and the "prevocalic" form, used only in derivation, is /vin⁺/. A freely constructed phrase like "bitter wine", with the modifying adjective /egr/ *aigre* "bitter", will always have the shape /vẽegr/ *vin aigre*. In the form meaning "vinegar", on the other hand, the construction is marked as a compound by the use of /vin⁺/, not /vẽ/: /vinegr/ *vinaigre*. Similarly, with the noun for "foot", spelled *pied*, the full or "prevocalic" form /pje^t/ is used only in derivatives like //pje^toⁿ// /pje^tõ/ *piéton* "pedestrian" and in a compound like /pje^tater/ *pied-à-terre* "(small) apartment in town, literally foot-on-the-ground". In a free phrasal combination involving these same elements, as in the expression *mettre pied à terre:* "to set foot on the ground", one would use the "preconsonantal" sandhi-alternant /pje^/, and would say /metrəpje^ater/. Historically speaking, such French compounds as these are survivals of old phrases, in which (at an earlier time) the "prevocalic" sandhi-variant was used much more freely; with the change in sandhi habits leading to general use of the "preconsonantal" variant in the free construction of phrases, these older fixed combinations with the "prevocalic" variant have become frozen into compounds.

When expressions like French /vinegr/ *vinaigre* and /pje^tater/ *pied-à-terre* become frozen in this way, another result of their fixity is that they often reflect older syntactic habits. French /fam/ *femme* means "woman", and /saʒ/ *sage* "wise"; in modern French, "a wise woman" would be /ynfamsaʒ/ *une femme sage*, with the adjective following the noun. On the other hand, the compound /saʒfam/ *sage-femme* "mid-wife" has the adjective preceding the noun, as was possible in Old French but much less likely nowadays. Archaic grammatical forms or meanings may likewise be preserved in compounds, as in English /dréd+nɔ̀t/ *dreadnought,* which combines a verb which is now rather poetical with an archaic negative pronoun; nowadays, the usual expression would be *not be afraid of anything.*

Likewise, compounds are normally unsplittable and cannot be fully expanded. I used to cause my friends considerable amusement by treating the compound /biwǽr/ *beware* as if it were a verbal phrase /bí wǽr/, and by urging them on occasion to /bí véri wǽr/ *Be very ware!*. In French, the phrase /ynfamsaʒ/ can be expanded by adding, say, the adverb /tre/ *très* "very" before the adjective, with the result /ynfamtresaʒ/ *une femme très sage* "a very wise woman". But the compound /saʒfam/ cannot be expanded in the same way. In German, one criterion for distinguishing compound verbs from verbs with "separable" prefixes or prefixed complements is the insertability of the past-participle-forming prefix /ge-/ *ge-*. Between a "separable" prefix or a prefixed complement and the verb to which it is attached, this past-participle-forming prefix can be inserted, as in /vék+gè:n/ *weggehen* "go away", past participle /vék+gegàŋen/ *weggegangen* "gone away"; /lí:p+hàben/ *lieb-*

haben "hold dear", past participle /lí:p+gehàpt/ *liebgehabt*. But in a compound like /líp+kò:zen/ *liebkosen* "fondle (lit. caress lovingly)", the element /ge-/ *ge-* cannot be inserted in this way, and must precede the entire compound: /gelíp+kò:st/ *geliebkost* "fondled".

In languages with extensive inflection and use of stem-vowels, compounds are frequently distinguished by the use of special connecting vowels. Thus, in Latin, a formation like /agrikola/ "farmer", consisting of the two stems /agr-/ "field, farm" and /kol-/ "cultivate" (literally, therefore, a "field-cultivator"), is marked as a compound by the use, not of the normal stem-vowel of /agr-/ (which, as a second-declension noun, has /-o/: /agro-/), but of the connecting vowel /-i/ (short), which occurs nowhere else in the inflection of this and other second-declension nouns. Italian, Spanish, French and other languages which have borrowed extensively from Greek and Latin, use the same type of device, as in d'Annunzio's coinage of Ital. /velívolo/ *velìvolo* "aeroplane" cited on p. 177. Sometimes these connecting elements are used in ways foreign to those of their source languages. The French association of taxi-owners wished to make, in the early twentieth century, a phrasal compound based on /taksametr/ *taxe à mètre* (lit. "fare as per meter"), to be pronounced in the same way but written as a single word, *taxamètre*. This form gained considerable currency in France and is still widely used there, but the French Academy (cf. Chap. 62) ruled that the "correct" classicizing formation should be /taksimetr/ *taximètre*, in which form it was borrowed from French into many other languages, and which is the basis for the world-wide abbreviated form *taxi*.

In languages with extensive inflectional systems, compounds can often be identified whenever their inflectional characteristics differ from those of the elements of which they are formed. Italian has a very wide-spread type of verb-plus-noun compound, of the type of /pórta+cé^nere/ *portacénere* "ash-tray" (= /pórta-/ "carry" + /čé^nere/ "ash"), or /stúccika+dénti/ *stuzzicadenti* "toothpick" (= /stúccika-/ "tickle, pick at" + /dénti/ "tee th"). No matter what the gender or plural formation of the noun comprising the second element of such a compound, however, the compound as a whole is always masculine and invariable, thus setting it apart morphologically from its component forms. Here, too, as in the case of the derivatives discussed on pp. 183–184, it is probably most convenient to recognize, concomitantly with the process of compounding, the addition of a zero-suffix /+∅-/, masculine and invariable, which has the effect of "immobilizing," as it were, the inflectional characteristics of the elements which are joined in the compound.

The contrast between endocentric and exocentric is present in compounds as well as in derivatives. If the function of the compound is the same as that of one of its elements, with no gross variation in meaning, it is to be classed as endocentric. A number of American Indian languages have a process often termed "noun-incorporation," whereby a noun object is combined with a verb-root into an endocentric verbal compound, as in Nahuatl, where the noun /naka+tl/ "meat" is combined with /kwa/ "eat" to make verb forms like /ni-naka+kwa/ "I meat-eat, i.e., I eat meat". We have a similar type of endocentric formation in our modern English "noun-incorporating" verb-compounds like /háws+kìp/ *house-keep*, /gét+kràʃ/ *gate-crash*, /hédʒ+hàp/ *hedge-hop*, and numerous others (without, of course, any historical connection between the American Indian languages and English with regard to this kind of compound).

On the other hand, if the compound belongs to a form-class or subdivision of one different from that of its elements (or of the head in the phrasal type on which it is founded), then it is of course exocentric, as in the case of French /ruʒgorʒ/ *rouge-gorge* (m.) "robin", compounded of /ruʒ/ *rouge* "red" (adj.) plus /gorʒ/ *gorge* "throat" (noun, f.). In English, we have compounds like /fájv+sènt/ *five-cent* (as in *a five-cent cigar*), /hǽf+màjl/ *half-mile* (as in *a half-mile walk*), which are adjectives, formed on phrases of adjective (attribute) plus noun (head); they are therefore exocentric. For semantic reasons, we will also class /réd+kæ̀p/ *red-cap* or /blú+nòz/ *blue-nose* as exocentric. Although they are nouns based on endocentric noun-phrases, they do not have the same meaning as the phrases, but mean rather "person or thing possessing or characterized by what is described by the phrase": a *red-cap* (luggage-porter) is not "a cap which is red", but "a man with a red cap", and a *blue-nose* (excessively puritanical person) is not "a nose which is blue", but someone who is caricatured as having a blue nose.

The detailed description of the compounds of any given language entails listing the various types of combinations, both syntactic and asyntactic, according to the elements comprised in each. For English, our list of compounds would include the following, all characterized by the presence of full stress /ˊ/ on the first element, internal disjuncture /+/, and intermediate stress /ˋ/ on the second element:

PHRASAL (SYNTACTIC):
Endocentric:
   Adjective + Adjective: /bítər+swìt/ *bitter-sweet* "bitter and sweet"
   Adjective (verb participle head) + Adverb (attribute): /kǽst+ɔ̀f/ *cast-off*
Exocentric:
   Noun = Adjective (attribute) + Noun (head): /réd+kǽp/ *red-cap*
   Noun = Adjective + Adjective: /bítər+swìt/ *bitter-sweet* (kind of plant)
   Noun = Noun (possessive, attribute) + Noun (head): /búlz+àj/ *bull's-eye*
   Noun = Verb (head) + Noun (object): /lík+spìtəl/ *lick-spittle*
   Noun = Verb (head) + Pronoun (object): /dréd+nɔ̀t/ *dreadnought*
   Noun = Verb (head) + Adverb (attribute): /rɔ́n+əbàwt/ *run about*
   Noun = Adjective (verb participle, head) + Adverb (attribute): /kǽst+əwè/ *cast-away*
                      etc.
NONPHRASAL (ASYNTACTIC):
Endocentric:
   Noun = Noun (attribute) + Noun (head): /bɔ́s+tìkɛt/ *bus-ticket*
   Noun = Verb (in *-ing* form, attribute) + Noun (head): /swímɪŋ+pùl/ *swimming-pool*
   Noun = Adverb (attribute) + Noun (head): /báj+lɔ̀/ *by-law*
   Adjective = Noun (attribute) + Adjective (head): /fájr+prùf/ *fire-proof*
   Adjective = Noun (attribute) + Verb Participle (head): /fláj+blòn/ *fly-blown*
   Verb = Noun (object) + Verb (head): /bébi+sìt/ *baby-sit*

Verb = Adjective (attribute) + Verb (head): /dráj+klìn/ *dry-clean*
Verb = Adverb (attribute) + Verb (head): /bái+pæs/ *by-pass*
Adverb = Indefinite Adjective (attribute) + Adverb (head): /sóm+hwæ̀r/ *some-where*

Exocentric:
Noun = Adjective (attribute) + Noun (head): /lóŋ+lègz/ *long-legs*
Noun = Noun (object) + Verb (head): /bút+blæk/ *boot-black*
Noun = Adverb (attribute) + Verb (head): /áwt+kràp/ *out-crop*
Pronoun = Indefinite (attribute) + Noun (head): /sóm+bàdi/ *some-body*
Pronoun = Indefinite (attribute) + Numeral (head): /sóm+wòn/ *some-one*
etc.

Even in the nonphrasal compound types, a great many of the combinations can be described as consisting of attribute plus head. Not all compounds have this structure, and we often find groupings of two (or even more) coordinate elements, especially primary bases of rather vague meaning, either repeated (e.g. /tʃú+tʃù/ *choo-choo*) or with only partial differentiation (as in /hə́gər+mə̀gər/ *hugger-mugger*). These coordinate compounds often belong to more than one form-class (e.g., /flím+flæm/ *flim-flam*, which can be a noun, an adjective, or a verb), and constitute one of the arguments in favor of recognizing overlapping form-classes like NAV etc. (cf. pp. 178–179), since it would be highly artificial to assign a word like *flim-flam* to any one specific part of speech (say, noun) as its "basic" part of speech and to treat its occurrence as a member of other form classes (say, adjective or verb) as derived from the noun by a zero-suffix.

It is not always easy to determine the constituent elements of a compound, and sometimes our decision must be left somewhat in abeyance. In Italian exocentric compounds of the type /pórta+čé^neri/ *portacéneri* "ash-tray" (p. 188), the first (verbal) element is in almost all instances identical with a second singular imperative, e.g., /pórta/ *porta!* "carry!" The 2.sg. imperative, however, is itself almost always the same as the "present stem" of the verb, e.g., /pórt-a-/, to the root /pórt-/. In a few instances, the verbal element of these compounds cannot be identified with an imperative, as in /fáči+dánno/ *facidanno* "harm-doer, evil-doer", in which /fáč-/ "do" is the root of the verb and /-i-/ is a connecting vowel or substitute stem-vowel which does not occur elsewhere in the inflection of this root; but the 2.sg. imperative of /fáč-/ is /fáˣ/ *fa'*, not */fáči/ *faci*. Hence it would seem best to take this type of compound in Italian as consisting, not of 2.sg. imperative plus noun object, but of verb-stem plus noun object. Yet many scholars object to this latter formulation, and would rather treat such an element as /fáči+/ in /fáči+dánno/ as a "substitute imperative" or the like. In a case like this, no decision can be reached until we reach a clear understanding on the limits of definition of terms like "imperative" and "stem"; *adhūc sub jūdice līs est.*

NOTES

Compounding: Bloomfield, 1933a, Chap. 14.
Noun-incorporation: Hall, 1956.
The type facidanno*:* Hall, 1948e.

31

Syntax

IN TRADITIONAL GRAMMAR, syntax is treated as the study of the way in which words are used, as opposed to morphology, which analyzes the way they are built. However, as we have seen, the border-line between morphology and syntax—although it certainly exists and should not be neglected—is not so sharp as to permit such a neat division. Especially in syntactic compounds (p. 186), syntactic constructions can be used as bases for morphological formations. On the other hand, especially in languages with extensive inflectional and derivational systems, single free forms contain a great deal of what we normally regard as syntactic material (e.g., in French and Eskimo, pp. 148–149). It will not do, either, to treat morphology as the branch of linguistics dealing with minimum free forms and their structure (Chap. 22), and syntax as dealing with the constructions in which they occur. Such a division rests on the unrealistic assumption that all bound forms occur only on the inflectional and derivational levels, and that once we have taken care of these levels, we can leave bound forms behind in order to study combinations of free forms. However, as we have seen (pp. 132–133), bound forms occur also on the phrasal and clausal levels. We must simply recognize that here, as elsewhere in the structure of language, there can be interpenetration of levels, and that it would be artificial to try to make an excessively sharp separation between morphology and syntax.

It is perhaps best to define syntax negatively, as the study of the combinations of such morphemes as are not bound on the levels of either inflection (as defined in Chap. 22) or derivation (Chap. 28). By this definition, most of the elements involved in syntactical combinations will indeed be free; but some, such as the definite and indefinite article in English and many other languages, the prepositions in Romance, conjunctions, etc., will be phrasally or clausally bound. In practice, this formulation gives approximately the same results as the earlier approaches, since we will still treat a sequence of morphemes like /dirájvz/ *derives* as an inflected form, /dèrɪvéʃən/ *derivation* as a derivative, and /ðədɛrɪvéʃən/ *the derivation* as a phrase. However, it is useful to realize that this identity of practical results is due to the false identification which traditional grammar and spelling give to syntactically bound forms by writing them as if they were independent "words" and thus enabling them to be discussed on the level of syntax as it is conventionally defined.

Syntactical constructions can be approached from two directions. We can approach them from "below" (in terms of the levels of linguistic structure shown in our Fig. 1, p. 31), i.e., from the direction of the morphological elements which they contain; or we can begin our syntactical description from "above," i.e. in terms of the syntactic positions which are to be filled, first stating these and then proceeding to treat the form classes which are "privileged" to occur in one position or another. Thus, a simple sentence like *The trains aren't running today* can be analyzed in terms of its phrasal constituents, as consisting of a noun-phrase (*the trains*) plus a negativized progressive verb-phrase (*aren't running*) which contains also an adverbial complement (*aren't running today*); the combination of these two endocentric phrases, in the function of noun and verb respectively, constitutes a clause consisting of subject (noun) and predicate (verb). In terms of its syntactic positions, we can describe it as consisting, first of all, of subject and predicate. The subject position, in English, is filled by a noun or pronoun, or equivalent phrase; the predicate position, by a verb or its equivalent. We then, in this approach, proceed to the lower level of phrase-structure, describing the successive expansions involved in the phrases as further attributive elements are added. The approach through morphologic constituents is the more basic of the two, as it is essential to the recognition of the elements which compose syntactic structures, and to their description in purely synchronic terms; that through syntactic positions underlies generative transformation grammar (Chap. 38).

There are a number of special terms for referring to features of syntactic structure. In accordance with the use of *-eme* and *allo-* expounded on pp. 24–26, if we take the element *tax-* to mean "syntactic combination", we might use *taxeme* "significant unit of syntactic combination", and *allotax* for "positional variant of a taxeme." Thus, in French, there is a significant combination of a verb plus one or two pro-complements (pp. 166–167) in what has been termed a *verbal core;* this combination, regardless of the order in which the elements occur, constitutes a taxeme. However, the position of the pro-complement(s) with respect to the verb differs according to the inflectional form of the latter. If the verb is a positive imperative, the pro-complement(s) follow, as in /rəgardəmwa/ *regarde-moi!* "Look at me!"; /alõzi/ *allons-y!* "Let's go to it!"; /donemã/ *donnez-m'en!* "Give me some!". However, if the verb is in any other form, the pro-complement(s) precede it:* /nəmadonepa/ *ne m'en donnez pas!* "Don't give me any!"; /nunvuzãdonrõpa/ *nous ne vous en donnerons pas* "We won't give you any"; /dəvuzãdone/ *de vous en donner* "of giving you some". We can, therefore, formulate the relationship between these French constructions as follows:

---

* In conventional spelling, the pro-complements are written as separate "words" if they precede the verb, but are joined to it by hyphens if they follow—another instance of the inconsistency and misrepresentation with which our traditional orthographies are rife.

TAXEME	ALLOTAXES	CONDITIONS OF OCCURRENCE AND EXAMPLES
verbal core = verb with one or two pro-complements (preceding or following the verb)	verb + pro-complement(s)	With verb in positive imperative: /donemã/ *donnez-m'en!*
	pro-complement(s) + verb	With verb in any other form: /nuvuzãdonrõ/ *nous vous en donnerons*

The terms *taxeme* and *allotax* are not widely used at present. Leonard Bloomfield, in his book *Language*, used *taxeme* in a rather different sense, that of "grammatical features by which immediate constituent forms are arranged"; but this use of the term has not been widely accepted, perhaps because its reference was too broad for convenience. "Allotax" has not been used widely, and is a new coinage for the specific meaning of "positionally determined variant of a taxeme (in the narrower sense we have given this latter term)." One reason for the neglect of this particular terminological problem is that our modern linguistic terminology has been developed chiefly in connection with English structure, and English has a great many taxemes with completely fixed orders and relatively few with variable order conditioned by predictable factors such as the form of the verb in the French verbal core discussed in the preceding paragraph. Instead of *taxeme*, many European analysts use the Greek term *syntagma* "something which is put together" (plural *syntagmata* or *syntagmas*), and for *allotax*, in the European tradition, one would simply say "syntactic variant."

In languages like English, with many taxemes involving completely fixed order, it is possible to distinguish not only units of combination, but units of syntactic position, i.e., of the place in a construction which elements can occupy with respect to each other. These significant positions are often compared to "slots" into which markers or cards are placed, as on a cribbage board. Thus, in *The trains aren't running on time*, there is a "subject slot" (occupied by the noun phrase *the trains*) and a "predicate slot" (occupied by the verb phrase *aren't running on time*). In *the trains*, the "determiner slot" is occupied by the definite article *the*, and the "head slot" by the noun *trains;* etc. Instead of the rather homely term *slot*, more learnèd terms have been proposed, of which *tagmeme* (used in a quite different sense from that in which Bloomfield used it) has been the most favored. A possible **allotagm(a)*, which might refer to a variant of a tagmeme, has not, to the best of my knowledge, been coined, probably because, by definition, a tagmeme is a fixed feature of relative position and hence is not subject to variation.

Syntactic analysis, whether in terms of taxemes (syntagmata) or of tagmemes, involves the abstraction of relative positions of forms, and their statement in terms of the elements which make them up or can be used in the particular "slots." In making such statements, we normally write the names of phrase- and clause-types, of form classes, or of "slots" in small capitals: e.g.

NOUN PHRASE = DETERMINER + ADJECTIVE + NOUN; MAJOR CLAUSE = SUBJECT + PREDICATE; etc. To save space, abbreviations are often used, e.g. S for SUBJECT, P for PREDICATE, etc., and quasi-algebraic symbols such as → and ← frequently take the place of such locutions as "is replaced by," "replacing," etc. It is also convenient to have special symbols to indicate forms which are bound on the phrasal or clausal level; I have found it convenient to use /ˌ/ before or after the transcription of phrasally bound forms, such as English /ðəˌ/ *the* or /ˌz ˌs ˌəz/ -'s (possessive suffix), and /‿/ before or after clausally bound forms like English /(ð)ət‿/ *that* (conjunction) or Italian /benkéˣ‿/ *benché* "although." The use of such abbreviations and special symbols permits the attainment, on occasion, of extreme compression, according to the stylistic preferences of the individual analyst. Some strive for concision at all costs, whereas others prefer to remain closer to everyday expository style even though it may demand more space and verbiage.

The advantage of modern methods of syntactic analysis lies in the establishment of structural units. Our traditional grammar analyzes syntax in terms of the "uses" to which the various "parts of speech" are put in sentences. For example, the "syntax of the noun" is customarily described in terms of its use as subject or as direct or indirect object of a verb, as object of a preposition, and so forth. Such an approach brings together many disparate types of structure: in these uses of an English noun, we have it functioning as a partner in an exocentric construction (subject of a clause, as in *the book is open*); as an attribute (direct or indirect object) in endocentric verbal constructions, e.g., *he gave his friend the tickets;* and as an axis in an exocentric phrase introduced by a preposition (*it's on the table*). Some of the same syntactic units are recognized in traditional grammar as in structural analysis, like phrases, modifiers, clauses, etc.; but traditional grammar does not do a satisfactory job of establishing units which can then be placed in relation to each other and to other levels of linguistic structure.

The term *syntax* is often extended to cover the study of semantic equivalences between constructions, both morphological and syntactical. Many studies have been made of "the syntax of such-and-such a form in such-and-such a language," such as the very competent monograph mentioned on p. 33, which was once written dealing with "The Syntax of the Imperative in Italian." But the Italian imperative itself has only three forms: e.g. *vieni:* "come (2.sg.)!", *veniamo:* "let's come", and *venite:* "come (2.pl.)!" Only a few pages at most, could be dedicated to the constructions into which the imperative itself can enter. All the rest of the monograph was devoted to an extensive treatment of synonyms for the imperative, such as the infinitive (*Tradurre il seguente brano in italiano:* "Translate the following passage into Italian"), the "future" (*Non farete nessun rumore:* "You will make no noise"), and combinations of various modal verbs with an infinitive (*dovete tacere:* "you are to be silent"; *volete tacere?:* "*Will* you shut up?"; *vogliate gradire questa tazza di caffè:* "Please be so kind as to accept this cup of coffee"; etc.), with their various social and emotional overtones. As a study of semantic connotations, this monograph was excellent, but it was badly misnamed, and should have been called something like "The Synonyms of the Imperative in Italian."

But if we have a technique for establishing units of syntactic construction, we can compare their relationships to one another within the same language, e.g., in stating which constructions can or cannot occur together or be included in larger constructions. We can contrast the syntactic units of different languages, as when we set the French verbal core over against its semantic equivalents in English (e.g., /ilmãnãvwa/ *il m'en envoie* "he sends me some") and point out the differences for the benefit of speakers of the one language who are learning the other. One of the greatest uses of taxemic analysis is in historical linguistics, where up to now we have had no adequate framework for tracing the development of syntactic structures over the course of time. By identifying specific phrase- and clause-types, we can follow their changes, as when a Latin combination of DEMONSTRATIVE (either *ipse*: "the same" or *ille*: "that") + NOUN (in either order) become either DEFINITE ARTICLE + NOUN in most Romance languages, or NOUN + DEFINITE ARTICLE, as in Roumanian. One of the major tasks of historical linguistics, and one which still awaits an extensive development, is the rewriting of historical syntax in taxemic terms (cf. Chaps. 56–58).

NOTES

General principles of syntactic analysis: Elson and Pickett, 1960; Nida, 1951d; Pickett, 1956.

Analysis of strings of elements: Harris, 1962; Longacre, 1960.

Syntax of English: Fries, 1952; Hill, 1958.

Taxeme and tagmeme: Bloomfield, 1933a, Chap. 10; Pike, 1958.

Verbal core: Hall, 1948d; Valdman, 1961.

Relation between syntax and semantics: Bar-Hillel, 1954; Garvin, 1954.

Development of Latin ille *and* ipse *to definite articles:* Trager, 1932.

32

Open and Closed Constructions

IN ANY GIVEN LANGUAGE, there are only relatively few types of syntactic structure, and these can be varied in many different ways by the substitution of one element for another or by the addition of new ones. This fact is what enables us, when speaking, to improvise virtually at will, within the framework of our syntactic habits. In extreme cases, we can even begin a sentence without any clear idea of how we are going to end it—and nevertheless come to a wholly clear, consistent termination. When we are writing, the process is even more obvious: as we write, we go back, cancel some words, substitute or add further words or phrases or dependent clauses, to obtain more satisfactory results. If this possibility of substitution and variation of our syntactic structures did not exist, every separate utterance would constitute an individual type of structure unto itself, and each language would have a myriad of independent, unrelated combinations. Such a situation would greatly restrict the learning and use of language. (Apparently, the communication systems of almost all nonhuman beings are of this latter type, without "interchangeable parts" and hence are limited to nonproductive structures, each consisting of a single morpheme.)

If a construction is susceptible of development by the substitution or addition of further elements, it is called *open*—if not, it is *closed*. This distinction applies even to minimum free forms. Thus, *ouch!*, *hey!*, and other interjections are closed from the outset, which is why they are to be set aside as a special clausal type (Chap. 36). On the other hand, the members of other English form-classes can be expanded, as when, say, *chairs* is preceded by an adjective like *wooden*, a numeral like *five*, or the definite article *the*. Likewise, an English imperative sentence like *Run!* can be optionally expanded by the addition of *you, you all*, or the likes: *You run!* or *You all run!*.

As in morphology, the principle of layering (pp. 168–172) is of fundamental importance in determining relationships. Any construction is to be regarded as being developed by the substitution or addition of further elements, not in equal order of importance or in meaningless sequence, but in a particular succession. Thus, we will regard such a phrase as *more brightly lit* as consisting of *lit* with an added element *brightly*, and this latter as having then been expanded to *more brightly*. Similarly, (*he*) *often works very hard indeed* will be treated as consisting of *works*, expanded by *hard* (which in its turn is replaced by *very hard* and this by *very hard indeed*) and the entire resultant phrase

196

then preceded by *often*. From the static point of view, we are following the principle of immediate constituents (Chap. 27); if we adopt the fiction of a necessary temporal sequence in the development of a construction, we are following the basic principle of transformation grammar (Chap. 38).

We must also take into account the direction in which a construction is open, i.e., whether further elements can be added before or after what is already present. If an element is added before what it modifies, we may speak of *anticipatory expansion*; if it comes after what it modifies, the process will be termed *sequential expansion*. This principle is often useful in deciding the nature of such form-classes as are determined (wholly or in part) by syntactic characteristics. Thus, in Neo-Melanesian, the forms to which we assigned the label "Class A" or "adjectives" (cf. pp. 145–147), such as /gudfɛlə/ "good", /nufɛlə/ "new", /trifɛlə/ "three", all precede the noun they modify: /gudfɛlə kajkaj/ "good food", /nufɛlə motokar/ "a new auto-mobile", etc. A noun is open to anticipatory expansion only if the added element belongs to the class of adjectives. We include such a form as /rəbɪš/ "without standing in the community" (p. 147) in this class because it is mutually substitutable, in this position, with adjectives which are morpho-logically marked by the suffix /-fɛlə/: /gudfɛlə mæn/ "a good man", /rəbɪš mæn/ "a man without standing in the community".

There are, however, other forms in Neo-Melanesian which we might, on the basis of their form and function in English, be tempted to assign to the adjective class: e.g., /tru/ "true", /nogud/ "bad, evil". But these Neo-Melanesian forms, even if they are monosyllabic, never take the adjectival suffix /-fɛlə/: we never find such a form as */trufɛlə/. Furthermore, they cannot take part in an anticipatory expansion of a noun, but only (like all other nonadjectival modifiers) in a sequential expansion: e.g., /frɛn tru/ "a true friend", /mæn nogud/ "an evil man". Forms of Class A never occur in adverbial constructions when provided with the suffix /-fɛlə/, but only when they are in their bare stem-form, as in /mekɪm gud/ "do it well". However, unlike forms of Class A, /tru/, /nogud/ etc. occur in adverbial constructions, modifying not only verbs, but also adjectives and adverbs, as in expressions like /tɔk tru/ "(to) speak truly"; /fajtɪm nogud/ "(to) beat (someone) up badly". Hence it is best, not to set up /tru/, /nogud/ and similar forms as a separate class of "adjectives," but to classify them with the adverbs. This decision is confirmed when we find, say, /nogud/ acting as a sentence-intro-ducing element, in such a sentence as /nogud ju mekɪm ɔlsem/ "don't act that way, lit. with undesirable results will you do it thus". (By a curious coincidence, this use of Neo-Melanesian /nogud/ is exactly parallel to that of the Old French adverb *mar:* "with sad results", in a negative command like *mar lo fereiz:* "don't do it, lit. with sad results will you do it"; but of course we do not allow the Old French situation to influence our decision in analyz-ing the Neo-Melanesian form and its use.)

If elements can be substituted for each other in a given syntactic position, they may be said to belong to the same *substitution-class* or *order-class*. Thus, in English, a construction can be closed to further anticipatory expansion (except with *all*) by the use of either the definite article *the*; the indefinite article *a, an*; the demonstratives *this, that* or the indefinites *some* or *any* when stressed (*there were some five hundred people in the room; I didn't see any five hundred people*); or the possessives *my, his, her*, etc. These various forms can be substituted for each other in this position, and hence belong to the same order-class, to which we give the name "determiner." The concept of order-class is most useful for languages with extensively fixed patterns of word-order like English and, to a lesser extent, the modern continental European languages. It is considerably less useful for a language like Latin, with relatively free word order; where the same construction can have many free order-variants which differ only in connotation: e.g., *hīs in rēbus:* "in these things" $\sim$ *in hīs rēbus:* "in these *things*" $\sim$ *rēbus in hīs:* "in *these* things".

By comparing the uses of apparently similar elements in parallel positions in different languages, we can often isolate subtle differences in the meaning of order-classes. In English, the possessives and the articles are mutually exclusive, and *my book* means "the book which belongs to me". If we wish to refer to "a book belonging to me", without a specific one being implied, we have to say *a book of mine*. In Italian, however, the possessives and the articles are not mutually exclusive. The normal possessive construction, equivalent in meaning to English *my book*, is DEFINITE ARTICLE + POSSESSIVE + NOUN: e.g., *il mio libro:* "my book", *la tua cravatta:* "your tie", *i nostri affanni* "our troubles". However, Italian possessive noun-phrases can also occur with numerals and indefinites instead of the definite article (e.g. *un mio libro:* "a book of mine", *alcune tue cravatte:* "some ties of yours"), or without any article or other element preceding the possessive. In the case of certain kinship terms (only when they are in the singular, unmodified, and not containing deriva- tional suffixes), the zeroing-out of the definite article is automatic and mean- ingless, as in *mia moglie:* "my wife", *tua zia:* "your aunt". Elsewhere, however, it is meaningful, since such a possessive phrase without definite article refers simply to unspecified objects: *tue notizie:* "news of you", as in *non abbiamo avuto tue notizie:* "we haven't had any news of you"; *la radice indoeuropea* g^wm- *e suoi derivati:* "the Indo-European root *g*ʷ*m-* and (some of) its derivatives" (if the author of the article had meant simply "its derivatives" as a whole, he would have said *i suoi derivati*, with the definite article). Hence we conclude that, in contrast to the English possessives, those of Italian mean simply "of—", e.g., *mio:* "of mine", *tuo:* "of yours", etc.; and that this semantic dif- ference is what underlies the Italian use of the definite article before a posses- sive phrase to indicate a specific object or person, as in *il suo àbito*, literally "the suit of his = his suit".

The details of expansion of open constructions differ markedly from one language to another, and order-classes are (as we have just seen) also different. In some languages, like German, anticipatory expansions may contain ele- ments which in other languages, like English or the Romance family, come only after what they modify, and vice-versa. Hence the difficulty which speakers of, say, English have in learning certain German patterns like those in which verbal complements precede participles used in adjectival function, as in *viele diesem Zweck dienende Einrichtungen:* "many this purpose serving arrangements = many arrangements which serve this purpose", or *diese auf den mündlichen Gebrauch beschränkten, aus den Schulen verbannten Idiome:* "these to the oral use limited, out of the schools banned languages". This type of anticipatory expansion is especially frequent in German verbal phrases consisting of AUXILIARY + PAST PARTICIPLE, in which all types of verbal complements precede the participle. Thus, in *sie müssen deshalb von Zeit zu Zeit mit einem Lappen, der gegebenenfalls mit Petroleum getränkt ist, gut abgerieben werden:* "they must therefore be rubbed off well from time to time with a cloth which has, if necessary, been soaked with oil", the phrase *müssen . . . abgerieben werden* "must be rubbed off" is interrupted by all the intervening complements of the participle *abgerieben:* "rubbed off". The same sentence contains an instance of a similar anticipatory expansion of a verb in a dependent clause, with *der . . . ist:* "which . . . is" interrupted by the predicate adjective (past participle) *getränkt:* "soaked", which is in its turn preceded by its complements *gegebenenfalls:* "if necessary" and *mit Petroleum:* "with oil".

On the other hand, certain elements (so-called "separable prefixes") that are prefixed to the infinitive and participles of German verbs (e.g. *angehen:* "to concern, lit. to go on") are placed, when the verb is inflected for person and number, at the end of the sentence: *die mancherlei übrigen Bedeutungsinhalte des Wortes "Sprache" gehen uns in dieser Abhandlung nichts an:* "the various other semantic contents of the word 'language' do not concern us in this treatise (lit. go us in this treatise nothing on)". These and similar differences in syntactic order between German and English have furnished extensive material for many humorists, especially Mark Twain in his essay "The Awful German Language" (in *A Tramp Abroad*) and his remarks about the propensity of "Sandy" (the heroine of *A Connecticut Yankee at King Arthur's Court*) to long-winded sentences.

In the Chinese-box-like structure of any phrase or clause of even moderate length, various types of constructions may be included. Such a sentence as *None of us believe all that nonsense that he's trying to peddle* consists, first of all, of an exocentric construction (SUBJECT *none of us* + PREDICATE *believe . . .*). The subject is an endocentric pronoun-phrase consisting of INDEFINITE PRONOUN (*none*) + EXOCENTRIC RELATION-AXIS PHRASE (= PREPOSITION *of* + PRONOUN OBJECT *us*). The predicate is an endocentric verbal phrase, containing VERB (*believe*) + DIRECT OBJECT, the latter being an endocentric noun-phrase made up of ATTRIBUTES *all* and *that* + HEAD *nonsense* + ATTRIBUTE, a relative clause. This relative clause is in its turn an exocentric construction, with SUBJECT *he* + PREDICATE *that . . . 's trying to peddle*, and this latter is an endocentric verb-phrase with anticipated direct object (the relative pronoun *that*). The flexibility of our syntactic structure derives largely from the possibility of almost any type of construction being included, in one way or another, in almost any other type.

NOTES

Neo-Melanesian phrases: Hall, 1943, Chap. 4.

33

Morphological Linkages in Syntax

ON THE BASIS of English alone, we might be tempted to think that syntactical relationships between forms were indicated primarily by tagmemic devices of relative position. The morphological indications of syntactical linkage in English are quite few; they are restricted to the combination SUBJECT + PREDICATE VERB, and even there, in all verbs except *be*, to the third person singular of the present: *I, we, you, they eat,* but *he eats.* Only in *be* do we have a difference between singular and plural in the past (*was, were*) and between first and third person in the singular of the present (*am, is*). In other languages, however, syntactical linkage is indicated much more extensively by morphological features of various kinds. If two or more syntactically linked forms are required to have some morphological characteristic in common, or if the presence of one form requires the other form to have a particular morphological feature, the forms are said to *agree*, and the phenomenon is called *agreement*. There are three main sub-types of agreement: *concord, government* and *cross-reference*.

In concord (also called *congruence*), there is a requirement that the forms which agree must be of the same subdivision of the form-classes to which they belong. This requirement may apply, in any given instance, to one or more of the categories of inflection (Chap. 25) of the particular language. The most familiar instance of concord is perhaps the requirement that, in Latin, an adjective modifying a noun must agree with the latter in gender, number, and case: *bonus homō:* "(a) good man", masculine singular nominative; *omnium deārum:* "of all goddesses", feminine plural genitive; *oppida italica:* "Italian towns", neuter plural nominative or accusative. Other attributes in Latin do not agree morphologically with their heads, but a subject and the verb of its predicate must agree in person and number, and an adjective in the predicate referring back to the subject must tell its number, gender and case. Agreement of subject and predicate are shown in *tu abūtēris:* "you (2.sg.) will abuse"; *absit ōmen* "may an evil omen be absent" (3.sg.); *exeunt omnēs:* "all go out" (3.pl.). Subject and predicate adjective agree in such sentences as *haec omnia mala sunt:* "all these things are evil", with *mala:* "evil" in the neuter plural nominative to correspond with *haec omnia:* "all these things".

In some types of agreement there is a further requirement that specific inflectional sub-classes be used according to the nature of the determiner, as in German phrases containing ARTICLE + ADJECTIVE + NOUN. Here, if the characteristic gender-number-case ending is present in the determiner, the following inflected adjectival forms take a special set of "weak" endings in which the categories of inflection are not so clearly marked. Thus, in *der gute Mann:* "the good man", the definite article has the nominative masculine singular ending *-er* and the adjective has the "weak" ending *-e*; in *das schöne Haus:* "the beautiful house", the definite article has the nominative or accusative neuter singular ending *-es*, and the adjective is again "weak." But the corresponding form of the indefinite article, *ein* (masculine nominative and neuter nom.-acc. singular) has no distinctive case-ending and hence in constructions like *ein guter Mann:* "a good man" or *ein schönes Haus:* "a beautiful house", the distinctive ending passes to the adjective, which is then said to have a "strong" ending.

Government involves the use of a particular case-form, which fits the element to which it is attached to enter into a construction with some other form. Usually, but not always, the constructions involved are verbal. In the Indo-European languages, for instance, a noun or pronoun form indicating the goal of the action is usually in the accusative case, and the verb is said to *govern* the accusative, as in Latin *Caesarem* (acc.) *vīdī:* "I saw Caesar". A few Latin verbs, however, govern other cases than the accusative. Five govern the ablative, e.g., *ūtī:* "to use" and its derivatives such as *abūtī* "to abuse", as in the famous initial sentence of Cicero's First Oration against Catiline: *Quō ūsque tandem, Catilīna, abūtēris patientiā nostrā* (abl.)*?:* "How far, after all, o Catiline, are you going to abuse our patience?" Other Latin verbs govern the genitive (as does *meminisse:* "to remember") or the dative (as does *nocēre:* "to harm"): e.g., *amīcōrum meōrum* (gen.) *meminī:* "I remember, am mindful of my friends"; *reī pūblicae* (dat.) *nocet:* "he harms the state". On occasion, adjectives (usually derived from verbs) also govern one case or another in their attributes, as in Lat. *reī pūblicae* (dat.) *infesta:* "harmful to the state"; from this peculiarity such adjectives are said to "have verbal force."

In English, the category of case remains, and hence government can be said to exist, only with regard to the personal and relative interrogative pronouns, with *I—me; he—him; she—her; we—us; they—them;* and (in conservative usage) *who—whom.* Since there is no morphological distinction in English between the goal of the action (direct object) and the beneficiary of the action (indirect object), grammarians often prefer to speak of *me—him*, etc., as manifesting the *objective* case: *he hit me* (direct object), *he wrote me* (indirect object) *a letter.* A similar two-case contrast existed in Old French and Old Provençal (Old South French), but throughout the substantive and pronoun system; for these languages, the non-nominative case is usually called the *oblique*, in that it filled all the functions not reserved to the nominative (which was in mediaeval grammar called the *cāsus rectus* or "upright case"). Thus, the same Old French form, /ré^i/ *rei* "king", would have been used to indicate direct object, indirect object and possessor, as in /limesáǧəs vé^it ləré^i/ *li messages veit le rei* "the ambassador sees the king"; /ləbriéf áðləré^idonǽð/ *le brief at le rei donét* "he has given the letter to the king"; /lakó^rtləré^i/ *la cort le rei* "the court of the king".

In subject-plus-predicate constructions, it is often required that the subject be in a particular case. In Indo-European languages, this is usually the same case as that used to name something or somebody in answer to a question (e.g., Latin *Quid est hoc?—Mēnsa* [nom.]: "What is this?"—"A table") and which is therefore called the *nominative* or "naming" case. In German, Old French, Latin, Greek, Sanskrit, etc., all nouns and adjectives, as well as pronouns, are in the nominative when acting as subjects or as predicate complements: e.g., German, *Der Zug* (nom.) *fährt ein:* "the train comes in"; Old French /čárləsliréis . . . sétánctócpléins áðestǽðenespáŋə/ *Charles li reis . . . set anz toz pleins at estet en Espagne* "Charles the king . . . full seven years has been in Spain"; Latin *faber est quisque suae fortunae:* "every man is the maker of his own fortune". Grammarians usually speak of the noun as "governing" the verb in the subject-predicate relationship. However, it would perhaps be better to say that the verb "governs" the subject and the predicate complement (no matter what the position of these latter), since in many languages the predicate can stand alone, and any subject or predicate complement is a simple amplification of and subordinate to the verb (cf. Chap. 36).

As already mentioned, case-forms occur also in nonverbal constructions. The best-known of such constructions is the possessive, in which, in the Indo-European languages, the noun indicating the possessor stands in the genitive case: e.g., German *ein Teil der Lokomotive* (gen.): "a part of the locomotive", or Latin *imperātōris* (gen.) *auctōritās:* "the personal prestige of the emperor". In some German dialects, the noun indicating the possessor is in the dative, not the genitive: *dem Schaffner sein Hut:* "the conductor's hat, lit. to-the conductor his hat"; this same use of the dative is found also in Hungarian, as in *Jánosnak kabátja:* "John's overcoat (lit., to-John overcoat-his)".

In cross-reference, a specific anticipation or repetition of one element of a construction is provided by another element. It is exemplified in the possessive elements with pronominal reference in the dialectal German and the Hungarian sentences just quoted (Ger., *sein:* "his", with cross-reference to *Schaffner:* "conductor"; the Hungarian possessive suffix *-ja:* "his", with cross reference to *János:* "John"). In French interrogative sentences with noun subjects, if one does not form the sentence merely by prefixing /eskə/ *est-ce que . . . ?* "is it that . . . ?" to the declarative sentence, the noun subject stays in its original position, but one must introduce after the verb a further subject-pronoun which refers back to the noun subject and agrees with it in person, number and gender: e.g., /ʃarlətravajtil?/ *Charles travaille-t-il?* "Is Charles working (lit. Charles works he)?" Many analysts consider that the agreement between subject and predicate discussed in the second preceding paragraph involves cross-reference, because they treat the person-and-number endings of verbs (e.g., Spanish *trabajo:* "I work", *trabajan:* "they work") as containing a pronominal reference with anaphora to a subject (expressed or implied). However, if we consider the verb as governing the subject rather than vice-versa, and this latter as being a subordinate adjunct to the verb, we can treat verbal endings as simply indicating gender and number of the actor and hence as not necessarily having pronominal reference at all. (We are, of course, distinguishing sharply between "actor" and "subject"; cf. Chap. 36.)

In a language like Latin, which makes extensive use of concord, government, and (if we consider it as being involved in the subject-predicate relation) cross-reference, the extensive interplay of these morphological linkages permits of very complicated syntactical relationships. Even a relatively simple

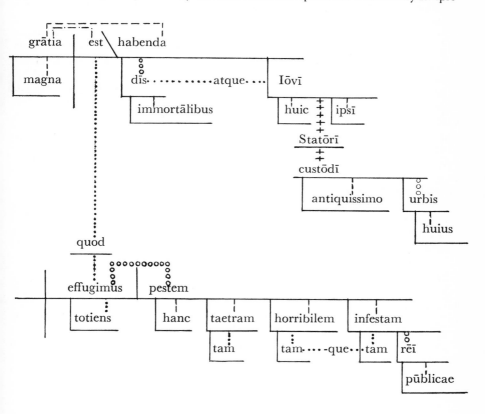

Linkages:

· · · · · · · ·   By syntactical relation alone
– – – – – –   By agreement
+ + + + +   By apposition (including agreement)
ooooooooooo   By government
— · — · — ·   By cross-reference

Fig. 18: Structure of a Ciceronian Sentence.

sentence can manifest a highly developed structure, as in the following (by no means exceptional) one from Cicero's First Oration against Catiline (sec. 10): *Magna dīs immortālibus habenda est atque huic ipsī Iōvī Statōrī, antīquissimō custōdī hūius urbis, grātia, quod hanc tam taetram, tam horribilem, tamque infestam rēī publicae pestem tōtiēns iam effūgimus:* "Great thanks must be given to the immortal gods and to this very Jove the Founder [in whose temple Cicero was speaking], the most ancient guardian of this city, because we have already escaped [at least] to this extent a plague so dire, so fearful, and so harmful to the body politic".

In Fig. 18, we diagram the Latin sentence in the traditional scholastic fashion, and indicate by various types of lines the different kinds of morphologic linkages which hold the sentence together. Note that only the adverbs *tam:* "so" and *totiēns:* "to this extent", and the conjunctions *atque:* "and", *-que:* "and" and *quod:* "because" are left out of the morphologically indicated relations; and they are the only elements whose position is relatively fixed. This widespread morphological linkage frees Latin word-order for the task of indicating emphasis, which in English has to be taken care of by suprasegmental features of stress and intonation. In Latin, the position of greatest emphasis in a phrase or clause was at the end; of next greatest emphasis, at the beginning; and of least emphasis, in the middle. Any English translation therefore inevitably loses the effect of Cicero's Latin style, which, by piling up unresolved problems of congruence, government and cross-reference and then solving them just at the end of a phrase or clause, hammers home his points with a force that cannot be reproduced in a language with fixed word-order like English.

NOTES

Morphological linkage: Hockett, 1958, Chap. 25.

34

Universal Combination-Types and Endocentric Phrases

BEFORE PASSING to the structure of phrases, we must examine certain types of combinations by which forms of any kind (minimum or expanded) can be grouped together. Since, in these combinations, each item normally has the same function, the items contained are said to be *coördinate*, and the elements (if any) which connected them are called *coördinators* (a slightly better term than the traditional expression *coördinating conjunctions*). Coördinate constructions can occur with single free forms, phrases, or clauses (in some instances, even with bound forms, as in *pre- and post-war*), and hence we may term them *universal combination-types*. Coördinators normally occur in specific positions in these combinations, of which there are often three, four, or more sub-types in a given language, according to the positions of the coördinator(s). In English, we have four main universal combination-types:

1. With the same coördinator (e.g., *and, or*) preceding every item but the first: *John or James or Mary or Evelyn; he eats and drinks and smokes; we eat and you drink and they are merry*.
2. With a coördinator only before the last element: *John, James, Mary, or Evelyn; he eats, drinks, and smokes; we eat, you drink, and they are merry*.
3. With no coördinator (zero-coördinator, in contrast to the two preceding types): *men, women, children, babies, all were howling their heads off at once*. In English, such combinations normally occur only with a string of several items; in other languages, they may occur with as few as two, e.g., Neo-Melanesian /mæn meri/ "men and women", /papa mama/ "father and mother", or Italian /dúetré^óre/ *due-tre ore* "two or three hours".
4. With two different coördinators (e.g., *both . . . and*, *either . . . or*), of which the first precedes the first item and the second occurs according to either pattern 1 or pattern 2: *either John or James or Mary or Evelyn; he neither eats, drinks nor smokes on fast-days*.

Other languages have somewhat different types of coördinators, often occurring in different positions. Latin and the Romance languages, for instance, have a universal combination type in which the same coördinator precedes each item in the construction, including the first: e.g., Latin *aut vivere aut morī:* "either to live or to die"; Spanish *ni éste ni aquél:* "neither this one nor that one". In our familiar modern languages, the coördinator is placed before (is *proclitic* to) the item it is related to, but in others it may be placed after (be *enclitic* to) the first element of the item, as with Latin *-que:* "and", in *Senātus Populusque Romānus:* "the senate and the people of Rome", or (in the sentence analyzed in Chap. 33) *tam taetram, tam horribilem, tamque rēī publicae infestam pestem:* "a plague so dire, so frightful, and so harmful to the body politic".

In approaching syntax "from below," we are first concerned with distinguishing the various types of nonmaximal constructions, or phrases. In analyzing the structure of phrases, the linguist's task is to determine and state their constituent elements and the relationships (obligatory or optional) among these latter with regard to tagmemic requirements of relative position and with regard to morphological linkage (cf. Chap. 33). We will distinguish, first of all, between endocentric and exocentric phrases; since the former are, in general, far more frequent and make up a larger proportion of the phrasal stock of a language, we will first analyze their structure and then (in Chap. 35) take up that of exocentric phrases.

Since, by definition (pp. 170–171), every endocentric construction has a head and one or more attributes, our analysis must start from the identification of the head in terms of the form-class to which it belongs. Normally, in any given language, there are endocentric phrases which take the place of each of its major form-classes, whether these latter be inflected or not. This holds true even for such parts of speech as prepositions and conjunctions. Prepositional phrases* are exemplified by English *because of, on top of, in spite of*; French /akoteˆdə/ *à côté de* "beside", /ãfazdə/ *en face de* "opposite", / ãrezõdə/ *en raison de* "on account of"; or Neo-Melanesian /wəntajm lɔŋ/ "together with", /antap lɔŋ/ "on top of, over", /ɪnsajd lɔŋ/ "inside (of)". Conjunctional phrases are represented by, say, English *inasmuch as* (really four elements, *in* + *as* + *much* + *as*), Italian *benché* "although (lit., well that)", or Neo-Melanesian /ɪnəf lɔŋ tajm/ "until (lit. sufficiently to the time [when])".

If the order of attributes in phrases is significant, this can be shown by means of one or more diagrams giving the relative position occupied by the various elements. For most languages, such a diagram and its exemplifications would be too long to list here; but Neo-Melanesian, with its reduced structure, may serve as an example. The Neo-Melanesian endocentric noun-phrase has a head, which occurs either with or without (±) one or more of the following attributes, in this order:

$$\text{adjective} \pm \underset{\text{(head)}}{\textbf{NOUN}} \pm \left[\begin{array}{c}\rightarrow\text{NOUN} \\ \\ \hookrightarrow\text{verb}\end{array}\right]\rightarrow \pm \text{adverb} \pm \begin{array}{c}\text{exocentric}\\\text{phrase}\end{array} \pm \text{predicate} \pm \text{clause}$$

Examples:

1. Adjective + Noun: /gudfɛlə mæn/ "a good man"; /dɪsfɛlə haws/ "this house"; /tufɛlə spir/ "two spears".

2. Noun + Noun, with the second noun (attribute) indicating either:

  a. A characteristic or purpose of what is referred to by the first: /ples balus/ "place for aeroplanes, i.e., air-strip"; /haws pepər/ "house characterized by paper = office".

* We are restricting our use of the term *prepositional phrase* to "endocentric phrase which fulfills the same functions as a single preposition". The term *prepositional phrase* is also widely used to mean "exocentric phrase introduced by a preposition", a use which does not agree with the terminological pattern which we follow in our discussion here.

b. A substance or thing, of which the first indicates the quantity (partitive construction): /hæf šel/ "a piece of shell".

3. Noun + Verb, with the latter indicating purpose:/haws kʊk/ "house for cooking = kitchen".

4. Noun + Adverb: /papa tru/ "really father, true father".

5. Noun + Exocentric phrase introduced by preposition: /haws bɪlɔŋ mi/ "house of me = my house".

6. Noun + Predicate, the latter being equivalent in meaning to an English relative clause introduced by a subject relative pronoun: /meri i-gat bɛl/ "a woman who has a belly = pregnant woman".

7. Noun + Clause, the latter being equivalent to an English relative clause introduced by an object relative pronoun: /tɔk dɪsfɛlə mæn i-gɪvɪm lɔŋ mi/: "what this man told me (lit., the talk [which] this man gave to me)".

If the elements which exclude each other in any given position are very numerous, or if their privileges of occurrence are very limited, the alternatives may be indicated by a "flow-chart." In the French verbal core (see below), when the sentence is not imperative, the pro-complements fall into

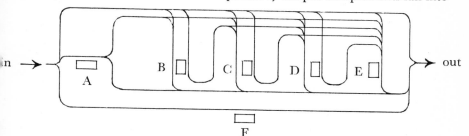

FIG. 19: Flow-Chart: Order of French Pro-Complements.

five order-classes; not more than one pro-complement from each order-class may occur in any given verbal core, and not more than two pro-complements altogether may occur. The five order-classes, with the pro-complements included in each, are as follows:

A. //m(ə)// *me* "me"; //t(ə)// *te* "thee"; //s(ə)// *se* "him-, her-, itself, themselves"; //nuᶻ// *nous* "us"; //vuᶻ// *vous* "you".

B. //l(ə)// *le* "him, it"; //l(a)// *la* "her, it"; //leᶻ// *les* "them" (direct objects only).

C. /lɥi/ *lui* "to him, to her, to it"; /lœr/ *leur* "to them".

D. /i/ *y*, pro-phrase (cf. p. 166).

E. /ãⁿ/ *en*, pro-phrase (cf. p. 166).

In addition, there is the pro-predicate-complement //l(ə)// *le*, invariable (cf. pp. 166–167), which may be regarded as a sixth order-class (F) which can occur only alone in a verbal core. Examples: /ilməvwa/ *il me voit* "he sees me"; /ilməldon/ *il me le donne* "he gives it to me"; /ilməlɥidon/ *il me lui donne* "he gives me to him"; /ilmivwa/ *il m'y voit* "he sees me there"; /ilmãdon/ *il m'en donne* "he gives me some"; /etilfatigue? wi, ille./ *Est-il fatigué? Oui, il l'est* "Is he tired? Yes, he is". Fig. 19 gives a flow-chart to show these relationships; it is to be read with the convention that one enters at the left, moves along any of the lines (with no reversing permitted), and at each of the "stations" picks up not more than one of the "passengers" waiting on the "platforms," and continues, eventually going out at the right.

Often, we must recognize more than one layer of phrasal construction within a phrase. Our familiar verbal phrases consisting of auxiliary + verbal form (past participle or *-ing*-form) afford an example: in *he was eating an orange*, the verbal phrase *was eating an orange* consists of *was eating* + the direct object noun-phrase *an orange*, with *was eating* as an inner layer of phrasal construction occupying the same position as a single verb-form (*he ate an orange*). In the Romance languages, a further inner layer is formed by the combination of verb plus one or two pro-complements (pp. 166–167), which we have termed a *verbal nucleus* or *verbal core* (cf. the French examples just given). A verbal core can take the place of a single verb-form, including an auxiliary in a "perfect" or passive phrase: e.g., French /ilparl/ *il parle* "he speaks", /ilmãparl/ *il m'en parle* "he speaks to me about it", /ilmãnaparle/ *il m'en a parlé* "he has spoken to me about it".

Traditional grammar has special terms for certain types of attributes, which we may keep as long as we redefine them carefully. Thus, an "adjectival" attribute may be understood to refer to any type of attribute which modifies a noun head, even the postnominal attributes (which are morphologically anything but adjectives) in the Neo-Melanesian noun phrase (p. 206). The term *complement*, for an attribute of any kind in a verbal phrase (e.g., direct object, indirect object, predicate noun or adjective, adverbial attribute) is also useful. On the other hand, when a term is confusing because it refers to more than one structurally distinct phenomenon, it must either be carefully limited or else discarded, e.g., the expression "adverbial modifier," which can refer in traditional grammar to adverbs modifying verbs, adjectives, and other adverbs.

All requirements of morphological linkage (agreement, government, cross-reference) must also be stated explicitly, as in the familiar rules for Latin noun modifiers ("an adjective must agree with the noun it modifies in gender, number, and case"), or for the verbs governing the ablative ("*utor, fruor, fungor, potior* and *vescor* govern an object in the ablative instead of the accusative"). Some linguistic analysts have tried to treat features of agreement (e.g., grammatical gender-classes) as if they were manifestations of separate morphemes; but such formulations are highly artificial and introduce more complications than they solve, and we will do better, in such instances, to keep to the more realistic procedure of stating linkage requirements in terms of purely phrasal structure.

NOTES

Neo-Melanesian phrase-structure: Hall, 1943, Chap. 4.
French verbal core: Hall, 1948d, §4.231.

35

Phrases—Exocentric

EXOCENTRIC PHRASES, since they do not consist of a head plus one or more attributes, are rather less unified and more scattering in the kinds of construction which appear in them, than are endocentric phrases. The most familiar type of exocentric phrase is that consisting of a form which indicates a relation (a preposition in Indo-European and some other language families, a postposition or similar element in others) together with another which indicates the direction or *axis* along which the relation lies (usually termed the *object* of the preposition or postposition). However, there are also various other types of exocentric phrase-construction.

In the relation-axis construction, the element indicating the relation may stand before, after, or even in the middle of the object or object phrase. If it always (or almost always) precedes its object, it is termed a *preposition*, as in our familiar English forms like *with*, *from*, *by*, *of*, and so forth. In some instances, a preposition may occasionally stand after instead of before its object: thus, most German prepositions regularly precede (e.g., *nach:* "after", as in *nach dem Abendessen:* "after the supper") but in certain fixed locutions *nach* follows its object (e.g., *meiner Meinung nach:* "according to my opinion"). Hungarian and other Finno-Ugric languages have *postpositions*, which follow rather than precede their objects, as in Hungarian *a ház elő'tt:* "in front of the house (lit., the house in-front-of)" or *könyv nélkül:* "without a book (lit., book without)." These Hungarian postpositions, like most of the pure-relational suffixes discussed on pp. 155–156, can take personal possessive (allocational) suffixes (e.g., *elő'ttem:* "in front of me", *nélküle:* "without him"), but they are separate words, as shown by their having independent stress. In some Latin phrases, the preposition can come in the middle between a modifier and its head, as in *hīs dē rēbus:* "concerning these things".

In most Indo-European languages, prepositions are phrasally bound forms, since the only place they occur is introducing a relation-axis phrase. In English, they are at least partly free, as shown by the fact that they can occur at the end of a sentence in certain constructions (relative and "infinitival"), e.g., *the firm I work for*; *he's a good man to work for*. English grammarians have condemned this construction (as stated mockingly in the formulation "A preposition is a bad thing to end a sentence with"), but their objections rest on the obviously false assumption that what is incorrect in Latin must *ipso facto* be incorrect in English.

The parts of speech which can be used as objects of a preposition (or postposition) vary from one language to another. In Indo-European languages, traditionally, substantives, pronouns and verbs are the only parts of speech occurring in this function, as in English *on the bed*, *for the rich*, *with me*, *by writing*. Other structures may also occur after a preposition, even in English, such as the clause object in *Forget about you haven't had your lunch yet;* a similar construction is found in Neo-Melanesian, e.g., /ples bɪlɔŋ pɪg i-stap/ "pig-pen = the place for the pig to be (lit., the place for the pig is-located)". Of this latter type is the "term of comparison" introduced by *than* in English: *he's bigger than I am*, in which *than* is a preposition and *I am* is its object.

There are often requirements of government in phrases introduced by prepositions. Frequently, these requirements are automatic and hence meaningless, as with Latin *ā* (*ab*): "from" or *dē:* "down from, concerning", which always take the ablative case: e.g., *ā Rōmā:* "from Rome"; *de vīris illustribus:* "concerning outstanding men". In other instances, the choice of governed case-form is meaningful, as with Latin *in*, after which an accusative indicates motion towards a place, whereas an ablative indicates location in a place, without motion: *in Galliam:* "into Gaul", but *in Galliā:* "in Gaul". With verbs, often a particular form of the verb is required. In Latin, a verb governed by a preposition had to be in the ablative of the gerund, as in *ā nōn lūcendō:* "from not shining". In the Romance languages, for the most part the infinitive is required after a preposition, as in Italian *senza parlare* or Spanish *sin hablar:* "without speaking", in French, after /ãⁿ/ *en* "in, during, while," the present participle in //-ãᵗ// -*ant* "-ing" is required, whereas all other prepositions take the infinitive: /ãparlã/ *en parlant* "while speaking", but /sãparleˆ/ *sans parler* "without speaking". In English, the verb is in the simple form after *to*, but in the *-ing*-form after all other prepositions: *to work*, but *while working*, *without working*.

The fact that in many (not all!) constructions the English preposition *to* plus a verb corresponds to the Latin infinitive has misled our traditional grammarians into equating the two throughout, and especially into promulgating their totally unfounded ban against the "split infinitive" (e.g., *to completely wreck the negotiations*). True, no Latin infinitive would ever be split by an intervening element; but a Latin infinitive is a minimum free form, whereas what is usually called an "infinitive" in English is actually a relation-axis phrase. This English construction may at best be termed an "infinitive phrase," and may of course be split like any other combination of preposition plus verb: *by completely wrecking the negotiations*. By now, so many emotional overtones of hostility and diffidence have been built up around the English "split infinitive" that it is probably best, stylistically, to use it sparingly and only for special emphatic effect; but its legitimacy as a normal English construction cannot be called into question.

Another taboo of English grammarians, that against the use of an objective case-form after *than*, is likewise founded on a misunderstanding, the equation of English *than* with its translation-equivalent, Latin *quam*. In Latin, *quam* was a conjunction, and in such a sentence as *melior est quam egō:* "he is better than I", *quam egō* was a transformation (with "ellipsis" or zeroing out of the verb) of *quam egō sum*: "than I am", with the subject naturally in the nominative. In English, however, as we have just seen, *than* is not a conjunction, but a preposition, and hence it is natural for it to take the objective form of a following pronoun: *he's better than me*. Such a construction is paralleled by the use of an objective form in many other languages, e.g., French /ilemejœrkəmwa/ *il est meilleur que moi*, Italian *è migliore di me*. Similarly, English *like* is a preposition, and as such can take either a single form, a phrase, or an entire clause as its object: *like me, like all of us*, or — *tastes good like a cigarette should*.

A special development in the Romance languages is the use of exocentric phrases introduced by forms reflecting Latin *dē*: "from, of" in *partitive* meaning, i.e., referring to a part but not all of whatever the noun object refers to ("some, any"). The normal construction of such phrases is PREPOSITION + DEFINITE ARTICLE + NOUN: e.g., Italian *della carne*: "some (lit. of the) meat", *degli sbagli* "some (lit. of the) mistakes". A peculiarity of French syntax is that under certain circumstances the definite article is automatically zeroed out, i.e., the preposition /də/ *de* is used alone, for instance when the phrase depends on a negative or when a plural adjective precedes the noun, as in /deˆsigaret/ *des cigarettes* "some cigarettes", but /patsigaret/ *pas de cigarettes* "no cigarettes"; /dybõtaba/ *du bon tobac* "some good tobacco", but /dəbõkrejõ/ *de bons crayons* "some good pencils". That these phrases are still exocentric, not simply normal endocentric noun-phrases, is shown by the fact that they take a special type of pro-complement as their replacement in the verbal core, the *pro-phrase* (cf. p. 166), French //ãⁿ// *en*, Italian *ne*.

Another type of exocentric phrase involves an expression of time past, such as English *six months ago*. In the Romance languages, this type of construction has grown out of a verbal phrase, which is still such in Spanish, as in *hace dos años que no lo veo:* "I haven't seen him for two years (lit., it makes two years that I don't see him)". In French and Italian, however, the verb-forms corresponding to Spanish *hace* "it makes" have become morphologically frozen, and separated syntactically from their original function, so that they now no longer determine the relationship of the construction: e.g., French /elevny iljadœˆsmen/ *elle est venue il y a deux semaines* "she came two weeks ago (lit., there is two weeks)", or the corresponding Italian sentence *è venuta due settimane fa* (lit., two weeks it-makes). That the verbal expressions have lost their morphological freedom here, is clear from the fact that, whereas in the Spanish construction one can still transform the verb into some other tense than the present, saying, for instance, *hacía dos años que no lo veía:* "it had been two years since I saw him (lit., it made two years that I wasn't seeing him)", such a transformation is not possible in the French or Italian constructions.

In Italian, there is a type of exocentric phrase, also involving verbal forms, composed of an imperative repeated two or three times, forming an adverbial phrase with durative meaning: *aspetta aspetta aspetta, vide che non compariva nessuno:* "after waiting a long time (lit., wait wait wait); he saw that no-one appeared"; *e scava scava scava, fece una buca profonda:* "and by dint of much digging (lit., dig dig dig), he made a deep hole". Here, as in the instance of the Italian verb-plus-noun exocentric compounds discussed on p. 190, it is problematical whether we have a true imperative here, or rather simply a stem-form which in almost all instances is homonymous with the imperative.

"Absolute" constructions, if they have no morphological indication of their function, or if their morphological structure does not determine their function, are likewise exocentric. The Latin "ablative absolute," in phrases like *hōc factō:* "this (having been) done = when this had been done", had an adverbial function, for which its ablative case fitted it by being an "ablative of condition." Classically-minded writers since the Renaissance have imitated this Latin construction, but necessarily without the morphological basis for its syntactical relationships, since the modern European languages have nothing corresponding to the Latin ablative and hence nothing comparable to the "ablative of condition." Hence we must class as exocentric such phrases as English *this done* or *this having been done*, or the corresponding phrases in French, /səsife/ *ceci fait*, Italian *ciò fatto* or *fatto ciò*, or Spanish *hecho esto*.

The English possessive, whose nature is so widely misunderstood, belongs here. Under the influence both of Latinizing grammar and of the earlier situation in English, grammarians have insisted on treating the English possessive suffix as inflectionally bound, and hence on presenting the English noun as if it had four inflectional forms:

	SINGULAR	PLURAL
Nonpossessive	ox	oxen
Possessive	ox's	oxen's

However, we have seen (p. 132) that the possessive suffix /-əz -z -s/ -'s can be added not only to single nouns, but also to noun-phrases, such as *the Lord Mayor of London's show, the girl I was telling you about yesterday's father.* It also occurs with pronominal phrases, such as *somebody else's.* Although purists used to (and some still do) object to such constructions, they are completely normal and natural in present-day English, and much less awkward than the pseudo-correct expressions which the purists recommend (such as *somebody's else*).

The clue to the problem is found in the fact that the possessive suffix is phrasally bound. By means of this suffix, a noun, pronoun, or equivalent phrase is transformed into a construction which acts as an attribute to another noun. Such a construction is exocentric, in that it is not inflectional and its function (of possessive attribute) is determined, not by any element in itself, but by something outside of itself, namely the suffix. The English possessive construction is quite parallel to the construction PREPOSITION + NOUN OBJECT, except that the phrasally bound form involved is not a preposition which precedes the noun or noun-phrase, but a suffix which follows it.

36

Clauses—Independent

THE MAXIMAL UNIT of utterance—i.e., the unit into which we can subdivide utterances taken as wholes—is the *clause*. Each clause is carried by a particular intonation-contour; however, since there is no direct correlation between the type of contour and the grammatic structure of the clause (cf. Chap. 19), we can "peel out" the intonational features and analyze the clause independently. Often, the structure of clauses differs according to whether they are not included in any further construction (are *independent*) or are included in a larger construction (are *dependent*). The latter are usually describable in terms of transformations of the former, as will be seen in Chap. 37.

Traditional grammar restricts the term "clause" or "sentence" to an utterance "which expresses a complete thought," as defined by its containing a subject and a predicate. However, a moment's thought will show that a "complete thought" can be expressed by many kinds of utterances that do not have subject and predicate, and which can in fact consist of as little as one word. No thought could be more "complete" than those expressed by the shouts *Fire!* or *Help!*. Many other utterances, somewhat longer but still not containing subject or predicate, are still perfectly complete in the meaning they express: *on the table, not before tonight, quite well,* etc. Rather, the traditional grammarian's definition of a "complete thought" stems from his emphasis (partly, but not wholly justified) on one particular type of clause, that consisting of subject and predicate.

In any given language, there is more than one type of clause, but certain types are more frequent or more consistent in their structure than others. In English, we have clauses that consist of SUBJECT (noun, pronoun, or equivalent phrase) + PREDICATE (verb or equivalent phrase): *John runs, the workers built the bridge, I'm tired.* We also have clauses that do not have that structure, such as *Yes. No. Why? Why not? Not at all. Where? In the garden,* etc. That type of clause whose structure, in each language, is most frequent and most consistent is known as its *favorite* clause-type or major clause. For English, the favorite clause-type is unquestionably the subject-plus-predicate structure, and the others (including those called "elliptical") are minor. In French, likewise, a major clause must have both subject and predicate: /ʒətem/ *je t'aime* "I love you", /mõfrervudremãʒeˆ/ *mon frère voudrait manger* "my brother would like to eat". Only in imperative clauses do we find English or French verbs without subjects: Eng. *eat!*, Fr. /mãʒeˆ/ *mangez!* "eat!".

In other languages, we find other types of major clauses. In many, a predicate alone suffices as basic element, without any subject being present; this is the case in the earlier stages of the Indo-European and of the Romance languages, and is still so in conservative varieties of Romance such as Italian, Spanish, Roumanian, or Sardinian: e.g., Latin *currō:* "I run", *canit:* "he sings", *dormīmus:* "we sleep", and the corresponding forms in Italian: *corro, canta, dormiamo;* or in Spanish: *corro, canta, dormimos.* Traditional grammars would say in this connection that the Latin, Italian, Spanish, etc., verbs have subjects which are "implicit" but unexpressed—a contradiction in terms, since if something is unexpressed in a linguistic utterance, it simply is not there. Such verbs as Latin *ninguit,* Italian *névica* and Spanish *nieva:* "it snows", or Latin *tonat,* Italian *tuona,* Spanish *truena:* "it thunders", cannot have subjects, and hence we must conclude that, for these and similar languages, the essential part of the major clause is the predicate alone. If a subject occurs with a Latin, Italian, or Spanish verb, it is only by way of furnishing a more detailed explanation for the person-and-number reference which is already inherent in the verb-ending. A subject in these languages is, therefore, simply an anticipatory or sequential expansion (Chap. 34) of the predicate, and in these instances we should speak of the predicate "governing" the subject rather than vice versa as does traditional grammar (cf. Chap. 33).

In this connection, we must distinguish sharply between *actor* and *subject.* We shall define the *actor* as the grammatical person- and number-reference of an inflectional verb-ending: e.g., the first person singular of Latin *amō:* "I-love", the first plural of Old French *chantoms:* "we-sing", or the third person plural of Spanish *descansan* "they-rest". We shall use the term *actor* in this specialized sense even if the verb is medio-passive or passive (cf. p. 158), as in Latin *amantur:* "they are loved". What the actor-reference of an inflected verb-form of this type tells us is simply that someone or something, of the person and number specified, is doing the action referred to by the verb (or is undergoing it). The term *subject,* on the other hand, will be reserved for specific forms which amplify the actor-reference of the verb, e.g., Latin *egō amō:* "*I* love", Old French *nos chantoms:* "*we* sing", or Spanish *los trabajadores descansan:* "the workers are resting". In this way, we avoid the contradiction inherent in speaking of the inflected verb as having an "implicit subject" or as having cross-reference to an "unexpressed subject." Needless to say, this distinction between actor and subject is useful chiefly for languages whose verb-forms contain inflectional actor-reference. For such languages as those of the Algonquian or Iroquoian family, whose verb-forms also contain references to goals or beneficiaries, we shall need to make a similar distinction between goals and direct objects, beneficiaries and indirect objects. In discussing English and French, however, we can continue to speak of the subject in much the same way as before.

In Russian, Hungarian, and many other languages, there is a type of major clause whose predicate contains, not a verb, but some other kind of minimum free form or its phrasal equivalent. If the predicate contains a noun or adjective, the meaning of the clause is "identity" or "equality," and such a clause is termed *equational:* e.g., Russian /éta kníga óčeŋ xoróša/ эта книга очень хороша "this book [is] very good", or the equivalent Hungarian sentence /eza kœŋv naɟon jo:/ *ez a könyv nagyon jó*, in which the predicates are simply /óčeŋ xoróša/ and /naɟon jo:/ "very good", respectively. If the predicate contains an adverb or equivalent phrase, its meaning may be that of "location," "manner," etc., as in Russian /ón zdéṣ/ он здесь "he [is] here"; Chinese Pidgin English /púsi tébɔl tapsajd/ "the cat [is] on the table"; Neo-Melanesian /tɪŋktɪŋk bɪlɔŋ mi i-ɔlsem/ "my opinion [is] thus = this is what I think". Still other types of major-clause structure are found in other languages. In some instances, it is better even to abandon our traditional terms *subject* and *predicate*, and to use more neutral expressions like *topic* and *comment*, especially where (as in Chinese) more than one element within a clause could be called "subject."

Major clause-types frequently, but not necessarily, have special transformations for negation, interrogation, exclamation, or other variations from straightforward exposition or narration. Traditional grammars lay so much emphasis on such transformations, in order to teach them, that we often lose sight of the fact that they are not always obligatory. Not only French, Italian, and the other Romance languages, but English as well, have the possibility of a subject-plus-predicate combination being used interrogatively, with a rising intonation contour, but without any change in order: English *You're going already?*; French *Vous partez déjà?*; Italian *Se ne va già?*; Spanish *¿Ya se marcha?*. There is, indeed, often a difference in connotation from one language to another, since such a sentence in English normally indicates surprise, whereas it has no such overtone in the Romance languages. Special interrogative particles, added to otherwise unchanged sentences, indicate in many languages that a question is being asked, e.g., Latin *-ne;* Russian /-li/ -ли; Chinese /ma/. Thus, in Latin, *-ne* was suffixed to the element being queried: *venisne?:* "Are you coming (lit.; you-come-huh)?", *nōnne venis:* "Aren't you coming (lit. not-huh you-come)?"; Russian /poŋimajiţi-ļi?/ понемаете-ли? "have you understood?"; Chinese /nǐ hǎw ma/ "are you well (lit. you well, huh)?".

Interrogative and other transformations involve various types of syntactical processes. The two to which English has accustomed us most are changes in word-order, especially inversion, and the use of expanded verbal phrases with special auxiliaries. Simple inversion of subject and verb, in English, is limited to a relatively few verbs (*be, have, do* as auxiliary, and the modal auxiliaries like *can, will,* etc.): *He is working* has the interrogative transformation *Is he working?* (represented with the quasi-algebraical symbolization → *Is he working?*); *He has only three books* → *Has he only three books?*; *He doesn't want to go home* → *Doesn't he want to go home?*. With other verbs, we do not normally invert subject and verb, although such questions as *Writes he often?* are still marginally comprehensible, at least to literate speakers who know something of older stages of the language. In other languages, such as German, inversion is far more frequent, e.g., Ger. *Schreibt er oft?:* "Does he write (lit., writes he) often?'''. In French, every specifically interrogative sentence not introduced by /eskə/ *Est-ce que . . . ?* "Is it that . . . ?" must contain an inversion, to be supplied by the addition of a pronoun with cross-reference (p. 200) if only a noun subject is present in the declarative sentence: e.g., /ile^krisuvã/ *Il écrit souvent* "He writes often" → /ekritilsuvã?/ *Écrit-il souvent?* "Does he write often?"; but /ʒãe^krisuvã/ *Jean écrit souvent* "John writes often" → /ʒãe^kritilsuvã?/ *Jean écrit-il souvent?* "John writes-he often = Does John write often?''.

For verbs other than *be, have* and the auxiliaries, English has an obligatory expansion to a phrase consisting of *do* + VERB (in its simple form) and then inversion, for the negative, interrogative, and negative-interrogative transformations: *He works* → *Does he work?, He doesn't work,* and *Doesn't he work?.* In negativization, some languages make no distinction between the negative minor-clause form (cf. below) and the element used to render a clause negative. Thus, Spanish and the several varieties of Pidgin English use /no/ for both "no" and "not," as in Spanish *No, se~or, no quiero trabajar:* "No, sir, I don't want to work", or Chinese Pidgin English /nó, mísi, máj nó hǽb lúki hí/ "No, madam, I've not seen him (her, it)''. In some languages, there are special negative verbs, with complete inflection for person and number, approximately equivalent to English "I don't, he doesn't," etc.: e.g., Finnish *en:* "I don't", *et:* "thou dost not", *ei:* "he doesn't", which can occur either independently or in verbal phrases with a following main verb, as in *en tunne:* "I don't know".

At the other extreme of complexity in negation, modern French has developed a double negativizer, composed of the inherited negative particle //n(ə)// *ne* plus one of several second elements such as //pa^ᶻ// *pas* "not", //pwẽᵗ// *point* "not at all", //ʒameᶻ// *jamais* "never", /ger/ *guère* "hardly", //rjẽⁿ// *rien* "nothing," and a number of others. These pairs of negativizers are sandwiched around the verbal elements of predicates, in various positions according to the form of the verb involved and the structure of the clause. With an infinitive, the negativizers both precede: /etr unpa^ zetr/ *être ou ne pas être* "to be or not to be". With an inverted order of verb + subject, /n(ə)/ *ne* comes before the verb and the second negativizer after the subject, e.g., /ʒãnetilpa^vny?/ *Jean n'est-il pas venu?* "Hasn't John come?''. Otherwise, the two negativizers are sandwiched around the finite form of the verb or auxiliary, as in /ʒãntravajʒame/ *Jean ne travaille jamais* "John never works", or /ʒãnaʒametravaje^/ *Jean n'a jamais travaillé* "John has never worked". Apart from verbs, however, the second negativizer normally occurs alone, without //n(ə)// *ne:* /pa^ mwa/ *pas moi* "not me"; /rjẽdytu/ *rien du tout* "nothing at all". In popular speech, //n(ə)// *ne* is normally lost entirely: /ʃkõprãpa^/ *j'comprends pas* "I don't understand". In the Creoles based on French (cf. Chap. 65), /pa/ is the only negativizer, and has passed in Haitian Creole to the status of a predicatively-bound prefix: /lipatravaj/ "he doesn't work (lit. he not-work)", or /lipaisit/ "he's not here (lit. he not-here)."

Not infrequently, there are special requirements as to the number or position of negativizers, which go contrary to what our school grammars teach us about "double negatives." In the conservative Romance languages, every negative major clause must have a negative element before the verb, no matter whether there is another negative following or not, and if there is no other negative before the verb, it must be *non:* "not" or its equivalent. Thus, in Spanish, if the adverb *nunca:* "never" comes before the verb, no further negativizer is needed, as in *nunca pierde:* "he never loses"; but if *nunca* follows, then *no* is required before the verb: *no pierde nunca:* "he never loses". In Afrikaans (the language which has grown out of Dutch, spoken in South Africa), the opposite requirement holds, and the negativizer *nie:* "not" must always follow the verb, whether any other negativizer precedes or not: *moei is de naam nie:* "the name is not beautiful", but *hij het nie naam nie:* "he has no name (lit. he has no name not)".

On the borderline between major and minor clauses are certain kinds of sentences which, although not as frequent as the favorite types, nevertheless share certain basic features with them. Latin had an equational clause of the type *beātus ille:* "happy [is] he", which was not very frequent (by no means so common as it is in Russian or Hungarian), but which had subject and predicate. English has a clause-type which has survived from earlier times and is used chiefly in proverbs and aphorisms (whence its name, the *aphoristic* clause), as in *First come, first served* or *Old saint, young sinner.* What is considered a major clause in one language may be less so, even to the extent of being considered a minor clause, in another; the classification of clause types as major or minor, or as borderline cases, differs from each language to the next, and depends wholly on the frequency and consistency of the use of each type in any particular language.

Minor clauses, by their very nature, do not lend themselves to a systematic classification as do major clauses. There are two main kinds of minor clauses: those which refer back to the context (either some feature of a preceding utterance or the real-life situation) and complete it, and those which do not. The former type is termed *completive,* and the latter *exclamatory.* Completive minor clauses can be of all kinds, including any forms which can stand alone, minimum or nonminimum. They are especially frequent in easy-going give-and-take dialogue, in which they often form a numerical majority of the clauses present: *Hello! Where're you going?—To eat.—What for? It's not time yet.—How so? It's noon.—No kidding?* In this brief dialogue, there is a total of eight clauses, of which only three are major and the other five are minor. Traditional grammarians often speak slightingly of completive minor clauses, calling them "elliptical sentences" (as if something had been left out of them), and imply that they are in some way incomplete or fail to convey meaning accurately. This is not true, since a minor clause has just as definite and accurate a meaning, in its context, as a major clause.

Among exclamatory minor clauses, some are no different in their makeup from other structures, and all kinds of syntactical types may be found as exclamations: *Drat it to heck!, By gum!, You darling!, How marvelous!.* On occasion, an exclamation may have a peculiar syntactical structure, as in

Land's sakes alive! or *My gracious!*. Many such peculiarities result from the intentional deformation, for euphemism (cf. Chap. 40), of expressions with normal structure but with meaning whose regarded as blasphemous or otherwise objectionable; in these instances, the originals of the sentences just given were a blending of *(for the) Lord's sake!* with *Lord alive!*, and *My God!*. If an exclamation is used only alone, without the possibility of its being included in some larger construction, it is to be considered as belonging to a separate form-class, the *interjection* or (a more general term) *minor clause form:* e.g., English *ouch!, hello, oh!, gosh!*. Interjections shade off into nonlinguistic noisemaking habits. In some instances, sounds which are part of the phonologic stock of a language are used in unaccustomed environments, e.g., English /ʃ/ *sh!*, or Spanish and Italian /pst/ (used to attract someone's attention). Such forms as these are usually considered part of the language, but aberrant in one respect or another. But if a sound is wholly outside of the phonologic system (like the voiced bilabial trill which we make when we are cold, and usually write *B-r-r-r!*, or the voiceless bilabial trill called the "raspberry" or the "Bronx cheer," cf. p. 56), most analysts would consider it simply a nonlinguistic noise, despite its classifiability in terms of our framework of phonetic analysis.

37

Clauses—Dependent

WHEN TWO OR MORE clauses come one after the other, with a nonfinal intona-tion-contour on all but the last, they are said to be in *parataxis* ("a putting next," i.e., one to another): *You're sick + You'd better go to bed → You're sick, you'd better go to bed.* Such constructions are termed *paratactic.* Parataxis can occur both with clauses that are structurally independent of each other, as in this example, and with a sequence of clauses of which one (the *subordinate* clause) is dependent on the other (the *main* clause). If, however, the de-pendent status of a clause is marked formally by the presence of some special element (a *subordinator*) it is said to be in *hypotaxis* ("a putting under"), or to be in a *hypotactic* construction. Subordination is, in many instances, marked by nothing beyond simple parataxis or the inclusion of some subordinator. It can also be marked by various types of special grammatic processes, such as the use of particular forms (especially of verbs) reserved for subordinate clauses, or the replacement of one verb-form by another, or the choice of special word-order.

Subordination by simple parataxis is more common than our Latinizing grammars lead us to think. It is optional in English with clauses that act as complements of such verbs as *say, think,* or that modify nouns with zero relative object: *He says + He's tired → He says he's tired; The man + I saw him → The man I saw.* The fact that this construction is optional in English, and alternates with the use of dependent clauses introduced by subordinators such as *that* or *whom* (*He says that he's tired; the man whom I saw*), has led our classicizing grammarians to speak of dependent clauses in parataxis as being "elliptical" and somehow less acceptable than those with subordinators. This is of course a nonsensical conclusion, since the clauses without subordina-tors are completely normal and acceptable on all levels of usage. In other languages, this type of paratactic construction is not optional, but required, as in Neo-Melanesian /ɛm i-tɔk/ "he says" + /i-no rɛdi jɛt/ "he's not ready yet" → /ɛm i-tɔk i-no rɛdi jɛt/ "he says he's not ready yet".

Subordinators are most familiar to us from our "subordinating conjunc-tions" *that, if, because,* and the like. Some subordinators, like those just cited and their counterparts in other languages (such as Spanish *que, si* and *porque,* respectively) have only the function of tying two clauses together: e.g., *He comes + I'll wait → If he comes, I'll wait;* Spanish *Dice:* "he says" + *No se puede hacer nada:* "nothing can be done" → *Dice que no se puede hacer nada:* "he says nothing can be done". This type of subordinator constitutes a separate form-class in itself. Many subordinating elements, however, belong to one form-class or another of the language, and play a double role, that of connecting two clauses and also that of fulfilling some syntactic function in the dependent clause. Such subordinating elements are termed *relatives*, and are assigned to the appropriate form-class on the basis of their form, function or both, as relative pronouns, adjectives, adverbs, etc. Thus, *The man + He killed Liberty Valance → The man who killed Liberty Valance; Then you're ready + I'll come → When you're ready, I'll come.* The details of position and morphologic linkage differ, of course, from one language to another: for instance, to an invariable relative in one language may correspond an inflected one in the next, as in Spanish *cuyo- -a -os -as* (relative adjective) over against English *whose:* e.g., *los autores cuyas poesías hemos leido:* "the authors whose poems we have read".

In many languages, the use of a special verb-form is enough to indicate that a clause is dependent, without any subordinator being necessary. In German, what is traditionally called the "present subjunctive" has been renamed the "quotative," because in modern German it is used almost exclusively to indicate that the contents of a dependent clause have been said by someone else than the speaker or writer: *Er sagt:* "he says" + *Es ist nichts zu tun:* "There is nothing to be done" → *Er sagt, es sei nichts zu tun:* "He says there is (lit., be) nothing to be done". A similar quotative construction ("indirect discourse") in Latin involved the replacement of any inflected form of a verb by the corresponding infinitive, and the concomitant replacement of the nominative form of the subject by the accusative: *Dīcit:* "he says" + *Rōma* (nom.) *ā barbarīs capta est:* "Rome has been captured by the barbarians" → *Dīcit Rōmam* (acc.) *ā barbarīs captam esse* (infin.): "He says Rome has been captured (lit. to have been captured) by the barbarians." In Old French paratactic constructions, the simple presence of a subjunctive verb indicated that its clause was dependent on another: e.g., /nəpuét muðǽr/ *ne puet muḍer* "he can't prevent" + /dəzuéḷc nəpló^rəð/ *des ueilz ne ploreṭ* "he doesn't weep from his eyes" → /nəpuét muðǽr dəzuéiḷc nəpló^rt/ *ne puet muḍer des ueilz ne plort* "he can't keep from weeping (lit., he can't prevent he doesn't weep) from his eyes", with the subjunctive form /pló^rt/ *plort* "(that) he weep" replacing the nonsubjunctive /pló^rəð/ *ploreṭ* "he weeps".

Such indications of subordination in parataxis can be used, in some languages, throughout long stretches of discourse to indicate their status as quotations or otherwise dependent elements. Those of us who, as school-children, plowed through Caesar or Cicero will remember the passages of indirect discourse marked by sequences of infinitives in clauses printed as independent sentences:

Locūtus est prō hīs Diviciācus Haeduus: Galliae tōtīus factiōnēs esse duās: hārum alterīus principātum tenēre Haeduōs, alterīus Arvernōs. Hī cum tantopere dē potentātū inter sē multōs annōs contenderent, factum esse, utī ab Arvernīs Sequanīsque Germānī mercēde arcesserentur. Hōrum prīmō circiter mīlia XV Rhēnum transīsse; postquam agrōs et cultum et cōpiās Gallōrum hominēs ferī ac barbarī adamāssent, trāductōs plūrēs; nunc esse in Galliā ad centum et XX mīlium numerum.

"On behalf of these, Diviciacus the Haeduan spoke, [saying that] there were in all Gaul two factions, [and that] the Haedui held the leadership of one of these and the Arverni that of the other. [He said that] when these groups had vied with each other so much for the hegemony for many years, it came to pass that the Germans were called in for pay by the Arverni and the Sequani. [He also said that] of these, at first about fifteen thousand had crossed the Rhine; [and that] after these men, wild and barbaric, had taken a liking to the Gauls' fields and farming and abundance, many had been brought over; [and that] now there were [Germans] in Gaul to the number of a hundred and twenty thousand."

Likewise, in German a reporter can quote someone else *in extensō*, but showing by the use of the quotative that the responsibility for what is said is not the reporter's: *Vor Studenten sagte Nehru, Indien befinde sich praktisch im Krieg mit China. Indien habe von einer Kriegserklärung abgesehen, weil sonst mit der Gefahr chinesischer Luftangriffe zu rechnen sei* "Before students, Nehru said [that] India was practically at war with China. [He said that] India had refrained from a declaration of war because [according to him] it would otherwise be necessary to count on the danger of Chinese air attacks".

Instead of or together with a modification in form, a modification in syntactic order may indicate dependence of one clause on another. Inversion of verb and subject, indicating that a clause has conditional meaning ("if . . . "), is common in the Germanic languages, e.g., German *Entgleist ein Fahrzeug, so schaltet der Kurzschlussschalter den Transformator aus:* "If a train goes off the track, the circuit-breaker cuts the transformer out (lit., Goes a train off the track, so cuts the circuit-breaker the transformer out)". In the Scandinavian languages, this construction is normal, as in Norwegian *Vil de røyke—se da først etter om røyking er tillatt:* "If you want to smoke (lit. Will you smoke), see first whether smoking is allowed".

The use of a special form, such as the "subjunctive" in verbs, together with some subordinating element, is well known to us from our familiar Indo-European languages: e.g., French /bjēkilswavny/ *bien qu'il soit venu:* "although he has come", or its Italian equivalent /benké^ssíavenúto/ *benché sia venuto*. English grammarians often speak of a "subjunctive form" of the verb (e.g., *come* or *be*) in such dependent clauses as (*It is not necessary*) *that he come or . . . that he be ready*. In English, however, we have no morphologically distinct "subjunctive" verb form. In these instances we have, rather, a verb in its simple form (*come, be*) used instead of an inflected form (*comes, is*). We could, if desired, speak of the "subjunctive use" of the simple form of the verb, with the understanding that this is a syntactical, not a morphological phenomenon.

In the use of special constructions in dependent clauses, it is often useful to distinguish between their automatic occurrence under given conditions (in which case their use is not meaningful) and, on the other hand, their nonautomatic and hence meaningful use under other conditions. In the Romance languages, the "subjunctive" must be used after many conjunctions, such as French /purkə/ *pour que* "in order that," or its Spanish equivalent *para que*—French /purkilləfas/ *pour qu'il le fasse;* Spanish *para que lo haga* "in order that he may do it". In French it is simply wrong to say, */purkilləfe/ *pour qu'il le fait,* or in Spanish **para que lo hace,* because no one ever uses those forms. Hence the use of the subjunctive with these conjunctions does not contrast with the use of any other form of the verb in the same positions, and is therefore meaningless.

On the other hand, in clauses depending on nouns in the Romance languages, there is a choice between subjunctive and nonsubjunctive forms. A nonsubjunctive simply describes an existing situation, as in Italian *un ragazzo che è cortese:* "a boy who is courteous (he already exists and is known to us)". A subjunctive, however, tells the hearer or reader that certain characteristics are not known for sure to exist, but are desired, and that the choice is limited to specimens showing the desired characteristics: *un ragazzo che sia cortese:* "a boy such that he is courteous (he is not known to us, and we are not even sure that he exists, but we don't want any boy who isn't courteous)". The latter type of adjectival clause, with subjunctive, occurs chiefly in contexts which refer to need, desire, etc.: *Occorre un ragazzo che sia cortese:* "We need a boy who is courteous"; nevertheless, it is not the context, but the choice of subjunctive vs. nonsubjunctive, that gives the clause the meaning of "limitation to desired characteristics."

Often, there are subsidiary choices within the subjunctive or other types of indication of subordination (e.g., in the tense of the verb), as in the pair of Italian sentences *Non credo che sia Corelli:* "I don't think it [an encore just played] is Corelli (with 'present subjunctive')" $\sim$ *Non credo che fosse Corelli:* "I don't think it was Corelli (with 'past subjunctive')". If these subsidiary choices are determined by features of the main clause, the relation between the two constitutes a *sequence.* The most familiar example of such subsidiary determination is our *sequence of tenses,* in which a main verb in a particular tense category requires a dependent verb to be in a corresponding category: e.g., *He said + I'm coming → He said he was coming.* Such requirements are, in some languages, quite extensive, as in Latin, where dependent infinitives and subjunctives must observe the sequence of tenses even where it seems irrational to us. A Latin verb dependent on an infinitive in indirect discourse must automatically go into the subjunctive and, if the infinitive is perfective, the verb must also be in a past tense. Hence, if the clause *quam diū iūre iūrandō hostium teneor:* "As long as I am held by my oath to the enemy" is made dependent on a perfective main verb in indirect discourse, then *teneor:* "I am held", in addition to going into the third person, must go into a past subjunctive tense: *Regulus dīxit quam diū iūre iūrandō hostium tenērētur nōn esse sē senātōrem:* "Regulus said that as long as he was held by his oath to the enemy he was not a senator". The Romance languages have similar sequence-of-tenses requirements in conditional sentences, as when an Italian main verb in the "conditional" requires the verb of the dependent "if" clause to be in the "past subjunctive": *Se non fosse vero, sarebbe ben trovato:* "If it weren't true, it would be a good invention". Our parallel construction in English, with *were* in "subjunctive" function, is by now literary and even archaizing; in normal speech, we would say, *if it wasn't true,* not *if it weren't true.*

Another type of conditioned subsidiary feature of dependence is the automatic replacement of one kind of structure by another, depending on the syntactic environment. In Italian, if a main clause and a dependent clause have two different actors, the two clauses normally remain as such: *Dice che sono stanchi:* "He says that they are tired". But a combination of two clauses, one dependent and the other a main clause containing a verb like *dire:* "to say" or *crédere:* "to believe", and having the same actor reference in both verbs, is normally replaced by a construction of MAIN VERB + PREPOSITION *di* + DEPENDENT INFINITIVE: *Dice:* "he says" + *è stanco* "he [the same person] is tired" → *Dice di èssere stanco:* "He says that he is tired (lit., he says of being tired)".

38

Transformations and Structures

IN THE CHAPTERS devoted to syntax, we have been referring to relations between structures as often involving transformations, for instance *It is necessary* + *he goes* → *It is necessary that he go.* It is often convenient to state grammatical relationships in this way, using the convention that we will regard the relation between two constructions as necessarily involving a grammatical process. This approach to grammatical relationships has been used for generations in teaching both English and foreign languages, for exercises of the type: "Transform the following active sentences into the passive, on the model of '*The dog bites the man*' → '*The man is bitten by the dog*'"; or: "Transform these declarative sentences into the negative, the interrogative, and the negative interrogative."

In the development of synchronic linguistics, the concept of "grammatical process" was accepted more or less without question and used widely in the description of linguistic structures, especially in the grammars of American Indian languages prepared by or under the direction of Franz Boas and Edward Sapir. Somewhat later, in an effort to exclude the time-factor entirely from linguistic description, the item-and-arrangement approach (p. 34) was favored by some scholars, who in extreme cases went so far as to ban item-and-process analysis, and even the term "grammatical process," entirely. This approach rested on the consideration that, at any given point of time, a system exists as an entirety, and on the fiction that it is possible to describe it as such all at once. An exclusive concentration on a fictitiously static situation, and the complications and artificialities which it introduced into linguistic description, led to a reaction in the opposite direction, in favor of an analysis exclusively in terms of grammatical processes (replacements of one kind or another—expansion, contraction, and the like). A grammar couched wholly in these terms is a *transformation(al) grammar*, and the processes involved are *transformations*.

Transformations can often be conceived of as proceeding in either direction, and indicated by ↔: thus, the active *The dog bit the man* ↔ the passive *The man was bitten by the dog*. However, it is in many instances convenient to take even bidirectional transformations as unidirectional. There are two main directions in which a transformational grammar can proceed. We can go from the complicated to the simple, by a series of successive reductions, as when a number of different English sentences are shown to have the same fundamental structure, e.g. NOUN (subject) + VERB (predicate). We can also go in the opposite direction, from the simplest possible fundamental structure (known as a *kernel*) to its various ramifications, by means of successive expansions. Thus, from the English kernel just mentioned, we can derive most of the more complicated structures of English; from that of VERB (predicate alone), those of Italian or Spanish. The latter type of transformation grammar, involving production or generation of structures from a kernel, is also known as a *generative grammar*.

In a complete generative grammar, there must be a succession of steps, in each of which the relation between the structure used as point of departure (the *input*) and the resultant transformation* (the *output*) is stated in a *rule*. Often, there is a considerable number of intermediate steps, and a corresponding number of rules, to be set up in order to describe a given relationship. Each successive transformation must involve the replacement of only one element; and, if alternative transformations are possible, they must be stated in terms of *binary choices*, i.e., only two alternatives are given and a choice must be made by taking one or the other. As in immediate constituent analysis (Chap. 27), the order of the intermediate steps is not a matter of indifference. On the contrary, they must be chosen as carefully and stated as precisely as possible, in order to avoid ambiguities and possible inaccurate outputs. Some rules will be obligatory, and others non-obligatory.

We may exemplify a relatively simple set of transformations by taking the generation of the Italian sentence *Mia moglie è bella:* "My wife is beautiful" from the utterance-kernel. In the following enumeration, we give first the abbreviations and then the successive steps:

Adj = Adjective
CV = Copulative Verb (one of a list including *èssere:* "to be")
DA = Definite Article
Det = Determiner (one of a list including DA)
KN = Kinship Noun (one of a list including *moglie:* "wife")
MajCl = Major Clause
MinCl = Minor Clause
N = Noun
P = Predicate
Poss = Possessive
Pron = Pronoun
Pres = Present
S = Subject
Sg = Singular
V = Verb
* = mark of a hypothetical intermediate construction, not found in actual usage because automatically replaced.

1. Utterance = MajCl or MinCl
2. MajCl → P (obligatory)
3. P → S + P or P + S

* The noun *transform* /trǽnsfɔrm/ is also used in this sense.

4. $S + P \rightarrow S + V_{sg}$ or $S + V_{pl}$
5. $S + V_{sg} \rightarrow S + V_{3sg}$ or $S + V_{non-3sg}$
6. $S + V_{3sg} \rightarrow N_{sg} + V_{3sg}$ or $Pr_{3sg} + V_{3sg}$
7. $N_{sg} + V_{3sg} \rightarrow N_{sg} + V_{3sgpres}$ or $N_{sg} + V_{3sg\ non-pres}$
8. $N_{sg} + V_{3sgpres} \rightarrow N_{fsg} + V_{3sgpres}$ or $N_{msg} + V_{3sgpres}$
9. $N_{fsg} + V_{3sgpres} \rightarrow *N_{fsg} + Adj_{fsg} + V_{3sgpres}$
10. $*N_{fsg} + Adj_{fsg} + V_{3sgpres} \rightarrow *N_{fsg} + Adj_{fsg} + CV_{3sgpres}$
11. $N_{fsg} + Adj_{fsg} + CV_{3sgpres} \rightarrow N_{fsg} + CV_{3sgpres} + Adj_{fsg}$
12. $N_{fsg} + CV_{3sgpres} + Adj_{fsg} \rightarrow *Det_{fsg} + N_{fsg} + CV_{3sgpres} + Adj_{fsg}$
13. $*Det_{fsg} + N_{fsg} + CV_{3sgpres} + Adj_{fsg} \rightarrow DA_{fsg} + N_{fsg} + CV_{3sgpres} + Adj_{fsg}$
14. $DA_{fsg} + N_{fsg} + CV_{3sgpres} + Adj_{sfg} \rightarrow DA_{fsg} + Poss_{fsg} + N_{fsg} + CV_{3sgpres} + Adj_{fsg}$
15. $DA_{fsg} + Poss_{fsg} + N_{fsg} + CV_{3sgpres} + Adj_{fsg} \rightarrow *DA_{fsg} + Poss_{fsg} + KN_{fsg}$
    $+ CV_{3sgpres} + Adj_{fsg}$
16. $*DA_{fsg} + Poss_{fsg} + KN_{fsg} + CV_{3sgpres} + Adj_{fsg} \rightarrow Poss_{fsg} + KN_{fsg} + CV_{3sgpres}$
    $+ Adj_{fsg}$
17. Substitution of specific morphemes (here given in morphophonemic transcription):
    $Poss_{fsg} + KN_{fsg} + CV_{3sgpres} + Adj_{fsg} \rightarrow$ //mía móḷḷe éˣ bélla//

This type of rule-giving can then be continued "downward" from the morphophonemic level to the realization of the utterance in phonemic units, and of these latter in sounds. Some analysts consider it possible to bypass the phonemic level entirely, but it is doubtful whether this is really possible. Some utterances are ambiguous, since the same sequence of phonemes can represent two or more sequences of morphemes. For instance, in English, /dʒəmékə/ is either the name of an island in the West Indies or the colloquial form of //d(ɪd) jə mék (h)ə(r)// *Did you make her?*: "Did you cause her (e.g. to go)?" In instances like these, one can perhaps by-pass the phonemic level going "downwards," but not going "upwards," because of many ambiguities of the type just exemplified. This fact is at the base of many puns and jokes which depend on multiple morphophonemic interpretation of phonemically identical utterances:

> A. My wife's gone to the West Indies.
> B. Jamaica?
> A. No, she went of her own accord.

The set of transformations just given for the generation of Italian *Mia moglie è bella* is only a brief sample; for an entire language, a great many thousands of such rules would have to be elaborated. They are easiest to develop for languages whose elements come in linear strings, with relatively few phenomena of morphologic linkage. For these latter, if we are to adhere strictly to the principle of a binary choice at every step, we must elaborate a number of intermediate rules which are often quite arbitrary and lead to the setting up of nonexistent constructions.

Transformational grammar is very useful for certain purposes, especially that of teaching either humans or machines to perform operations with linguistic materials. For humans, transformation exercises are helpful, particularly at the elementary level, in foreign language learning, and also in clarifying certain relationships in our native language that traditional grammar does not make clear (e.g., the identification of the subject of a sentence). It is also useful as a basis for programmed instruction in either native or foreign language, in connection with "teaching machines." Although it is not a direct outgrowth of work on machine translation, it is extremely helpful in this connection, affording a technique for formulating an input in one language so as to produce a given output in another.

However, transformational grammar is not, as some have claimed, a more complete or powerful technique for linguistic description than previous types of analysis. As already suggested (pp. 34–35), the item-and-process approach, on which transformational grammar is built, is most useful for making the equivalent of a guide-book, with instructions as to which path to follow at each point. Such a set of instructions presumes, however, that the territory to be covered is already known and has already been mapped; it contributes nothing to the exploration of the territory, nor to determining the nature of the relationships that exist among the features of the territory. At its best, a transformational grammar is a helpful—though, occasionally, somewhat artificial—guide for those unacquainted with the language through whose mazes it leads them. At its worst, it can degenerate into an arid, artificial game of inventing rules for constructing series of abstract formulae, pure "hocus-pocus" (cf. p. 123), with little necessary relation to the facts of language as it is spoken and as a functioning aspect of the behavior of humans living and interacting in society. And when the apriorism inherent in its analytical procedures is used as a pretext for returning to rationalism, idealism, or normativism, the transformational-generative approach becomes inimical to scientific method in linguistics.

NOTES

Transformational grammar: Chomsky, 1957; Harris, 1957, 1962; Lees, 1957.

The best exemplification of transformational grammar, so far, as applied to a large section of a specific language: Lees, 1960.

Critiques of transformation theory: Reichling, 1961; Uhlenbeck, 1963.

39

Meaning

So FAR, we have been using the term *meaning* without extensive definition or discussion, more or less taking it for granted. The analysis and description of linguistic structure must be based on form, rather than meaning (as pointed out on pp. 31–33). Yet the factor of meaning must always be kept in mind, as a decisive criterion for determining whether a sound or a form has functional significance or not. Some linguistic analysts consider that it might be possible, in theory, to study and formulate the structure of a language without any reference to meaning; but, even if it were possible to do so, it would take so much effort and energy as to involve a tremendous waste. In its social context, language derives its usefulness—and its very reason for existence—from meaning. Humans are not parrots, and no-one would waste time juggling with so complicated a system of vocal habits, unless they were able to convey meaning by it and thus profit by their use of it.

The meaning of any linguistic form is the situations in respect to which it is used. The phrasing *in respect to which*, rather than "in which," is necessary in order to cover situations of displaced speech. As mentioned on p. 6, we can often use linguistic forms to convey meanings even when what they refer to is not present in the actual situation between speaker and hearer. It is apparently possible to teach some types of apes to respond to linguistic stimuli and even to speak—but they see meaning in linguistic forms only when the object referred to is present in the immediate situation. If something out of sight (e.g., a toilet seat) is referred to, the ape is puzzled and cannot understand the displaced reference. The fact that we humans can use displaced speech is what gives language its tremendous effectiveness as a means of achieving a most intricate social coördination. We can relay messages from one person to another, almost indefinitely, until in the end we achieve some desired goal, such as receiving a shipment of rails from a country halfway around the globe—and almost wholly by the use of displaced speech.

Our basic assumption in linguistic analysis is that in every speech community some utterances are alike as to form and meaning. Otherwise, of course, if the speakers of a language could never depend on similarity of form and meaning for any given combination of sounds, from one moment to the next, communication would be impossible. But we have already noted that linguistic form is far more nearly constant, and more easily identifiable, than linguistic meaning. This is because of the relatively limited range—of phonemes, morphemes, taxemes—which linguistic forms cover, and because of the immense range which is covered by the situations with respect to which almost any form is used. That is, when we analyze all the factors in any human situation, even the simplest, in which language serves as a means of communication, we find that their ramifications are enormous. Even such an apparently clear meaning as that of *pie* is much more complicated than we might think at first sight. There are quite a number of different kinds of pie (e.g., apple, blueberry, chicken, "Eskimo" pie; shallow, deep-dish; covered, open-top; and so on), and not the same in the various parts of the English-speaking world. The chemical and physical constituents of *pie*, simple though they may seem, are very complex, and, even in the present state of our scientific knowledge, by no means wholly definable.

Moreover, the meaning of the word *pie*, like that of every other word, differs for each situation in which it occurs—depending on the state of mind, attitude, and so on, of the speaker and the hearer—and no two situations are ever alike. The term *pie*, for instance, may cause me pleasure or disgust, or leave me indifferent, according to how I am feeling, how hungry I am, the previous experiences I may have had with pie, and so forth. Emotional factors such as these last are usually left out of dictionary definitions (it would be hard to include them), but they are very real factors in the total meaning of any linguistic signal in each specific situation in which it is used. To give a complete definition even of *pie* would be a tremendous task, and it would be much harder in the case of admittedly more elusive terms such as *justice, love* (noun and verb), or *matter*.

But the meaning of any specific linguistic form is purely arbitrary. There is no underlying connection, no inherent and inescapable relationship, between any linguistic form and what it signifies. The same animal is referred to in English as *dog*, in French as /ʃjẽ/ *chien*, in German as *Hund*, in Hungarian as *kutya*, in Russian as /sabáka/ собака, in Armenian as /šun/, and so on. From the point of view of pure logic, there is no relationship between any of these combinations of sounds and the animal "canis familiaris" to which they refer. It is wholly a matter of social convention; the meaning of words is determined only by the usage of the speakers of the language, not by some divine fiat. The only reason we make the word *dog* refer to an animal of the species "canis familiaris" and the word *cat* refer to one of the species "felis Lybica domestica," rather than vice-versa, is that we, as speakers of modern English, are in the habit of doing so, and have learned this habit from other speakers of English. On the other hand, different languages use the same combinations of sounds with entirely different meanings: the English word /dú/ *do* means "perform, act" and is a verb, whereas French /du/ *doux* (pronounced nearly like English *do*) is an adjective meaning "sweet," and German /dú/ *du* is a second person singular pronoun meaning "thou."

All meaning reflects our experience of the universe we live in. It is a commonplace to say that if we have had no experience of something, we do not know what it means—not only linguistically, but also emotionally and in our social adjustment. Yet our experience of the universe is something which, in itself, is indivisible, and any division we set up in our experience—as the meanings of our language inevitably lead us to do—is of necessity conventional. The spectrum, for instance, is a continuous scale of light-waves, whose length ranges from 40 to 72 hundred-thousandths of a millimeter; but our language and its meanings cut the spectrum for us into various shades, from *violet* through *indigo, blue, green, yellow, orange* to *red*, thus segmenting our experience for us into quite arbitrary divisions. For colors which the human eye cannot perceive and hence experience directly, our language simply offers no terms—and hence physicists had to coin the new terms *ultra-violet* and *infra-red*. Terminology referring to kinship ought, theoretically, to be quite easy and simple, and yet even in English our kinship terminology shows surprising quirks and gaps. We have, for instance, the words *brother* and *sister*, but no popular term for "persons born of the same parents" without reference to sex. The anthropologist uses the term *sibling* in this meaning, but it still remains a learned term.

When we go from one language to another, it is immediately obvious that the segmentation of experience differs, in the meanings which different languages ascribe to forms. This is true even (and especially) in what we might think the most simple and self-evident words and meanings: *be, get, have, do*. No two languages have exactly the same range of meanings, covered by comparable forms. In Spanish, the meaning of English *be* is covered by three verbs: *ser* referring to identity or "being" that adheres to a fixed norm; *estar*, referring to "being" in a given location or not adhering to a fixed norm; and *haber*, used in contexts comparable to English "for there to be". To translate our word *get* into any other language, we have to resort to half a dozen or more different equivalents, as we can see from the various meanings of *get* in such expressions as *to get* (obtain) *some money, I got* (became) *sick, he got* (arrived) *home after midnight, he got* (received) *a prize, I've got to* (must) *go home*, or *do you get* (understand) *me?*. For the speaker of French, the verb *se promener* (literally "to promenade oneself") covers all that segment of experience involving making an excursion or short pleasure trip, no matter by what means. If he looks for a single, simple English equivalent, he will be disappointed, and will have to resort to various expressions like *take a walk, go for a ride*, etc., which force him to specify what means of locomotion are involved, whether he wants to or not. When we get to "exotic" languages (e.g., Japanese or an American Indian language), the entire classification of experience, even in the grammatical categories of experience, is totally different from what we are accustomed to.

Yet, despite all the difficulties in the way of analyzing meaning, the study of meaning (*semantics*) has made considerable progress, and linguistic analysts have been able to note certain facts of considerable importance. One is that a great many linguistic forms have more than one meaning, that is, they are used in more than one type of situation. The word *pie*, as just pointed out (p. 229), can have several different meanings, and many other instances could be cited, such as these chosen at random: "try" (*I'll try to do it; I'll try it* [meaning "I'll sample it"]; *they're going to try him for murder; it's enough to try anybody's patience; I'll try out the fat*)—or "party" (*a wild party; the Republican party; a party line* [on the telephone]; *he was party to the crime; the party of the first part; this party* [meaning "this person"]). Whenever a form has two or more meanings, its users almost always regard one of them as the *central* meaning (also called the "literal" meaning) and the others are considered *marginal* (or "transferred" or "metaphorical") meanings. Sometimes it is hard to tell whether a given combination of phonemes represents a single form with two or more widely divergent meanings, or two or more distinct forms, as in the case of *ear* (*the human ear* vs. *an ear of corn*). In general, the central meaning of a form is the meaning in which we use it most consistently, and which we assume it has unless there is some special reason to look for a transferred or marginal meaning. As Leonard Bloomfield says (*Language*, p. 149):

> Sometimes the practical feature that forces us to take a form in a transferred meaning, has been given by speech: *Old Mr. Smith is a fox* is bound to be taken in transferred meaning, because we do not call real foxes *Mr.* or give them family-names. *He married a lemon* forces us to the transferred meaning only because we know that men do not go through a marriage ceremony with a piece of fruit.

The existence of transferred meanings and their relation to the central meaning of any given form is a thing which of course varies from one language to another, and also, within the same language, in the course of time. Many metaphors which we think are normal and self-explanatory seem quite foreign to speakers of other languages; no speaker of French would ever use /wazo/ *oiseau* "bird" in such transferred meanings as "fellow, guy" (*He's a queer old bird*) or "a Bronx cheer, or other kind of derisive reception" (*He gave me the bird*). Some metaphors common in earlier English seem out-of-date to us now, like Mark Twain's frequent use of *party* as a facetious term for "person," and some which are very common now, like *off the beam* or *in the groove*, would have been incomprehensible in Mark Twain's time—partly because the practical situations on which they are based (radio, phonograph records) did not exist.

NOTES

Meaning: Bloomfield, 1933, Chap. 9; Nida, 1951b; Fries, 1954, 1962; Read, 1955; Sperber, 1930; Ullman, 1957, 1962.

The colors of the spectrum: Brown and Lenneberg, 1954; Gleason, 1961, Chap. 1; Lenneberg, 1953.

40

Lexicon

THE LEXICON of a language—its stock of contentives—does not lend itself to division into functional units, as do the functors. For this reason, the term *lexeme* ("functional unit of word-like form"; p. 134) has not been of any practical usefulness in analytic procedure. In presenting a lexicon as a whole, especially in a reference work, centuries of experience have shown that it is best to adopt some wholly arbitrary order, usually that of the alphabet, rather than to try to follow some principle of organization according to the meaning of the items listed. This is because a conventional order like the alphabetical is easily learned and followed by everyone, whereas no two people are likely to agree concerning the order of semantic groupings to be followed (should we start with the most generic terms and end with the most particular, or vice versa? with the most philosophical, such as "God," "angel," "mankind in general"? with the most important things for our daily living, such as "shelter" and "food")? Here, opinions would vary, not only from culture to culture, but from one individual to the next, and any objective, scientifically valid basis would be undiscoverable.

This is not, of course, to deny that the study and classification of lexical items according to their semantic characteristics is possible and desirable, even though it cannot be done with the sharpness and precision possible for structural characteristics of language on the emic level. It is quite practicable to group the contentives of a language according to the areas of meaning which they cover, and to analyze the manner in which a given "semantic field" is segmented in a particular language, either in itself or as contrasted with one or more other languages. Such an analysis is not so useful for practical purposes, however, as it is for theoretical studies, and especially for investigating the way in which one facet or another of a culture is reflected in the lexical stock of the corresponding language. In such a study, the behavior and attitudes of a cultural group must be studied in as much detail as possible, in order to see in what contexts each lexical item occurs, and hence how its semantic field is related to that of each other lexical item. If we are lucky enough to be working on a language spoken at present, we can make our observations at first hand, either *in situ* or on as large a body of texts as we can amass. For languages no longer spoken, or for earlier stages of a language, we have to depend on such texts as may chance to have survived. Especially for an earlier stage of a language which is still spoken, we must be on our guard against assuming that the culture and hence the semantic patterns of other places or times are necessarily the same as those which are familiar to us. The ethical attitudes reflected in the lexicon of the Old French epic *La Chanson de Roland*, for instance, are very different from those of modern French culture, and the Old French words referring to this semantic area have quite different meanings from those of their modern descendants. Such words as /barón/ *baron* and /vasál/ *vassal* were not, as we might think, primarily terms referring to juridical relationships within the feudal system. The former meant, rather, "strong man, brave man," in general, and the latter "one who fulfilled faithfully his duties towards his overlord, especially in fighting." Many terms which, especially since the Counter-Reformation, have a strongly Christian and even pietistic overtone, meant something quite different for the mediaeval aristocracy whose ideals were reflected in the *Roland*. Old French /duél/ *duel* did not mean "sorrow, mourning" like Modern French *deuil*, but "chagrin", the feeling one has when one's self-esteem has been outraged; and /orguél/ *orguel* "pride" did not have the unfavorable connotations that attach to Modern French *orgueil*, but referred rather to the justifiable feeling of self-esteem that each *baron* was expected to have, rather equivalent to the Spanish and Hispano-American concept of *dignidad*. The entire picture of the mediaeval French aristocracy and of its attitudes that emerges from a study of its ethical vocabulary is one of a decidedly non-Christian culture motivated, not by a feeling of guilt and need for atonement, but by a desire to avoid shame and to emphasize personal standing by self-assertion, especially by bravery in war.

Many semantic groups are unified by the fact that they have a special connotation. Analysts of meaning distinguish between *denotation*, or the meaning a form has for all those who use it, and *connotation*, or the special additional meaning the same form may have for some one speaker or for certain speakers. In general, our dictionaries give us only the denotation of a form—as much of its meaning as can be stated objectively and for all the speakers of the language. Mathematicians and scientists strive to avoid all connotations in the meaning of their terms—a perfectly valid and attainable goal in the specific and carefully delimited type of work they are doing. Sometimes purists tell us we should do likewise in everyday speech, but such an aim is hardly realistic or feasible in view of the complexity of any human being's life and environment—and, even if it could be attained, it would remove from our speech much that makes it interesting and living, including all poetry and imaginative use of language.

Connotations may be individual in their extent—that is, only one speaker may have a special connotation for a form—or they may extend to whole groups of speakers or even the majority of those who use a form. Each of us has some words which convey a special flavor, for us alone. The word *swerve*, for example, has for me a very unpleasant connotation, due to its use in connection with a childhood accident. On the other hand, because I happen to be an electric railway enthusiast, the words *street-car* (*tram-car*), *elevated*, *subway* fill me with a much warmer glow of pleasure than they give to the majority of their users. An individual or private connotation of this type is just as real as a more widespread one, but, because it is restricted to one speaker, it has little or no communicative value.

Of the more widespread types of connotation, perhaps the most common are those which ascribe words to cultural (social) levels and to functional varieties, of the types discussed on pp. 21–22. A form like *ain't* or *I seen* has the same denotation as *isn't* or *I saw*, but quite a different connotation: many people think that the first pair connote undesirable characteristics, such as ignorance or illiteracy or carelessness, whereas the second pair carry a connotation of desirable characteristics. Our functional varieties of speech are likewise differentiated by the degree of familiarity they connote. There is a whole range of different situations, from the purely formal through the semi-formal (as in a university lecture) to the wholly informal (private correspondence or familiar conversation); and, to a certain extent, we feel that some forms are suited to one type of situation and not to another. There are some words or turns of speech which we would use only in a formal situation, such as the "subjunctive use" of *be* in *unless this be so*, or the expression *busy though he may be*, or such items of vocabulary as *vociferation* for "yelling", *contingency* for "chance", *enumeration* for "listing", and so on. Most of our formal vocabulary has been taken over from Greek or Latin by men of letters or others with special learning, and hence is called *learnèd* vocabulary. At the other extreme, such an expression as *he has bats in his belfry* is extremely informal, and would be quite inappropriate in a formal oration or sermon. Most of our vocabulary and usage falls in between these two extremes.

Other types of connotation, often on the formal or learnèd side, are those of *archaisms, foreignisms,* and *technical terminology.* It sounds either Biblical or Shakespearean to use the *-th* ending in the third person singular of a verb: *he goeth, she cometh;* and even more archaic to use *ye* (as in *Hear ye!*) or the second person singular pronouns *thou, thee* and the corresponding verb forms in *-(e)st: thou singest,* or *I tell thee.* If we use a sprinkling of foreign words or phrases in our speech or writing, we convey to our hearers the impression that we know more than one language, and also (often) the idea that we are seeking the exact term to refer to some strange thing or concept, as when we speak of Russian *sputniks,* of an Israeli *kibbutz* (or even, using the Hebrew plural, of *kibbutzim*), or of Puerto Rican *jíbaros* (hillbillies) and *campesinos* (peasants). Borrowings from other dialects of our own language also convey special connotations; for instance, for most Americans, certain specifically British vocabulary items suggest slight affectation, e.g. *cove* for "guy, fellow", *petrol* for "gasoline", or *lift* for "elevator". Technical terms have all kinds of different connotations, which depend essentially on the social standing of the calling they are associated with, such as *swing* and *riff* from jazz, *rumble* and *shiv* "knife" from juvenile delinquency, or *schistosomiasis* and *beta-haemolytic streptococcus* from medical terminology.

We can also give a humorous twist to our speech, by making use of *mock-forms,* which have a purposely ridiculous connotation. We make fun of learnèd or formal vocabulary by inventing and using such words as *dis-*

combobulate, busticate, ruction or *rambunctious* (and the verb formed on the last-mentioned, *rambunct*). Students plowing their way through Shakespeare or Milton often intentionally add the ending *-est* where it does not belong, together with humorous use of *thou* and *thee*, as when high-school students ask *Wiltest thou comest to the officest with me-est?* The Romance languages are close enough to Latin so that a mixed type of language, known as *macaronic Latin*, can be constructed combining Latin functors with contentives from Latin, one or more of the standard Romance languages, and local dialect. Macaronic Latin was very popular during the sixteenth and seventeenth centuries, especially in Italy, where the greatest mock-epic of the century was the *Baldus* (1519) of Teòfilo Folengo, a long poem in macaronic hexameters. Here are three lines exemplifying Folengo's macaronics, taken from his diatribe against monks:

> Unde diavol, ait, tanti venere capuzzi?
> Non nisi per mundum video portare capuzzos.
> Quisque volat fieri frater, vult quisque capuzzum.

> "Where the devil," said he, "did so many cowls come from? I don't see anything but cowls in the whole world; everybody flies to become a monk, everybody wants a cowl."

We can make fun of foreign languages, or of foreign speakers' accent in English, as in the following quotation from P. G. Wodehouse's *Psmith, Journalist:*

> Pugsy . . . appeared to have a fixed idea that the Italian language was one easily mastered by the simple method of saying "da" instead of "the", and tacking on a final "a" to any word that seemed to him to need one.
> "Say, kid," he began, "has da rent-a man come yet-a?"

Slang is distinguished as such by its connotations, which are those of extreme familiarity (sometimes substandard, sometimes not) and of very recent introduction. On the margin of the standard language, there are always new words of new meanings for old words; these are always being introduced, and at the time of their introduction have a strongly slangy flavor. Very often these new usages do not become permanent, or they linger in the speech-habits of only one age-group. When I was a child, my parents would often tell me to *skidoo!*, but persons of my generation rarely use that word, preferring to tell someone to *scram!*. I later found that *skidoo!* and *twenty-three!*, both in the meaning of *"get out!"*, were slang usages current in the early 1900's; the first of them I remember from my childhood in the 1910's and '20's, and the second I never heard in normal speech. Similarly, the expressions *funny ha-ha* and *funny peculiar*, as slightly jocular ways of distinguishing the two meanings of *funny*, were current in the 1930's and still are in my own usage; they seem out-of-date to younger persons. On the other hand, some slang expressions "catch on" and we soon forget that they began as slang: we now speak of *jazz* music, eating a *sandwich* at a *snack bar*, or riding in a *jeep*, without realizing that *jazz, snack, sandwich, bar* in the sense of "eating or drinking place", and *jeep* were slang at one time or another.

Also coming under the head of connotations are the factors of taboo on terms referring to sex or evacuation of bodily waste. Here, too, there are various degrees of taboo or impropriety; I can, under certain circumstances, speak or write the word *whore*, but there are some other words which I (together with 98 percent of our speech-community!) know, but which I would rarely speak and never write. Of this same type, essentially, are the connotations of *ominous* meaning that we attach to some words, so that we replace them by other, less strongly connotative expressions (*euphemisms*). In our society, with our intense fear of death, we are often afraid to say *if I should die*, and instead we say *if something should happen to me*. Some people are afraid to mention such words as *syphilis* or *venereal disease*, and substitute them by *social disease* or similar less meaningful terms. To a certain extent, these ominous connotations are irrational survivals of older superstitions to the effect that a name has some magical power of its own, and hence that naming some evil thing or spirit might bring its evil workings upon us. This was why, for example, the Greeks called the goddesses of revenge, the Furies or *Erinnyes* ("Furious Ones"), not by their real names, but *Eumenides* "Gracious Ones".

Observations of this general type, concerning the classes which words fall into as determined by their semantic field and their connotations, are all that the linguistic analyst can make about meaning, because it lies largely outside his field of analysis. The linguist can simply define linguistic forms and their approximate meaning, but he cannot do the work of the chemist, the physicist, the anthropologist, etc., in analyzing and defining the further ramifications of ultimate physical and social structure involved. To define meaning completely and exactly, even that of the simplest linguistic form, we should have to have a complete knowledge of the structure of the universe, and also of everything going on inside the body and head of every speaker and every hearer. This is manifestly impossible. Meaning remains something approximate and indefinite, much more so than linguistic form; and yet we are left with the paradox that meaning, even with the difficulties it presents us (both the analyst and the unreflecting speaker of a language), is what makes language effective in human society. Perhaps future scholars will discover a way in which linguistic analysts can state meaning as precisely and as concisely as they can do for form. When this is done, we shall be able to correlate form and meaning without running the risk, as we do at present, of losing sight of the simple essentials of form in the maze of meaning.

NOTES

The description of lexicon (lexicography): Householder and Saporta (eds.), 1962.
The "field of meaning" pertaining to ethics in the Song of Roland: Jones, 1962.
Slang and taboo words are treated more discursively in Hall, 1960b.

PART II

LINGUISTIC GEOGRAPHY

41

Regional and Social Variation

LANGUAGE VARIES, not only from one individual to the next, but from one subsection of a speech-community (family, village, town, region) to another. People of different social classes, occupations, or cultural groups in the same community will show variations in their speech. These variations are not random, but can be correlated with regional and social factors, and their study constitutes one of the links between linguistics and anthropological–sociological analysis. Almost any type of division among humans is likely to be reflected in a linguistic difference; the analysis of these differences and of their geographico-social correlates is known by the general term *linguistic geography*, even when nonspatial relationships are involved.

We are perhaps most familiar with variation "on the flat," from one place to another. Even in the United States and Australia, where settlement has been relatively recent and the population is quite mobile, there is considerable regional variation, and not only between Tennessee mountaineers or Ozark "hill-billies" and the rest of the country. A *milk shake*, east of the Alleghenies, does nor normally include ice cream in the mixture of milk and syrup; to get ice cream in the drink, one has to ask for a *frosted chocolate*, a *frappe* /fræp/, a *velvet*, or a *cabinet*, depending on the part of the country. West of the Alleghenies, a *milk shake* includes ice cream, in greater quantity the farther west one goes. If we ask for *tonic* outside Eastern New England, we are likely to get some kind of hair restorative or other liquid for improving our health or bodily condition. However, in an area centering on Boston and extending outward for about fifty or a hundred miles, a request for *tonic* will bring a bottle of ginger ale, root beer, or some other soft drink of the kind that else-where is called "soda pop." Nor is regional variation limited to lexicon; it can occur in any aspect of linguistic structure, including phonology, as when American speakers from (roughly) south of the 40th parallel use the form /grízi/ *greasy* in contrast to those from farther north, who normally use /grísi/.

In other parts of the world, where the population has been established for a longer time and is less mobile, regional variation is even greater. If we were to take a walking or bicycle tour from one end of any large European country to the other (say, in Germany, France, Italy, or Spain), we should find differences between each village and the next one we came to. On arriving at the other end of the country, the local speech would be so different from that of our starting-point that the two would not be mutually comprehensible. Even in such a simple expression as that for "let's go!" (standard Italian *andiamo!*), in Milan we would find /andóm/, in Emilia /andém/, in Tuscany /ņámo/, in Rome /annámo/, in Naples /iámmə/, and in Sicily /ğámu/. Nor are such differences limited to local dialects; even in the standard language there can be extensive variations. The terms for "barber-shop" vary markedly in the Italian national language, from *salone:* "saloon" or *salone da barba:* "beard-saloon" in the south, *barbieria:* "barber establishment" in some parts of the center, and simply *barbiere:* "barber" in some other regions.

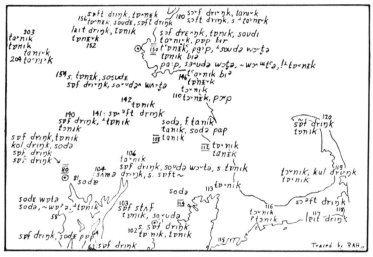

MAP 1: Words for "Soda Pop" in Eastern New England.

If differences of this type are marked on a map, we can identify the areas in which various linguistic phenomena are manifested. Map 1 shows a part of the New England area, with the expressions for "soda pop" as they were obtained at selected points from two, three, or four specially chosen persons who acted as sources of information ("informants") at each point. On such a map, we can draw a line around any area which we wish to set off from other areas because of a particular linguistic characteristic which it manifests. Such a line is known as an *isogloss*. Note that an isogloss is not a line connecting two or more points, as are isobars, isotherms, and many other lines whose names begin in *iso-*; it is a boundary line, marking an approximate division between points or areas. Usually, regions are characterized by the presence of a number of features at the same time, and hence a corresponding number of isoglosses must be traced to show the spread of these features. For a small region, a relatively small number of isoglosses will often do to characterize it (five, ten, twenty or so); for a larger area, such as a country as a whole, a much greater number of isoglosses must be established in order to determine its dialectal divisions and sub-divisions. Over the last century, it has been found most convenient to present the necessary materials in the shape of a collection of maps, known as a *linguistic atlas*. To collect, edit, and publish the materials of a linguistic atlas for a country or large region is a major undertaking, usually requiring extensive funds and a staff which includes the scholar who directs the project and one or more assistants.

The gathering of linguistic atlas materials is a lengthy process, usually carried on *in situ* by an interviewer or *field-worker* who must, above all, be endowed with keen hearing and carefully trained in phonetic analysis and notation. The number of places at which the investigations are carried out will differ according to the extent of the regional variations that are to be traced, and the financial resources available. For the study of only one or a few features (such as the words for "soda pop" in New England, or the developments of the Latin consonant clusters /mb/ and /nd/ in Italy or Spain), speakers from a great many places can be interviewed, thus giving a close or *fine-meshed* network of localities investigated. In order to cover a great many separate items (as in a linguistic atlas), it is usually necessary to restrict the number of places, so that the resultant network is *wide-meshed*. The accuracy of the isoglosses which are established will depend, of course, on the closeness of the network of points investigated: the wider the mesh, the more approximative are the boundaries which the isoglosses represent. In some studies of lexical distribution, for which phonetic accuracy is irrelevant, the field-worker technique has been dispensed with and a very fine-meshed network has been obtained by sending postcards to thousands of correspondents, who fill in the requested data in conventional spelling and return the cards to the project director.

Before the detailed work of gathering the atlas materials gets under way, a preliminary survey is normally made to determine what regional differences exist and are worth studying. On the basis of this survey, a questionnaire is drawn up, carefully planned so as to waste as little as possible of the field-worker's time in his interviews with his informants. Since the informants are often farmers or peasants, and since many of the items to be recorded are terms of rural life, it is usually best to hold the interviews in the informants' home environment, so that the context of normal everyday life will be available to refresh their memory. The field-worker will choose his informants carefully, to make sure that their speech is completely representative of the locality. At the interviews, the field worker takes down the informants' replies in as detailed and narrow a phonetic transcription as possible, usually making one or two carbon copies for safety's sake, and sends the results of each interview back to the project office. Tape-recorders and other sound-recording devices are useful adjuncts to such interviews, but not essential, and the "hi-est" of hi-fi equipment will not take the place of a trained field-worker's ear and phonetic notation.

Once the materials have all been sent to the home office, they are carefully edited and prepared for publication. A linguistic atlas can be published in any one of various typographic presentations. The transcriptions can be printed on an ordinary page, in columns, like a set of logarithmic or similar tables, with, say, a single column for each informant whose speech was investigated, and all the responses to a single question printed across the page on the same line. Or the page can be arranged in the shape of a map, with the informants' responses placed on the map in the relative positions of their localities, as shown in Map 1. This latter way of reproducing the material is perhaps the best, and certainly the easiest to use and interpret at a glance, but it is quite costly, since the lettering usually has to be done by hand and the printing costs are very high. A linguistic atlas is an extremely valuable source of information for present-day speech and its past history. There are linguistic atlases either completed or in process of planning or completion for many countries (Germany, France, Italy, Corsica, Roumania, Catalonia, Spain and Portugal, the Mediterranean basin, etc.). For the United States, a three-volume atlas of New England (over 600 maps) was published in 1940–43, and gathering and editing of materials for the rest of the country has nearly been completed.

The earliest studies in linguistic geography were made from an almost wholly spatial point of view, considering dialectal phenomena in a two-dimensional light, with little or no reference to differences in the speech of generations or of social groups. In more recent work, considerable care has been expended on the choice of at least two informants for each locality, to represent an older generation with little or no education and which has stayed very close to home, and a younger generation with a certain amount of education and also of mobility. In larger urban areas, as many as five or ten informants may be chosen, to represent various parts of town and also different socio-economic levels. With such an expanded approach, the older conception of linguistic geography as dealing only with the distribution of rural terminology "on the flat" has given way to a multidimensional study of socially, as well as geographically, determined variations in language, in city as well as country.

It is of course possible to study social variations without any regard to their spatial distribution. Perhaps the best-known (one is tempted to say "notorious") of such studies is that made by Ross on upper-class ("U") versus non-upper-class ("non-U") usage in England, which was made very widely known by the novelist Nancy Mitford. Ross enumerated and discussed a large number of differences in British usage which are correlated with the social level of their speakers, such as the contrast between /jú/ and /ú/ in words like *tune*, *duke*, *new* (in England, /tjún djúk njú/ are "U" and /tún dúk nú/ are very "non-U"), or the use of *lunch* ("U") versus *luncheon* ("non-U"). Such preoccupations seem strange to Americans, most of whom lay much less stress on social distinctions (in language or other matters) than do Englishmen, but Ross's study, as popularized by Miss Mitford, was widely read in England, and his distinctions between "U" and "non-U" were objects of extensive discussion and often of agonizing self appraisal.

The findings of geographico-social analysis of language can on occasion be helpful to scholars in more specifically social studies, such as sociology, in both its theoretic and its applied aspects. In Spanish, the most prestige-bearing variety of the standard language ("Castilian") distinguishes between /θ/ and /s/, as in /káθa/ *caza* "hunt" vs. /kása/ *casa* "house"; but many dialects of peninsular Spanish and almost all of American Spanish merge these two phonemes into /s/, and say /kása/ for both "hunt" and "house". Throughout Spanish America, however, the use of /θ/ (a practice called "ceceo" /θeθéo/) is widely considered a mark of superior social standing, whereas "seseo" (use of /s/ instead of /θ/) is often looked down upon; hence those who aspire to being looked on as elegant and upper-class will affect "ceceo." Purists encourage "ceceo," and close their own and others' eyes to the fact that its use gives connotations of social climbing. Yet geographico-social studies on Spanish-American usage and attitudes connected therewith have shown clearly that, among the lower classes and peasants, "ceceo" is regarded as snobbistic. This question comes to be quite important on a practical level when university-trained personnel, e.g., on a land-improvement project, are attempting to convey information to peasants or Indian tribesmen. A prerequisite to any successful communication in such a situation is that university-trained people, with their intellectual and social prejudices, should learn to avoid "ceceo," whose use antagonizes their hearers and provokes, not admiration, but hostility and closure of minds to the reception of any information that might come from a "ceceo"-using person.

NOTES

Linguistic geography in general: Bloomfield, 1933a, Chap. 19 (the best discussion of linguistic geography in relation to the rest of linguistics); Pop, 1950.

A sociologically-oriented study: Putnam and O'Hern, 1955.

"U" and "non-U" in England: Ross, 1954.

North American linguistic geography: Atwood, 1953, 1962; Kurath, 1939, 1939–43, 1949; Kurath and McDavid, 1961; McDavid, 1949, 1961; McDavid and McDavid, 1956.

42

Geographic Distribution

WHEN THE MATERIAL of a linguistic atlas has been gathered and recorded in maps or tables, the analyst can set to work studying its geographic distribution. His first and most important task is to draw isoglosses, either identifying particular areas or setting off one area against another. No isogloss is ever more than an approximation, and those that are drawn on maps must not be thought of as absolute or comparable to such sharp lines as those separating political areas. Every linguistico-geographical study represents only a sampling of localities and informants. Even if we were somehow able to obtain data on the speech of every single speaker in an area, we could still not trace absolute lines of demarcation, since humans are not plants or trees and therefore are continually on the move from one point of time to the next. An isogloss may represent either the outer limit attained by a particular feature, or the inner limit within which competing forms are not found.

Since it would be, in general, undesirable to mark up atlas maps—a linguistic atlas is an expensive thing, which very few people can own for themselves and which an individual would not like to spoil even if it were his own property—the analyst usually makes his marks on blank maps or *base-maps*, which are outline maps of the region covered by the atlas involved, with numbers to correspond to each of the atlas's numbered localities. One can simply draw isoglosses on the base-map as one looks at the materials contained in the atlas, or one can make conventional marks of all kinds (squares, circles, triangles, plus-signs, x's, etc., in various colors) to represent whatever features are being studied—contrasting sounds, word-types, etc. Map 2 ("*Tonic* in New England") shows the use of conventional marks (in this instance, unfilled and filled-in circles); Map 3 ("Latin -*r̨*- in Tuscany") gives isoglosses. If maps are to be printed in black and white, it is often necessary to use supplementary devices, such as different kinds of lines, or number or letter names for the lines, to take the place of different colors.

Detailed study of the distribution of linguistic phenomena shows three main kinds of areas. A certain feature may be manifested over a solid block of territory, without any competitors. In Map 2, *tonic* is virtually the only term for "soda-pop" in Boston and the area within thirty or so miles around. In Map 3, all but one of the words shown have -*i̯*- from Latin -*r̨*- in a zone including Florence (point 523), Pisa (530) and Siena (532), central Tuscany, and the coastal region. Even *macellaio:* "butcher" shows -*i̯*- in the central part of this area. When a given sound or form is universally prevalent, in a compact region centering around a specific point or focus, it is said to constitute a *focal area*.

In other regions, such a feature as *tonic* for "soda-pop" is present only sporadically and at certain points, in competition with other features (different terms for the same concept, different grammatical forms having the same function, or divergent developments of the same earlier sound). In Map 2, *tonic* is shown as occurring only scatteringly in regions more than a

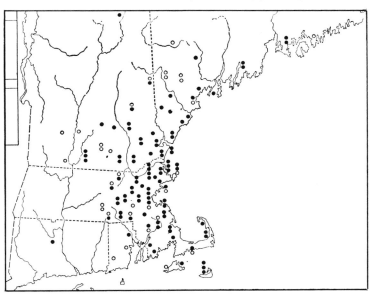

MAP 2: *Tonic* in New England.

• spontaneous response: the term is regularly used by the informant
○ prompted response: the term is familiar to the informant but not his customary one
Tonic in the sense of "soda-water" is confined to the wholesale trade area of Boston. The subsidiary trade centers of eastern New England (Providence, Worcester and Portland) appear to be passive in this instance.

hundred or so miles away from Boston; in Map 3, there is an extensive spread between the isoglosses for the various words, in the outlying regions of Tuscany and in Umbria. This spread shows, in shorthand fashion, that any given point within the spread (say, 556 in Umbria) certain words will show -*i̯*- (e.g. *cuoio:* "leather", isogloss B) and others (e.g. *macellaro:* "butcher", isogloss A³) will show other developments such as -*r*- rather than -*i̯*- from Latin -*ri̯*-, whereas still others manifest both treatments (e.g., *aia, ara:* "threshing-floor", isogloss E).

In such regions, the various isoglosses cross and recross each other; especially where communications are well developed, the isoglosses flare or fan out. The best-known instance of such flaring is the so-called "Rhenish fan" (Map 4). In South Germany, earlier /k/ has become /x/ in such a word as North German /máken/ "make" ∼ South German /máxen/; /p/ > /f/ in

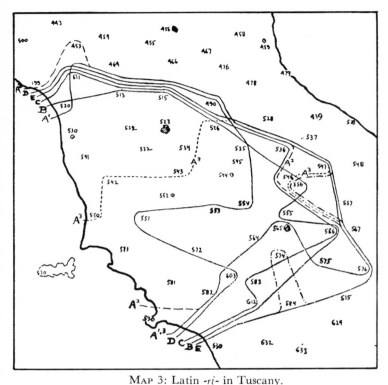

MAP 3: Latin -r̯i̯- in Tuscany.

A¹   outer limit of -aio in *mugnaio:* "miller" (AIS 251) ——
A²   "   "   " -aio in *carbonaio:* "coal-dealer" (AIS 211) — —
A³   "   "   " -aio in *macellaio:* "butcher" (AIS 244) — ·· —
B   "   "   " -i̯- in *cuoio:* "leather" (AIS 1568)
C   "   "   " " *acciaio:* "steel" (AIS 401)
D   "   "   " " *cucchiaio:* "spoon" (AIS 982)
E   "   "   " " *aia:* "threshing-floor" (AIS 1468)
       ara within outer limits of *aia* — · —

/dórf/ ∼ /dórf/ "village"; and /t/ > /s/ in /dát/ ∼ /das/ "that". The lines dividing the southern from the northern region run fairly close together in eastern Germany, but they separate and fan out just east of the Rhine near Cologne. Areas which show this kind of spreading or flaring isoglosses are called *graded* areas or *transitional* zones.

If a feature is present only in a region which is cut off from communication in one way or another, the area is said to be *marginal*. In the distribution of *tonic* in New England (Map 2), Cape Cod is marginal to the focal area of Boston. It is not necessary that the "marginal" areas be geographically on the edge ("lateral" areas, as in Map 5); they can also be isolated in other ways, as in mountainous regions like the Massif Central of France, or in islands, such as Sardinian with respect to the rest of the Romance-speaking territory. A "marginal" speech-community may be formed by a "speech-island" even in the midst of a large urban area; it need not even be isolated geographically at all, but may be set off simply by voluntary or involuntary isolation,

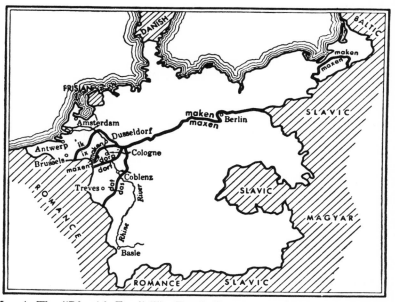

MAP 4: The "Rhenish Fan." The Dutch-German speech-area, showing the isogloss of (k) versus (x) in the word *make*, and, in the western part, the divergence of three other isoglosses which in the east run fairly close to that of *make*. (After Behaghel.)

as are the Mennonites and Amish in southeastern Pennsylvania, or women in the more conservative part of the Arab world.

In broader studies of the relationships of regions to each other, other types of area are often identified. On occasion, sounds or words are borrowed through regions of easy communication, cutting apart lateral areas and forming *corridor*-like areas, as in the long strip between Tuscany on the northwest and the rest of Italy to the southeast shown in Map 6 ("The Papal States in Italian Linguistic History"). An area may be "central" with respect to other areas, as is Italy among the Romance-speaking lands. The date of settlement of an area will often determine its relation to regions from which it was settled; we then speak of *later-settled* and *earlier-settled* regions.

Studies of geographical distribution can be carried out on any aspect of linguistic structure—phonetic characteristics, phonemic contrasts, inflectional or syntactic features, or lexical items. At the time when modern linguistic geography was being developed, around the beginning of the twentieth century, in the work of Jules Gilliéron (1854–1926) and his followers, the

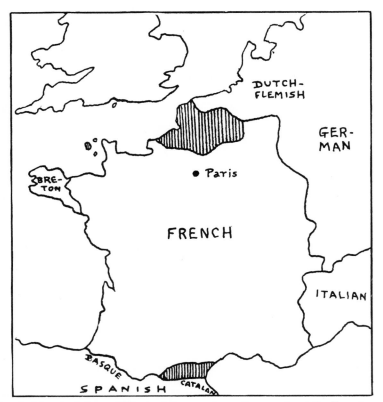

MAP 5: Marginal Areas. The shaded areas show those parts of the French speech-areas in which /k/ has not been shifted to /c/ or /ts/, or later developments thereof, in *cheval:* "horse" from Proto-Romance /kabállu/. (After Map 269 of the *Atlas Linguistique de la France.*)

detailed study of phonetics had already been extensively developed, and is reflected in the careful, ultra-narrow transcription that it has become customary to use in linguistic atlases. The principle of phonemic contrast was not explicitly stated until later (in the 1920's and '30's) and has tended to be neglected in linguistic geography. Consequently, some structuralists, considering phonemically significant contrasts the only aspect of phonology worth taking into account, have criticized linguistic geographers for what

MAP 6: The Papal States in Italian Linguistic History. Elements of Vocabulary.
Words for "now" (1533).

▲ adesso   ○ ora   ✕ qui
⊿ asse(a)   □ mo'

Lines (representing outer limit of areas):
A   stracciaro-aio "ragman"   204
B   fora "outside"   356
C   somaro "donkey"   1066
———somara f. (∼ asino m.)
D   (di- im-) panatoio -tura "reel" 1507

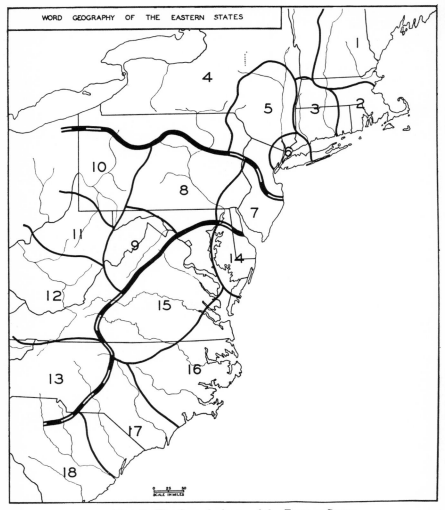

MAP 7: The Speech Areas of the Eastern States.

The North

1   Northeastern New England
2   Southeastern New England
3   Southwestern New England
4   Upstate New York and W. Vermont
5   The Hudson Valley
6   Metropolitan New York

The Midland

7   The Delaware Valley (Philadelphia Area)
8   The Susquehanna Valley

seemed an "excessive" concentration on phonetic facts. However, linguistic areas are set off from each other by nonsignificant features just as much as by significant contrasts, the prime instance being the difference in lip-rounding in [o] and [u] which constitutes the single most important isogloss between the English of North America and that of the British Commonwealth (except Canada). Lexicographical distribution is the main concern of most linguistic geographers, and a frequent near-synonym for "linguistic geography" is *word-geography*.

The findings of phonological or morphological studies do not always coincide with those of word-geography, with regard to the divisions of a particular area. The most notorious instance is that of the United States and its major linguistic divisions. Primarily on the basis of phonetic characteristics (especially the treatment of "post-vocalic r," as in *hard, heard*), earlier students of American English had divided it into three main varieties: New England, the South-East, and the rest of the country, calling the speech of this latter "General American." The term "General American" has become widely known and used in reference-works such as dictionaries and treatises on pronunciation. Later studies, based primarily on lexicon, have shown a different division of American English, into three distinct zones: the North, the Midland, and the South (cf. Map 7). The earlier classification and the term "General American" have therefore tended to fall into perhaps undue disfavor, because their critics have not realized that phonologically-based divisions can be different from those based on lexical studies, but equally valid.

Closely connected with the study of word geography has been that of the geographical distribution of nonlinguistic phenomena, particularly with regard to the artifacts and customs of rural life (what kind of pails are used? what kind of roofs do houses have? what kind of serenades do people give newly married couples?). The combination of these two orientations, linguistic and nonlinguistic, has been known as the *Wörter und Sachen* ("Words and Things") movement. On the synchronic plane, the *Wörter-und-Sachen* approach is very helpful in establishing correlations between the names given to things and the things themselves, e.g., the special types of huts known as *baite* (sg. *baita*) which shepherds build in the Italian Alps for shelter during

---

9   The Upper Potomac and Shenandoah Valleys
10 The Upper Ohio Valley (Pittsburgh Area)
11 Northern West Virginia
12 Southern West Virginia
13 Western North and South Carolina

The South

14 Delamarvia (Eastern Shore of Maryland and Virginia, and southern Delaware)
15 The Virginia Piedmont
16 Northeastern North Carolina (Albemarle Sound and Neuse Valley)
17 The Cape Fear and Peedee Valleys
18 South Carolina

the winter. In historical linguistics, it has been of major service in explaining otherwise unclear semantic developments and etymological relationships, as when Rudolf Meringer (1859–1931) showed that German *Wand:* "wall (of a room)" was related to the verb *wenden:* "to turn" through its having referred earlier to wattle-and-daub walls, made with twisted withes.

NOTES

Latin -rị- in Tuscany: Hall, 1942b.

Papal States: Hall, 1943c.

Some scholars consider areas in which genetically nonrelated languages manifest similar phenomena (e.g. nasalization, palatalization, postposition of the definite article, etc.) as deserving of special consideration, and term them *Sprachbünde* or "linguistic areas": cf. Jakobson, 1931; Trubetzkoy, 1931.

43

Historical Implications

IN GENERAL, the geographical distribution of a linguistic feature has historical implications, in that it enables us to make suppositions concerning the earlier status of the feature. In the simplest cases, the presence of a word (or a sound or a grammatical feature) in a focal area like that of *tonic* around Boston (Map 2), or of -*i̯*- from -*ri̯*- in Tuscany (Map 4) tells us that it has been there for a long time, long enough to have become thoroughly customary in the whole area and to have edged out all competitors. Nevertheless, the presence of a given phenomenon in a focal area is not, in itself, a guarantee that it has been there since earliest times, or that it has resulted from an "indigenous" development, i.e., one which took place on the spot. The phenomenon now occupying a focal area may itself have been imported from outside at some earlier stage (as was, say, the loss of "post-vocalic *r*" into New England from the southern part of England) and have become firmly implanted over the course of time. If we are lucky, we may find scattered survivals of its earlier competitors in relic areas (cf. below); or they may have all been eliminated, as has been the case with the descendants of Latin *ignis:* "fire" in the Romance languages, which have replaced this word entirely with forms developing out of Latin *focus*, originally "hearth".

The existence of a graded area or transitional zone (like the outer edges of the *tonic* area or that of Tuscan -*i̯*-) tells us that there is a spread taking place, or that there has been one in recent times. Simply from the static representation afforded by the map alone, we cannot tell in which direction the spread is taking place, and whether, say, *tonic* or Tuscan -*i̯*- from Latin -*ri̯*- is gaining or losing ground. Often, we are tempted to think that a graded area on the edge of a focal area must represent a current stage of the expansion of the latter, and many times this is true. Sometimes, however, the informants give the field worker specific comments as to whether a form is archaic or recent; in such instances, our expectations are on occasion deceived. The forms *ara* corresponding to Tuscan *aia:* "threshing floor" and *macellaro* instead of *macellaio:* "butcher" (Map 3) were specifically labelled "new" by the Italian atlas' informants. In this instance, the old focal area of Tuscany is apparently losing its force of expansion, and the forms with -*r*- are being borrowed back into the transitional zone from the southeast.

If, however, we find a feature only in marginal areas, such as those shown in Map 5 for nonpalatalized /k-/ in words from Proto-Romance /kabállu/

"horse", with some other competing form or sound (in this instance, /č-/ or /ts-/ or their later developments) occupying most of the region, the conclusion is that the feature now evident only in the marginal areas was formerly more widespread and used to cover most or all of the territory. Such a feature is, from the historical point of view, a *relic* or *archaism*, and the territory in which it is preserved is a *relic area*. Especially in phonology, archaic features may be preserved in different lexical items in different places; when the geographic distribution of a number of such items is charted all together on the same map, a broad band constituting a large relic area may result, as shown in Map 8 ("Preservation of Non-Palatalized /k/ before /a/ in Gallo-Romance"). For this reason, and especially in studying the extent of a phonologic or morphological archaism, it is most unwise to take one single word as representative of a particular development (e.g., the descendants of /kabállu/ for nonpalatalized /k/ before /a/).

Yet just the presence of a feature in a marginal position does not necessarily prove that it must be a relic. Many centers which are active foci of linguistic diffusion are on the edge of their territories, as are Boston, Lisbon, or Rio de Janeiro. It can also happen that very remote and superficially "marginal" points are subjected to modernizing influences before points which are nearer the centers of radiation. Thus, certain places at the very head of Alpine valleys are often less conservative than points farther down the valleys, owing to such contacts as those with through traffic along international lines of communication (e.g. the Simplon or Gotthard passes and tunnels) and with urban patrons of the Alpine tourist industry.

Linguistic geography teaches us, above all, that language is constantly *on the move:* features of speech are spreading from one place to another. The instance of *tonic* in New England is instructive. We can see from the map that its extent, in the meaning "soda pop," correlates closely with the wholesale trade area centering on Boston. When this type of drink was introduced in Boston, it was termed *tonic water*, presumably to induce customers to favor it because of supposed medicinal values, or else to avoid restrictions of one type or another; and, along with its distribution to wholesale dealers who bought from Boston jobbers, the term *tonic* spread. Together with this type of drink, customers in the Boston wholesale trade area became familiar with the name *tonic*, both the drink and the name being at first importations from Boston. Importations of this kind are known as *borrowings* (though this type of spread is by no means the only mechanism through which borrowing can take place). A very great number of linguistic features originate in a given place—usually a cultural center such as Boston or New York in America, or London, Paris, Madrid, Florence in Europe—and then are borrowed into other, outlying areas, from the cultural and linguistic focus of diffusion.

A feature which originates in a given place is at first an *innovation* in contrast to whatever preceded it, as was *tonic* meaning "soda-pop" at one time in Boston, or -*i̯*- taking the place of -*ri̯*- in the speech of Tuscany. The innovation is then borrowed, i.e., imitated by the speakers of the surrounding territory; the cause of the imitation usually, though not always, lies in the prestige or

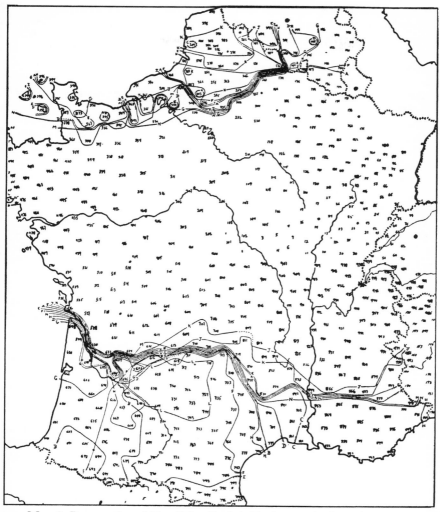

MAP 8: Preservation of Non-Palatalized /k/ before /a/ in Gallo-Romance.

A	blanche	ALF	135	H	cher	ALF	268
B	chaîne	ALF	221	I	cheval	ALF	269
C	chambre	ALF	224	J	chier	ALF	280
D	champ	ALF	225	K	choses	ALF	282
E	chandelle	ALF	229	L	fourchette	ALF	604
F	changer	ALF	230	M	tache	ALF	1275
G	charpentier	ALF	244	N	vache	ALF	1349

K is also attested for *fraîche* (ALF 617) and *sèche, sécher* (ALF 1209, 1210) at 879; for *chienne* (ALF 279) at 965, 966, 975, 978, 979, 985, 986, 987, 988.

higher social standing of such a cultural center as Boston or Florence. As the innovation spreads, the outer edge of its area presents the appearance of a graded area, and in the inner core of the region it eventually replaces all its competitors so that the central part of its territory comes to be a focal area. Finally, the defeated competitors survive only in marginal areas; and eventually, if the process of spread is carried through to its conclusion, even the marginal areas are wiped out and the innovation is solidly evidenced throughout the entire territory.

Innovations do not normally spread evenly throughout a speech-community, travelling directly across country as do migratory insects or plant-spores. Rather, linguistic innovations are adopted by individuals from other individuals, not indiscriminately, but to a greater or lesser extent in accordance with the frequency or *density of communication*. A Maine farmer is more likely to imitate someone from Maine or Massachusetts than someone from California, simply because he has much more frequent and intense contacts with other New Englanders than with Californians. Simple density of communication is not the only factor involved in borrowing; the prestige of those who act as sources for borrowing is also important. Our Maine farmer is more likely to borrow from someone whom he considers worthy of imitation— a politician from Augusta, a successful business man from Portland, a visitor from Boston—than to take over innovations from someone he considers no more than his equal, or below him. The politician from Augusta or the Portland business-man, in his turn, will have gotten some new word or pronunciation on his last trip to Boston, and will serve as an effective intermediary in its distribution.

With ever-increasing mobility, innovations are likely to travel very fast and far, and to be diffused first to secondary and then to tertiary centers of radiation, often by-passing many geographically intermediate but more isolated places, in a manner reminiscent of military "island-hopping" and capture of advanced outposts by parachute troops before the "mopping-up" operations carried out by the main body of an army. Since each innovation will have different connotations for those who take it over, and will receive acceptance in different degrees, the resultant isoglosses will be different for each word involved. This fact is summed up in the well-known maxim that "every word has its own history."

The density of communication is in many instances conditioned by political and economic factors. People tend to get their fashions in language (as in other matters) from the centers to which they look for governmental direction and aid, and where they go to buy and sell their wares. In many cases, isoglosses reflect old territorial boundaries; it has been shown that the spreading lines of the "Rhenish fan" (Map 4) continue the pre-1789 frontiers of the duchies of Jülich and Berg and the electorates of Cologne and Treves (Trier). Similarly, in Italy, the long stretch of territory known as the Papal States (extending from Parma down through Emilia, Romagna, the Marche and Umbria to the area around Rome) served as a corridor for travel and the introduction of new fashions, primarily spreading southward from the

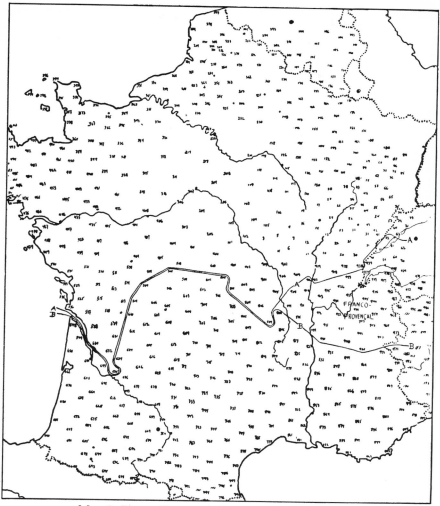

MAP 9: Franco-Provençal (Traditional Presentation).

A   enterrer   ALF   467
B   changer   ALF   230

north. In language, forms showing the voicing of earlier voiceless intervocalic consonants, and various North Italian lexical items, were borrowed southward along this route (as shown in Map 6).

Not only smaller dialect areas, but entire languages may be compared with each other on a geographic basis; in our view of their relationships, we should take into account both their relative positions and the nature of the isoglosses

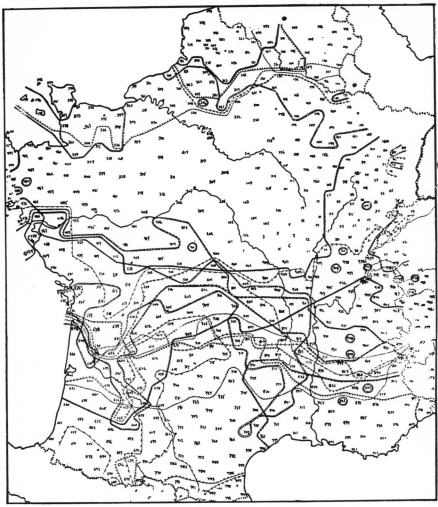

MAP 10: Transitional Zones in Central Gallo-Romance.

Heavy line with hachures: á > é after non-palatal.
Double line with spaced blocks and hachures: á > é, í after palatal.
Line with barbed circles: en > an.
Line with open wedges: k palatalized before a.
Line with spaced teeth: g palatalized before a.
Double line with hachures: Ī delateralized.
Scalloped line: s desibilized.
Light line with hachures: -d- (< -t) lost.

which divide them. Sardinian shows a number of notable archaisms in contrast to the rest of Romance, especially the preservation of high-front quality in the vowel-phoneme continuing Proto-Romance lax /í/ over against /é^/ in the other Romance languages, as in Sardinian /píske/ "fish" vs. Italian /pé^šše/ *pesce* or Old French /pé^is/ *peis*. Clearly, the large-scale preservation of such archaisms is connected with the marginal (isolated, though spatially central) position of Sardinia in the Romance territory. Because of the large number of isoglosses dividing Sardinian from the rest of Romance, we shall consider it a separate language, and not merely a dialect of some other Romance language such as Italian.

In other instances, the nature of the isoglosses may lead us to consider an ensemble of dialects which is often set up as a separate "language," as being really only a great transitional zone. This is the case with Franco-Provençal, which is usually classed as an independent Romance language, on the basis of two isoglosses normally exemplified in only one word each (Map 9). A more extensive examination of the boundary between North and South Gallo-Romance shows plainly, however (cf. Map 10), that a great many individual features show widely separated and flaring isoglosses across the whole east central region of France and French-speaking Switzerland. In the light of these isoglosses, Franco-Provençal is not a unified region at all, linguistically, but is an immense graded area between the focal area of North French and the more conservative regions of southern France and the rest of the Romance territory.

Attempts have been made to codify the principles of linguistic geography, setting up "norms" for the interpretation of the spatial relationships between speech-areas. In a body of doctrine to which he gave the name *Neolinguistica* (cf. Chap. 50), M. G. Bàrtoli (1873–1946) established six such norms, according to which one of two competing forms was to be considered older if it was attested (1) earlier, (2) in an isolated area, (3) in a lateral area (taken in the strictly spatial sense), (4) in the larger of two areas, (5) in a later-settled area or one into which the feature has been borrowed, or (6) if it was obsolete or obsolescent. These norms are useful pointers if they are taken in a relative sense, if it is understood that they do not always apply in every instance, and if they are taken as rules of thumb rather than basic scientific principles. However, such norms cannot take the place—as some have tried to make them do—of more fundamental postulates, especially that of regularity of sound-change (cf. Chap. 50), in historical linguistics.

NOTES

Alpine valleys: Jaberg, 1928.
Density of communication: Bloomfield, 1933a, Chaps. 3–4.
Franco-Provençal: Hall, 1949a.
Bàrtoli's "Neolinguistica": Bàrtoli, 1925; Hall, 1963b, Chap. 1.

PART III

WRITING AND LANGUAGE

44

Graphemics

Up to this point, we have been discussing the structure of language as it is spoken, with no theoretical consideration of writing except as a means for affording as exact a representation of speech as possible, in phonetic or phonemic transcription. Especially when discussing linguistic structure from the synchronic point of view, the analyst often minimizes the importance of writing and particularly that of conventional spelling. Our culture's misconceptions on the relation of writing to speech are so great that it is best, on first approaching synchronic linguistics, to free ourselves from misleading notions which arise from the orthographical representation of language.

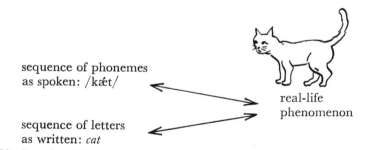

sequence of phonemes
as spoken: /kǽt/

real-life
phenomenon

sequence of letters
as written: *cat*

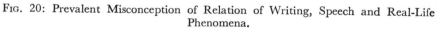

Fig. 20: Prevalent Misconception of Relation of Writing, Speech and Real-Life Phenomena.

Yet writing is a very important adjunct of our use of language, especially in our complex modern society, and it affords the only type of direct attestation we have had (until the invention of sound-recording devices) for the language of past generations. Hence this will be the best place for a discussion of the nature and function of writing, after our treatment of synchronic linguistics and before passing to the historical aspect of language study.

It is widely, but erroneously, believed that a sequence of letters—a written or printed word—represents a "meaning" in the same way and with the same type of direct relationship as does a sequence of phonemes (as shown in Fig. 20). This conception of writing and speech as having an equally direct relationship to the meanings of the real-life world is at the base of the extremely widespread habit of speaking of *written language* as opposed to *spoken language.* However, this conception of the relation between speech and writing rests on an inaccurate analysis of the nature of the "meaning" of what is written. To arrive at a better understanding of the nature and function of writing, we must establish a clear distinction between *real-life meaning* and *linguistic meaning.* '

Language is of course not the only type of symbolism used by humans to convey meaning. Visual symbols are quite widely used, as when a red-and-white pole tells us that the shop in front of which it stands belongs to a barber, or when a colored piece of cloth or bunting stands for a state or nation. In cases of this kind, the visual symbol is related directly to a feature of the world around us, of real life, and so may be said to have real-life meaning. In general, nonlinguistic symbols with real-life meaning are not organized into systems, although there do exist a few instances of such systems; the best-known of these is the European international road-sign code. In this, there are clearly defined structural features, such as the use of a circle to indicate something forbidden, a triangle for danger, a square for something

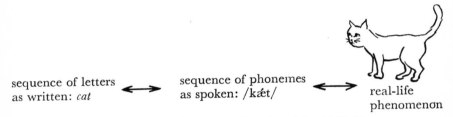

| sequence of letters as written: *cat* | ⟷ | sequence of phonemes as spoken: /kǽt/ | ⟷ | real-life phenomenon |

Fɪɢ. 21: Actual Relation of Writing to Speech and Real-Life Phenomena.

called to the motorist's attention, etc., combined with conventional signs indicating the presence of schools, level crossings, and so forth. Either systematic or nonsystematic visual symbols of this type can be read off in any way desired, since they are not correlated with features of any particular language.

In writing, however, the relation between the visually perceived marks and the real-life situation is never direct. It is always indirect, because the written notation symbolizes one aspect or another of linguistic structure. The letters, characters, or other features of writing do not, in themselves, have real-life meaning, but only linguistic meaning, i.e., a reference to linguistic phenomena. The relation of writing to real-life meaning is that shown in Fig. 21: writing symbolizes speech, and speech in its turn stands for real-life meaning. Some linguistic analysts have tried to salvage the term *written language,* by giving it a narrow, carefully defined meaning of "written representation of language"; but popular misunderstanding on this subject is so great that it is best to discard this misleading term entirely, and to restrict the term *language* to its fundamental manifestation in speech.

In systems of writing, as in language, we can distinguish between functional units and nonsignificant variants. A functional unit of visual shape is a *grapheme*, and a positional variant of a grapheme is an *allograph;* if desired, we can use the marks ⟨ ⟩ to enclose a graphemic symbol. In our printed form of the Roman alphabet, there are few allographic variations in the shapes of the letters, except for minor variants like the dotless allograph of ⟨i⟩ in the ligature *fi*. In the Greek alphabet, the grapheme ⟨σ⟩ "sigma",

SYLLABARY
a
i
u
kᵃ
kᵘ
xᵃ
gᵃ
gᵘ
cᵃ
jᵃ
jⁱ
tᵃ
tᵘ
θᵃ
çᵃ
dᵃ
dⁱ
dᵘ
nᵃ
nᵘ
pᵃ
fᵃ
bᵃ
mᵃ
mⁱ
mᵘ
yᵃ
rᵃ
rᵘ
lᵃ
vᵃ
vⁱ
sᵃ
šᵃ
zᵃ
hᵃ
IDEOGRAMS
XŠ = xšāyaθiya
BU = būmiš
DH = dahyāuš
AM = Aura-mazdā
BG = baga
AMmaiy
WORD DIVIDERS

FIG. 22: Part of the Old Persian Syllabary.

corresponding to our ⟨s⟩, has the two allographs ς (occurring only at the end of a word, before space) and σ (used elsewhere): e.g., *σωφία* /so:phí:a:/ "wisdom", but *ἄνθρωπος* /ánthro:pos/ "man". Capital letters in some writing systems constitute simply allographs of the small letters, but in others (such as most of the West European orthographies) capitals constitute a separate closely related sub-system, as do also italics, small capitals, bold-face letters, and other systematic variations affecting the entire alphabet. Accent marks such as the acute ⟨´⟩, the grave ⟨`⟩, and the circumflex ⟨^⟩, or superscript elements like the diaeresis ⟨¨⟩ and subscript elements like the cedilla ⟨¸⟩, are added to ordinary graphemes in a manner reminiscent of suprasegmental phonemic features (p. 84).

It is, in theory, possible to analyze graphemes purely in terms of the structure of their visual shapes, identifying their graphic components such as vertical strokes, horizontal strokes, curves, etc.; an analysis of this type is very useful in palaeography (the study of ancient manuscripts). For our purposes, however, the only useful analysis of a graphemic system is in terms of the symbolization it affords to features of linguistic structure, i.e., in terms of its linguistic meaning. The linguistic feature to which a grapheme refers is its *referent*. The referents of a system of writing can be the phonemes, the morphophonemic alternations, or the morphemes of a language, or more than one of these at the same time.

In our modern world, we are most familiar with writing which represents units of sound—phonemes or morphophonemes. A writing system whose graphemes correspond to phonemes is an *alphabet*. It is rare for an alphabet to afford representation to sub-phonemic (allophonic) variations, if it has been developed by native speakers of the language. We do not, for instance, give separate representation to the aspirated [p'] of English ['p'ɪt] *pit* and the unaspirated [p] of ['spɪt] *spit*. If anyone were to propose doing so, the innovation would hardly be successful, because, as native speakers of English, we are normally unaware of the existence of the difference between these two sounds; indeed, we have been trained to ignore it ever since childhood. If non-native speakers devise an alphabet for a language, they often provide special representation for allophonic variants which have significance in their own native language. In Japanese, the sounds [tˢ], [č] and [t] are all allophones of one phoneme /t/, and [ʃ] and [s] are allophones of /s/; but Romaji (the normally accepted orthography used for writing Japanese in Roman characters) provides separate representation for each of these sounds, because for the Westerners who devised this romanization they seemed phonemically distinct, and so, for instance, /mitubisi/ [mitˢubiʃi] is Romanized as *Mitsubishi*.

In representing phonemes, *compound graphemes* are often used: examples are quite widespread, such as our use of ⟨sh⟩ for /ʃ/, ⟨ph⟩ for /f/, or ⟨th⟩ for both /θ/ and /ð/. In Italian spelling, ⟨ci⟩ and ⟨gi⟩ stand for /c/ and /g/, respectively, before ⟨a o u⟩: e.g., *mancia* /mánča/ "tip", *mangio* /mánǧo/ "I eat", whereas ⟨ch⟩ and ⟨gh⟩ represent /k/ and /g/ before ⟨e i⟩, as in *cheto* /kéˆto/ "quiet", *ghermito* /germíto/ "crowded". French orthography uses ⟨ch⟩ for /ʃ/, as in *chanter* /ʃateˆ/ "to sing". Compound graphemes can be discontinuous, a situation with which we are very familiar in English orthography, with the use of a "mute *e*" at the end of the spelling of a word to indicate that the preceding vowel letter has "long value": *a . . . e* stands for /e/, as in *hate* /hét/, *waste* /wést/, and similarly for *e . . . e* /i/, *i . . . e* /aj/, *o . . . e* /o/, and *u . . . e* /(j)u/: *Mede* /míd/, *tide* /tájd/, *rode* /ród/, *tune* /t(j)ún/. A double consonant letter, if it stands for a single phoneme, is a compound grapheme, as is ⟨pp⟩ in English *happy* /hǽpi/, *jolly* /dʒáli/. Combinations of three or more graphemes are occasionally found representing single phonemes, as in German ⟨sch⟩ for /ʃ/: *Schelm* /ʃélm/ "rogue". The opposite phenomenon, use of a single grapheme to stand for a cluster of phonemes, is somewhat less common, but not rare, as in the use (in Latin, French, English, etc., orthography) of ⟨x⟩ for /ks/, Greek ⟨Ψ⟩ (psi) for /ps/, and Russian ⟨щ⟩ for /šč/.

If we were to keep on pronouncing /ənǽpəl/ and /əbúk/, but were to write the indefinite article as *an* throughout; *an apple* and **an book*, the use of *an* for both /ə/ and /ən/ would be morphophonemic writing, since in this instance the letter *n* would stand for the alternation between the phoneme /n/ and zero. The occurrence of graphemes with morphophonemic reference is, in English spelling, limited mostly to instances of (more or less optional) alternations of full (stressed) vowel phonemes with reduced (unstressed) vowels: e.g., ⟨a⟩ standing for /ǽ/ in *organic* /ɔrgǽnɪk/, but for /ə/ in *organize* /ɔ́rgənàjz/. Russian orthography affords widespread morphophonemic representation to alternations between full vowels under stress and reduced vowels not under stress: the first five phonemes of the root for "good" are spelled хорош— in both хорошо /xarašó/ (neuter sg. nom., acc.) and хороший /xaróši/ (m. sg. nom.). French orthography affords extensive representation to morphophonemic alternations in sandhi-variants (cf. Chap. 22). The "regular" plural suffix of substantives is /z/ before vowels and zero before pause or consonants, but both of these allomorphs are represented by *s* in conventional spelling; the /leˆz/ of /leˆzarbr/ "the trees" and the /leˆ/ of /leˆgarsõ/ "the boys" are both spelled *les: les arbres, les garçons*. Especially since French is usually taught on the basis of its conventional spelling, one of the major problems of the non-native learner is to know when a final consonant letter stands for a phoneme ("is pronounced") and when it represents phonemic zero ("is silent").

Intermediate between alphabetic and morphemic representation, but still with specifically phonologic reference, is the use of graphemes to represent syllables. Such use is found sporadically in our Western European tradition, such as *&* standing for /ɛt/ (in English, only in *&c.* /ɛtsétərə/). For various non-European languages, however, complete sets of graphemes with syllabic referents have been devised; such a set of graphemes is a *syllabary*. The earliest syllabaries were those used to represent the languages spoken two to three thousand years ago in the Middle East: Sumerian, Akkadian, Old Persian. Two distinct, though related, syllabaries, known as katakana and hiragana, are used for Japanese, either independently or conjointly with Chinese characters. One of the most famous syllabaries was that invented in 1821 for Cherokee by a native speaker named Sequoyah; his syllabary did yeoman service for nearly a century. A syllabary is especially useful for languages with a simple phonological structure and a restricted number of syllable-types, so that the total number of syllables to be represented is relatively small; for such languages, a syllabary may be more economical than an alphabetic writing system.

Not all the elements of an orthographical system are letters of the alphabet. All our familiar West European orthographies and many others include nonalphabetical marks of *punctuation;* for the most part, these signal suprasegmental features of stress, juncture, or intonation. It is relatively rare for an orthography to be thoroughly consistent in symbolizing even one of these prosodic aspects of a language. Spanish orthography is highly consistent in its representation of stress, using an acute accent-mark whenever a word ending in *l* or *r* is not stressed on the last syllable, and whenever any other word is not stressed on the next to the last: *cantar* /kantár/ "to sing", *Alcázar* /alkáθar/, *canto* /kánto/ "I sing", *cantó* /kantó/ "he sang", *lástima* /lástima/ "pity". Most other orthographies are either incomplete in this respect (e.g., Italian) or give no representation at all to stress (English, German, and so forth). Internal open juncture is occasionally represented, by a hyphen or some such device; especially in English spelling, however, the use of the hyphen in words like *tram-car* or *speech-sound* is most haphazard, and dictionaries give us, in this respect, nothing but the codification of complicated and irrational inconsistencies. Punctuation marks (comma, period, etc.) stand primarily for features of intonation, but here again, no orthography provides more than a sketchy representation. In our Western European tradition, the use of punctuation has further been confused by rules of pseudo-logic and prescriptions couched in terms of meaning ("nonrestrictive clauses are set off by commas," etc.) which have served only to becloud the issue and render our use of punctuation less effective than it would otherwise be.

The other chief use of graphemes is to represent morphemes. When we write an Arabic numeral like *2, 3, 4,* or a mathematical symbol like $+$, or a chemical symbol like Fe or Na, these graphemes (simple or compound) stand for morphemes of English or some other language, and are "read off" with the morphemes (usually, but not always, "words") they represent: /tú/ *two*, /θrí/ *three*, /fór/ *four*, /plás/ *plus*, /ájrn/ *iron*, /sódiəm/ *sodium* for the six graphemes given above. In other languages, these same symbols will be read off with the equivalent morphemes in each language, and arithmetic or mathematic formulas will correspond to different syntactic types in different languages: *3 x 3 = 9* stands for English *three times three equals* (or *is*) *nine*, French *trois fois trois font neuf*, German *dreimal drei macht neun*, or Italian *tre volte tre fanno nove*. In instances like these, our folklore about language tells us that the symbols stand for abstract "ideas" or "meanings"; but this is not the case, since in every instance there is a specific morpheme in each language to which the grapheme corresponds. This is true also for writing systems where, as in the case of Chinese characters or Egyptian hieroglyphs, a large set of characters is used, each character corresponding to a morpheme of the language. Such characters are often termed *ideographs*, because of the inaccurate notion just referred to. However, even though both Chinese characters and Egyptian hieroglyphs grew out of rebus-like pictures with real-life meanings, by the time they were used in complete graphemic systems, they had ceased to have such real-life meanings and had acquired, instead, purely linguistic meanings. As against alphabetic writing, a set of characters with morphemic reference has the grave disadvantage that there must be a far greater number of characters, since every language has tens of thousands of distinct morphemes, and the users of such a set of characters are subjected to a much heavier burden on their memory than are those whose languages are represented alphabetically. One advantage of a set of characters like those of Chinese, however, is that a message written in characters can be read off in any one of a group of related dialects, even though the phonologic differences between these latter may be (as they are in the varieties of Chinese) in some instances so great as to render them mutually unintelligible when their speakers meet and try to talk together.

NOTES

Graphemics: Bloomfield, 1933a, Chap. 17; Gleason, 1961, Chap. 25; Hall, 1962.
History of writing: Cohen, 1958; Diringer, 1944; Gelb, 1952.
Old Persian syllabary: Kent, 1950.
Non-linguistic visual symbols: Buyssens, 1943; Moulton, 1956.

45

Sound and Spelling

THE DEGREE of correlation between two systems of any kind is known as the *fit* which they manifest (the extent to which one *fits* the other). The closer the correlation, the more perfect the fit. In the relation between orthographies and the linguistic phenomena they represent, the fit is usually considerably less than perfect. There are two purposes that a writing system can have: to provide a complete representation of a linguistic sub-system (e.g. phonology), for analysts or learners of the language; or to serve simply as a mnemonic device, to recall some (not all) of the salient features of the language for those who already know it. It is this latter service that users of an orthography, who are normally native speakers of the language in question, require of it; this fact makes them, not only content with an imperfect fit between sound and spelling, but often impatient with a fit which is more nearly perfect but not in accord with their intrained and ingrained orthographic habits.

It is of course possible to attain a perfect fit between sound and spelling; linguistic analysts, who want as complete and accurate a representation as possible, consider it highly desirable to design their transcriptions for this purpose. In a phonetic transcription, it is hard to devise enough symbols to cover all the possible shadings of sound that may occur, even though this was the original ideal of the founders of the IPA (cf. p. 76); disappointment over the unattainability of this ideal was one of the motives underlying the development of phonemic theory. In a complete phonemic transcription, we can give a thorough and accurate representation for all of the significant units of sound, on both the segmental and supra-segmental levels; such a transcription is indispensable for further work on the levels of morphology and syntax.

The ordinary speaker of a language, however, is not concerned with its analysis, and requires of an orthography only that it give him enough indication of what has been said so that he can supply the rest as he reads. The redundancy of language (pp. 105–107) is such that a great deal can be omitted without a correspondingly great loss in the conveyance of the message. This is why our conventional punctuation is so sketchy, since, for everyday purposes, only an approximate indication of intonation is necessary; hence also the need for novelists to give a more detailed indication of how their characters speak, by describing them as *growling, screaming, snorting,* etc. In their familiar correspondence, speakers of French, Czech, Spanish, and other languages whose orthographies use accent-marks, often omit these latter, since for a native speaker of (say) French, the accent-less *J'ai deja ete au theatre* "I've already been to the theater" is fully as comprehensible as the official spelling with accent marks *J'ai déjà été au théâtre*. In the Semitic languages (e.g. Hebrew and Arabic), the vowel phonemes bear primarily the indication of inflectional variation, such as number and tense, and are much less important for conveying "dictionary meaning" than are the consonant phonemes. Hence the earliest forms of Hebrew and Arabic writing indicated only the consonants, and signs to represent the vowels were not added until considerably later, thus giving rise to considerable difficulty in the interpretation of the sacred scriptures of the Old Testament and the Koran. Since English has a similar use of vowel-phonemes in many forms, its orthographic representation would not be too incomprehensible if the vowel letters were omitted in the same way: *sh- s-ngs th- s-ngs h-r m-th-r t-ght h-r*, or even *sh sngs th sngs hr mthr tght hr*.

In a perfect fit between grapheme and phoneme, there are exactly as many graphemes as there are phonemes. Imperfections of fit can be caused either by an insufficient number of graphemes for the phonemes to be represented; or by an excess of graphemes over phonemes; or by inconsistent use of graphemes. English orthography suffers from all three of these defects. We have somewhere between thirty-four and forty linear phonemes in English (depending on the formulation one accepts; cf. Chap. 20), and only twenty-six letters of the Roman alphabet to represent them. By using combinations of letters as compound graphemes (pp. 266–267), it would be possible to devise an adequate, wholly consistent phonemically-based orthography to cover both British and American English; such orthographies (not to be confused with naive varieties of "reformed spelling" à la Bernard Shaw!) have been devised, notably by Bloch and Joos. However, our spelling lacks adequate representation for a number of phonemes, especially /ə a ɔ/ among the vowels, and /ð ʒ/ among the consonants. Among European orthographies, similar inadequacies are found most extensively in the spelling of French, which gives poor representation to its mid-back vowels /o/ and /oˆ/, and to its nasalized vowels; that of Italian does not distinguish adequately between the lax mid-vowels /e o/ and the tense mid-vowels /eˆ oˆ/. Minor inadequacies of this kind are to be found even in the orthographies of German, Spanish, or Russian.

On the other hand, an orthography may have too many graphemes for a particular phoneme, even at the same time as it affords inadequate representation to other phonemes. In English spelling, we do not need both the simple grapheme *f* and the compound grapheme *ph* for /f/. Either one would afford an unambiguous representation: we could perfectly well write *Filadelfia*, *filosofy*, *fosforus*, using only *f* (as is done in Italian and Spanish, in which the corresponding forms are written *Filadelfia*, *filosofia*, *fósforo*); or, conceivably, we could use *ph* throughout, which would give us *phorty-phive*, *phitphul*, or *awphul*. The former possibility does not strike us as too unreasonable although of course many of us are too conservative to feel really happy about it; the latter strikes our risibilities because it has been used for centuries as a device of eye-dialect (cf. below). Likewise, we do not need both *k* and *c* to stand for /k/, nor both *s* and *c* to represent /s/ (in fact, the letter *c*, as a unit grapheme, is not put to any effective use in English orthography), nor yet *x* for /ks/.

A special case of excessive use of graphemes in proportion to phonemes is the representation of phonemic zero. The only sensible representation for phonemic zero is, of course, graphemic zero—not writing a letter where it does not correspond to anything pronounced. In both English and French orthography, however, there are a number of "silent letters" which, from the point of view of phonemic representation, are quite unnecessary, like the *b* in English *debt* /dét/, the *c* in *indict* /ındájt/, the *g* in *paradigm* /pǽrə-dɪm/ or /pǽrədàjm/, or the *h* in French *théâtre* /teˆaˀtr/. We will not include the final *n* of *damn* /dǽm/ or the *g* of *phlegm* /flɛ́m/, because these letters are morphophonemic in their representational function: /n/ reappears in *damnation* /dæmnéʃən/, and /g/ in *phlegmatic* /flɛgmǽtık/. For the most part, these "silent letters" are a heritage from the late Middle Ages and the Renaissance, when scribes (who were paid by the page) used to add extra letters in order to pad out the text and increase the number of pages, and learnèd men would copy the spelling of Latin and Greek to show off their knowledge and thus distinguish themselves from the vulgar herd. On occasion, their efforts to be learnèd would lead them to introduce letters that were never present in the Latin or Greek originals, as in English *author*, earlier *autor*, a borrowing from Old French *autor*, in its turn borrowed from Latin *auctōrem*. Later generations have, in some instances, taken to pronouncing these historically unjustified additions in their normal values, so that we now say, for instance, /ɔ́θər/; such a reinterpretation on the basis of spelling is a *spelling-pronunciation*.

Another source of imperfect fit between sound and spelling is alternate representation for a single phoneme. In English, the tense vowels /i e o/ each have several representations, e.g., *e . . . e*, *ee*, *ea* for /i/, as in *Mede*, *meed*, *mead*, all standing for /míd/ in its different meanings. From a structural point of view, this superfluity of representation is haphazard, since it corresponds to no functional characteristics of the words which are pronounced the same but spelled differently: there is nothing about /míd/ "a drink made from honey" which should determine its being spelled with *ea*, and nothing about *ee* which should cause it to be used in the spelling of /míd/ "reward". If every word pronounced the same were spelled the same, there would still be no more ambiguity than there is in speech, since the context normally makes their meaning clear. The chief use of these alternate spellings in English and French is for morphemic distinction, giving a quick means of telling at a glance and out of context (e.g., in lists or dictionaries) which meaning a word has: if we see the spelling *mead*, we know at once that it refers to "a drink made of honey", not "reward" or "an ancient Persian". Such morphemic distinctions by means of alternate graphemic representation are a grave impediment to the learner at the initial stages of developmental reading, since they require a considerable extra investment of effort in memory to keep the spelling of homonyms distinct. However, they are probably a help to the experienced reader, enabling him to identify words by their peculiarities of spelling and thus reducing his dependence on the total context, so that he can increase his speed in reading.

Many of the quirks of the inadequate fit between sound and spelling are consecrated in our official orthography, and are codified in dictionaries, which, for a large part of the public, serve as the official sanctuaries where they may be venerated. Other possible inconsistencies have, however, not been thus canonized, and serve for occasional indication of special connotations, often with disapproval from purists who approve only the irregularities that have received official sanctification. An extra "mute *e*" makes *Ye Olde Gifte Shoppe* appear quainte or the like to its patrons; use of *k* instead of *c* seems "snappy" to the buyers of *Kustom Klothes on Kredit*. Use of an "incorrect" spelling which in actuality represents the facts of pronunciation better than does the "correct" spelling, is known as *eye-dialect*, as when we write *wimmin* instead of *women* for /wímən/, or *vittles* rather than *victuals* for /vítəlz/. Eye-dialect serves as a device to make fun of someone whom the writer wants the reader to consider ignorant or illiterate. If we represent someone's speech with such spellings as *wimmin* or *vittles*, we are telling the reader "this character is the kind of person who, if there were a substandard pronunciation for *women* or *victuals*, would use it." In earlier centuries, when schools and typists were less insistent on unified spelling, alternations in spelling were much more widespread than they are now, and apparently without arousing the hostility which they provoke today, e.g., *cloke* and *cloak*, *smoke* and *smoak*.

English orthography shows a nearly perfect fit between sound and spelling in a great many words, particularly those with lax ("short") vowels: *cat*, *fat*, *hat*, *rat*, *bid*, *ten*, *but*, *sop*, and thousands of others whose spelling is completely regular. In many others, there is less than perfect fit, but the irregularities show a certain amount of patterning, as in *meat*, *seat*, *feat*, *neat*, *beat*, etc., all with *ea* for /i/, or in *physics*, *epitaph*, *photo*, *telephone*, and all the others which show *ph* for /f/. The really irregular spellings such as *choir* /kwájr/ and *laugh* /lǽf/ are relatively few. In other words, English orthography is not, as is often thought, wholly irregular and haphazard; there is a gradation in the fit between sound and spelling. A very large number of our words are spelled quite regularly, and another large number are only semi-irregular, in that their irregularities fall into patterned sets; only a small percentage of our words show patternless irregularities in their spelling. As we shall see in Chaps. 73–74, these facts should be taken into account in our teaching of reading and spelling, although our educationists have in general neglected them, with disastrous results for our children's ability to read and spell.

NOTES

Fit of orthographies and sound-systems: Gleason, 1961, Chap. 25; Hall, 1961.
A phonemically-based orthography for English: Joos, 1960.

PART IV

LINGUISTIC CHANGE

46

Child Language

Human language, as we have already observed (p. 34), is constantly changing, both in each person's idiolect and in the usage of the speech community. It is only by a necessary fiction that we treat linguistic systems, for the purposes of synchronic analysis, as if they were static and unchanging. The linguistic analyst's first task is the synchronic description of linguistic structures; his second task is to formulate the changes that take place in language with the passage of time, through irreversible alterations. That such changes take place, is generally realized by the public at large, in our culture; what is not so widely known is that they are steadily and inevitably at work altering the structure of every language, so much so as to render successive stages of a language very different both in structure and in vocabulary. If a Roman of 0 A.D., a speaker of the Old French of 1000 A.D., and a speaker of Modern French could be brought together, no one of them could understand the other two without studying their speech as he would a pair of foreign languages. Just to take one word as an example, for the eighth month of the year the Roman would have said /augustu(m)/, the speaker of Old French /aúst/, and the modern Frenchman /u/ août.

People often wonder how human language began, and what its earliest stages of development were. In the early nineteenth century, before the Darwinian revolution in scientific thought deepened our time-perspective on human history by millions of years, and while the Biblical chronology was still thought to limit the origin of the human race to perhaps 6000 B.C., one of the main reasons for the comparative study of the Indo-European languages was the hope that it would enable us to reconstruct the speech of "primitive" man. This expectation has long since been abandoned as illusory, since reconstructed Proto-Indo-European (cf. Chap. 51) was simply a language like any other, and the period to which we can go back by the most daring reconstruction—say, perhaps five or six thousand years ago—represents only the merest scratch on the surface of human history. The only way by which we can obtain at least an idea of how human speech may have acquired its basic characteristics (cf. pp. 6–7) is by observing its development in the ordinary person, on the well known principle that ontogeny (the life-history of each individual) recapitulates phylogeny (the development of the species). From this point of view, the early development of language in the child, up through adolescence, is of especial interest, and furnishes another avenue of transition from the synchronic to the diachronic approach in linguistics.

A new-born baby has the innate ability to make noises with its vocal organs, and from birth it cries and babbles. Its babbling is quite random, but is essential to linguistic development in that it provides the baby with its initial practice in managing and coördinating its organs of speech. All during the time the baby is making aimless noises, its parents and others who come in contact with it are talking to it and about it; its conditioning to a particular linguistic environment begins at birth. The normal parent or nurse is actively concerned in helping the child to learn to talk, and from a very early stage, it is told "This doll for baby. Baby see doll? Baby play with nice doll," etc., often in a special variety of *baby-talk*, with reduced grammatic structures, which adults think suitable for the baby's limited understanding. Proud parents, especially, listen for the infant's first word, and are often ready to interpret some fragment of its babbling as if it were a meaningful utterance—taking, say, a repeated [mamama] as the word *mama*, or [dada-dada] as if it were *dada, daddy*, or the like.

The first stage in the child's development of linguistic habits comes when it imitates the speech of those around it with a certain degree of recognizability, and with a firm correlation between the utterance and some phenomenon of the environment, i.e., with a definite meaning. At this stage, there are always at least two phonemes (if there were only one phoneme, there would be no phonemic contrasts and hence no system); often there are more, although they may not correspond very closely to those of the adults' language. Some scholars consider that there is a definite order in the development of phonemic contrasts, first between labial and nonlabial (oral) in the consonants, and then with further differentiation in oral consonants between dental and nondental, and similarly for vowel contrasts. However, our data are still too scanty to permit of such generalizations, and some evidence would seem to indicate that not all children's systematic contrasts develop in the same order. For instance, the writer's son developed three "first words" at the same time, ['baba] "doll", ['bebi] "baby", and ['naw] "now", with three vowel phonemes /a e i/ and three consonant phonemes /b n w/. At this stage, each utterance constitutes a separate morpheme (is *monomorphemic*), without any necessary similarity to the rest of the stock of morphemes; as each new utterance is learned, it constitutes a further separate morpheme. Duality, in the existence of a set of phonemes and also of a set of morphemes, starts as soon as the child has two distinct, meaningful utterances that he habitually uses; productivity does not start until later.

Cultural transmission thus begins from the earliest stages, through the child's contact with the linguistic and nonlinguistic behavior of those around him, and his imitation thereof. Some psychologists consider that the ability to imitate is an inborn trait of humans, whereas others consider that imitation is itself learned rather than innate. It seems certain, in any case, that there is an optimum stage at which children learn their first language through direct imitation of other humans. If this stage is passed without language habits being acquired, the individual's ability to do so may be gravely impaired. There are well-authenticated cases of children who have been brought up by wolves or other animals in India (à la Mowgli) and who have come to live in human society only at the age of thirteen or fifteen; the extent to which they are, by then, able to learn speech and other human behavior patterns is still a subject of debate.

As the child's stock of morphemes grows, so does his phonemic inventory; but, especially in the first two or two-and-a-half years, his range both of sounds and of phonemes is usually rather restricted and often markedly different from those of the adults around him. The actual sounds he uses frequently do not correspond to those of the adults: he may use nasalized vowels where adults have vowel + nasal consonant, as in one child's [ˈtehõ] for /télǝfòn/ telephone, or he may have palatalized [kʲ] where adults have [t] and [k], as in another child's [ˈkʲikʲi] for /kíti/ kitty. In a case like this latter, the child's phonemic structure was unquestionably different from that of the adults: corresponding to their /t/ and /k/, he had only one phoneme, which could be transcribed with either symbol, as it was intermediate between the two. Every child's phonemic system, in the course of its expansion, passes through a number of stages of development, often with defective contrasts in one part of the system or another, and one or more resultant archiphonemes (Chap. 20). Childish mispronunciations, or adults' interpretation of them, often become part of the family dialect and remain in use for years or decades, such as the name Kiki for a cat in the instance just cited, or another child's tumpy for tummy, itself orginally a childish word of the same kind for stomach. In one family, such forms as /múgɪs/ for music, /ǽkɪt/ for attic, and /sílo/ for cereal have become virtually regular; almost every family could furnish parallels. Our familiar nicknames such as Meg or Peg for Margaret, Doll(y) for Dorothy, etc., which show considerable distortion as compared with their prototypes, were originally childish forms of this kind which eventually passed from one or more family dialects into general usage.

The decisive step in the child's linguistic development comes when the closed system of his monomorphemic utterances becomes open, i.e., productive, in that he begins to combine the elements of his already-learned utterances into forms that he has not heard from others. If he has learned, say, daddy come, mommy come, and daddy all gone, and then produces, on his own, mommy all gone without any other speaker as a model, he has reached the stage of productivity. This productivity is attained through analogical new-formation: the child has learned to make new formations on the analogy of already existing combinations: if he has elements a, b, c, d in the combinations ac, ad, and bc, he makes bd on the analogy ac : ad = bc / x, where x = bd. This ability to analogize, to meet new situations with new combinations of already known elements, is perhaps the human being's most valuable intellectual asset, and it is manifested first and most extensively in his use of language.

As soon as the child has learned to analogize, the expansion of his linguistic system goes ahead by leaps and bounds, usually between the ages of around one-and-a-half to five or six years old. This is a period of tremendous learning, especially in the acquisition of functors and their combination patterns. The child builds up his idiolect by a process of continuous trial and error, normally in a completely unreflecting way, as he plays and, in fact, as a major part of his play-activity. This trial-and-error process consists primarily of the exploration of paths of analogy, in the course of which the child learns by experience which new-formations are acceptable to those around him and which are not. He thus learns that he can, for instance, form regular plurals like *bushes*, *hats*, *tables*, and so forth by the thousands, with almost any new nouns he learns, but that for certain ones the regular plural formation is not acceptable: he must say *men*, *feet*, *geese*, *sheep*, not *mans*, *foots*, *gooses*, *sheeps*. Every family has its own stock of stories about its children's analogical errors. In one family, a child, obviously treating *please excuse me* as if it consisted of **pleasex* plus **cuse me*, would say after a meal "Pleasex cuse me; pleasex take off my bib." In her third and fourth year, the writer's daughter made such formations as *sambals:* "sandals", *ondions:* "onions", and *balloons:* "loons". When the writer was in the third grade, his teacher would say "Class, be seated", pronouncing *be seated* very prissily as [biˈsit+ɪt], and, on the model of *beat it!* and *cheese it!*, he interpreted this injunction as *beseat it!*.

By the sixth or seventh year, the "blood and bone" of a child's linguistic system, i.e., the grammatical core of his idiolect (cf. Chap. 21), is almost fully formed. There may still be various minor divergences from the community's usage that remain to be ironed out, especially one idiosyncrasy or another with regard to analogical formations like *foots* (*feets*) or *wroten*. Normally, these irregularities are eliminated in the next few years. Nevertheless, sporadic analogical formations continue throughout every individual's life. When we are tired, rattled, or talking too fast to notice what we are doing, we may make "slips of the tongue" such as *mans*, *writed*, or *intelligenter*. On occasion, such unusual formations serve humorous purposes (as when Lewis Carroll has Alice remark "Curiouser and curiouser!"), or are features of a recherché literary style, as in Joyce's analogical coinages in *Ulysses* and *Finnegan's Wake*. In other words, each individual's grammatical core always retains a certain degree of capacity for analogical new-formation, and never becomes completely ossified as long as he remains an active participant in his community's speech-activity.

Even after the fifth or sixth year, the capacity for acquiring completely new linguistic habits does not decrease immediately. Children are able, especially if moved into a new linguistic environment, to learn a new language, even one of entirely different structure from their first one, in a very short time. In our culture, at least, this ability continues until around the age of ten or twelve; in other cultures it seems to last longer. There is some evidence that the well-known difficulties which our adolescents have in learning a second language is connected, not with physical maturation, but with inhibitions which are limited to our culture. Boys, especially, more than girls, seem to learn from those slightly older than themselves, when they come into adolescence, that it is unseemly to distinguish oneself by being skillful at making "funny noises" with one's face. This comes to be a matter of mores, quite literally a question of morality, and differing only in degree from such equally immoral behavior as killing one's grandmother. Most individuals remain adaptable to regional variations for a rather longer period of time—perhaps because such variations are farther removed from conscious analysis—and a person moving to a new part of the country (e.g., going off to college), up to the age of twenty or so, adapts easily to the local speech-patterns.

Lexicon is the last aspect of language to slow down in its development, and it never completely stops growing. Each of us keeps on learning new contentives, even into old age. The exact extent of any individual's lexicon at any given time is hard to estimate, because, although some words that he learned in the past may have gone out of his active use, there is never any telling when, even up to the day of his death, some quirk of memory may bring them back into use again. Particularly in derivatives and compounds, new combinations are constantly being made, and this fact introduces a still further aspect of indeterminacy into lexical growth and structure.

Each individual thus builds up his own idiolect, but of course not out of his own inner consciousness. On the contrary, he forms it almost wholly by imitation of those with whom he comes into contact: first his parents or those who take care of him in childhood, and later his playmates, those who are slightly older than himself, and other persons whom he esteems enough to take as models. Until recently, the mass-communication media were not by any means as strong an influence on an individual's speech as was the usage of his age-mates, with their local peculiarities. In recent years, there has been some evidence that nation-wide radio and television are acting as models, not for the active elimination of local dialects, but for the establishment of a national variety of pronunciation and usage free from marked local characteristics.

There is no possibility of ever recapturing the details of the first prehistoric development of human language, because it lies too many hundreds of millennia in the past. We shall never know, even, whether language developed only once in the history of the race, at one specific time and place (according to the *monogenetic theory*), or at several times and places, and among different groups of incipient humans (as the *polygenetic theory* holds). However, if linguistic ontogeny can be taken as a suggestive parallel, it would seem likely that the first stage must have been the growth of firm correlations between certain sequences of sounds and what they referred to, i.e., their meanings. For how long a period such correlations kept arising and lasting only a short time, without being taught to the young, we have no way of knowing; but cultural transmission must have set in soon, if, indeed, it did not already exist in a rudimentary form for nonlinguistic behavior patterns. The next step must have been the development of productivity, with the formation of new utterances by analogy; until this stage was reached, utterances may have had duality (in the existence of a phonemic and a morphemic level), but can only have been monomorphemic, as children's earliest utterances still are.

At this earliest stage of language development (hundreds of thousands of years ago), there must have been extensive *creation* of new relationships between functors in the grammatic cores of nascent languages, and between contentives and their meanings. However, these early stages lie so far back in history that all developments that took place then have long since been completely obliterated by myriads of later changes. Some overly optimistic investigators have hoped to find, surviving in modern languages, primitive elements of original human speech, such as universal root-forms. Such expectations are now recognized by all competent scholars to be completely illusory, and only untrained persons or fanatics ride this hobby-horse any longer. Nor is there any really "creative" activity going on in language change at present, nor has there been for as far back as we can reconstruct linguistic history. In the last few thousand years (and probably for tens of thousands of years before that, or even longer), linguistic change has consisted simply of the reshuffling of already existing elements and of their combination-types, with nothing truly new being created. The best formulation of the nature of linguistic development at the present stage of human history was given by Dante in the *Divine Comedy:*

> Opera natural è ch'uom favella,
> Ma così o così, Natura lascia
> Poi fare a voi, secondo che v'abbella.

"It is an inborn characteristic that man speaks; but whether this way or that, Nature leaves it up to you, as best suits your fancy."

NOTES

Bibliography of child language: Leopold, 1952.

Linguistic ontogeny: Hockett, 1958, Chap. 41; Jespersen, 1922, Chaps. 5–10; Osgood and Sebeok, 1954-§6.1.

The most extensive single study of a child's speech: Leopold, 1939–47.

Development of syntax in children's speech: Braine, 1963.

Children brought up by animals: Brown, 1958, Chap. 5.

Family dialects: Read, 1962.

47

Innovations and Competition

AT ANY GIVEN POINT of time, most of a linguistic system is in equilibrium, without alternate possibilities in usage; if it were not mostly in equilibrium, its users would not be able to communicate as they do. But no system is in complete equilibrium: there are always some points on which there are oscillations in usage. These oscillations can occur on any level of linguistic structure. They can be of phonetic nature: do you use [ɹ] or [ř] as the allophone of /r/ after /t/ in, say, *train*, or after /d/ in *drain*? On the phonemic level, some speakers distinguish between /e/, /ɛ/ and /æ/ in such a set as *Mary, merry, marry*, while others neutralize the contrast (pp. 121–122). In morphology, some use forms like *dived, awaked* while others use *dove, awoke;* in syntax, the intransitive use of a verb like *identify* (as in *He doesn't identify with a group very easily*) is in competition with the transitive-reflexive use of the same verb (*He doesn't identify himself with a group very easily*). Moot points of this type are present in all languages at all times; change (from which no living language is exempt) takes place through the rise of innovations which enter into competition with existing habits, and the gradual favoring of an innovation as opposed to the older alternative, until the latter finally becomes obsolete and disappears.

Normally, we cannot document the very first appearance of any given innovation, because minor innovations are taking place all the time in our everyday speech, without anyone paying any attention to them. "Slips of the tongue" such as *breaked* or *swimmed*, casual variations in pronunciation like an aspirated [pʼ] in ['spʼʌn] under emphatic stress, deliberately humorous coinages on the order of *wibble* ("wobble and wiggle")—all of these are part and parcel of normal linguistic behavior. Even if a particular individual becomes so fond of an innovation of his own that he adopts it as part of his regular speech-habits (e.g., a certain person's fondness for the spelling-pronunciation /pǽrədɪgəm/ for *paradigm*), it still has very little likelihood of becoming anything more than just an idiosyncratic peculiarity of one idiolect. Occasionally, if an innovation catches on quickly enough and is identified as the coinage of a particular individual (e.g., in commercial use or through literary authorship), we can date it precisely. The stock examples are the word *gas*, coined by the Dutch chemist van Helmont ca. 1600; *galumph* and *chortle*, the two fanciful coinages of Lewis Carroll in his poem *Jabberwocky* that have passed into general usage (*Through the Looking-Glass*, 1872); Gelett

Burgess' *blurb* "a noise made by a publisher", 1907; and George Eastman's *kodak*, 1888.

If an individual's innovation is taken over by other members of the speech-community, this may be due to various factors, most of them nonlinguistic. Often, the adoption of an innovation corresponds to some more or less clearly felt need. In scientific research, many fields have a tradition of word-coinage according to fairly clearly established patterns, so that newly discovered phenomena (e.g. chemical compounds) receive new names that are immediately intelligible. In other fields, especially those in which commercial publicity is extensively practised, new terms are brought into general use, under modern conditions, in a relatively short time, as is the case with trade names like *Vel*, *Dreft*, or *Metrecal*. Apart from an active force (scientific research, advertising) impelling rapid public acceptance of innovations, the chief situation in which a new coinage spreads rapidly is that of slang (p. 235), which has the specific connotation of novelty and (normally) rapid obsolescence. In most situations, however, an innovation takes a considerable length of time—years, decades, even centuries—to find acceptance with a large enough sector of the speech-community so that it comes to constitute an alternative in general usage.

When a variation in usage has arisen in this way, there is, over a shorter or longer period, a *fluctuation* in the frequency of the competing phenomena. In theory, if we had perfect means of observation, we could chart the number of times each single speaker used each one of the alternatives (e.g., *it's me* versus *it's I*), and could note the conditions under which each use took place, especially the social relations between speaker and hearer. Such detailed observation is of course impossible, and we have to resort to approximations, based primarily on written documentation from previous periods (cf. Chap. 48), supplemented by deductions from such aspects of the phenomena as their geographic distribution (cf. Chap. 43). A count of the occurrence of two competing phenomena over a period of time, in a chosen sample of texts, will reveal the approximate frequency of their occurrence, so that we can measure the rise of one and the decline of the other. Thus, the use of the definite article with the family name in Italian, of the type *il Machiavelli* "Machiavelli" (cf. pp. 15–16), arose in the sixteenth century, became universal from the seventeenth to the nineteenth centuries, and in the twentieth century has declined again. In French, the older type of construction *je le veux voir* "I want to see him" (with the pro-complement placed before the combination of modal verb + infinitive) was replaced by the construction *je veux le voir* (with pro-complement directly preceding the infinitive) during the seventeenth century. The older construction was predominant in the first part of the century, both were in active competition in the middle of the century, and the newer construction rapidly forced the older one out from 1660 onwards, chiefly under puristic pressure.

The factors which cause a given alternant to be favored or disfavored are in part linguistic, but mostly nonlinguistic. The chief linguistic factor leading to the replacement of one form by another is *homonymy*, the existence of two or more forms with different meaning but identical phonologic structure. Not all homonymy leads to replacement, as is shown by the fact that all languages have homonyms existing side by side for centuries, e.g., English /bǽr/ bear: "the animal ursus", bear: "carry" and bare: "naked"; or French /set/ cette: "this (f. sg.)," sept: "seven", c'est: "it is" (in liaison before a vowel), and Cète (Sette): "name of a town in southern France". Homonymy does not seem to be troublesome if the forms involved have different enough meanings so that they occur in different contexts, or if they belong to different form-classes, as in the English and French examples just cited. But if the form-class or meaning of the homonyms does not keep them sufficiently apart, difficulty in communication arises, and speakers will cease using one of the two forms that are causing trouble. A classic instance of troublesome homonymy is that which arose between the developments of the two Old English verbs /lǽ:tan/ "allow" and /léttan/ "hinder". As long as they were kept apart by the difference between /æ:/ and /e/, and by the difference in consonant length, no trouble arose; but when, by phonological change, they became homonyms in Early Modern English (sixteenth century), confusion could easily arise between let "hinder" and let "allow". The former has gone out of everyday use, and survives only in the expression a let ball in tennis (one which has been impeded by the net in its passage); even this is unclear to many modern speakers, and is often replaced by the semantically clearer a net ball.

When a homonym becomes troublesome in this way, its place is taken by less ambiguous synonyms, which are often slightly different in denotation or connotation at the outset of the process, but which lose their special meaning as they replace the obsolescent form. In Old French, /yi/ ui (from Latin hodiē) was the normal word for "today", and continued to be so until it came to be nearly homonymous with a new expression, /ui/ oui "yes", which had developed out of earlier /o il/ "yes, he", generalized from an affirmative answer to a question involving a third-person singular verb. Here again, trouble could arise if, for instance, some-one were to ask /vjentil?/ "is he coming?" and the answer /ui/ "yes" was scarcely distinguishable from /yi/ "today". The latter form was then replaced, in the Middle French period (fourteenth and fifteenth centuries) by a synonymous expression which had grown up in the stilted, formalized language of bureaucracy and the law courts, /oʒurdyi/ au jour d'hui "on the day of today". As it entered into general usage, /oʒurdyi/ lost its special bureaucratic and legalistic connotations, and became the normal expression for "today". In present day French spelling, it is written as a single word but with an apostrophe before the last three letters: aujourd'hui, and very few speakers of modern French connect the first part with au jour de: "on the day of" any longer. Another example of such replacement was that which took place in an area of southwestern France, where earlier /ll/ became /t/ at the end of a word, and hence Proto-Romance /gállu/ "rooster" became /gat/, homonymous with /gat/ from /gáttu/ "cat". Homonymy in the names of these two domestic animals could easily cause trouble, and /gat/ "rooster" was replaced in this region by various synonyms, which had originally had somewhat different connotations, e.g. /azan/ "pheasant" or /begej/ "vicar" (from the rooster's habit of strutting and preening himself like a conceited churchman).

In some instances, forms come to be markedly shorter than the average for the language of which they are a part; this happens particularly as a result of extensive phonemic reduction (cf. Chap. 52). Some scholars have considered that excessive shortness will cause one word to be replaced by another; Jules Gilliéron ascribed to this cause the replacement of Old French /ef/ *ef* "bee" (from Proto-Romance /ápe/) by /abéɟ̞ə/ *abeille*, Modern French /abej/ (from Proto-Romance /apíkula/), since Old French /ef/ would have developed into a Modern French word consisting of a single phoneme, /eˆ/. Yet other one-phoneme words exist in Modern French, such as /o/ *eau* "water" (from Proto-Romance /áku̯a/) and /u/ *août* "August" (from /au̯gústu/), so that merely the possible reduction to a single phoneme would not account for the replacement of */eˆ/ by /abej/. The familiarity and frequency of the term, especially in city-dwellers' usage, may have been a factor; it is worth noting that /ef/ survived in country regions, where bees are a normal feature of daily living, better than in urban areas.

It might also be thought that irregularity in a morphological or syntactical construction would be conducive to its replacement by a more regular form. This has certainly been the case in a number of instances. In Old English, the plural of /bo:k/ "book" was /be:č/, and that of /ku:/ "cow" was /ky:/; these forms would have given Modern English */bítʃ/ *beech* and */káj/ *kye*, respectively, but they were replaced by the analogical new-formations *books* and *cows*. Yet many even more irregular formations have not been subjected to analogical levelling in this way, as in the instances of English plurals like *men, women;* the Italian plural /uómini/ "men" (singular /uómo/), or the verbs meaning "be" and "have" in almost all Indo-European languages. Factors of frequency in everyday speech play a rôle in inhibiting the replacement of irregular by regular forms; the more often a form is used, apparently, the greater is its resistance to replacement.

Among the nonlinguistic factors leading to replacement of linguistic features, change in social status is one of the most important. Early Modern French had a diphthong /we/ in words like /rwe/ *roy* "king", /twe/ *toit* "roof", /bwerə/ *boire* "to drink", /twelə/ *toile* "cloth", and it had a palatal lateral /ɟ̞/ in such words as /fiɟ̞ə/ *fille* "daughter", /travaɟ̞/ *travail* "work", /muɟ̞e/ *mouillé* "soaked". As a result of sound-change, /we/ became /wa/ and /ɟ̞/ became /j/ in the seventeenth century, but at first only in the speech of the urban lower classes. At the time of the French Revolution, many behavior patterns which had previously been regarded as vulgar rose in social standing, and /wa/ and /j/ replaced /we/ and /ɟ̞/, respectively, in acceptable usage. The time of active competition between /we/ and /wa/ came right at the time of the Revolution. There is a story of a woman who narrowly escaped being guillotined on suspicion of royalist sympathies, because neighbors overheard her saying /uemõrwe? ʒəvœˆmõrwe./, which they interpreted as *Où est mon roi? Je veux mon roi:* "Where is my king? I want my king", whereas she insisted she had been asking for her /rwe/ *rouet* "spinning-wheel", not for her /rwa/ *roi* "king". The diphthong /we/ and the consonant /ḷ/ thus came to have aristocratic overtones, and were so disfavored during the Revolutionary and Napoleonic periods as to have become obsolescent by the time the Bourbons were restored to the throne in 1815; Modern French has /rwa twa bwar twal/ and /fij travaj muje/ in the forms cited above.

Another strong factor causing forms to be replaced is *taboo*. In many "primitive" societies, it is believed that mentioning the name of some animal (e.g., when going out to hunt it), or of some other type of thing or person, will bring bad luck, and a taboo is placed on mentioning the word involved, for part or all of the year. It is thought that this was the reason why the Indo-European word for "bear" (Proto-Indo-European */arktós/) was replaced in the Balto-Slavic languages by words which originally meant "honey-eater", such as Russian /meḍyét/. In our own society, we consider that we are beyond such superstitions, but we impose a strong taboo on informal or jocular mention of certain activities (sexual reproduction, elimination of bodily waste) which many "primitive" societies would not be worried about at all. If a word comes to be homonymous with some taboo term, it is often subjected to an equally strong (and often rather more effective) taboo. Thus, the Old French term for "rabbit", /koníḷ/ *conil*, and the English word borrowed from it, /kóni/ *coney*, have both gone out of general use because of their similarity to an obscene word which is still extensively found in sub-standard speech in both languages; the present-day New Yorkers who go to *Coney Island* have no awareness of the earlier meaning of the first part of this place-name.

The basic "how" of linguistic change involves, as we have just seen, the rise of alternative features, their competition with older features, and the eventual replacement of the latter. As to why language changes, there is no agreement among scholars, and a great many different causes have been suggested, ranging from "spiritual activity" to the persistence of features of childish speech, to a desire to conserve energy, and to the influence of the physical environment such as climatic conditions. It would seem, however, that the structural characteristics of human speech and the way in which we use language are sufficient in themselves to explain why language changes. As we have seen, language is a low-energy system (p. 16) which serves, not to perform actions, but to trigger them; and redundancy, which is an essential feature of linguistic structure (cf. Chap. 17), provides unavoidable fluctuation on all structural levels. People acquire their linguistic habits in childhood (Chap. 46), through a process of whose nature they are not analytically conscious at the time, and which they do not usually remember in later life, except for minor details (usually comic) which distort their view and understanding of language. In every language, as a child learns it and gets in the habit of using it, there are alternatives which he either accepts as of equal value or learns to evaluate in accordance with their nonlinguistic (especially social) standing. To the absence of complete equilibrium in the linguistic system is added the fact that the nonlinguistic world is constantly changing, and hence also the attitudes of speakers towards features of their own and other speech. At the same time, almost all normal speakers pay very little attention to variations in language which are not topics of debate. They consider that they have more important matters to worry about than which sound or which form to use; in fact, a large part of learning a language involves growing insensitive to meaningless variations. Hence changes are going on under our noses every day, without our paying any attention to them; but when they have taken place, even though the total result may displease us (as when we dislike some widespread innovation such as *identify* used intransitively or [tř] as the phonetic realization of /tr/), it is too late to do anything about it. Under these conditions, the surprising thing is, not that language changes, but that its rate of change is as slow as it is.

NOTES

Fluctuation in frequency: Bloomfield, 1933a, Chap. 22.
Innovations and linguistic change: Osgood and Sebeok, 1954, §6.3.
Conflict of homonyms: Menner, 1936.
French type je le veux voir*:* Dabbs, 1948.
French aujourd'hui*:* Nyrop, 1914–30, Vol. 4, §156.
Southwest French words for "cat" and "rooster": Gilliéron and Roques, 1912, Chap. 12.
French abeille*:* Gilliéron, 1918.
Story of "Où est mon /rwe/?": Nyrop, 1914, Vol. 1, §158.

48

Historical Documentation

EFFECTIVE SOUND-RECORDING devices have existed only since the end of the nineteenth century. We can listen to recordings of the voices of Theodore Roosevelt, Taft, and Wilson, but not of Lincoln, Madison or Washington. In earlier times, the lack of such recording devices was felt very keenly; the entire first part of Alfred de Musset's *Stances à la Malibran* is a lament over the underdeveloped state of technology in the nineteenth century, which did not permit a great singer's art to be preserved for posterity as were the works of painters or sculptors. So far as the language of earlier periods is concerned, we are somewhat better off, in that written records are available for the speech of the past four or five thousand years. Even these written records, however, are considerably less than perfect evidence, both because of the nature of graphemic systems (which, as we saw in Chap. 44, always give an incomplete representation of the languages they represent) and because, inevitably, the farther back we go in time, the less extensive the documents become.

As we go backwards in time, our written documents become more and more difficult to interpret, in all respects. The language of a nineteenth-century text in a standard European language seems virtually identical with that of our own time; if anything, we are tempted to consider that no change at all has taken place. In eighteenth- and seventeenth-century material, we find strange spellings, such as English *cloke*, *smoak*, and *mee:* "me", or French *roy* instead of *roi* "king", *sçavoir* instead of *savoir:* "know". Rhymes are occasionally strange, and seem to point to different pronunciations from those of today, as when Pope rhymes *tea* with *say*. As we proceed back to Shakespeare or Rabelais, there are more spellings, forms, and constructions that seem strange to us, and by the time we come to fourteenth-century texts like those of Chaucer or Charles d'Orléans, the language is so different as to be virtually foreign to us. In both English and French, the dividing line is around 1450 or 1500; since roughly the end of the fifteenth century, when the spelling of these two languages was fixed, their phonological systems have changed while orthography has not. Hence we tend to assume, falsely, on the basis of conventional spelling, that there has been little or no change in phonology, and we blithely read off Shakespeare's or Milton's poetry without realizing that our pronunciation is markedly different from what theirs must have been. More than one literary critic has made egregious blunders by finding in, say, Milton's or Donne's poetry, aesthetic values and sound-symbolism based entirely on modern phonological characteristics, without relevance for the actual speech of earlier times and hence for these authors' poetry as they must have spoken it.

The interpretation of old texts, a study known as *philology*, has a broader and a narrower aspect. In its broader aspect, it involves the investigation of the entire background, cultural and historical, out of which a document grew, and a reconstruction of a culture in the light of all the surviving evidence, linguistic and nonlinguistic. This type of study is best exemplified in *classical philology*, the integrated reconstruction of the cultures of ancient Greece and Rome, for which we have relatively extensive documentation, the best available for any period before modern times. In the narrower sense, philology involves the detailed analysis of documents, primarily from the graphemic and linguistic points of view.

Before the invention of printing in the fifteenth century, all documents were written by hand, and of course a great many informal communications, down to the present time, are still handwritten. In our West European tradition, we are most accustomed to documents either written with pen and ink (or with pencil) on paper or some similar material (parchment, papyrus), or else incised with hammer and chisel on stone. These are not the only type of materials that can be used; in other cultures, palm-leaves and similar organic matter is used instead of paper, and in the ancient civilizations of the Tigris and Euphrates valleys, bricks or other small slabs of clay served as carriers for wedge-shaped indentations made in their surface by triangular styli (whence the name of *cuneiform*, or "wedge-shaped," given to this type of writing). The study of manuscripts, *palaeography*, involves the analysis of the scribal tradition (i.e., the styles of writing, especially as determined by the instruments and materials used) and the establishment and interpretation of the graphemes used by the scribe. In the course of centuries, the style of handwriting changes, so that it is often possible to date a manuscript reasonably accurately (at least to the nearest century and often even closer) by the kind of letters used and other features of the scribal tradition. In preparing modern editions of mediaeval or ancient texts, editors transcribe the manuscripts into present-day Roman characters, frequently regularizing the orthography in the process, so that the ordinary reader is often unaware of the extensive difference between the text as he reads it and its form in the original manuscript (cf. Fig. 23).

The extent to which we are able to decipher a text depends largely on the continuity of the scribal tradition or on the correlation which we can establish between the graphemes of the text and those of some other orthography which we are already able to interpret. In some instances, it is possible to identify the graphemes of one or more texts without having a correspondingly clear idea of what phonemes they stand for or of what the texts mean. The ancient Etruscans used an alphabet derived from the Greek, and we can decipher and transcribe Etruscan texts. On the assumption that their graphemes corresponded to phonemes, we know that there was a contrast between the phonemes which we transcribe from the Etruscan alphabet as *p* and *φ*, *t* and *θ*, *k* and *χ*, but we have no idea what phonologic feature (aspiration? fricativization? something else?) was involved in the contrast. On the other hand, a set of characters such as the hieroglyphs used by the Maya Indians of Yucatan in pre-Columbian times, or those used by the former inhabitants of Easter Island in the Pacific, remains a riddle because the direct tradition of interpretation has been lost, and we have no bilingual texts of which we know the meaning for one of the languages.

The same considerations hold for our knowledge of the meaning of old texts. For some languages, there is a direct tradition of interpretation and translation going back to the time when they were the native languages of their respective speech-communities, as is the case with, say, Latin, Greek, Hebrew, or Classical Arabic. Even in such instances, however, we must be

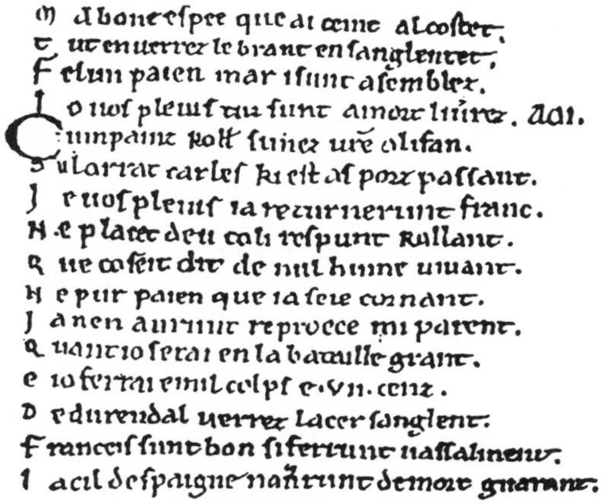

Fig. 23: A Page of a Mediaeval Manuscript (The Oxford Ms. of *La Chanson de Roland*, Digby 23, folio 20, a, verses 1066–81).

on our guard against inaccuracies of interpretation which may have crept in, as when, through faulty insertion of "vowel-points" at a later stage in the Hebrew scribal tradition, the prophet Elijah was thought to have been fed in the desert by "ravens" (I KINGS 17:4–6) instead of by nomads. In the absence of direct tradition, bilingual texts are usually necessary for any extensive interpretation; the ancient Egyptian hieroglyphs were undecipherable until the finding in 1799 of the Rosetta Stone, which had three versions of the same text, in two varieties of Egyptian writing and in Greek. It is very rare that internal evidence alone will suffice for establishing the meaning of a text; the closest approach to such interpretation was made by Georg Friedrich Grotefend, who in 1802 laid the foundations for deciphering the Old Persian inscriptions of Darius, through careful detective-work starting with only a few hints given in Herodotus' remarks about Persian history—a feat which has remained unduplicated in philological research. Otherwise, we are condemned to remain in ignorance; we can "read" the ancient Etruscan texts insofar as we can equate their letters with those of the Roman and Greek alphabets, but, in the continued absence of bilingual texts, we have only a fragmentary idea of their meaning.

The linguistic historian uses earlier texts as sources for the history of a language. In doing so, he must not assume *a priori* that texts can be taken at their face value, in their documentation of sounds, forms, or lexical items. In many—perhaps most—instances, old texts are inconsistent in their graphic representation of linguistic phenomena. In the Oxford manuscript of the Old French *Song of Roland* (somewhat after 1100 A.D.), some words, which in Modern French have /y/ *u*, are consistently written with *u*, e.g., *mur:* "wall", *tu:* "thou"; but others, which in Modern French have /u/ *ou*, are written part of the time with *u* and part with *o:* *tur* or *tor:* "tower", *nus* or *nos:* "we, us", *vus* or *vos:* "you". From these discrepancies, we conclude that two different phonemes were involved, and on the basis of their origins in Latin and Proto-Romance and of their later developments, we interpret the first-mentioned as /u/ and the second as /oˆ/: /mur/, /tu/, but /toˆr/, /noˆs/, /voˆs/. Inconsistencies of this kind are often helpful in the relative dating of linguistic changes. In Old English writing, the compound grapheme *gh* stood for a phoneme /γ/: *light* /líγt/, *night* /níγt/. From Old French, the speakers of Middle English borrowed the word /dəléitə/ "pleasure", spelled at the time *deleite;* this word never had any /γ/-phoneme. Hence when we find the spelling *delight* for later /dəléit/, we can be sure that by this time *light* and *night* must have lost their /γ/ and become /léit/ and /néit/ respectively, rhyming in sound with /dəléit/; otherwise the spelling in -*ight* would not have been used for /dəléit/ *delight*.

Closely allied to this type of evidence is that afforded by *overcorrections* and similar mistakes. Latin had a consonant cluster /ns/, in words like *mensa:* "table", *sponsa:* "bride", or *prehensum:* "taken (past participle, m. sg. acc.)". The Romance languages show, in words which can safely be traced all the way back to Proto-Romance (cf. Chap. 51), no trace of this cluster, and for Proto-Romance, corresponding to the Latin words just cited, we reconstruct /méˆsa/, /spóˆsa/, /préˆsu/. If, in a Late Latin document, we find the word *thesaurus:* "treasure" written *thensaurus*, with an intrusive letter *n* which never belonged there, we conclude that the person who wrote the word knew that he said /méˆsa/, /spóˆsu/ and /préˆsu/, and that he was supposed to write them with *ns;* he then carried his "correct" spelling too far, and decided that his /tesáurus/ also ought to be written with *ns* for /s/. In instances of this sort, we must not be so naïve as to think that every letter which a scribe wrote always stood for some feature of his pronunciation. Some scholars who work on Late Latin documents are prone to make this error, and hence ascribe to Popular Latin many features of pronunciation which it never had.

In some types of literary composition which are marked by special prosodic characteristics like meter or rhyme, these features often give us information which is not available in ordinary prose. Latin and Greek verse depended on a regular alternation of long and short syllables, arranged according to predetermined patterns. The syllable was long or short depending on the actual length of time it took to pronounce it; a syllable was long if it was checked (ended in a consonant) or if it was free (did not end in a consonant) and contained a long vowel or a diphthong; otherwise it was short. For most words, the only evidence we have as to whether their vowels were long or short is their occurrence in poetry. Thus, from the prosodic structure of a verse like the first line of Vergil's *Aeneid:*

Armă vĭrumquĕ cănō, Trōiae quī prīmŭs ăb ōrīs

we know that the *-a* of *arma,* the *i* of *virum,* the *e* of *-que* and the other vowels here marked with the breve (ˇ) were short, and that those marked here with the macron (⁻) were long. In some instances, where a vowel was in a checked syllable (e.g., the first *a* in *arma*), or where the word is not attested in poetry, we do not know from internal evidence whether the vowel was short or long, and hence have to depend on chance external evidence or on reconstruction from later stages.

In addition to internal evidence, we occasionally have data from outside sources which can help us to reach a conclusion as to earlier stages. The optimum situation is that in which we have a first-hand description by a competent observer. For most languages, we do not possess such data from times earlier than the Renaissance, at which time there were several highly intelligent analysts, such as Antonio de Nebrija (1446–1522) working on Spanish, Claudio Tolomei (1492–1555) on Italian, Louis Meigret (ca. 1510–ca. 1560) on French, and John Hart (?–1574) on English. Before this time, most theoretic discussions of pronunciation and grammar were couched in terms which are very difficult to interpret, and it is rare to find an exception such as the anonymous eleventh-century Icelandic "First Grammarian" who provided an excellent phonemic analysis for the Old Norse of his time. Ancient descriptions, likewise, are often difficult to interpret, as when Late Latin grammarians speak of there being two kinds of [l]-sound in the speech of their day, *l pinguis* or "fat *l*" and *l exīlis* or "thin *l*." These impressionistic terms probably refer to apico-dental and dorso-velar laterals, respectively, but we cannot be absolutely sure.

Nontechnical writers also furnish valuable information on occasion, often in other connections than those of formal grammatical analysis. From the historian Suetonius, we learn that the emperor Vespasian was once criticized by the grammarian Florus for using a substandard pronunciation /plo:stra/ "wagons" instead of /plau̯stra/, and that the next day Vespasian got back at the grammarian by calling him *Flaurus.* This anecdote tells us that there existed, in popular Latin, a substandard development of /au̯/ into /o:/, which might have been expected also for such a word as /kau̯da/ "tail", popular */ko:da/, and thus confirms our reconstruction of the Proto-Romance ancestor of the Romance words for "tail" as /kóˆda/ (with Proto-Romance vowel tenseness /ˆ/ corresponding to Latin vowel length /:/). The Roman poet Catullus wrote a venomous poem satirizing a certain parvenu named Arrius for dropping his aitches and then overcorrecting by inserting /h/ where it did not belong, as in *chommoda* for *commoda*, *Harrius* for his own name *Arrius*, and *Hionia* for *Ionia*. Catullus thus confirms our reconstruction of Proto-Romance without any /h/-phoneme, in contrast to the presence of this phoneme in Classical Latin.

Linguistics and philology often furnish mutual aid to each other. On occasion, a difficult word or passage in an ancient text serves to cast light on a problem of historical linguistics. Isidore of Seville (6th–7th centuries A.D.), in his *Etymologies*, a book of presumed word origins written in the Latin of the time, has a heretofore unintelligible passage involving a term for "to put fertilizer (on a field)"; this passage was rendered intelligible by assuming that a copyist had mistranscribed *fimāre*: "to fertilize" (to Latin *fimus*: "fertilizer"). At the same time, this emendation provided direct attestation for a word which Romance scholars had already had to postulate as an ancestral form for verbs meaning "to fertilize" in several Romance dialects.

The data furnished by linguistics are frequently decisive in settling questions concerning the period of composition or the authorship of old literary monuments. There has been, for over a hundred years, a dispute as to whether the *Iliad* and the *Odyssey*, traditionally ascribed to the poet Homer, were the work of one man or more than one. The linguistic characteristics of a number of lines which were "athetized" (considered spurious) by ancient critics such as Aristarchus have definitely shown that they cannot be of the same period and hence by the same author as the rest of the poems, and therefore that the poems cannot be the work of one man. In the same way, linguistic evidence shows that the Old French *Song of Roland* consists of at least two strata, one of material written before ca. 1100 A.D., and the other of material written after that date; in this instance too, the poem cannot possibly be (as some, especially the French scholar Joseph Bédier [1864–1938] have maintained) the result of a unified conception, no matter how much genius we ascribe to the presumed author. The differences in linguistic strata in the *Roland* coincide, furthermore, with very marked differences in the two or more authors' conceptions and attitudes towards their subject matter and the cultural backgrounds out of which their reworkings of the Roland legend sprang.

NOTES

Philology: Bolling, 1929.
Palaeography: Bischoff, 1956.
The letters o *and* u *representing* /oˆ/ *in the* Chanson de Roland: Jenkins (ed.), 1924.
Renaissance grammarians: Kukenheim, 1932.
Nebrija: Alonso, 1949.
Meigret: Shipman, 1953.
John Hart: Jespersen, 1907.
"First Grammarian": Haugen, 1950.
Romance *fimare: Spitzer, 1940a.
Strata in the Iliad: Bolling, 1944; *in the* Chanson de Roland: Hall, 1963a, Chap. 1.

49

Sound-Change

THE MOST IMPORTANT aspect of linguistic history is sound-change: the fact that, to a given phoneme at one point in the history of a language, there correspond at a later stage one or more different phonemes which have developed out of that which was present earlier. That not only words, but sounds, change, has been known for centuries; however, until the beginning of the nineteenth century, it was not generally realized that sound-change could be analyzed in a reasonable and profitable way. An eighteenth-century witticism (often ascribed, like many other wise-cracks of the time, to Voltaire) described etymology as "a science in which the vowels count for very little and the consonants for nothing." At the time, this wise-crack was fully justified; since then, however, linguistic analysts have arrived at a far more satisfactory understanding of the role and nature of sound-change.

Phonological development is to be divided into two aspects: phonetic change and phonemic change. The former involves simply change in speakers' habits of making sounds; the latter, change in the structural units of sound and in their relationships. Since, as we have seen (cf. Chap. 14), allophonic variations do not, by definition, make any difference in meaning, they can arise, last for a shorter or longer time, and disappear again without, in themselves, affecting the phonemic structure of the language. Of this type is, say, the fricativization of voiceless stop consonants between vowels in Tuscan (pp. 25 ff.): [-k-]* became [-h-] at some time in the past (opinions differ as to the exact date; cf. Chap. 63) and, in a parallel development, [-t-] became [-θ-] and [-p-] became [-Φ-], as in /čokkolátokáldo/ [tʃok:o'laθo-'haldo] *cioccolato caldo:* "hot chocolate", or /dipépe/ [di'Φe:Φe] *di pepe:* "of pepper". As long as a change of this sort remains within the limits of allophonic variation and has no meaning for the speakers of the language, they normally pay no attention to it in their everyday behavior (even though such a variation may on occasion arouse the ire of purists or the mockery of speakers of other dialects).

A subphonemic change may affect the allophones of a phoneme in every position in which they occur; in this case, it is known as a *nonconditioned* change.

---

* A hyphen written before and after a letter or a phonetic or phonemic symbol indicates, in discussions of phonological history, that the sound which it represents stands between two other sounds. Similarly, a hyphen before a symbol indicates that the sound for which it stands is in final position; after a symbol, it indicates initial position.

Of this type was the change by which Proto-Gallo-Romance /u/ (from Proto-Romance /uˆ/) became [y] throughout in French, so that Proto-Romance /múˆru/ "wall" is represented in Modern French by /myr/ *mur*, /rekepúˆtu/ "received" by /rəsy/ *reçu*, and similarly in hundreds of other examples. If on the other hand, the allophonic variation arises only under certain circumstances—as in the Tuscan examples cited in the preceding paragraph or in the case of English [ř] taking the place of [ɹ] after [t] in ['tře^{i}n] *train*, ['dře^{i}n] *drain*—it is known as a *conditioned* sound change. Some scholars consider that all sound changes start as conditioned change, i.e., as allophonic variations taking place only under some conditions and not under others, and then become generalized so as to be no longer conditioned. Definite proof of this contention has, however, not been furnished to date.

As long as an allophonic variation remains confined to a single phoneme, and there is no alteration in the phonological environment in which the allophone occurs, the change has remained on the purely phonetic level. If, however, the phonological environment itself changes, what was formerly an allophonic variant may no longer be determined by its environment, and hence—since, by definition, a sound feature not determined by its environment is significant—acquires phonemic standing. Thus, we find that the Proto-Gallo-Romance vowels /eˆ e a o oˆ/ in free syllables are represented in Old North French by raised vowels (most of which developed into diphthongs), whereas the same vowels in checked syllables remained unchanged:

PROTO-GALLO-ROMANCE		OLD NORTH FRENCH	
In Checked	*In Free*		
Syllable	*Syllable*		
/méˆt-to/ "I put"	/kréˆ-do/ "I believe"	/méˆt/	/kréˆiθ/
/fés-ta/ "feast"	/bé-ne/ "well"	/fés-tə/	/bién/
/pás-ta/ "paste"	/tá-le/ "such"	/pás-tə/	/tǽl/
/pór-ta/ "door"	/bó-nu/ "good"	/pór-tə/	/buón/
/móˆl-tu/ "much"	/flóˆ-re/ "flower"	/móˆlt/	/flóˆur/

Note the symmetry of the developments in free syllables: the high-mid vowels /éˆ/ and /óˆ/ changed into /éˆi/ and /óˆu/ respectively; the low-mid vowels /é/ and /ó/ changed into /ié/ and /uó/; and the low-central vowel /á/ developed into a front, slightly raised vowel which we may write as /ǽ/, and which was undoubtedly intermediate in sound between /a/ and /e/, with which latter it eventually merged.

How does phonemic, as opposed to phonetic, change take place? Both of these questions have worried linguistic analysts and laymen, ever since our science became aware of phonemic change. By now, we are at a stage where we can give a reasonably good answer to the first, but not as yet to the second. As to the "how" of phonemic change, the usual idea of nineteenth-century scholars was that sounds changed more or less by themselves, much as plants or other organisms evolved. The idea of the phoneme had not yet been elaborated, and linguistic analysts tended to think of individual sounds as the building-blocks of a language; sounds were thought of as undergoing a kind of spontaneous evolution in the course of time. Later, when we had arrived at the notion of the phoneme—not an individual sound, but a functional unit comprising one or more sounds—it was evident that the important thing was change in phonemes, and that in some way the sounds comprised in a phoneme gradually changed. Bloomfield, in 1933, said "Historically, we picture phonemic change as a gradual favoring of some nondistinctive variants and a disfavoring of others." Recent theoretic discussion has cleared up our idea of the relation between phonetic and phonemic change. Phonemic change involves some displacement, not in pronunciation, but in the function of sounds—whereas phonetic change precedes phonemic change, and involves nonsignificant, nonfunctional displacement in the speakers' habits of articulation. As W. F. Twaddell has observed:

> Through any one change, either pronunciation or structure remains stable. A pronunciation changes by the development of allophones, while the phonemic structure is maintained; the differences in pronunciation are slight (that is, allophonic). Then the pronunciation stays constant, while the determinant is changed or loses importance, perhaps for the very reason that the allophones themselves now share in the distinction. The pronunciation is maintained, and the differences are those of structure (assignment of a given pronunciation to different phonemes) and hence unobtrusive.

In the instance of the Old French diphthongization and raising of stressed vowels in free syllables, for example, we must assume that at first there took place a nonsignificant, nondistinctive change in articulation, conditioned by the position of the vowel in a free syllable. As long as the syllable remained free, the difference in pronunciation was determined by and statable wholly in terms of surrounding sounds, and the diphthongs or raised vowels met all the requirements for still being classes as allophones of the simple vowels out of which they had developed. (For convenience, we may refer to this intermediate stage as Pre-French.) But somewhat later, one of the changes which took place was the loss of all final vowels except /a/, which became /ə/. This loss of final vowels caused many consonants which had previously been between vowels to come at the end of words, and to belong to the syllable of the preceding vowel (since there no longer was a following vowel). With this change, there now came to be, in Old French, a contrast between simple vowel and diphthong, or between low and raised vowel (/a/ vs. /æ/) before a consonant in checked syllable; and since we can no longer state, for Old French, that the diphthongs or raised vowels occur under specific conditions, we have to treat them as phonemically distinct from the vowels out of which they originally developed.

The following table gives a more detailed picture of the transition, phonetically and phonemically, from Proto-Gallo-Romance to Old French, in the words listed on p. 296. Each word is now given in phonemic and phonetic transcription. Note that in the Pre-French stage, the diphthongization or raising of the vowel has no phonemic significance, and hence is indicated only in the phonetic transcription, between square brackets; in the Old French stage, the diphthongization has acquired phonemic significance, and so is shown between slant lines as well.

PROTO-GALLO-ROMANCE	PRE-FRENCH	OLD FRENCH
/méˆt-to/ [ˈmeˆt-to] "I put"	/méˆt-to/ [ˈméˆt-to]	/méˆt/ [ˈmeˆt]
/kréˆ-do/ [ˈkreˆ-do] "I believe"	/kréˆ-do/ [ˈkreˆi̯-ðo]	/kréˆi̯θ/ [ˈkréˆi̯θ]
/fés-ta/ [ˈfɛs-ta] "feast"	/fés-ta/ [ˈfɛs-ta]	/fés-tə/ [ˈfɛs-tə]
/bé-ne/ [ˈbɛ-ne] "well"	/bé-ne/ [ˈbjɛ-ne]	/bién/ [ˈbjɛn]
/pás-ta/ [ˈpas-ta] "paste"	/pás-ta/ [ˈpas-ta]	/pás-tə/ [ˈpas-tə]
/tá-le/ [ˈta-le] "such"	/tá-le/ [ˈtæ-le]	/tǽl/ [ˈtæl]
/pór-ta/ [ˈpɔr-ta] "door"	/pór-ta/ [ˈpɔr-ta]	/pór-tə/ [ˈpɔr-tə]
/bó-nu/ [ˈbɔ-nu] "good"	/bó-nu/ [ˈbwɔ-nu]	/buón/ [ˈbwɔn]
/móˆl-tu/ [ˈmoˆl-tu] "much"	/móˆl-tu/ [ˈmoˆl-tu]	/móˆlt/ [ˈmoˆlt]
/flóˆ-re/ [ˈfloˆ-re] "flower"	/flóˆ-re/ [ˈfloˆu̯-re]	/flóˆur/ [ˈfloˆu̯r]

To the question "Why do phonemes change?", therefore, we can answer "Because habits of articulation change, and then are reinterpreted in a different function from that which they had before." The question then becomes, naturally, "Why do habits of articulation change?", and to this, no one has as yet found a satisfactory answer. By "satisfactory answer," we mean valid correlation between change in habits of articulation and other aspects of human culture or environment. All kinds of suggestions have been made—correlation with climate, with race, with national psychology, and so forth—but none that will hold water. It is very tempting, for instance, to think that climatic conditions must in some ways influence the state of people's vocal organs and hence of their habits of pronunciation, and it has been suggested, for instance, that the clear, sharp habits of articulation of Italian and Spanish must reflect the bright, sunny climate of the Mediterranean with its blue skies and clear air, whereas the more complicated phonetic habits of French and above all the presence of nasalized vowels would be due to the mists and fogs of northern France. Unfortunately for such a theory, Portuguese also has a more complicated set of vowels (including nasals), and yet has a bright, sunny, dry type of climate.

At present, it looks as if we must simply say that habits of articulation are subject to changes in fashion, just like habits of dress, eating, and so forth—and, just as these latter vary with no apparent reason, so do habits of pronunciation. We have historical records of some fashions which arose, lasted for a while, and then disappeared again. In sixteenth-century Tuscan, there was apparently a fashion of using an allophonic variant [γ] between vowels for the /g/-phoneme, parallel to the use of [x] (later [h]) for the /k/-phoneme; but the voiced allophone [γ] has gone out of use, whereas the voiceless [h] has stayed in fashion (but, up to now, no change in the environment has taken place to render it phonemically significant). Dante, the first great thinker on the subject of linguistic change, said:

> Since, therefore, every human language . . . has been re-made in accordance with our whims since the confusion of the Tower of Babel . . . and since man is a most unstable and variable being, language cannot be long-lasting or stable; but like other human things, such as customs and dress, it has to vary in space and time.

This is as good a statement of the situation with regard to phonetic (not phonemic!) change as has yet been made. As long as scholars considered only the purely phonetic aspect of sound-change, it could seem chaotic and totally irregular; not until the phonemic approach, from the point of view of functional units of sound, was made at least implicitly in the work of nineteenth-century scholars, could order be brought out of the apparent chaos.

NOTES

Phonological change: Bloomfield, 1933a, Chap. 20; Hill, 1936; Jakobson, 1931; Lehmann, 1962, Chap. 10; Martinet, 1955.

Relation of pronunciation and phonological structure: Twaddell, 1948b.

Old French material: condensed somewhat from Hall, 1960, Chap. 10.

50

The Regularist Postulate

LINGUISTIC CHANGE has been going on for hundreds of thousands of years; and yet, except for a handful of anticipations in the last few centuries, only in the past hundred and fifty years have scholars made any start in its analysis. This delay is due to several causes. In the first place, no one had a satisfactory technique for describing linguistic habits, until the Greek grammarians developed a technique for their own language, and the Sanskrit grammarians developed one for theirs. Even then, the Greeks and the Romans, and also the ancient Hindus, were primarily interested in their own language alone, in that of their own times, and from the point of view of "correctness." They had little sense of historicity, and little interest in things plebeian or barbarian. And, most important of all, even though they had techniques for description of their own language, they had none for comparison of different languages or for analysis of historical change.

This situation was made more or less permanent by a widespread misunderstanding of a condition that was present from the late period of the Roman Empire onward: the coexistence of Latin, as a fixed form of speech and writing learned in the schools and used in the Church, and the currently-spoken and rapidly developing everyday speech of the common people. Those who, like priests, monks, and lawyers, learned Latin were taught to regard it as the only correct form of language, in fact as "grammar" *par excellence* (cf. p. 124), and to see in the everyday vernacular nothing but a "corruption" of Latin, which—as Dante put it—was "acquired without any rules, as one sucked one's mother's milk." Both Latin and the vernacular were regarded as having coexisted at all times, and very few people saw any historical relation between them. Intellectual prejudice played a part here, too: the pride of the educated and the grammarians led them to despise the untutored speech of the illiterate, naïve common folk.

During the sixteenth century, however, some scholars began to see that there was a historical development from Latin to the modern Romance tongues, and that these latter were not mere corruptions due to "ignorance" or "mental laziness" of lower-class speakers, but the result of normal, regular, inevitable change, whereas the apparent correctness of modern Latin was due simply to its being kept artificially alive in Church and schools. The truth of this assumption was made evident in the fifteenth and sixteenth centuries in Italy, when the gap between Latin and vernacular was made even wider by the humanists' reform of Latin writing, and reintroduction of strict adherence to the norms of the Golden Age of Latin literature. To a sixteenth-century Italian, Claudio Tolomei (1492–1555), goes the honor of first stating clearly the basic principle of what we would now call *regular phonemic change*, which he deduced from observing the Italian (Tuscan) words derived from Latin words beginning in *pl-*. He noticed that most Latin words beginning in *pl-* were continued in Italian by words beginning in *pi-*, such as Italian *pieno:* "full" from Latin *plēnus*, Italian *piano:* "level" from Latin *planus*, Italian *più:* "more" from Latin *plūs*, and many others. On the other hand, some Italian words had *pl-* representing Latin *pl-*, as in *plora:* "he weeps" from Latin *plōrat*. Tolomei explained this difference in development by assuming that the normal continuation of Latin *pl-* in Italian was *pi-*, saying:

> . . . and I would be so bold as to say that in the original and pure speech of Tuscans, this was a universally valid rule [i.e. that Latin *pl-* gave Italian *pi-*], and that all those words which are now used and written differently, such as *plora:* 'he weeps', *implora:* 'he implores', *splende:* 'it is resplendent', *plebe:* 'populace' and the like, were not taken from the middle of the town squares of Tuscany [i.e., from everyday speech], but were set up by writers, and by someone who wished to enrich the language, preferring to use them in the form in which he found them written in Latin, without giving them the form of Tuscan speech [i.e., without substituting *pi-* for *pl-*] . . . because without a doubt the common usage of earlier times would, had it inherited these words, have said *piora, impiora, spiende* and *pieve*, and we have manifest evidence of this latter in that in the vernacular we call *pieve* a church devoted to the religious services of the common people.

This passage from Tolomei is very important; it contains, not only in germ, but fully developed, all the essential features of modern historical linguistic methodology. Tolomei starts out by making one basic assumption: that phonemes change regularly, and hence explains the Italian words with initial *pi-* like *pieno:* "full", *piano:* "level", and *più:* "more", as being the normal representatives of Latin *plēnus*, *planus* and *plūs* respectively. That leaves a group of forms, a *residue*, which show, not *pi-* as we would expect according to the formula just set up, but *pl-*, apparently unchanged from Latin. The older approach would have shrugged off the discrepancy as mere happenstance, since there was not supposed to be any historical relation between Latin and Italian anyhow. Tolomei, however, is forced by his basic assumption to find an explanation for exceptions to his rule; and he finds it in a further assumption, that the residue showing the discrepant treatment *pl-* is due to some other factor than phonemic change: in this particular instance, to direct borrowing from Latin, of the kind we now call *learnèd borrowing* (cf. Chap. 53). Tolomei thus distinguishes between two kinds of words in modern Italian: those which developed in everyday speech (like *pieno, piano, più*) and those which were not developments in everyday speech but were taken directly from Latin by learnèd men (words like *plora, implora, splende, plebe*). He notices and comments on the existence of pairs of words, both from the same source, but one of which developed in everyday speech (*pieve*) and the other of which was taken directly from Latin (*plebe*)*;* such pairs of words are now called *historical doublets.*

Tolomei, over four hundred years ago, hit on the basic elements of historical linguistics; unfortunately, after his time, no one continued or improved on his method, and grammarians were too concerned with prescribing "correct" speech and with forcing all languages into the mould of Greek and Latin grammar, to make any real progress in studying languages from a historical point of view. Real, enduring progress towards a scientific approach was not made until the end of the eighteenth and the beginning of the nineteenth century. Scholars' horizons had been steadily broadening, so far as their knowledge of the world's languages was concerned, until by 1800 something was known of a number of exotic languages, the most significant of which were Sanskrit (Old Indic, the language of the ancient hymns of India) and Finnish. When these languages became known, it was quite evident that there must be some relationship between them and the better-known languages: between Sanskrit and a number of European languages, and between Finnish and Hungarian (and various languages spoken in eastern Russia and Siberia). For a while, and due to the old confused notions about the relationship of languages, people thought that all the other languages related to Sanskrit must be derived from it. Soon scholars began to see, however, that Sanskrit was not a "mother" but a "sister" language to Latin, Greek, the Germanic, Celtic, and Slavic languages, and so on. The first person to state this relationship clearly was Sir William Jones, one of the first great Western Sanskritists, in 1786, pointing out that Sanskrit in relation to Greek and Latin

. . . bears a stronger affinity, both in the roots of verbs, and in the forms of grammar, than could possibly have been produced by accident: so strong, indeed, that no philologer could examine them all three without believing them to have sprung from some common source, which, perhaps, no longer exists; there is a similar reason, though not quite so forcible, for supposing that both the Gothick and the Celtick, though blended with a very different idiom, had the same origin with the Sanskrit.

During the first half of the nineteenth century, a great deal of work was done by scholars to reconstruct the parent language from which Sanskrit, Latin, Greek, Germanic, Balto-Slavic (the intermediate ancestral stage of the Slavic languages such as Russian, Polish, etc., and of the Baltic languages like Lithuanian) and Celtic must have originated. Similar reconstructions were made for Finno-Ugric, the ancestral language of Finnish, Hungarian and others. Between the languages of each of these groups there are a great many correspondences, in sounds, forms, syntax, and vocabulary, which simply cannot be due to mere chance nor yet to borrowing (no matter how widespread), but can be explained only on the hypothesis of differentiation from a single earlier source. Take such sets of words as these, showing correspondences between Sanskrit, Greek, Latin, Old Church Slavonic, Gothic (the earliest attested of the Germanic languages) and Old Irish:

	"brother"	"carry"	"flee, bend"	"split, bite"	"beech"
LAT.	frātr-	fer-	fug-	find-	fāgo-
GREEK	phrātr- "member of a religious brotherhood"	pher-	phyg-	pheid- "save, spare"	phēgo-
SKT.	bhrātar-	bhar-	bhuj-	bhind-	—
OCHSL.	bratr-	ber- "gather, take"	—	—	—
GOTHIC	brōθar	ber-	biug-	beit-	OHG buohha, OEng. bōc
OIR.	brāthir	ber-	bocc "bow (n.)"	—	—

The first scholars to notice these wide-spread correspondences (which run into the thousands) were, for the Finno-Ugric languages, the Hungarian S. Gyarmathi in 1799, and for the languages we now call Indo-European, Rasmus Rask of Denmark in 1814 and the German scholar Franz Bopp in 1816. By comparing related languages, they were able to make statements concerning correspondences of sounds—not merely isolated, but in whole sets—which enabled them to reconstruct the phonemic and grammatical systems of the ancestor language from which the later languages had developed. Thus, in the sets of forms given in the above table, we notice the correspondence of Latin *f*-, Greek *ph*-, Skt. *bh*-, and Old Church Slavonic, Gothic, and Old Irish *b*-. Because of these and similar correspondences in all the other sounds in the forms given in the table, we set up for the ancestor language, Proto-Indo-European, the hypothetical forms:

bhrātr- "brother" bher- "carry" bhug- "flee, bend" bhi(n)d- "split, bite"

and, with somewhat less certainty (because it is not found in all the related languages) *bhāg*- "beech".

After the time of Rask and Bopp, many others worked on the historical grammar of the Indo-European languages, notably Jakob Grimm (1785–1863), August Pott (1802–1887) and August Schleicher (1821–1868); on the Romance languages, the most outstanding work was done by Friedrich Diez (1794–1876). These scholars took more or less for granted the principle of regular phonemic change, without stating it explicitly. In the 1870's, however, a group of scholars centered on the University of Leipzig carried to their normal conclusion the principles on which historical linguistics had been based since the beginning of the century, and which Tolomei had prefigured so clearly in the passage cited on p. 301. These scholars—of whom the two most important were the Slavicist August Leskien (1840–1916) and the comparativist Karl Brugmann (1849–1919)—made an overt, categorical statement of the principle that phonemes change regularly, under the form "Phonetic laws admit of no exceptions" (*die Lautgesetze kennen keine Ausnahmen*, Leskien, 1876). Because of their rigor in procedure, and perhaps because of the brusqueness and apparent overconfidence of their manner in announcing and adhering to this principle, Leskien and Brugmann and their group were not universally liked; they were given the name of *Junggrammatiker* ("young grammarians" or, as it is usually translated into English, *Neo-Grammarians*), at first as a nickname, and the nickname stuck.

Although competent scholars had been using the basic assumption of regular phonemic change as their guiding principle since Tolomei's, and especially since Rask's and Grimm's time, it had not been stated explicitly. Immediately it was stated, it aroused opposition, both from some older men such as the Hellenist Georg Curtius (1820–1885), and also from younger men like Johannes Schmidt (1843–1901) and the Romance scholar Hugo Schuchardt (1842–1927). To a certain extent, the rigorous assumption that phonemes change, without reference to the meanings of the words in which they occur, and apparently blindly and mechanically, aroused the hostility of people who were emotionally attached to the idea that speech must of necessity "mirror" and follow human thought, not determine it. To a much greater extent, the dispute—which in some instances reached extremes of bitterness and developed into a true quarrel—was due to the poor way in which Leskien made his statement of principle. Furthermore, the term *law* was applied to statements of phonetic developments, on the analogy of such "laws" of physics as "Boyle's law" or "Watt's law." Thus, for instance, the scholar Karl Bartsch (1832–1888) was the first to observe and state the fact that Latin stressed /á/ developed, when no consonant followed in the same syllable, into Old French *ié* /iǽ/ after a palatal but into *é* /ǽ/ otherwise: from *mare:* "sea" we have OFr. *mer* /mǽr/, but from *carum:* "dear" we have *chier* /čiǽr/. This statement is known as "Bartsch's law." But the "laws" of historical linguistics are statements, not of general relationships, but of specific historical developments, each of which took place at a certain time and place in a certain language. Thus, "Bartsch's law" is a statement of a phonemic change which took place under certain conditions, and at a certain time—not earlier than the 7th century and not later than the 9th—and in a certain language, the dialect of the region around Paris. It is about as sensible to talk about "Bartsch's law" as it would be to talk about "the *law* of Gettysburg," referring to the historic event of the battle of Gettysburg.

The assumption that phonetic "laws" suffer no exceptions, or, better stated, that phonemes change regularly, is an assumption, not a statement of fact; it is a guiding principle which we assume in order to help us discover and explain exceptional developments. So, for instance, in Modern English we find *f*- as the normal representative of Middle English *f*-, as in *fox, full, foot* (from Middle English *fox, ful, foot*) and a host of other words. However, we find *v*- instead of *f*- in the word *vixen* "female fox" (from Middle English *fixen*). Does this invalidate our assumption of regular phonemic change, here of the continuation of Middle English *f*- by Modern English *f*-? By no means. We look for another explanation of the aberrant *v*- of *vixen*, just as Tolomei did for the aberrant *pl*- of *plora, plebe;* and we find that *vixen* is borrowed from a dialect of Southern English speech in which *f*- regularly became *v*-. But it is only our assumption of regular phonemic change that permits us to isolate exceptions and establish a residue of this kind, and which forces us to seek and find explanations for it. The assumption of regular phonemic change is a fruitful one, because it helps us to analyze, classify and explain developments that we would otherwise regard—as did almost all people before about 1800— as an inexplicable welter of criss-cross and meaningless correspondences.

Workers in linguistic geography (Chaps. 41–43) have been especially given to confusion on this score. Since the results of dialect investigation show that "each word has its own history," and since local dialects show as much irregularity in phonetic developments as do standard languages, many linguistic geographers (especially M. G. Bàrtoli and his followers [p. 259]) have concluded that the Neo-Grammarians' principle of regular phonemic change must be unfounded. This conclusion is due to a very superficial kind of reasoning, without realizing that the assumption of regularity in phonemic change is the only thing that gives any foundation to whatever inferences we make concerning dialect borrowing. The principle of regular phonemic change is an assumption of the same type as Newton's "first law of physics," that every body remains in a state of rest or of uniform motion in a straight line unless it is compelled to change that state by force acting upon it. This "law," like the principle of absolutely regular phonemic change, is something we never see in nature, because there are always other factors entering in; but it is, nevertheless, the assumption of regularity that enables us to sort out the various factors that cause irregularity.

For nearly a hundred years, the assumption of regular sound-change has been called, after its initial promulgators, the "Neo-Grammarian postulate." However, the term *Neo-Grammarian* has been so widely misunderstood—in some quarters coming to be little more than a cuss-word—that it is best to reserve it (and its German equivalent *Junggrammatiker*) for use as a historical term, to refer only to Brugmann, Leskien and their immediate followers. For the postulate of regular phonemic change, it is best to use a more general and emotionally neutral term, *regularist*. We will therefore speak of this basic assumption of historical linguistics as the *regularist postulate*, and of those who accept it (no matter what generation they belonged to) as *regularists*. Tolomei (p. 301) was the first regularist; Rask, Grimm, Bopp, Brugmann, Leskien, Bloomfield were all regularists—as, indeed, are all scholars with any competence in historical linguistics, whether they admit to being regularists in theory or not. For such linguistic geographers and others as oppose the regularist postulate in their theoretical elucubrations but observe it in practice, the term *crypto-regularist* will perhaps be most suitable.

NOTES

Tolomei: Hall, 1942a, Chap. 4.
History of comparative linguistics: Bloomfield, 1933a, Chap. 1; Pedersen, 1931.
Phonetic "law": Hall, 1963b; Pulgram, 1955.
Comparative method and the realism of its result.. Hall, 1960; Pulgram, 1959, 1961; Nehring, 1961.

51

Comparative Reconstruction

We know, from historical sources, that Latin was spoken in a small area of central Italy, particularly in Rome and the area around the mouth of the Tiber, from ca. 800 B.C. onward. We know also that, as the dominion of the Romans expanded, the Latin language spread along with it; not only references in historical and literary works, but also inscriptions on tombs and monuments, give evidence that during the time of the Roman Empire (ca. 0–400 A.D.) Latin was used throughout the Mediterranean basin and northwestern Europe. The present day Romance languages, from Portuguese on the west to Roumanian on the east, show so close a resemblance to each other

	"CHEST"	"CLOTH"	"TO SLEEP"	"A HUNDRED"
Classical Latin	pektus	te:la	dormi-re	kentum
Proto-Romance	péktus	té^la	dormí^re	kéntu
Sardinian	péttus	téla	dormíre	kéntu
Roumanian	piépt	teárə	durmí	—
Italian	pétto	téla	dormíre	čénto
Rhaeto-Romance	péč	táila	durmír	sént
Old North French	píc	té^ilə	dormír	cént
Old South French (Old Provençal)	piéits	té^la	dormír	sént
Catalan	pít	té^la	dormír	sént
Spanish	péčos (OSp.)	téla	dormír	ciénto
Portuguese	pé^ito	té^la "web"	dormír	cént (OPort.)

Fig. 24: Selected Pan-Romance Lexical Correspondences.

that we can apply to them, *mutatis mutandis*, Sir William Jones' dictum about the relationships of the Indo-European languages (quoted on p. 302). Furthermore, this resemblance to Latin, although close, nevertheless does not permit us to assume that the Romance languages evolved directly out of the classical Latin used by the authors of the Golden Age such as Cicero, Vergil, Horace, Ovid and Caesar. We must assume, rather, that the Romance languages were evolved out of a common ancestral form which was somewhat different from Classical Latin, a form which we call Proto-Romance. We can reconstruct this Proto-Romance by working backwards from the attested forms of the Romance languages; for this purpose we can use over ten thousand related lexical items, such as those shown in the table in Fig. 24.

A table such as this contains essentially a set of predictions: each of the forms marked "Proto-Romance" in the list given across the top implies a prediction that if historical documentation were available, we should find for the common ancestral language a form with essentially this phonemic shape and meaning. (Note that the term *prediction* can apply to backward- as well as forward-looking discoveries.) For the Romance languages, these predictions are confirmed by our attestations of Latin, to such a large extent that we can consider our assumption of a historical relationship between Latin and Romance as completely confirmed. Where the reconstructed Proto-Romance forms differ from those of Classical Latin, we conclude, not that our reconstruction is wrong, but that the ancestral language belonged, in this respect, to a different variety of Latin from that used in elegant literature. Often (though not always) there is direct historical evidence for the validity of this conclusion. The anecdote of the emperor Vespasian and the grammarian Florus (p. 293) confirms our reconstruction of a Proto-Romance /kóˆda/ "tail". We reconstruct Proto-Romance forms without final /-m/ (cf. the form for "a hundred" in the table in Fig. 24); this is confirmed by the fact that, in classical versification, final syllables ending in -*m* did not count in establishing the meter, and hence it is evident that even in elegant pronunciation final -*m* must not have been pronounced as a consonant (though it may have been present as nasalization of the preceding vowel). Every so often a form postulated for Proto-Romance, on the basis of comparative reconstruction, is attested in newly-discovered documents; this has happened in the instances of /abánte/ "in front" (= Classical Latin *ab ante:* "from in front"), /abantiáre/ "to go ahead", and many other words.

To refer to reconstructed ancestral languages, we normally use the name of the language family, preceded by the element *Proto-:* thus, *Proto-Romance* for the common ancestral form out of which the Romance languages grew by differentiation, and similarly *Proto-Indo-European, Proto-Finno-Ugric, Proto-Athapaskan*, etc. The corresponding German prefix *ur-* means "original, primitive," and on occasion we find writers in English referring, say, to *Primitive Indo-European*. It is, however, advisable to avoid the term *primitive* in this connection, since it is open to misinterpretation as referring to a more "primitive" state or type of language; but, as we saw in Chap. 46, there has been no really "primitive" language spoken for many thousands of years. To save space, the prefix *Proto-* is abbreviated *P*, followed by the customary abbreviation for the name of the language family, e.g., *PRom.* for "Proto-Romance," *PIE* for "Proto-Indo-European," or *PAth.* for "Proto-Athapaskan." The term *Proto-*, as applied to a language, applies only to the ancestral language as reconstructed by the comparative method. Proto-Romance, especially, is not to be confused with "Popular Latin" or "Vulgar Latin;" these latter terms refer to a much broader concept, that of all the everyday language of the Latin speech-community, whether continued in the Romance languages or not.

The comparative method has to deal, not only with instances of perfect correspondences between related languages, but also with discrepant correspondences, where one language shows a given feature (phoneme, morpheme, taxeme) and another shows a different phenomenon. Thus, there are four series of correspondences among the Romance languages which entitle us to reconstruct, without much difficulty, the PRom. phonemes /iˆ eˆ uˆ oˆ/, as shown in the first four columns of the table in Fig. 25. The fifth and sixth columns show us forms in which there are discrepant correspondences: Sardinian and Roumanian have /ú/ where the other Romance languages point to /óˆ/, and Sardinian has /í/ where the others have vowels going back to /éˆ/.

For discrepant correspondences of this type, there are various possible explanations. One of the discrepant phenomena may be due to analogical new-formation, as when a speaker of English forms *thunk* on the analogy of *drunk;* we would not use this analogical *thunk* as a datum in our reconstruction of the earlier shape of the past of *think*. Or it may be due to borrowing between dialects, in which case it is equally invalid as a basis for comparative

PRom.	"WINE"	"CLOTH"	"WALL"	"KNOT"	"FISH"	"THROAT"
	u̯íˆnu	téˆla	múˆru	nóˆdu	píske	gúla
Sardinian	vínu	téla	múru	nódu	píske	gúla
Roumanian	vín	teárə	múr	nód	péš	gúrə
Italian	víno	téˆla	múro	nóˆdu	péˆšše	góˆla
Rhaeto-Romance	vín	téˆla	múr	nóˆd	péˆs	góˆla
Old North Fr.	vín	téˆilə	múr	nóˆuθ	péˆis	góˆulə
Old South Fr.	vín	téˆla	múr	nóˆd	péˆis	góˆla
Catalan	vín	téˆla	múr	nóˆd	péˆis	góˆla
Spanish	víno	téla	múro	nódo (OSp.)	péc (OSp.)	góla
Portuguese	víno	téˆla	múro	nódo	péˆiše	góˆla

FIG. 25: Romance Vowel Correspondences.

reconstruction. When all such instances are eliminated, however, there still remain, in any group of related languages, a number of discrepant correspondences which cannot be explained as due to analogy or borrowing. For such correspondences, we reconstruct a special feature of the ancestral language; in the instance just cited, we reconstruct PRom. lax /í/ and /ú/, as opposed to tense /íˆ/ and /úˆ/, for /píske/ "fish" and /gúla/: "throat" respectively, to take care of the discrepancies evidenced in Roumanian and Sardinian. Our reconstruction is confirmed by "looking in the back of the book" and finding that Latin did have just such a pair of phonemic features, except that in Classical Latin the contrast was one of length versus shortness, /i:/ vs. /i/ and /u:/ vs. /u/, rather than of tenseness versus laxness. In the instance just discussed, there are a number of lexical items for which we reconstruct PRom. lax /i/ and /u/; but it is not necessary that there be a great many such items. One or two will suffice to justify our reconstructing a special feature of the ancestral language, provided no other explanation suffices and the resultant reconstruction fits into the pattern of the proto-language.

Scholars in the Romance field are in the fortunate position of being able to "look in the back of the book" and check most of their findings against attested Latin materials. For almost all other language families, no such confirmation is available, since, by historical accident, the speech-communities of the proto-languages were nonliterate. Yet the example of the Romance languages shows that reconstructed proto-languages can be accepted as valid representations of a reality that must have existed, even though we may have no written attestations for them. Some scholars have thought that comparative reconstruction could be carried out only for languages some of whose earlier history was known, or only for "languages of civilization" such as the Indo-European, the Finno-Ugric or the Semitic families. However, comparative work on many American Indian, African and Asian language families has shown that the languages of so-called "primitive" peoples are no exception to the general applicability of the regularist principle (cf. Chap. 50) and of comparative reconstruction. The definitive proof of this assertion was furnished by Leonard Bloomfield in his reconstruction of a

	"HE IS OLD"	"FIRE"	"MOCCASIN"	"MY GRAND-MOTHER"	"HE KICKS HIM"	"HE IS RED"
PCA cluster	čk	šk	xk	hk	nk	çk
PCA form	kečkjeewa	iškuteewi	maxkesini	noohkuma	tankeškaweewa	meçkusiwa
Fox	kehkjeewa	aškuteewi	mahkeseehi	noohkumesa	takeškaweewa	meškusiwa
Ojibwa	————	iškudee	mahkizin	noohkumis	tangiškawaad	miskuzi
Menomini	kečkiw	eskoteew	mahkeesen	noohkumeh	tahkeeskaweew	mehkoon
Plains Cree	————	iskuteew	maskisin	noohkum	tahkiskaweew	mihkusiw

FIG. 26: Proto-Central Algonquian Consonant Clusters.

special consonant-cluster */çk/ for Proto-Central Algonquian (PCA), at first on the basis of a discrepant correspondence between Menomini and Cree on the one side and Fox and Ojibwa on the other, in the forms for "he is red" (the sixth set in the table given in Fig. 26).

After the cluster */çk/ had been set up for Proto-Central Algonquian, an outlying Algonquian dialect, Swampy Cree, was found to agree with Plains Cree in the first five correspondences, but to have a special cluster /htk/ in this morpheme and only in this morpheme: /mihtkusiw/ "he is red". This Swampy Cree form thus furnished complete justification for Bloomfield's postulation of a special PCA cluster */çk/, since Swampy Cree /htk/ could come from no other source. Later investigators, working through old dictionaries and other materials prepared by missionaries, uncovered further correspondences pointing back to PCA */çk/; but the assumption of this cluster for PCA would have been justified on the basis of the one correspondence in the words for "he is red" alone. Since it furnished the final, unquestionable proof of the validity of comparative reconstruction based on the postulate of regularity in sound-change (Chap. 50), it is no exaggeration to say that Swampy Cree /mihtkusiw/ has been the most important single form in the development of historical linguistics.

Languages do not develop out of a common source by a process of simultaneous splitting; rather, they undergo differentiation by the rise and spread of successive innovations, each of which introduces a new isogloss and hence a new dialectal division into the speech-community. (Nor must proto-languages themselves be thought of as absolutely unified; no speech-community that ever existed was without dialectal divisions of some kind, and our reconstructions often point to the existence of such divisions, as when the Romance languages show both /íll-/ and /íps-/ as the stems to be set up in Proto-Romance for the predecessor of the definite article.) Successive innovations will have different origins and will spread to different extents, so that eventually the proto-language will be broken up into a number of related varieties, no two of which will show exactly the same developments. The extent and distribution of the changes enable us to set up a relative chronology for their origin and hence for the splitting off of the different varieties. Thus, for the developments of PRom. lax /i/ and /u/, all scholars assume that the change of /í/ to /é^/ antedated that of /ú/ to /ó^/, because the former change spread to Roumanian and the Romance of the Balkans before they were separated from the rest of the Romance-speaking world, whereas the latter did not. We can thus set up three successive stages:

1.   píske   gúla   (Sardinian then splits off, preserving /i/ and /u/ as such)
2.   pé^ske gúla   (Balkan Romance shares in this stage and then splits off)
3.   pé^ske gó^la (Italian and the Western Romance languages continue this stage)

Convenient labels can always be devised for the successive stages of differentiation; for the three stages set up above, we can use the terms *Proto-Romance*, *Proto-Continental Romance*, and *Proto-Italo-Western Romance*, respectively.

On the basis of these and similar successive splits, we can establish a "family tree," or diagram showing the relations of the languages which are derived from a common source. Figures 27 and 28 show such diagrams for the Germanic and the Romance languages. It must not be thought, however, that the divisions shown in such diagrams were sharp or absolute, except in cases of actual migration and hence permanent separation of speech communities (as when the Angles, Saxons and Jutes left the mainland of Germany and invaded Britain in the fifth century A.D.). In general, speakers of the different varieties which have arisen out of a common source remain in more or less contact with each other, and hence often borrow forms from each other, thus overlaying to a greater or less extent the results of an earlier differentiation. In extreme cases, as pointed out long ago by Johannes Schmidt, an apparent sharp split between two languages—let us call them A and H—may be the result of the obliteration, through dialectal borrowing, of earlier intermediate varieties, B, C, D, E, F and G. Some scholars have thought that this observation of Schmidt's and his followers (known as the "wave theory") invalidates the "family tree" and the principle of comparative reconstruction. In fact, however, these two approaches complement each other. The wave theory serves always to remind the comparativist that he must always, at every stage, eliminate from his reconstructive procedures all

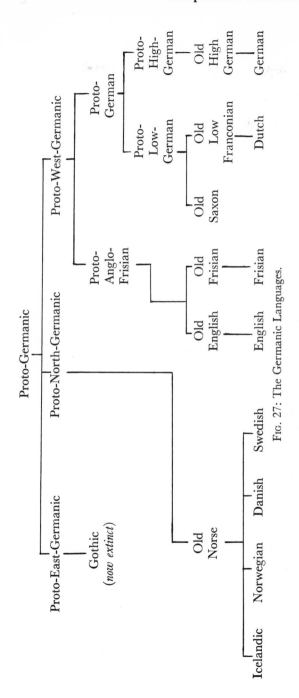

Fig. 27: The Germanic Languages.

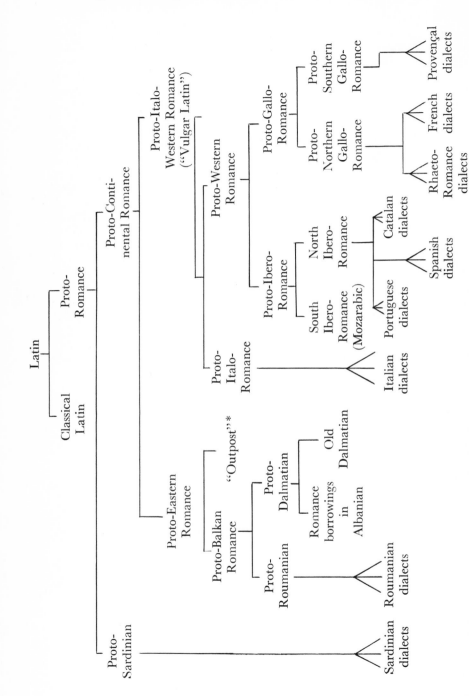

Fig. 28: The Romance Languages.

elements that are under suspicion of borrowing; for instance, we will not project back into Proto-Romance, under the form /aduentúˆra/, an ancestral form for It. *avventura*, Sp. *abentura*, and Fr. /avãtyr/ *aventure:* "adventure", since the history of mediaeval culture shows us that the Italian and Spanish words, as well as English *adventure* and German *Abenteuer*, were borrowed from French.

Two further cautions are in order at this point. Reconstructed forms such as those given in this and the preceding chapter are purely linguistic reconstructions. We set them up on the basis of correspondences of phonemes in the languages which are obviously derived from a common source, and they tell us nothing at all about either the kind of people who used them or the place where they were used. With regard to Proto-Indo-European, there are certain inferences which we may perhaps make from the presence of some words in all of the related languages, e.g., the word for "snow" (reconstructed PIE/snigʷhs)/, which leads us to suppose that the speakers of that language knew of snow and hence did not live in an extremely hot region; but even such inferences as these are tentative. Certainly there is no justification for the exaggerated conclusions concerning the physical race (supposedly "Nordic") and the dwelling place (often ascribed to Northern Europe or more specifically Germany) in which some scholars—mostly, but not exclusively, German—have indulged on the basis of purely linguistic data concerning Proto-Indo-European.

There also exists a very widespread custom of using the terms *mother language* and *daughter language* for an earlier stage (e.g., Latin) and a later stage (e.g., Spanish, French, or Italian), respectively. This metaphor is dangerous, since it implies that there is some type of reproduction involved. In actuality, languages are sets of habits, not plants or animals, and they do not reproduce either sexually or asexually. The modern Romance languages, for instance, are the direct continuation of the Latin of the Roman Republic, handed down from one generation to another through a tradition of first-language learning. Hence, if we speak of "ancestral" or "descendant" languages, of "family trees" and of "genetic relationship," it must be with full consciousness of the metaphor involved, and without letting ourselves be deceived by false biological parallels.

NOTES

Principles of comparative reconstruction: Bloomfield, 1933, Chap. 18; Lehmann, 1962, Chap. 5.

Proto-Romance: Hall, 1950.

Proto-Algonquian */çk/*:* Bloomfield, 1928, 1933a, Chap. 20; Geary, 1941; Hockett, 1948.

The spread of Old French aventure *through cultural borrowing:* Mever-Lübke. 1936. Introd.

52

Types of Sound-Change

WHEN A PHONEME CHANGES, it may do so in one of three ways. It may split, what was formerly one phoneme becoming two. Proto-Romance had a single voiceless stop in the velar region, /k/, as in */ké^na/ "dinner", */kása/ "house", */kó^da/ "tail"; through a conditioned sound change, /k/ > /č/ before front vowels and remained /k/ elsewhere, as in Proto-Italo-Western Romance forms which corresponded to those just cited and which have continued unchanged in Italian /čé^na/, /kása/, /kó^da/. A phoneme may merge with another, through loss of contrast. For Proto-Italo-Western Romance we assume (on the basis of Italian evidence) that there were two phonemes in contrast, /č/ [tʃ] and /c/ [ts], as in */bráčču/ "arm" and */póccu/ "well". For Proto-Western Romance, however, we need set up only */c/[ts], since the western Romance languages (Gallo- and Ibero-Romance) show no traces of a contrast between */č/ and */c/. In this instance, between Proto-Italo-Western Romance and Proto-Western Romance, */č/ merged with */c/. A special type of merger occurs when a phoneme is lost (i.e., merges with zero), as when final /-m/ was lost in popular Latin speech (p. 307). A third type of change is that in which a phoneme is neither split nor merged, but simply continues as a separate unit in the phonological system of the language, but with different allophones from those it had previously, in a different relation to the rest of the system, so that it must be considered as having changed its function and hence its nature and symbolization, as when Proto-Gallo-Romance /u/ became /y/[y] in French, e.g., in /myr/[myr] "wall".

Phonemic split takes place through the mechanism discussed in Chap. 50: first an allophonic variation arises, then there is a change in the conditions under which the variation originally arose so that it is no longer conditioned by them, and under the new conditions the phonetic variant is not predictable and hence has phonemic status. In the split of PRom. /k/ into /č/ and /k/, there was first an allophonic variation of /k/ to [kˈ], [kʲ] and [tʃ] before front vowels, but not elsewhere; as long as these sounds occurred only before front vowels and [k] elsewhere, they were still allophones of /k/, and [ˈkˈe^:na], [ˈkʲe^:na] or [ˈtʃe^:na] were still phonemically /ké^na/. But then the /ki̯/ of a word like */brákki̯u/ "arm", which would also have been allophonically [kˈi̯], [kʲi̯] or [tʃi̯], lost its [i̯], and people got into the habit of saying [ˈbrat:ʃu] instead of [ˈbrat:ʃi̯u]. As soon as this second change took place, [tʃ] now occurred before back vowels as well as front, and the [tʃu] of ['brat:ʃu] was in contrast with the [ka] of, say, ['sik:u] /síkku/ "dry". At this stage, therefore, [tʃ] had separate phonemic status, and the word for "arm" ['brat:ʃu] was phonemically /braččíu/ and hence also that for "dinner", ['tʃeˆ:na], was phonemically /čéˆna/. This shift in the phonemic status of the former allophone [tʃ] left a vacant spot in the phonemic inventory, since there was no longer any /k/[k] before front vowels. This spot was then filled by the cluster /ku̯/ losing its /u̯/ before front vowels, so that, for instance, /ku̯íˆ/ "who" became /kíˆ/. This development then left the cluster /ku̯/ before front vowels unrepresented, and other combinations changed to fill this vacant slot, as when the combination /ékku (h)íˆk/ "behold here" became /(ek)ku̯íˆ/, Italian /kuí/ "here".

Phonemic merger, on the other hand, takes place through a subtle process of reinterpretation of allophones which have become closely similar through nonsignificant variation. In my own speech, *train* /trén/ and *drain* /drén/ are ['tɹeˆⁱn] and ['dɹeˆⁱn], respectively, with no palatal characteristics at all; after the tip of the tongue has struck the gum ridge for [t] or [d], the back of the tongue goes up to make the bunched dorsal fricative [ɹ]. In many other people's usage, however, the tip of the tongue makes contact rather behind the gum ridge, and immediately thereafter the top (not the back) of the tongue approaches the front part of the palate to form [ř]. The resultant [t'ř] and [d'ř] sound to my ears extremely close to [tʃ] and [dʒ], respectively. I feel no desire to imitate this latter pronunciation, but if I were to do so (because of some feeling, perhaps, that it was more elegant or prestigious than my own), I might very likely do so by using my own [tʃ] and [dʒ] in words where I had previously used [tɹ] and [dɹ], respectively, I would thus end up by saying ['tʃeˆⁱn] /tʃén/ and ['dʒeˆⁱn] /dʒén/ for *train* and *drain*, and similarly in all other words containing /tr/ and /dr/. In such a case, I would have merged /tr/ with /tʃ/, and /dr/ with /dʒ/, through misinterpretation of other speakers' allophones.

Loss of phonemes takes place in much the same way. The loss of /-m/ in popular Latin speech came about through upper-class speakers substituting a nasalized vocoid in final position for vocoid + [-m], e.g., in /dominum/ ['dominũ] "master". Other speakers, hearing the nasalization, did not interpret it as involving an allophone of /-m/, but equated a nasalized final vowel with their own oral final vowels, and imitated ['dominũ] with their own ['dominu], which was, of course, phonemically /dominu/. Similarly, speakers of present day Romance languages expect to hear a full release on a final consonant (cf. p. 68); when they hear speakers of English pronouncing unreleased final consonants, as in ['hwat] /hwát/ *what*, they think that no final consonant has been pronounced, and imitate the speakers of English by leaving off the final consonant altogether, saying, for example, ['hwa] instead of ['hwat].

Phonemes can change with regard to any of their distinctive phonologic features. Vowels can undergo *raising* or *lowering* in the position of the tongue, as when Proto-Gallo-Romance /á/ in a free syllable, not after palatal or before nasal, became first /æ/ and then /é/ in Old North French (cf. p. 296), in such a word as PGRom. /máre/ "sea" > OFr. /mǽr/ > mér/.* An example of lowering is the development of PRom. lax /í/ to /éˆ/ and lax /ú/ to /óˆ/, discussed on p. 308. A vowel sound may undergo *fronting* or *backing;* the latter phenomenon is exemplified in some modern varieties of Swedish, in which /a/ has moved back to /ɔ/, as in the town-name /jeliváre/ *Gällivare* > /jelivɔ́re/. Fronting is rather more common, e.g., the development of Proto-Gallo-Romance /u/ to French /y/ discussed on p. 296. A single vowel may be replaced by a diphthong, in the process of *diphthongization* or *breaking,* exemplified in the Old French developments shown in the table on p. 298. Rather less frequently, diphthongs undergo *monophthongization* or *simplification;* some scholars consider that modern Florentine and Tuscan simple vowels in /bóno/ "good" or /véne/ "he comes", as opposed to older /buono/ and /viéne/, are the results of such a process. Oral vowels may be subjected to *nasalization,* as when Old French /an/ became Modern French /ã/, in such a word as /ban/ *ban* "summons" > /bã/. The opposite process, *denasalization,* is rarer, but is exemplified in the loss of nasalization that took place in Early Modern French nasal vowels before nasal consonants, e.g., in /grãmer/ *grammaire* "grammar" > /gramer/ (cf. the comic scene of the servant-woman Martine in Molière's *Les Femmes Savantes,* when she confuses the old-fashioned pronunciation of *grammaire* "grammar" with /grãmer/ *grand'mère* "grandmother"). The general term "weakening" is often applied to a *centering* of vowel articulation, as when PGRom. /-a/ became /-ə/ in Old North French, for instance in /kantáta/ "sung (past part. f. sg.)" > /čantǽðə/ *chantede.*

Consonants, likewise, may show changes in place or manner of articulation, or in voicing. They may undergo *palatalization,* as in the case of PRom. /k/ before front vowels becoming /č/ cited on p. 314, or *aspiration,* as when earlier [k] became [h] between vowels in Tuscan (cf. Chap. 5). *Fricativization* is frequent, with such examples as Spanish intervocalic /b d g/ becoming [β ð γ]: e.g., /ába/ "bean" ['aβa] from earlier /hába/ ['haba]. A passage of /s/ or some other consonant to /r/ is known as *rhotacism,* and to /l/ as *lambdacism:* e.g., for the former, Old Latin */au̯so:sa/ "dawn" > /auro:ra/ "dawn", and for the latter, the development of intervocalic /-d-/ to /-l-/ in some varieties of Latin, from which such forms as /konsilium/ "a sitting together, council" (< */konsidium/, to the root /sed-/ "sit") were borrowed into the standard language. *Voicing* is one of the most frequent developments, as in the modern American treatment of the intervocalic tongue-flap allophone of /t/, which has merged with the corresponding voiced tongue-flap allophone of /d/, [r], in such words as *letter,* formerly /létər/ and now /lédər/ ['lerɹ], or *meeting,* formerly /mítɪŋ/ and now /mídɪŋ/ ['mirɪŋ].

Certain directions of sound-change are more frequent than others; for instance, vowel-raising is more common than vowel-lowering. Plosive consonants becoming palatals, assibilates or affricates is a far more common

---

* In historical linguistic discussion, the symbol > means "becomes, becoming," and < means "comes from, coming from."

process than the reverse. On the basis of these observations, we are often able to judge the likelihood of a development assumed by linguistic historians where direct evidence is lacking. A few scholars have objected to assuming, for Latin, a plosive pronunciation [k g] for /k g/ before front vowels, arguing that the church pronunciation of written *c g* as [tʃ dʒ] in this position and the evidence of most of the Romance languages render it probable that the ancient Romans had /č ǧ/ as separate phonemes in Classical Latin. The presence of /k/[k] and /g/[g] in such Sardinian words as /kéna/ ['kena] "supper" and /gélu/['ge^lu] "cold",* they explain as the result of "reintegration" or "hardening" of /č ǧ/ to /k g/. Among the reasons for rejecting this point of view is the extreme unlikeliness of such a process taking place, since consonantal change normally takes place in the direction of stop to assibilate and almost never vice versa.

Not to be confused with the type of sound-change we have been discussing are instances of sudden replacement of one phoneme by another. Under this heading come *dissimilation, assimilation,* and *metathesis.* In dissimilation, one of two successive phonemes is replaced by another, often with the same general type of articulation; the liquids and nasals /l r m n ŋ ŋ/ are especially subject to dissimilation, as when Old Italian *canònico:* "canon (of a cathedral)" was replaced in popular speech by *calònico,* with /n . . . n/ > /l . . . n/. Sometimes the dissimilation takes the shape of complete loss of one or more phonemes; to Latin /kụi:nkụe/ "five" correspond Romance forms derived from PRom., /kí^nkụe/, e.g., Italian /čínkue/ *cinque,* French /sɛ̃k/ *cinq,* Spanish /θinko/ *cinco.* If a whole syllable is repeated in the earlier form of a word and comes to be lost by dissimilation, the process is known as *haplology,* as when Latin *idololatria:* "worship of idols" appears as *idolatria:* "idolatry": one historian of language exemplified this process in his terminology by calling it *haplogy* instead of *haplology.* Assimilation involves the replacement of one phoneme by another more similar to a preceding or following phoneme, as when Proto-IE */peŋkʷe/ appears in Latin as /kụi:nkụe/. In metathesis, two phonemes exchange their position; for instance, Latin *capitulum:* "chapter" appears in Spanish as /kabíldo/ *cabildo,* which presupposes an intermediate stage */kapílodo/; Latin *philosophus* appears in Old Italian as *fisòlafo.* Changes of this type obviously do not involve gradual allophonic variations followed by phonological restructuring. They are more closely akin to "slips of the tongue," which are going on all the time on the fringe of our linguistic behavior, and represent generalizations (frequently humorous) of such occasional variants.

Phonemic change does not take place simply at random, with one phoneme developing in one direction and another in another direction. Just as the phonemes of a language fall into a certain pattern, so do their changes fall into patterns, which we often call *shifts.* When the long vowels of Middle English changed, for instance, they all shifted in the same direction, towards

---

* In Sardinian, /é/ and /ó/ vary allophonically according to the nature of the final vowel of the word they are in: they are higher when the final vowel is /i u/, and lower when it is /e a o/.

a higher position of articulation in the mouth; this change was known as the "great English vowel-shift." In two instances, the shifted vowels have given diphthongs in modern pronunciation according to the IPA-Kenyon-Pike analysis; according to the Bloomfield-Trager-Smith analysis (Chap. 20) they all gave diphthongs:

MIDDLE ENGLISH	MODERN ENGLISH CONVENTIONAL SPELLING	IPA-KENYON-PIKE TRANSCRIPTION	TRAGER-SMITH TRANSCRIPTION
/ná:me/	name	/ném/	/néjm/
/dé:d/	deed	/díd/	/díjd/
/gé:s/	geese	/gís/	/gíjs/
/wí:n/	wine	/wájn/	/wájn/
/stɔ́:n/	stone	/stón/	/stówn/
/gó:s/	goose	/gús/	/gúws/
/hú:s/	house	/háws/	/háws/

Another instance of patterned shifting is found in the raising of Old French vowels in free syllables (not after palatals or before nasals) as shown on p. 296; here all vowels except /i u/ (which could hardly be raised any higher) were articulated in a higher position in the mouth, with accompanying diphthongization of the mid vowels.

The comparative method enables us to reconstruct the earlier stages of families of related languages, and to make predictions looking backward in time, as to what may be found (and, on occasion, is found) if new attestations come to light. There is no similar technique for looking forward in time and predicting the changes that will take place in the phonologic structure of a language; there are too many variables, both linguistic and nonlinguistic, at work, whose relative influence cannot be foreseen. In this respect, linguistics is similar to such a science as geology, rather than to physics or chemistry, which operate within a much more restricted and hence more easily controlled and predicted framework of variables. At the present time, all we can say with regard to sound-change in the future is that, since it is an integral part of linguistic history, it will be continue to go on, although we cannot tell which specific changes will take place, in what dialects or when.

NOTES

Classification of types of sound-change: Bloomfield, 1933a, Chap. 21.
Phonemic split and merger: Hoenigswald, 1960.
Development of vowel pattern as a whole in Romance: Hall, 1955a.
Allophones of /e o/ *in Sardinian:* Wagner, 1941, pp. 11, 12, 249.
Exemplification of haplogy: Pei, 1941.

External Borrowing

SOUND-CHANGE is one of the major factors in the continual alteration of language, and probably the most fundamental factor. As a result of sound-change, morphemes and syntagmata can undergo change, either by being levelled through the merger of phonemes, or having morphophonemic alternations introduced when phonemes split. In the development of Italian out of Latin and Proto-Romance, final /-s/, /-m/, and /-t/ were all lost; hence, between Late Latin times and the earliest attestations of Old Italian, the forms of the imperfect singular of first-conjugation verbs developed as follows:

	LATIN	PROM. AND PITWROM.	PRE-ITALIAN
1.sg.	kanta:bam: "I was singing"	kantába	kantáva
2.sg.	kanta:ba:s: "you were singing"	kantábas	kantáva
2.sg.	kanta:bat: "he was singing"	kantábat	kantáva

In this instance, the distinctive endings of the three persons of the imperfect singular were all lost (merged with zero) as a result of the loss of the final consonants. In the plurals of noun-stems ending in /-k-/, however, the palatalization of this phoneme before front vowels (cf. p. 316) introduced into the stem an alternation between /k/ and /č/ which had not been there before:

PROTO-ROMANCE	ITALIAN
sg. /amí^kus/: "friend", pl. /amí^ki/	sg. /amíko/, pl. /amíči/
sg. /médikus/: "doctor", pl. /médiki/	sg. /médiko/, pl. /médiči/

Phonemic change, and changes in forms and constructions which result therefrom, can be termed *evolutionary* or *organic* change. This is the kind of linguistic change of which the speakers of a language are least aware, because it takes place so gradually, and is conditioned by phonologic habits, to which the ordinary speaker has in general little or no conscious reaction. He is usually far more aware of the other major factor in linguistic change, *borrowing*. When any part of the structure of a language is changed by importation of features, whether from some other part of the language or from some external source, the imported features are said to be *borrowed*. We distinguish between two types of borrowing: *external* and *internal*, depending on the source of the borrowing.

Under the heading of external borrowings come those from one dialect to another (*dialectal* borrowings), those from an earlier stage of the same language (*archaisms*) and those from other languages (*loans*). It is very frequent for a language to borrow forms from related dialects (regional, social, occupation) for various reasons: distinctive meanings, humor, or pleasant or unpleasant connotations of one sort or another. The Northerner who has come in some contact with the social structure of the Southern states may use the term *po' white trash*, with an approximation of the Southern pronunciation *po'*, although in all other situations he will use his normal pronunciation for *poor*. Such expressions as *thar she blows!* (originally from whalers' jargon), *hoot mon!* (Scottish), or *petrol* or *lift* (British English) have the flavor of the regional or social types of speech from which they were taken. A good example of dialect borrowing for favorable connotation is French /amur/ *amour* "love". As this word goes back to PRom. /amóˆre/, we should normally expect Modern French */amœ r/ *ameur* just as PRom. /óˆra/ "hour" gave /œˆr/ *heure* and /dolóˆre/ "pain, sorrow" gave /dulœˆr/ *douleur*: but we actually find /amœˆr/ only in rustic dialects and with the meaning "rut (period of sexual excitement in animals)". The French form has the vowel /u/, not /œˆ/ as we would expect; it is clearly a borrowing from Provençal (South French), in which the development /u/ is to be expected in this word. We know that in the Middle Ages Provençal was the prime literary language of love, and that the Provençal poets formulated and expressed doctrines of courtly love which found widespread acceptance throughout the European upper classes; we conclude that Northern French (on which modern standard French is based) took over the form /amur/ *amour* from Provençal because of the literary and social prestige of the form, and that the indigenous /amœˆr/ was then relegated to the meaning of "animal love, rut".

If there are written records of an earlier stage of a language, those who read them may find old words in them and reintroduce them, either to refer to phenomena of earlier times which have later gone out of use, or for special effect. In discussions of the history of fortification, we must use such terms as *casemate* (from Italian *casamatta*, originally "movable house or shelter for artillery"), *machicolation*, *portcullis*, and similar archaisms; treating of the history of fighting, words like *mace*, *harquebus* or *javelin;* and similarly in other fields. Writers of historical fiction find it helpful to introduce archaisms to give "atmosphere", e.g., *guerdon:* "reward", *forsooth:* "indeed", *methinks*, or exclamations like *by my halidom!* or *'od's bodkins!*. Occasionally, a writer may misinterpret a passage in an earlier author, as when Sir Walter Scott took a verbal phrase in Edmund Spenser's *Faerie Queene*, *derring do:* "to perform acts of daring", and treated it as a noun, *derring-do:* "heroism"; such an unjustified use of an archaism is a *ghost-word*. It was primarily to archaisms that Horace was referring when he wrote in his *Ars Poetica* ("Art of Poetry"):

Multa renascentur quae iam cecidere, cadentque
Quae nunc sunt in honore vocabula, si volet usus

"Many words which have gone out of use come back to life again, and words which are now in honor fall into disuse, if usage so wills it."

External borrowing is not limited, of course, to related dialects. Borrowings between mutually unintelligible languages are also very frequent. We are all familiar with such foreign words in English as *blitzkreig, kamikaze, sputnik, spaghetti, smörgåsbord, chile con carne, fortissimo, au revoir*. A very large part of the vocabulary of English, over fifty per cent, is of Latin or Greek origin, either borrowed directly from those languages by scholars (*learnèd words*), or through the intermediary of French (mostly in Middle English times, in the fourteenth and fifteenth centuries). Of the first type of Graeco-Latin borrowings in English are such terms as *interpretation, particular, vocabulary, marginal;* of the second, words like *chair* (from Latin *cathedra* through Old French *chaire*) or *table* (from Latin *tabula:* "board"). From more remote languages, we have in English such words as *sugar*, from Arabic, and ultimately from Sanskrit *çarkara:* "gritty substance"; *thug* from an East Indian word; or *squaw, moccasin, squash, tomahawk*, from American Indian languages.

If a form is taken over directly (with more or less phonological and mor-phological adaptation), it is known as a *loan-word*. In some instances, the foreign form itself is not taken over, but the meaning of a native form or combination of forms is shifted to correspond to that of a foreign expression; in this case we have a *loan-shift*. Strong emotion was regarded by Greek Stoic philosophers as something morbid, and was called by them /pathós/ "suffering, disease"; the Romans translated this by *passiō:* "suffering", from which our term *passion* was later borrowed. We use the term *passion* in the meaning "suffering" only in connection with the *passion* of Jesus Christ, and otherwise use it in the meaning of the Latin loan-shift *passiō* "deep emotion". In French, *ça va sans dire* means literally "that goes without saying", and figuratively "that's obvious"; in English we often use the loan-shifted expres-sion *that goes without saying*, and likewise *a marriage of convenience* for French *un mariage de convenance*, or *a superman* for German *Übermensch* (given currency by the philosopher Nietzsche). Only a few loan-shifts achieve general accept-ance in any language, and other literal translations of foreign idiomatic expressions sound strange or ridiculous; such an expression as *I'm in train of writing* makes no sense in English unless the hearer is familiar with French *je suis en train d'écrire:* "I'm in the act, the process of writing". If a part of a loan is reshaped to resemble a native form, while the rest remains more or less in its initial shape, the result is a *loan-blend*, as when English *pocketbook* was reshaped in Pennsylvania German into /bókabùx/ *bockabuch*, with the latter part adapted to German /búx/ *Buch* "book".

Single words are most easily borrowed from one language to another; and when they are borrowed, they are normally adapted to the structure of the borrowing language, in sound and in form. Thus, *garage* is pronounced in French fashion as /gəráʒ/ only by some who know a certain amount of French. Most speakers of American English say /g(ə)rádʒ/; in England, the stress has—in accordance with normal English patterns—been shifted to the first syllable, and the word is pronounced by upper-class speakers as /gǽraʒ/ with a French-type ending, but by lower-class speakers it is wholly Anglicized into /gǽrɪdʒ/. Loan-words, once assimilated into the body of a language, serve as bases for further formations just like all other words: for instance, on the noun *chauffeur*, borrowed from French, we now have the verb *to chauffe* /ʃóf/ (as in *I had to chauffe my mother around all day*)*;* and a suffix like *-able*, originally used only in Latin or French loan-words like *inevitable*, *amiable*, has now become so general that it can be added to any English verb, in such formations as *eatable*, *seeable*, *loveable* (cf. Chap. 56).

Not only individual words, however, but sounds, phonemic distinctions, and syntactic patterns may spread across language-boundaries and be borrowed from one language into another of different origin. In most of the Romance languages, the *r*-sound is a tap made with the tip of the tongue against the inside upper front teeth (a voiced dental flap); but since the seventeenth century, a uvular trill has become fashionable, first of all in French, originating in Paris and spreading from there to other urban centers. It was imitated in languages other than French, spreading along with French courtly behavior in the seventeenth and eighteenth centuries; it has become the normal urban representative of /r/ in German, and is widespread in Spanish and Portuguese as a variant of the /r:/ phoneme. The suffix *-eteria* was present originally in the one word *cafeteria* (a borrowing from Italian /kaffetería/ *caffeteria* "coffee-shop") and then generalized from that word, with the meaning—peculiar to English—of "place where one serves oneself", as in *groceteria*, *hatteteria*. Even the whole structural pattern of a language may be affected in this way; for instance, Armenian, originally a language related to English and the other Indo-European languages, has gradually favored more and more those regularized structural patterns which resemble those of the neighboring Turkish, until Armenian is now far more similar in pattern to Turkish than it was formerly.

All these different types of borrowing are of course not made in a void; as the Italian scholar P. G. Goidànich once said sarcastically, they are not "packed up in boxes and shipped across country by rail," to be opened and distributed impersonally at the receiving end of the line. The intermediary in all cases of borrowing is someone who is bilingual, to the extent of having at least some slight knowledge of both the source of borrowing and the language into which the borrowing is made. The New England farmer who goes to town and hears a new pronunciation for *road* and takes it back home with him; the soft-drink salesman who travels out from Boston and sells *tonic* to the country stores in neighboring New England; the journalist or radio commentator who knows and uses such words as *kolkhoz* or *kibbutz*—all these are active helpers in the borrowing and transmission of loan-words to the community at large.

NOTES

General theory of borrowing: Haugen, 1953; Weinreich, 1953.
Italian casamatta*:* Hall, 1962b.

54

Internal Borrowing (Analogy)

INTERNAL BORROWING, or analogy, involves the transfer of a linguistic feature from one part of a system to another part of the same system. We are all familiar with analogical new-formations from child language (Chap. 46), when children make combinations like *foots, mans* instead of *feet, men*, on the analogy of regular plurals like *hats, cans*. Such analogical new-formations, on all levels of linguistic structure, are not limited to child language, but are present at all times in the history of all languages, and form an essential part of the mechanism of linguistic change, as much as do sound change and external borrowing.

Analogical changes of this kind are often presented in the shape of proportional formulae, with *x* standing for the new-formation, thus:

$$hat:hats \quad = foot:x$$
$$box:boxes \quad = ox:x$$
$$kick:kicked = stick:x$$
$$rake:raked \quad = break:x$$

On occasion, objections are made to the statement of analogical replacements in proportional formulae; critics say that naïve speakers would not be capable of exact enough reasoning to make up a formula of this kind and apply it. There are two answers to these objections. Analogy is not a process which involves analytical reasoning; experiment has shown that even chickens are capable of distinguishing lighter from darker colors on a basis of analogical proportion. Hence we need not assume that analogical new-formation requires analytical reasoning; even the most stupid human has more reasoning-power than a chicken and hence is capable of making this type of formation. The Danish linguist Otto Jespersen (1860–1943) tells of a Danish child who should, according to normal Danish usage, have said *nikkede:* "nodded" as the past of *nikker:* "nod", but said *nak* instead, on the analogy of *stak:* "stuck", whose present is *stikker*. When corrected, the child immediately retorted *"Stikker—stak, nikker—nak"*, showing that he knew perfectly well on what analogy he had made the new past form, and stating it in the form of a proportion.

On the phonological level, analogy involves the transfer of allophones from their "normal" environment to other positions where their occurrence is no longer automatic; this is one of the mechanisms whereby allophones acquire phonemic status. The classical example of phonetic analogy is Puerto Rican Spanish [h]. In those varieties of Puerto Rican Spanish where [x] is still a voiceless velar fricative [x], the status of the aspirate [h] has been simply that of an allophonic variant of /s/ in syllable-final position: /losómbres/ [lo-'sombreh] *los hombres* "the men", /lostíteres/ [loh'titereh] *los títeres* "the marionettes". In this variety of Puerto Rican Spanish, the plural ending /-s/ has two allophonically conditioned (though phonemically identical) allomorphs: [-s] before vowel in close juncture (which is the only place where it occurs in syllable-initial position), and [-h] before consonant or pause (where it is in syllable-final position). However, many speakers have come to transfer the allomorph of the plural suffix [-h] to prevocalic position, and form plurals like [lo'hombreh] "the men", [lo'hotroh] *los otros* "the others". For these speakers, [-h-], by coming to stand between vowels, has acquired phonemic status, since it contrasts with intervocalic [-s-] in such forms as ['oso] /óso/ *oso* "bear", ['weso] /uéso/ *hueso* "bone"; and for them, [lo'hombreh] is phonemically /lohómbreh/, [lo'hotroh] is /lohótroh/, [loh'titereh] is /lohtítereh/, and the plural suffix has only one allomorph, /-h/, occurring in all positions.

On the phonemic level, analogy leads to *over-correction*, in the extension of phonemes to positions where they are historically unjustified, often creating new phonemic combinations in the process. Speakers of modern English who have /ú/, not /jú/, in stressed position after a dental consonant are frequently criticized and told to say /njú/ instead of /nú/ *new;* /tjún/, not /tún/ *tune;* /djúk/, not /dúk/ *duke,* and so forth. On the analogy of these equivalences, radio announcers have been known to produce such forms as /njún/ for /nún/ *noon* ("The news at newn") and even /mjún/ for /mún/ *moon* ("The mewn was shining brightly"). When speakers of a given dialect fail to understand the conditions under which a given sound change has taken place in a related dialect, they often make such over-corrections. At least some of the spread of diphthongization under stress in the Romance languages is to be traced to this type of misinterpretation. In Castilian Spanish, all open /é/ and /ó/ vowels, whether in free or in checked syllable, have been diphthongized to /ié/ and /uó/ (later /ué/) respectively, as in Proto-Ibero-Romance /bónu/ "good" > Cast. /buéno/, /béne/ "well" > /bién/, /pónte/ "bridge" > /puénte/, /sénto/ "I feel" > /siénto/. There are historical grounds for suspecting that this diphthongization (which took place in the ninth and tenth centuries, at a time when French influence was strong in the kingdom of Old Castile) may have come about through Castilian speakers' imitation of Old French diphthongization of open vowels in free syllable (cf. p. 296); but, not realizing the conditions under which the diphthongization took place, they diphthongized their own open /é/ and /ó/, not only in free syllable, but in checked syllable as well.

We are most familiar with analogical extension of allomorphs and morphemes on the morphological level, as in the examples cited at the beginning of this chapter. In addition to simple transfer, analogy can lead to new combinations and divisions in morphemes, through the processes of *back-formation* and *recutting*. If a speaker is familiar with the verb *to back-bite* and the noun derived therefrom, *back-biter*, and also with the noun *type-writer*, he can form, by analogy, the back-formation *to type-write*, and also *to house-keep*, *to baby-sit*, *to gate-crash*, etc.:

$$
\begin{aligned}
\text{back-biter:back-bite} &= \text{type-writer:x} \\
\text{``} \qquad \text{``} &= \text{house-keeper:x} \\
\text{``} \qquad \text{``} &= \text{baby-sitter:x} \\
\text{``} \qquad \text{``} &= \text{gate-crasher:x}
\end{aligned}
$$

Most of our modern English "noun-incorporations" (cf. p. 189) are back-formations made on nouns in *-er* (such as those just cited) or in *-ation* (e.g. *to noun-incorporate* based on *noun-incorporation*).

Recutting takes place when a stem that has inherited a given phonemic shape through organic change (p. 319) is divided in a different place from where its original morphological division lay. The inherited form of the PRom. derivational suffix /-áriu/ "person connected with a given thing or substance" is, in French, //⁺je^r//, as in /otəlje/ *hôtelier* "hotel-keeper" (to /otel/ *hôtel*) or /kutyrje/ *couturier* "dress-designer" (to /kutyr/ *couture* "sewing"). A number of the French derivatives in //⁺je^r// are made on stems ending in //-t//, e.g. /arʒãtje/ *argentier* "silver-smith" to /arʒã^t/ "silver", or /ʃarpãtje/ *charpentier* "carpenter" to //ʃarpãt// *charpente* "beam". On the analogy of these latter, the suffix has been given a /t/ which, historically, was part of certain stems to which //⁺je^r// was added and not of the suffix itself; thus, new-formations in //⁺tje^r// have been made on /biʒu/ *bijou* "jewel" and /ferblã/ *ferblanc* "tin (literally 'white iron')", neither of which ever had any /-t/ as stem-final consonant: /biʒutje/ *bijoutier* "jeweller" and /ferblãtje/ *ferblantier* "tinsmith".

Syntactical analogies are also frequent. The use of *like* as a conjunction, for instance, is due to an analogy such as:

$$
\begin{aligned}
\text{to do better than Judith} &: \text{to do better than Judith did} \\
\text{to do like Judith} &: \qquad \text{x.}
\end{aligned}
$$

The widespread use of *I* instead of *me*, *he* for *him*, etc., as the object of a preposition, is due to analogical over-correction. People have so often been told that they must not say *him and me are going to the movies*, but *he and I are going to the movies*, that they conclude they must replace *him and me*, *you and me*, etc., by *he and I*, *you and I* and the likes in all positions, and end up by saying *between you and I*, *for he and I*, and so forth. On occasion, this pattern is extended even to a single pronoun standing after a preposition; in one family, a time-worn anecdote concerns a boy who said to his brother, asking for a certain toy: *Now, Hornell, be a good boy and give it to I.*

Changes in the meaning of words are also due to analogy, i.e., to the extension of the situations with respect to which the words are used. There is a shift in the central meaning of the word, and what was formerly a marginal meaning becomes central, whereas the old central meaning becomes marginal or eventually disappears. In Old English, for example, the word *bede* meant "prayer" (it is ultimately related to German *beten:* "to pray"); however, in saying one's prayers, one used a rosary, a succession of little spheres on a string, as part of the process. Counting one's *bedes* gradually came to mean, not so much counting the prayers, as counting the little spheres on a string; and the word *bead* thus came to mean, not "prayer" any longer, but what it does now, a "little sphere" of one kind or another—by now, no longer necessarily connected with a rosary at all and even usable in connection with bead-like, spherical shapes such as *beads* of perspiration. Similarly, Middle High German *kopf* (related to English *cup*) meant "cup, bowl, pot"; during the late Middle Ages, its meaning shifted to that of "head", which it has in Modern German. The word *kopf* was used in the meaning "head", first of all in a special situation; it is found in texts which describe battle scenes, in which one warrior smashes another's *kopf*. At first, this usage was probably a loan-shift under the influence of Old French *teste*, which had developed the meaning "head" out of an earlier meaning "pot, potsherd"; it was then extended analogically from situations referring to head-smashing in battle to other situations in which heads were referred to. The proportional formulas for developments like those of English *beads* and Middle High German *kopf* would be set up more or less like this:

to count pearls : to string pearls = to count beads : x
to smash a head : to nod one's head = to smash a kopf : x

There has long been a debate, among theoreticians of linguistic history, over the relation between sound-change and analogy. The established point of view is that sound-change is fundamental, in that its effects underlie all other happenings in organic change; and that borrowing—especially analogical or internal borrowing—serves to build up again those portions of linguistic structure which have been "eroded," as it were, by organic change (as in the instance of the Italian imperfect cited at the beginning of Chaps. 53 and 55). Matters are more complicated than this, however: in many instances, analogical changes take place without there being any apparent phonological need. In the case of French /ferblätje/ *ferblantier* "tinsmith" cited on p. 325, for instance, there is no phonological reason why this formation should have taken the place of a possible */ferbläkje/ which would have resulted from a combination of Old French /ferblánk/ "tin" + the suffix //⁺jer⁺//, or a possible */ferbläſje/ which would have been the development of a Proto-Gallo-Romance */ferrublankáriu/ "worker in white iron". In Modern Greek, a great many final consonants, especially /-n/, have been lost, in a process which is so widespread and nearly universal, that it simulates a nonconditioned sound-change; but closer examination has shown that it is really the result of numerous analogical replacements. In view of such phenomena, some theorists have sought to reverse the usual formulation and to consider analogy as more fundamental to linguistic history than sound-change.

From the point of view of the basic characteristics of language, sound-change would seem to be essentially a product of the inevitable structural looseness resulting from redundancy (pp. 105–107) and from duality (p. 6), so that the phonologic units of a language can change independently of its forms and their combinations; analogy is the direct manifestation of productivity (p. 6) and the mechanism whereby new combinations are produced. Both sound-change and analogy are, therefore, immediately related to the innermost nature of language, and to dispute which came first is as futile as the traditional debate over the priority of the hen and the egg. From the point of view of analytical method, however, sound-change must be analyzed first, since it is only in the light of our knowledge of the sound-changes which a linguistic system has undergone that we can identify and formulate the analogical and other borrowings which have been made. The traditional approach to the relation of sound-change and analogy is, therefore, justified, not so much because of their inherent relation to the structural characteristics of language, as from the point of view of analytical methodology.

NOTES

Analogy in relation to sound-change: Bloomfield, 1932; Hermann, 1931; Kuryłowicz, 1945/49; Mańczak, 1958.

Danish child's nikker—nak: Jespersen, 1922, Chaps. 7.4.

English bead: Bloomfield, 1933a, Chap. 24.7.

German Kopf: Sperber, 1930.

55

Change in Inflection

As A RESULT of evolutionary change (p. 319) and borrowing (Chaps. 53–54), the morphology, syntax, and lexicon of every language are undergoing constant alterations, each of which undoubtedly seems insignificant to the speakers at the time it takes place, but the sum total of which may bring about major restructuring in the language in the course of the centuries. On, the level of inflection, these changes may extend to the inflectional markers, the attribution of individual morphemes to form-classes or their sub-divisions, and the loss or rise of form-classes themselves.

On p. 319, we saw how loss of final consonants could cause a contrast in the endings of a tense to disappear, with Latin /kanta:bam -ba:s -bat/ "I, you, he-she-it was singing" giving Pre-Italian /kantáva/ in all three persons of the singular of the imperfect. In a situation of this type, one of two things can happen: the contrast may be restored through analogic borrowings from some other part of the system, or—if the loss takes place throughout a large enough segment of the system—the contrast may be eliminated entirely or almost entirely by further analogical loss. In the instance of the Italian imperfect, the first of these possibilities took place, as shown in the following table:

	LATIN	PRE-ITALIAN	OLD ITALIAN	MODERN ITALIAN
1.sg.	/kanta:bam/	/kantáva/	/kantáva/	†/kantávo/
2.sg.	/kanta:ba:s/	/kantáva/	†/kantávi/	†/kantávi/
3.sg.	/kanta:bat/	/kantáva/	/kantáva/	/kantáva/

In the columns of Old Italian and Modern Italian forms, a dagger has been placed before those containing analogical replacements. The second person singular had already, by the time of our earliest attestations of Old Italian (10th–11th centuries A.D.), received a distinctive ending /-i/, taken over by analogy from the present tense 2.sg. of verbs like /ódi/ "thou hearest" from Lat. /audi:s/. During the sixteenth and seventeenth centuries, the 1.sg. also received a distinctive ending, /-o/, also from the present tense (as in /kánto/ *canto* "I sing", /ódo/ *odo* "I hear"). In this instance, since the distinction between the three persons of the singular had not been lost in the other parts of the verbal system, it was restored by analogy in the imperfect. In such cases, one is justified in speaking of *pattern-pressure,* i.e., of a pressure exerted by parts of a pattern to preserve distinctions which have been lost in other parts.

Yet not all pattern pressure works towards the preservation of contrasts in a system, nor are we justified in speaking, as do some scholars, of a teleological drive (conscious or unconscious) on the part of speakers to preserve "necessary" distinctions. (There is always a circularity in such arguments: why was a distinction preserved?—because its users felt it was necessary; how do we know they felt it was necessary?—because they preserved it.) Ever since Proto-Indo-European times, there has been a steady over-all reduction in the inflectional forms of the Indo-European languages, in either substantival or verbal categories or both. Proto-Indo-European had eight cases; Latin had six; Old French had two; Modern French has entirely lost the contrast of case in nouns and adjectives, as have all the other Romance languages except Roumanian.

	LATIN		OLD FRENCH	MODERN FRENCH
Singular:				
Nominative	/muːrus/		/myrz/ *murs*	
Genitive	/muːriː/			
Dative	/muːroː/			/myr/ *mur*
Accusative	/muːrum/	Oblique	/myr/ *mur*	
Ablative	/muːroː/			
Vocative	/muːre/			
Plural:				
Nominative-Vocative	/muːriː/		/myr/ *mur*	
Genitive	/muːroːrum/			/myrᶻ/ *murs*
Dative	/muːriːs/			
Accusative	/muːroːs/	Oblique	/myrz/ *murs*	
Ablative	/muːriːs/			

FIG. 29: Development of Case-Systems from Latin to French.

We can follow the gradual loss of case-distinctions best in the development from Latin to Modern French, in the word for "wall," as shown in Fig. 29. The six cases of Latin were, by Old French times, reduced to two, through the loss, in final unstressed syllables, of all vowels except /-a/, which became /-ə/. The nominative retained a distinctive form, in contrast to the single case form known as *oblique* which combined the functions of all the non-nominative Latin cases which it had replaced. The distinction between nominative and oblique came to rest wholly on the final sibilant /-z/ (automatically replaced, in Old French, by the voiceless /-s/ before pause or voiceless consonant); this consonant carried all the functional load of the contrast in case and also of that in number, singular versus plural. In early Middle French (late fourteenth and early fifteenth centuries), however, /-z/ and /-s/ were lost through a conditioned sound change (at first, only before a following consonant) and resultant further analogy; with them, the entire case- and number-system of Old French lost its underpinning, and underwent extensive changes.

In later Middle French and early Modern French, the loss of final /-s/ brought about the complete disappearance of case, within a very short time—so short, in fact, that the poet François Villon, writing in the mid-fifteenth century, when he attempted to write a poem "in the Old French style" with case-distinctions which had been prevalent less than a century previously, had no feel at all for these contrasts and made an unholy mess of them. In general, only the forms of the old oblique survived, and those of the nominative were lost; only a few old nominatives have been continued into modern French (such as /pretr/ *prêtre* "priest", from Old French /prestrə/ *prestre*, whose oblique was /prəvé^i̇θrə/ *preveiḍre*). If both nominative and oblique forms have been preserved, they have simply split into two separate lexical units in modern French. Thus, of the pair consisting of oblique sg. /empərəðó^ur/ *empereḍour* "emperor", nom. sg. /empərǽðrə/ *empereḍre*, only the former is continued in Modern French /ãprœr/ *empereur* but of the pair consisting of obl. sg. /seŋó^ur/ *seignour* "lord", nom. sg. /sirə/ *sire*, the former is now the normal term for "lord" and the latter is restricted to the vocative form for addressing a king, "sire".

Number has not wholly disappeared from Modern French; it is universally marked with the letters -(e)s in conventional spelling, but in speech it is only scantily indicated. The plural morpheme, in pronunciation, has three allomorphs, which in Early Modern French (sixteenth century) were phonologically conditioned: /-z/ before vowels, /-s/ before pause, and zero before consonant. Of these three, however, /-s/ now occurs with only two substantives, and in all phonological positions: /tus/ *tous* "all (m. pl.)", only when used pronominally; and /mœrs/ *moeurs* "manners, customs, mores". Outside of very formal oratory or poetry reading, the allomorph /-z/ is used only before vowels and only with attributes which precede the head of a noun-phrase, as in /le^zo^tgarsõ/ *les autres garçons* "the other boys", /le^bo^zarbr/ *les beaux arbres* "the beautiful trees", /le^zo^tzami/ *les autres amis* "the other friends".

Forms are continually shifting from one sub-division (declension, conjugation) of a form-class to another, through all kinds of analogies. One theological student announced proudly, after having led a service at a country church, *Well, I sure praught 'em a bang-up sermon this morning*, with *praught* /prɔ́t/ as past tense of *preach*, clearly on the model of *taught*, past of *teach*. In the Romance languages, the Latin verb-roots /pot-/ "be able" and /u̯ol-/ "wish" have undergone extensive regularization, passing from the conjugation characterized by zero stem-vowel (Latin /posse/ "to be able" = /pot-/ + /-se/; /u̯elle/ "to wish" = /u̯el-/, allomorph of /u̯ol-/, plus /-se/) to that characterized by stem-vowel /e^/: PRom. /poté^re/, /u̯olé^re/. Other verb-roots shifted from the /e/-conjugation to the /e^/-conjugation and vice-versa: thus, Latin /arde:re/ "to burn" and /ri:de:re/ "to laugh" appear in Romance as /árdere/ and /rí^dere/, but Latin /kadere/ "to fall" and /sapere/ "to be wise, to know" appear as /kadé^re/, /sapé^re/.

In each separate language, there are a great number of such transfers taking place over the centuries, involving, of course, different morphemes in each language. It is not uncommon for nouns to pass from masculine to feminine grammatical gender or vice-versa; but in French this passage took place for /dã/ *dent* "tooth" (f.), from PRom. /dénte/ (m.), whereas in Spanish it affected the word for "milk", /léče/ < PRom. /lákte/ (m.). All the Romance languages have two major classes of adjective: those with distinctive forms for masculine and feminine (e.g., Old French /viéḷ/ *vieil* "old" [m.], /viéḷə/ *vieille* [f.]), and those with only one form for the two genders (e.g., OFr. /póvrə/ *pauvre* "poor"). Only in Old French, however, was there extensive analogical formation of new, morphologically distinctive feminines for adjectives which had previously had none, thus causing the passage of these adjectives from the first of the types mentioned above to the second. Thus, such previously nondistinctive forms as /gránt/ *grant* "large", /fórt/ *fort* "strong", /vért/ *vert* "green" or /tǽl/ *tel* "such" received the new feminines /grándə/ *grande*, /fórtə/ *forte*, /vértə/ *verte* and /tǽlə/ *tele* respectively. The morphology sections of the historical grammars of single languages consist very largely of the detailed enumeration and classification of the shifting of individual morphemes from one sub-class to another.

Morphemes can change, not only their sub-class, but also their form-class, although this type of passage is relatively infrequent. Latin /trans/ "across, beyond" was a preposition, as are its continuators Italian /traˣ/ "among" and Spanish /tras/ "behind"; but in French, through being used very frequently before adjectives and adverbs (e.g., Proto-Gallo-Romance */trás bónu/ "beyond good, extremely good"; */trás béne/ "beyond well, extremely well"), it came to be an adverb, continued in Modern French //treᶻ// *très* "very". Old English /dú:n/ was a noun meaning "hill" (and still survives as such in the British English geographical term referring to certain hills of South England, e.g., the *Suffolk Downs*); but, through being used adverbially in the meaning "along (down) the hill", it passed to being an adverb, in Modern English *down*. The Latin adverbs /ibi/ "there" and /inde/ "thence" were the ancestors of modern Romance pro-phrase particles (p. 166) such as French /i/ *y* and //ã ⁿ// *en*, Italian /vi/ *vi* and /ne/ *ne*, respectively. When the Old French nominative singular /on/ *on* "man" was left isolated by the disappearance of the category of case (p. 201), it ceased being used to refer to specific individuals, but continued in the meaning of "man in general, people in general, an indefinite actor, 'one'" (as in Modern French /õdi/ *on dit* "people say, one says") and thus passed to the status of an indefinite subject pronoun.

Categories of inflection and form-classes themselves can disappear or arise. One of the best-known instances of disappearance of a category of inflection is the loss of the Latin future, which took place in Late Latin times, primarily because such future tense forms as /ama:bo:/ "I shall love" or /re:gam/ "I shall rule" became, with the loss of final consonants, homonymous with either the imperfect or the subjunctive. The Romance languages preserve no trace of the Latin future, and hence we set up no simple future tense for Proto-Romance. In popular Latin speech, there were verbal phrases consisting of MODAL AUXILIARY (such as /avéˆre/ "to have", /debéˆ-

re/ "to be scheduled to", /u̯olé^re/ "to want") + VERBAL INFINITIVE, which were roughly synonymous with the simple future and which were ready to step in and take over its semantic function when it was lost. When these synonymous phrases replaced the simple future semantically, they of course lost their overtones of special emotional connotation. For Proto-Romance, we set up a phrase-type consisting of MODAL AUXILIARY + INFINITIVE (in either order) with future meaning: e.g., /ábi̯o kantáre/ or /kantáre ábi̯o/ "I shall sing" (or with /dé^bo/ or /u̯óli̯o/ in place of /ábi̯o/). This is still the state of affairs in the most conservative Romance languages: Sardinian has /áppo kantáre/, Roumanian has /vóju kintá/ voiu cînta.

At a later stage, however, the Western Romance languages developed a new simple future (often misnamed the "synthetic" future in historical grammars), wherever the phrase type INFINITIVE + MODAL AUXILIARY /avé^re/ came to be a set combination which could no longer be broken up freely by the intercalation of other elements, such as pro-complements. This process began first in Gallo-Romance; in the Strassburg Oaths of 843 A.D. we find forms like /salvarái/ salvarai "I shall aid", /pre^ndrái/ prindrai "I shall take", consisting of infinitives (/salvár/ "to aid", /pré^ndrə/ "to take") with forms (or parts of forms) of the verb "to have" which have become inflectional endings, here /-ai/, first person singular. From Gallo-Romance, the new simple future spread to Italy and Iberia, but did not become completely dominant in the latter area: in the earliest Old Spanish (Auto de los Reyes Magos, 11th century A.D.), we find forms like /veér lo é/ veer lo he "I shall see it", where modern Spanish would have only /loberé/ lo veré. In modern literary Portuguese, the older phrasal type of construction is still possible: /veré^i/ verei "I shall see", but /veloé^i/ ve-lo-hei "I shall see it". Not only the endings of the present of /avé^re/ "to have" were fused with the infinitive of the main verb, forming a simple future, but those of a past tense (imperfect or preterite) were used to form a "past of the future" or "conditional," such as Old French /čantəré^iə/ chantereie "I would sing", or /salvəré^iə/ salvereie "I would aid". There were thus formed, not only two new tenses, but a new stem (the so-called "future stem," whose basic meaning is that of probability, cf. p. 157). This new stem originated from the infinitive, but in some instances assumed a different allomorphic shape from that of the infinitive, as in the case of Old French /enve^iiǽr/ enveiier "to send" (infinitive), but "future stem" /enverr-/ enverr- (e.g., in /enverrái/ enverrai "I shall send").

A wholly new form-class may arise, if a sub-division of a previously existing class acquires sufficiently distinctive morphological or syntactic characteristics to effect a complete separation. In Neo-Melanesian, the predicate-marker /i-/ occurs before any third-person predicate, as in /dɪsfɛlə kajkaj i-gu̯dfɛlə/ "this food is good", or /ɔl i-go bu̯š/ "they go (went) to the bush". This form, which has to be set up as a separate form-class in Neo-Melanesian on the basis of its syntactic function, originated in the English pronoun he, but by now has lost any pronominal function, and simply serves to tell the hearer that a third-person predicate is coming, even when no subject is present or could be present (e.g., /i-ren/ "it's raining"). The Romance definite article grew out of a Latin demonstrative pronoun, the stem /ill-/ in most varieties of Romance and /ips-/ in others (e.g., Sardinian and pre-literary South French). Here again, the process of separation between definite article and demonstrative has gone farthest in Gallo- and Italo-Romance, where the definite article (French /lə/ *le*, Italian /il/ *il* and their respective allomorphs) occur only in proclitic position before noun-phrases and never occur alone. In Ibero-Romance, on the other hand, the definite article still preserves certain pronominal characteristics, in that it can often be used as the head of a phrase as can demonstrative pronouns: e.g., /laskamísas demipádre/ *las camisas de mi padre* "the shirts of my father" can be trans-formed, by omission of the noun /kamísas/ *camisas* "shirts", into /lás demipádre/ *las de mi padre* "the ones of my father = my father's (i.e., shirts)".

By successive changes of this sort, the entire inflectional type of a language can gradually change over the centuries and millennia. In the Indo-European family, the general trend has (as already mentioned on p. 322) been one towards inflectional simplification; this trend has been observable in docu-mented materials for a period of roughly three and a half millennia (i.e., back to ca. 1500 B.C.), and can be projected further back into prehistoric times for another fifteen hundred years or so. From this, some scholars have concluded that the general direction of linguistic change was towards simpli-fication of inflection and resultant compensatory complication of syntax, as exemplified especially in English and in a comparable though unrelated instance, that of Chinese. However, in other (especially American Indian) families, the opposite trend seems to be at work, leading to increase rather than decrease in the number and complication of inflectional phenomena. It does not seem justified, at present, to speak of any one trend as dominant in all inflectional change, although specific languages and language families do manifest what Sapir called "drift" in certain directions.

NOTES

Old French case-distinctions: Ewert, 1938, §§182–184.
Development of French sandhi-classes: Ewert, 1938, §§101, 125.
Origin of Romance future: von Wartburg, 1958, Chap. 1.4.

56

Change in Derivation

SINCE, by definition, all derived forms belong to one form-class or another, the elements which determine their membership in form-classes and their relation to the rest of the utterance are covered under inflectional features, and all changes in these latter are covered in the history of inflection. In other words, the history of the plural ending in, say, *baby-sitters* or *jack-in-the-pulpits*, or that of the past-tense markers in *baby-sat* (*baby-sitted*) or *authorized* does not concern us when we are dealing with change in derivation. Under this heading, we treat rather of the loss of old elements and patterns of affixation and compounding, and the origin of new ones.

Evolutionary development can, through the change of the phonemic shape of elements, cause simple replacement in their constituent phonemes or can bring about new morphophonemic relationships. The Proto-Romance substantive-forming suffix /⁺ár̦u-/ "one who deals with, is connected with . . ." (as in /karpentár̦u/ "a beam-maker, carpenter" or /kaballár̦u/ "one who deals with horses") has given Italian /⁺áio/, French //⁺jeʳ// *-ier*, Spanish /⁺éro/ and Portuguese /⁺éˆiru/ *-eiro*, because of diverse phonological developments in the history of each of these languages. Hence we have French /ʃarpãtje/ *charpentier*, Spanish /karpintéro/ *carpintero* and Portuguese /karpĕtéˆiru/ *carpenteiro* "carpenter"; and Italian /kavallaio/ *cavallaio* "ostler", French /ʃəvalje/ *chevalier* "knight", and Spanish /kabal̦éro/ *caballero* "gentleman". The suffix itself, however, has retained its basic function as a substantive-forming element, and its fundamental meaning, even though there have been individual semantic developments in the various languages (as when, through its connection with feudalism and chivalry, the term developed the meaning of "knight" in Gallo-Romance).

If enough phonemes are lost, a derivational element may be reduced to zero or even to a morphophonemic process involving the loss of one or more phonemes (p. 142). For instance, the past participle formation of Proto-Romance on the root /ab-/ "have" was /abúˆtu/ (taking the place of Latin /habitu-/). With the reduction of unstressed /a/ to /ə/ and that of intervocalic /b/ first to /v/ and then, before /u/, to zero (after which /u/ became /y/), this past participle became, in Old French, /əýð/ and later /əy/, with simply /ə/ representing the root of the verb. In Middle French, /ə/ in hiatus (i.e., before another vowel) was assimilated to the following vowel, with resultant lengthening thereof, so that the past participle /əy/

became /y:/ (though the old spelling *eu* has been kept until the present day). In this last-mentioned stage, the root itself is represented in this derivative by zero. Because of these and similar extensive sound-changes, especially the loss of final consonants in Middle and Modern French, there are by now many derivatives in French involving the loss of final consonants as a grammatical process (p. 142), such as the nouns /abri/ "shelter" on the verb root /abrit-/ "to shelter", or /dõ/ "gift" on /don-/ "to give".

Divergent phonemic development may bring about extensive morphophonemic alternations in the allomorphs involved in derivation, either in affixes or in the derivationally-bound variants of base-morphemes. On English /sím/ *seam*, we have the derivative /sémstrɛs/, which is in conservative usage spelled *seamstress* but often respelled *sempstress;* similarly, /lájf/ *life* has now only one phoneme in common with /lív/ *live*. In Old French, phonemic change had split up such originally similar pairs as Proto-Romance /bréɥe/ "short" and its derivative /abbreɥiáre/ "to shorten", giving /briéf/ *brief* and /abrĕğiæ̃r/ *abregier*, respectively. In extreme cases, if the phonemic and semantic divergence is wide enough, two originally related forms can become quite unrelated to all eyes except those of the historian of the language. Very few speakers of modern English connect *ferry* "to set some-one across a river" with *fare* "travel"; the former, however, goes back to an earlier /fárjan/ "to cause to travel," derived with a causative suffix /⁺j-/ from /fáran/ "to travel".

Any syntactic combination which becomes frozen in usage can survive in derivation, either as a base or as a compound. This syntactic "freezing" can occur through extreme frequency of use, so that an expression becomes a fixed locution, as in the inelegant but very widespread sentences in Italian and French meaning approximately "I don't give a damn", /ʒmãfu/ *je m'en fous* and /menefré^go/ *me ne frego* respectively. Both of these have served as bases for suffixal derivatives: French /ʒmãfutism/ *je-m'en-foutisme* and Italian /menefregísmo/ *menefreghismo* "I-don't-give-a-damn attitude"; French /ʒmãfutist/ *je-m'en-foutiste* and Italian /menefregísta/ *menefreghista* "one who takes an I-don't-give-a-damn attitude". It is also possible for a given syntactic combination-type to lose its productivity so that it is no longer a living pattern for new improvised utterances; locutions following these outmoded patterns can then survive as fixed expressions. A number of the compound-types of English and many other languages continue old, no longer productive phrase- or clause-types, e.g., French /grãmer/ *grand'mère* "grandmother" or /pje^tater/ *pied-à-terre* "small apartment in town", which continue old and no longer operative sandhi-habits (cf. pp. 186–187). In English, a compound like *devil-may-care* (used as an adjective, e.g., *a devil-may-care attitude*) continues an old sentence-type, in which the subject could occur without determiner.

All kinds of changes in derivational relationships can be brought about by borrowing, both internal and external. Analogic extension is probably the most common mechanism for the spread of derivational types, especially in connection with affixes. Our suffix /⁺ər/ *-er*, forming nouns of agents on verbs, has by now become so common that it can be added to practically any verb in the language, whether it be of Germanic or of Romance or Latin origin; we can form not only *eater, drinker, singer,* but also *organizer, commander* or *telegrapher.* (Rudyard Kipling, in his *Stalky & Co.,* has one of his characters describe a type of Japanese wrestling which he calls *shibbuwichee,* and then refer to a certain schoolmaster as a *shibbuwicher.*) The rapid extension, in the last few decades, of the "noun-incorporating" type of verb compound has been due to the analogy of such relationships as *back-biter : back-bite* (cf. p. 325). A similar process took place with the extension of the originally feminine suffix *-ster* (as in *spinster* "a woman spinner") to all kinds of formations in which it no longer had feminine meaning (e.g., *webster:* "weaver", *huckster, jokester, songster, punster*).

False analogy is at work in the process of recutting (p. 326), in the formation of new allomorphs such as French //⁺tjeʳ// *-tier* from earlier //⁺jeʳ// *-ier,* in words like /ferblãtje/ *ferblantier* "tinsmith" or /biӡutje/ *bijoutier* "jeweler", on the model of formations like /ʃarpãtje/ *charpentier* "carpenter". A similar case of recutting is found in the German abstract noun-forming suffix /⁺kajt/ *-keit,* parallel to /⁺hajt/ *-heit;* the former originated in a false analogy based on the occurrence of /⁺hajt/ *-heit* after adjectives ending in /k/, e.g., in /tráurik+kàjt/ "sadness", to the adjective /traurik/ *tráurig* "sad".

If a suffix loses its former identity or acquires a new function, it can in its turn receive the addition of another suffix, with which it may fuse to form what, from the historical point of view, is a double suffix. After it had lost its specifically feminine meaning, the English element *-ster* (discussed above) served as a base for feminine formations in *-ess,* a suffix borrowed from French, as in /sémstrɛs/ *seamstress.* In this last-mentioned word, the suffix /⁺strɛs/ therefore contains two elements, both of which earlier indicated femininity: the element /⁺str⁺/ (allomorph of /⁺stər/) and /⁺ɛs/. Needless to say, this consideration is valid only from the historical point of view; present-day speakers who use words like *seamstress* or *songstress* are not aware of the presence of two historically distinct elements in what for them is a single suffix, /⁺strɛs/ *-stress.*

Derivational elements can be introduced from outside sources, either regional dialects or foreign languages. Simply the borrowing of one or two words with a foreign derivational element is not enough, because in such a case the derivational element is not recognized as such and the word simply remains, for the speaker of the borrowing language, a single lexical unit. This is the case with such a German loan in English as /gezúnt+hàjt/ *Gesundheit!,* literally "(your) health!", said to some one who sneezes; speakers of English who do not know German are not normally aware of the presence of the suffix /⁺hajt/ *-heit* in this form. The borrowings containing the new derivational element or pattern must be present in a large enough number of individual loan-words for the ordinary processes of analogical new-formation to become operative, so that then the new element spreads by a process of internal borrowing. This is what has happened with a great many prefixes and suffixes contained in our loan-words from French and Latin; a suffix like /⁺ɛs/ -ess was at first present only in loans like *duchess, countess,* or *hostess,* but later came to be added to such pre-existing bases as *hunter,* giving *huntress,* and the like.

Once it is present in enough forms, an originally borrowed element may lose all connotations of foreign or learnèd origin, and receive very wide extension, even, on occasion, acquiring popularity for more or less slang-like new-formations, as has been the case with English /⁺ét/ -ette, in coinages like /fàrmərɛt/ *farmerette* or /əʃərét/ *usherette.* The modern popularity of this suffix seems to have begun in the early 1900's with /səfrədʒét/ *suffragette*; that its productivity has not yet been lost is shown by the coinage /nìmfét/ *nymphette,* first introduced to the general public in a pornographic novel of the 1950's. In some languages, specific learnèd suffixes serve to "acclimatize" foreign loans, as it were; thus, German /⁺íren/ -i(e)ren is freely added to elements of almost any foreign language to make verbs that can be inserted into German syntactical combinations, e.g. /ruiníren/ *ruini(e)ren* "to ruin" (on Latin *ruin-*), /kapíren/ *kapi(e)ren* (Italian /kap-/ *cap-,* especially in the infinitive /kapíre/ *capire* "to understand") or /publicíren/ *publizi(e)ren* "to publish."

By the influx of new elements over the course of time, or by the loss or replacement of older elements, the entire derivational pattern of a language may change. Old English had a number of freely and widely usable derivative elements and compound types, some of which (like our suffix /⁺ər/ -er) had earlier been borrowed from Latin. This situation was changed with the importation of a great many loan-words and their derivatives from Old French and from Latin and Greek. As a result, we are now accustomed to having, in the derivational relationships of our words, far more morphophonemic alternation (of the type /dʒɔ́jnt/ *joint* ∼ /dʒəŋkt⁺/ *junct-,* e.g., in /dʒə́ŋktʃər/ *juncture* "a joining") than was familiar to our linguistic ancestors of a thousand years ago. Hence our derivational pattern is richer, but far more irregular, than that of Old English. Probably the very presence of such a large amount of morphophonemic variation makes us, as speakers of present-day English, more ready to accept aberrant morphological characteristics in new loan-words, and hence more open to all kinds of borrowings, than are speakers of languages with a greater degree of regularity in their derivational patterns such as Italian and Spanish.

Old French also had an extensive and productive set of derivational elements, particularly in such suffixes as /⁺et/ -et (m., with f. /⁺etə/ -ete), diminutive, which could be added to almost any morpheme of the class(es) with which they were normally associated. This fact was widely recognized and even used as a basis for humor, as when one poet said that, among those who took part in a certain tournament, there were *Richardet* "little Richard", *Jeanneret* "little John", and "all the other -et's." From the early seventeenth century onwards, however, under the pressure of neoclassical academicism and puristic absolutism (cf. Chap. 62), habits of free word-formation were banished from literary French. A great many older derivatives, especially diminutives and other formations with emotional overtones, fell into desuetude as a result of puristic condemnation. Modern French has, in the nineteenth and twentieth centuries, recovered a certain amount of freedom in word-formation, but even now it is far from having as rich and varied a series of derivational patterns as did the Old French of, say, seven or eight hundred years ago.

NOTES

Old French -et's: Jenkins, 1933, Chap. 11.

57

Change in Phrase-Types

STUDIES IN HISTORICAL syntax have, up to the present time, been relatively rare, inasmuch as no adequate framework has been available for analyzing the development of syntactic constructions. Most works have attempted to deal with historical syntax in terms of changes, either in the use of individual parts of speech, or in their possible semantic equivalents and paraphrases. Now that a more adequate framework is available for formulating the structural combination-types of languages, it is clear that historical syntax should deal with changes in these combination-types in the course of time. In this and the next chapter, we shall sketch briefly the main kinds of changes which take place in phrase-types and clause-types.

For the most part, syntactic changes are the result of evolutionary development and of alteration by internal borrowing (analogy). A good example of evolution due to phonological change is the development of the Romance verbal core. The various Romance pro-complements (p. 166) go back to elements which in Latin were independent: the demonstrative pronoun /illu-/, which was the source of the third person direct and indirect object pronouns like French //l(ə)//, Italian and Spanish /lo/ "him", or French, Italian and Spanish /la/; the personal pronouns like /me:/ "me", /te:/ "thee"; and certain adverbs of place like /hi:k/ "here", /ibi/ "there", /inde/ "from there". These forms were capable of receiving full stress, and could occur in freely variable position with respect to the verb they modified: e.g., /me: u̯idet/ "he SEES me" or /u̯idet me:/ "he sees ME"; /inde u̯enit/ "he COMES from there" or /u̯enit inde/ "he comes FROM THERE". Emphasis came, in these phrase-types as generally in Latin, from position in the expression, the most important place being at the end. For Latin, therefore, we set up a single phrase-type for the combination of VERB ǂ OBJECT PRONOUN,* and another for VERB ǂ ADVERB.

In Proto-Romance, however, stress became phonologically significant. With this change came a difference in the degree of stress which could be placed on the above-mentioned pronominal and adverbial elements, so that they could occur either stressed or unstressed. Each of the two phrase-types mentioned above split, therefore, into two, one with a stressed element modifying the verb and one with an unstressed element. The latter type would be exemplified by Proto-Romance */u̯ídet meˆ/ or /meˆ u̯ídet/ "he

---

* We use the sign ǂ to mean "plus, in either order".

SEES me". This latter type developed into the Romance verbal core (pp. 166–167) with a special "conjunctive" element modifying the verb and forming with it a kind of "super-conjugation." In most of the Romance languages, the unstressed conjunctive elements underwent different phonological developments from the corresponding stressed forms: e.g., Italian unstressed /mi/ "me" but stressed /mé^/, or French unstressed /mə/ versus stressed /mwa/, from Proto-Romance /mé^/. In this way, these unstressed forms of what were earlier pronouns and adverbs have developed into distinct, phrasally-bound elements, and have come to form a morphologically distinct category of "pro-complements."

At first, the choice of the two possible orders in the verbal core, PRO-COM-PLEMENT + VERB or vice versa, was still determined by considerations of emphasis. In the mediaeval Romance languages, the initial and final elements of an utterance had to be stressed (a continuation of the earlier situation in which those were the emphatic positions in the sentence) and hence an unstressed element like a pro-complement could not stand at the beginning of a sentence. In Old Italian, for example, we find such contrasting pairs of verbal cores as the combinations of /vé^de/ "he sees" with /mi/ "me (conjunctive, unstressed)" in the two sentences /ó^ra mivé^de/ "now he sees me" but /védemi ó^ra/ "he sees me now". Up to this point, the development of the Romance verbal core was entirely conditioned by evolutionary change working on inherited material, both in word-order and in morphological constituents. Since the Middle Ages, however, through the working of analogy, the unstressed pro-complements have come to be used in initial position as well as elsewhere: in modern Italian, one normally says both /mivé^de ó^ra/ and /ó^ra mivé^de/. In Italian, Spanish, and French, the place of the pro-complements has come to be determined, not by their position relative to the beginning or end of the utterance, but by the sub-category of the verbal form to which they are attached. There has been a somewhat different development in each of these languages, but they all agree in placing the pro-complements after a positive imperative (e.g., French /donləmwa/ *donne-le-moi*, Italian /dámmelo/, Spanish /dámelo/ "give it to me!") and before all nonimperative finite forms (e.g., French /ilmələdon/ *il me le donne*, Italian and Spanish /melodá/ "he gives it to me").

Phrase-types can also disappear through evolutionary change, when their basis in morphological distinctions is lost by phonological development (cf. p. 319). Old French had a phrase-type consisting of NOUN (head) ++ NOUN (possessive modifier, in the oblique case): e.g. /lakó^rt ləré^i/ *la cort le rei* or /laré^ikó^rt/ *la rei cort:* "the king's court". When the contrast between oblique and nominative cases was lost in Middle French, there was no longer any morphological indication of the relation between the two elements of such a phrase. It went out of productive use, its place being taken by a competing phrase-type in which the possessive element was introduced by /də/ *de* "of", forming a modifying phrase following the head, as in Modern French /lakur dyrwa/ *la cour du roi* "the court of the king". In present-day French, the old NOUN + NOUN possessive phrase (no longer, of course, showing any contrast in case) survives only in a few set phrases like /oˆteldjœˆ/ *hôtel Dieu* "alms-house" (literally "hostel [of] God") and place names of the type /marli lərwa/ *Marly-le-Roi*, literally "King's Marly". A similar loss of the Latin and Proto-Romance possessive phrase-type NOUN ++ NOUN (in the genitive) took place in Italo- and Ibero-Romance because of the early loss of case distinctions in those varieties of Romance, but before our earliest attestations of the mediaeval vernaculars, so that we cannot follow the replacement of one phrase-type by the other in detail as we can in Old and Middle French.

Analogical influence is frequently at work in the development of new phrase-types even when it is not involved in reshaping the effects of evolutionary change. A well-known example of purely analogical replacement not motivated by evolutionary change is the German phrase-type /aintrúŋk váser/ *ein Trunk Wasser* "a drink of water", whose present-day structure is NOUN (head) + NOUN (attribute), the second being uninflected and having partitive meaning. Earlier German had a noun in the genitive in the second position: /aintrúŋk vásers/ *ein Trunk Wassers* "a drink of water", with the structure NOUN (head) + NOUN (attribute in the genitive). The replacement of the second element by a non-genitival form is due to the analogy of instances where (as in feminine nouns) the genitival and nongenitival forms were identical, both seemingly uninflected, as in /mílx/ *Milch* "milk". The relationship was phrased by Leonard Bloomfield in the following proportional formula:

Milch trinken: "to drink milk" : *ein Trunk Milch:* "a drink of milk"
Wasser trinken: "to drink water" : *x.*

Phrase-types may originate through the break-up of combinations which were formerly more closely united. Latin compounds, especially in preclassical times, were apparently loose enough to permit of such splitting. The poet Ennius (ca. 259–169 B.C.) made experiments of this type such as breaking up the noun *cerebrum* "brain" in the phrase *cere- comminuit -brum:* "he smashed his brain". Such a procedure was regarded as an exaggeration, but a similar division was a productive grammatic process in the breakup of Latin compounds consisting of *per-* "very" + ADJECTIVE such as *permagnus:* "very big". The split of this kind of compound was continued in the Old French phrase-type consisting of /par/ "very" + ADJECTIVE, which occurred for the most part with a verbal element intervening between the two parts of the phrase: e.g., /móˆlt pár fúð béls/ *molt par fuṭ bels* "he was most extremely handsome". This particular phrase-type lasted through the Old and Middle French periods, and disappeared in the Renaissance, partly under the regularizing pressure of purism and partly because of conflict with the growing requirement that a subject be the only element of a clause to precede a verbal core (cf. Chap. 58).

The omission of connecting elements may lead to the rise of new phrase-types. In the modern Romance languages in general, one noun is placed in syntactic dependence on another by being included in a following attributive phrase introduced by a preposition: e.g., French /ləproblemdyravitajmã/

le problème du ravitaillement "the problem of providing food", or Italian *assicurazioni sulla vita:* "life insurance (lit. assurances on the life)". At first in telegrams and newspaper advertisements (to save money where charges are imposed by the number of words) and headlines (to save space), the habit arose, in nineteenth-century France and Italy, of omitting the connecting prepositions, as in French /ləproblemravitajmã/ *le problème ravitaillement* or Italian *assicurazioni vita*, corresponding to the phrases with preposition given above. In modern Italian, especially, this process has gone so far as to create a new phrase-type, NOUN (head) + NOUN (attribute indicating purpose or characteristic), and as to introduce into Italian structure, for the first time, the principle of significant word order alone, as a feature of syntactic construction. Many modern Italian phrases of this kind are normally used without any intervening preposition, and it would be hard to determine in a strictly transformational type of grammar which preposition had been omitted, as in *scalo merci:* "freight station" or *campo pròfughi:* "refugee camp". On occasion, especially in signs and advertisements, three or four nouns in a row may occur in a sequence of this type, and sometimes amusing misunderstandings may result, as in a Florentine shoe-store window-sign which announced *Vasto assortimento uòmini e bambini:* "Extensive assortment . . . ", obviously intended to mean "*for* men and children", but which could also be re-expanded as if it were a transformation of "OF men and children".

Borrowings from extraneous systems are not infrequent in the field of phrasal structure. When they occur, it is in the form of loan-shifts (p. 321): the morphological and semantic structure of a phrase-type in the language which serves as a model is reflected in the choice of the morphological elements and their order in the imitating (borrowing) language. French has served as a model for many English innovations of this type in phrase-structure. Even before the First World War, French exclamations consisting of /me/ *mais* "but" + ADVERB were imitated in English: e.g., *but yes!*, *but certainly!*, reflecting French /mewi/ *mais oui!* and /mesertenmã/ *mais certainement!* respectively. A more recent syntactic borrowing from French involves the combination of two nouns in a phrase naming an operation or activity, such as *Operation Crossroads* or *Operation Bootstrap*. During the Renaissance, a number of Latin constructions were imitated in this way in the modern European languages, even when the morphological bases for the constructions were absent in the structures of the imitating languages. This was the source of the "nominative absolute" construction of NOUN + ADJECTIVE (especially PAST PARTICIPLE), such as English *this having been done*, French /səfe/ *ce fait*, Italian *fatto ciò*, or Spanish *hecho esto*, all imitations of the Latin ablative absolute /ho:k fakto:/ *hōc factō*. As in morphology, successive syntactic borrowings of this type can, if continued long enough, bring about extensive change in the structure of the imitating language, as has happened with English under the influence, first of Old French and then of Latin and Greek.

NOTES

The proportional formula: Bloomfield, 1933, Chap. 23.

58

Change in Clause-Structure

THE CHIEF SOURCE of change in clause-structure is borrowing, both internal (analogic) and external. Analogical change often intervenes, here as in other parts of linguistic structure, to replace losses occasioned by evolutionary developments. A classical instance of this kind of change in clause-structure is the development, in Middle and Modern French, of the obligatory use of a pronoun subject, if no noun subject is present, in the normal nonimperative clause. In Latin, Proto-Romance, and the more conservative Romance languages, the favorite clause-type consists of PREDICATE alone = VERB or equivalent phrase (p. 214), since the person and number of the actor is automatically indicated in the verb form: e.g., Latin /u̯enit/ "he comes", and similarly Italian /viéne/, Spanish /biéne/ *viene*, Portuguese /vẽ́/ *vem*, all from Proto-Romance /u̯énit/. Old French had this same type of clause, since its verbs likewise indicated the person and number of the actor; hence, for instance, /viént/ *vient* "he comes", /pórtas̸/ *portes* "thou carriest", /pórtəð/ *portet* "he carries", /cantǽc/ *chantez* "you sing", were complete clauses in themselves. The phoneme /ð/ was lost around 1100 A.D., so that in the first conjugation the first and third persons of the singular came to be identical, e.g., later Old French /portə/ *porte* "I carry, he carries". However, this merger took place only in the first conjugation, and these persons continued to be distinguished in other conjugations, e.g., Old French /dórs/ *dors* "I sleep", but /dórt/ *dort* "he sleeps".

In the Middle French period, however, many final consonants were lost before the initial consonant of a following word, and, by phonological analogy, before pause as well. There was, as a result, extensive homonymy in nonprevocalic verb forms, especially in the singular and third person plural, when, say, /ʃantə/ came to be the continuator of /ʃantə/ *chante* "I sing, he sings", of /ʃantəs/ *chantes* "thou singest", and of /ʃantənt/ *chantent* "they sing". Old French had, like the other Romance languages, the possibility of using a subject personal pronoun with a verb, but only for emphasis: /íl čántəð/ *il chantet* had meant "HE [not somebody else] sings". To relieve the troublesome homonymy caused by the levelling of verbal endings, speakers of Middle and Early Modern French came more and more to use the subject personal pronouns, thus clarifying the person and number reference of the verb. Together with this increased frequency of use, there came a lessening of the emphasis implicit in the subject personal pronouns, so that they became simply indicators of the person and number of the actor: Modern French

/ilʃãt/ *il chante* is the semantic equivalent of Old French /čántəð/ *chanteṭ*. The modern semantic equivalent of Old French emphatic /íl čántəð/ is either /ilʃãt, lɥi/ *il chante, lui* (literally "he sings, him") or /selɥikiʃãt/ *c'est lui qui chante* (literally "it's him who sings"). The first and second persons of the plural had (and still have) distinctive endings, Modern French //-õᶻ// and //-eᶺᶻ// respectively, as in /(nu)ʃãtõ/ *(nous) chantons* "we sing" and /(vu)ʃãteᶺ/ *(vous) chantez* "you sing". Significantly, these persons of the verb could be used without subject pronoun much longer than the others, down through the sixteenth and into the early seventeenth century. The present state of affairs, in which all verbs must be accompanied by a subject— i.e., in which the clause-type SUBJECT + PREDICATE has completely replaced the Old French and general Romance type consisting of PREDICATE alone— was definitely crystallized in the seventeenth century, partly as a result of normal analogical development and partly under the pressure of regularizing academic purism (cf. Chap. 62).

Not all analogical replacements in clause-structure are necessarily the result of levelling through evolutionary change. English, up through the Early Modern period (sixteenth and early seventeenth centuries), normally asked questions by an inversion of subject and verb: e.g., *Know ye this man?* or *Why sings he so loud?*. In more modern times, this inversion has ceased to be permissible except with *be* and *have*, among verbs used independently: e.g., *Is he here yet?; Have you anything to say?*. All other verbs except auxiliaries (but including *do* when it is used as an independent verb) must replace the verb itself by an expansion involving the auxiliary *do* and then the inversion of AUXILIARY + SUBJECT: *Does he usually work late?*; *What does he do for a living?*. This replacement of the interrogative clause-type INFLECTED VERB + SUBJECT by the other clause-type AUXILIARY *do* + SUBJECT + VERB (SIMPLE FORM) represents the generalization of a structure which was used, at an earlier stage, only for emphasis. However, there was no phonological or morphological necessity for this replacement; it seems to have been connected, rather, with a growing syntactic habit of avoiding the use of stressed non-interrogative elements at the beginning of a question.

External borrowing in clause-structure is best known, iñ our West European languages, as the result of learnèd influence. Thus, the paratactic type of subordination (pp. 220–221) was normal in Old French, in sentences like /niáðcəlúi nəplóᶺurt ninəkríðəð/ *n i aṭ celui ne plourt ni ne criḍeṭ* "there is not a one (lit. not the one) [such that he] does not weep and cry". In this construction, the subordination is clearly enough indicated by the subjunctives /plóᶺurt/ *plourt* and /kríðəð/ *criḍeṭ*, so that no overt subordinating element is necessary. However, well before the partial obliteration of the distinction between subjunctive and nonsubjunctive forms by the loss of final consonants in Middle French (cf. p. 329), learnèd men were introducing hypotaxis in constructions of this type. Knowing Latin, in which a subordinate clause must be introduced by a specifically subordinating element, they preferred the Latinizing use of relative pronouns such as /ki/ *qui* "who, whom". Such a sentence as the one just cited came to have, more and more, a different type of subordinate clause, with hypotactic construction effected by an introductory relative element: /niáðcəlúi kinəplóˆurt ninəkríðəð/ *n i aṭ celui ki ne plourt ni ne criḍeṭ.* In the same way, persons who know English are borrowing the conjunction /bɪkɔs/ "because" into Neo-Melanesian, and with it the use of subordinate clauses: where, previously, Neo-Melanesian would have said /ɛm i-sɪk, na i-no kəm/ "he was sick, and he didn't come", the habit is now spreading of saying /ɛm i-no kəm, bɪkɔs i-sɪk/ "he didn't come, because he was sick".

In general, however, it has been a commonplace of historical linguistics to observe that syntactic structures, and particularly clause-types, are less open to borrowing from outside than are other structural elements such as phonology and lexicon; most syntactic change is due to readjustment after there have been alterations in phonology and morphology. Linguistic structure is often compared to a coal pile, in which the lumps rest, one upon the other, in a complicated and delicate equilibrium. When a shovelful of coal is taken away from the bottom, the equilibrium of the rest of the pile is disturbed, and lumps start rolling downward, first from the middle of the pile to take the place of those removed from the bottom, and then from higher up down towards the middle.

We can follow this process in detail in the effects of the conditioned sound-change in Middle French by which, as already mentioned (p. 329), /s/ was lost, first of all before a consonant. Like all phonological changes, this one began with an allophonic substitution: fifteenth-century speakers of French got into the habit of not making complete contact with their tongues against the roof of their mouths when pronouncing [s] and [z] before a consonant, and thus of producing an aspirate [h], as is the habit of modern speakers of Caribbean Spanish (p. 324). In earlier Middle French, [h] occurred nowhere else in the system, and hence it was still an allophone of /s/, in a word like /pastə/ ['pahtə] "paste", or at the end of a form like /ʃantəs/ ['ʃãⁿtəh] *chantes* "thou singest". This stage is attested both by grammarians of the period instructing foreigners how to pronounce contemporary French, and by loan-words in other languages, such as German /ʃáxtel/ *Schachtel* "box", from Middle French /ʃastel/ [ʃah'tɛl] *chastel* "castle".

In later Middle French, however, this [h] underwent two further developments. If a vowel preceded, [h] was lost but the vowel was lengthened (i.e., the [h] was assimilated to the vowel): e.g., ['pahtə] became ['pa:tə]. The resultant vowel length was not an allophone of /s/, since in late Middle French there was another source of vowel length: /ə/ before or after another vowel was assimilated thereto with compensatory lengthening, as when /əaʒə/ *eage* "age" became /a:ʒə/ *âge** and /ʃanteə/ *chantée* "sung (past part. f. sg.)" became /ʃante:/. But after a consonant, [h] was simply lost, so

---

* The orthography of the period symbolized vowel length in non-final syllables by a circumflex accent written over the vowel letter, no matter what the source of the long vowel: /pa:tə/ *pâte*, /be:tə/ *bête* "animal" (from earlier /bestə/ *beste*) and /a:ʒə/ *âge*. The use of the circumflex in such words has survived into modern French orthography, long after the disappearance of vowel length as a significant phonological feature.

that earlier /s/ now had three developments: preservation before pause or vowel; change to /:/ after vowel and before consonant; and loss between two consonants. Such a phrase as late Old French /dœsmylsfors/ *deus muls for(t)s* "two strong mules (oblique pl.)" gave, in late Middle French, /dœ:mylfors/.

This threefold development of /-s/ brought a further complication into the already involved morphology of the Old French substantive and into the second person singular and plural endings of all verb-forms. As pointed out on pp. 329–330, the distinction between nominative and oblique case rested almost entirely on the phoneme /s/, variously distributed in the different declensions, as in the following examples (in phonemic transcription representing the pronunciation of ca. 1200 A.D.):

	"WALL"		"PRIEST"		"WOMAN"	
	sg.	pl.	sg.	pl.	sg.	pl.
Nom.	myrs	myr	prestrə	prəvoˆirə	famə	faməs
Obl.	myr	myrs	prəvoˆirə	prəvoˆirəs	famə	faməs

In addition, some nouns ending in /-s/ were invariable in all four forms, e.g., /nes/ *nés* "nose".

When /-s/ broke up, giving three different phonological results, there was a corresponding split in every morpheme which had /-s/ as one of its elements, depending at first on its phonological position in each individual phrase. In the Middle French phrase /dœ:mylfors/ "two strong mules", for instance, the (formerly oblique) plural ending was represented by /:/, by zero and by /-s/ in the three successive elements of the phrase; but if the order of the noun and adjective were to be reversed, the phrase would have been /dœ:formyls/. The widespread presence of zero as one of the new allomorphs of the nominative singular and oblique plural endings, together with its extensive use in other parts of the paradigms, led to its further analogical extension. In the end, the old case-distinction could no longer be maintained, because so much of the indication of case had become zero, and hence the occurrence of clearly identifiable case-markers was no longer consistent or predictable.

The extensive alternation which thus arose between /s/, /z/ and zero has remained down into Modern French, in the plural of substantives and the personal endings of verbs. Since its occurrence is no longer phonologically conditioned, it, together with the alternations arising from a number of other sound changes, has given rise to a new category of inflection, sandhi-alternation (p. 159). The loss of /-s / in the second person endings of the verb might not, in itself, have occasioned further perturbations, except that it was soon followed by the loss of other final consonants. As pointed out on pp. 343–344, the disappearance of these consonantal endings caused troublesome homonymy in verbal forms, by largely destroying the indication of person and number of the actor within the forms themselves, thus leading to the generalization of the clause-type SUBJECT + PREDICATE. An originally non-significant allophonic change, therefore, has had profound effects on the entire structure of the French language, by leading to the loss of distinctive endings, thus provoking the loss of one category of inflection and the rise of another; and the realignments thus caused have, in their turn, brought about a major syntactic readjustment. The process has so far lasted five hundred years or more, and the end is not yet in sight; it will probably take another three to five hundred years for the fragmentary remainders of the old system to be completely eliminated, by processes of analogy, from the structure of French.

NOTES

French subject pronouns: Blinkenberg, 1928; Franzén, 1939. For an analogous development in Lombard, cf. Spiess, 1956; Hall, 1958b.

Neo-Melanesian /bɪkɔs/: Hall, 1955c.

Middle French /s/ [h]: Nyrop, 1914, Vol. 1, §462.

Middle French loss of /ə/: Ewert, 1938, §62.

59

Change in Meaning

NOT ONLY the phonemes, morphemes and syntagmata, but also the meanings of every language are subject to change. As we saw in Chap. 39, linguistic forms have *central* and *marginal* meanings, as in the examples of *try*, *party*, *fox*, etc., discussed there. However, the relation between the central or "literal" and the marginal or "transferred" meaning of any form is never wholly stable. This situation is, in the last analysis, inherent in the nature of human speech-communities; each individual speaker has differences (even though they may be only slight) from every other speaker with regard to the overtones of meaning which he attaches to a given form. What for one speaker or group of speakers belongs to the marginal sphere of meaning of a form, may for another speaker or group be closer to its central meaning. Thus, for instance, for speakers of Italian who came to maturity under Fascist rule in the 1920's and '30's, all words connected with the special institutions of that period, such as *littorio:* "lictorate", *littoriale:* "Lictorial (a special Fascist celebration)," and *littorina* "diesel rail-car (first developed and named in this epoch)" all have ineradicable connotations of Fascism. After the Second World War, all the specifically Fascist terms of this word-group went out of use, but *littorina* survived as a popular name for "rail-car" (the technical term is *automotrice*); for younger speakers, it has no Fascist overtones, and is simply a sequence of phonemes like any other form in the language.

The process by which semantic shifts take place is basically one of analogical extension or contraction of the practical situations in which a form is used. How well we can document this process for individual words depends very largely on the vagaries of historical accident; it is rarely as well attested as the shift of German *Kopf* from the meaning of "cup" to that of "head", at first in the context of head-smashing in battle (pp. 325–326). For the most part, these shifts occur in homely situations involving everyday speech, to which no-one pays attention until they are *faits accomplis*. They are perhaps most easily observable in child language, when, through inexperience, children "misuse" words which they have heard only in particular contexts, taking for the central meaning what for the rest of the community is only a marginal meaning. We are all familiar with the story of the city child who knew *pig* only as a term meaning "dirty, ill-mannered person" and who, on his first visit to a farm, exclaimed, on seeing the animals rooting around and wallowing in the pig-sty, how right it was that they should be called *pigs*.

Students of semantic change group shifts in meaning into various classes. The most inclusive of these are *expansion, contraction,* and *splitting* of meanings. A term may, at one point of time, have a relatively limited sphere of reference, as when Latin *caballus* referred to a particular kind of horse, relatively little prized, probably "nag" or "work-horse", in contrast to the general term for "horse", *equus.* Probably as the result of a troublesome homonymy arising from the change of /aịkụus/ *aequus* "even, fair, just" to /ekụus/, this latter in the sense of "horse" became obsolete and was replaced, in more general reference, by *caballus.* Other classical examples of expansion of reference include Classical Latin *virtūs:* "manliness" becoming in Mediaeval Latin "good quality in general, virtue", and in Renaissance usage (both in Latin and in the Italian loan-word *vertù*) "ability, skill"; Middle English *bridde:* "young birdlet" giving our *bird;* and Middle English *dogge:* "a particular breed of dog" becoming modern *dog.*

That such changes are not limited to "languages of civilization" is shown by similar developments in many other language-families, and even in pidgins and creoles (Chaps. 64–65). Two examples from Neo-Melanesian: before the aeroplane was introduced into New Guinea, the meaning of /pĭgɪn/ was expanded to cover any kind of bird; for "pigeon", the term was a borrowing from the native language of the Gazelle peninsula, /balus/. With the coming of the aeroplane, this latter term was applied also to the new means of transport, and underwent a great expansion, being used not only to refer to the flying-machine itself, but also in phrases like /ples balus/ "airstrip (lit. place [for] aeroplanes)". Another technological innovation, the radio, when it first reached New Guinea in the 1930's, was referred to by the English loan-word /wajrlɛs/. The meaning of this term was soon expanded to include any type of communication by invisible means, and hence "gossip, whispering campaign, slander", and phrases were formed such as /tɔk wajrlɛs/ "slander", as in /ɛm i-tɔk wajrlɛs lɔŋ mi/ "he is conducting a whispering campaign against me, is slandering me".

The opposite process, contraction, is equally prevalent. In Old English, *mete* meant "food" of any kind, and this earlier meaning survives as an archaism in expressions like the Biblical *meat and drink* or as a marginal meaning in such a compound as *sweetmeat.* Its field of reference has been restricted, in Modern English, to "edible flesh", so that naïve persons are often puzzled as to why *sweetmeat* should refer to candies that have no "meat" (in our modern sense) in them. The Germanic terms related to our English *deer*—e.g., German *Tier,* Swedish *djur*—mean "animal (in general)"; our word has undergone a narrowing, to refer to a particular kind of animal, the family of the *Cervidae.* In Classical Latin, *necāre* meant "to kill" in general; but in popular usage, it became restricted to "kill in water, drown", as shown by its Romance continuators in this latter sense: Roumanian /aneká/ *aneca*, Italian *annegare*, French /nwaje/ *noyer*, Provençal *negar*, Ibero-Romance (Catalan, Spanish, Portuguese) *anegar.* Similarly, Latin *orbus* meant "deprived (of anything, especially one's parents); orphan"; but for Proto-Romance, we must reconstruct /órbu-/ "deprived of eyesight, blind", on the basis of

Roumanian /órb/, Dalmatian /vuárb/, Italian /órbo/, Friulian /uárb/, and Old French and Old Provençal /órp/.

A referent constituting a unified field of meaning can, on occasion, split, so that the earlier connection between the parts of the semantic field becomes obscure or disappears, and as a result of a form becomes *isolated* from others to which it was earlier related, especially by derivation. In Classical Latin, *plicāre* meant "to fold", but in popular speech it developed two opposite meanings, both derived from specialized contexts in which *plicāre* was used. In military parlance, "to fold (one's tents)" came to mean "to depart", as it still does in Roumanian /pleká/ *pleca*; but in nautical terminology, it referred to arrival at a shore (first in the derivative *applicāre* and later in the simple form), and has survived in this sense in Ibero-Romance: Spanish /ʎegár/ *llegar*, Portuguese /ʃegár/ *chegar*. Often, such splits are favored by phonological developments which give different phonemic shapes to originally related forms, as we have seen for Old French /ómə/ *ome* "man" (oblique case), with its nominative /óm/ *om*; the former is continued in Modern French /om/ *homme* "man", whereas the latter has become the term for "an indefinite actor" and has passed from the status of noun to that of pronoun (cf. p. 331). Other instances of pairs which were earlier related in form and meaning but have become separated are English *straw* and *strew*, *fare* and *ferry*, *ride* and *ready* (from Old English /jeræ:de/ *geraede* "prepared for riding"); German /ʃǿ:n/ *schön* "beautiful" and /ʃón/ *schon* "already", or /fést/ *fest* "firm" and /fást/ *fast* "almost". It occasionally happens that semantic shifts of this type are not correlated with any differentiation in phonemic shape, but that literate speakers take advantage of a loose fit in spelling-habits (cf. pp. 270–273) to indicate the semantic split by a difference in spelling: e.g., /fǽntəzi/ spelled *fantasy* when used as a term of literary criticism, but *phantasy* in psychoanalytical reference.

Other classifications of semantic change involve the type of alteration which the meaning undergoes, or the relative social standing of a linguistic form before and after the change. If a term passes from referring to a concrete situation to a reference that has some feature in common with its earlier meaning but is no longer to be taken literally, the new meaning is called *metaphorical* or *transferred*. Most of our abstract terminology, especially that borrowed from Latin or Greek, was formed in this way, as when Latin *spīritus*, originally "breath", was used metaphorically for "spirit". It has for hundreds of years been a commonplace to observe that the metaphors of Latin abstract terminology involved chiefly comparisons derived from rustic life and the farming interests of the Romans in early Republican times. Thus, *dēlīrāre* "to rave" was derived from *līra:* "furrow", and meant at one time "to go out of the furrow (when plowing)"; *dēfīnīre* "to define" meant earlier "to set bounds to" (related to *fīnis* "boundary, e.g., of a field"). Latin *ēlīmināre* was derived from *ē, ex:* "out of, out from" and *līmin-:* "threshold", and at the time of its formation meant simply "to put out over the threshold, i.e., throw out of the house"; our modern use of *eliminate* has arisen by metaphor from the earlier literal meaning. In some languages, whole classes of forms have come to have transferred meaning, as in Neo-Melanesian ADJECTIVE + NOUN compounds, such as /bɪgnem/, not "large name" but "generic name" or "reputation"; /bɪgmaws/, not "large mouth" but "a large-mouthed gun; insolence"; /hɔtwara/, not "hot water" but "sago pudding" or "hot springs".

Related meanings are often regarded as "stronger" or "weaker." If the meaning of a word becomes weaker than formerly, the process is called *hyperbole*, as in our widespread use of *awfully, frightfully, terribly* for "very", or French /formidabl/ *formidable* for "remarkable" in general. It is not common to experience true difficulty in breathing because of deep absorption and emotional tension when attending a drama, hearing a musical performance, or looking at a landscape; yet we frequently use *breathtaking* to refer to anything of this kind which excites our admiration. The opposite of hyperbole is *litotes* or understatement, when a term is used in a stronger meaning than it had previously: e.g. our English *kill*, a development of a Proto-Germanic /kwalljan/ "torture" (which is still the meaning of German /kve:len/ *quälen*).

A form may, on occasion, pass from lower social status to higher or vice-versa. We have already mentioned (p. 349) the passage of Latin *caballus* from the decidedly plebeian meaning of "nag" or "work-horse" to the much loftier meaning of "horse" in general; in this latter sense, its Old French continuation /čəvál/ *cheval* served as the base for the derivatives /čəvaliǽr/ *chevalier* "horseman, knight" and /čəvaləríə/ *chevalerie* "knighthood, chivalry". Similarly, in popular Latin speech, /testa/ "potsherd" came to mean "head", first as a jocular expression (one's head being one's "pot", cf. our expressions "noggin", "noodle", "bean", "nut", and so forth), but later losing its humorous connotation. Such a passage of meaning is referred to as *elevation*, and its opposite as *degeneration*, when a term with high social standing comes to refer to something lower in the scale. An example of the latter development is our word *knave*: Old English /knáfa/ *cnafa* meant simply "boy", as its German cognate /kná:be/ *Knabe* still does; but *knave* has come by now to mean "rogue, scoundrel".

An interesting case of semantic split involving both degeneration and elevation is the development of Latin /baro:n-/ (nominative /baro:/), originally meaning simply "strong man" (perhaps of Etruscan origin). In Classical Latin, this word underwent a change to pejorative meaning, as intellectuals, with their contempt for a man who had more brawn than brain, used it in the sense of "lout"; the nominative was continued in Italian /báro/ *baro* with a further pejorative development to "scoundrel, knave, card-sharper". But in Romance, the descendants of Proto-Rom. /baró^ne/ either continued the basic meanings of strength and masculinity (as in Spanish /barón/ *varón* "man" and dialectal Portuguese /varáu/ *varão* "husband") or acquired, under feudalism, such highly favorable connotations as to become the name of a rank of nobility (Old French /barón/ *baron*, whence the borrowing of this title in many other modern Romance and non-Romance languages). For a parallel semantic development, we need look no farther than the usage of gang-land of our own day, in which *strong man* is a term of praise and admiration.

We must not make the mistake of thinking that a particular situation which, through its special connotations, gives rise to shifts in meanings lasts or is remembered by later generations. No normal speaker of modern English is aware of the earlier situations in which the ancestral forms of *knave*, *kill*, *bird*, *dog*, etc., were used; the modern German does not know that his linguistic ancestors used *Kopf* for what he would call *eine Tasse:* "a cup" or *ein Kelch:* "a goblet". Hence it is a bad methodologic mistake to read historical considerations of a form's earlier meaning into its later use. Italian *rifiutare:* "to refuse" is best explained as coming from Latin *refūtāre*, of the same meaning, with its phonemic shape influenced by *fiutare:* "to sniff" (from *flautāre:* "to breathe"), as a dog does when it smells and turns disgustedly away from something it does not like. This semantic developments took place before our earliest attestations of Italian, in the context of hunting, from which the new form spread into general use. However, a certain scholar objected to this explanation, on the grounds that it had too undignified a connotation, especially in connection with such lofty poetical passages as Dante's *Vidi e conobbi l'ombra di colui / Che fece per viltà il gran rifiuto* "I saw and recognized the shade of him / Who made through cowardice the great refusal" (Pope Celestine V, who abdicated the papacy in 1294; *Inferno* 3.59–60). Such an objection, however, unrealistically reads into later generations' usage an awareness of a semantic shift that was probably forgotten within a generation or two after it took place. Here, as elsewhere, we must not allow irrelevant historical considerations to influence our understanding of the state of a language at any given point of time, or vice-versa.

NOTES

Semantic change: Sperber, 1930; Ullmann, 1957. Extensive Indo-European materials collected in Buck, 1949.

Romance words from Proto-Romance /baró^n-/: Hall, 1947.

Italian rifiutare: Spitzer, 1940; Hall, 1963b.

60

Change in Lexicon

NOT ONLY MEANINGS (as we saw in the previous chapter), but also the lexical units of the language, its contentives, are continually undergoing change. So far as the single words are concerned, the processes involved are those of obsolescence and replacement, for the types of reasons examined in Chap. 47. However, the various lexical groups of a language are also subject to change, so that over the millennia their composition and hence the semantic character of the language's vocabulary may vary markedly. Of all its parts, the lexicon of a language is the most responsive to changes in the surrounding non-linguistic culture, and hence the cultural development of a speech-community is reflected in the history of its vocabulary. We may best examine such development over a relatively long time in the history of a single language, and for this purpose we shall choose French in its development out of Latin, from the earliest times at which the latter is attested.

Latin had a certain number of inherited Indo-European words relating to fundamental human activities, relationships, and features of daily living, such as *pater:* "father", *māter:* "mother", *ignis:* "fire", *equus:* "horse". In addition to these, the earliest stratum of Latin vocabulary included a great number of derivatives; of these, some had direct semantic relationships to their bases, such as *fēmina:* "woman" (formed on the Indo-European verb-root *dhē-:* "to give suck"), but many involved metaphorical transference of meaning (cf. pp. 330–331). In addition to *dēlīrāre, dēfīnīre* and *ēlīmināre*, we may cite such forms as *comprehendere:* "to understand < to take together" and *pecūnia:* "money" (derived from *pecū* "cattle"); most of these early Latin terms were of homely or rustic origin, evidencing the nonurban nature of the older Roman culture. From the earliest contacts of the Romans with neighboring groups came loan-words of various types. Etruscan furnished terms of religion and the theater (e.g., *haruspex:* "soothsayer", *persōna:* "mask"), and—since a large part of the early Roman aristocracy was of Etruscan origin—a number of family names, such as *Arruns, Tarquinius, Brūtus*, and perhaps *Caesar*. From the other languages of Central Italy, and especially from the distantly related Oscan and Umbrian languages, came a number of rather more popular terms, such as *popīna:* "rustic eating-house," and some more widely accepted words like *rūfus:* "red", recognizable as non-Latin because they show phonetic developments characteristic of the Italic dialects.

The expansion of Latin vocabulary owed more to Greek, perhaps, than to any other single language. There are several strata of Greek loans in the Latin lexicon, each with its own characteristics in the phonological and semantic spheres depending on the period and social level of the contact. The earliest stratum includes a group of words borrowed in relatively early times, beginning with the first contacts of the expanding Roman Republic with the colonies of Magna Graecia in southern Italy and Sicily, from the third century B.C. onwards. These words reflect, in general, the interests and activities of a relatively low social group, the mechanics and technicians, who borrowed terms pertaining to their specializations from the technologically more advanced Greeks. The Latin word *machina:* "machine" itself is an early borrowing from Greek /ma:khaná:/ μᾱχανᾱ́, the Doric form corresponding to Attic /me:khané:/ μηχανή; the word was taken over early enough to share in the weakening of Latin unstressed vowels in medial syllables, as shown by the reduction of the medial *-a-* to *-i-* (parallel to the development of, say, */kekadit/ "he fell" to /kekidit/ *cecidit*). Other such technologic borrowings include terms from nautical vocabulary, such as *campsāre:* "to sail around" from /kámptein/ κάμπτειν, and *calare:* "to lower" from /khaláein/χαλάειν; from culinary terminology, such as *mālum:* "apple" from Doric Greek /mâ:lon/ μᾶλον and *butyrum:* "butter" from /bútyron/ βούτυρον; and from other fields such as boxing (*colaphus:* "blow" from /kólaphos/ κόλαφος) and new fashions in living (*platea:* "town-square" from /platêia:/ πλατεῖα, *camera:* "room" from /kamára:/ καμάρα, and *cathedra:* "arm-chair" from /kathé:dra:/ καθήδρα).

A second stratum of Greek vocabulary, more aristocratic and intellectual in its connotations, consists of somewhat later borrowings, made during the last century of the Republic and the early centuries of our era, in philosophy, the language arts (rhetoric and grammar) and medicine. Classical authors like Cicero, Quintilian, Horace, Vergil, Ovid, etc., borrowed Greek terms by the hundred, beginning with *philosophīa:* "the love of wisdom" and including *rhētorica:* "the art of oratory", *grammatica:* "the art of writing", *thesaurus:* "treasure; collection of words, vocabulary", *hēmicrānia:* "migraine (headache affecting half the head)", and a host of others. In many instances, the Greek influence was manifested in loan-shifts, e.g., Latin *objicere:* "to cast in front of; to reproach, accuse (someone for something)" on the model of a similar combination of meanings in Greek, /probállein/ προβάλλειν; or *cāsus:* "a fall; (grammatical) case," modelled on Greek /ptô:sis/ πτῶσις, the cases being thought of as involving a "falling away" from the "upright" or nominative form. Some of these loan-shifts involved what seem to us ludicrous misunderstandings, especially in grammatical terminology: for instance, the Latin adjective *accūsātīvus*, as the name for a particular case, is a derivative of *accūsāre:* "to accuse (in a law court)", because it is modelled on the Greek adjective /aitia:tikós/ αἰτιατικός "connected with the act of accusing or pointing out (e.g. a direct object)". Many of these Greek loans never entered popular usage, or if they did, they died out soon, leaving no traces in the Romance languages; but they survived in classical texts, serving as a reservoir for later learnèd borrowings (cf. below).

During the Imperial period, with the spread and eventual official adoption of Christianity, a third wave of Hellenisms entered Latin in connection with the special concepts and organizational patterns of the new religion. Two Greek words competed throughout the Romance territory as terms for the church itself, *basilica* (which had already entered Latin as an architectural term) and *ecclēsia* (from /ekkle:sía:/ ἐκκλησία). Names of church dignitaries were in general of Greek origin, such as the "overseer" or *episcopus* (from /epískopos/ ἐπίσκοπος) and the "elder" or *presbyter* (Greek /presbýteros/ πρεσβύτερος), and also the names of supernatural beings such as the "slanderer" (*diabolus:* "devil", from /diábolos/ διάβολος) and the "messenger" (*angelus*, from /ángelos/ ἄγγελος). Many religious concepts were expressed either by direct borrowings, such as *parabola:* "comparison; parable; speech, word" and *chrisma:* "unguent (used in anointing with oil)," or by loan-shifts, as in *grātia:* "favor > grace" under the influence of Greek /khárisma/ χάρισμα.

After the conquest of Gaul by Julius Caesar (58 B.C. ff.), the Latin language was widely used there by the Roman conquerors—at first their soldiers and administrators, and later their merchants and settlers—and, during the first four or five centuries of our era, replaced the local languages of the region, chief among which was Gaulish, a Celtic tongue. The speakers of Gaulish, on learning Latin, carried over into it certain of their local terms, as did all the speakers of various regional languages which were given up in favor of Latin throughout the Empire. From Celtic, a certain number of terms entered the popular Latin of Gaul, especially words for non-Roman customs and artifacts, such as *bracae:* "breeches, pants" (the Romans did not wear trousers) and *carrus:* "a four-wheeled wagon"; and also a number of rural or agricultural expressions, of the type of *alauda:* "nightingale" (which has survived in French /aluet/ *alouette*), *carrūca:* "plough" (French /ʃary/ *charrue*), *cerevisia:* "beer" (Old French /cervé^izə/ *cerveise;* Spanish /θerbéθa/ *cerveza*), *glenāre:* "to glean" (French /glane^/ *glaner*), and *veltragus:* "greyhound" (Old French /véltrə/ *veltre*). Many place names contain Celtic elements, especially terms for "fortified place" such as *dūnum* in *Châteaudun, Verdun; dūrum* (as in *Altessiodūrum* > /oser/ *Auxerre*); and *briga* (e.g. in *Scaldobriga* > /eskodœvr/ *Escaudoeuvres*).

Even before the political collapse of the Roman Empire in the West, an ever-increasing number of Germanic immigrants had entered Gaul and Italy, first as soldiers and then as settlers, bringing their wives and families. From the period of the late Empire on through the great German migrations, and for some time thereafter, Germanic languages were spoken widely in Iberia, Gaul, and Italy. Some Germanic words entered Romance while there was still substantial (though of course dialectally differentiated) unity in the Romance-speaking world, and were widely diffused into all the western varieties; among such were /wérra/ "war" (French /ger/ *guerre*), /hosa/ "hose, leg-coverings" (Old French /uézə/ *huese*), and /hélm/ "helmet" (Old French /hélmə/ *helme*, Modern French /'o^m/ *heaume*).

Most Germanic words in Gallo-Romance entered, however, from the language of the Franks, who settled in northwestern Germany and northern

France, and from whom the modern name of the country is derived (*Frank-ia:* "Frank-land"). These borrowings were related to many semantic spheres, but particularly those of war, dress, and administrative activities. Terms connected with war include such words as /gúnd+fànon/ "battle-flag" > Old French /gonfanón/, modern /gõfanõ/ *gonfanon;* /want/ "glove" > Old French /gu̯ánt/, modern /gã/ *gant;* /skák/ "booty" > Old French /esči̯ǽk/ *eschiec;* and /bléttjan/ "bleed, wound" > Old French /bleci̯ǽr/ *blecier,* modern /bleseˆ/ *blesser.* The Franks introduced such furnishings as the /fálda+stò:l/ "folding-stool", which, in a form with arms, became a seat for distinguished persons (at first on military campaigns and later in permanent dwellings as well) and gave Old French /faldəstuél/ *faldestoël* and modern /foˆtœˆj/ *fauteuil* "arm-chair". Articles of dress included /rauba/ "booty; cloth" > /robə/ *robe* "(woman's) dress"; /skérpa/ "scarf" > Old French /esčarpə/ *escharpe,* modern /eˆʃarp/ *écharpe;* and /wímpel/ "wimple" > Old French /guimpə/, modern /gẽp/ *guimpe.* The feudal system, which reached its highest development between ca. 750 and 1000 A.D., included many offices which were referred to by Frankish terms, such as /márah+ skàlk/ "master of the horse" > Old French /maresčál/ *mareschal,* modern /mareˆʃal/ *maréchal* "marshal", and many others.

Of these manifold Germanic words which entered the French lexicon between the third and tenth centuries A.D., not more than half, at the most, survive in the modern language, and those have often undergone an extensive shift in meaning, as in the case of Old French /faldəstuél/ giving modern /foˆtœˆj/ *fauteuil.* Even as early as the first attestations of French literature (late ninth century, in the *Sequence of St. Eulalia*), Latin loan-words began appearing in French, e.g., *colombe:* "dove", *nones* (a particular church service), or *essample:* "example" (from *columba, nonas,* and *exemplum* respectively). These borrowings continued in ever greater number, especially in the work of the translators, who, from the twelfth century onward, were turning classical Latin (and later also Greek) works into the vernacular, and, wherever they could not find a suitable popular term, took over a classical word, often giving it only a popular-sounding ending, as in *philosophie, pontife, restauration,* etc. Beginning in the fourteenth century, and rising to a peak in the fifteenth and sixteenth, there developed the orthographical habit of introducing useless extra letters in imitation of classical spellings, as in *aultre:* "other" (imitating Latin *alter*) for what was at the time pronounced /ɔtrə/, and *doubter:* "to doubt" (cf. Latin *dubitāre*) representing /duter/. Sometimes these Latinizing spellings represented wrong interpretations on the part of the learnèd men who introduced them, as when /poˆis/ *pois:* "weight" was respelled *poids* under the delusion that it came from Latin *pondus,* whereas it actually came from Proto-Romance /péˆsu/, a derivative of /peˆsáre/ "to weigh".

In the sixteenth century, the flood of Latin and Greek loan-words was at its height, not only in belles-lettres, but in technical fields such as the sciences and medicine. During the sixteenth century, Italy, though politically dis-united, was a source of many cultural influences, especially in the fields of art, architecture, war, and elegant living. These are reflected in a great number of sixteenth-century Italian loans such as /freskə/ *fresque* "fresco", /fajansə/ *faïence* "a kind of ceramic made at Faenza", /styk/ *stuc* "stucco", /fasadə/ *façade*, /kazəmatə/ *casemate*, /solda/ *soldat* "soldier", /kolonel/ *colonel*, /kurtizan/ *courtisan* "courtier (m.)" (and the feminine /kurtizanə/ *courtisane* in the pejorative sense which it had already acquired in its Italian original *cortigiana*), and a host of others. In the seventeenth century, Italian continued to be a source of new terms in music and theatrical matters, which were Italy's principal export at the time, e.g., /virtyoˆzə/ *virtuose* "virtuoso (highly skilled performer)", /sonatə/ *sonate:* "sonata", /kantatə/ *cantate* "cantata", /opeˆra/ *opéra*, and the names of *commedia dell'arte* characters such as /poliʃinelə/ *Polichinelle* (from It. *Pulcinella*, whence English *Punch*) and /skapen/ *Scapin* (from It. *Scappino*). During the first part of the seventeenth century, however, the major cultural influence on France was that of Spain, with resultant borrowings such as /dyeɲə/ *duègne* "duenna (chaperone)", /enfantə/ *Infante* "Infanta (princess)", and /mantiɟə/ (later /mãtij/) *mantille* "mantilla".

The major development of the seventeenth century in the French lexicon was a severe pruning, both of terms which had survived from Old French (such as *ains:* "however" and *ores:* "now") and of many Latinisms which happened not to please the purists of the time such as François Malherbe (cf. Chap. 62). As a result, the literary language of the seventeenth and eighteenth centuries suffered extreme impoverishment, both in lexicon and in structure. Latin and Greek borrowings did continue in the fields of science and medicine, to cope with the new discoveries that were being made, especially after the development of techniques for investigating beyond the reach of the naked eye (with microscope and telescope) at the beginning of the century.

Since the middle of the eighteenth century, the largest single influence on French vocabulary has been that of English. At first, the borrowings reflected English customs and habits as they became known and imitated, e.g., the /bulẽgrẽ/ *boulingrin* "bowling green" and the /rədẽgot/ *redingote* "riding-coat", the /rosbif/ *rosbif* "roast-beef" and the /biftek/ *bifte(c)k* "beef-steak", and such political institutions as the /ʒyri/ *jury* and the /pãfle/ *pamphlet*. Later, however, the technological discoveries and social developments of the Industrial Revolution spread outward from England, bringing with them many nineteenth- and twentieth-century borrowings in many fields, e.g., those of the railway (/raj/ *rail*, /tender/ *tender*, /vagõ/ *wagon*), of elegant life (/fivoklok/ *five o'clock* "afternoon tea", /smokiŋ/ *smoking*, "tuxedo", /flirt/, /klyb/ or /klœb/ *club*, /blœf/ *bluff*, /snob/), etc. etc. Sports, especially, have furnished a large number of new terms to French and other European languages, under Anglo-American influence: /futbol/ *football*, /boks/ *boxe* "boxing", /gol/ *goal*, and a host of others. The flood is still continuing, and shows no sign of diminishing.

In this rapid survey of the development of French vocabulary, we have seen the different ways in which the elements constituting the lexicon of a language can develop, giving it a different consistency at different times. The percentage of words from any given source which are in active use will vary from one period to the next: for instance, the number of Greek words in Latin increased steadily from ca. 250 B.C. until ca. 400 A.D., and then diminished considerably with normal obsolescence and with the decay of intellectual life after the fall of the Roman Empire. The same can be said of the proportion of Germanic words in Old French in the earlier Middle Ages, of Italian words in the Renaissance, and of Spanish words in the seventeenth century. The two major sources of lexical innovations in modern times, Graeco-Latin scientific borrowing and Anglicisms, seem to have been increasing the percentage of their contributions without cease down to the present. The various segments of a language's lexicon show innovation (principally by borrowing), retention, and obsolescence, as do the individual lexical items. Since, in normal nonpuristic behavior, the ordinary man is fairly ready to adopt new terms from any necessary source, the lexicon of a language is able to adapt itself without difficulty to the exigencies of changing situations, often (as in modern technological developments) in the span of a very few years indeed. As the Florentine shoe-maker and philosopher of language, G. B. Gelli (1498–1563) said in the sixteenth century, referring primarily to lexicon, "All languages are suited to the needs of the people who use them; and if they are not, their users make them so."

NOTES

History of Latin vocabulary: Devoto, 1939.
History of French vocabulary: Nyrop, 1914–30, Vol. 4.
Etymology as a discipline: Malkiel, 1962.

61

The Rise of Standard Languages

IN A HOMOGENEOUS community, without major social distinctions, such dialectal divisions as exist do not have overtones of an invidious kind. This is the case in most small "primitive" tribes, such as those of Australia, New Guinea, or Central Asia. In societies marked by class distinctions, however, one of the major marks of status is the use of a particular variety of speech, that of the dominant social group serving as a standard against which the usage of other groups is measured. In complicated societies like ours, the number and relation of levels of usage can become quite highly involved (cf. Chap. 4), with a hierarchy of prestige correlated with the (real or imagined) standing of their speakers.

Our modern standard languages have not existed and enjoyed their present status since time immemorial, as the naïve present-day speaker often tends to think. After the fall of the Roman Empire, Europe was in a state of near-anarchy for some centuries; national states were almost nonexistent or very weak, and the largest effective political unit was the duchy or province, or in some regions (e.g., Italy) the city-state. Correspondingly, the largest linguistic unity was the regional dialect, and before about 1200 or 1300 most writings in the vernacular were specifically identifiable, not as "French" or "Italian" or "Spanish," but as Norman, Picard, Leonese, Asturian, Milanese, Genoese, Venetian, Neapolitan, and so forth. But during the following three or four hundred years the various national states (France, Spain, England) became essentially unified politically and economically; and in each, one particular region (normally that of the capital: Paris, Madrid, London) set the pattern for the rest of the country, its language going along with its political, economic and cultural dominance. Significantly enough, Italy was not unified politically until 1870, considerably later than the rest of the countries of Western Europe. Up to 1870, Italy was divided into small fragmentary city-states, duchies and minor kingdoms; and its linguistic development went along with its political history—a single national standard language did not find universal acceptance until after political unification in 1870. Even the economic importance of Florence from about 1250 on, and its cultural supremacy from about 1350 on, were not able to bring about the unquestioned dominance of its language—on which modern Italian is based—as the political sway of Madrid, Paris and London did in their respective countries.

Before a single standard language has arisen in any given country, the local dialects are of equal social standing: in the early Middle Ages, the speech varieties of Northeastern England, of Scotland, of Southern England were all equally acceptable, and each person spoke and wrote without hesitation in his own dialect. Likewise in France, Spain, Italy and the other countries of Europe; in Italy, for instance, thirteenth- and fourteenth-century writers used their own local speech, very little modified under the influence of other Italian dialects: Bonvesin da Riva of Milan wrote in Milanese, Jacopone da Todi of Umbria wrote in Umbrian, the anonymous Roman author of the famous Life of Cola di Rienzo (the fourteenth-century republican rebel, hero of Wagner's early opera *Rienzi*) used his native Roman dialect, and so forth. But as soon as the dialect of any particular place or region comes to acquire special prestige for nonlinguistic reasons such as political, economic or cultural dominance, then speakers of other dialects begin to have an inferiority-complex concerning their normal native speech, and want to use instead the dialect whose use carries greater prestige. This situation then forces the local types of speech into an unfavorable position vis-à-vis the standard language, and use of a local dialect comes to have the connotation of lower social or cultural standing.

In the European countries in general, the process just described took place by stages. There first arose regional standard languages—in France, those of the region around Paris (the so-called Île de France, whose language is termed *Francien*), of Picardy, of Normandy, of Champagne, of Southern France (*Provençal*, itself based on the speech of several subregions); in Italy, those of Sicily, of Tuscany, of Lombardy, etc. Then a single region acquired political, economic, or cultural dominance over the others, and consequently linguistic superiority as well, so that the various regional standards were in their turn relegated to the status of inferior social acceptability. Francien became the basis of modern standard French, because Paris became the capital of France, and likewise with Castilian as the basis of standard Spanish and with the speech of London and Middlesex as that of standard English. Finally, with the development of literature in the standard language, a split occurs in this latter itself, a more formal or literary variety being distinguished from the less formal, everyday, colloquial variety. For some whose ideal is that of static perfection defined by a set of rigid norms, the literary language (or, in some instances, even a particular sub-dialect of the literary language, such as poetic usage) becomes the exclusive standard, in contrast to which even colloquial standard is unacceptable.

In the meanwhile, especially in large urban areas such as those of Paris and London, innovations have gone on arising, as they always do—but they have arisen too late to be included in the standard language as it was at the time of its rise to dominance. So, for instance, the cockney of London "drops his *h*'s," that is, no longer has word-initial /h-/, saying *'ouse* instead of *house*, *'Arry* instead of *Harry*, *'eat* instead of *heat*, and so forth. The lower-class speaker of Parisian French merges the phonemes /a/ (normally spelled *a*) and /aˑ/ (usually spelled *â*) and generalizes the latter in all positions. He converts the element /-t-il/ *-t-il* (roughly equivalent to "does he . . . ?"), in such a question as *donne-t-il?:* "does he give?" into an interrogative particle /ti/—whose structure is misunderstood by upper-class speakers, who write it *-t'y*—and adds it to all statements to turn them into questions, as in /tyvati?/ *tu vas-t'y?* "Are you going?". The Florentine develops fricative allophones [Φ θ h] for /p t k/ when they are single and between vowels, and says [la'ha:sa] for /lakása/ "the house". Other speakers of the standard language—from the dominant center or from other regions—then feel that these later, obviously lower-class innovations are not socially acceptable, and reject them as "vulgarisms"; witness the attitude of the ordinary speaker of British English towards "dropping one's aitches," or of the ordinary American towards the New Yorker's pronunciation of, say, *bird*.

The conflict that then arises has two further consequences: 1) misunderstanding of the nature or conditions of the unwelcome innovation; 2) overcorrection. For instance, the non-Tuscan speaker of standard Italian often misunderstands the conditions under which the Tuscan substitutes a fricative for a plosive, and thinks that the Tuscan would say also [a'ha:sa]: "to (the) house, at home" where standard Italian would write *a casa*; actually, the Tuscan speaker would say [la'ha:sa] /lakása/, but [ak'ka:sa] /akkása/. Likewise, the ordinary American thinks that lower-class New Yorkers say *boid* for *bird*, *hoid* for *heard*, etc., and, taking his cue from the approximate spellings *boid*, *hoid*, thinks that the New Yorker uses /ój/ in such words. Actually, the New Yorker shares this particular feature of pronunciation with a good part of the East and South; it is to be heard from natives of New Jersey, Pennsylvania, Virginia, Tennessee, and Texas, as well as from many upper-class New Yorkers. Such speakers pronounce *bird* as /bə́jd/, with a very short [ʌ'] and with the tongue somewhat to the rear in the mouth; their naïve hearers equate this back [ʌ'] with their own [ɔ], and think, wrongly, that the New Yorkers are saying /bɔ́jd/.

People are also often likely to misunderstand the social extent and acceptability of such a later innovation in the regional dialect on which the standard language is based. The supposedly "vulgar" pronunciation written *boid*, *hoid*, etc., is normal in all of New York City and wide areas on the Eastern seaboard, and I have heard it from such obviously acceptable speakers as heads of departments in Hunter College and Princeton University. Many Frenchmen will tell you that the merging (they call it "confusion") of /ẽ/ and /œ̃/ (e.g., in /brẽ/ *brun* "brown" or /parfẽ/ *parfum* "perfume"; cf. p. 90) or of /eˆ/ and /e/ (as in /le/ [leˆ] *lait* "milk") is vulgar and characteristic of extremely low-class speech in Paris. But in fact all we need to do is to keep our ears open, to realize that these phonemic mergers are to be heard from all Parisians of whatever class, even from such as will insist vehemently that they never merge the phonemes in question.

Then, the speakers of nonacceptable regional or social dialects try (as is natural) to acquire more acceptable speech patterns. But neither they nor their critics have the requisite linguistic training to analyze the situation objectively and accurately, and all the nonstandard speaker has to go by is a blanket condemnation—often based on misunderstandings such as those we have just been discussing—of some particular feature of his speech. The cockney who has been told he must not "drop his aitches" comes to the conclusion that he ought to put a /h-/ at the beginning of every word where he pronounces only a vowel; since he has been condemned for saying *'Arry*, *'Erbert*, *'Ounslow* for standard *Harry, Herbert, Hounslow*, he puts in an *h* in such words as *Anna, Alice*, or *Ealing*, and makes them into *Hanna, Halice, Healing*. This process is known as *over-correction* or *hyper-urbanism*. We have already mentioned (p. 293) Catullus' satirical poem on Arrius, who over-corrected on his aitches, pronouncing *chommoda* for *commoda* and *hinsidias* for *insidias;* finally he left Rome for Syria, and everybody's ears had a rest, until the frightful news came from the East that the Ionian sea was now the *Hionian* sea. Catullus implies that Arrius was a social parvenu, whose ancestors had been slaves; and, in fact, over-correction is a thing we find very often among people who are insecure about their normal speech and go too far in imitating what they take to be "better" usage. In the same way, a person from the country who said *Marthy* for *Martha*, or *Ameriky* for *America*, in his native dialect, once he had been taught that the final vowel in his pronunciation of these words was "incorrect," would easily go too far, and say *Cincinnata* for the standard form *Cincinnati*, or *Missoura* for *Missouri*, substituting in such words a final /-ə/ for an actually quite normal and correct /-i/. In some instances, as in the local pronunciations of *Cincinnati* and *Missouri*, such an over-correction becomes established as the regional standard.

Once it is established, a standard language becomes obligatory in many aspects of a community's activities. It is normal for it to be required in law courts, government offices, parliamentary sessions, and on formal occasions such as official ceremonies, speech-making, and the like. In many countries, the use of nonstandard speech in such circumstances is prohibited by law, and speakers of dialect have to accommodate themselves as well as possible to standard usage or else have an interpreter. In the Middle Ages in Europe, as in many underdeveloped regions nowadays, the great majority of the populace were illiterate and ignorant of the standard language; this fact gave an immense advantage to the favored few. The latter often used this linguistic advantage to cheat the innocent but ignorant peasants who did not understand the official language; this situation, portrayed by Manzoni in the episode of the lawyer Azzeccagarbugli in *The Betrothed*, is still common in such places as Haiti and the South American countries. This is one of the major incentives for nonstandard speakers to learn the standard language, so that they too may share in the advantages which accrue to those who know and use it.

The standard language comes also to be preferred for use in belles-lettres, often after a period of hesitation in which various local dialects are used for literary productions. In twelfth-century France, Norman, Picard and Champenois (the dialect of Champagne, east of Paris) vied with that of the Île de France; in thirteenth-century Italy, poetry was written in a somewhat Latinized and stylized variety of Sicilian, in Lombard, and in Bolognese, before Tuscan became the standard vehicle of poetical expression. When a particular dialect comes to be the literary standard, this happens only in part through the merit of works written in the dialect concerned (e.g., Dante's *Divine Comedy*, Petrarch's lyrics, and Boccaccio's *Decameron* in fourteenth-century Tuscan). Political and economic factors play just as large a role, if not larger, than do literary and aesthetic considerations in assuring the supremacy of one dialect over another. The coinage of the first gold florin in 1254 assured Florentine commercial and banking supremacy for the following centuries, thereby carrying the prestige of Florentine speech and authors to the rest of Italy. In cases of this kind, it is social prestige (based either on political or economic domination or both) that causes a particular dialect and its literature to be thought beautiful, not vice versa. It is safe to say that, had Dante written the *Divine Comedy* in the Roman, Neapolitan, or some other less prestigious dialect of his time, his work would have been much less famous and his reputation would not have been as great as it became through his having written in the economically and socially dominant Tuscan.

In some instances, standard languages have been created, not by a process of gradual development out of some one regional dialect such as those we have been discussing, but more or less artificially through a combination of features from several dialects. The earliest of the Romance standard languages, Old Provençal (Old South French) was the creation of a group of eleventh- and twelfth-century poets and minstrels, who wandered the countryside from one castle to another and sang their songs to audiences with slightly differing dialectal backgrounds. Consequently, Old Provençal included forms with varying phonological and inflectional characteristics, such as *leis, lieis* or *liei* for "her" (< PRom. /(il)léi/) and *chaudal, caudal, cabdal* or *captal* for "chief" (< PRom. /kapitále/). A deliberate mixture of primarily rustic dialects was made in the *Landsmål* or "country language" developed for Norway in the nineteenth century by Ivar Åsen (1813–1896) as a substitute for the official Dano-Norwegian *Riksmål* or "national language," which by that time was relatively far removed from the actual speech of Norwegians, especially those not residing in the capital city of Oslo. A similar standard language, Serbo-Croatian, was developed in the nineteenth century by Vuk Stefanovitch Karadjich (1787–1864) for what is now Jugoslavia. In general, such artificially created standard languages do not find easy popular acceptance, and tend to remain the property of an educated minority. If they do come to be established as national languages, they soon become modified in the direction of the speech of the dominant region or city; for instance, the Norwegian *Landsmål* has in recent decades come increasingly closer to Oslo urban speech, and is now called *Nynorsk*.

In our modern West European culture, the school is regarded as the normal place for inculcating standard behavior in many respects, not the least of which is the use of language. Hence the standard language comes to be the object of ambition on the part of all parents who want their children to have the benefits of a proper education, especially in democratic societies. This legitimate concern opens the door to exaggerations of many kinds, particularly to insistence on unrealistic and unachievable norms, and to exclusive attention paid to the formal as opposed to the informal standard language. This general lack of understanding of the problem of teaching standard usage is greatly aggravated by our society's peculiar concern with "pure" language. Such a concern is not general throughout human speech-communities, but is a product of the special conditions of the last four hundred years in Western Europe and North America, as we shall see in the following chapter.

NOTES

Standard languages: Ferguson, 1962; Ray, 1962. *The rise of new Germanic-based standard languages:* Kloss, 1952.

Over-correction on Tuscan [h]: Fiorelli, 1953.

Merger of French /ẽ/ *and* /ǽ/: Valdman, 1953.

62

Academicism and Purism

EVER SINCE the early Middle Ages, persons desiring to achieve social standing have been concerned with the elegance of their language. A twelfth-century French poet, Garnier de Pont-Sainte-Maxence, assures his readers *Mis langages est buens, car en France fui nez:* "My way of speaking is good, for I was born in the Île-de-France", and another, Conon de Béthune, complains (in very good French) that he was snubbed at court for not being a native speaker from the Île-de-France. This type of concern has lasted from the Middle Ages down to the present day; one of the major precepts of the Italian theorist of court life, Baldassare Castiglione (1478–1529), is that the aspiring courtier should avoid affectation of any kind and should use the up-to-date, socially acceptable language of the court to which he is attached.

One of the most attractive features of Renaissance intellectual life was the growth and spread of discussion-groups, which in sixteenth-century Italy and seventeenth-century France gathered, at first in private homes, to take up problems of all kinds connected with literary creation and scientific investigation. As they assumed an increasingly important role in each country's intellectual development, these groups were often granted official status and converted into *academies*, with their own rooms or buildings, and a regular organization and schedule of meetings. By the seventeenth century, academies pullulated throughout western Europe. On occasion, the discussion in the academies became inflated, empty or futile, and this situation caused a somewhat pejorative or contemptuous connotation to become attached to the adjective *academic*. In general, however, the academies performed a highly meritorious service in advancing research and furthering its publication.

In linguistic matters, the academies began by furnishing men of letters an opportunity to discuss problems connected with the use of the literary languages, which were still far from having achieved the supremacy or unity which they have today. This was the prime function of the informal gatherings which took place, for instance, in the gardens of the Rucellai family (the Orti Oricellari) in Florence in the mid-1500's, or in the house of one Valentin Conrart in Paris in the 1620's and '30's. The ideal which dominated these meetings was that of neo-classicism, the belief that for each language and each literary manifestation there was an ideal fixed for all time, already reached by the classical writers of Greece and Rome, and which could be attained in modern times only by imitating certain authors who were to be regarded as models of perfection. The Roman poet Horace had already enjoined such an attitude towards Greek literature, telling the readers of his *Ars Poetica* or "Art of Poetry"

> . . . vos exemplāria Graeca
> Nocturnā versāte manū, versāte diurnā.
> "Turn your Greek models over in your hands, night and day."

Carried over to the modern vernaculars, it meant the selection of archaic models to be considered classic and hence imitated, such as Petrarch and Boccaccio in Italy. This neo-classic ideal of perfection was adumbrated, on occasion, even in the names given to the academies, such as the Italian *Accademia della Crusca* or "Bran Academy" (because it was to sift the bran out of the linguistic wheat) which grew out of the gatherings in the Orti Oricellari in Florence.

To the neo-classicist ideal were added, at the end of the sixteenth and in the seventeenth century, the nonlinguistic elements of absolutism and authoritarianism. During this period, two major attitudes were in conflict throughout western Europe, conformism and nonconformism. The former attitude held up a single ideal for every aspect of human behavior and insisted on its being followed as an absolute which did not admit of dissidence or opposition. This motive underlay the belief in a single ideal of purity for language, as it did the insistence on absolute unity of belief in religious matters (in both Roman Catholic and Protestant countries) and unity of loyalty to a single political ruler (the "divine right of kings" in seventeenth-century Stuart England, and the absolutist ideal of *un roi, une loi, une foi:* "one king, one law, one faith" in the France of Louis XIII and Louis XIV). Under absolutist governments, such as that of the Mèdici dukes in sixteenth-century Florence, and that of Cardinals Richelieu and Mazarin in seventeenth-century France, the language academies, born as free discussion groups, were transformed into government-supported law-giving bodies, in the belief that it was possible to "regulate" a literary language both in its structure and in the use made of it by the community. The Florentine *Accademia della Crusca* was officially founded in 1546, and Conrart's group was officialized as the *Académie Française* in 1635. The latter was established as a group of exactly forty, to represent the best writers of the country (whence their unofficial title, "The Forty Immortals"), who were to legislate and sit in judgment on all matters of language (note the belief that creators of literature were *ipsō factō* the most qualified of all to decide questions pertaining to linguistic analysis, a superstition which has lasted in many quarters down to the present).

To enforce the precepts of absolutism, seventeenth-century governments had recourse to authoritarian procedures. In the last analysis, authoritarianism rested on the unscrupulous use of force, especially as increased by recent technological developments in offensive weapons (firearms, artillery) which tilted the balance of power in favor of an aggressor. In political and religious matters, force was widely used, creating an atmosphere of insecurity in which authoritarianism could easily prevail in other matters. No one was executed or jailed for nonconformity in his use of language in, say, seventeenth-century France, but strong forces of condemnation and ridicule could be and were brought to bear on nonconformists. Such a situation always creates a power-vacuum, into which unscrupulous persons may step and seize control for their own purposes and the gratification of their own egos. Such a person was at hand in early seventeenth-century France, one François Malherbe (1555–1628), who, through sheer force of unpleasant personality and readiness to be nasty to anyone that disagreed with him, succeeded (even before the establishment of the Académie Française) in becoming the linguistic dictator of France. Malherbe's authority was informal, and his pronouncements on language matters rested on no basis beyond his own say-so (based on the principle of *ipse dīxit* "[the master] himself said so"). Yet Malherbe's influence and that of his successors such as Claude Favre de Vaugelas (1585–1650) and Nicolas Boileau-Despréaux (1636–1711) was so strong as to create a centuries-long *libīdō serviendī*, a desire to be slaves, in linguistic matters, that has been handed down from one generation of French intellectuals to another ever since then.

The absolutist government of Cardinals Richelieu and Mazarin aspired to total control over every aspect of life, of course including language and literary expression. This was Richelieu's main purpose in founding the Académie Française, and in encouraging it to flex its muscles, as it were, in its first trial of strength in 1637, by condemning the highly popular new play *Le Cid* (1636) by Thomas Corneille (1606–1684). Corneille answered the Academy's criticisms, but thereafter showed that he had learned his lesson by following the Academy's official neo-classical line in the language and content of his plays. The Academy was entrusted with the task of "fixing" the French language in a dictionary and a grammar. The dictionary came out in 1694, only sixty years after the foundation of the Academy, and has ever since enjoyed a veneration, at all levels of French society, far out of all proportion to its modest merits; in its successive editions, it has normally been from fifty to a hundred years behind the times, and has never been noted for lexicographic competence or accuracy. The Academy's grammar appeared nearly three hundred years late (1932), and created a scandal because of the incompetence manifested in its analysis of the language—though little else could have been expected from forty "immortals" chosen for their merits as *littérateurs* and devoid of competence in the technical analysis of language.

This neo-classical, academic, absolutist and authoritarian ideal of purism rests on insecurity as its psychological foundation. Its chief effect on language is negative: to reduce richness of expression by condemning as "impure," "incorrect," etc., any usage which does not strictly conform to preconceived rules as codified in a narrow, inflexible grammar and a restrictive dictionary. Consequently, those who follow the dictates of purism remain ignorant of a great part of the language, and especially of the subtle overtones and connotations of synonymous modes of expression. There are many such differences, between standard and nonstandard, between formal and informal levels of usage—as, for instance, between simple *Wait!* and *Wait up!* "Wait until I catch up!". From this ignorance of the purists arises their insensitivity to the value of such differences. These "three I's of purism"—insecurity, ignorance, and insensitivity—can bring only impoverishment of the means of expression in both everyday and literary language, and any corresponding "improvement" of the language is quite illusory.

The worst harm done to any speech-community by the "three I's of purism" was in France, where the tyranny of the seventeenth and eighteenth centuries as extended to the language resulted in permanent impoverishment, which has never been fully remedied, not even by the re-expansion of its structural and lexical resources since the Romantic period in the early nineteenth century. While it was at its height, the prestige of the French Academy made a deep impression on the ruling and intellectual classes of other nations, some of which founded similar academies such as the Royal Spanish Academy (*Real Academia Española*, 1714). Some eighteenth-century English purists wished for a similar institution to "regulate" our language, but fortunately no such "English Academy" was ever established. Its place was taken by the works of individual grammarians such as Bishop Robert Lowth's *A Short Introduction to English Grammar* (1762), and by the famous dictionary (1755) of Samuel Johnson (1709–1784). The latter, especially, with all its merits but also with its expression of its author's personal likes and dislikes purely on the level of "ipse dixit," came to be regarded as an authority, and its dicta were accepted and followed by generations of Englishmen. The acceptance of purism was facilitated by the insecurity of the rapidly rising newly rich of eighteenth-century England, and kept alive since then by the class-consciousness and desire to maintain social barriers that have characterized much of English life even to the present day.

In America, puristic attitudes have been inculcated in our schools as if they were an essential prerequisite to learning. As with "grammar," however (cf. Chap. 21), the American brand of purism was based primarily on a desire to extend the supposed benefits of "good" or "pure" language to the entire population through universal schooling. Webster's and other dictionaries have been enthroned as if they were "authorities," and the public has been taught to be unhappy if a dictionary does not claim absolute infallibility. In modern times, there is no need for an Academy to "regulate" the language, because—particularly with regard to spelling—its place has been taken by the dictionary, which is expected to give an unequivocal and definite answer to every question raised by typists, proof-readers and others whose knowledge of the facts of the language is incomplete and whose insecurity is correspondingly great. On the basis of the immense expansion of universal education and on the insecurity of many semi-literate persons, there has grown up a tremendous vested interest in "correctness-mongering," which is the main force keeping purism alive in the America of our day.

Aside from mere ignorance of the facts, there are only three psychological bases for purism: sadism, masochism, and desire for personal aggrandizement. Authoritarianism in any field (including language matters) is based primarily on sadism, the desire to force one's will on others and to cause unhappiness while doing so; most purists are, consciously or unconsciously, sadists. Some people do get pleasure out of masochistically yielding to the will of others and obeying puristic precepts—an attitude which the Roman historian Tacitus characterized two thousand years ago as the desire to *ruere in servitūtem:* "rush into slavery". Most contemptible of all are those who adopt puristic attitudes because they find that, by truckling to prevailing superstitions, they can impose themselves as "authorities" on that part of the public who know no better (incidentally selling books on "how to improve your language" and the like, and fattening their bank accounts in the process).

NOTES

The grammar of the French Academy: Brunot, 1932.
Malherbe: Brunot, 1891.
American purism: Pyles, 1952.

63

Substratum and Superstratum

EXCESSIVE PURISM has brought in its wake a strong reaction on the part of linguistic analysts, who have found that puristic attitudes cause great harm, not only in practical matters, but in theoretical linguistics itself. In the nineteenth century, purism was especially harmful in limiting the point of view of many historical linguists, who, starting from the concept of "pure" languages, neglected or even denied the possibility of mixture taking place in linguistic structure. Yet, as we have seen in our discussions of borrowing (cf. Chaps. 53 and 55 ff.), no language is absolutely pure, in the sense of being free from imported elements, no matter what purists may say. Every language has noninherited features, most obviously in vocabulary, but also in other aspects of its structure. However, there has been considerable discussion as to the extent to which linguistic structure is open to outside influence. Every competent linguistic analyst at present agrees that to paraphrase Orwell's famous dictum in *Animal Farm*—all languages are mixed, but some are more mixed than others; but to what extent, and in what part(s) of their structure? Furthermore, from what kind of sources can language mixture come, and by what specific process? For answers to these questions, linguistic analysts have turned their attention more and more to instances in which languages show a very large admixture of unmistakably foreign elements.

In some instances, it has been difficult even to establish the genetic affiliation of certain languages, because of their having a very heavy overlay of borrowed elements. Such a language is Albanian, which has a large number of vocabulary items which were taken over from the popular Latin speech of the Balkans, such as /émtə/ "aunt", /kusbrí/ "cousin", /kál/ "horse"; only on the deeper levels of grammatical structure is it evident that Albanian is not a Romance language, but is a separate member of the Indo-European stock. Such elements as the numerals are thought, in general, to be the most tenacious and resistant to replacement by borrowed forms; but Chamorro (the Malayo-Polynesian language spoken on Guam and in the Marianas), in addition to having borrowed even terms of close relationship like /pariéntes/ "relative" from Spanish, has taken over the entire Spanish numeral system from /ún/ "one" on upwards. Yet Chamorro is unquestionably Malayo-Polynesian, not Romance, as is shown by its grammatical structure, especially the widespread use of grammatical processes like infixation and reduplication (p. 181).

That vocabulary can be mixed, is by now a commonplace in linguistic analysis; outside influence on the phonological and grammatical structure of a language is still a matter of debate. Mixture in phonology has been discussed primarily in connection with the influence of *substratum* and *superstratum*. The former term refers to a language spoken by a group who then give it up in favor of another tongue, as in the instances of Gaulish (p. 355), replaced by Latin in Gaul; Etruscan, replaced by Latin in Tuscany; Oscan and Umbrian, whose successor was the popular Latin of central Italy; and the various African languages whose place was taken by English, Spanish and Portuguese in the speech-habits of the Negroes brought from Africa to the Americas, from the sixteenth to the nineteenth centuries. The term *superstratum* refers to the speech of a group of conquerors who invade and settle a country, but then give up their earlier language in favor of that of their subjects. The most frequently cited instances of superstrata are the languages of the Germanic tribes which established kingdoms in western Europe on the ruins of the Roman Empire, and which were spoken, together with the nascent Romance dialects, in these kingdoms for several centuries before the Germanic conquerors finally merged linguistically with the speakers of Romance.

Substratum and superstratum are most frequently invoked to explain developments in historical phonology. Many scholars have considered that French /y/ < PRom. /uˆ/ (p. 296) was a change due to Celtic substratum. Other alleged substratum influences have been that of Etruscan in causing the development of intervocalic voiceless fricatives from plosives in modern Tuscan (cf. pp. 25–26, 316); that of Oscan and Umbrian in *-nd-* > *-nn-* and *-mb-* > *-mm-* in the modern dialects of Central Italy, e.g., in Roman *quanno:* "when" from PRom. /kuándo/, or *gamma:* "leg" corresponding to standard Italian *gamba*; or that of Basque or Iberian in the replacement of Proto-Ibero-Romance /f/ by Old Castilian /h/, e.g. in /fába/ "bean" > OCast. /hába/, or /fabláre/ "to speak" > /hablár/. The influence of Germanic, more specifically Frankish, superstratum has been invoked to explain the diphthongization of mid-vowels in Old North French (pp. 296, 298). These are only a few of the many substratum influences that have been suggested, in order to explain almost any phonologic development that was not obviously traceable to some internal structural cause.

In general, one of two attitudes tends to prevail with regard to supposed substratum influences: either to accept them *en bloc*, or to deny them in equally all-inclusive fashion. The "substratomaniacs" often ascribe the influence of substratum languages to physical heredity—alleging, for instance, that there was something in the way the Etruscans' or the Gauls' vocal organs were shaped that gave them a propensity to pronounce certain sounds in a particular way—or to a general, rather mystical "tendency" to return constantly to certain kinds of articulation which is supposed to hover over a speech-community. The "substratophobes," on the other hand, deny the possibility of such influences, either from heredity or from some kind of supernatural source, and point to the acquisition of perfect American English speech-habits on the part of the second or third generation of immigrants to the United States. The debate has been going on for many decades, and has reached a point of stagnation because neither "substratomaniacs" nor "substratophobes" have put their arguments on a realistic basis or have taken all the facts of human speech-behavior into account.

Any arguments based on presumed hereditary factors can be dismissed out of hand; if anything is certain about human language, it is that speech habits are—especially in details like the very minute adjustments involved in features of pronunciation—wholly acquired and quite independent of physical heredity. A Chinese baby brought up from earliest infancy in an entirely English-speaking community, and never hearing a word of Chinese, will know only English, and will speak it in exactly the same way as those from whom he learned it, so that over the telephone, say, or speaking from behind a screen, he will be indistinguishable from any other member of that speech-community. Similarly with a child of English-speaking parents brought up speaking nothing but Chinese. This phenomenon is to be observed in millions of instances, such as those of the Nisei Japanese in California and Hawaii, and of American Negroes brought up in the northern part of the United States. Hence it is completely unrealistic to argue that, for example, the Celts of ancient Gaul or the Etruscans must have had inherited physical characteristics (e.g., in the shape of their jaws or the conformation of their tongues) which caused them to be unable to pronounce certain sounds and to substitute them by others. We can of course dismiss as completely fantastic any mystical theory of occult influences or atavistic return to the habits of remote tribal ancestors whose spirits still hover over the region where a given language used to be spoken.

However, the influence of a substratum (or, for that matter, of a superstratum) becomes perfectly plausible if we view it in the light of the bilingualism that must intervene as an intermediate stage in any language transfer. If a population abandons one language for another (as did, say, the speech-community of ancient Gaul when they left off speaking Celtic and thenceforth spoke only the popular Latin of their time), there must be a period during which a large number of the population are bilingual, having a certain command of both the languages involved. Bilingualism is, however, rarely (if ever) perfect; any given speaker almost always has a better command of one of his two languages than he does of the other. This has been repeatedly observed with the bilingualism of successive generations of immigrants to the Americas: the first generation speaks the new language (English, Spanish, Portuguese) quite imperfectly and with a strong accent; the second generation shows only some traces of foreignisms in the new language; and the third and successive generations are completely native-like in the new language but have an increasingly poor command of the old, until finally the original immigrants' descendants have no knowledge at all of their ancestors' tongue.

There are also social factors involved in the process of complete assimilation of a new language: in some situations, pressure to acquire complete accentless, native-like speech-habits is much stronger than in others. In the United States, it has been very strong, furnishing a great incentive for immigrants and their descendants to get rid of non-English-sounding speech as soon as possible; a foreign accent has been a sign of "coming from the wrong side of the tracks," something to be un-learned and replaced by completely Americanized English. In other situations, the pressure is by no means as strong or is even nonexistent. According to what the writer has been told about the pre-1918 Austro-Hungarian Empire, and observed himself in Budapest in the 1930's, the ordinary Hungarian man-in-the-street did not care in the slightest whether his neighbor spoke with a foreign accent or not. In some instances, a foreign accent can even enjoy prestige and be imitated by native speakers of a language, as has happened with the spread of the "French *r*" in Italy, where among some groups it is considered elegant to use a uvular trill instead of the normal dental flap or trill for /r/; and with the imitation of an English accent in the pronunciation of Afrikaans in South Africa.

We can therefore easily postulate a situation free from puristic and nationalistic concerns of the type that beset our own society; in such a situation, those who learn a new language, and eventually use it exclusively, learn it well enough to speak it effectively, but never get rid of their "foreign accent," and transmit it to their linguistic descendants, not by physical heredity but by serving as models for the successive generations to imitate in everyday life. This is the situation that must be hypothesized for a realistic view of both substratum and superstratum influences. The former type of influence involves a carrying-over of speech-habits from the language of those who were already living on the spot when a group of conquerors imported the new language, as in the case of the various pre-Latin languages which were replaced by Latin. The latter would presume that the "foreign accent" of a conquering group, such as the Frankish aristocracy in Merovingian and Carolingian times, would have enjoyed such social prestige as to have been taken over by other speakers in place of their own "native" accent.

The question of a possible substratum influence depends, therefore, on the possibility of there having existed a period of bilingualism whose effects have not been eradicated by more accurate imitation of the new language on the part of later generations. It also depends on the existence, in the old language, of those features to which the later developments are ascribed. For instance, there certainly was a period of bilingualism in the Oscan and Umbrian regions of Italy, in which the population spoke both Oscan (or Umbrian) and Latin; we have proof of this in the wall inscriptions of Pompeii, in which three languages (Latin, Greek, Oscan) were being used simultaneously on the day when the eruption of Vesuvius buried the city. Oscan and Umbrian had the passage of -*nd*- to -*nn*- and of -*mb*- to -*mm*-, as shown in such forms as Oscan *upsannam:* "to be worked", corresponding to Latin *operandam*, with Oscan -*nn*- from an earlier -*nd*-. That the Latin of the region did have this feature, carried over from Oscan, is shown by the presence, in the inscriptions of Pompeii, of spellings like *qvanno* for *qvando:* "when". The influence of

Osco-Umbrian substratum in this development in the modern Central Italian dialects can, therefore, be considered as amply demonstrated.

Not every alleged instance of substratum influence is as well documented as that of Osco-Umbrian in the development just discussed; each instance has to be considered on its own merits, and our decision may be positive in one case, negative in another, and the question may have to be left open in still another. That Etruscan substratum played a part in the substitution of voiceless fricatives for intervocalic stops in modern Tuscan (p. 371) is quite doubtful; the territory of [h] from [k] is approximately that of ancient Etruria, but the extension of [θ] from [t] is much less, and that of [φ] from [p] is very restricted, although the phenomenon as a whole is expanding rather than contracting. We know that in ancient Etruscan there was a contrast between the phonemes represented by the LETTERS *p* and *φ*, by *t* and θ, and by *k* and *χ*; but of what nature this contrast may have been, we have no indication (cf. p. 291). Nor do we know by what strata or by what proportion of the population of ancient Etruria the Etruscan language was used, even at the time of its greatest extension, and hence we know nothing as to what kind of period of bilingualism may have existed at the time of the language transfer or as to what its extent may have been. The first historical reference to the Tuscan fricative allophone [x] or [h] from [k] is from the sixteenth century, in the writings of Claudio Tolomei (1492–1555; cf. pp. 301–305); even Dante, who condemned the Florentine dialect bitterly, does not mention this characteristic. On the other hand, the last sure mention we have of Etruscan is from the period of the Emperor Claudius, in the first century A.D., and even at that time it seems to have been well along the road to extinction. Even if, for the sake of the argument, we consider Etruscan not to have become extinct until around 400 A.D. at the latest, there is still an unfillable gap of around a thousand years during which there is no proof that any fricativization existed in Tuscan speech, and considerable *argumenta ex silentio* that it did not exist until the sixteenth century. At the most, all that we can say for Etruscan substratum influence in this case is "not absolutely impossible, but very far from proved."

The instances we have been discussing are all in the realm of phonology. Other alleged instances of sub- or superstratum influence involve morphology or syntax, as when the extension of Old French /fors-/ "out" (from Proto-Romance /fóris/) to the meaning "wrongly, mis-", e.g., in /forsfáire/ "to do wrong, harm", is traced to the influence of the Germanic prefix /fer-/, of like meaning. Here again, there have been extensive discussions, and many scholars have considered the "inner form" of a language (cf. Chap. 21) as less susceptible to outside influence than its phonology. In this connection, it is rewarding to examine the most extreme instances of language mixture that are known, in pidgin and creolized languages, which are interesting both in their own right and as limiting cases of the most that is known to happen in the carrying-over of habits from one language into a structure derived from another. We shall accordingly dedicate the next chapter to pidgin languages, and Chap. 65 to their outgrowths, creolized languages.

NOTES

General substratum theory: Terracini, 1938.
Chamorro: Safford, 1905; von Preissig, 1918.
Substratum in Italy: d'Ovidio, 1903; Pulgram, 1949; Rohlfs, 1930.
Etruscan substratum in Tuscan: Hall, 1949c; Heinimann, 1955; Merlo, 1926, 1954.
Osco-Umbrian substratum in central Italy: Hall, 1949b.
Iberian substratum in Spain: Menéndez Pidal, 1950.
Germanic superstratum in French diphthongization: von Wartburg, 1950; 1958, Chap. 22.

64

Pidgin Languages

EVERY SPEAKER of a normal or "full-sized" language has, in his idiolect, at least some 25,000 lexical items, a phonological system with sixteen to forty or more phonemes, and an extensive system of morphological elements and syntactic arrangements thereof (no-one has yet succeeded in devising a method for counting them exactly). On the margin of normal linguistic activity, however, in certain types of situations there arise systems of a greatly reduced type, known as *pidgin* languages. From the fact that they are normally used to help out in specific situations of social contact, they are often called *auxiliary* or *contact* languages, and from their status on the edge of ordinary language behavior, they have also been termed *marginal* languages. An auxiliary language used chiefly in commercial relations (as between two tribes of different speech) is often called a *trade jargon*. We shall reserve the expressions *creole* and *creolized language* for one which has grown out of a pidgin and has become the first language of a speech-community (cf. Chap. 65).

There exists so much confusion and indeterminacy in the general use of the term *pidgin* that we must restrict our use of it to one specific type of language, to be carefully defined according to one criterion of a linguistic nature and another of a sociological nature. A pidgin language is one whose structure and lexicon have been drastically reduced, and which is not the native language of any who use it. Take the instance of an Italian guide who shows his charges around a museum: when he stops in front of a picture he says to them such things as *Questo èssere molto bello pittura Michelàngelo:* "This be very beautiful picture [by] Michelangelo", and the tourists reply to him in the same way, e.g., by asking *Quando Michelàngelo dipìngere questo pittura?:* "When Michelangelo paint this picture?". The structure of the language is reduced, by such processes as using the infinitive instead of inflected forms of the verb; not having agreement between adjective (*bello:* "beautiful" or *questo:* "this", m.) and noun (*pittura* "picture", f.); and omitting the preposition *di:* "of, by". It also involves a loan-shift in the meaning of *pittura* from "(act of) painting" to "picture", under the influence of English *picture*. It is not the foreign tourists' native way of talking, nor does the Italian guide speak this way with other Italians; we therefore have here an instance of Pidgin Italian.

It takes two sides to make a pidgin. If I, as a native speaker of English, ask an Italian *Quando Michelángelo dipíngere questa pittura?* and he answers me in normal Italian, making no concessions in reducing his grammatical or lexical structure, no pidgin is involved; I have simply asked a question in broken Italian. Reduction of linguistic structure must also be present in a pidgin. If a group of, say, parliamentarians or business-men, none of them native speakers of English, are gathered in New Delhi or Manila and, having no other language in common, are all conversing in English, with excellent pronunciation and full command of all its resources, no pidginization is involved. In this latter instance, English is serving as a *lingua franca*, i.e., as a means of communication among people of different linguistic backgrounds. The term *lingua franca* (pl. *lingue franche*) is more inclusive than *pidgin:* every pidgin is a lingua franca, but not all lingue franche are pidgins.

Pidgin languages have arisen repeatedly in the course of the centuries. There were probably pidginized varieties of Greek and Latin in the Mediterranean in ancient times, though no attestations of such have survived and there is no reason to ascribe any features of modern Greek or of the Romance languages to pidginization. In the Middle Ages, the original *lingua franca* was a pidginized variety of the Romance spoken along the Riviera from Genoa to Marseilles, which was used by West Europeans in the Near East (Palestine, Egypt, the Byzantine Empire) in their contacts with the Levantines in trade and other activities. In modern times, the "expansion of Europe" since the fifteenth century has been accompanied by a continual growth of pidgins, based on the languages of the European conquerors and colonizers. Portuguese has perhaps been the most extensively used of all as a base for pidgins and creoles; it has been said that there is or was a Portuguese-based pidgin or creole in every one of the present or former Portuguese colonies. English has run Portuguese a close second, and there have been English-based pidgins in the Americas, China, West Africa, New Zealand, Australia, and the South Pacific. Spanish and French have also served as bases for some pidginization and ensuing creolization, the former in Papiamentu (spoken in Curaçao, Aruba and Bonaire off the coast of Venezuela) and the latter in numerous creoles in Louisiana, the Caribbean, and the islands of Réunion and Mauritius. Non-European languages have also given rise to pidgins, perhaps the best-known of which are the Chinook Jargon of the Northwest Pacific coast, and the Police Motu of Papua (south-east New Guinea).

A pidgin arises, normally, out of relatively casual, short-term contacts between groups which do not have a language in common. It therefore does not, properly speaking, have a speech-community of its own. These contacts may be of various types, involving all kinds of social relationships: between equals, e.g., when two or more groups meet for trade or similar purposes (as in the Pacific Northwest, in the formation of Chinook Jargon); between sightseer and guide, as in our example of the Florentine or Roman cicerone's simplification of Italian; between master and servant, as in New Guinea and the South Seas; or between owner and slave, as in Africa and on the American plantations. It is not accurate to ascribe the formation of all pidgins to inequality of social relationship and hence to condemn them out of hand, as is often done, as products of colonialistic expansion. Rather, a pidgin can arise—on occasion, even in the space of only a few hours—whenever an emergency situation calls for communication on a minimal level of comprehension. For this reason, Jespersen rightly termed pidgins "minimal" languages, and, from their basically improvisatory character, "makeshift" languages. In the contact situation, by our very definition of the term *pidgin*, all its speakers already have full-sized "normal" languages which they customarily use in their everyday relationships with the members of their own speech-communities, and hence the pidgin is (as mentioned on p. 376) a socially *marginal* language.

A pidgin is formed by a series of successive approximations, in which each side imitates the other's attempts at speaking. The native of whatever region is involved hears the European use a certain word or combination of words, and imitates as best he can; the European then, on hearing an inevitably imperfect imitation on the part of the native, concludes that that is the best the native can do, and replies to the native in the same way. In this conclusion, the European is often strengthened by his preconceived notion that all non-Europeans are his intellectual inferiors and have a "child-like" mentality; so he speaks to them with the same kind of simplified structure that he uses in "baby-talk" (Chap. 46). The native believes, at this point, that this is the Europeans' true language, and learns it as well as he can, but of course making loan-shifts on the basis of his native language, as do all language learners at the elementary stage (as when students of French form a non-existent *paille-chapeau* through a literal translation of English "straw hat").

In normal language learning, the elementary stage is soon passed, and the learner goes on to acquire a more extensive and detailed knowledge of the niceties of the language; but a pidgin represents a petrification of the rudiments of language structure at a very elementary stage. This petrification may take place simply because of insufficient contact (e.g., infrequent meetings for trade and barter), or it may be due to the desire of at least one side to hold the other at arm's length. (In the case of Chinese Pidgin English, each side looked down upon the other, the Chinese upon the "foreign devils" and the Westerners upon the "heathen Chinee"; the Chinese forbade the teaching of their language to foreigners, and were not willing to learn the latter group's official tongue, but did deign to use what they knew to be a reduced version of the Westerners' speech.) From this point on, the user of the newly-formed pidgin is working within a narrowly limited framework of structural and lexical resources, and often resorts to ingenious combinations and extensions of meaning to expand the semantic range of the pidgin. In Neo-Melanesian, for instance, /gras/ "grass" has been used in such formations as /gras bɪlɔŋ hed/ "hair", /gras bɪlɔŋ fes/ "beard", /gras bɪlɔŋ maws/: "mustache"; in this way, the meaning of /gras/ itself has been extended to: "anything which projects, blade-like, from a surface".

Contrary to popular belief, a language formed in this way, although reduced, has a clearly formed and describable structure. At the beginning of Chap. 24 (p. 145 ff.) we listed the four bound forms of Neo-Melanesian and described the determination of the form-classes on the basis thereof. Likewise, any pidgin language has a definite set of patterns of syntactic combinations, in phrase- and clause-structure. Often, these patterns are different from the ones we are accustomed to, as when Neo-Melanesian has the phrase-type NOUN (head) + NOUN (attribute indicating characteristic or purpose) (e.g., /haws məni/ "house [for] money; bank"), and clause-types such as SUBJECT + (nonverbal) PREDICATE with equational or locational meaning (e.g., /ɛm i-mæn bilɔŋ nədərfɛlə bænɪs/ "he is a man of another totemic group"). The phonology of pidgin languages involves a certain amount of free variation, since there are no native speakers to act as models; even here, however, there is no more uncertainty as to the phonemic structure of the language than there is with any major language which has several dialectal varieties. The cry of "no grammar!" which is often directed against pidgin languages is due in large part to a very narrow, puristic notion of "grammar," which does not recognize the existence of other structural features than those provided for in our Latinizing tradition (cf. pp. 124–125). The lexicon of a pidgin language, also, is normally capable of meeting all the needs of the contact situation, especially by periphrases of the type mentioned on p. 349. Neo-Melanesian has around two thousand separate lexical items, and Mihalić's Neo-Melanesian vocabulary lists some six thousand English expressions for which there are equivalents (single words or phrases) in Neo-Melanesian.

In the formation of a pidgin language, there are normally two "ancestral" languages involved: that on which the pidgin is fundamentally based (e.g., English, Portuguese, Chinook, Motu), which we shall term the *source* language, and that of the other groups which learn the reduced variety of the source language, who are usually (though not always) the inhabitants of a region to which the speakers of the source language have come for trade or conquest, and whose speech we shall therefore call the *local* language. These two, the source language and the local language, do not have an equal part in the formation of a pidgin. In theory, it might be possible for the contribution of the two to be so nearly equal that it would be impossible to determine to which of them the pidgin was more closely related. In practice, however, we find that every pidgin has a closer relationship to one than to the other of the languages involved in its formation, but also has heavy carry-overs from the other. These carry-overs can be found at all levels of linguistic structure, as well as in many items of vocabulary.

In phonology, we find that the influence of the local language is generally more evident in the phonetic raw material of pronunciation than in its phonemic organization. Many Melanesian languages have a contrast, not between voiced and voiceless stops, but between stops with prenasalization (cf. p. 59) such as [ᵐb ⁿd ᵑg] and nonprenasalized stops ([b d g] between vowels, [p t k] elsewhere). Neo-Melanesian has an English-type phonemic contrast between voiced and voiceless stops, as in /pæs/ "letter" vs. /bæk/ "back", but Melanesian speakers are likely to realize the voiced stops phonetically with prenasalization, pronouncing /bæk/ as [ᵐbæk], /tabak/ "tobacco" as ['taᵐbak], or /sɪdawn/ "sit" as ['sɪⁿdaun]. In phonemics, the most noticeable effects of the local language are found in the loss of certain contrasts of a type unfamiliar to its speakers: especially such phonemes as English /θ ð/ are likely to become merged with /t d/, as in Neo-Melanesian /dɪsfɛlə/ "this" from English /ðɪs/, or /tɪŋktɪŋk/ "think; opinion" from English /θɪŋk/ (reduplicated).

In morphology, the transformation and restructuring of elements of the source language often takes place through loan-shifts based on the semantics of the local language. This was the case with the Chinese Pidgin English numeral suffixes /-pisi/ and /-fɛlə/, e.g., in such numerals as /wɔ́npisi/ "one (inanimate)" and /wɔ́nfɛlə/ "one (animate)": in the classical nineteenth-century form of Chinese Pidgin English, "one house" was /wɔ́npisi háws/, "one man" was /wɔ́nfɛlə mǽn/. In Chinese Pidgin English, these forms were bound, occurring only suffixed to numerals; but they developed out of the English nouns *piece* and *fellow*, respectively, on the model of the Chinese use of numeral classifiers, e.g., *sān kwài chyán:* "three hunk money", *yí wèi syānsheng:* "an honorable gentleman". Note especially that in Chinese these numeral classifiers are for the most part independent nouns, as are their equivalents (like *two head of cattle*) in English; but in Chinese Pidgin, their number was reduced to two, and the English nouns themselves were restructured to become numeral suffixes in Pidgin. In twentieth-century Chinese Pidgin English, the suffix /-fɛlə/ went out of use, and with it went the syntactical contrast between animate nouns (those which required modifying numerals to use the suffix /-fɛlə/) and inanimate (those which required /-pisi/ on modifying numerals); in its later stages, Chinese Pidgin English had only the one numeral suffix /-fɛlə/. Derivational patterns (which are more fundamental to the "inner form" or grammatical core of a language than are its inflectional patterns) remain, in general, those of the source language.

Syntactical patterns likewise can show, on occasion, very heavy carry-overs from the local languages. Chinese Pidgin English has exocentric phrases with the structure AXIS + RELATION, such as /tébəl tápsajd/ "on the table (lit. [with respect to] the table on-top)", or /níŋ-pó mó fár/ "beyond Ning-Po (lit. [with respect to] Ning-Po more far)", which is a loan translation from Chinese phrases with the same meaning. In Neo-Melanesian the use of /i-/ as a third-person phrase-marker is a reflection of a similar phenomenon in Melanesian and Micronesian languages, such as Marshallese, in a sentence like *e-bat a-m jerabal:* "it-slow property-your work, i.e., your work is slow, you work slowly", with a special third-person predicate-introducing pronoun form /e-/. Not infrequently, a morphological phenomenon of the local language will be reflected in the syntax of the pidgin, or vice versa. Thus, the dual, trial and quadral numbers in the pronominal system of the Melanesian languages are represented in Neo-Melanesian, not by inflectional features, but by the pronominal phrase-type PRONOUN + NUMERAL, as in /mi trifɛlə/ "the three of us", /ju forfɛlə/ "the four of you", /ɛm tufɛlə/ "the two of them".

In lexicon, the borrowings from the local language(s) range anywhere from moderate to very few. Neo-Melanesian has approximately 80 percent of its vocabulary from English, and not over 10 percent of its words are from local languages, particularly from the Kuanua language of the Gazelle peninsula of New Britain (where Melanesian Pidgin was first standardized). In Chinese Pidgin English, on the other hand, there are only a very few Chinese words, such as /má+fú/ "groom (lit. horse-man)", forming not over one or two percent of the total vocabulary of around seven hundred words. Some of the detractors of pidgin languages consider them as "jumbles" of words taken from every possible source—a gross exaggeration, since even Neo-Melanesian has only 20 percent of its vocabulary from non-English sources, whereas English itself has over 50 percent of its words of non-Anglo-Saxon, especially French, Latin and Greek origin. The opposite extreme, of declaring that a pidgin language is simple "the local language (e.g., Chinese) spoken with English words," is also an exaggeration. The syntax of the pidgin is not a reflection of that of the local language, but represents a reduction of the structure of the source language in the direction of what is common to the two "ancestral" languages.

From this rapid survey, it is evident that the habits of a previously spoken language can easily be carried over into a newly acquired one, on any level of structure. Their survival and transmission to later generations, however, is another matter, and will be discussed in a separate chapter devoted to creolized languages.

NOTES

Pidgin languages: Bloomfield, 1933a, Chap. 26; Hall, 1943a, 1944a, 1953b, 1953c, 1955b, 1955c, 1961a; Jespersen, 1922, Chap. 12; Reinecke, 1937.
Lingue franche in Africa: Samarin, 1962.
Neo-Melanesian vocabulary: Mihalić, 1957.

65

Creolized Languages

A PIDGIN LANGUAGE normally lasts as long as the situation which called it forth and in which it became crystallized. Where opportunity permits, the local users of the pidgin usually prefer to acquire a more extensive knowledge of the source language, or else of the language of the administratively dominant power, and the pidgin goes out of use. This is what happened in New Zealand, where the Maoris have long since abandoned New Zealand Pidgin English and learn standard English in the schools, and in Australia, where the aborigines now learn a somewhat substandard English on the plantations or on the cattle and sheep stations. In some instances, the situation is resolved in the opposite direction, by speakers of the source language learning the local language, as when missionaries who have begun their evangelizing work in a pidgin (especially among mixed groups of natives who have no other language in common, e.g., in the populous centers of New Guinea like Lae, Madang or Rabaul) pass to using the native languages of the region. Pidgins are enabled to survive the situations in which they arise only in case they become the native language of a speech-community, through the process of *creolization*.

A pidgin becomes creolized when a generation of speakers learn it from their earliest childhood, and grow up using the pidgin as their first language. This normally happens when the parents are of different linguistic backgrounds, and have only the pidgin as a common language in which to carry on their everyday family conversation. Usually, this situation prevails in a number or in all of the families of a given community, so that the new generation hear the pidgin, not only from their parents, but from their age-mates as well. On the plantations of the southern United States and the Caribbean area, slaves imported from Africa were systematically separated from their fellow-tribesmen and put together with slaves from other tribes, with whom they had only the pidgin of the particular plantation (whether it was based on English, French, or Portuguese) in common; their owners intended, in this way, to diminish the likelihood of slave plots and revolts. In Melanesia, since the Second World War, a number of new communities have been formed by the voluntary amalgamation of older villages, whose members use Neo-Melanesian in all their domestic life, inter-family relations, and community activities. Note that, whereas a pidgin is defined by two criteria, one linguistic and one social (pp. 376–377), the criteria used in defining a creole are social and historical, and are linguistic only insofar as they concern the type of structure (pidginized) from which the creole takes its start.

The linguistic needs of a speech-community are normally considerably greater than those that can be met by a pidgin language, even though the structure and vocabulary of the latter are considerably greater than is usually thought (cf. p. 379). Hence, when the pidgin becomes creolized, there is a considerable re-expansion of its resources, both from within and by borrowing from an outside source. This latter is normally the European power which is dominant in the area concerned, often (but not always) the source language out of which the original pidgin developed. Thus, Neo-Melanesian is now expanding its syntactic resources (e.g., by the use of subordinate clauses introduced by such conjunctions as /bɪkɔs/ "because", which was not previously part of the language), and is taking over many hundreds of new words, especially referring to modern technology and other new developments, such as /græmofon/ "gramophone", /kawnsɛl/ "council", etc. In Sranan (the English-based creole of Dutch Guiana), most of the recent borrowings have been from Dutch, the official language of the colony, e.g., /xúlde/ "guilder", /amtenár/ "official", /éxi/ "own (adj.)", and a great many others. In this way, a creolized language rapidly becomes as qualified as any other language to serve as a means of communication in its speech-community, with all the structural and lexical resources of any "major" language. As the borrowings from the culturally dominant language continue, if this latter is the original source language for the pidgin out of which the creole developed, they may become so numerous as to form a heavy stratum overlaying the earlier pidginized characteristics. In Jamaica, for instance, the local "creole" is, by now, not a sharply defined, unitary linguistic system contrasting with standard English, but an entire spectrum of possibilities ranging from the "bongo talk" of the isolated Maroon communities in the hills, to the almost (but not quite!) wholly assimilated sub-standard English of the urban lower classes in Kingston. In the same way, the speech of American Negroes ranges from the still markedly creolized structure of Gullah (spoken on the Sea Islands off the coast of Georgia and South Carolina) to urban standard English.

Yet, as long as the underlying grammatical structure of the creole is not overlaid by more recent borrowings from its source language, its origins in a pidginized structure remain clearly evident. In Haitian Creole, for instance, the morphology and syntax of the language still show a drastic restructuring, such as it would have taken thousands of years to produce by the normal slow processes of linguistic change. The familiar Indo-European categories of inflection (such as gender, number, case) have disappeared: /jũ bel fij/ "a beautiful girl", /deˆ bel fij/ "two beautiful girls", /deˆ bel gasõ/ "two handsome boys". Verbal inflection does not involve suffixation at all, as in French and the other Romance languages, nor the categories of person, number, and tense; it involves prefixation of elements indicating aspect, such as /ap-/ continuative and /fek-/ terminative, as in /m-ap-ʃãteˆ/ "I'm singing", /m-fek-ʃãteˆ/ "I've just sung". The phrase- and clause-structure is fundamentally Indo-European; yet there are many specific types of phrases which reflect an African substratum and must clearly have been carried over through a stage of pidginization, since there is no other way in which they could have arisen in the short space of two or three centuries during which Creole has been spoken. Such phrase-types are the comparative phrase with the term of comparison introduced by /pase^/ "surpass"; the combination of several verbs, especially those indicating motion; and the use of /ba(j)/ "give" in dative sense. These constructions are exemplified in /li fo pase^ mwẽ/ "he is strong, surpassing me = he is stronger than I am", and in /l-fek-sot rive^ ke^yi ņu kok vin bã mwẽ/ "he has just gathered a nut for me, lit. he has just come [from] arriving [to] gather [a] nut [to] come [to] give [to] me". It is the presence of sharp reduction and restructurings of this type that justify us in treating pidgin and creole languages together in our consideration of substratum languages and their effects.

The question has often been raised as to whether the regularist principle of historical linguistics (Chap. 50) and the comparative method (Chap. 51) are applicable to pidgins and creoles, since they are extreme instances of language-mixture. The answer is definitely in the affirmative. Even with the data available at present, it is evident that the ancestral form of any given group of related pidgins and creoles can be reconstructed, using the accepted techniques of comparative linguistics, and that the "proto-Pidgin" which we reconstruct in this way shows a reasonable correspondence with certain features of the source language which we already know from other materials. The following lists show sample correspondences between several English-based pidgins and creoles (Neo-Melanesian, Chinese Pidgin English, Sranan, Gullah) on the basis of which a kind of Proto-Pidgin-English can be set up.

Proto-PE Phoneme	Meaning	Neo-M.	CPE	Sranan	Gullah	Proto-PE
/i/	"he, she, it"	i- pred-mkr	hí	i-	i-	hí
	"three"	tri(fɛlə)	θrí	drí	trí	θrí, drí
/e/	"table"	tébəl	tébəl	—	tébəl	tébəl
	"make"	mék(ɪm)	méki	mék(i)	mék	mék(i)
/ɛ/	"red"	rɛd(fɛlə)	réd	réd	réd	réd
/æ/	"be able"	kæn	kǽn	kán	kán	kǽn
	"axe"	ǽkɪs	—	áksi	áks	ǽks
/a/	"hot"	hát	hát	háti	hát	hát
/o/	"no"	no	nó	nó	nó, nə	nó
	"break"	brok(ɪm)	brók	bróko	brák	brók
/ʊ/	"good"	gʊd(fɛlə)	gúd	gúdu	gúd	gúd
	"foot"	fʊt	fút	fútu	fút	fút
/u/	"you"	ju	jú	unu	unə	jú(nə)
	"do"	du(ɪm) "rape"	dú	dú	dú	dú
/m/	"me"	mi	máj	mí	mí	mí, máj
	"mouth"	maws	máwθ, máwf	mófo	máwt	máwθ, máwf
	"time"	tajm	-tajm suff.	tém	tájm	tájm
/n/	"name"	nem	ném	ném	ném	ném
	"man"	mæn	mǽn	mán	mán	mǽn·
/ŋ/	"with"	loŋ	lóŋ	náŋa	—	lóŋ
	"sing"	sɪŋsɪŋ	síŋ	síŋ	síŋ	síŋ

For this proto-language, as for other proto-languages, as reconstructed solely on the basis of this type of comparative evidence, we should have to set up certain alternate forms, for which (if we did not have other attestations) we should simply have to say "non liquet" in attempting to decide between them. In cases where both Chinese Pidgin English and Sranan show a final /-i/ vowel (as in /méki/ "make"), we might consider it desirable to set up a proto-form having an optional final /-i/; for the alternate form /dri/ in Proto-Pidgin-English (necessitated by Sranan /drí/), it is only outside evidence that tells us that this in reality represents the Dutch numeral *drie* rather than English *three*. Further analysis would show us that the unstressed /-ɛm -ɪm/ which we would have to set up for the direct object suffix in Proto-Pidgin-English was simply the pronoun /hɛm hɪm/ "he, him; she, her; it" used in unstressed position after a verb form. As with the Romance languages, we are here in a position to "look in the back of the book" (cf. pp. 307–309) and check on the accuracy of our reconstruction, which we find to be, by and large, valid; in its turn, this finding confirms the validity of the comparative method.

It is often thought that the comparative method is not valid unless it enables us to arrive at, not only features of the linguistic system of the presumed proto-language, but also the geographical location and the complete structure of the system. The example of pidgins and creoles demonstrates that neither of these last-mentioned aspects is of the essence of reconstruction. The Proto-Pidgin-English that we reconstruct on the basis of such correspondences as those just listed is essentially an approximation of such features of lower-class seventeenth-century English as its speakers saw fit to use in their contacts with non-Europeans in the course of their trading, colonizing, recruiting of indentured labor, and slave-marketing activities. If we have to assign a specific locality to our Proto-Pidgin-English, it will have to be somewhere in the lower reaches of the Thames, below Tower Bridge, in the docks and settlements of Bermondsey, Rotherhithe, Wapping, Shadwell and Limehouse. This locality could never be guessed on the basis of the world-wide distribution of historically attested English-based pidgins and creoles in the Americas, Africa, the Far East and the South Pacific. Nor is any physical heredity involved at all—quite the opposite: the linguistic ancestors of the speakers of present-day Sranan, Gullah, Krio (the creolized English of Freetown, Sierra Leone), Neo-Melanesian, etc., were quite unrelated to them physically.

We naturally have no way of knowing how many times pidginization and creolization may have taken place in earlier linguistic history. One instance of possible pidginization in prehistoric times, however, is of interest to us as speakers of English. As is well known (cf. Chap. 51), English and the other Germanic languages have developed out of a common source, Proto-Germanic, which was spoken in the first millennium B.C., probably in southern Scandinavia and nearby parts of northern Germany; Proto-Germanic was, in its turn, one of the Indo-European languages. Now in Proto-Germanic, as contrasted with Proto-Indo-European, we find certain striking developments, particularly the great shift in the consonant pattern known under the names of "Grimm's Law" and "Verner's Law," and the use of vocalic alternation (as in *sing—sang—sung* or *drive—drove—driven*) which in Proto-Indo-European had been automatic and hence meaningless, as a means for indicating changes in the tense of verbs. These developments seem to show the same kind of brusque restructuring that we find in pidgin and creolized languages. Furthermore, Germanic has lost many of the words characteristic of Indo-European, and uses in their stead a number of words of unknown, but presumably non-Indo-European, origin, such as *wife, hand, leg*. On the basis of these phenomena, it has been suggested that Proto-Germanic may well have originated as a pidginized variety of Indo-European, which arose along the amber trade route from the Mediterranean to the Baltic in the first millennium B.C., and which then became creolized, replacing the native languages of the tribes around the lower Baltic.

NOTES

Creolization: Bloomfield, 1933a, Chap. 26; Hall, 1953b, 1953c, 1962a.
Creoles in the Caribbean area: Stewart, 1962.
Haitian Creole: Hall, 1953b.
Dominican Creole: Taylor, 1947, 1951.
Jamaican Creole: Cassidy, 1960; LePage, 1957–58; LePage and DeCamp, 1960.
Sranan (Taki-Taki): Hall, 1948c; Voorhoeve, 1953, 1958, 1961, 1962.
The historical implications of creoles and their "genetic relationships": Hall, 1958a; Taylor, 1956.
Possible origin of Germanic languages in a creolized variety of Indo-European: Feist, 1932.

66

Measurement of Linguistic Change

WITH OUR MODERN EMPHASIS on quantification wherever possible in scientific analysis, it is natural that attempts should have been made in this direction in studying language and the changes which take place therein. From the synchronic point of view, quantitative measurement takes the form of a statistical count of the relative frequency of competing features (phonemes, forms, constructions; cf. Chap. 47). For any given feature, samples can be taken at successive points of time, thus giving an approximate picture of the shift in its frequency and hence of its rise and/or decline, as in the instances of the Italian construction DEFINITE ARTICLE + FAMILY NAME (type *il Machiavelli*) and of the position of the pro-complements with respect to the verbal core in modal verb phrases (type *je le veux voir*) in seventeenth-century French (cf. p. 284). When combined with the philological investigation of old texts (Chap. 48)—including, for the Romance languages, attestations of Romance elements in Latinized form in medieval documents—and with linguistico-geographical analysis, this type of study often casts light on otherwise unsuspected earlier distributions of grammatical and lexical phenomena. In present-day Romance, the continuations of PRom. /ípsu-/ (from Lat. *ipsu-* "him-, her-, itself") as definite article are attested only in Sardinian; but counts carried out on mediaeval Latin texts have shown *ipsu-* in a number of other Romance-speaking regions (Provence, Catalonia) which were also settled early in the expansion of Roman rule. This type of study can of course be done for vocabulary items also, by counting the relative frequency of the words for any given concept, e.g., *ignis* vs. *focus* for "fire", or *equus* and *caballus* for "horse", in Late Latin. For instance, the origin of French *bois*, Italian *bosco*: "wood, forest" was problematical (was it from Greek /pýksido-/ πύξιδο- or from Germanic */busk-/, akin to English *bush*?), until palaeo-graphical-geographical-statistic studies showed that it is attested earliest and most frequently in regions where Germanic settlements had taken place, and that hence these words are best regarded as borrowings from Germanic into Romance.

Such studies concern only individual structural or lexical features of any given language or family. Scholars have also attempted to determine the degree of relationship between two or more languages by various types of statistical counts, involving, in general, the assignment of numerical values to selected structural features and then the determination of the relative proportion of these features present in each of the languages being compared.

An over-all attempt to determine mutual intelligibility of a group of related dialects was carried out on several languages of the Iroquoian group and on several of the Algonquian group. In this instance, one or more native speakers of each language were asked to listen to recordings of the other languages, and then to indicate which aspects they understood or did not understand. A rough count was thus obtained, enabling the investigators to establish approximate figures, showing, for instance, that between Sauk-and-Fox and Kickapoo there was 79% mutual comprehensibility, between Kickapoo and Shawnee 6%, and so forth. In this type of counting, which depends on reactions of naïve native speakers, a great deal will obviously depend on the subjects' perceptivity and even on their mood of the moment, and hence not more than a rough approximation can be obtained.

Especially in connection with the "family-tree" type diagram of relationship among languages (cf. Figs. 27 and 28, p. 312), the question has been raised as to whether statistical counts would verify or disprove the validity of this type of formulation. Here again, it is difficult to decide how much weight to assign to any given difference in linguistic structure, i.e., to any given isogloss between two related languages. Is the difference between /b/ and /gu/ (as in Sardinian /ébba/ "mare" vs. Spanish /iégua/) to be considered as greater than that between /k/ and /č/ (as in Sardinian /kéna/ "supper" vs. Italian /čé^na/) or not? Any attempt at assigning different values to one such difference as opposed to another would inevitably depend on the subjective impressions of the researcher. In such studies, therefore, it is customary to assign an arbitrarily equal value to each isogloss which is taken into consideration. A count of the respects in which each of a group of related languages differs from each of the others gives a series of percentages, which can be expressed in tabular form (cf. Fig. 30 for a table of the relationships between the Romance languages). Statistical counts of this type have normally confirmed the formulations made in conventional family-tree diagrams—which is not surprising, since both types of analyses are usually made on the basis of the same isoglosses. Most linguistic historians come, through working with sets of related languages, to have a "feel" for the closeness of relationships, e.g., that Fox is about as close to Proto-Central-Algonquian as Italian is to Proto-Italo-Western Romance ("Vulgar Latin"); statistical studies simply serve to give an apparent quantitative confirmation of what the historian already "feels" on the basis of empirical observation.

The most ambitious effort at quantifying historical relationships and at ascribing approximate dates to the latest times at which common ancestral tongues were spoken is *lexicostatistics*, of which the most important branch is *glottochronology*. The glottochronological method is based on a count, not of structural, but of lexical items. Its basic assumption is that, from the long-range point of view, over the millennia, the basic vocabulary of human speech tends to be replaced at a constant rate. Hence, by determining the proportion of basic vocabulary which a language has in common with a related language, it should be possible, according to glotto-chronology, to determine the degree of relationship and also—by applying a formula which represents the standard rate of change—to calculate how long any two languages have been separated. The method was first worked out in connection with the Indo-European languages, whose times of separation and development were already approximately known, and where a correlation could be established with some degree of certitude. The formula for finding the rate of retention was $t = \log c / \log r$, in which $t =$ the period of time between two stages of a language, $c =$ the fraction of common forms on the test list, and r is the rate of retention. It was found, on the basis of this formula, that r was approximately 80 or 81 percent per thousand years. To apply this finding to languages whose earlier chronology is unknown, and hence to discover approximately how far back their time of separation must have lain, one takes the formula $min\ t = \log C / 2 \log r$, where $min\ t$ is the minimum divergence time, C is the fraction of corresponding test-list equivalents that are cognate between the two languages involved, and r is the (already known) retention rate.

Portuguese:	Sp.	Ca.	Fr.	It.	Rou.	Sa.
Spanish:	Po.	Ca.	Fr.	It. —— Rou.		Sa.
Catalan:	Sp.	Po.	Fr.	It.	Rou.	Sa.
French:	Ca.	Po.	Sp.	Rou.	It.	Sa.
Italian:	Rou.	Sa.	Ca.	Po.	Sp.	Fr.
Roumanian:	It.	Ca.	Sa. —— Po.		Sp.	Fr.
Sardinian:	It.	Ca.	Rou.	Sp.	Po.	Fr.

FIG. 30: Quantitative Relationships Among the Romance Languages.

"This table gives a simple ranking which shows for each language which languages are closer to it and which are farther from it. The table is to be read: The languages related to Portuguese (or whatever language appears in the left-hand column) are Spanish, then Catalan, then French, Italian, Roumanian, and Sardinian, in that order of closeness. Languages linked by a dash differ by exactly the same amount from the language at the left end of the row. Boxes enclose subgroupings.

The table shows the following results: (1) Sardinian and French are at opposite poles of the group: this suggests a deep cleavage of the Romance languages into a Western group (those farthest from Sardinian), with a high degree of similarity, and all the rest. (2) The Iberian languages and French group together consistently, even where Roumanian and Sardinian are about as far from each other as they both are from Western Romance (see the last two rows). (3) Catalan is grouped with the Iberian languages: even though it is the closest of these languages to French (fourth row), it is still closer to Spanish and Portuguese (third row). In short, the figures arrived at by applying the computations we have proposed agree with what we already know about the sub-groupings in the Romance family."

—J. Grimes and F. B. Agard, Language 35.604 (1959).

The originators of glottochronology have been well aware of certain of the problems facing its application. The vocabulary of a language is normally the part which is most subject to change, and for which the rate of change is most likely to vary from one semantic field to another. Slang can come in and go out in a matter of years or even months; technologic terminology comes in with mechanical innovations and goes out when they are superseded. Cultural influences, particularly those of fashion, can determine the unpredictable popularity or impopularity of any given word, as when it suddenly becomes fashionable to talk of a person's or a nation's *image* in others' eyes, or when Italian *gabinetto:* "toilet" comes to be considered less elegant than the more recent French borrowing *to(e)letta*. To overcome these difficulties, it was proposed to limit the glottochronological calculations to a very small group of words which might be considered free from cultural influences, and universally applicable to all human experience, of the type of *hand, foot, head, water, rain, earth*. The first list contained two hundred such items; a later revision weeded out a number of terms which had proved, after all, to be subject to cultural influence, reducing the list to one hundred; and a second revision brought it down to only sixty-seven items.

Another problem concerns the periods for which the glottochronological calculations can be considered valid. As with other types of dating (e.g., radioactive carbon 14), a glottochronological estimate can be considered only approximate, and valid within plus-or-minus a given period of time—normally, several centuries. Glottochronology is therefore of little use for short term periods of much under a thousand years. On the other hand, the effects of mere chance are likely to produce a certain percentage of similarity between languages which we know to be quite unrelated historically. Thus, Modern Greek /máti/ and Malay /mata/ both mean "eye"; but the former is from an ancient Greek diminutive /ommátion/ "little eye", formed on /ómma/ "eye", whereas the Malay word is related to forms of much the same shape in other Malayo-Polynesian languages and seems to have had much the same phonemic shape for many centuries. Chance resemblances between the vocabularies of any two languages may run as high as five or six percent. Hence, when the percentage of words that are similar in form and shape—even in the basic, supposedly "culture-free" vocabulary—drops below a certain percentage (say, two or three percent), there is little or no guarantee that the resemblances may not be the result of fortuitous convergence rather than of a common origin of the linguistic structures involved. The glottochronologists have, in general, recognized these dangers, and do not claim that their method is valid for periods of less than, say, a thousand years, nor more than about twelve or fifteen thousand.

The difficulties do not stop here, however. It is problematical whether any item of vocabulary can really be considered free from cultural influences. Any term referring to the physical environment can be subject to various types of reinterpretation, as when, in Italian and Spanish dialects, the term which in the literary language means only "water" (Italian *acqua*, Spanish *agua*) comes to be used for both "water" and "rain" (Italian *pioggia*, Spanish *lluvia*). Even those terms which would seem to be most essential to refer to the human body and its parts can be subject to unexpected cultural taboos and other types of replacement: not only our usual "taboo-words" (pp. 10, 236), but many others can be given one kind of reinterpretation or another that will lead to their rapid replacement. Furthermore, two competing terms may survive side by side for centuries or even millennia, as have *capo:* "head" (from Latin *caput*) and *testa* (from Latin *testa:* "potsherd > head") in Italian. Nor does it do any good to attempt to distinguish between "learnèd" or "literary" on the one hand and "popular" on the other, because usage and attitudes will differ from one part of a country to another, with, say, *testa* being popular and *capo* literary in northern and central Italy, and vice-versa in southern Italy. This difficulty leads to the further one of deciding what type of language (standard or nonstandard; regional variety of standard, such as Florentine, Milanese, Roman, etc., for Italian) is to be taken into account in making the calculations. This problem is not relevant for the comparative method, which depends purely on data of linguistic structure, but it becomes serious for glottochronology.

Furthermore, it is at least open to doubt whether the vocabulary of one language family changes at the same rate as that of another. The coefficient of change of 80 percent was first established for Indo-European languages, and then, on being tentatively extended to other families such as Algonquian, Athabaskan, etc., or certain Central American stocks, seemed to yield satisfactory results. When applied to other language families whose history is relatively well known, however, it has not always been satisfactory. In the dialectal varieties, amounting to separate languages, which have developed out of Arabic, it would seem that a coefficient of 89 to 92 percent is indicated, and hence that the lexical stock of this group is subject to a much lower rate of replacement than glottochronology has assumed (on the basis primarily of Indo-European) to be normal. In other words, the rate of lexical replacement itself may well be culturally conditioned.

This suspicion is confirmed when we examine the relationship of at least some pidgin and creole languages to the source languages out of which they have developed. In some instances, the "culture-free" lexicon of a pidgin language shows only a slight percentage of replacement: among the 700 or so words of "classical" Chinese Pidgin English (cf. Chap. 64), only ten percent at the most were different from English, and those were mostly of the environmentally conditioned variety (e.g. /má+fú/ "groom" from Chinese, or /sǽvi/ "know" and /ğós/ "god" from Portuguese). Other pidgins, however, show a much greater rate of replacement: the vocabulary of Neo-Melanesian has a retention rate of between 60 and 69 percent, depending on the items one chooses to include in the count. Or, if one takes the 80–81 percent retention rate as already and universally valid, these figures would seem to indicate, not the hundred and fifty years of divergence which we know to have existed, but somewhere between one and three thousand years. The lexical statistics here correspond to the impressionistic evaluation that the analyst would make on the basis of the structural changes that have taken place, in a much shorter time than is usually considered necessary.

It may be argued that the formation of a pidgin language is something which involves so abnormal a cultural situation—as contrasted with the use of language and its handing down from generation to generation in a normal society—that it should not be taken into account. In itself, this objection is valid; however, the instance of the pidgin language has a more far-reaching implication. In the instance of languages whose history we do not know, there is no telling whether (as may be the case in Germanic, cf. pp. 385–386) or how many times they may have undergone pidginization and subsequent creolization. If pidginization has intervened as a stage in the development of a language (a phenomenon which might occur any time, and is not dependent on nonlinguistic, e.g., socio-economic, factors), it may have induced a far more rapid restructuring of the lexicon, as well as of the grammatical core, than would otherwise have taken place, and the time perspective will thus have been radically altered. We can allow for this in the case of Neo-Melanesian (which, as pointed out in Chap. 65, is already rapidly becoming creolized), but how can we tell whether or not it may have taken place in other instances where we know nothing of its possible occurrence? Creolization is frequent enough for it to be a factor to be reckoned with in the possible prehistory of any language, and some scholars have suggested that it may be especially frequent in certain parts of the world (notably Melanesia).

We are therefore justified in being cautious with regard to the degrees of relationship and the time perspectives which glottochronology may seem to indicate. There are too many possible variables entering into the situation; the structure of human speech as a whole (and especially that of lexicon, which is one of its most easily changeable parts) is too flexible to be as rigid in its rate of change as, say, an individual radioactive element. To arrive at even an approximately valid measurement of any aspect of linguistic change, we would have to have far more extensive and accurate data for a number of related languages, and over many more centuries, than there is any hope of our ever having. In all probability, any hope of being able to apply valid statistical techniques to the measurement of linguistic change is illusory, and had best be abandoned; our best approach to language history is still through comparative reconstruction, which does not depend on arithmetical or mathematical measurement of any kind.

NOTES

Measurement of linguistic diversity: Greenberg, 1956.
French bois, *Italian* bosco: Aebischer, 1939.
Proto-Romance /ípsu-/ *in mediaeval documents:* Aebischer, 1948.
Mutual intelligibility in Iroquoian languages: Hickerson, et al., 1952; Voegelin and Harris, 1951.
Mutual intelligibility in Algonquian languages: Pierce, 1952.
Quantification of linguistic relationships: Ellegård, 1959; Gleason, 1959; Grimes and Agard, 1959; Kroeber, 1960; Kroeber and Chrétien, 1937; Pei, 1949.
Glottochronology: Hymes, 1960. *Critiques of the basis of glottochronology:* Chrétien, 1962; Bergsland, 1958.
Neo-Melanesian and glottochronology: Hall, 1959b.

PART V

LINGUISTICS AND RELATED FIELDS

67

Linguistics and Anthropology

LINGUISTICS OCCUPIES a position intermediate between the social sciences and the humanities. Language derives its function and its very existence from human social activity, and as a group phenomenon it belongs with the subject-matter of the social sciences. At the same time, it has its place of existence only in the individual idiolect, and its use conveys meanings connected with the life and activities of the individual person using it; the analysis of language can, therefore, not be separated from the humanities, particularly the study of literature and of music. The next five chapters will treat of the relations of linguistics with the fields most closely related to it: in the social sciences, anthropology and psychology; in the humanities, philosophy, literature, and music. Rather less close, but still deserving a brief discussion, are the relations of linguistics with the natural sciences, particularly physiology and biology.

The term *anthropology* is used with several referents. In its broadest sense, it refers to the study of mankind in general; as such, it covers any subject-matter connected with man and his activities, including such widely disparate fields as economics, linguistics, literature, and even aesthetics. Frequently, however, it is limited in practice to the study of primitive societies or of prehistoric man. The main sub-divisions usually established are physical anthropology, covering primarily the classification of humans by their somatic characteristics and their relation to the nearest branches of the simians; cultural anthropology, dealing with human culture in general; and archaeology, concerned with nonlinguistic evidence for human activity in prehistoric times. Linguistics is a branch of cultural anthropology; by definition, it has no direct relation with archaeology (except insofar as artifacts with inscriptions may be dug up). The chief finding of physical anthropology that has a bearing on linguistics is negative: that there is no correlation between heredity or minor racial differences in bodily structure, and linguistic structure or the changes which it undergoes. This conclusion may seem obvious, but it is important because it goes counter to a widespread belief about language. Some persons still believe that one aspect or another of linguistic structure is determined by physical heredity; the *reductiō ad absurdum* of this belief was reached in a nineteenth-century German philologist's statement that it would be a crime, from the genetic point of view, for a man whose language was "inflecting" (cf. p. 148) to marry a woman of "agglutinative" speech. On a slightly—but only slightly—more sophisticated level is the belief of many scholars in a physical basis for substratum and superstratum influence (cf. Chap. 63), as shown most recently in a naïve attempt to demonstrate correlation between presence or absence of the dental fricatives [θ] and [ð], and the dominance of one or another blood-type in national groups.

The chief contribution of cultural anthropology, as a whole, to the study of language has been the broadening of scholars' outlooks so that their horizons include, not only languages, but cultures of many different types. The study of language has, in our West European tradition, grown out of classical philology, along with whose techniques there has too often come a restrictive, puristic approach, so that even the somewhat broader outlook afforded by the contrast between the ancient and the modern languages has not been so beneficial as it might otherwise have been. Negatively, this increased awareness has led to the abandonment of many old myths concerning the superiority of one language over another, since it is now realized that no linguistic structure is inherently more "meritorious" than another. The time is past when it might seem reasonable or intelligent to ask the rhetorical question "Is it quite fair to treat a language like French, which is the vehicle of a great culture and civilization, exactly as we treat some little-known tongue of central Africa that has no literary, cultural, or aesthetic values, or even a written form?" The answer which the author was clearly calling for was "no"; the answer which must be given, in the light of modern linguistics and cultural anthropology, is equally obviously "yes." It makes no difference in the merit of a language, as a language, whether it has a writing system connected with it (a "written form") or not. Just as obviously, it makes no difference in the merit of a language, as a language, whether it has a literature connected with it or not. When we speak of the literary or cultural "values" of a language, we are really not talking about the language itself at all; we are talking about the social standing, the prestige, of nonlinguistic things such as culture and literature.

The positive contribution of cultural anthropology to linguistics lies in furnishing data for the interpretation of meanings, on both the grammatical and the lexical level. Often, the meaning of a set of grammatical forms can be understood only in the light of their social function; this is especially true in pronouns of direct address and related phenomena, which frequently reflect complicated social distinctions. In Italian, there are four forms used for addressing people: the second person singular *tu:* "thou", the second plural *voi:* "you", the polite third singular *Lei:* "you" and the polite third plural *Loro:* "you". The earliest Latin usage was simple; it involved using *tu* to any one person (regardless of social status) and *vos,* the ancestor of *voi,* to more than one person. Beginning with the Roman Empire, the habit grew of using the second person plural, in Latin and the Romance languages, first to an emperor or king, and then to any individual to whom one wished to show respect or from whom one was separated by a social barrier. In the sixteenth century, and probably in imitation of Spanish *Usted* /ustéθ/ (from *Vuestra*

Merced: "Your Mercy"), north and central Italians took on the habit of using *La Signorìa Vostra:* "Your Lordship, Your Ladyship" and the corresponding plural *Le Signorìe Vostre.* These noun phrases came to be replaced by the subject pronouns *Ella* and *Elle,* respectively, and by the corresponding conjunctive object pronouns *La* and *Le.* By now, *Ella* and *Elle* are completely obsolete in everyday conversation, surviving only as pronouns of direct address in very stiff, formal letter-writing; in everyday speech they have been replaced by the disjunctive object forms *Lei* and *Loro.* The use of *Lei* in formal direct address has become universal in northern and central Italy, and is at present spreading to southern Italy and Sicily as well, especially among upper-class and professional people. The Fascist government tried, in the late 1930's, to decree by law the abolition of *Lei* and the use of *voi* in its place, and tried to enforce the decree by monitoring telephone conversations and telling people *Date del voi:* "Use *voi!*", etc., but this effort was totally unsuccessful. To understand the use of *Lei, voi,* and *tu* in modern Italian, one must take into account factors, not only of linguistic structure, but also of history, geography, politics, and social relationships.

The contribution of linguistics to anthropology is both practical and theoretical. For any cultural anthropologist working in the field, in first-hand contact with the culture he is studying, a knowledge of the language of the group would seem to be indispensable; yet a surprisingly large number of ethnologists have contented themselves with working through interpreters, on a level at which no analyst of a modern European culture would ever be satisfied with remaining. Simply for a practical command of the language, the techniques of working with a native speaker as informant and of analyzing linguistic structure which are now widely applied in the language-teaching field (cf. Chap. 77) can be used to acquire at least an elementary working knowledge of any language in a few weeks of intensive study. (In fact, these techniques were first developed in the field of American anthropology, and spread from this to other fields just before the Second World War.) Some anthropologist-linguists, notably Edward Sapir and Leonard Bloomfield, became fluent speakers of at least some of the languages of the tribes with which they worked, as do many missionaries. The problem is to a considerable extent one of available time and money; but it is questionable whether insights attained without a thorough knowledge of the language involved are likely to be valid bases for further work or comparison.

On a more theoretical level, linguistics has made a very valuable contribution to the methodology of the social sciences, through the concept of the functional unit and the distinctive feature of behavior, on the one hand, and of the subfunctional, nondistinctive variation on the other. It has been possible to establish this distinction with relative ease in linguistics, because linguistic structure is a relatively self-contained aspect of human behavior, not directly correlated (except of course through lexical meaning) with other aspects of human existence such as physical heredity or nonlinguistic culture. Once analysts of language had ceased introducing irrelevant criteria (especially those of meaning, including connotations of social and intellectual standing) and had developed the distinction between "emic" and "etic" levels of behavior (cf. pp. 28, 31), it became evident that this concept could fruitfully be extended to other types of behavior as well. Patterns of dress, of food consumption, of work, of worship, etc., can all be analyzed in terms of their emic structure and etic variation. A number of neologisms in -eme have been coined, some of them humorously and some of them not; even if cravatteme: "functional unit of necktie-wearing" is slightly jocular, dieteme: "functional unit of diet" and behavioreme: "functional unit of behavior" is not. Although they may perhaps be displeasing to purists, such new terms and the meanings attached to them are quite useful for the structural analysis of human activity in general, and it may yet prove possible to formulate all of human beings' life and its structure in terms of emic units and etic variations.

Another aspect of human behavior that has been clarified by an approach developed in linguistics is the relation between individual and social group. There has been an extensive discussion of the nature of "culture" (not in the sense of the prestige culture of a particular social group, but in the broad sense in which the term is used in anthropology). This term generally covers all behavior which is transmitted from one generation to another through the learning process, without its being determined by heredity (as are, for instance, skin-color, physical functioning of the parts of the body, or susceptibility or inheritance of certain diseases) or by physical environment (e.g., falling, due to the force of gravity). The exact location of culture and its nature, however, have been a subject of extensive debate: does it exist only in the group as a whole, or in each individual as well? This is more than an academic question, since on the answer depends our treatment of cultural innovations and hence our understanding of the way in which cultures change and develop. Some analysts maintain that an innovation (e.g. a new invention or even a previously nonexistent combination of two or more features of cultural behavior) is not part of culture until it has been transmitted by its originator to his fellow-men and has become part of the behavior of an entire group. It will be seen that this view of culture implies that the group is paramount, and that the activities or innovations of an individual have little or no significance in themselves until they have passed to the level of group acceptance.

The fallacy of considering culture as a purely group phenomenon, however, is evident when we examine the parallel with language. As mentioned in Chap. 4, language has its locus existendi in the totality of speech-habits, the idiolect, of each individual speaker. A dialect or language does not have a separate existence in and for itself, floating, as it were, above the community as a whole; it is only an abstraction consisting of as much as is common to two or any greater number of speakers. In the same way, it is useful to realize that cultural behavior exists only in the habits of each individual; a culture is not something hovering in some supernatural fashion over and above the community which shares it. It might be helpful to have a term, parallel to idiolect, to cover all the cultural patterns of an individual, defining these latter negatively as everything in his behavior which is not conditioned by heredity or physical environment; *idiocult* seems awkward, but may do until some-one can suggest a better term. A "culture," in the sense of the behavior of a community, is only as much as is common to two or more idiocults. A cultural innovation is, therefore, part of cultural behavior from its inception, insofar as it forms part of the idiocult of its inventor; then, of course, it becomes part of the "culture" of the group as soon as at least one other person has taken it over. The concept of the idiolect can thus help to establish the parallel notion of "idiocult" and relieve anthropology of a perennial, but needless logomachy over the nature of "culture" in the abstract.

NOTES

Language and "culture" in the narrow sense: Hall, 1944c.
History of Italian Lei, voi, tu: Grand, 1930; Migliorini, 1946.
Use of native languages in anthropological field-work: Mead, 1939.
General theory of functional units of behavior: Pike, 1954–55–60.
Ethnolinguistics: Olmsted, 1950.

68

Linguistics, Philosophy and Psychology

THE STUDY OF LANGUAGE has traditionally been closely related to philosophy and psychology, ever since the inception of each of these latter fields. The Greek philosopher Plato (427–347 B.C.) devoted one of his dialogues, the *Cratylus*, to the question of language, and especially of the extent to which there might exist an inherent connection between words and their meanings; and problems of language are treated, explicitly or implicitly, in many of his other dialogues. Plato reached the conclusion that the meanings of words were determined "by nature" (φύσῃ); most later philosophers, from Aristotle onwards, in the Graeco-Roman tradition reached the opposite conclusion, that meaning is determined θήσῃ, "by convention." If one accepts the Platonic theory that words are inherently derived from the things for which they stand (as formulated in the mediaeval aphorism *Nomina sunt consequentia rerum:* "names are the consequences of things"), this opens the door to all kinds of irresponsible pseudo-etymologizing of the type in which all ancient and mediaeval philosophers engaged, and which reached its climax in the *Etymologies* of Isidore of Seville, who derived *caelebs:* "a bachelor" from *caelum:* "heaven" because an unmarried person's life was like heaven. The Platonic theory of the origin of words, underlying ancient, mediaeval, and Renaissance etymology, was perhaps the greatest single impediment to the development of a scientific attitude towards the historical study of language.

One of the major concerns of Greek and Roman philosophers was to determine the nature of being and the categories into which it fell. Beginning with Aristotle, it was customary to establish three main "categories of predication," things or "substances," qualities, and actions. As has been repeatedly pointed out in modern times, these categories are simply reflections of the three major form-classes of the Greek language. Without knowing it, Aristotle was simply observing that whatever is referred to by a noun is usually called a "thing" or a "substance"; similarly, the referents of verbs are called "actions," and those of adjectives, "qualities." Later generations in Roman times and in the modern West European culture area have accepted the Aristotelian categories unquestioningly, because Latin and our modern languages have the same Indo-European part-of-speech system as does Greek. It has been remarked that if Aristotle had been a native speaker of a non-Indo-European language (e.g., one belonging to the Bantu family) his

400

categories would have been very different. This type of unfounded deduction from unrealized linguistic bases gave rise to Leonard Bloomfield's remark that "a good deal of what passes for 'logic' or 'metaphysics' is merely an incompetent restating of the chief categories of the philosopher's language."

Another instance of a grandiose pseudo-philosophical structure built up, without realizing it, on a purely linguistic basis was Descartes' supposed proof of the reality of existence, summed up in his famous maxim *Cogitō, ergō sum* (French *je pense, donc je suis*): "I think, therefore I exist", which has impressed many generations as containing the profoundest of wisdom. It has rightly been observed, however, that Descartes was actually doing nothing but pointing out the identity of the first person singular in two verbal expressions; in Latin, this finds its expression in the morphological structure of the two verbs involved, and in French and English it is contained in the pronoun used with the respective verbs. So far as the cogency of the demonstration is concerned, Descartes might just as well have said "I eat, therefore I exist," or "I stand on my head, therefore I exist;" the only significance of any of these examples is that the philosopher deduces the reality of his own existence from the fact that his language has a first person singular form with which he can refer to himself. The choice of *cogitō, je pense*, or *I think* was obviously dictated by the socio-intellectual prestige of the abstract reason in seventeenth-century French culture.

Considerations of this type have led some analysts of language to suspect that there may be a closer correlation that has hitherto been suspected between the structure of a language and the way in which its speakers are likely to analyze the world about them. With his customary felicity of phrasing, Edward Sapir remarked "It is almost as though at some period in the past the unconscious mind of the race had made a hasty inventory of experience, committed itself to a premature classification that allowed of no revision, and saddled the inheritors of its language with a science that they no longer quite believed in nor had the strength to overthrow." Developing this insight of Sapir's still further, one of his pupils, Benjamin Lee Whorf, established numerous comparisons between the structures of our familiar Western European languages and those with widely different organization such as Hopi and Maya. Hopi, a language of Arizona, has in its verbs a special pattern of derivation to indicate that the action takes place in repeated segments. In the following table of Hopi verbs, the left-hand column contains forms referring to action taking place at a single point of time, and the right-hand form to action taking place in repeated segments:

hóʻci: "it forms a sharp acute angle"	*hocícita:* "it is zigzag"
wála: "it (e.g., a liquid) makes one wave, gives a slosh"	*walálata:* "it is tossing in waves, it is kicking up a sea"
ríya: "it makes a quick spin"	*riyáyata:* "it is spinning, whirling"
hέro: "he (or it) gives out a sudden hollow gurgle from within"	*hεrórota:* "he is snoring"
yóko: "he gives one nod of the head"	*vokókota:* "he is nodding"
rípi: "it gives a flash"	*ripípita:* "it is sparkling"

Concerning this distinction in Hopi punctual and segmentative verbs, Whorf said:

All this . . . is an illustration of how language produces an organization of experience. We are inclined to think of language simply as a technique of expression, and not to realize that language first of all is a classification and arrangement of the stream of sensory experience which results in a certain world-order, a certain segment of the world that is easily expressible by the type of symbolic means that language employs. [That is to say, a grammatical process of one kind or another serves as a symbol for—in this instance— vibratory phenomena.] In other words, language does in a cruder but also in a broader and more versatile way the same thing that science does. We have just seen how the Hopi language maps out a certain terrain of what might be termed primitive physics. We have observed how, with very thorough consistency and not a little true scientific precision, all sorts of vibratile phenomena in nature are classified by being referred to various elementary types of deformation process. The analysis of a certain field of nature which results is freely extensible, and all-in-all so harmonious with actual physics that such extension could be made with great appropriateness to a multiplicity of phenomena belonging entirely to the modern scientific and technical world—movements of machinery and mechanism, wave process and vibrations, electrical and chemical phenomena—things that the Hopi have never known or imagined, and for which we ourselves lack definite names. This is simply because their language establishes a general contrast between two types of experience, which contrast corresponds to a contrast that, as our science has discovered, is all-pervading and fundamental in nature. According to the conception of modern physics, the contrast of particle and field of vibrations is more fundamental in the world of nature than such contrasts as space and time, or past, present, and future, which are the sort of contrasts that our own language imposes upon us. The Hopi aspect-contrast which we have observed, being obligatory upon their verb forms, practically forces the Hopi to notice and observe vibratory phenomena, and furthermore encourages them to find names for and to classify such phenomena. As a matter of fact the language is extraordinarily rich in terms for vibratory phenomena and for the punctual events to which they are related.

Extending these considerations to other aspects of our grammatical system, it has been suggested that our Western European concern with time—which is a specific characteristic of our culture, not at all innate to the human race as a whole—may be due to the presence, in our grammatical systems, of a contrast between past and nonpast tenses (with also a specifically future tense in Greek and Latin, in which our philosophical systems were elaborated). Other languages have no tense-contrasts at all, but (like Hopi or the Slavic languages) lay much more emphasis on aspect (e.g., completed vs. incomplete action) or verified vs. unverified status (as when a statement must be given as being on either the speaker's or some one else's authority). Similarly, our insistence on exactitude in counting (with all its ramifications in technological development) may well be rooted in the persistence of a sharply defined number-system in Indo-European inflection, as opposed to other languages (e.g., Chinese, Japanese, Malayo-Polynesian) in which number does not exist as a grammatical category.

The "Whorfian hypothesis" (as it is often called)—that the structure of a language influences the view which its speakers have of the world around them, their *Weltanschauung*—has often been misinterpreted, as if Whorf had declared that a language formed a kind of strait-jacket from which it was impossible to free one's outlook. In fact, the most that Whorf can be considered to have held is that a naïve person's attempts at philosophizing and categorizing his experience are likely, if he is not careful, to be mere reflections of the structure of his language. If the Hopi had developed a system of physics independently of the West European tradition, their linguistic structure would have been likely to induce them to lay more emphasis at the outset on vibratory phenomena and less on those of time. In actual fact, the Hopi of course never developed a scientific analysis of their own; and Western European science has learned to be less time-bound by emancipating itself from the naïve outlook imposed by the structure of our languages. Whorf's lesson is, rather, that both science and philosophy must be emancipated from any distortions that may be imposed by linguistic structure; this has been one of the major tasks of modern science and scientific philosophy.

Another problem inherited from ancient philosophy by both psychology and linguistics has been that of "mind." In order to explain many phenomena which did not seem to be due to observable natural causes, it has for millennia been customary to postulate supernatural agents—e.g., for phenomena located outside the individual like lightning and thunder, and for those inside the individual like bodily sickness, sensations, and thoughts. For the last-mentioned, our culture traditionally postulates a special supernatural entity connected with each individual and termed the "mind." The seat of the mind is popularly thought to be in the brain, since it is easily observable that when the brain undergoes physical damage, "mental" functions are impaired or stopped. Language has always been one of the human activities which are interpreted as being "mental" rather than physical in nature. Any given phenomenon of language or its historical development has been regarded as explainable in terms of "mental" causes. Thus, the loss of the future tense in Late Latin has been ascribed to a special mentality of the decadent Roman Empire, in which the populace considered that there was no more future for the world and therefore that future tense-reference in verbs was unnecessary.

In the last three centuries, it has been seen that, for a very large number of phenomena which were previously ascribed to supernatural agents, it is not necessary to postulate any but physical causes. The major dividing line in the history of scientific inquiry was the early seventeenth century, when the field open to investigation and research was immeasurably expanded through the development of new techniques for extending observation beyond the reach of the naked eye. We no longer ascribe lightning to the flash of Zeus' spear, nor thunder to the pounding of his staff on the ground; nor do we consider sickness as due to the evil influence of unappeased ghosts. In psychology and linguistics, likewise, major advances have come as investigators have eliminated the necessity for postulating supernatural factors of "mind." In the instance just discussed, the loss of the future in Late Latin is to be ascribed, not to some peculiarity of its speakers' "mentality," but to sound-change and troublesome homonymy resulting therefrom (cf. pp. 284–286).

We are of course still far from having a full understanding of the functioning of the human brain with respect to speech and the storage of linguistic habits. However, considerable indirect and some direct evidence has made it increasingly clear that, with regard to language as to many other activities, some of the brain's functioning is analogous to that of a servo-mechanism, operating on a very low supply of energy, storing information by means of something analogous to circuits that afford a "circulating memory," and directing the expenditure of a much larger amount of energy with the help of "feedback" on the progress of its activities. Some of the most helpful indications have come from the study of *aphasia*, the derangement of speech due to brain damage. Recent experiments in this field seem to show that there is no one specific area of the brain devoted to linguistic activity (not even "Broca's cortex," which was thought to be such), but that the use of language is related to the flow of weak electric currents over the entire surface of the brain.

The elimination of mental factors as necessary postulates for explaining linguistic phenomena has not taken place without arousing a great deal of protest. The person who has been brought up to believe that lightning is due to the flash of a god's spear-point is greatly offended when a nonspiritualist approach demonstrates its electrical nature. Similarly, those who have been taught to regard language as explainable only in terms of "mental" causes have their emotions deeply hurt when it, too, is analyzed in a nonmentalistic frame of reference and when advances are made through eliminating a presumed factor of "mind." Such persons often regard a nonmentalist approach to language as next door to blasphemous, and accuse linguistic scientists of neglecting large segments of human language behavior, particularly meaning. When it is suggested that what are popularly termed "ideas" are very largely nothing more than linguistic phenomena, the proponents of this theory are termed "mechanists" or "materialists," often with the added adjective "crass," or even "subversives" or "anarchists." It must be realized, however, that the nonmentalistic assumptions of modern linguistics are no different from the basis on which all other scientific work rests, and that a scientific attitude towards one's subject matter (even if it be human beings and societies) implies no negation of whatever ethical or religious standards one's community may have.

In recent decades, linguistics has become somewhat estranged from both philosophy and psychology, because forward-looking analysts of language have been dissatisfied with the mentalistic approach which still dominates in large areas of these two fields. There have been some efforts on the part of philosophers to take into account the findings of the scientific analysis of language, especially in the movement known as "linguistic philosophy." Similarly, joint efforts on the part of psychologists and linguists have established the interdisciplinary field of *psycholinguistics*. Such collaboration is especially desirable in the field of educational psychology, where language factors are normally not taken into sufficient consideration in measuring intelligence and forecasting scholastic progress. The fruitfulness of such collaboration has already been demonstrated in both normal and abnormal psychology. In experimental psychiatric work, the contrast between normal and abnormal speech-habits has been correlated with differences in other types of behavior. For normal persons, also, it has been demonstrated by several types of experiments that sense of personality and security is far more closely tied up than has hitherto been suspected with satisfaction with and command of one's means of linguistic expression, and hence that disturbance of a person's language or disparagement of it coming from outside sources is likely to cause severe personality derangements. This consideration is especially important when government and educational policy is to be determined with regard to the languages of minority groups and to varieties of speech which are the object of social disfavor (e.g. creoles; cf. Chap. 79).

NOTES

Linguistics and philosophy: Carroll, 1953, Chap. 5.

Aristotle's "categories" and Greek "logic" in general, as dependent on the form-classes of Greek: Bloomfield, 1933a, p. 270; this view goes back at least as far as Sayce, 1880, Vol. 2, p. 329.

Descartes: Read, 1949.

"Premature" classification implied in linguistic categories: Sapir, 1921, Chap. 5.

Hopi verbs: Whorf, 1936.

Discussion of the "Whorfian hypothesis": Hoijer, 1951, 1954.

Loss of future tense in Late Latin: Vossler, 1955.

Language and "ideas": Bloomfield, 1936, 1939; Hockett, 1948.

Aphasia: Jakobson, 1941; Penfield and Roberts, 1959.

"Mentalism" and "mechanism": Hall, 1946b; Pei, 1946; Spitzer, 1946.

Psycholinguistics: Osgood and Sebeok, 1954.

Linguistics applied to psychoanalytic interviews: Pittenger, Hockett and Danehy, 1960.

69

Linguistics and Literature

THE NATURE of language is of vital concern to those who study literature, because language is the medium in which literature is written, just as the chemistry of paint and the science of optics are important for historians of art. It is a mistake to think that the "creative artist," whether in literature, painting, sculpture, music or any other field, is wholly free and untrammelled by "material" considerations. Every artist's work is conditioned by the limitations of the medium within which he works, by the cultural background in which he has grown up, and by the demands which his culture makes on his art. Hence the literature written in any given language is of course channelled, insofar as its possibilities of expression are concerned, by the structure of the language. This latter determines what can and cannot be said in the language, and limits the means at the literary artist's disposal, just as his cultural background determines the semantic content of his work. This influence is exerted at every level of linguistic structure, from the phonological through the syntactic, and of course in lexicon as well.

The phonology of the language in which a work of literature is written determines the type of aesthetic effect which the author can obtain, especially in verse. The major characteristic of versification is that the author undertakes in advance to observe certain conventions concerning the more or less regular recurrence of specific phonological characteristics. These latter may include such features as verse-length (measured in the number of recurrent stresses, syllables, or "feet" of syllabic length); rhyme (the use of the same sequence of phonemes in a given distribution, normally at the end of each verse, in a sequence of verses); or assonance (each verse ending in the same vowel phoneme, though not necessarily the same consonant or consonants). Since English and the other Germanic languages are stress-timed (cf. pp. 64–65), the meter of our verses is determined by the number of recurrent stresses in the line:

Hópe sprĭngs ĕtérnăl ín thĕ húmăn bréast:
Măn névĕr ís, bŭt álwăys tó bĕ blést.

In these famous lines of Pope's, as in all others written in so-called "iambic pentameter" in English, there are five main stresses to the line; in other types of line, there may be three, four, or six main stresses. In irregular verse-forms, the number of stresses differs from line to line, as in the limerick:

> Thĕ límĕrĭck's shíftў ănd méan;
> Yoŭ mŭst kéep hĕr ĭn clóse quărăntíne,
> Ŏr shĕ snéaks tŏ thĕ slúms
> Ănd prómptlў bĕcómes
> Dĭsórdĕrlў, drúnk, ănd ŏbscéne.
> —Morris Bishop, *Sonnet and Limerick*

Even apparent instances of breaking metrical rules prove, on closer inspection, to be only exaggerations, which stretch principles of versification but do not really break them, as in the limerick cited on p. 64.

In the Romance languages, which are not stress-timed, but syllable-timed (cf. pp. 64–65), a system of versification depending on recurrent stresses is not possible because of the phonological structure of the language. Romance versification depends on the number of syllables in the line, coupled (in the more conservative type of Romance structure) with the occurrence of a main stress at one or two points (depending on the length of the verse), before the caesura and at the end, as in the initial lines of the eleventh- and twelfth-century Old French *Song of Roland* (given here both in the normalized orthography of T. A. Jenkins' edition and in a reconstructed phonemic transcription):*

> Charles li reis, | nostre emperedre magnes, ||
> Set anz toz pleins | aṭ estéṭ en Espagne. ||
>
> /čárləs liré^is | nóstrémpərǽðrəmáɲəs
> sétánctó^cplé^ins | aðestǽðenespáɲə./
>
> "Charles the king, our great emperor,
> Full seven years has been in Spain".

Ever since late mediaeval times, when French lost phonemically significant stress entirely, the use of a regular number of syllables and of rhyme has been the only characteristic distinguishing French verse from prose, as in the well-known line of Racine (*Phèdre*, Act 1, Sc. 4)

> C'est Vénus toute entière à sa proie attachée
> /seve^nys tutãtjer asaprwe ataʃe^/
> "It is Venus, entirely intent on her prey".

The relative slightness of the distance between verse and prose in French poetry, plus the understatement characteristic of Racine's style, justifies Sainte-Beuve's famous remark about Racine, *Il rase la prose, mais avec des ailes:* "He skims lightly above the level of prose, but with wings [of inspiration]."

In other languages, where syllable length is phonemically significant, the nature of the verse is determined by the number of units of length (*morae*, sg. *mora*) present in each line. This was the case in Latin, Greek, and Sanskrit

---

* In this and other quotations of poetry, | will represent the caesura (half-break in the middle of the verse), and || the end of the verse.

poetry, as in such Vergilian lines as

Parcere subjectīs et dēbellāre superbōs

/parkere subjekti:s | et de:bella:re superbo:s/
"to treat kindly the conquered and to hurl the proud from their power"
—Vergil, *Aeneid* 6.853

If attempts are made to imitate classical Latin and Greek meters in stress-timed languages such as English or German, the result, no matter how pleasing it may sound, is still fundamentally determined by the principle, not of the mora, but of recurrent stress, as in Longfellow's well-known first line of *Hiawatha:*

Thís ĭs thĕ fórĕst prĭmévăl, | thĕ múrmŭrĭng pínes ănd thĕ hémlŏcks ‖

Attempts at imitating classical meters in syllable-timed languages like Italian or French (such as those made in Renaissance times, e.g., by the Italian poet Annìbal Caro [1507–1566] and the French poet Antoine de Baïf [1532–1589]) are forèdoomed to worse failure than those made, say, in English or German, because there is nothing at all in a syllable-timed language that can be made to correspond to the mora of Latin or Greek.

We have already discussed (pp. 126–8) the role of the functors in determining the effect of literary style—a role far greater than is normally realized by many critics, who often take the structural features of language for granted. A language like Latin, which does not have any articles at all, definite or indefinite, is of course incapable of the particular literary effects made possible in English by the presence of the article; on the other hand, its special structural characteristics make possible its own peculiar literary effects which, say, English cannot attain. The existence of an extensive range of inflection in Latin nouns, adjectives, and verbs, and of far-reaching concord between them, made it possible for Roman orators to construct involved but perfectly balanced and rhetorically effective sentences such as the one analyzed on pp. 203–204. At the other syntactic extreme, very great compression was possible in Latin, as exemplified especially in the style of the historian Tacitus, in such sentences as the one in which he described the emperor Otho in six words, as *omnium consensū capax imperiī, nīsī imperāsset:* "by general agreement capable of exercising the imperial power, if only he had not tried to exercise it". A similar concision is achieved in Tacitus' five-word sentence in which he described the break-up of the romance between the emperor Titus and his mistress Queen Berenice: *Titus Berenicēn invītus invītam dīmīsit:* "Titus, although he did not wish it, sent away Berenice, although she did not wish it"; and these five words served as the basis for an equal number of acts in Racine's play *Bérénice* (1670).

Word-formation can often be used as a source for particular literary effects. Elizabethan writers were especially fond of transferring words from one form class to another, and would use *happy, malice* or *foot* as verbs, *fair* or *pale* as nouns, or *seldom* as an adjective. On occasion we find modern speakers engaging in the same kind of play, as when a certain kind of archness is affected by using *fun* as an adjective (*it's a fun thing to do*). In his writings, the humorist P. G. Wodehouse has such formations as *butlerine*, an *eel-jellier* (one who prepares jellied eels), *re-sunshining* a pal's life, or someone *de-dogging* the premises or ambling off *pigwards*. In more serious literature, word-formation is a source of many more or less startling effects, especially in ultra-modern poetry, e.g.,

> River-marsh-drowse
> and in flood
> moonlight
> gives sight
> of no land.
> —Lorine Niedecker, *Poetry* (Aug. 1963)

Much of the surprise force which readers feel in the work of James Joyce and Ezra Pound comes from their having carried English word-formation up to and well beyond the limits of normal usage, as in *Finnegan's Wake:*

Sir Tristrem, violer d'amore, fr'over the short sea, had passencore rearrived from North Armorica on this side the scraggy isthmus of Europe minor to wielderfight his penisolar war . . .

In a similar way, the syntax of literary style makes use of the resources of the language with, on occasion, a straining of these resources to or beyond their normal limits. The most effective use of syntactic resources is made by those authors who stay within the boundaries of everyday speech, but combining independent and dependent, major and minor clauses, and expanding or contracting the attributive elements so as either to coïncide with the reader's expectations or (where it will produce a striking effect) to differ from them. The choice which an author makes among the possibilities available to him, in the way of syntactic framework and lexical elements, is the subject-matter of *stylistics*. In every speech-community—including those most supposedly "primitive," such as American Indian tribes—there are differences from one individual to the next with regard to effective style. Some speakers or writers will arrange the elements of their utterances (spoken or written) so as to hold the attention of their hearers or readers: in Menomini, for instance, a successful user of the language will use the conjunct mode in the right place in story-telling, will keep his proximative and obviative ("third" and "fourth" person, p. 156) references clear, and so forth. Others are ineffective, because they do not use the resources in a clear or attention-holding way: a poor speaker of Menomini will confuse his modes or get mixed up in his pronominal references. Effective style is not a matter of school-book "correctness" and obedience to prescriptive grammarians' rules, but of effective use of the resources of whatever variety of language the hearer is ready to respond to. Many of the most successful demagogues, such as the late Huey Long and Adolf Hitler (to mention no living examples) have used decidedly nonstandard speech, but so skillfully as to play on the emotions of hearers who responded to them far more readily than they did to "correct" but stylistically inappropriate exhortations from less unscrupulous persons.

Critics and aestheticians, dealing with the use of language in literature, have tended—as does any person with no knowledge of linguistic structure— to observe the choices which authors make within the resources of a language, to think of the choices as being wholly free, and to ignore the limitations placed on style by the language. In fact, any speaker or writer (even those with the most elegant literary pretensions) is limited to the potentialities which his linguistic structure affords him. Nor does a literary artist, even the greatest, change the linguistic medium in which he works; a language is the habits of an entire speech-community, not the property of any one speaker, no matter how gifted he may be. As has been remarked, not even Dante could have made Tuscan into a tone-language. An author's contributions to the language in which he works are usually limited to a few proverbial expressions (e.g. *to flourish like a green bay tree* or *the lilies of the field, which toil not, neither do they spin,* and many similar expressions from the King James Bible, or *caviar to the general, to tear a passion to rags and tatters,* or *the sheeted dead, which did squeak and gibber in the Roman streets a little ere the mightiest Julius fell,* from Shakespeare) and to a few lexical coinages, such as d'Annunzio's *velìvolo* for "aeroplane" (cf. pp. 177, 188). Even in word-formation, however, an innovation that does not conform with the normal habits of the speech-community has little or no chance of catching on; such coinages as Dante's *immiarsi:* "to make itself part of me" or *intuarsi:* "to make itself part of thee" were not normal in fourteenth-century Tuscan and hence were not accepted into everyday usage.

Literature is dependent on its medium, language, far more than is customarily realized; most critics, being native speakers of the language whose literature they are discussing, tend to forget its existence in much the same way in which (as pointed out at the beginning of this book) we forget the existence of the air we breathe. The language itself, however, being the habits, not only of a few *littérateurs* but of an entire community of humans of all kinds, has an existence and a function which goes far beyond that of even the most exalted literature, and which does not depend thereon at all.

NOTES

Linguistics and literature: Hockett, 1958, Chap. 63; Sapir, 1921, Chap. 11.

The borderline field of stylistics is too extensive to treat here; for the structural relations of style and language, cf. especially Sebeok (ed.), 1960.

Differences in style in "primitive" communities: Bloomfield, 1927.

70

Linguistics and Music

THAT LANGUAGE has much in common with music, has been evident almost since the beginning of the organized analysis of linguistic structure in ancient Greek times. Both are media for expression of "meanings," and both have effects on the behavior of listeners. The ancient Greeks considered that each of their different musical "modes" (whether these were scales or other types of structural organization, is not clear) had a different effect on the emotional and even the ethical outlook of the hearer. In modern "common practice" of the last three centuries, the modes have been reduced to two (major and minor), and they do not seem to us to have inherent ethical implications; but we all recognize the immediate emotional effect of martial rhythm or languid sentimental harmonies.

However, there is a major difference between music and language, which is immediately evident when we consider the relations of the two with the world around us. In linguistic structure, all contentives and most functors have "dictionary meaning," i.e., reference to specific features of the external world, which can be defined, if not exhaustively or (in most instances) with absolute precision, nevertheless with a reasonable degree of clarity, at least in most instances and for the purposes of everyday life. We know by experience or can find out by checking with other speakers (including writers of reference books) what kind of object is referred to by *table*, *chair*, *ink*; what kind of behavior is meant by *fair play*, *justice*, *decency*; what time-reference is involved in *he ate* or *he has eaten* vs. *he eats*. In addition to these denotations, linguistic forms also have connotations (p. 233) or emotional "overtones" which are associated with the denotation, but which may vary from one individual, one group, one community, one era to the next, and which are always (by definition) vague and indefinable. In music, however, there are no denotations at all; the only meaning that any melody, harmony or succession of harmonies, or instrumental timbre can have is a connotative one.* Denotation is absent from all except the most outspoken program music (e.g., the bleating of the sheep in Richard Strauss' *Don Quixote*), and this latter type of "realism" is not considered at all appropriate in "pure" music.

Both language and music have in common the use of successive but different pitches, with possible variations in length, intensity, and timbre. This

---

* We are of course speaking here only of the sequences of pitches and timbres themselves, not of any words which may be associated with a given tune.

means that the prosodic aspects of linguistic structure (cf. Chaps. 18–19) will be those having the closest possibilities of correspondence with musical structure. Any given language develops the possibilities of variation in prosodic features only to a relatively small extent, with perhaps four or five relative levels or directions of pitch, not more than four distinctive levels of stress, and normally not more than a two-way contrast in length at the most (long vs. short), although a three-way contrast (short, long, over-long) is reported for Esthonian. However, all native speakers of the language learn completely whatever prosodic distinctions it has, and use them effectively. In fact, these are the earliest linguistic contrasts that children normally learn, and hence are both most deep-rooted and most unanalyzed in the ordinary speakers of a language. If a person does not learn the prosodic features of his language as do the other members of the community, it is a sign of either feeble-mindedness or deep-seated psychic disturbance. As we pointed out on p. 73, at least to the extent that he responds to the distinctive prosodic features of his native language, no normal person is truly tone-deaf. If anyone claims to be tone-deaf, the best test is to see if he hears the difference between *You're coming?* and *You're coming.* If he does, then he is not tone-deaf.

In music, on the other hand, the range of possible variation in pitch, intensity (both loudness and stress, with accompanying developments in rhythm) and length is exploited to a far greater extent than in ordinary speech. In our Western European musical practice, the relative levels of pitch have been organized with our familiar division of twelve intervals in the octave, although of course many other types of organization are possible and are found in other musical systems. The length of notes, which may vary widely, has likewise been organized into extensive divisions and sub-divisions (whole notes, half-notes, quarter-notes, etc.). In loudness, an almost infinite variation is possible from *ffff* to *pppp*, and in the suddenness of onset of loudness ("accent" in musical, "stress" in linguistic terminology). Especially with groups of singers or players, or with instruments on which more than one note can be sounded at a time, the complexity of the possible combinations becomes, if not infinite, at least enormously greater than those available to any one speaker of a language. The degree to which an individual is aware of and sensitive to these variations in music varies greatly, from the bare ability to carry a simple tune to the acute sensitivity and perceptivity of a great orchestral conductor like Walter or Beecham. In common parlance, being "tone-deaf" refers, not to physiological inability to distinguish levels of pitch, but to insensitivity to more complicated musical phenomena.

Given at least this extent of correspondence between linguistic and musical structure, it might be expected that some correlation would exist. Theories of such a relation have been prevalent ever since the seventeenth century, and have been developed in considerable detail by some theorists; the most extensive system of musical-linguistic relations was developed by Jean-Philippe Rameau (1683–1764), the eighteenth-century French composer. In Rameau's and other systems of his time, each pitch-relationship was thought to have a specific emotional meaning, and eighteenth-century recitative follows such theories far more than is customarily realized nowadays. To a certain extent, these theorizings were vitiated by their proponents' having started from the (more easily analyzable) facts of music and proceeded to those of language, rather than vice versa. Most of the details of Rameau's and similar systems have long since been discarded as untenable, and, if anything, theories of the relation between music and language have fallen into too great disrepute.

Yet it is reasonable to expect that there would be a certain foundation for the musical structure of a community's practice in the intonation, the other prosodic features, and the basis of articulation of its speech. Here we must distinguish clearly between indigenous and imported musical styles. In the United States, for instance, American English patterns are reflected, not in "art song" nor even in conservative hymns (which represent importations from Europe and England), but in folk song, the less inhibited "gospel hymns," rock-and-roll, and similar unprestigious music. Our international Western European musical style of the last three centuries has been an import from seventeenth-century Italy, of which it was the principal commercial export; its melodic patterns reflect those of Italian speech, and the prestigious style of singing inculcated by singing-teachers and choral directors involves essentially the Italian basis of articulation.

Certain composers, such as Bach, Mozart, Beethoven and Schubert (and, to a lesser extent, Wagner and Brahms), are universally popular wherever the common Western European style of the last three centuries has been accepted. Other composers, however, enjoy a rather remarkable popularity in their own countries and far less in others, as in the cases of Edward Elgar in England, Gabriel Fauré in France, or Anton Dvořák and his followers (e.g., Josef Suk, Zdeněk Fibich, Vitězslav Novák, Josef Foerster) in Czechoslovakia. In these instances, we may suppose that the former composers have developed the potentialities of the international style with a minimum of local peculiarities (hence giving the illusion that they have a "universal" appeal); and that the latter reflect the characteristics of their own speech-communities to a much greater extent, so that they are not liked elsewhere (or, in some instances, are actively disliked, as is Elgar by many Americans).

A cursory examination of the characteristics of Elgar's and Fauré's styles seems to bear out this hypothesis. The intonation of British English, as opposed to American, has at least two major characteristics: a wide spread between high and low pitch, and a greater incidence of falling melodies (because of the prevalence of 3-2-1 or 4-2-1 patterns on yes-or-no questions, such as *Are you coming?* or *Is this the right place?*); and it is just these differences which irritate speakers of American English. Both of these characteristics are richly represented in Elgar's music. For the wide range of pitch, cf. the main themes of the "Enigma" Variations, of the first movement of the second symphony, or of the 'cello concerto; and it has been widely remarked that, whereas the themes of his contemporary Richard Strauss are predominantly rising, Elgar's are predominantly falling. In Fauré's music, on the other hand, there is little or no contrast in stress (cf. especially the *Requiem*) and the intervals in his melodies are normally small—two features which are quite characteristic of French intonation. It is likely that similar—as yet unanalyzed—characteristics of Dvořák's and his successors' music are what causes Czechs to feel that there is something special about it which speaks directly to them as no other music does.

If our hypothesis is correct, these differences in the linguistic substratum (as it were) of various composers' music would exert their influence in a largely unanalyzed fashion, of which both the composers and their listeners would be almost wholly unaware. This would explain such apparently nonsensical remarks as that of Elgar concerning the sources of his musical inspiration, when he said that music was "floating in the air all around" and that "all one needed to do was to reach out and grasp it." If this is taken to refer to general musical inspiration, it is a sentimental banality, rather uncharacteristic of Elgar's personality; but if it refers to the British English speech which was going on around him all the time, it becomes a highly relevant observation. It would be extremely valuable to analyze both Elgar's and Fauré's music and the intonation patterns of their respective languages in greater detail, especially with regard to the local speech of the regions where they grew up (Worcestershire in Elgar's case, Paris in Fauré's), to test this hypothesis further.

It must be emphasized that this influence, if it exists, is exerted by the fundamental prosodic patterns of the language on the composer's style, and not vice versa. After all, as pointed out in the previous chapter (p. 410) à propos of literature, the members of a speech-community are many and its musical composers, like its *littérateurs*, are few in comparison; and speech-habits are too deeply rooted and too widespread to be influenced by one or the other individual's style of musical, any more than literary, composition. On the other hand, certain habits of intonation in our everyday speech are so fundamental that they will probably stand in the way of the widespread popular acceptance of any musical style which runs counter to them. Our /2-3-1)/ intonation contour, or its equivalent in the rising-falling contour of the Romance languages, involves a fall of approximately a major third, a perfect fifth or an octave, which tells the hearer "this is the end of what I have to say." The "common practice" of West European harmony is built on just this type of terminal cadence, especially in the dominant-tonic relationship, which is based on the fall of a perfect fifth (from *sol* down to *do*) or its equivalent, the rise of a perfect fourth (from *sol* up to *do*). It would seem very questionable whether any harmonic system which denies the validity of even the dominant-tonic relationship (as does, for instance, the dodeca-phonic or "twelve-note" style of Schönberg and his followers) can ever obtain acceptance as long as the normal speech-habits of the community affirm the validity of this relationship every time any speaker brings a sentence to a normal close.

To a certain extent, the musical practice of earlier centuries can give indirect information concerning intonation and other prosodic features which are not indicated in our linguistic documents. Investigation of eighteenth-

and seventeenth-century French songs has shown that the French of that period had essentially the same type of intonation-contours and stress-patterns as does modern French. Very little work has been done in this field, unfortunately, and many interesting hypotheses remain to be tested. It would be interesting to know, for instance, whether the contrast between long and short vowels (which sixteenth-century French grammarians tell us was significant at the time) received any reflection in the musical settings of the poems of Ronsard, Du Bellay and other poets of the time. We suspect that the junctural habits of Elizabethan English were quite different from those of later times (cf. p. 111), and that close juncture between (say) determinant and noun must have been much more prevalent than now, as shown by false separations like *an adder* from *a nadder* /ənǽdər/, or, in the opposite direction, the nickname *nunk, nunky* from *nuncle*, separated out from *mine uncle* /majnə́ŋkəl/ reinterpreted as *my nuncle*. Was stress likewise less heavily marked in Elizabethan English, as would seem to be indicated by the smoothly-flowing polyphonic style of Morley, Byrd, and Gibbons? This style became very rapidly obsolete in a remarkably short period of time (less than fifty years) between Charles the First's and Charles the Second's reigns, and the latter is said to have called for "music that he could stamp his feet to." Was this change in musical taste due to a change in the prosodic features of the language, and to the emergence of a stress and juncture system more closely approximating those of modern times? These and similar problems await detailed investigation by someone skilled in the analysis and history of both linguistic and musical structure.

NOTES

Relation between linguistic and musical structure: Weingart, 1929.
Elgar and the intonation of British English: Hall, 1953a.

71

Linguistics and the Natural Sciences

LINGUISTICS TOUCHES on the natural sciences at several points: on physics, through acoustics; on physiology, through the structure of the human vocal organs; and on zoölogy, through the comparative study of the communicative systems of living beings. These, with the exception of the last-mentioned, are marginal concerns, with respect to linguistics proper; in addition, however, there are general problems of methodology, involving the position of linguistics with respect to both the natural and the social sciences.

Inasmuch as the "expression" of linguistic structure (to use the terminology of Louis Hjelmslev) is manifested in sound, the acoustic characteristics of this latter are of interest to linguistic analysts. The actual molecular displacements involved in the formation of the sound-waves themselves are quite marginal, but, at least in theory, the characteristics of the sounds might be expected to be as important as the physiological mechanisms by which they are formed. In practice, however, despite the development of accurate instruments for measuring the characteristics of sounds, such as the sound-spectrograph (p. 39), the acoustic approach has contributed only refinements of detail to what was already known from earlier investigation on a primarily physiological basis. This was no more than might have been expected, since there must be a close correlation between the mechanism with which any given speaker produces sounds and that with which he perceives and interprets what he reacts to as the "same" sounds coming from other speakers. In any case, it can never be determined from any acoustic record what the speakers of a language treat as distinctive features of sound and what they treat as nondistinctive; the factors which determine distinctiveness of sound features reside, not in any acoustic characteristics of the sounds themselves, but in the habits of reaction which have been built up in each speaker's brain by his experience of growing into his speech-community from earliest childhood.

As we emphasized in Chaps. 7–10, a fairly detailed knowledge of the organs of speech is of major usefulness in the classification of sounds. It must be emphasized once again, though, that on occasion very similar sounds may be produced by different organs of speech, as when some speakers of English are able to produce [u], or speakers of French to produce [y], without rounding the lips as is usually done for these sounds. When we describe, say, [y] as a "high-front-rounded" vocoid, we are therefore essentially referring simply to whatever vocoid is produced by imitating a sound formed in this position. This is why we refer (as on p. 40) to the physiological approach to phonetics as involving an "imitation-label" technique. The minute details of physiological structure involved (e.g., the exact type of tissue found in the tongue, or the kind of cartilage in the larynx) are not normally considered necessary for linguistic analysis, because what we must analyze is the distinctive points at which sounds are formed, in order to have a basis for the imitation-labels of which the terminology of physiological phonetics is formed.

An aspect of physiology of which it would be very desirable to have more detailed knowledge (if such should ever become possible) is that of the brain and the central nervous system. If it were possible to know from direct evidence how the brain reacts to incoming auditory and visual stimuli, how it sorts them out, and how it organizes the information received thereby; if we could know how the brain functions in preparing to send out a message and in actualizing the morphemes in phonemes and the phonemes in sounds—we should have a much clearer picture of the way in which language functions inside the individual human organism. However, up to now, such knowledge as we have of the way in which the brain functions in language matters has had to be gained from indirect evidence, especially that of speech-disorders (p. 404), and by deduction from analogy with servo- and similar mechanisms, and the way in which feed-back functions therein. It is possible to construct abstract diagrams of the probable types of reaction systems that we think must exist, in some shape or other, in the brain, labelling them "morpheme-box," "phoneme-box," "phonetic actualizer," and so on. A more exact knowledge of these and similar functions, however, must wait upon the development of more satisfactory techniques of accurate observation of the brain itself.

A more general connection between linguistics and zoölogy lies in the relation of human language to the communicative systems observed in other living beings. It is well known that many types of animals communicate in various fashions, and the communicative systems of some have been studied in considerable detail. (We are here following Hockett's definition of *communication*, in a very broad sense, as any kind of behavior whereby one organism triggers another into activity.) There are various types of communicative systems, differing very widely in the nature of the signals involved and in their complexity; but none of them approach human language in all of the respects mentioned on pp. 6–7. In the most elementary type of communication, one animal simply gives a signal to another, which then responds in a particular way (e.g., in a courtship or mating procedure). Here, one characteristic or another, such as a particular color on a part of the male, or a particular cry, serves as a signal for action of a specific kind; no symbolism is involved (since there is no substitution of one phenomenon for another) and the mechanism of communication is determined by heredity. In other, more advanced types of communication, symbolism (as opposed to mere signalling) is involved, e.g., in the "dances" whereby bees tell each other of the location of nectar; but here, there is a direct iconic representation of a relation in the real world, and the habits of communication and response are still inherited, not learned. Many groups of animals, e.g., deer, utter warning cries, love calls, and the like; but apparently only certain communities of apes may possibly acquire some of their habits of communication by learning, i.e., cultural transmission, rather than heredity. Even so, the "language" of these apes is limited to a few stereotyped calls (danger, play, group cohesion) which are not productive and do not have the duality of human language nor its use in displaced situations.

These considerations are of major importance in determining the relation of humans to other living beings, and in suggesting the way in which the human race may have come to its present position in the world. Many lines have been suggested along which the difference (and presumed superiority) of the human race, as opposed to the animal kingdom, may be formulated. Some of these lines of distinction involve the human possession of presumed "mental" or "spiritual" characteristics of which other living beings are supposed to be devoid; others relate to the greater complexity of human behavior in one respect or another, e.g., use of fire, elaborations of techniques for meeting innate drives (shelter, food, reproduction, etc.). Yet all of these characteristics are reducible, in the last analysis, to one facet or another of the fact that humans have culture and transmit it from one generation to the next by teaching and learning. But, in its turn, the very existence of culture, as defined especially in its transmissibility, depends on the existence of language, with the various characteristics which make linguistic communication so flexible as the indispensable vehicle for cultural continuity. It is well known that the human race, in contrast to others, shows markedly infantile characteristics in its bodily development, i.e., that physical evolution has not taken place with humans as it might normally have been expected to do. Culture (made possible by language) has taken the place of biology, and man's adaptation to his environment has been along cultural rather than physical lines.

It is thus clear that communication is at the center of man's special position in the universe, since language has made it possible for him to gather, preserve and spread information that no other type of living being has at its disposal. As Hockett has said, paraphrasing Jesus' saying, "Man does not live by bread alone; his other necessity is communication." This paraphrase of Hockett's has seemed more than faintly blasphemous to some, because it seems to equate the word of God with human language. Yet it is through linguistic channels alone that the Divine Word—both in the narrow sense of the Biblical text and in the broader sense of our understanding as much as possible of the universe around us—can come to mankind. Communication of such an understanding is one of the senses that can reasonably be given to the *Logos* or Divine Word; and from this point of view, the beginning of the Gospel according to St. John, *In the beginning was the Word, and the Word was with God, and the Word was God*, has very deep significance with respect to the central position of the communicative function of language in mankind's existence and relation to the universe in which we live.

Human communicative ability is also central to the problem of a "special creation," as narrated in the first chapter of Genesis, and as hotly debated ever since the middle of the nineteenth century and the dominance of Darwinian theories of evolution. For a century, it has been the normal habit of scientists to deny the possibility of a sudden, special creation of mankind, as incompatible with the generally prevalent theory of slow, gradual evolution. However, some anthropologists (notably Loren Eiseley) have recently returned to the possibility of a relatively rapid development of the human race out of the Hominoids, and this possibility is not unreasonable when viewed in the light of language as the major distinguishing feature of the race. It is clear that greatly enlarged brain-capacity and the development of linguistic communication must have gone together, but there is no telling which came first; it is perfectly possible that command of language may have contributed to natural selection of those with larger brain-capacity. Language itself may have developed fairly rapidly as a human institution, once the basic step was taken, of developing duality and productivity; and this development may have been so rapid (relatively speaking) as to justify, at least in a figurative sense, the formulation of human creation as having taken place "in a single day" (as viewed *sub specie aeternitatis*).

In its methodology, linguistics is intermediate between the natural and the social sciences. In certain respects, the subject matter of linguistics—since it involves human behavior—is far more complicated, involves many more variables (especially the factor of meaning; cf. Chap. 39) and is much less predictable in detail than is that of any of the natural sciences. Due to these complexities, linguistics is not able to predict the future course of events either in detail with regard to any single language or in general with respect to human language as a whole (no one can tell what developments will take place in human communicative behavior in the next hundred thousand or half a million years). Hence linguistics is, in general, more comparable to a descriptive-historical science like geology than it is to a predictive one like physics or chemistry. Techniques of detailed measurement, especially mathematical or statistical, are in general not applicable in linguistics except on a fairly low level of counting the relative frequency of competing phenomena (cf. Chaps. 47, 66), and linguistics has little in common with mathematics. On the other hand, linguistics deals with the simplest subject matter of all the social sciences, specifically because it eliminates from its initial consideration (though not from its ultimate concern!) the factor of meaning, which is the principal concern of the social sciences in general. Meaning then returns at a later stage in linguistic analysis, after the functional units and their groupings have been determined; by serving as a model for procedure in this respect, linguistics can make a highly useful contribution to the methodology of the other social sciences.

NOTES

Encoding and decoding: Joos, 1948; Osgood and Sebeok, 1954.
Position of humans in world: Hockett, 1958, Chap. 64.
Development of mankind: Eiseley, 1960; Hockett and Ascher, 1964.

PART VI

THE USES OF LINGUISTICS

72

The Folklore of Language

In every culture, the people at large have widely diffused but erroneous notions concerning many matters about which they have no detailed or accurate knowledge, but think themselves competent to hold opinions. (Usually, the less competent a person is on any given topic, the more firmly held and unshakable are his notions.) Of this nature were the prescientific theories that the sun goes around the earth, that "nature abhors a vacuum," or that if a woman is frightened during pregnancy her child will be born deformed. Even notions of this type, which have been thoroughly discredited by scientific observation, still have a surprising number of adherents. In fields other than the natural sciences, folkloristic notions are still widely held. Human relations are the subject of many deeply entrenched superstitions, which it is most difficult to dethrone (especially when they are supported by vested interests of finance or prestige), e.g., that there is a necessary, inborn correlation between intelligence and physical race. In no field is there such an extensive and inaccurate folklore, prevalent among such wide circles of the public, as in matters of language. The misconceptions about language to which our society holds with such tenacity are, for the most part, relics of seventeenth-century absolutism and authoritarianism (cf. Chap. 62) and have become firmly entrenched in our schools. The paradoxical result is that the more educated a person is, the less accurate his or her notions with regard to language are likely to be. People with little or no formal education have far more open minds and are much more able to adopt a scientific attitude than are those who have acquired our society's traditional scholastic lore about language.

Probably the most widespread misconception that our society holds concerns the relation between writing and language. We learn to speak long before we are able to analyze what we do when we speak, and our attention is turned to language matters only when we come to deal with writing, at the age of five or six, well after the essential task of acquiring our linguistic structure is finished. Hence we learn, in school, only about letters and their combinations, and are taught to think of the latter as being "words" *par excellence.* One well-known *littérateur,* writing in an issue of a review devoted to children's books, said of his nephew: "This fall, Ronald will go to school and, for the first time, will come in contact with words." (What had Ronald been using to make himself understood before his sixth year—mute gestures?) We are taught in school to describe words only in terms of the letters with which they are written, and to think of sounds only as the way in which letters are "actualized" in speech. Of an accurate analysis and description of sounds, or even of the possibility of such (as set forth in our Chaps. 7–20), we are given no hint in school, and hence find it difficult or impossible to conceive of when introduced to it later. Even the shapes of the twenty-six letters of the Roman alphabet come to be regarded as virtually sacred; some persons have violently hostile emotional reactions on their first contact with graphic shapes like ŋ, ʃ or ʒ. The only technique we learn for distinguishing different sounds is the use of impressionistic (and virtually meaningless) adjectives modifying letter-names, e.g. "flat *a*," "broad *a*," "dark *l*," "hard *c*," and so forth. I was once told by an Australian that his fellow countrymen had great trouble with their *o*'s; it turned out that he was referring to their pronunciation of words like *now*, *cow* and *brow*.

Our schools, regarding written words as the only constituent elements of language, place a horrendous over-emphasis on spelling, from the very outset of every child's training. In accordance with the tyrannical outlook of our inherited linguistic absolutism, every word is regarded as having one and only one "correct" spelling, any variation from which is regarded as completely inadmissible. There are social, as well as pseudo-intellectual, reasons for this intolerance of variations; as the economist and sociologist Thorstein Veblen observed at the beginning of the twentieth century:

> As felicitous an instance of futile classicism as can well be found, outside of the Far East, is the conventional spelling of the English language. A breach of the proprieties in spelling is extremely annoying and will discredit any writer in the eyes of all persons who are possessed of a developed sense of the true and beautiful. English orthography satisfies all the requirements of the canons of reputability, under the law of conspicuous waste. It is archaic, cumbrous, and ineffective; its acquisition consumes much time and effort; failure to acquire it is easy of detection. Therefore it is the first and readiest test of reputability in learning, and conformity to its ritual is indispensable to a blameless scholastic life.
> —*Theory of the Leisure Class*, Chap. 14

If the spelling of a word does not represent its pronunciation as accurately as another, less accepted spelling might do, our folklore calls the former "correct" and the latter "phonetic." By a natural semantic transition, *phonetic*, as applied to the spelling of English, comes to mean "inaccurate", e.g., *roat* for *wrote* or *nite* for *night*. When the term *phonetic* is then applied to pronunciation in the sense of "incorrect," it produces such gems as the reference which a certain writer on Pidgin English made to "phonetic pronunciation," which turned out to be a reference to such approximations as *esker vooz avay* (his spelling) for French /eskəvuzaveˆ/ *est-ce que vous avez?* "Do you have?". It also produces the widespread description of languages like Italian or Spanish as "phonetic languages" (yet since every language is by definition spoken, how can any language be anything but phonetic?). What the users of such an expression mean, of course, is that the orthographies of Italian or Spanish are closer to their respective phonologies than is the spelling-system of English to the sounds it is intended to represent.

Spelling is only one of the many respects in which our Western European culture has an extensively developed folklore about "correctness." Any given linguistic manifestation can be condemned as "incorrect," "bad English," "corrupt" or the likes, if it is displeasing for one reason or another to somebody. The language is thought to have an ideal form, embodied in "authoritative" grammars and dictionaries, whose prescriptions have the force of law, and any departure from these "laws" is thought to constitute a breach of custom virtually equivalent to sin, even if not to crime in the legal sense of the term. Hence some self appointed "defenders of the language" have not hesitated to condemn, say, Shakespeare or Milton for their supposed "mistakes" such as split infinitives or the *it is me* construction, saying "even the greatest authors make these mistakes." The adjective *authoritative* apparently has such magic selling-power as to cause advertisers to use it to describe even dictionaries and grammars which specifically reject authoritarianism, and, if a dictionary's editors change from a prescriptive to a descriptive approach, ignorant and incompetent critics behave as if there were a conspiracy to commit rape upon the body of the English language.

Since language is thought of only in terms of writing, it is widely held that the languages for which no writing system exists must of necessity be in some way or other "primitive," "incomplete" or in some other way inferior to "languages of civilization." Casual conversations on pidginized and creolized languages (Chaps. 64, 65) inevitably lead up, eventually, to questions as to whether such languages are written or have a literature (as if either of these points were in any way relevant to their nature as languages). To remedy these defects of a "primitive" language, all that is thought necessary is to devise some system of writing for them, preferably as close to English spelling as possible. One United States senator was very proud of having invented a "universal alphabet" which would make it possible for users of English to learn any language on earth, even Chinese, in only a few days. An even more serious obstacle to the improvement of "primitive" languages, however, is said to be their lack of vocabulary, since, according to the notion given currency by F. Max Müller in the nineteenth century (p. 13), they have at the most three hundred words in their lexicon, and their speakers have to eke out their limited vocabularies with grunts (*Ugh! How!*) and gestures. The only way to remedy these deficiencies, it is thought, is to enrich them with words taken over from English or some other "civilized" language, of course spelled with all the inconsistencies and confusions of the orthography of the source language. Thus, /kawnsəl/ is taken over into Neo-Melanesian with the spelling *council* rather than *kaunsel*. The latter spelling is more rational and the former causes confusion to the native (who is tempted to read it off as /sonsɪl/ or /sawnsɪl/), but these considerations are brushed aside as less important than fidelity to the "real" spelling of the word, because *kaunsel* would be more "phonetic" and hence of course "incorrect," "wrong," and virtually sinful.

Foreigners, when they learn a language, normally learn it from prescriptive grammar-books (and, of course, a certain amount of prescription is inevitable as part of the process of teaching the new language; cf. Chap. 77). The stage of the language presented in such grammar-books is usually from fifty to a hundred years behind the times; as such, it has the prestige, with the native speaker of the language, that often accrues to phenomena which are out-of-date, useless, a hindrance rather than a help to true understanding, and are therefore "classical." Foreigners who learn such an archaic form of the language may not be able to understand what they hear or make themselves understood very easily, and their pronunciation may be very unlike that of a native, but they are often complimented on the "purity" of their language, and told that they speak "better _____ (English, French, etc.) than the natives." Anyone who teaches a foreigner the current, normal, everyday, useful form of a language (e.g., French /japatkwa/ instead of /ilniapa'dəkwa/ *il n'y a pas de quoi* "you're welcome") is accused of "corrupting" the language and of teaching the foreigners "bad _____ (French, English, or whatever the language may be)."

The notion of "corruption," as applied to language, is extremely widespread. Children's speech and that of the lower classes has, ever since the Renaissance, been considered a "deformation" of the language as it "ought" to be. The change of language in the course of time is also thought of almost exclusively in terms of "debasement"; we are often told that a given form, e.g., English *goodbye* or French /u/ *août* "August", is a "corruption" of an earlier stage such as *God be with you* or Latin *Augustum*. This notion is a carry-over from the philological study of manuscripts and from the history of literature. As applied to the transmission of manuscripts, the term *corruption* has a specific, objective meaning, i.e., the inaccurate copying of one or more elements (letters, words) in a passage, and the confusion and misinterpretation which may result therefrom. In literature, it is generally held that some epochs show a "lower" level of achievement and taste than do others (e.g., Late Latin literature in contrast with that of the Golden or even of the Silver Age), and hence that both the content and the style of authors writing in periods of decline may be called "corrupt." However, none of these considerations are applicable to language: one phoneme, morpheme or construction, in successive stages of a language, is just as good as another, and to praise or condemn a language because of the literature written in it is like saying "The stone they used for building in the Middle Ages was much better than that used nowadays; look at the wonderful cathedrals they built then, and at the frightful modernistic architecture we have now" (or vice-versa).

How fantastically mistaken all these folkloristic notions are, will be evident to anyone who has read and understood our exposition of linguistics up to this point. Their continued prevalence, however, has caused and is causing our society a tremendous waste of time, effort, and money. Our misapprehensions concerning the relation of writing to language cause reading and spelling to be taught with incredible inefficiency in our schools; similarly, because of our folklore about the structure of language, grammar and usage are taught with equal incompetence. It has been estimated that about two

years of every American school child's life are wasted because of the ineffective teaching he receives in English; this accounts, to a large extent, for the
two-year lag which our children show in their education as compared with
those of virtually every other country. Foreign languages, despite some recent
advances, are generally taught so poorly as to represent an almost total waste
of time. Lack of knowledge of the facts of language leads some idealists down
the garden path, to the utopistic dream of an international language; and, in
practical matters concerning government and official policy on linguistic
questions, our legislators are so ignorant as to be utterly unable to deal with
the problems which arise. How we can most effectively deal with these and
related matters will be discussed in the next seven chapters.

NOTES

Widespread misconceptions: Bloomfield, 1944, an article which represents the reaction
of a scientist when badgered beyond endurance by ignorance and incompetence.

73

Reading

As WE SAW in Chap. 44, our Western European writing systems are essentially alphabetic; English orthography has, however, a number of instances (of the type of *meat, mete* or of *light*) in which the correlation between grapheme and phoneme is loose. Our orthography has only a very few elements in which graphic shapes stand directly for morphemes, without any reference to the phonemes involved, e.g., *lb.* for /páwnd/ "pound" or the ampersand *&* for /ǽnd/ "and". Hence the main problem, in teaching anyone to read the orthography of a European language, is, first of all, to establish as much correlation as possible between graphemes and the phonemes for which they stand. In terms of the distinction established on p. 264, the *linguistic* meaning of a written word must be learned first, without any necessary reference to the *real-life* meaning of the word as spoken. The learning of this latter is a separate problem, which has nothing to do with learning to read off the letters with which the phonemes are represented.

In the elementary (or "developmental" or "basal") readers used in the British Commonwealth and in American schools in the nineteenth century (e.g., the famous McGuffey series), this problem was recognized and met reasonably successfully. The major technique used was that of presenting words to be learned by "families," i.e., groups which rhymed, having the same graphemes to represent the same phonemes (e.g., *can, Dan, fan, man, Nan; fight, light, night, sight*). Even though they were not necessarily presented to the learner in the exact order of their difficulty, these "word-families" helped him to recognize the similarities between the spellings of words, and gave him a basis for interpreting unfamiliar spellings on the basis of those already learned. A child who had learned the pronunciation of *camp, damp, lamp* and *tamp* would have no difficulty in reading off such an unfamiliar word as *gamp* or a name like *Hamp*. On the other hand, a person who has learned to read by this method can on occasion, especially if he is slow-witted or has little experience of the world of real-life meanings, fail to develop beyond a fairly slow rate of reading, needing to read out loud or *sotto voce* in order to grasp the real-life meaning of what he is looking at.

Observing the slowness of reading manifested by some learners—whose number grew as education was extended to the totality of the American population—and desiring to increase the speed of reading (a laudable aim in itself), educationists sought, in the 1920's and '30's, to find new ways of teaching elementary reading. Unfortunately, they knew nothing of the relation of writing to language, and hence nothing of the problem which they were trying to solve. The "reading specialists" saw that adults who read rapidly do so, not by interpreting the spelling of each word one after the other, but by taking in whole words or sequences of words at a time. From this observation, the erroneous conclusion was drawn that "rapid readers" must proceed directly from the written word to its real-life meaning (the misconception portrayed in our Fig. 20, p. 263), not realizing that there are two steps, instead of one, involved: understanding first the linguistic meaning of the written word, and then the real-life meaning of the word itself (as shown in Fig. 21, p. 264). The self-styled "reading experts" also thought that it is possible to read in true silence, deriving "ideas" directly from the written word without going through the process of speech at all. In reaching this erroneous conclusion, they neglected the all-important phenomenon of subvocalization or nonexternalized speech (pp. 16–17), without which no reading or writing at all ever takes place. What actually happens in rapid reading is that the reader moves his or her eyes very fast over the written or printed page and "reads" (normally with subvocalization) only the high spots, supplying the rest by extrapolation. Naturally, this process is successful only insofar as the reader is already familiar with the subject matter and is able to supply what is likely to have come in between the points which he has perceived by direct reading; it is much less successful with material whose subject matter is unfamiliar (e.g., advanced or technical exposés of difficult topics) or which does not follow predetermined patterns (e.g., modernistic poetry).

Not knowing these elementary facts, and thinking that children could be taught from the beginning to read as rapidly as adults, the "reading experts" developed a method known variously as the "word-method," the "global method" or the "see-and-say" technique. This involved presenting the first-grader with a series of books, each one containing only a very few words, chosen on the basis of their supposed frequency and interest in the life of American six-year-olds, without any consideration of the ease or difficulty presented by the degree of correspondence between grapheme and phoneme. Such texts therefore jumble together, haphazardly, spellings which are regular (*can* or *met*), semi-irregular (*Pete, meat; bear, bare*) and quite irregular (*laugh, money*). The writers of these books start from the unjustified assumption that, since some English spellings are illogical, the entire system is illogical, and that there are no similarities at all between the spellings of any words. The child is expected to learn the spelling of each word as if it had a purely morphemic referent, as Chinese characters do (pp. 268–269). To take the place of learning by analogy, as it is used in the "word-family" method, the constructors of these texts rely on the brute force of repetition. The slogan of the "see-and-say" method was "reading for meaning" (the real-life meaning, of course, since the existence of the linguistic meaning of writing went unrecognized); the real-life meaning is given by copious illustrations occupying half or more of each page. The resultant texts contain fascinating reading material like "Oh, oh! Jane, Jane! Look, look! Funny, funny Spot! Oh, look! Oh, Spot! Oh, Jane! Oh, look, Jane, Spot! Oh, oh, oh, look, Jane, look, Spot, look, look, Jane, Spot, Jane, Spot, look . . . !" with pictures presenting a conventionalized version of middle-class American suburbia in its most insipid form.

To oppose to the "word-method," all that the nineteen-twenties and 'thirties had to offer was an attempt to correlate letter and sound in an approach known as "phonics." The basis of this method was essentially valid, in that it did recognize the existence of a dependence of grapheme upon phoneme (although not explicitly in those terms). Unfortunately, however, the proponents of the "phonic" method were often ignorant of the elementary facts of phonetics (to say nothing of phonemics), and confused the issue by trying to teach the six-year-old to pronounce the sounds of his native language, which he has already learned how to do well before entering school. Writers of "see-and-say" texts would often pay lip-service to "phonics" by including a few nearly useless exercises on elementary relations between letters and sounds, usually only in word-initial position. There arose and became widespread among the general public an unfortunate polarization of the problems in terms of "word-method" versus "phonics," and all attempts to correlate graphemes and phonemes (no matter whether well or ill founded in linguistic analysis) came to be lumped together under the heading of "phonics."

The results of the dominant "word-method," as they spread to virtually all American elementary education by the nineteen-fifties, were completely disastrous. There grew up a generation of Americans who had either not learned to read effectively or, if they had learned, had done so in spite of, not because of, the way they had been taught. The educationists' misguided attempts at teaching rapid reading from the first grade onwards had produced only the ability to skim a text superficially and guess wildly at its possible contents, thus depriving the learner of the ability to read and understand any text thoroughly, even the simplest. Still worse, children were systematically taught to disregard any possible correlation between sounds and letters, so that at a later stage they found it difficult to realize that such a correlation exists. Consequently, the child taught in this way was deprived of much-needed training in analogical reasoning, such as is involved, say, in interpreting *ban* on the basis of a previous knowledge of *bat*, *cat*, and *can*. An ever-increasing number of children have come to have difficulty with reading and hence also with learning all subjects that are taught through printed texts. An entire problem of teaching "remedial reading" has arisen, and the educationists have made extensive studies of the supposed causes of retardation in reading—emotional disturbance, family maladjustment, etc.—without ever realizing the existence of the central problem of establishing in the learner a relation between grapheme and phoneme. It has been remarked that, with regard to problems of reading, the educationists developed marvelous peripheral vision and a tremendous blind spot at the center.

In the middle nineteen-fifties, protests against this increasingly unsatisfactory state of affairs began to be heard, especially with the publication of

Rudolf Flesch's *Why Johnny Can't Read* (1955) and the ensuing controversy. This provocative book sparked a storm of protest against the prevailing unscientific way of teaching reading, but in a few years the outcry died down and Flesch's book had little permanent effect. This was largely because professional educationists and publishers, with many millions of dollars invested in existing series of readers, conducted a tremendous anti-Flesch campaign to convince the public that his attacks on current teaching methods were unfounded. In doing so, Flesch's opponents dragged in such irrelevancies as the question of whether the "Johnny" of Flesch's book was a real or a fictional child, and insinuated that to question the efficiency of our teaching of reading was to cast doubt on the validity of democratic education. On the specific question of teaching-techniques, they countered his basically sound arguments with unsound ones, e.g., the logical fallacy that written words are perceived as units by adult readers and should therefore be taught as such to child learners. Unfortunately, the general public did not have enough linguistic knowledge to detect the unsoundness of such arguments, and Flesch, although his negative criticisms were quite valid, had not supplied his readers with enough linguistic theory to evaluate his opponents' replies. Consequently, the Flesch revolt fizzled out and proved to be a kind of Wat Tyler's rebellion, in which an embattled group with a very just grievance and with right on their side were defeated by forces that had both greater material power and more tactical skill. Other publications had even less success in breaking the hold of the multimillion dollar publishing interests in the field.

A satisfactory reading text—of which several have been made available commercially—must be based on our knowledge of the relation between grapheme and phoneme. Since, as we saw in Chap. 45 (pp. 270–273), there is a gradation in the fit between sound and spelling in English orthography, this gradation must be taken into account in presenting the material to be learned, in accordance with the fundamental principle of passing from what is easier to learn to what is more difficult. Hence the first part of the text will contain almost nothing but words with completely regular spellings (*bat, cat, fat; Ben, den, fen, men; but, cut, nut;* etc.); a few irregularly spelled words like *a, the, is* can be introduced to facilitate the construction of connected text, but they must be kept to a minimum. Only after the regularly spelt words have been presented, should the semi-irregulars (*date, fate, gate; bait, gait, wait*) be introduced; and only after these, in the last sections, the real irregulars (*boatswain* /bósən/, or *fuchsia* /fjúʃə/). Whether each of these three major types of words is presented by word-families (as is done in some books), or in a less structured order (as in others) is a minor question; the most important problem is to present the three levels of difficulty in successive stages, not all at once.

At this point, it is often objected that "meaning is being left out of account." Such an objection of course loses sight of the already-mentioned fundamental distinction between linguistic and real-life meaning. All that a linguistically-oriented elementary reading text is doing is to take into account the primacy, AT THIS STAGE, of linguistic over real-life meaning when it comes to learning to read. Linguistic meanings—the phonemic referents of the sequences of graphemes—come first, and no harm is done even if a child learns to read off some words (e.g., *ramp*, *hack*, *jag*) whose real-life meaning he may not know. Educationists like to sneer at children who have acquired enough mastery of our spelling-system to read off words without knowing their real-life meaning, and term such children "word-callers." In fact, however, such a child is, in his understanding of the principles of our orthography, far ahead of others who are baffled by any word (no matter how regularly spelled) which they have not already met in a text. The ultimate test of any method of teaching reading is whether the learners can deal with nonsense-syllables; if a child cannot read off *glump*, *trib*, or *donk*, not caring whether these syllables have a real-life meaning or not, the method has failed.

Since the only immediate problem in teaching reading is to establish the grapheme-phoneme correspondences, all distracting elements should be kept out of the material used. Any kind of picture or other illustration, especially, will never help and can often hinder the learning process. If a picture of a vessel is shown above the word *ship*, there is always the likelihood that the beginner will interpret the picture and the four letters as standing for /bót/ *boat* rather than for /ʃíp/—in which case, nothing has been learned, and the important correspondences between *sh* and /ʃ/, *i* and /ɪ/, and *p* and /p/ have not only not been established, but rendered less likely to be established than before. A satisfactory elementary reading text should never have pictures or illustrations of any kind; on the other hand, special devices for emphasizing irregularities (e.g., special colors for silent letters or for those used in unusual values) might well be incorporated, at least at the initial stages. In programmed instruction for use in "teaching-machines," use might well be made of recorded tapes, with spaces left for the learner to repeat out loud the words whose spelling he sees in front of him and whose sound he hears coming over the tape recorder at the same time.

From what has been said, it should be evident that learning to read is a special aspect of the English-speaking child's schooling, which should be kept carefully separated from the rest of the learning-process at the elementary level, because it must be programmed in a different way from the rest of the subject-matter—specifically in order that it may be accomplished as rapidly as possible and integrated as effectively as possible at a slightly later stage (from, say, the third grade onwards). For this reason, reading and spelling should never be introduced in connection with so-called "global experience" programs (in which the children visit, say, a bakery or a grocery-store and report on their experiences), because there is every likelihood that the words which come up in such connections will not fit at all into the orthographical patterns which must form the basis for quick and effective learning of reading. However, if reading is taught independently of other topics and on a linguistically sound basis, the essentials of our orthography can be mastered by any child of normal intelligence within a maximum of two years, and from the third grade onwards the reading-matter can be on a far more advanced level than it is customary to assign at present.

NOTES

The bibliography on methods of teaching reading is enormous, but very few of the educationists' publications on the topic take any of the findings of linguistics into account. For general references on the relation of linguistics to the teaching of reading, cf. Bloomfield and Barnhart, 1961; Fries, 1963; Hall, 1961; Smith, 1963.

Sub-vocalization: Edfeldt, 1960.

74

Spelling

IN LEARNING to read, a child is acquiring an essentially passive skill, the interpretation of graphemes in terms of the phonemes that he already knows (though unanalytically) and uses as part of his normal native speech. Learning to spell involves an active skill: the learner must be able to start from the way he speaks and write down the corresponding letters. Since passive comprehension and response to a problem normally precedes the acquisition of active habits, it is reasonable that learning to read should precede learning to spell. On the other hand, there is no need for postponing active drill on spelling until full completion of learning to read; the analysis and practice of spelling any given word or word-family can come immediately after learning to read it. In other words, learning to read and learning to spell can proceed nearly *pari passu*, with the latter following the former with only a slight delay.

Reading can be learned with a minimum of overt analysis, since all that is necessary is for the learner to respond to what he sees written or printed. If spelling is to be learned in a wholly unanalytical way, however, much time has to be wasted in brute memorization, especially of exceptions and alternate types of graphic representation (e.g., *boat*, not *bote; wrote*, not *roat*). It is therefore very desirable that the teacher have enough knowledge of the phonology of the language whose spelling is being taught—and also of the local dialect of the learners, where this differs from the standard—in order to give them as many helpful hints as possible concerning the principles of spelling, and especially how far these principles may be applied. Such a teacher, for instance, would not berate a child for spelling /mɔ́ni/ as *munny*, on the analogy of /fɔ́ni/ *funny*; on the contrary, she would praise him for being intelligent enough to see the analogy, and would then point out the existence and nature of the exception. Of course, in order to do this, the teacher herself would have to know the regularities and the exceptions of English spelling, and would have to be able to explain them in simple, comprehensible language to a class of second- or third-graders.

There then arises the problem of what to do with mistakes in spelling, which may range all the way from the omission of "silent" letters (e.g., *dout* for *doubt*), to use of alternate means of graphic representation of phonemes (*procede* for *proceed*), to misrepresentation of phonemes (*sedimental* for *sentimental*). The tendency of teachers of spelling is to think of all mistakes as being equally bad, no matter to which of these types they belong, and hence to consider, say, *dout* for *doubt* as being just as "wrong" as *sedimental* for *sentimental*. It should be obvious, however, that there are degrees of difference in the "wrongness" of spelling. The purpose of a spelling is, after all, to signal a given pronunciation and, on occasion, a given morpheme as opposed to another. We can set up a series of degrees of harmfulness in spelling errors, with at least the three following levels:

1. Those not creating confusion as to the phonemes or morphemes signalled, e.g., *dout* for *doubt* or *fait* for *fate*: venial, hardly harmful.

2. Those not creating confusion as to the phonemes, but signalling the wrong morpheme, as in *bare* for *bear* (*In Yellowstone we saw a grizzly bare*) or *feat* for *feet* (*he washed his feat with soap*): not venial, but more likely to cause confusion when the word is cited in isolation than when it is used in context. Sometimes, of course, the context can be ambiguous, as when a certain town in Indiana advertised that it had "excellent home sights."

3. Those which signal the wrong phonemes and hence inevitably either a nonexistent morpheme or the wrong one, e.g. *bology* for *biology* or *sedimental* for *sentimental*. These misspellings are the most harmful, since they are likely to cause real confusion on the part of the reader.

The essentials and the difficulties of our orthography can best be taught for spelling in the same way as for reading (cf. the previous chapter), with a carefully organized progression from regular to semi-irregular to wholly irregular. Many state or city boards of education provide lists of words whose spellings are to be mastered by a given stage (sixth grade, seventh grade, etc.). These lists are normally constructed in connection with the subject-matter being studied at the particular level involved, and hence on a purely semantic basis, with no reference at all to the structural problems involved. Thus, we may find *county, court, room, judge, jury, witness, box*, etc., with some words that present little or no problems (like *room*) and others of much greater difficulty (like *judge*), all jumbled together. If lists of this kind were replaced by others arranged according to structural principles, a very large part of the spelling-difficulties which now beset students even at the high-school or college level could be eliminated.

Much of the trouble associated with spelling—which bothers even a great many adults in the English-speaking world—is to be traced to our culture's overinsistence on absolute uniformity at all costs. This is a relatively recent development, dating only from the last two hundred or so years. As mentioned on p. 8, in earlier times there was considerably more latitude in the use of alternate spellings such as *smoak* or *smoke*, *cloak* or *cloke*, *cloathes* or *clothes*. No harm was done by the existence of such alternatives, nor would it be done at present. The current insistence on complete orthographical uniformity comes from several sources. One is social, in a desire to separate the sheep from the goats by the facile criterion of "correctness" in spelling (cf. our quotation from Veblen on p. 424). One is psychological, in the sadistic desire of some purists to enforce uniformity. Another is scholastic, in the desire of many teachers to have something which can easily be marked "right" or "wrong," with reference to an absolute authority, the dictionary. Still another is economic, in the desire of unscrupulous dictionary-makers to have something to sell a gullible public as "authoritative," and the need of secretarial and similar schools to have something to teach. By now, there are substantial vested financial interests in maintaining public belief in a unitary, sacrosanct spelling for each word in the language—a situation which is far from being functionally necessary or even beneficial.

At this point, there always arises the question of spelling-reform: would it not be better to replace the present inconsistent, confusing, and wasteful spelling of English by a rational, phonemically-based orthography? Such a spelling-reform, it is argued, would save even more years of school-children's lives, would remove most (but, as we shall see, not absolutely all) of our spelling-problems, and would eliminate the anxiety which now besets many of us because, even as adults, we still cannot spell correctly. This is an old proposal, and has attracted the enthusiasm of many. The late George Bernard Shaw, for instance, first came in contact with the problem of spelling-reform in the late nineteenth century (especially through the phonetician Henry Sweet, some of whose traits he incorporated in Henry Higgins in *Pygmalion*) and became a lifelong advocate of reformed spelling, eventually leaving a large part of his fortune to further its cause.

Here, we must distinguish sharply between partial and complete spelling-reform. Many—perhaps most—proposals for spelling-reform envisage only the removal of certain inconsistences—such as the use of the "silent letters" *gh* in *light, night, fight* and the like, or of *s* in *aisle*—but not the elimination of all inconsistencies or alternative spellings. A certain Midwest newspaper once began a campaign for what it called "reformed spelling," writing *lite, nite, fite,* and *aile* (for *aisle*), without its editors realizing that they had indeed removed certain inconsistencies but had simply introduced others in their place (the representation of /aj/ by *ai* in *aile,* instead of by *igh* in *fight,* etc.). This type of incomplete reform is of no use, since it does not go to the root of the problem, i.e., it does nothing really effective towards reducing the number of inconsistencies that beset our orthography; at the same time, it serves only to irritate and render hostile those who are emotionally attached to the present spelling-system.

A thorough-going reform would involve making English spelling completely phonemic. This could be done, by using the IPA alphabet or any other set of characters which were found most useful and acceptable. Such orthographies have been devised, e.g., the one proposed by Bernard Bloch and Martin Joos, and exemplified below:

Az Wijk haz pointed aut, wön wei tu introdiús a radikali niu speleng reméinz oupen íven tudéi: it kan bi iuzd alóun in dhe ërliest skûleng, sjifteng tu tradisjonal speleng after dhe habits ov fliuent rîdeng hav bin estáblisjt, sei a thërd ov dhe wei thrû dhe sekond jir.

Such a radical reform would at first arouse intense hostility in most of us who have painfully and with great difficulty acquired the habits of traditional spelling. But later generations, once they had acquired it from the outset, and without any emotional attachment to an older system, would take to it like ducks to water, and the whole spelling-problem would have disappeared.

However, one problem would have to be recognized and met in one way or another; that of regional variations in standard speech. How would we represent, say, the three words which we now spell *marry*, *merry*, and *Mary?* People east of the Alleghenies have three different vowel phonemes in these three words: /mǽri/, /méri/, and /méri/ respectively; Mid-Westerners, on the other hand, neutralize the contrast of /ǽ/, /ɛ́/ and /é/ before /r/, and use only one vowel in all three of these words, making them all /méri/. We would have to adopt and teach one of two attitudes: either taking one particular regional variety and basing our new spelling on that—preferably the variety which made the greatest number of distinctions—or else allowing for a variation in spelling to correspond to the variation in speech-patterns. The latter procedure would definitely be more realistic and more scientific; if we based our completely reformed spelling on one particular variety of speech, people who used a different variety would find such a spelling unrealistic and artificial, and we would be back where we started. Recognizing regional varieties in spelling as well as in speech would, it is true, require more attentiveness to what we read, and would deprive us of the convenience of having a single graphic representation to cover divergent pronunciations. But it would be more in accord with the facts, and would force us to recognize the existence and nature of linguistic differences far more than we do now.

The whole question is somewhat academic, anyhow; such a radically reformed spelling for English would be highly desirable, but at the present time it is a quite unattainable goal. The obstacles are not linguistic in nature, but political, economic and cultural. To put such a reform across, and to reduce the transitional difficulties and dislocations to a minimum, would take a far more centralized political system than we have or want to have in the United States. It could be done by governmental order in some such country as Russia, or even France and Italy, where the central government's say-so counts for much more both in the school-system and out of it, and where people are willing to follow an official ukase of this sort. It was done in Turkey in the 1920's, under the dictator Kemal Atatürk, when the Roman alphabet was substituted for the older Arabic writing. In the United States, with its loose organization of school systems, with control of the schools in the hands of individual local boards, and with Americans' normal attitude of distrust and rebellion against centralized authority and orders coming from above, it just could not be put across by the fiat of the central government. On the other hand, any other than authoritarian means would be quite ineffective; even if people could be persuaded of its worth (an almost impossible task in the present stage of the English-speaking public's knowledge concerning linguistic matters), it would take so long to adopt that the language would have changed and the reform would be out of date even before it was fully adopted.

There are also economic and cultural factors standing in the way of a really thoroughgoing spelling reform. Even aside from the existence of vested financial interests in journalism and the book trade, the trouble involved in reprinting all our books would be enormous, and the expense (even with governmental subsidy) staggering. Such a complete change in orthography would virtually wipe out the continuity of our present-day culture with that of the past—a continuity which is already gravely threatened from many other sides, but which is hardly to be rejected out-of-hand. A great many important, but not popular, books might go unreprinted and fall into undeserved oblivion; within fifty years, everything that is now in print would be as obsolete and unreadable as the English of Chaucer's time is to us. The gain in convenience and efficiency would be at least fully balanced (and in many people's view far outweighed) by the cultural loss which a radical spelling reform would entail.

We are faced with a paradoxical situation, from which, in the present state of affairs, there seems to be no escape. Our spelling system was crystallized in its present form in the mid-eighteenth century, with a host of irregularities which were specifically designed to make it difficult and inaccessible to those without the leisure and upper-class standing which were then necessary in order to receive the requisite education. Irrational use of alternations such as *oa* and *o* . . . *e* for /o/ or *ee*, *ea* and *e* . . . *e* for /i/, etc., demanded the availability of time to waste on learning them, and etymological spellings such as *debt* or *damn* called for a knowledge of Latin and Greek in order to write them correctly. In our modern civilization, however, we are forced (for the reasons set forth in the immediately preceding paragraphs) to continue the use of this wasteful system, because in changing it we would stand to lose more than we would gain; but we have to teach it as effectively as we can to the totality of our population. The only way out of this dilemma is to abandon all methods of teaching reading and spelling that are not in line with the facts of language and of the relation of writing thereto, and to place our teaching henceforth on a sound, linguistically-oriented basis.

NOTES

Spelling reform: Joos, 1960.
Spellers based on linguistic analysis: F. A. Hall, 1962; Hall and Brenes, 1960.

75

Grammar

OF ALL THE SUBJECTS we normally study in school, "grammar" is perhaps that which is least loved; in many people, as a result of their youthful experiences, the very word *grammar* arouses strongly hostile emotional reactions, so that it is often avoided by textbook-writers who wish to remain in public favor. This aura of antagonism attendant on the term *grammar* is the inevitable result of the confused and incompetent way in which the subject is usually presented. As pointed out in Chap. 21, our culture by now uses *grammar* in a number of different senses, all of which (except, of course, the scientific analysis of language and the presentation of its structure) are jumbled together without rhyme or reason in our schools. The prescriptive, authoritarian approach is still almost universally dominant, and the schools teach (or try to teach) our children that *he ain't*, *it's me*, or *like* used as a "conjunction" (e.g., in ——— *tastes good like a cigarette should*) are "bad grammar," "not English," or the likes. Any child with even the most ordinary intelligence can see that what goes under the name of "grammar" has very little relevance to what is actually said in acceptable speech or written in literary English, and hence very many persons in our society have a fully justified contempt for this subject, since they have found it quite useless in any real-life connection.

As a result, some educational reforms have involved the abandonment of grammatical instruction, and especially the products of "progressive" schools have been sent forth without much or any knowledge of traditional grammar. This type of remedy has proved, however, to be worse than the cure, in that it throws the baby out with the bath. A person who goes through school without learning any way of analyzing language will pass the optimum point for acquiring a knowledge of his or her own linguistic structure (which is between ten and fourteen years of age) and will come to maturity with no understanding of either the facts or the need for knowing them. This gap in one's education can be very harmful both in dealing with one's own language and in trying to learn another. It can at least be argued that the total absence of any grammatical instruction is even worse than the traditional type of "grammar," since the person who has received instruction in the latter at least knows that a way of analyzing language exists, and he or she has a basis (no matter how erroneous) for eventual learning of a more adequate approach and analysis.

An argument of this type can go on, however, until Doomsday, without any definitive solution being reached. When this type of dead center is reached in a discussion, it is normally because the question itself has been posed in inadequate terms. If the present teaching of grammar is hopelessly unsatisfactory, the only effective remedy is, not to abolish it, but to reform it so as to make it useful and helpful to ordinary people in their everyday use of language. In order to do this, the sixth and last type of grammar mentioned on p. 125 must be brought into play, i.e. the study of language must be placed on a scientific basis from the beginning of the child's contact with it in the fourth or fifth grade. This calls, of course, for a staff of English teachers who know something about the language they are supposed to be teaching, i.e., who have had adequate training in linguistic analysis. At the moment of writing (1963) this would seem to be a Utopian ideal, but it is to be hoped that the latter part of the twentieth century will see a marked rise in the level of linguistic competence on the part of teachers of English.

An adequate program for teaching English structural grammar in elementary schools would involve, first of all, making our children aware of what they do when they speak, as opposed to what they do when they write. Any normal child is capable of understanding the nature of the sounds which he or she makes, when they are explained accurately in a clear, rational way and without needlessly technical terminology. The important thing is that children should first realize the existence of functional units of sound in their speech, as opposed to and differentiated from the units of graphic shape they use in writing. They can be brought to this realization at the third- or fourth-grade level; a more detailed analysis of their phonologic structure can be given to seventh- or eighth-graders. After all, the terms *phoneme* and *phonemic* are no harder to learn than are *atom* or *element*, and even *fricative*, *alveolar* or *voiceless* are no more difficult than terms of elementary chemistry such as *ferrous*, *ferric*, *oxide*, *sulphate*. If (as has been demonstrated in experimental programs) it is possible to teach set-theory in mathematics to fifth-graders, the elements of phonemic theory (which is certainly no harder) should offer no difficulty to pupils in the seventh and eighth grades. Even a phonemic transcription—hard though it may be for older persons to learn and use consistently once they have become set in the habits of English orthography— would not be at all difficult for youngsters who are still linguistically open-minded and not "sot in their ways."

Special care must be used in analyzing the prosodic aspects of our speech, and in calling the learner's attention to the ways in which they are and are not represented in our system of punctuation. Many of the difficulties which writers of English (on all levels, from school children to adults) have with punctuation are due to insufficient realization of its relation to intonation and juncture. A perennial problem like that of the use of commas with "nonrestrictive clauses" can easily be solved, once it is realized that punctuation marks represent primarily pause-points in intonation. In such a case as this, both teachers and pupils need to learn how to keep their ears open and listen to their own speech, and to punctuate accordingly. Similarly with the use of hyphens in compounds: as soon as it is realized that a hyphen represents a "plus-juncture" /+/ in such words as *speech-sound, pause-point, night-rate*, most of the problems connected with using the hyphen disappear. If teachers and pupils can learn to observe their own behavior with respect to supra-segmental (prosodic) features of phonology, a great deal of futile running to the dictionary for "authoritative" pronouncements on when to use hyphens, etc., can be avoided.

The same considerations apply to the study of morphology and syntax. The fourth grade is not too soon to begin a presentation of the elements of morphology; but the old definitions of the parts of speech, based on pseudo-philosophical concepts, must be replaced by new descriptions in terms of their actual functioning in everyday speech, which the learner can observe and understand for himself. Thus, we will no longer tell our children that "a noun is the name of a person, place or thing," but that it is "any word that you can put *the* in front of," like *name, house, man, electricity* or *justice*; not that "a verb indicates action or a state of being," but that it is "a word that shows, in its variation in form, a difference between present and past (*eat—ate, run—ran, organize—organized*) or that behaves in the same way as one of these (*put, cut*)." Likewise, the essential concepts of syntactic structure can be taught with reference to the linguistic behavior of their elements. For instance, the subject and object of a sentence are most easily presented by starting from syntactic frames in which they are clearly marked morphologically (*he sees him, they hate her, we like them*, etc.) and the nonmorphologically-marked occurrence of subjects and objects (*John sees Mary, the Turks hate the Armenians*) can then follow on the analogy of the first type.

For the analysis of language, even on the elementary-school level, technical terms are just as necessary as they are for analyzing any other topic. There is no need of resorting to simple-minded, pseudo-elementary terms like "thing-word" for *noun* or "action-word" for *verb*; such presumed simplifications normally define their referents no better and, in many instances, create more problems than the supposedly more difficult terms which they are intended to replace. We need not be afraid either of retaining old-established technical terms or of introducing new ones in case the older ones are no longer adequate or need to be supplemented. Thus, we need not hesitate to bring in such a term as "pro-verb" (with the pronunciation /pró+vᵊrb/ and the spelling with a hyphen, as distinguished from *proverb* /právᵊrb/), for the use of, say, *do* to replace another verb, e.g. in *You really like rhubarb?—Yes, I do.* Here again, conservative teachers, using their own reactions as a basis for judgment, tend to over-estimate the extent of student resistance to new terminology; for a beginner, a term like *pro-verb* fits into a series like *pro-noun, pro-consul, pro-tempore* etc., just as easily as *sulphide* does with *chloride, iodide*, and so forth.

To present the material of linguistic analysis, any technique is valid which will hold attention and arouse interest, as long as it does not unduly distract the students from the subject matter to be learned or leave them with inaccurate notions. This is especially true of historical considerations, which are often introduced to give presumed "spice" to material which, it is feared, will otherwise be uninteresting (e.g., the former pronunciation of *tea* as /té/ or the survival of "Elizabethan" forms like /hólp/ *holp*, past of *help*, in some outlying American English dialects). As a reaction against uncalled-for historicism, a strict descriptivism has on occasion been preached, even for use in the classroom; but this, too, can prove counter-productive if too static an approach is used. A transformational approach is very helpful for introducing beginners to grammatic analysis; this, as pointed out in Chap. 38, is one of the major uses of transformational grammar, provided that, in its turn, it is not presented with excessive formalization or made the object of exclusivism or fanaticism.

Needless to say, a new approach to English grammar, such as that suggested above, inevitably implies a radical house-cleaning in the actual material to be presented. There are a great many rules of old-fashioned prescriptive grammar that need to be swept into the dust-bin: not only antiquated shibboleths like the notorious "shall-and-will" rules, but a great many other prescriptions which are simply out of accord with the facts of present-day English. Some of these out-dated rules represent unwarranted carry-overs from Latin grammar, like the prohibitions against the "split infinitive," against the use of a "plural" pronoun (*they, them, their*) to refer to an indefinite (e.g., *somebody left their hat on this table*), or against the placing of a preposition at the end of a sentence (*a preposition is a bad thing to end a sentence with*). Still others represent faulty conclusions drawn from insufficient observation, or instructions designed to help a pupil "play it safe" in case of doubt, as in the "rule" that, with names of towns and cities, one should use *at* with names of smaller places and *in* with those of larger places: *at Elmira*, but *in New York*. (There is a shade of difference in meaning between *at* and *in* which this puristic prescription overlooks: *at* indicates general vicinity and *in* location within the boundaries of a place, so that I can say *I live at Ithaca, N.Y., but I live in Cayuga Heights* [which is a suburb of Ithaca].)

Charles C. Fries pointed the way towards an accurate reassessment of the facts of grammar, in his American English Grammar (1941). In this book, he analyzed a large number of letters written to the U.S. War Department during the First World War, to discover the actual facts of their writers' behavior with respect to a great many moot points of grammatical structure such as *It's me* vs. *It is I*, or *due to* in the sense of "because of". He did not start from a preconceived notion of what was "right" and "wrong" in the grammatical constructions themselves; instead, he determined the social standing of the writers of the letters in advance, quite independently of their linguistic behavior as manifested in the letters, and setting up the three categories of "formal," "standard," and "vulgar" into which each person fitted. He then analyzed statistically the occurrences of each moot point in correlation with the social standing of the letter-writers using the possible variants. As might be expected, a number of firmly-established notions were upset by Fries's findings; for instance, he discovered that *due to*, as a prepositional phrase, was by no means limited to the "vulgar" group, but was characteristic of all levels. However, language-structure does not stand still, and (as pointed out in Chap. 47) there can be changes in the relative frequency and acceptability of grammatical features over even relatively short periods of time, even twenty-five or thirty years. Hence the work begun by Fries should be carried on by studies repeated at least three or four times every century, in order to keep our knowledge of the facts of the language up to date.

The desirability of keeping our grammatical information up-dated is only one aspect of the general need for members of our culture to be more actively and accurately aware of the actual facts of their own linguistic behavior. This does not mean that we have to turn the entire population into skilled linguistic analysts; but it does mean that they can be and should be furnished with a reasonably accurate framework into which to fit their perception and evaluation of their own and others' linguistic behavior. Such a framework is now available, and is constantly being developed and refined in the findings of modern linguistics. The problem now is, rather, to get these findings incorporated, effectively and rapidly enough, into the text-books used in our schools, and, even more important, how to give our teachers both an understanding of the facts and an ability to take an objective, nonprescriptive attitude. In detail, this involves the introduction of elementary linguistics as an absolute prerequisite in training anyone who wishes to teach English in our schools; in general, it merges into the over-all problem of giving our teachers an open-minded, inquiring, scientific approach to whatever subject-matter they are dealing with.

NOTES

At the time of writing (1963), no satisfactory detailed discussions of the problems of teaching first-language grammar have yet appeared; Pooley, 1957, is quite unsatisfactory (cf. Sledd, 1958). The best practical application of linguistic method to the preparation of an English grammar-textbook is Roberts, 1956.

76

Usage

UNDER THE GENERAL heading of usage come all questions of "correctness," in the choice of both lexical items and constructions. "Correct" language is one of the major concerns of our society, and (as pointed out in Chap. 2) misunderstandings on this topic are so widespread as to be one of the prime obstacles to our comprehension of the nature and functioning of linguistic systems. In societies such as ours, language is used not only for its normal purpose of communication, but also as a means of social discrimination, since it affords a facile criterion for separating the sheep from the goats, the people who are socially acceptable (no matter how we define this term) from those who are not. Under these conditions, it is natural for people to be concerned about their language, just as a girl is concerned with her hair-do and the other aspects of her appearance. Yet it is desirable for us to know what are the real problems of social acceptability, so that we can be in a position to defend ourselves against the impostures and frauds which are often practised by correctness-mongers.

In no culture is "correctness" or "incorrectness" of usage determined by any criterion except that of social acceptability. Even in those countries where an official academy was set up to "regulate" the language (as in France, Italy or Spain; cf. Chap. 62), in reality all that the academy has ever done has been to grant its approval to uses of language already firmly established in the behavior of dominant social groups, especially the aristocracy and the urban upper classes (what seventeenth-century French critics used to call *la cour et la ville*, "the court and the town"). In England, likewise, acceptable usage, in the absence of any specific approval-giving body, has been a matter of upper-class sanction, as made clear especially by Ross's study on "U" and "non-U" usage and by the extensive interest shown in the topic after it was popularized by the novelist Nancy Mitford. America has never, even in Boston or Philadelphia, had the sharp class-cleavage that (especially earlier) characterized English or European society, and our criteria of acceptability have, in language as in other matters, been correspondingly broad in comparison. To a considerable extent, American standards of usage—in fact, if not always in text-book prescriptions—involve largely a number of avoidance-patterns: there are certain words, locutions or constructions which are thought of as "vulgar" or unsuited for polite discourse and hence to be shunned. The intersection of the divisions of standard vs. nonstandard and of formal vs. informal creates a four-way contrast (pp. 21–22), in a situation which is far more complicated than the simplicistic "right" vs. "wrong" of the purists might lead us to believe.

What can be a satisfactory guide to usage? There is nothing in human use of language that makes it subject to "laws" promulgated from any source. In this respect, language habits are to be classed with customs like those governing our use of knife and fork, our wearing of various types of clothes, etc., rather than with matters of morality and permissible behavior which can be regulated by legal sanction. Hence language can never be subject to the dicta of any one person, no matter how much of an "authority" he may claim to be, as Malherbe did (p. 367), nor of any group, no matter by whom constituted, even by a cardinal of France. Even the most drastic "language reforms" instituted by governments have been effective only if they concerned superficial, only partially linguistic matters, such as the orthography of Turkish, which was changed from Arabic to Roman by the dictatorial fiat of Kemal Atatürk in 1922 (p. 437). The very confusing use of the third person singular feminine pronoun *Lei* for "you (polite address)" in Italian (p. 396) causes trouble to natives and foreigners alike; but not all the official injunctions, exhortations, spying, telephone-monitoring and other measures taken by the Fascist government in the late 1930's (p. 397) were able to eradicate the use of *Lei* in favor of the simpler and clearer *voi*. For legislation of this type to be really effective in any speech-community, the human race would have to have different characteristics from those which it has, especially in being far more docile and given to instant mass obedience than it is or shows signs of ever becoming.

From these considerations, it should be evident that no-one has any right, not only to set him- or herself up as an "authority," but also to claim to give guidance on "right" or "wrong" in language for financial compensation. At the most, all that any-one can give in such matters is advice and counsel, of a general kind and without any claim to ultimate validity. Some self-styled "authorities," in person or through advertisements, ask "How many of the following common mistakes do YOU make?", inspiring their hearers or readers with insecurity over perfectly acceptable pronunciations like /kjúpàn/ "KEW-pon" or /ǽdvərtájzmənt/ "adverTISEment" or constructions like *it's me*, and offer to "improve" their audience's English—for a consideration, of course. Since such offers are based on valueless claims to "authority," and since what is offered has no worth in "improving" anyone's language, this type of correctness-mongering constitutes just as much of a fraud as does the promotion and sale of patent medicines, fake cancer-cures, or other types of quack doctoring. Advertisements for fraudulent medicines were finally banned from reputable newspapers and magazines, despite the financial loss involved, because it was realized how much harm this kind of product causes the public. It is perhaps not Utopian to hope that some day the harm done by language frauds will also be widely enough recognized to cause responsible publishers to refuse to carry the advertisements of correctness-mongers, no matter how many thousands of dollars in advertising revenue may be lost thereby.

Nor can we take as our guides the dicta of any particular professional group, especially not those of authors, whether of poetry or prose. Literary men use their own especial variety of language, which—particularly in the hands of true masters—is an effective medium for their artistic expression. However, just by virtue of its being a special variety of language, adapted only to a narrow purpose, literary usage is not suitable as a guide or model for the much broader needs of the speech-community as a whole. Every so often, some naïve person interrogates or otherwise encourages a famous writer to pronounce himself on matters of language, or, still worse, some author (e.g., James Thurber or George Orwell) behaves as if he had a special right to hold forth on the topic. Usually, when an author or man of letters without any particular training in linguistics undertakes to make pronouncements on language, he succeeds only in bringing forth an assortment of folklore (of the various kinds discussed in Chap. 72), often made even worse by prejudices peculiar to writers, e.g., that literature is the highest form of linguistic expression possible. Obviously, an artist who uses language as his medium of expression is qualified to discuss the particular problems that he has had to meet and solve, but he is no more qualified to hold forth on nonartistic aspects of language than is, say, a painter on the chemistry of paint, the science of optics, or the social significance of one color-combination or another.

Nor do more abstract considerations, such as those of logic or beauty, have any relevance to the determination of usage. Because of its inherent and necessary redundancy (p. 105), no language constitutes or can ever constitute a completely logical or rational system. In fact, if everyday, ordinary language were to be reduced to being completely logical or rational (as are, for example, mathematic and philosophic discourse), this would constitute a major loss, not a gain, since language would thus lose its flexibility and adaptability to all kinds of situations. At the opposite extreme, aesthetic considerations—considering one way of speaking as either more or less "beautiful" than another—are too completely variable to serve as guides to usage, since they inevitably differ from one individual to another. In language, as in every other matter, "beauty is in the eye of the beholder" (in this instance, in his ear!), and all of our aesthetic preferences are conditioned either by the culture in which we live or by our own personal likes and dislikes which have grown out of our experience as individuals. "The beautiful," in the abstract, does not exist, and hence affords us no basis on which to praise one linguistic phenomenon and condemn another.

Even considerations of the social standing of words or constructions are not absolute, and there can be no excuse for snobbism based on linguistic criteria. There is no inherent characteristic in any phonological feature (e.g., the use of /ʃ/ instead of /s/ before another consonant) or in any particular sequence of phonemes (e.g., /hél/) that makes it objectionable, and the social standing of such features differs from one speech-community and from one sub-group to another. In German, /ʃ/ instead of /s/ before consonant is characteristic of the most highly acceptable language, as in /ʃpréxen/ *sprechen* "to speak"; in Italian, it is part of a Neapolitan accent, and stamps its user as vulgar, e.g., in /ʃtánko/ instead of /stánko/ "tired". The double superlative, frowned upon by modern purists, was normal in Shakespeare's day (*the most unkindest cut of all*) and still is in large segments of our speech community. It is well known that what is acceptable and "correct" for some subgroups is not so for others; this consideration holds not only for upper-class attitudes towards lower-class usage, but also vice versa. By now, many persons have had the same type of experience as the university-trained man who, on working in a Houston shipyard during the Second World War, found his fellow workmen hostile until he gave up saying *those things* and took to saying *them things* instead. The social standing of lexical items and of constructions is, like everything else in language, constantly undergoing change; what was once favored by any given group or region can become disfavored (e.g., the pronunciation /líʒər/ for *leisure* in England), and what was formerly frowned upon may come into repute (e.g., /ǽdəlt/ *adult* stressed on the first syllable). We can never claim to prescribe or regulate usage on the basis of supposedly fixed standards.

All these considerations do not necessarily imply, as some have thought, that "all barriers are now down," that linguistic analysts deny the validity of any standards, or that they favor the abolition of all teaching or advice with regard to the acceptability or otherwise of usage. On the contrary, linguistic analysts recognize, as well as does any one else, the existence of standards and the desirability of teaching their observance in school. However, the findings of linguistics show us clearly that all standards of usage are relative, not absolute; that description on a wholly objective basis must take the place of prescription, and must serve as a necessary foundation for advice; and that any advice given can be valid only for a single given level and functional variety of usage (e.g., formal standard, informal standard), in a particular part of the English-speaking world (North America, England, Australia) and region thereof, and for the present time (as distinguished from earlier periods of the language whose standards of usage are no longer necessarily valid).

Rebus sic stantibus, it is evident that the teaching of usage in our schools needs to be placed on a far broader base than has normally been the case heretofore. A knowledge of formal standard usage is of course necessary in many situations, especially in expository writing; but it is not the only variety, nor yet the most important variety, of usage that should be taught explicitly. In many types of presentation (fiction, oral composition, speeches), a variety of styles, combining both formal and informal, standard and nonstandard, must be used to achieve whatever effects are desired. The greatest twentieth-century master of English style, the humorist P. G. Wodehouse, has based his use of the language on a thorough command of formal standard usage, skillfully varied at the most telling points by the inclusion of informal or nonstandard elements. Our aim should be, not to restrict our children to one level or one style of expression in their native language, but to make them capable of observing and reproducing speech and of expressing themselves in as many different ways as possible.

Our animadversions in the last four chapters have perforce been primarily negative, directed towards breaking down the restrictive attitudes which still dominate the teaching of English. However, the presentation of the actual facts of the language, and the pupil's introduction to scientific exploration in a field hitherto thought impervious to such investigation, can be made into a positive contribution to his education, interesting and exciting in its own right. In our modern world, with nearly universal literacy, the general public is increasingly impatient, and rightly so, with pretentious, empty purism as applied to nonliterary use of the language. In literature, with continually growing markets for all levels of creative authorship, no amount of schoolmarmish purism is going to restrain adventurous writers from using the language as they see fit, and have been seeing fit for the last century. However, if our schools are to make any positive contribution to training future users of English (literary or nonliterary), they must prepare themselves to do so on a basis of positive knowledge of the language and constructive advice as to its use, such as only linguistics can furnish.

NOTES

A whimsical but stimulating presentation of our problems in connection with usage: Joos, 1962a.

77

Foreign Languages

IF ANYONE wishes to learn a foreign language, the normal procedure, that has been customary since time immemorial, is to spend as much time as possible with someone who talks that language (preferably, of course, a native speaker), to imitate that person's way of talking, and to learn the language by reproducing it as well as possible. Especially at the outset, the learner is sure to make mistakes, on all levels of linguistic structure, by carrying over features of pronunciation, grammar or meaning from his or her native language; but with sufficient practice, at least the major errors are overcome, and some learners are able to go a very long distance towards completely accurate, native-like use of the language being learned (the *target language*). There is considerable difference among individuals in their ability to master a new language. It is well known that children under, say, ten or twelve have much less difficulty than do adults in foreign-language learning; recent experiments would seem to indicate that there is a physio-logical basis, in the structure of the brain of the growing child, for the relative ease with which a new language is acquired before puberty and adulthood. However, some adults retain the ability to learn a second language more than do others, normally through remaining adaptable, having a reasonably good memory, and having few or no inhibitions against making strange noises and unusual combinations of grammatical elements or meanings. In our culture, women seem to have these prerequisites more frequently than men; from adolescence on, most males are less adaptable, think other things more worth remembering, and are too self-conscious about making spec-tacles of themselves, to be as good language-learners as they might other-wise be.

In Western Europe, however, there has arisen over the last thousand years a different tradition of language-learning, which is still dominant in our schools and in many persons' thinking on the matter. In mediaeval schools, where Latin was the only language used in teaching or allowed in conversa-tion, it was perforce spoken; but it was taught to beginners through rote memorization of rules (such as "the ablative is governed by five verbs: *utor, fruor, fungor, potior* and *vescor*") and of paradigms, of the type of:

SINGULAR	PLURAL
dominus "master"	*domini* "masters"
domini "of a master"	*dominorum* "of masters"
domino "to a master"	*dominis* "to masters"
dominum "master"	*dominos* "masters"
domino "from a master"	*dominis* "from masters"
domine "O master!"	

Some learners (the present writer included) enjoy learning such paradigmatic sets, and do not find them a hindrance to effective fluency in the target language; but for many others, the memorization of paradigms is a stumbling-block, serving not as a help but as an obstacle in the learning process.

From the seventeenth century onwards, as the students' native language took the place of Latin in elementary teaching, translation came to be more and more important, at first in the study of Latin and Greek. In general, modern foreign languages were not extensively taught in schools until the nineteenth century; when they were, the techniques for doing so were borrowed from the teaching of the classical languages, both in the learning of rules and paradigms ("grammar" in the second and fifth senses mentioned on pp. 124 and 125), and in insistence on translation. In nineteenth-century American education, foreign-language learning was, in general, restricted to the leisure classes, and was not intended to serve much of any practical purpose. In accordance with our culture's folk belief that the "written language" is primary and the "spoken language" unimportant, not only Latin and Greek but the modern languages as well were approached almost wholly from the point of view of reading and writing, with virtually no attention paid to understanding and speaking. This "grammar-and-translation" method produced, usually, only the ability to upset the individual words of the target language into their equivalents in the learner's language, as when such a German passage as *Nun werden draussen die Tropfen an den Bäumen hängen, und wir werden in der Veranda Kaffee trinken* (Thomas Mann, *Buddenbrooks*) is rendered as "Now will out there the drops on the trees hang, and we will in the veranda coffee drink". A few people did manage to become reasonably fluent in languages studied in this way, but only after many more years' study than necessary, and in spite of the way they were taught rather than because of it.

Even in the nineteenth century, there were revolts against the "grammar-and-translation" method of foreign-language teaching; the first and best-known was that embodied in the "direct method," which was founded on the assumption that adults could learn to speak a new language by direct imitation of a native speaker, without ever using their own language in the process, "learning as a child does." After physiological phonetics had been developed in the late nineteenth century, its findings were applied to foreign-language teaching in the "phonetic method," developed by the German Wilhelm Viëtor and the Frenchman Paul Passy, and championed in America by the Italianist and Dante scholar Charles H. Grandgent. The phonetic method laid great stress on exact description of the processes of pronunciation

nd an extensive use of IPA phonetic symbols; some of the earliest restate-
nents of grammatical structure in modern terms (e.g., Passy's of French)
vere made in connection with this approach. After the First World War,
owever, language study declined in the United States, in large part as a
esult of the isolationist mood of the 1920's and '30's. The proportion of a
tudent's time available for foreign-language study was continually cut
irther and further by unsympathetic or hostile administrators, and all that
eemed possible was to achieve an elementary ability to read a text, not for
omplete translation, but for over-all comprehension. Many teachers who
ould not speak the language they were supposed to be teaching used the
reading objective" as an excuse for complete neglect of the auditory and oral
spects of the target language. As a result, most persons who were exposed to
 foreign language in school found that, even after three or four years' study,
hey could still neither understand, speak, read or write it at all.

Even before the entry of the United States into the Second World War, a
enewed effort was made, in the Intensive Language Program (ILP) of the
merican Council of Learnèd Societies, to apply the findings of modern
nguistics to foreign-language teaching. The principles of the ILP were
pplied extensively in the Army Specialized Training Program (ASTP) of
943–44, which in its turn had a limited effect on post-war civilian teaching
though largely blocked by the inertia of conservatism and by vested inter-
sts). Widespread understanding of the need for placing language teaching
n an oral-auditory (or, as it later came to be called, "audio-lingual") basis
vas not attained until use of mechanical means of sound-reproduction,
specially tape-recorders, became general in the 1950's and '60's. When the
eaching of a foreign language is placed on an oral basis, the need for reana-
yzing its structure in the light of the way it is spoken and for utilizing the
ndings of contrastive grammar (p. 125) become self-evident, and it is seen
hat linguistic analysis has a vital contribution to make in this connection.

The teaching material used in presenting a foreign language cannot be
rganized haphazardly or confusedly; in the oral approach especially, mere
asual conversation of the pure "direct method" type causes a tremendous
vaste of time and effort. The material must follow a carefully structured
rder, being divided into lessons or units which present a graded increase in
ifficulty of grammatical and lexical problems. In the work to be done in
ach unit, there are four main stages: *memorization* of a certain number of
entences; *analysis* of patterns in the target language; *practice* on the new
atterns; and training in *improvisation*. Each of these four stages depends on
he previous one(s) for its effectiveness, and they should therefore come in
he order stated. All language-learning inevitably involves a tremendous
mount of memorization, far more than we usually realize, since most of us
o not remember the immense effort we put in on learning by heart the
unctors and contentives of our native language and their patterns in early
hildhood. The best way to do this for a second language is to start each unit
vith a group of sentences to be learned by heart—so thoroughly that they
re "over-learned." The *basic sentences*, as they are often called, should be

sentences (whether major or minor clauses), not individual lexical items or phrases, for people do not talk in isolated words. Especially at the outset, the basic sentences should constitute conversations in ordinary, everyday language, since human linguistic intercourse normally involves the give-and-take of two or more persons talking together in a not overly formal way. The equivalent in the learner's language should be given along with the basic sentences, since the work of memorization must not be converted into a task of puzzle-solving.

Before the learner has reached linguistic adulthood, i.e. the age of around twelve or so (cf. p. 280), he can learn a new language without inhibitions, without reflection, and "as a child does" without conscious analysis of the structural differences between his first language and the new one he is learning. From twelve or so onwards, the patterns of the learner's first language are more and more likely to interfere with those of the target language, and if he is not made consciously aware of the nature and source of the interferences, he is likely to continue having difficulties without being able to overcome them, or else he will have to waste considerable effort in needless trial-and-error procedures. Each unit of an oral-approach language text should therefore contain, after the basic sentences, a section devoted to accurate description and discussion of the problems he is likely to meet at this stage with regard to pronunciation, spelling, and grammatical patterns. The discussion should be in the learner's language; there is no need to waste his time and energy in making him decipher a discussion of a language which he does not yet know, in the very language he is trying to learn. The topics taken up should come out of already memorized material, and the analysis should be deductive (formulating principles on the basis of what is known) rather than inductive (setting up principles and expecting the learner to apply them to hitherto unknown material). There always has to be a certain amount of prescription, in telling a learner what is and is not permissible in using the foreign language, but it must be based on the facts of the language and an accurate description of them. It is often thought that, because the oral approach eliminates memorization of rules and of paradigms, "grammar" has been thrown out of the window; but this is true only of the second and fifth meanings of *grammar* as set forth on pp. 124–125. Grammar in the sense of an accurate description of the structure of the target language, as contrasted with that of the learner's language, has become not less, but more important than ever before.

It is not enough merely to memorize basic sentences, nor yet to study a theoretical discussion of the grammatical structure of the target language; the learner must have practice in acquiring, as automatic, unreflecting habits, the patterns of the new language. He must learn how far he can go in extending the patterns which he is acquiring, and where are the boundaries of analogical formation that he cannot overstep—where, that is, irregularities occur that he must be aware of and observe in using the target language. In English, for instance, we can say *I extend, I extended; I organize, I organized; I fish, I fished*, in our "regular" past-tense formation, but the learner has to know that he cannot say *I *eated* or *I *goed*, and he must be given extensive practice in both regular and irregular formations on every point of the target language which is likely to offer him difficulty. Hence the next section of each unit must contain *pattern-practices* of various kinds, involving both substitution of one item for another in a set frame (*substitution-drill*), and changes which involve modification of other parts of the sentence than merely the item substituted (*correlation-drill*). Simple substitution is done in a drill like this:

TEACHER	LEARNER
I like this house.	I like this house.
Hotel.	I like this hotel.
Restaurant.	I like this restaurant.
Park.	I like this park.
House.	I like this house.

A drill involving the correlation of one part of the utterance with another would be like the following, which gives practice on German verb forms:

TEACHER	LEARNER
Ich komme.	Ich komme: "I come".
Wir.	Wir kommen: "we come".
Er.	Er kommt: "he comes".
Sie.	Sie kommen: "they come".
Du.	Du kommst: "thou comest".
Ihr.	Ihr kommet: "you come".
Ich.	Ich komme: "I come".

Pattern-drill, however, is not enough, even coming after well-memorized basic sentences and well-learned structural analysis. When the learner is in contact with native speakers of the language, they will not be talking to him only in whatever basic sentences he has learned; he must be prepared to understand different combinations from those which he has memorized, and as they come at him unexpectedly, not in the fixed framework of a pattern-drill. For passive understanding of new combinations, the best teaching device is the *review dialogue*, which presents—again in real-life situations, characteristic of the culture in which the target language is spoken—the material already learned, but in fresh arrangements. For active command, the learner must be trained to improvise, since virtually all of our ordinary linguistic activity involves improvisation, and in order to converse freely and easily in the target language one must be able to talk right "off the bat" without hemming-and-hawing or searching one's memory for the proper form of, say, the past subjunctive. Topics are assigned for an improvised but structured conversation between two or more members of the class, on material already covered in the units studied previously: one takes the rôle of, say, a ticket agent and another takes that of a traveller, or one is a sales-person and another a customer. Imagination is called for, of course, in acting out these improvised conversations in front of a class, but students find that stage fright and hesitation soon disappear and that this type of practice gives them ability to understand and respond quickly in a conversational situation.

Clearly, the best model to imitate when learning a new language is a native speaker, because he or she has been familiar with it from earliest childhood and can resolve any problem as to normal usage without any hesitation. In an ordinary situation, a speaker of the standard informal variety will be preferred if available—someone who speaks naturally, as normal socially acceptable people do, neither pedantically nor vulgarly. If no such person is available, then a pedant or a vulgarian can be used as model, but with caution. A non-native speaker is acceptable only as a third choice, and only if his or her speech is a reasonable approximation of that of a native. Until the spread of mechanical reproducing devices, it was hard to obtain native speakers under ordinary American conditions, and many non-native language teachers could get by with highly un-native-like pronunciation and even virtually no fluency in the language at all. With the voices of natives available on tapes for use in language laboratories, there is no excuse for such a situation to be perpetuated. There is still, however, plenty for the non-native teacher to do, in directing the class activities and in leading the class through contrastive structural analysis and pattern drills based thereon. But to be effective in such work, the teacher must be sufficiently conversant with the methods and findings of contrastive linguistics to use its results as presented in textbooks.

For the findings of linguistics to be most effectively utilized, it is not enough for the class-room teacher to know them in theory, and then to go along using the same old textbooks and procedures. New books, organized along the lines we have just discussed, must be prepared, and new procedures must be devised to implement them. During the Second World War, an entire series of such texts, with detailed instructions for their use, was prepared in connection with the U.S. Armed Forces Institute's language-teaching program. In more recent times, perhaps the most detailed methodology for class-room teaching has been worked out by the Centre de Recherche et d'Étude pour la Diffusion du Français (CREDIF) in Paris, and applied in their series of texts for teaching French.

Reading is by no means banished, as some have thought, from language courses conducted by the oral approach; its beginning is simply postponed for a short time (a few weeks in the case of modern European languages), until the beginner has had a chance to learn enough of the phonology of the language to understand and interpret its orthography. Starting from a command of the present-day language, the learner can, at a slightly later stage, read intermediate and advanced texts more rapidly than heretofore, and with at least an approximation of the same approach to earlier literary monuments that the modern native speaker of the target language brings to them. Experience with oral-approach courses in which extensive reading is introduced at the later stages has shown that learners trained in this way are able to read at least as well as those who have learned by the "grammar-and-translation" method, and have the ability to understand what they hear and to converse freely as well. Writing—either set translation into the foreign language or free composition—is the most complicated of all the language skills, and rightfully belongs at the intermediate and advanced, rather than the elementary, level.

In the second half of the twentieth century, the United States (and the English-speaking world in general) needs a tremendous expansion of language-teaching competence in general, so that speakers of English can both learn other languages and act as models or teachers of English as a foreign language (it has been estimated that, by 2000 A.D., there will be two million persons engaged in teaching English to non-native speakers of the language!). The oral approach, reinforced by the use of audio-visual aids such as the tape-recorder, is the only successful path to solution of the problems of second-language teaching; but, to be fully effective and to avoid the dangers of mere toying with machines and empty gadgetry, it must embody at its core the findings of linguistics in contrastive structural grammars and pattern-practice based thereon.

NOTES

General bibliography on language-teaching: Brooks, 1960; Moulton, 1961.

Psycholinguistic aspects of second-language learning: Osgood and Sebeok, 1954, §6.2. Cf. also Carroll, 1963.

International Languages

THERE IS a very widespread belief that difficulties between nations are caused by linguistic diversity, and that if all mankind talked the same language it would be easy to reach agreement on points of difference. This belief is very old; it is expressed symbolically in the legend of the Tower of Babel, according to which all mankind did talk one language from the time of Adam until Nimrod presumed to build a tower to reach Heaven—and, to impede the completion of the tower, the Lord created diversity of speech among the peoples working on it. This legend is significant because it recognizes the basic role of language in human coöperation, and implies that if all mankind were to work in complete harmony together, there would be no secret of the universe that they would be unable to unveil (symbolized by the tower reaching Heaven). The legend also indicates how far back our desire for linguistic unity reaches in thinking and folklore; but interest in a universal language has become especially strong in the last two hundred years or so, and many plans have been made to bring one into existence.

There is a very good reason why interest in an international language should have become stronger in recent centuries: the linguistic fragmentation of the West European intellectual world, due primarily to the continually increasing force of political and cultural nationalism. Things were not ever thus: in the Middle Ages, all intellectual activity was carried on with the use of Latin as a lingua franca, with which one could correspond or travel from England to Italy, from Spain to Poland. Mediaeval Latin was not spoken as anyone's native tongue; all its users learned it in school as a second language, and for them it was "grammar" *par excellence* (cf. p. 124). Nevertheless, it was a living language, not exactly like the Latin of Cicero in "purity" or "correctness," but constantly changing and developing to meet new situations and needs. Its use was restricted to a select few—members of the clergy, lawyers, and a few other intellectuals—and it had a strong intellectual tradition in back of it, with an extensive literature, which kept its use alive. Under these conditions, it was possible to keep Latin in active use long after its popular developments, in the Romance tongues, had changed so far as to become independent languages. But for such artificial preservation of a dead language, two things are necessary: 1) a very small, highly trained number of users, with a conservative attitude; and 2) a highly respected literature and intellectual tradition. The first of these prerequisites has disappeared in modern times, and the second has become weakened; hence modern efforts to revive its use or to popularize an artificially simplified form (*Latino sine flexione*, "Latin without inflection") have fallen through, more or less of their own weight.

The chief alternative to use of a dead language as an international lingua franca is the adoption of some modern language. French fulfilled this function from the seventeenth through the nineteenth centuries, as a result of the dominant position which France occupied in political and intellectual matters. This was due, not to any particular inherent merit of French as opposed to other languages, but purely to nonlinguistic considerations; only after French had risen to a dominant position did myths begin to arise about its being especially "intellectual," "clear," "precise," and the like. During the past two hundred years, English has gradually been taking the place of French, due to first English and then American leadership in commerce, industry, and science. This is the natural way in which languages become predominant and widely used: people adopt the language out of whose use they can get the most benefit. The poorly-fitting orthography of English does not seem to be as much of an obstacle to its spread as might *a priori* be expected; rather, the wide use of English seems to be carrying along with it an increase in the prestige of wasteful, inaccurate spelling as applied to other languages (e.g. German, Italian) as well. A greater obstacle is modern nationalism, with its self-centered, ingrown, parochial group egocentrism, for which the language of each country serves the people of that country as a symbol of their political and cultural autonomy; even this, however, has not been able to constitute a barrier against the spread of English.

In order to avoid the hostility which nationalistic feelings arouse against the use of one real language or another, many people have considered it desirable to create an artificial language which might serve as a lingua franca. For the last hundred years and more, this idea has exercised great fascination, and it has been estimated that well over a hundred such artificial languages have been invented, averaging something like a language a year. Their inventors have given them all kinds of names, like Kosmos, Occidental, Parla, Spokil, Universala, Frater, and so forth. The three most successful to date have been Volapük (which first appeared in 1879), Esperanto (1887), and a modified version of the latter called Ido; of these three, Esperanto is the only one which has become really well-known and which comes to mind immediately when international languages are mentioned. These artificial languages normally have markedly simplified grammatical structures: for instance, in Esperanto all nouns are made to end in -*o* and all adjectives in -*a*. Structurally, Esperanto and Ido are Romance-based pidgins, which have come into being through deliberate creation instead of having grown "like Topsy" under the natural conditions of cultural contact (pp. 376–378). Their vocabularies, however, are much more extensive than those of ordinary pidgins; that of Esperanto is primarily Latin and Romance in its origin, with some words taken from Germanic, Greek, and other sources.

It was the original hope of the creators of such artificial languages that they would spread, through the obvious desirability of having a single means of communication available to all mankind, and would eventually replace the present national languages and their dialects. These hopes have revealed themselves as unrealistic, for several reasons. Almost all the artificial international languages that have been constructed so far have been essentially designed for and by Western Europeans. A language like Esperanto, although supposedly simplified from our point of view, still keeps the essential parts of speech (noun, adjective, verb, etc.) of Indo-European, and the concepts and categories of meaning that our languages have made us familiar with. A speaker of, say, Chinese or Telugu or some American Indian language would have as much difficulty with Esperanto as he would with French or English or German. It would be a well-nigh impossible task to find a common denominator of linguistic material for all the three thousand or so languages of the world; and yet to base one's artificial language on any particular language-type (whether Indo-European, Semitic, Sinitic or any other) is invidious and inevitably implies a value-judgment of some kind which is hardly complimentary to the speakers of other types of languages.

It has also been pointed out that, if Esperanto or any other artificial language were to become so widespread as to be the native language of any sizeable speech-community, it would immediately become subject to the normal principles that govern language development, and would start to be differentiated and to change as all other languages have done. Everyone who speaks Esperanto does so with a certain "accent" due to the substratum of his native language, and this effect would be tremendously magnified in the case of whole speech-communities passing to Esperanto as the speakers of pre-Latin languages did in taking over popular Latin speech (cf. Chap. 63). There are by now a few people who are actually native speakers of Esperanto, having been brought up by Esperantist parents and using Esperanto as the normal family language from their earliest childhood; and in these people's usage, changes have already begun to take place. But by and large, the speakers of Esperanto have some other tongue as their native language, and use Esperanto only by intention and with conscious effort; and in this fact lies a further difficulty. There are so few native speakers of Esperanto that they are not enough to set a standard for usage; and there is no body of material, oral or written, to serve as a canon, such as there is in classical Latin or Greek, or such as naturally grows out of the situation for any living language.

Deliberate reductions of existing tongues have been even less successful than artificially created international languages; the worst such fiasco in modern times has been Basic English, a restricted variety of English constructed by the philosophers C. K. Ogden and I. A. Richards. This language is strictly limited in vocabulary to 850 words, chosen by the sponsors of the language, plus 18 special auxiliary verbs or "operators" such as *get, do, be,* etc. The lexical items were chosen with a view to their use in expressing (no matter with how much circumlocution) every possible idea, rather than to their frequency or practicality in everyday usage. Ordinary English spelling is used, and little attention has been paid to the phonetic side of the problem; apparently it was assumed that foreigners' difficulties in learning English sounds were of little or no weight, and the language seems to have been envisaged primarily as a means of written communication. Despite its professed limitation to 850 words, the actual number of possible combinations and the range of meaning covered by Basic English vocabulary is very great, and they all follow the patterns of standard English. The auxiliary verbs or "operators" constitute one of the hardest parts of Basic English for any non-native speaker of English, since such words as *get* and *do* are among the trickiest things in the English language. In short, Basic English is quite without the ease and simplicity that has been claimed for it, and has been put together naïvely and without realization of the linguistic problems involved.

In recent years, it has come to be realized that the role of any artificial language has to be much more restricted than that of eventually replacing all the rest of the world's tongues, as was often the dream of such men as Schleyer (the inventor of Volapük) or Zamenhof (who constructed Esperanto). A group called the International Auxiliary Language Association (IALA) has for some years had an ambitious program for the construction of still another auxiliary language, using all the available resources of linguistic analysis, in studying the types of concepts that are most frequently found, the frequency of occurrence of the most important word-roots of the European languages, and so forth. The IALA language will undoubtedly be essentially a Latin-and-Romance-based artificial pidgin, as are Esperanto and Ido; but its proponents envisage it primarily as an auxiliary language for quick and extensive intercommunication on a scientific level. Basic English, likewise, is coming to be used more and more as simply an initial stage in the learning of English as a second language, from which the learner can pass to a fuller comprehension of the standard variety as soon as possible. On this basis, and for these limited aims, international auxiliary languages can have a certain utility.

Perhaps the major reason why the international language movement has, on the whole, been losing momentum is that more and more members of the general public are coming to realize that the ideal of "one world, one language" is so unrealistic as to be quite unattainable, and is in addition quite unnecessary. It is now known that the diversity of the world's linguistic structures is so great that no one language, or even language-type, could ever take their place except by a type of tyrannically world-dominant power which is abhorrent to most people; furthermore, the loss of this diversity would constitute, not a gain, but a loss to the human race as a whole, since each different linguistic structure represents a different way of organizing and interpreting human experience. Learning one or more foreign languages is not the extremely difficult task which it is often thought to be; improved methods of language teaching, with the help of contrastive linguistics (cf. Chap. 77), have made it clear that any ordinary person can, with proper motivation and application of time and energy, acquire a second language without waste or inefficiency. The problems besetting the world are nonlinguistic in nature, and use of a single language would not help solve them in the slightest; a willingness to agree, no matter what language is used, is far more important than the use of a single language to agree in. Multilingualism is with us to stay, as it has always been, and there are good reasons for not regarding it as a curse and trying to get out of it, but, quite the contrary, for accepting it as a blessing and trying to turn it to our best advantage.

NOTES

Discerning advocates of international auxiliary languages no longer take the position of over-enthusiastic advocacy that called forth such strong reactions as Collitz, 1926; the latter is still, however, a valuable corrective for starry-eyed naiveté.

79

Glottopolitics

NOT INFREQUENTLY there arise, on the level of political decisions and government policy, problems which involve language matters. It has been customary for politicians and bureaucrats to deal with such problems on a basis of "common sense," i.e., of our culture's folklore about matters of language (Chap. 72); the results have rarely been satisfactory and have often ranged from unsatisfactory to disastrous. With the development of linguistics, it has become evident that in language matters, as in other aspects of the functioning of our society, the findings of the social sciences could profitably be applied to solving some of the problems of official policy. The branch of applied linguistics dealing with such problems has been termed *glottopolitics*; it finds its most immediate applications in such fields as the relation of the standard language to the dialects, the treatment of minority language groups, and policy with regard to bilingualism. The chief government branch involved is normally the education department, but the court system, the forces of public order, and the legislative organs (especially the parliament) may also be involved insofar as they are concerned with the use of one language or one variety of a language as opposed to another.

In Western Europe, it has always been assumed, more or less axiomatically, that the standard language was to be preferred to local dialects in any kind of activity involving social prestige—not only the conversation of elegant people and the writing of belles-lettres, but also the teaching carried on in schools, the sessions of law-courts, and the activities of governmental bodies and bureaus. When Francis I of France decreed in 1539, in the ordinance of Villers-Cotterets, that law courts were thenceforth to use the "langue françoyse," it was standard French that was referred to, not (as a few have thought) the local dialects. Where the standard language is not very different from regional speech (as is the case in the United States and Canada), not much trouble arises in this connection; at the most, there is some friction over problems of "correct" language. In other instances, however, where the standard language is markèdly different from the local dialects, undue or premature insistence on the former can cause incomprehension, decreased efficiency on the part of schools, and malfunctioning of courts and governmental bodies. In mediaeval times, when the only language of the courts was Latin, the ordinary peasant was at the mercy of any unscrupulous lawyer who wanted to take advantage of his ignorance of that language (cf. p. 362);

a similar situation prevails even today in Spanish America and in Haiti, where the *nèg mòn* ("man from the hills" or hillbilly) knowing only Creole is likely to be defrauded because he does not know standard French. A child going to school and being taught from the first day in a language which he does not know is likely—especially if his family are poor and he is underfed and underclothed anyhow—to lose interest and drop out very rapidly.

Normally, those who determine governmental policy in regard to local dialects consider them to be simply "corruptions" of the "real language" and, as such, to be accorded no consideration, in fact to be stamped out as soon as possible. Whether the dialects can be eradicated easily or not makes no difference, nor does the question of what (if anything) is to take their place. This unrealistic attitude on the part of legislators and bureaucrats is to a considerable extent a survival of the notions of the French revolutionaries of 1789, who thought that local dialects were the product of aristocratic discrimination against the peasants, who were thus being deprived of their right to "good" language. On the other hand, an intelligent policy, based on the findings of linguistics, would suggest that if the local dialect is very different from the standard language, the dialect should be used in the earliest years of schooling, and should serve as the basis on which to build up a knowledge of the standard language. It is rare, however, to find such a policy put into practice; the only instance known to the present writer is the reform instituted in the Italian schools in the 1920's by the philosopher-educationist Giovanni Gentile. In the Gentile reform, the first- and second-graders were first made literate in their local dialect and then provided with texts especially constructed on a contrastive basis to enable them to learn standard Italian more rapidly. Unfortunately, Gentile's name and work were closely associated with the Fascist régime; he himself was assassinated by anti-Fascists in 1945, and the principles of his reforms were discarded after the Second World War.

In many countries, both in Europe and in America, there are minority groups of various sizes, whose mark of identity is normally their language; we may think of the French Canadians, the Puerto Ricans in the New York City area, the Pennsylvania Germans, and the Mexicans in the American Southwest, to mention only the most obvious instances in North America. Popular attitudes towards such minority language-groups vary markèdly, as does their juridical status; in instances where they are citizens of the country involved, there is a strong tendency on the part of the majority to insist that the minority must conform in many ways, among which language-patterns are among the most obvious. Reactions of the minority groups differ, depending largely on their social and economic position and their ability to resist pressures. In the United States we are perhaps most familiar with immigrant groups for whom the language of the old country has symbolized all that they wished to leave behind them, and which they and their descendants have therefore hastened to abandon as soon as possible. In many other instances, however, preservation of the minority language has been a mark of independence and of opposition to domination by a majority group; such attitudes have been found, not only among the upper classes of, say, the Philippines in their attachment to Spanish and of Louisiana with regard to their variety of standard French, but also in disfavored but tenacious groups like the Jews or the Navaho in all their enforced migrations.

Governmental policy with regard to minority groups likewise varies widely. The normal American official attitude—that of disregarding them entirely except where complete ignorance of English might make official interpreters a contemptuously accepted necessity—has been facilitated by the frequent desire of the immigrant minorities themselves to discard the old language. At the other end of the scale is the recognition, in Switzerland, of four national languages, of which three (French, German, Italian) are universally recognized throughout the country and the fourth (Romansh, in the Engadine) has been added largely out of motives of nationalistic pride so as to have at least one language that is distinctively Swiss. Coupled with this recognition, however, is the strict requirement that, in each region, only the language of that region is to be taught in the schools and used in governmental and judicial affairs; there are in Switzerland no French-minority schools in German-speaking areas or vice versa. Some observers have, paradoxically, attributed some of the famous Swiss tolerance in linguistic matters to the absence of the persecution-complexes that normally accompany the institution of special schools and other governmental agencies for language minorities. Most countries with minority-problems resort to solutions somewhere in between that of complete indifference and complete recognition; the difficulties of purely linguistic nature are usually complicated by nonlinguistic attitudes, especially persecution-complexes.

The most obvious solution to the problems caused by the presence of two or more language groups in a single political unit would be a more or less complete bilingualism, i.e., a situation in which every speaker had an effective command of the languages involved. That such a solution can be attained, at least in small, compact countries, is demonstrated by the widespread prevalence of bilingualism in Switzerland and Belgium. That bilingualism is in itself no cure for political and cultural tensions is also demonstrated by the example of these two countries: marked harmony among speakers of the four languages of Switzerland, and marked disharmony between Walloons and Flemings in Belgium. In other countries, certain regions are marked by greater or less bilingualism, e.g., the Upper Adige (South Tyrol) in Italy, the Basque regions of France and Spain, or Transylvania (which has scattered German-speaking enclaves within a larger Hungarian-speaking enclave) in Roumania. Here, too, attitudes and policies vary, from the broad tolerance accorded to Basque on the French side of the Pyrenees to the extreme repression practised against the same language on the Spanish side, and, in between, the rather grudging recognition accorded to German in the Upper Adige by the Italian authorities.

Considerable attention has been given to problems of bilingualism by linguistic analysts, psychologists, and educationists, with attention especially to the relation of bilingualism to intelligence. There are two sharply divided schools of thought on the matter: those who hold that bilingualism is beneficial, and those who consider it harmful, especially for a growing child who is having to learn more than one language and the regular subject-matter of the school curriculum at the same time. The proponents of bilingualism draw most of their examples from countries with high standards of living such as Switzerland and Belgium, and cite the achievements of brilliant individuals such as former Premier St. Laurent of Canada. Their opponents have worked chiefly with underdeveloped regions (India, Africa, Central and South America) and with the underprivileged classes in such countries, whose members often have low I.Q.'s and great economic difficulties. The conclusion that seems to have emerged from the mass of studies on bilingualism is that its desirability is related to the general symbolizing-ability of the individual. It is apparently a help to intelligent persons to have more than one way of symbolizing what they know and learn; but people of less intelligence, who already have trouble mastering the symbolization afforded by one language, have their difficulties increased when they are called on to do the job simultaneously in two or more languages. For mass education, therefore, it seems desirable to avoid forcing a bilingual situation (especially one where the elementary classes are conducted in some language other than the children's native speech) on a population which is not intellectually equal to it. This conclusion is reinforced by the observation (pp. 404–405) that every speaker's ego is intimately bound up with his or her native speech, and that devaluation of a person's mother-tongue, especially at an early age, is more harmful than is usually realized.

In many situations, more than one of the factors we have discussed (attitudes towards dialects, minority groups, and bilingualism) is present at the same time. The worst situations of all, perhaps, are found in countries such as Haiti, Curaçao and Aruba, Mauritius, Réunion, or Sierra Leone, where the population as a whole speaks a creolized language (Chap. 65) and the language of administration is a European "language of culture." In such areas, folkloristic notions about language, social prejudices, economic interests and political oppression often combine to create a highly unrealistic appraisal of the language situation on the part of the dominant classes. In Haiti, for instance, although virtually everyone learns Creole from earliest infancy, upper-class speakers will deny that they have any knowledge of it; in their discussion of its origin, they will seek to minimize the African element and to maintain that it is only a "corruption" of seventeenth-century Norman French dialect. Although in reality Creole is as far from French as modern French is from Latin, the ruling classes of Haiti do not wish to see this fact recognized or Creole used in elementary schooling, even as a basis for the teaching of standard French. Several literacy campaigns have begun, using an easily-learned phonemically-based orthography, but have been allowed to lapse, not for lack of support, but because of changes in government and the opposition of the ruling classes, who wish to see Creole either not written at all or written with a Gallicizing orthography which will be hard to learn. Creole is, in general, treated as if it were the dialect of a despised minority, although it is actually the mother-tongue of the entire population, of whom only the upper tenth are bilingual in Creole and French. The basic reason for this attitude is the fear on the part of the dominant minority that, if Creole were written with an easily-learned orthography and were admitted in schools and public life, their power would be taken from them by the majority as soon as the latter were educated and aroused to the injustice of their position.

In situations involving the political status of language phenomena and requiring the solution of linguistic problems, the linguistic analyst can study the facts, analyze them, and place his findings at the disposition of the government and the public. In Haiti, for instance, he can recommend that a phonemically-based Creole orthography be taught widely and used for achieving general literacy; and he can point out that the most effective educational policy would be to use Creole as a starting-point for imparting a soundly-based knowledge of standard French. In New Guinea, he can urge the importance of Neo-Melanesian as a "linguistic cement" for the Territory of Papua and New Guinea, and can point out the fallacies in the United Nations' Trusteeship Mission's demands for the immediate "abolition" of Neo-Melanesian. As with other branches of applied anthropology, however, the acceptance of the linguistic analyst's recommendations depends, not on rational considerations of intelligent policy, but on the strength of non-linguistic forces such as social and financial interests. In some instances, a reasonably enlightened government may take his recommendations seriously and adopt a policy calculated to maximize the effective use of the languages involved (e.g., Quechua in relation to Spanish in Perú). In others, however, a reactionary upper class, with a strong interest in maintaining their own dominance at all costs, may be too powerful to permit liberalization of governmental policy (e.g., towards Creole in Haiti); in such instances, glottopolitical consultation and advice is of little or no use.

NOTES

Governmental policy concerning Neo-Melanesian: Hall, 1959b.
The social and political position of Creole in Haiti: Efron, 1954.
Bilingualism and applied linguistics: Hall, 1952a.

80

Linguistics in Society

IN OUR NECESSARILY brief presentation of the methods and findings of linguistics, we have seen that it enables us to analyze and describe the structure of language, with more exactitude than is possible for the subject-matter of any other social science. It casts light, not only on the interpretation of such historical documents of earlier speech as remain to us, but (through the extrapolation rendered possible by the comparative method) on even earlier periods of human speech. It enables us, by clarifying the nature of our systems of communication in contrast with those of other living beings, to have a clearer understanding of the place of man in the world around him. It has direct applications in a number of fields, in which it can help us to improve unsatisfactory educational procedures and to reach realistic conclusions with regard to governmental policy. In addition to these theoretical and practical uses, however, linguistics has broader implications for our daily living, as members of human society, and for our attitudes towards many language-based problems that beset us. To a greater extent than we normally realize, the difficulties with which modern society has to contend are the result of unfounded and unrealistic notions which its members have about their own and other people's language.

On this score, linguistics has a message which is largely in direct opposition to the folklore which we acquire formally from schools and other sources of opinion (newspapers, magazines and the like) and informally by observing other people's behavior, from our earliest childhood onwards. Many people consider that it is "common sense" to insist on "correct" speech, and to exert one kind of sanction or another against those who do not speak "correctly." Untutored and natural speech is very often made an object of reproach and condemnation; the general attitude towards talking naturally, the way we learn our language from family and playmates without benefit of schoolmastering, is usually that it shows ignorance, neglect, carelessness, or stupidity. A person who talks a nonstandard dialect is, as a result of such condemnation, apt to have an attitude of self-depreciation—usually serious, sometimes humorous—which is, in the long run, harmful to his or her personality and relations with other persons.

The amount of snobbery and social discrimination which goes on in the name of "correctness" is enormous; each one of us can think of many instances in our own experience. One of the features of his behavior that was strongly held against Al Smith in his campaign for the presidency in 1928 was his pronunciation /rǽdio/ instead of /rédio/ for "radio," which was widely considered "vulgar"; more recently, there have been strong objections to /éwɔl/ as a pronunciation for *A.W.O.L.* "absent without leave" and to such transitive verbs, formed on nouns, as *to contact* or *to clearance*. Plenty of people have been turned down for jobs just because they said *ain't* or *Armitice*, and others of inferior worth accepted because they used *is not* or *Armistice* as the school-books and dictionaries prescribe. Linguistics demonstrates quite clearly, however, that there is no basis other than social prejudice for considering, say, *ain't* inferior to *isn't*, *et* to *ate* or *eaten*, or /rǽdio/ to /rédio/, nor for snubbing or discriminating against someone on the ground that "their speech reflects their personality." Shibboleths of this kind constitute only an artificial, superficial, meaningless basis for separating some of the sheep and goats from others, rather than using more thorough and rational criteria to determine people's real merits. Our society uses such empty criteria only because they are 1) easy to apply, and 2) soothing to the egos of those who are in a position to apply them.

Linguistics points out that such standards, although they have a perfectly real existence in people's behavior, have nothing to do with language itself, and are imposed from the outside, for motives of laziness and snobbery. The harm done to nonstandard speakers by this type of condemnation is far greater than we normally realize. On occasion, it can produce deep psychologic effects of resentment and hatred. One speaker of Papiamentu (the Spanish-based creole of Curaçao), who had acted as informant in a linguistic investigation of that tongue, was greatly surprised to discover that it was regarded as a "real language" by linguistic analysts; he asked that a copy of the grammar might be given him when it was ultimately published, so that he might take it and ram it down the throat of the teacher who had told him and his classmates that Papiamentu was not a language at all, but only a base corruption. It is not exaggerated to suspect that much of the resentment and bitterness manifested in present or former colonial areas, especially on the part of the lower classes, stems from the unjust contempt in which their way of speaking has been held.

In any given social situation, it is often enough necessary for the non-standard speaker to make changes in his way of speaking, so as to bring it more in line with standard usage. He is usually at a disadvantage for economic reasons, and finds that he has to change his natural speech-patterns to conform to those of people who have more social and economic prestige and hence have power over him. But when he tries to conform, he finds that it is by no means easy. Very few people can tell him accurately and clearly what to do in order to change his speech effectively, and those who do try to tell him, do so by invective ("your English is bad," "your language is not English") and by preaching ("Saying *it ain't me* shows that you are neglectful and careless and sloppy in your speech; you should say *It is not I*") rather than by telling him objectively what is not acceptable in his speech and in what way it needs to be changed. The over-corrections to which nonstandard speakers are prone, such as *between you and I* or what the *New Yorker* magazine calls "the omnipresent *whom*" (as in *Senator Blank, whom it is well known is opposed to the proposal . . .*), are due to their insecurity and their incomplete comprehension of what actually constitutes standard usage.

For nonstandard speakers, the implication of the findings of linguistics is that, if we find it necessary to change our speech from nonstandard to standard, we should not meddle ignorantly with our language, but should change it by objective and rational means, with a clear-eyed recognition that we are thereby trying to change our social status, without false humility or needless self-depreciation. For those whose usage is already standard, however, the message of linguistics is that they need to be less snobbish, less overbearing, and less insistent on a false "correctness." The merit of what a person says or does is not in any way affected by the way in which they say or do it, provided it is the most efficient way of saying or doing it; to insist on "correctness" for its own sake is, in the last analysis, to uphold the criterion of conspicuous waste that characterized the leisure classes of a bygone age. Those of us who are brought up on standard speech have no right to lord it over nonstandard speakers just because of our language; we would do better to take an attitude of true humility towards our own speech and tolerance towards others', with a willingness to accept deviations from our own practice.

It is often objected that by destroying absolute standards, we will remove all barriers to anyone's talking any way they wish, and that if strong, conscious efforts are not made to preserve the language from "corruption," within a short period of time we will all be talking so differently from each other that no-one will understand anyone else. Such an argument fails to take into account the cohesive, centripetal forces of society that are always at work, and can be expected to outweigh the disintegrative, centrifugal forces. Abandonment of absolute standards does not necessarily imply abandonment of all standards; just because we tolerate deviations from our own practice, we need not expect everything to fly apart immediately. The pressure of human need for communication will always ensure people's keeping their speech reasonably uniform; the difficulty arises mainly over certain moot points (like *he did it* vs. *he done it*, *it's me* vs. *it is I*) which normally do not make any difference in communication and which serve simply as indicators of socio-economic standing. Relaxation of over-rigid and absolute standards brings no harm at all to mutual communication and understanding; on the contrary, it improves it by removing sources of needless disagreement and friction.

The elimination of absolutism with regard to the meaning of words, and the abandonment of dictionary-worship, brings a greater realization that not everyone means the same thing in using the same word, and that we must therefore pay more attention than we are often accustomed to doing, to possibilities of divergent interpretation. The movement known as "General Semantics" has laid especial emphasis on the necessity for taking semantic differences into account: for instance, a term like *socialism* has not only different connotations, but also widely varying denotations. To use such a term in an undefined fashion, and to deliberately obscure the possible differences in interpretation (as was done in California by unscrupulous persons who placed posters in shop-windows and on automobiles with the blanket identification "Socialism Is Communism"), is to utilize existing misconceptions for dubiously honest motives. The semantic analysis of words leads to a clearer recognition of often widely divergent meanings, so that we must recognize, say, in this instance that *socialism*₁ may be the kind envisaged by pre-Marxian theorists, *socialism*₂ that which Marx and Engels preached, *socialism*₃ the Fabian variety, and so forth through a whole range of variations. Together with a recognition of the differences between individuals in their personalities and experiences, these considerations lead to the conclusion that Edmund Burke stated in his oration on the American Revolution, "One cannot condemn an entire people," nor yet reach sweeping, over-all conclusions concerning any group or class of people or phenomena simply because they happen to be referred to by one and the same linguistic label, e.g. *Negro, Japanese, Italian, Jew, socialism*, etc.

These considerations concerning differences within a single language also apply, on a larger scale, to differences between languages. When we substitute a relativistic for an absolutistic point of view, we begin to realize that our language is nothing special in comparison with others, nothing particularly God-given or superior or peculiarly fitted for higher intellectual activity, any more than our own dialect of our language is better than any other dialect. Our own language, whether it be English or French or Italian or German, and all the other so-called "civilized" languages, are civilized only in that they happen to be spoken by particular groups of people who have achieved enough technological progress along certain lines to build "civilizations," that is, more complicated cultures. Many so-called "primitive" languages, as shown by the investigations of Whorf and others (cf. pp. 401–402), have grammatical structures which symbolize other and just as important contrasts in the world around us as do the structures of our "languages of civilization." When a widely-read weekly refers to Hindi as "a relatively primitive language, sadly deficient in scientific and technical vocabulary," its editors are simply revealing their ignorance and reliance on folkloristic value-judgments, which have no place in either scientific or popular discussion of the differences among languages.

Once we realize that all languages are equal in merit, nationalism based on linguistic differences loses any cogency that it might have. It is a common habit of modern man to think that difference in speech must necessarily imply difference in national allegiance and loyalty, and that hence the first thing to do to assure national unity is to enforce linguistic unity. Many nations, especially those of Central Europe, have made strenuous efforts to ensure the spread of their own languages at the expense of others spoken within their borders: the old Austro-Hungarian Empire, the pre-1914 German Empire, and the "successor states" of the post-1918 settlement all engaged in ruthless campaigns to force their official languages on subject groups. The resentment thus engendered was a major factor in aggravating the international tensions that led to the Second World War. Yet the example of Switzerland (pp. 463 proves that there is no necessary connection between language and nationality or patriotism. The popular notion that there is such a connection is quite mistaken; to win and hold the affection of its citizens, a government does not need to ram the majority language down the throats of all its minorities. Actions, here as elsewhere, speak louder than words, and decent, fair treatment is essential rather than enforced linguistic unity.

Linguistics in itself does not, of course, constitute a panacea for the world's ills, any more than any other single branch of human knowledge. It can, nevertheless, make a highly significant contribution to the improvement of society, both by placing the actual facts concerning language at the service of mankind, and by pointing to conclusions based on these facts which, if intelligently applied, can greatly reduce misunderstandings and tensions due to linguistic causes; and it can aid in developing a positive basis for constructive coöperation between individuals and groups—thus enabling language to fulfill more adequately its primary function in human society.

NOTES

The contribution of linguistics to determining attitudes towards language: Hall, 1960b, Chap. 14.

Current orientations in linguistics: Haugen, 1951; Joos (ed.), 1957, especially the introduction and the remarks appended to each reprinted article; Malmberg, 1959.

Reference to Hindi: Newsweek, April 25, 1963, p. 24.

BIBLIOGRAPHY

In the following are listed the books and articles referred to in the notes at the end of each chapter. It is not a complete bibliography of linguistics (such a work would require a great many volumes in itself). For the period before 1933, the bibliography given by Bloomfield (1933a) is quite full; for the essential works which appeared between then and 1960 cf. the bibliography given in Gleason (1961). Mohrmann (ed.) (1947 ff.) gives a very full year-by-year listing of current publications in linguistics.

Frequently occurring names of periodicals or series are abbreviated, and the abbreviations themselves are listed and explained in their appropriate alphabetical position.

AcL = Acta Linguistica. Copenhagen, 1939 ff.

Aebischer, Paul, 1939. Les origines de l'italien *bosco*. Etude de stratigraphie linguistique. Zeitschrift für romanische philologie *59:* 417–430.

———, 1948. Contribution à la protohistoire des articles *ille* et *ipse* dans les langues romanes. Cultura Neolatina *8:*181–204.

Albright, Robert William, 1958. The International Phonetic Alphabet: its backgrounds and development. Bloomington, Indiana: Indiana University Research Center in Anthropology, Folklore, and Linguistics, Publication 7.

Alonso, Amado, 1949. Examen de las noticias de Nebrija sobre antigua pronunciación española. Nueva Revista de Filología Hispánica *3:*1–82.

AnL = Anthropological Linguistics. Bloomington, Indiana, 1959 ff.

ArL = Archivum Linguisticum. Glasgow, 1949 ff.

AS = American Speech. A quarterly of linguistic usage. New York, 1925 ff.

Atwood, Elmer Bagby, 1953. A survey of verb forms in the eastern United States. Ann Arbor: University of Michigan Press. (University of Michigan Studies in American English, No. 2.)

———, 1962. The regional vocabulary of Texas. Austin, Texas: University of Texas Press.

Austin, Herbert Douglas, 1945. A suggestion as to the origin of *sundae*. MLN *60:*534.

Bar-Hillel, Yehoshua, 1954. Logical syntax and semantics. Language *30:*230–237.

Bàrtoli, Matteo Giulio, 1925. Introduzione alla Neolinguistica (Princípi—Scopi—Metodi). Genève: Olschki. (Biblioteca dell'Archivum Romanicum *II:*12.)

Bergsland, Knut, 1958. Is lexico-statistic dating valid? Proceedings of the thirty-second international congress of Americanists 654–675 (Copenhagen, 1956: Ejuar Munksgaard).

Beyer, Franz, and Paul Passy, 1893. Elementarbuch des gesprochenen Französisch. Cöthen.

Bischoff, Bernhard, 1956. Paläographie. 2. überarbeitete Auflage. Berlin: E. Schmidt.

Blinkenberg, Andreas, 1928. L'ordre des mots en français moderne. Copenhague: Andr. Fred. Høst & søn.

BLOCH, BERNARD, 1948. A set of postulates for phonemic analysis. Language *24:*3–46.
BLOCH, BERNARD, and GEORGE L. TRAGER, 1942. Outline of linguistic analysis. Baltimore: Linguistic Society of America.
BLOOMFIELD, LEONARD, 1926. A set of postulates for the science of language. Language *2:*153–164. Reprinted in IJAL *15:*195–202 (1949) and in Joos (ed.), 1957, pp. 26–31.
——, 1927. Literate and illiterate speech. AS *2:*432–441.
——, 1929. A note on sound change. Language *4:*99–100.
——, 1932. Review of Hermann: Lautgesetz und Analogie. Language *8:*220–233.
——, 1933a. Language. New York: Henry Holt and Co.
——, 1933b. The structure of learnèd words. A commemorative volume issued by the Institute for Research in English Teaching on the occasion of the tenth annual conference of English teachers 17–23 (Tokyo).
——, 1939. Linguistic aspects of science. Chicago: University of Chicago Press. (International Encyclopaedia of Unified Science *1:*4.)
——, 1944. Secondary and tertiary responses to language. Language *20:*45–55.
BLOOMFIELD, LEONARD, and CLARENCE L. BARNHART, 1961. Let's read: a linguistic approach. Detroit: Wayne State University Press.
BOAS, FRANZ, 1911. Handbook of American Indian languages. Washington, D.C.: Bureau of American Ethnology—Bulletin No. 40.
BOLLING, GEORGE MELVILLE, 1929. Linguistics and philology. Language *5:*27–32.
——, 1944. The athetized lines of the Iliad. Baltimore: Linguistic Society of America.
BRAINE, MARTIN D. S., 1963. The ontogeny of English phrase structure: the first phase. Language *39:*1–13.
BROOKS, NELSON E., 1960. Language and language learning. New York: Harcourt Brace and World.
BROSNAHAN, L. F., 1961. The sounds of language. Cambridge, England: Heffer.
BROWN, ROGER, 1958. Words and things. Glencoe, Illinois: The Free Press.
BROWN, R. W., and ERIC LENNEBERG, 1954. A study in language and cognition. Journal of Abnormal and Social Psychology *49:*454–462.
BRUNOT, FERDINAND, 1891. La doctrine de Malherbe d'après son commentaire sur Desportes. Paris: G. Masson.
——, 1932. Observations sur la Grammaire de l'Académie Française. Paris: E. Droz.
BUCK, CARL DARLING, 1949. A dictionary of selected synonyms in the principal Indo-European languages. Chicago: University of Chicago Press.
BÜHLER, KURT, 1931. Phonetik und Phonologie. TCLP *4:*22–53.
BULL, WILLIAM E., 1960. Time, tense, and the verb. Berkeley and Los Angeles: University of California Press. (UCPL, Vol. 19.)
BUYSSENS, ERIC, 1943. Les langages et le discours. Essai de linguistique fonctionnelle dans le cadre de la sémiologie. Bruxelles: Office de Publicité.
CARROLL, JOHN B., 1953. The study of language. Cambridge, Mass.: Harvard University Press.
——, 1963. Linguistic relativity, contrastive linguistics, and language learning. IRAL *1:*1–20.
CASSIDY, FREDERIC GOMES, 1961. Jamaica Talk. London, Macmillan and New York: St. Martin's Press.
CHAO, YUEN REN, 1934. The non-uniqueness of phonemic solutions. Bulletin of the Institute of History and Philology, Academia Sinica, *4:4:*363–397. *Reprinted in* Joos (ed.) 1957, pp. 38–54.
CHERRY, E. COLIN, MORRIS HALLE, and ROMAN JAKOBSON, 1953. Toward the logical description of languages in their phonemic aspect. Language *29:*34–47.

CHOMSKY, NOAM AVRAM, 1957. Syntactic structures. The Hague: Mouton & Cie. (Janua Linguarum, No. 4.)

CHRÉTIEN, C. DOUGLAS, 1962. The mathematical models of glottochronology. Language 38:11-37.

COHEN, MARCEL, 1958. La grande invention de l'écriture et son évolution. Paris: C. Klincksieck.

COLLITZ, HERMANN, 1926. World languages. Language 2:1-13.

COUSTENOBLE, HÉLÈNE, and LILIAS ARMSTRONG, 1934. Studies in French intonation. Cambridge, England: Cambridge University Press.

CLS = CREOLE LANGUAGE STUDIES. London: Macmillan and New York: St. Martin's Press, 1960 ff.

DABBS, JACK AUTREY, 1948. The pattern je le veux voir in 17th-century French. Language 24:267-279.

DANEŠ, FRANTIŠEK, 1960. Sentence intonation from a functional point of view. Word 16:34-54.

DARLINGTON, C. D., 1947. The genetic component of language. Heredity 1:269-286.

——, 1961. Speech, language, and heredity. Speech Pathology and Therapy (April, 1961).

DE SAUSSURE, FERDINAND, 1916. Cours de linguistique générale. Paris: Payot. English translatiom, Course in general linguistics (tr. Wade Baskin), New York: Philosophical Library, 1959.

DEVOTO, GIÀCOMO, 1939. Storia della lingua di Roma. Bologna: L. Cappelli. (Istituto di Studí Romani: Storia di Roma, Vol. 23.)

DIRINGER, DAVID, 1949. The alphabet. New York: Philosophical Library.

D'OVIDIO, FRANCESCO, 1903. Reliquie probabili o possibili degli antichi dialetti italici nei moderni dialetti italiani e negl'idiomi romanzi in genere. Atti della reale accademia di scienze morali e politiche (Nàpoli) 24:13-50.

EDFELDT, ÅKE W., 1960. Silent speech and silent reading. Chicago: University of Chicago Press.

EFRON, EDITH, 1954. French and Creole patois in Haiti. Caribbean Quarterly 3:199-214.

EISELEY, LOREN C., 1960. The firmament of time. New York: Atheneum.

ELLEGÅRD, ALVAR, 1959. Statistical measurement of linguistic relationship. Language 35:131-156.

ELSON, BENJAMIN, and VELMA B. PICKETT, 1960. Beginning Morphology—Syntax. Santa Ana, California: Summer Institute of Linguistics.

ERVIN, SUSAN M., 1962. The connotations of gender. Word 18:248-261.

ESTRICH, ROBERT M., and HANS SPERBER, 1952. Three keys to language. New York: Rinehart and Co.

FEIST, SIGMUND, 1932. The origin of the Germanic languages and the Indo-Europeanising of north Europe. Language 8:245-254.

FERGUSON, CHARLES A., 1962. The language factor in national development. In Rice (ed.), 1962, pp. 8-14.

FIORELLI, PIERO, 1953. Gorgia toscana e gorgia beota. LN 14:57-58.

——, 1958. Del raddoppiamento da parola a parola. LN 19:122-127.

FRANZÉN, T., 1939. Étude sur la syntaxe des pronoms personnels sujets en ancien français. Uppsala: Almqvist & Wiksells Boktryckeri.

FRIES, CHARLES CARPENTER, 1925. The periphrastic future with shall and will in modern English. PMLA 40:963-1024.

——, 1941. American English grammar. New York and London: Appleton-Century.

——, 1952. The structure of English. New York: Harcourt Brace.

——, 1954. Meaning and linguistic analysis. Language *30:*57–68.
——, 1960. The teaching and learning of English as a foreign language. Ann Arbor: University of Michigan Press.
——, 1962. The Bloomfield "school." Trends Volume 196–224.
——, 1963. Linguistics and Reading. New York: Holt, Rinehart, and Winston.
GARVIN, PAUL L., 1954. Delimitation of syntactic units. Language *30:*345–348.
GEARY, JAMES A., 1941. Proto-Algonquian *çk: further examples. Language *17:* 304–310.
GELB, IGNACE J., 1952. A study of writing: the foundations of grammatology. Chicago: University of Chicago Press.
GILLIÉRON, JULES, 1918. Généalogie des mots qui désignent l'abeille, d'aprés l'Atlas Linguistique de la France. Paris: Champion.
GILLIÉRON, JULES, and MARIO ROQUES, 1912. Etudes de géographie linguistique. Paris: Champion.
GLEASON, HENRY ALLAN, JR., 1959. Counting and calculating for historical reconstruction. AnL *1:2:*22–33.
——, 1961. An introduction to descriptive linguistics. Revised edition. New York: Holt, Rinehart and Winston.
GRAND, CAMILLE, 1930. *Tu, voi, Lei:* etude des pronoms allocutoires en italien. Ingenbohl: Impr. du P. Théodore.
GREENBERG, JOSEPH E., 1956. The measurement of linguistic diversity. Language *32:*109–115.
——, 1962. Is the vowel-consonant dichotomy universal? Word *18:*73–81.
GRIMES, JOSEPH E., and FREDERICK B. AGARD, 1959. Linguistic divergence in Romance. Language *35:*598–604.
GROOTAERS, WILLEM, 1958. New approaches in the field of Japanese dialectology. Transactions of the International Conference of Orientalists *8:*71–74.
GUNDERSON, ROBERT G. (ed.), 1962. Webster's Third New International Dictionary: a symposium. QJS *48:*431–440.
HAAS, W., 1957. Zero in linguistic description. Studies in Linguistic Analysis 33–53 (Oxford: Basil Blackwell).
HÁLA, BOHUSLAV, 1960. Autour du problème de la syllabe. Phonetica *5:*159–168.
——, 1961. La syllabe, sa nature, son origine et ses transformations. Orbis *10:*69–143.
HALL, FRANCES ADKINS, 1962. Twenty steps to perfect spelling. New York: Bantam Books, No. H2519.
HALL, FRANCES A., and ELEANOR H. BRENES, 1960. Spelling patterns. Ithaca, N.Y.: Linguistica.
HALL, ROBERT A., JR., 1941. Definite article + family name in Italian. Language *17:*33–39.
——, 1942a. The Italian Questione della Lingua: an interpretative essay. Chapel Hill, N.C.: University of North Carolina Press. (University of North Carolina Publications in the Romance Languages and Literature, No. 4.)
——, 1942b. Review of Jaberg and Jud: Sprach- und Sachatlas Italiens und der Südschweiz. Language *18:*282–287.
——, 1943a. Melanesian Pidgin English: grammar, texts, vocabulary. Baltimore: Linguistic Society of America.
——, 1943b. Occurrence and orthographical representation of phonemes in Brazilian Portuguese. SiL *2:*6–13.
——, 1943c. The Papal States in Italian linguistic history. Language *19:*125–140.
——, 1943d. The unit phonemes of Brazilian Portuguese. SiL *1:15:*1–6.

——, 1944a. Chinese Pidgin English: grammar and texts. Journal of the American Oriental Society *64:*95–113.

——, 1944b. Hungarian Grammar. Baltimore: Linguistic Society of America. (Language Monograph No. 21.)

——, 1944c. Language and superstitition. French Review *17:*377–382.

——, 1945. Progress and reaction in modern language teaching. AAUP Bulletin *31:*220–230.

——, 1946a. A note on bound forms. Journal of English and Germanic Philology *45:*450.

——, 1946b. The state of linguistics: crisis or reaction? Italica *23:*30–34.

——, 1947. Proto-Romance *baró^ne* strong man. SiL *5:*65–68.

——, 1948a. Benedetto Croce and "idealistic" linguistics. SiL *6:*27–35.

——, 1948b. Descriptive Italian grammar. Ithaca, N.Y.: Cornell University Press.

——, 1948c. The linguistic structure of Taki-Taki. Language *24:*92–116.

——, 1948d. Structural Sketch No. 1: French. Baltimore: Linguistic Society of America. (Language Monograph No. 24.)

——, 1948e. Ancora i composti del tipo *portabandiera, facidanno.* LN *9:*22–23.

——, 1949a. The linguistic position of Franco-Provençal. Language *25:*1–14.

——, 1949b. Nasal + homorganic plosive in central and south Italian. ArL *1:*151–156.

——, 1949c. A note on "gorgia toscana." Italica *26:*64–69.

——, 1950. The reconstruction of Proto-Romance. Language *26:*6–27. *Reprinted in* Joos (ed.) 1957, pp. 303–314.

——, 1951a. Idiolect and linguistic super-ego. StL *5:*21–27.

——, 1951b. Sex-reference and grammatical gender in English. AS *26:*170–172.

——, 1951c. Terminologia linguistica: il suffisso *-ema* e problemi affini. LN *12:* 52–54.

——, 1952a. Bilingualism and applied linguistics. Zeitschrift für Phonetik und allgemeine Sprachwissenschaft *6:*17–30.

——, 1952b. Terminologia linguistica: pro-complementi. LN *13:*22–24.

——, 1953a. Elgar and the intonation of British English. The Gramophone *31:*6–7.

——, 1953b. Haitian Creole: grammar, texts, vocabulary. Menasha, Wisconsin: American Anthropological Association (AAA Memoir No. 74; *also issued as* American Folklore Society, Memoir No. 43).

——, 1953c. Pidgin English and linguistic change. Lingua *3:*138–146.

——, 1955a. The development of vowel pattern in Romance. Lingua *4:*394–406.

——, 1955b. Hands off Pidgin English! Sydney, N.S.W.: Pacific Publications Pty. Ltd.

——, 1955c. Innovations in Melanesian Pidgin (Neo-Melanesian). Oceania *26:* 91–109.

——, 1956. How we noun-incorporate in English. AS *31:*83–88.

——, 1958a. Creole languages and "genetic relationships." Word *14:*367–373.

——, 1958b. Review of F. Spiess: Die Verwendung des Subjektpersonalpronomens in den lombardischen Mundarten. RPh. *11:*395–398.

——, 1959a. Colonial policy and Neo-Melanesian. AnL *1:3:*22–27.

——, 1959b. Neo-Melanesian and glottochronology. IJAL *25:*265–267.

——, 1960a. Italian [z] and the converse of the archiphoneme. Lingua *9:*194–197.

——, 1960b. Linguistics and your language. (Second, revised edition of Leave your language alone!.) New York: Doubleday Anchor Books, No. A-201.

——, 1960c. On realism in reconstruction. Language *36:*203–206.

——, 1960d. Thorstein Veblen and linguistic theory. AS *35:*124–130.

——, 1961a. Pidgin. Encyclopaedia Britannica *17:*905–907.

——, 1961b. Sound and spelling in English. Philadelphia: Chilton Books.

——, 1962a. The determination of form-classes in Haitian Creole. Zeitschrift für romanische Philologie *78:*172–177.

——, 1962b. The etymology of Italian *casamatta*. Language *38:*270–273.

——, 1962c. Graphemics and linguistics. Symposium on language and culture (Proceedings of the annual spring meeting of the American Ethnological Society) 53–59.

——, 1962d. The life-cycle of pidgin languages. Lingua *11:*151–156.

——, 1963a. Cultural symbolism in literature. Ithaca, N.Y.: Linguistica.

——, 1963b. Idealism in Romance linguistics Ithaca, N.Y.: Cornell University Press.

——, 1964. Moot points in Italian grammar. III. Definite article + family name (masc.). Italica.

HALLE, MORRIS, 1962. Phonology in a generative grammar. Word *18:* 54–72.

HARRIS, ZELLIG S., 1944. Simultaneous components in phonology. Language *20:* 181–205.

——, 1945. Discontinuous morphemes. Language *21:*121–127.

——, 1951. Methods in structural linguistics. Chicago: University of Chicago Press. (Reprinted 1960 by same publisher, under title Structural linguistics.)

——, 1957. Co-occurrence and transformation in linguistic structure. Language *33:*283–340.

——, 1962. String analysis of sentence structure. The Hague: Mouton & Co.

HAUGEN, EINAR, 1950. First Grammatical Treatise: the earliest Germanic phonology. Baltimore: Linguistic Society of America. (Language Monograph No. 25.)

——, 1951. Directions in modern linguistics. Language *27:*211–222.

——, 1953. The Norwegian language in America. Philadelphia: University of Pennsylvania Press.

HEFFNER, ROE-MERRILL SECRIST, 1937–40. Vowel length in American English. AS *12:*128–134; *15:*74–79 (*with* W. N. Locke), 377–380 (*with* W. Ph. Lehmann).

——, 1952. General phonetics. Madison: University of Wisconsin Press.

HEINIMANN, SIEGFRIED, 1955. Noch einmal zum "Substrat" in Mittelitalien. Orbis *4:*114–115.

HERMANN, EDUARD, 1931. Lautgesetz und Analogie. Berlin: Weidmann. (Abhandlungen der Gesellschaft der Wissenschaften zu Göttingen, Philosophisch-Historische Klasse, NF: *23:*3.)

HERZOG, GEORGE, 1934. Speech-melody and primitive music. Musical Quarterly *30:*452–466.

HICKERSON, HAROLD, GLEN D. TURNER, and NANCY P. HICKERSON, 1952. Testing procedures for estimating transfer of information among Iroquois dialects and languages. IJAL *18:*1–8.

HILL, ARCHIBALD A., 1936. Phonetic and phonemic change. Language *12:*15–22.

——, 1952. A note on primitive languages. IJAL *18:*172–177.

——, 1955. An analysis of "The Windhover:" an experiment in structural method. PMLA *70:*968–978.

——, 1958. An introduction to linguistic structures: from sound to sentence in English. New York: Harcourt Brace and World.

HJELMSLEV, LOUIS, 1953. Prolegomena to a theory of language (tr. F. J. Whitfield). Baltimore (IJAL Memoir No. 7).

HOCKETT, CHARLES FRANCIS, 1942. A system of descriptive phonology. Language *18:*3–21.

——, 1948a. Biophysics, linguistics, and the unity of science. American Scientist *36:*572.

——, 1948b. Implications of Bloomfield's Algonquian studies. Language *24:*117–131. *Reprinted in* Joos (ed.), 1957, pp. 281–289.

——, 1948c. A note on structure. IJAL *14:*269–271.

——, 1954. Two models of grammatical description. Word *10:*210–234. *Reprinted in* Joos (ed.) 1957, pp. 386–399.

——, 1955. A manual of phonology. Baltimore: Indiana University Publications in Anthropology and Linguistics. (IJAL Memoir No. 11.)

——, 1958. A course in modern linguistics. New York: Macmillan.

——, 1959. Animal "languages" and human language. *In* J. N. Spuhler (ed.): The evolution of man's capacity for culture, pp. 32–39 (Detroit: Wayne State University Press).

HOCKETT, CHARLES F., and ROBERT ASCHER, 1964. The human revolution. American Scientist *52:*70–72.

HOENIGSWALD, HENRY M., 1959. Some uses of nothing. Language *35:*409–420.

——, 1960. Language change and linguistic reconstruction. Chicago: University of Chicago Press.

HOIJER, HARRY, 1951. Cultural implications of some Navaho linguistic categories. Language *27:*111–120.

—— (ed.), 1954. Language in culture. Menasha, Wisconsin: American Anthropological Association (AAA Memoir No. 79).

HOUSEHOLDER, FRED WALTER, JR., 1952. Review of Z. S. Harris: Methods in structural linguistics. IJAL *18:*260–268.

HOUSEHOLDER, FRED W., JR., and SOL SAPORTA (eds.), 1962. Problems in lexicography. Bloomington, Indiana: Indiana University Research Center in Anthropology, Folklore, and Linguistics, Publication No. 21.

HUBER-SAUTER, MARGRIT, 1951. Zur Syntax des Imperativs im Italienischen. Bern: A. Francke AG Verlag. (Romanica Helvetica Vol. 36.)

HYMES, DELL H., 1960. Lexicostatistics so far. Current Anthropology *1:*3–44.

IJAL = INTERNATIONAL JOURNAL OF AMERICAN LINGUISTICS. New York (later Bloomington, Indiana), 1917 ff.

IRAL = INTERNATIONAL REVIEW OF APPLIED LINGUISTICS IN LANGUAGE TEACHING. Heidelberg, 1963 ff.

ITALICA. The quarterly bulletin of the American Association of Teachers of Italian. Menasha, Wisconsin, etc., 1924 ff.

JABERG, KARL, 1928. Der Sprachatlas als Forschungsinstrument. Halle an der Saale: Max Niemeyer Verlag.

JABERG, KARL, and JAKOB JUD, 1928–40. Sprach- und Sachatlas Italiens und der Südschweiz. Zofingen: Ringier & Co.

JAKOBSON, ROMAN, 1931a. Prinzipien der historischen Phonologie. TCLP *4:*247–267.

——, 1931b. Über die phonologischen Sprachbünde. TCLP *4:*234–240.

——, 1941. Kindersprache, Aphasie, und allgemeine Lautgesetze. Uppsala.

JAKOBSON, ROMAN, GUNNAR FANT, and MORRIS HALLE, 1952. Preliminaries to speech analysis. Cambridge, Mass.: Acoustics Laboratory, Massachusetts Institute of Technology.

JAKOBSON, ROMAN, and MORRIS HALLE, 1956. Fundamentals of language. The Hague: Mouton & Co.

JENKINS, THOMAS ATKINSON (ed.), 1924. La Chanson de Roland: Oxford version. Revised edition. Boston: Heath.

——, 1933. Word-studies in French and English. First series. Baltimore: Linguistic Society of America. (Language Monograph No. 14.)

JESPERSEN, OTTO, 1907. John Hart's pronunciation of English (1569–1570). Heidelberg: Carl Winter Verlag. (Anglistische Forschungen, Heft 22.)

——, 1922. Language: its nature, development, and origin. London: George Allen and Unwin.

JONES, GEORGE FENWICK, 1963. The ethos of the Song of Roland. Baltimore: The Johns Hopkins Press.

JOOS, MARTIN, 1948. Acoustic phonetics. Baltimore: Linguistic Society of America. (Language Monograph No. 23)

—— (ed.), 1957. Readings in linguistics. Washington, D.C.: American Council of Learnèd Societies.

——, 1960. Review of A. Wijk: Regularized English. Language 36:250–262.

——, 1962a. The five clocks. Bloomington, Indiana: Publications of the Indiana University Research Center in Anthropology, Folklore, and Linguistics, No. 22.

——, 1962b. Linguistic prospects in the United States. Trends Volume 11–20.

KAISER, L. (ed.), 1957. Manual of phonetics. Amsterdam: North-Holland Publishing Company.

KENT, ROLAND GRUBB, 1950. Old Persian grammar, texts, lexicon. New Haven, Connecticut: American Oriental Society. (American Oriental Series, Vol. 33.)

KENYON, JOHN S., 1948. Cultural levels and functional varieties of English. College English 10:31–56.

KLOSS, HEIZ, 1952. Die Entwicklung neuer germanischer Kultursprachen. München: Pohl & Co. (Schriftenreihe des Goethe-Instituts, Vol. 1.)

KROEBER, ALFRED L., 1960. Statistics, Indo-European, and taxonomy. Language 36:1–21.

KROEBER, ALFRED L., and C. D. CHRÉTIEN, 1937. Quantitative classification of Indo-European languages. Language 13:83–103.

KUKENHEIM, L., 1932. Contributions à l'histoire de la grammaire italienne, espagnole et française à l'époque de la Renaissance. Amsterdam: Nord-Hollandsche Uitgeverij Maatschappij.

KURATH, HANS, 1939. Handbook of the linguistic geography of New England. Providence, R.I.: Brown University Press.

—— (ed.), 1939–43. Linguistic atlas of New England. 3 Vols. in 6. Providence, R.I.: Brown University Press.

——, 1949. A word geography of the Eastern United States. Ann Arbor: University of Michigan Press. (Studies in American English, No. 1.)

KURATH, HANS, and RAVEN I. McDAVID JR., 1961. The pronunciation of English in the Atlantic states. Ann Arbor: University of Michigan Press. (Studies in American English, No. 3.)

KURYLOWICZ, JERZY, 1945/49. La nature des procès dits "analogiques." AcL 5:15–37.

LANGUAGE. Journal of the Linguistic Society of America. Baltimore, 1925 ff.

LEES, ROBERT B., 1957. Review of N. Chomsky: Syntactic Structures. Language 33:375–408.

——, 1960. The grammar of English nominalizations. Bloomington, Indiana: Indiana University Research Center in Anthropology, Folklore, and Linguistics, Publication No. 12.

LEHISTE, ILSE, 1960. An acoustic-phonetic study of internal open juncture. Basel and New York: S. Karger. (Supplement to Phonetica, Vol. 5.)

LEHMANN, WINFRED PHILIPP, 1962. Historical linguistics: an introduction. New York: Holt, Rinehart, and Winston.

LENNEBERG, ERIC, 1953. Cognition in ethnolinguistics. Language *29:*463–471.
LEONARD, STERLING ANDRUS, 1929. The doctrine of correctness in English usage, 1700–1800. Madison: University of Wisconsin Press. (University of Wisconsin Studies in Language and Literature, No. 25.)
LEOPOLD, WERNER FRIEDRICH, 1929. "Inner Form." Language *5:*254–260.
——, 1939–49. Speech development of a bilingual child: a linguist's record. 3 Vols. Evanston, Illinois: Northwestern University Press.
——, 1948. German *ch.* Language *24:*179–180.
——, 1952. Bibliography of child language. Evanston, Illinois: Northwestern University Press.
LE PAGE, ROBERT B., 1957–58. General outlines of Creole English dialects in the British Caribbean. Orbis *6:*373–391; *7:*54–64.
LE PAGE, ROBERT B., and DAVID DE CAMP, 1960. Jamaican Creole. London: Macmillan, and New York: St. Martin's Press. (CLS Vol. 1.)
LINGUA. International Review of General Linguistics. Haarlem (later Amsterdam), 1948 ff.
LL = LANGUAGE LEARNING. Ann Arbor, 1948 ff.
LN = LINGUA NOSTRA. Florence, 1939 ff.
LONGACRE, ROBERT E., 1960. String constituent analysis. Language *36:*63–88.
LOTZ JÁNOS, 1939. Das ungarische Sprachsystem. Stockholm: Ungarisches Institut.
McDAVID, RAVEN IOOR, JR., 1949. American dialect studies since 1939. Philologica *4:*43–48.
——, 1961. Structural linguistics and dialect geography. Orbis *10:*35–46.
McDAVID, RAVEN IOOR, JR., and VIRGINIA GLENN McDAVID, 1956. Regional linguistic atlases in the United States. Orbis *5:*349–386.
MacDONALD, DWIGHT, 1962. The string untuned. The New Yorker, March 10, 1962, pp. 130–160.
MALÉCOT, ANDRÉ, 1958. The rôle of releases in the identification of released final stops. Language *34:*370–380.
MALKIEL, YAKOV, 1962. Etymology and general linguistics. Word *18:* 198–219.
MALMBERG, BERTIL, 1959. Nya vägar inom språkforskningen. Stockholm: Svenska bokförlaget.
MAŃCZAK, W., 1958. Tendances générales des changements analogiques. Lingua *7:*298–325, 387–420.
MARTINET, ANDRÉ, 1936. Neutralization and archiphoneme. TCLP *6:*46–57.
——, 1949. Phonology as functional phonetics. London: Oxford University Press.
——, 1955. Économie des changements phonétiques. Berne: Éditions A. Francke S.A. (Bibliotheca Romanica I.10.)
MAURER, THEODORO HENRIQUE, JR., 1951. A unidade da România ocidental. São Paulo: Universidade de São Paulo, Faculdade de Filosofia, Ciencias e Letras.
MEAD, MARGARET, 1939. Native languages as field-work tools. American Anthropologist NS. *41:*189–205.
MEILLET, ANTOINE, and MARCEL COHEN, 1952. Les langues du monde. 2nd Ed. Paris: H. Champion.
MENÉNDEZ PIDAL, RAMÓN, 1950. Orígenes del español. 3ra Ed., muy corr. y adicionada. Madrid: Espasa-Calpe.
MENNER, ROBERT J., 1936. The conflict of homonyms in English. Language *12:* 229–244.
MERLO, CLEMENTE, 1926. Lazio sannita ed Etruria latina? L'Italia Dialettale *3:*84–93; also in Studí Etruschi *1:*303–311 (1927).
——, 1954. Del sostrato delle parlate italiane. Orbis *3:*7–21.

MESSING, GORDON M., 1951. Structuralism and literary tradition. Language 27:1–12.
MEYER-LÜBKE, WILHELM, 1936. Romanisches etymologisches Wörterbuch. 3. vollständig neubearbeitete Auflage. Heidelberg: Carl Winter Verlag. (Sammlung romanischer Elementar- und Handbücher III.3.)
MIGLIORINI, BRUNO, 1946. Primordi del Lei. LN 7:25–29. Reprinted in Migliorini, Saggi linguistici 187–196 (Florence, 1957).
MIHALIĆ, FRANCIS, 1957. Grammar and dictionary of Neo-Melanesian. Techny, Illinois: Mission Press.
MLN = MODERN LANGUAGE NOTES. Baltimore, 1885 ff.
MOHRMANN, CHRISTINE (ed.), 1939/47 ff. Bibliographie linguistique des années . . . (beginning with 1939/47). Utrecht and Antwerp: Spectrum.
MOULTON, WILLIAM GAMWELL, 1947. Juncture in modern standard German. Language 23:312–326.
——, 1956. Introduction to F. A. Hall: Sounds and Letters. Ithaca, N.Y.: Linguistica.
——, 1961. Linguistics and language teaching in the United States 1940–1960. Trends Volume 82–109. Reprinted in IRAL 1:21–41 (1963).
——, 1962. Dialect geography and the concept of phonological space. Word 18:23–32.
MÜLLER, FRIEDRICH MAX, 1862. Lectures on the science of language. 3rd Ed. London: Longmans, Green, Longman, and Roberts.
NEHRING, ALFONS, 1961. Zur "Realität" des Urindogermanischen. Lingua 10:357–368.
NIDA, EUGENE ALBERT, 1949. Morphology: the descriptive analysis of words. Second edition. Ann Arbor: University of Michigan Press. (University of Michigan Publications in Linguistics, Vol. 2.)
——, 1951a. Outline of descriptive syntax. Glendale, California: Summer Institute of Linguistics.
——, 1951b. A system for the description of semantic elements. Word 7:1–14.
NORMAN, HILDA LAURA, 1937. Reduplication of consonants in Italian pronunciation. Italica 14:57–63.
NYROP, KRISTOFFER, 1902. Manuel phonétique du français parlé. Deuxième édition traduite et remaniée par Emmanuel Philipot. Copenhagen: Det Nordiske Forlag.
——, 1914–30. Grammaire historique de la langue française. 6 Vols. Copenhagen: Gyldendalske Boghandel—Nordisk Forlag.
O'CONNOR, J. D., and J. L. M. TRIM, 1953. Vowel, consonant, and syllable—a phonological definition. Word 9:103–122.
OLMSTED, DAVID L., 1950. Ethnolinguistics so far. Norman, Oklahoma: Battenburg Press. (SiL Occasional Papers no. 2.)
ORBIS: bulletin international de documentation linguistique. Paris, 1952 ff.
OSGOOD, CHARLES E., and THOMAS A. SEBEOK (EDS.), 1955. Psycholinguistics: a survey of theory and research problems. Bloomington, Indiana: Indiana University Publications in Anthropology and Linguistics (IJAL Memoir No. 10).
PEDERSEN, HOLGER, 1931. Linguistic science in the nineteenth century: methods and results. Trans. by John Webster Spargo. Cambridge, Mass.: Harvard University Press. Reprinted under title The discovery of language, Bloomington: Indiana University Press, 1962.
PEI, MARIO A., 1941. The Italian language. New York: Columbia University Press.
——, 1946. The state of linguistics: reply to a mechanist. Italica 23:237–240.
——, 1949. A new methodology for Romance classification. Word 5:135–146.
——, 1962. The dictionary as battlefront: English teachers' dilemma. Saturday Review, July 21, 1962, pp. 44–46, 55–56.

PENFIELD, WILDER, and LAMAR ROBERTS, 1959. Speech and brain mechanisms. Princeton, N.J.: Princeton University Press.

PEPE, GABRIELE, 1942. Introduzione allo studio del medio evo latino. Milan. (2nd ed., Nàpoli, 1949: Edizioni scientifiche italiane.)

PICKETT, VELMA BERNICE, 1956. An introduction to the study of grammatical structure. Glendale, California: Summer Institute of Linguistics.

PIERCE, JOE E., 1952. Dialect distance testing in Algonquian. IJAL 18:208–218.

PIKE, KENNETH LEE, 1943. Phonetics: a critical analysis of phonetic theory and a technic [sic] for the practical description of sounds. Ann Arbor: University of Michigan Press. (University of Michigan Publications in Language and Literature, Vol. 21.)

——, 1946. The intonation of American English. Ann Arbor: University of Michigan Press. (University of Michigan Publications in Linguistics, Vol. 1.)

——, 1947. Phonemics: a technique for reducing languages to writing. Ann Arbor: University of Michigan Press. (University of Michigan Publications in Linguistics, Vol. 3.)

——, 1948. Tone languages: a technique for determining the number and type of pitch contrasts in a language, with studies in tonemic substitution and fusion. Ann Arbor: University of Michigan Press. (University of Michigan Publications in Linguistics, Vol. 4.)

——, 1954–55–60. Language in relation to a unified theory of the structure of human behavior. 3 Vols. Glendale, California: Summer Institute of Linguistics.

——, 1958. On tagmemes, née [sic] grammemes. IJAL 24:273–278.

PITTENGER, ROBERT E., CHARLES F. HOCKETT and JOHN J. DANEHY, 1960. The first five minutes. Ithaca, N.Y.: P. Martineau.

PMLA = PUBLICATIONS OF THE MODERN LANGUAGE ASSOCIATION OF AMERICA. Baltimore (later Menasha, Wisconsin), 1886 ff.

POOLEY, ROBERT C., 1957. Teaching English grammar. New York: Appleton-Century-Crofts.

POP, SEVER, 1950. La dialectologie. Louvain: chez l'auteur.

PREISSIG, EDWARD R. VON, 1918. Dictionary and grammar of the Chamorro language of the island of Guam. Washington, D.C.: Government Printing Office.

PULGRAM, ERNST, 1949. Prehistory and the Italian dialects. Language 25:241–252.

——, 1955. Neogrammarians and sound laws. Orbis 4:60–65.

——, 1959a. Introduction to the spectrography of speech. The Hague: Mouton & Cie.

——, 1959b. Proto-Indo-European reality and reconstruction. Language 25:421–426.

——, 1961. The nature and use of proto-languages. Lingua. 10:18–37.

PUTNAM, GEORGE N., and EDNA M. O'HERN, 1955. The status significance of an isolated urban dialect. Baltimore: Linguistic Society of America. (Language Dissertation No. 53.)

PYLES, THOMAS, 1952. Words and ways of American English. New York: Random House.

QJS = QUARTERLY JOURNAL OF SPEECH. Official publication of the Speech Association of America. Columbia, Missouri, 1915 ff.

RAY, PUNYA SLOKA, 1962. Language standardization. In Rice (ed.), 1962, pp. 91–104.

READ, ALLEN WALKER, 1949. Linguistic revision as a requisite for the increasing of rigor in scientific method. New York (mimeographed).

——, 1955. The term "meaning" in linguistics. ETC: a review of general semantics 13:37–45.

——, 1962. Family words in English. AS 37:5–12.

——, 1963. That dictionary or the dictionary? Consumer Reports 28:488–492.

REED, DAVID W., and YOLANDA LEITE, 1947. The segmental phonemes of Brazilian Portuguese, standard Paulista dialect. *In* Pike, 1947, pp. 194–202.

REICHLING, ANTON, 1961. Principles and methods of syntax: cryptanalytical formalism. Lingua *10:*1–17.

REINECKE, JOHN E., 1937. Marginal languages: a sociological study of the creole languages and trade jargons. New Haven: Yale University dissertation (typewritten).

RFE = REVISTA DE FILOLOGÍA ESPAÑOLA. Madrid, 1914 ff.

RICE, FRANK A. (ED.), 1962. Study of the rôle of second languages in Asia, Africa, and Latin America. Washington, D.C.: Center for Applied Linguistics.

ROBERTS, PAUL McH., 1956. Patterns of English. New York: Harcourt Brace.

ROBINS, R. H., 1952. Noun and verb in universal grammar. Language *28:*289–298.

ROHLFS, GERHARD, 1930. Vorlateinische Einflüsse in den Mundarten des heutigen Italiens? Germanisch-Romanische Monatsschrift *18:*37–56. *Reprinted in* G. Rohlfs: An den Quellen der romanischen Sprachen 61–79 (Halle, 1952).

ROSETTI, AL., 1959. Sur la théorie de la syllabe. The Hague: Mouton & Cie.

ROSS, ALAN S. C., 1954. Linguistic class-indicators in present-day English. Neuphilologische Mitteilungen *55:*20–56. *Partially reprinted under title* "U and Non-U: an essay in sociological linguistics" in Encounter, Nov. 1955, pp. 11–20, *and in* N. Mitford (ed.): Noblesse Oblige, pp. 9–34 (Penguin Books, 1959).

RPh. = ROMANCE PHILOLOGY. Berkeley, California, 1947 ff.

SAFFORD, WILLIAM EDWARD. 1905. The Chamorro language of Guam. Washington, D.C.: W. H. Lowdermilk & Co.

SAMARIN, WILLIAM J., 1962. Lingua francas, with special reference to Africa. *In* Rice (ed.), 1962, pp. 34–53.

SAPIR, EDWARD, 1921. Language: an introduction to the study of speech. New York: Harcourt Brace. (*Reprinted 1955:* New York, Harcourt Brace, Harvest Books No. HB-7.)

——, 1925. Sound patterns in language. Language *1:*37–51. *Reprinted in* Joos (ed.), 1957, pp. 19–25.

——, 1933. La réalité psychologique des phonèmes. Journal de Psychologie Normale et Pathologique *30:*247–265. *Reprinted* (*in English*), *under title* "The psychological reality of phonemes") *in* Sapir, 1949, pp. 46–60.

——, 1949. Selected writings of Edward Sapir (ed. David Mandelbaum). Berkeley and Los Angeles: University of California Press.

SAPON, STANLEY S., 1958/59. Étude instrumentale de quelques contours mélodiques fondamentaux dans les langues romanes. RFE *42:*167–177.

SAYCE, ARCHIBALD H., 1880. Introduction to the science of language. London: Kegan Paul.

SEBEOK, THOMAS A. (ED.), 1960. Style in language. Cambridge, Mass.: Technology Press of M.I.T.

SHIPMAN, GEORGE RAYMOND, 1953. The vowel phonemes of Meigret. Washington, D.C.: Georgetown University Press. (Monograph Series on Languages and Linguistics, No. 3.)

SiL = STUDIES IN LINGUISTICS. Washington, D.C. (later: Buffalo, N.Y.), 1943 ff.

SLEDD, JAMES HINTON, 1958. Review of Pooley, 1957. Language *34:* 139–144.

——, 1959. A short introduction to English grammar. Chicago: Scott Foresman.

SMALLEY, WILLIAM ALLEN, 1961–62. Manual of articulatory phonetics. Tarrytown, N.Y.: Practical Anthropology.

SMITH, HENRY LEE, JR., 1956. Linguistic science and the teaching of English. Cambridge, Mass.: Harvard University Press.

——, 1963. Review of Bloomfield and Barnhart, 1961. Language *39:*67–78.

SOMMERFELT, ALF, 1931. Sur l'importance générale de la syllabe. TCLP *4:*156–159.

——, 1936. Can syllable divisions have phonological importance? Proceedings of the Second International Congress of Phonetic Sciences, pp. 30–33.

SPERBER, HANS, 1930. Einführung in die Bedeutungslehre. 2nd Ed. Leipzig.

——, 1960. Linguistics in a strait-jacket. MLN *75:*239–252.

SPIESS, FEDERICO, 1956. Die Verwendung des Subjekt-Personalpronomens in den lombardischen Mundarten. Bern: A. Francke AG Verlag. (Romanica Helvetica Vol. 59.)

SPITZER, LEO, 1940a. *Fimare* in Isidore. American Journal of Philology *61:*357.

——, 1940b. Ital. *rifiutare.* Italica *17:*148–149.

——, 1946. The state of linguistics: crisis or reaction? MLN *71:*497–502.

STETSON, RAYMOND HERBERT, 1936. The relation of the phoneme and the syllable. Proceedings of the Second International Congress of Phonetic Sciences, pp. 245–252.

——, 1945. Bases of phonology. Oberlin, Ohio: Oberlin College.

——, 1951. Motor phonetics: a study of speech movements in action. 2nd edition. Amsterdam: North-Holland Publishing Company.

STEWART, WILLIAM A., 1962. Creole languages in the Caribbean. *In* Rice (ed.), 1962, pp. 34–53.

StL = STUDIA LINGUISTICA. Lund, 1947 ff.

SWADESH, MORRIS, 1934. The phonemic principle. Language *10:*117–129.

——, 1937. The phonemic interpretation of long consonants. Language *13:*1–10.

TAYLOR, DOUGLAS MACRAE, 1947. Phonemes of Caribbean Creole. Word *3:*173–179.

——, 1951. Structural outline of Caribbean Creole. Word *7:*43–59.

——, 1956. Language contacts in the British West Indies. Word *12:*399–414.

TCLP = TRAVAUX DU CERCLE LINGUISTIQUE DE PRAGUE. Prague, 1929–1939.

TERRACINI, BENVENUTO ARON, 1938. Sostrato. Scritti in onore di Alfredo Trombetti 321–364 (Milan). *Reprinted in* Terracini: Pagine e appunti di linguistica storica, pp. 407–448 (Florence, 1957).

TRAGER, GEORGE LEONARD, 1932. The use of the Latin demonstratives (especially *ille* and *ipse*) up to 600 A.D., as the source of the Romance article. New York: Institute of French Studies.

——, 1958. Phonetics: glossary and tables. Buffalo, N.Y.: University of Buffalo, Department of Anthropology and Linguistics. (Studies in Linguistics, Occasional Papers, No. 6.)

TRAGER, GEORGE LEONARD, and HENRY LEE SMITH JR., 1951. An outline of English structure. Norman, Oklahoma: Battenburg Press. (Studies in Linguistics, Occasional Papers No. 3.)

TRENDS VOLUME = TRENDS IN EUROPEAN AND AMERICAN LINGUISTICS 1930–1960 (ed. Christine Mohrmann, Alf Sommerfelt and Joshua Whatmough). Utrecht and Antwerp, 1961: Spectrum.

TRUBETZKOY, NICHOLAS, 1931a. Gedanken über Morphonologie. TCLP *4:*160–163.

——, 1931b. Phonologie und Sprachgeographie. TCLP *4:*228–234.

——, 1958. Grundzüge der Phonologie. 2nd Ed. Göttingen: Vandenhoek und Ruprecht.

TWADDELL, WILLIAM FREEMAN, 1935. On defining the phoneme. Baltimore: Linguistic Society of America. (Language Monograph No. 16.) *Reprinted in* Joos (ed.), 1957, 55–80.

——, 1948a. Meanings, habits, and rules. Education *49:*75–81. *Reprinted in* LL 2:4–11 (1949).

——, 1948b. The prehistoric Germanic short syllabics. Language *24*:139–151.
UCPL = UNIVERSITY OF CALIFORNIA PUBLICATIONS IN LINGUISTICS. Berkeley and Los Angeles: University of California Press.
UHLENBECK, E. M., 1963. An appraisal of transformation theory. Lingua *12*:1–18.
UŁASZYN, HENRYK, 1931. Laut, Phonema, Morphonema. TCLP *4*:53–61.
ULDALL, ELIZABETH, 1960. Attitudinal meanings conveyed by intonational contours. Language and Speech *3*:223–234.
ULLMANN, STEPHEN, 1957. The principles of semantics. 2nd ed. Glasgow: Glasgow University Publication, No. 84.
——, 1962. Semantics. An introduction to the science of meaning. New York: Barnes and Noble.
VALDMAN, ALBERT, 1959. Phonologic structure and social factors in French: the vowel "un". French Review *33*:153–161.
——, 1961. French. In S. Belasco (ed.): Manual of Applied Linguistics (Boston: Heath).
VOEGELIN, CHARLES F., and ZELLIG S. HARRIS, 1951. Methods for determining intelligibility among dialects of natural languages. Proceedings of the American Philosophical Society *95*:322–329.
VOORHOEVE, JAN, 1953. Voorstudies tot een beschrijving van het Sranan Tongo. Amsterdam: Bureau for Linguistic Research in Surinam.
——, 1958. Structureel onderzoek van het Sranan. De West-Indische Gids *37*:189–211.
——, 1961. Linguistic experiments in syntactic analysis. CLS *2*:37–60.
——, 1962. Sranan syntax. Amsterdam: North-Holland Publishing Company.
VOSSLER, KARL, 1955. Einführung ins Vulgärlatein (ed. Helmut Schmeck). München: Max Hueber Verlag.
WAGNER, MAX LEOPOLD, 1941. Historische Lautlehre des Sardischen. Halle an der Saale: Max Niemeyer Verlag. (Zeitschrift für romanische Philologie, Suppl. No. 93.)
WARTBURG, WALTHER VON, 1950. Die Ausgliederung der romanischen Sprachräume. Bern: A. Francke AG Verlag. (*Spanish translation:* La fragmentación lingüística de la Románia, Madrid, 1952: Editorial Gredos.)
——, 1958. Évolution et structure de la langue française. Berne: Éditions A. Francke S.A.
WEINGART, MILOŠ, 1929. Étude du language parlé suivi du point de vue musical. TCLP *1*:170–242.
WEINREICH, URIEL, 1953. Languages in contact: findings and problems. New York: Linguistic Circle of New York.
WEIR, RUTH HIRSCH, 1962. Language in the crib. The Hague: Mouton & Co. (Janua Linguarum No. 14.)
WELLS, RULON SEYMOUR, III, 1945. The pitch phonemes of English. Language *21*:27–39.
——, 1947a. De Saussure's system of linguistics. Word *3*:1–31. *Reprinted in* Joos (ed.), 1957, pp. 1–18.
——, 1947b. Immediate constituents. Language *23*:81–117.
——, 1947c. Review of Pike, 1946. Language *23*:255–273.
WENTWORTH, HAROLD, 1941. The allegedly dead suffix -*dom* in modern English. PMLA *56*:280–306.

WHORF, BENJAMIN LEE, 1936. The punctual and segmentative aspects of verbs in Hopi. Language *12:*127–131.
——, 1956. Language, thought, and reality: selected writings. Cambridge, Massachusetts: Technology Press of M.I.T.
WISE, CLAUDE MERTON, 1957. Applied phonetics. Englewood Clifls, N.J.: Prentice-Hall.
WORD. Journal of the Linguistic Circle of New York. New York, 1945 ff.

THE INTERNATIONAL

(Revised

		Bi-labial	Labio-dental	Dental and Alveolar	Retroflex	Palato-alveolar
CONSONANTS	Plosive..............	p b		t d	ʈ ɖ	
	Nasal	m	ɱ	n	ɳ	
	Lateral Fricative........			ɬ ɮ		
	Lateral Non-fricative....			l	ɭ	
	Rolled			r		
	Flapped..............			ɾ	ɽ	
	Fricative..............	ɸ β	f v	θ ð | s z | ɹ	ʂ ʐ	ʃ ʒ
	Frictionless Continuants and Semi-vowels	w | ɥ	ʋ	ɹ		
VOWELS	Close	(y ʉ u)				
	Half-close	(ø o)				
	Half-open	(œ ɔ)				
	Open	(ɒ)				

(Secondary articulations are shown by symbols in brackets.)

OTHER SOUNDS.—Palatalized consonants: ʈ, ɖ, etc.; palatalized ʃ, ʒ: ʆ, ʓ. Velarized or pharyngalized consonants: ɫ, đ, z, etc. Ejective consonants (with simultaneous glottal stop): p', t', etc. Implosive voiced consonants: ɓ, ɗ, etc. ɼ fricative trill. σ, ʚ (labialized θ, ð, or s, z). ꞁ, ꙟ (labialized ʃ, ʒ). ʇ, ʗ, ʖ (clicks, Zulu c, q, x). ɺ (a sound between r and l). ŋ Japanese syllabic nasal. ʄ (combination of x and ʃ). ʍ (voiceless w). ɪ, ʏ, ɷ (lowered varieties of i, y, u). з (a variety of ə). ɵ (a vowel between ø and o).

Affricates are normally represented by groups of two consonants (ts, tʃ, dʒ, etc.), but, when necessary, ligatures are used, (ʦ, ʧ, ʤ, etc.), or the marks ⌒ or ‿ (t͡s or t‿s, etc.). ⌒ ‿ also denote synchronic articulation (m͡ŋ = simultaneous m and ŋ). c, ɟ may occasionally be used in place of tʃ, dʒ, and ʒ, ʑ for ts, dz. Aspirated plosives: ph, th, etc. r-coloured vowels: eɹ, aɹ, ɔɹ, etc., or eʴ, aʴ, ɔʴ, etc., or ҽ, ą, ǫ, etc.; r-coloured ə : əɹ or əʴ or ɹ or ą or ɚ.

PHONETIC ALPHABET

to 1951.)

Alveolo-palatal	Palatal	Velar	Uvular	Pharyngal	Glottal
	c ɟ	k g	q ɢ		ʔ
	ɲ	ŋ	N		
	ʎ				
			R		
			R		
ɕ ʑ	ç j	x ɣ	χ ʁ	ħ ʕ	h ɦ
	j (ɥ)	(w)	ʁ		

	Front	Central	Back		
	i y	ɨ ʉ	ɯ u		
	e ø		ɤ o		
		ə			
	ɛ œ		ʌ ɔ		
	æ	ɐ			
	a	ɑ ɒ			

LENGTH, STRESS, PITCH.— ː (full length). · (half length). ' (stress, placed at beginning of the stressed syllable). ˌ (secondary stress.) ˉ (high level pitch); _ (low level); ′ (high rising); ˌ (low rising); ˋ (high falling); ˌ (low falling); ˆ (rise-fall); ˇ (fall-rise).

MODIFIERS.— ˜ nasality. ₒ breath (l̥ = breathed l). ˌ voice (ş = z). ' slight aspiration following **p, t,** etc. ᴗ labialization (n̮ = labialized **n**). ₙ dental articulation (t̪ = dental **t**). ˙ palatalization (ż = ʒ). ˌ specially close vowel (ẹ = a very close e). ˌ specially open vowel (ę = a rather open e). ˈ tongue raised (e˕ or ẹ = ẹ). ᴛ tongue lowered (e˕ or ẹ = ẹ). + tongue advanced (u̟ or y = an advanced **u,** t̟ = t̟). - or ˗ tongue retracted (i- or i̠ = ɨ˖, t̠ = alveolar t). › lips more rounded. ‹ lips more spread. Central vowels: ï(= ɨ), ü(= ʉ), ë(= ə˕), ö(= ɵ), ɛ̈, ɔ̈. ˌ (e.g. n̩) syllabic consonant. ˇ consonantal vowel. ʃˢ variety of ʃ resembling **s,** etc.

INDEX

ablative, 155, 201, 208, 210, 212, 342
absolute construction, 212, 342
abstract terminology, 350–351, 354
academicism, 337–338, 365–369
academies, 10, 188, 365–368, 444–445
Accademia della Crusca, 366
accent: 71, 373; "d'intensité," 108
accent-mark, 71, 108, 109, 265–266, 268, 270–271, 345
acclimatization, 337
accusative, 155, 163–165, 201, 220, 354
"Ach-Laut," 54, 112
acoustic phonetics, 24, 37, 39–40, 67, 416
acoustics, 416
active, 158–159, 224
actor, 203, 214, 343–344, 346
actualization, 80, 417, 423–424
"Adam's apple," 42
addition, 135–136
adjectival, 147, 208
adjective, 127, 134, 136, 141–142, 146–147, 153–154, 157, 171, 178, 182, 197, 200, 206, 211, 213–214, 220, 225–226, 331, 341, 346, 351, 400, 408
adjective-and-verb, 179
adverb, adverbial modifier: 126, 147, 171, 178, 197, 204, 206, 208, 212, 214, 220, 331, 339–340, 342; phrase, 211–212
Adyge, 85
aesthetics, 406–410, 446
affix, affixation, 135–136, 181–185, 334–338
affricate, 58, 95
African languages, 14, 37, 58–59, 86, 309, 371, 383–384, 396
Afrikaans, 217, 373
Agard, Frederick Browning, 389
agglutinative, 148–149, 153, 155, 395–396
agreement, 169–170, 174, 200–204, 208
Akkadian, 267
Albanian, 312, 370
Algonquian, 85–86, 149, 152–153, 156–157, 214, 309, 387–388, 391
Alighieri, Dante, 282, 298, 300, 352, 363, 374, 410

allo- (prefix), 25–26, 192
allocation, 156–157
allograph, 26, 265–266
allomorph, 12, 26, 132, 138–167, 177, 182–184, 324–326, 330, 332, 335–336
allophone, allophonic variation, 26, 77–102, 112–113, 266, 283, 295–299, 314, 323–324, 345, 361, 374
alloseme, 26
allotax, 192–193
allotone, 26, 114
alphabet, 36, 38, 79, 122, 232, 266–273, 424; *see also* International Phonetic Alphabet
alternation: 26, 121–123, 138–144, 319, 346; in orthographical representation, 272–273, 434, 438
alternative formulations, 119–123
alveolar, 41, 56–57, 77–78, 94–95, 440
alveolum, 43, 76
Amahuaca, 85
ambiguity, 225–227
ambisyllabic, 63
American Anthroposogical Association alphabet, 38
American Council of Learnèd Societies, 541
American English, 10, 20, 38–39, 42, 49, 52, 56, 66–67, 75, 116–117, 120–122, 239–259, 271, 321–322, 360–362, 368, 370, 373, 413, 441, 444
American Indian languages, 14, 21, 38, 41, 58, 62, 86, 149, 154, 157, 188–189, 230, 309, 321, 333, 409, 458
American Negro English, 383
American Spanish, 243, 362, 462
Amish, 20, 247
analogy, 279–280, 286, 308, 323–327, 330, 335–337, 339–352, 430, 434
analysis of patterns, 451–452
"analytic" languages, 148–149
analytical techniques, 24–28
anaphora, 146–167, 202
ancestral forms, languages, 306–313
Anglicism, 357

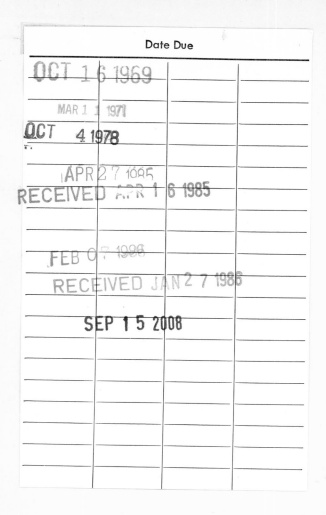